SOCIETY AND NATURE

A Sociological Inquiry

By

HANS KELSEN

THE LAWBOOK EXCHANGE, LTD.
Clark, New Jersey

ISBN-13: 978-1-58477-064-0 (cloth)
ISBN-10: 1-58477-064-3 (cloth)
ISBN-13: 978-1-58477986-5 (paperback)
ISBN-10: 1-58477-986-1 (paperback)

Lawbook Exchange edition 2000, 2009

The quality of this reprint is equivalent to the quality of the original work.

THE LAWBOOK EXCHANGE, LTD.
33 Terminal Avenue
Clark, New Jersey 07066-1321

*Please see our website for a selection of our other publications
and fine facsimile reprints of classic works of legal history:*
www.lawbookexchange.com

Library of Congress Cataloging-in-Publication Data

Kelsen, Hans, 1881-1973.
　　Society and nature : a sociological inquiry / by Hans Kelsen.
　　p. cm.
　　Originally published : London : K. Paul, Trench, Trubner, 1946, in series: International
library of sociology and social reconstruction.
　　Includes bibliographical references and index.
　　ISBN 1-58477-064-3 (cloth : acid-free paper)
　　　1. Ethnophilosophy. 2. Primitive societies. 3. Philosophy of nature. 4. Causation. 5.
Religion. I. Title.

GN451 .K4 2000
301'.7—dc21   99-054869

Printed in the United States of America on acid-free paper

SOCIETY AND NATURE

A Sociological Inquiry

By

HANS KELSEN

LONDON

KEGAN PAUL, TRENCH, TRUBNER & CO., LTD.

BROADWAY HOUSE, 68-74 CARTER LANE, E.C.4

First published in England 1946

THIS VOLUME IS DEDICATED TO THE

ROCKEFELLER FOUNDATION

BY ONE OF THE MANY EUROPEAN SCHOLARS
WHO OWE TO THIS NOBLE INSTITUTION
—THE SYMBOL OF AMERICAN GENEROSITY—
THE PRIVILEGE OF CONTINUING THEIR SCIENTIFIC WORK
IN A FREE COUNTRY

TABLE OF CONTENTS

INTRODUCTION

Our thinking is characterized by a fundamental dualism and by the tendency to overcome this dualism in establishing a monistic view of the world. The dualism manifests itself in various forms. The distinction between society and nature is only one of them.

Society and nature, if conceived of as two different systems of elements, are the results of two different methods of thinking and are only as such two different objects. The same elements, connected with each other according to the principle of causality, constitute nature; connected with each other according to another, namely, a normative, principle, they constitute society.

Causality is not a form of thought with which human consciousness is endowed by natural necessity; causality is not, as Kant calls it, an "innate notion." There were periods in the history of human thought when man did not think causally—that means, that man connected the facts perceived by his senses not according to the principle of causality but according to the same principles which regulated his conduct toward other men. The law of causality as a principle of scientific thought first appears at a relatively high level of mental development. It is unknown to primitive peoples. Nature, and that means the facts which civilized man conceives of as a system of elements connected with one another according to the principle of causality, is interpreted by early man according to a totally different scheme. The primitive interprets "nature" according to social norms, especially according to the *lex talionis*, the norm of retribution. To him "nature" is an intrinsic part of his society. The dualism of society and nature, so characteristic of the thinking of civilized man, is thoroughly foreign to primitive mentality. Modern science, on the other hand, tries to realize its monistic aim by conceiving society as part of nature and not nature as part of society.

This book undertakes the task of investigating on the basis of ethnographical material how primitive man interprets the surrounding nature and how from the fundamentals of this interpretation, especially from the principle of retribution, the idea of causality, and therewith the modern concept of nature, have developed. This development signifies the separation of nature from society in human mind.

If the insight gained into the origin of the concept of causality proves to be correct, then the controversy which recently has flared up in natural science about this concept appears in a new light, and then the tendency to eliminate or modify the idea of a causal law determining with absolute necessity all events shows its true meaning. The so-called "crisis of causality," the alleged revolution of our conception of the universe, can be understood as a last step of an intellectual process the significance of which is the gradual emancipation of the law of causality from the principle of retribution. It is the emancipation from a social interpretation of nature.

This process shows a relation between social and natural science which is very important from the point of view of intellectual history. This work is intended as a sociological contribution to this problem.

PART I

PRIMITIVE CONCEPTION OF NATURE

CHAPTER I

PRIMITIVE CONSCIOUSNESS

1. PREVALENCE OF THE EMOTIONAL COMPONENT

THE consciousness of primitive man is essentially characterized by the fact that with him the rational component, which is aimed at objective cognition, lags far behind the emotional component, which arises from feeling and volition; originally this emotional component almost exclusively dominated the mind of early man.[1]

A consideration of the peculiarity and function of these two fundamentally different attitudes of man toward his environment[2] is extremely important for a comprehension of primitive mentality. One leads to the idea of an objective connection between things, to reality as determined for civilized man by the laws of causality, to nature; the other leads to ideas which neither describe the world nor satisfy our curiosity and desire for knowledge but which serve subjective non-cognitive interests. These latter ideas, because they are related to objects which we desire or fear, are formed rather by productive fantasy than by receptive observation; ambivalent throughout, they decrease as well as increase the initial emotion, satisfy as well as re-excite desire, and allay as well as stir up fear. Upon these ideas are based concepts of value: of what is useful because desired, of what is harmful because feared, of what is morally good or bad because it is the expression of a group, rather than an individual, interest. These ideas are not concerned with explaining phenomena but with the need which primitive man feels for reacting to natural events, the justification of which action is the specific function of these ideas. Hence evaluations are expressed which establish a normative order of human behavior. Just as the rational attitude leads to nature governed by laws of causality, so the emotional attitude leads to society governed by norms. For civilized man these are indeed two different worlds, corresponding to fundamentally disparate mental attitudes.

It goes almost without saying that the emotional component is the

1

older or, at least, originally the stronger element.[3] This fact has been
well expressed by saying that in the beginning man's behavior was
essentially determined by desire.[4] Thence can be explained the pre-
eminent position which so-called "magic" has in the life of primitive
man. For it consists mainly in the fact that the less man technically
dominates nature, the more he turns with his wishes, expressed in a
peculiar sign-language, to superhuman beings. Especially because he
hopes that their power will satisfy his needs does he imagine these
beings.[5] There is no reason to suppose among primitive men either a
developed tendency to cognition or a direct desire for an objective explanation of the world—an explanation, that is, independent of his
wishes or his fears and free of any evaluation; for even the average
civilized man strives in a lesser degree after objective cognition than
after judgments of value and thus after a justification of his individual
interests in the light of collective interests (which present themselves
ideologically as norms).[6]

The mentality of primitive man is characterized by a lack of curiosity.[7] The best-informed ethnologists agree in depicting him as an individual who cannot easily be brought to that state of astonishment
which is the first impulse to investigation. The quest for deeper causes
is foreign to his nature.[8] The new arouses in him fear,[9] not curiosity.[10]
His mind, unlike that of civilized man, is not sensitive, so far as logical
contradiction is concerned. Dudley Kidd writes:

> With regard to the Kafirs, we must try and grasp the fact that they are capable of
> entertaining contradictory ideas at the same moment. Until some one points out the
> contradiction, a Kafir sees no difficulty in believing that his grandfather "went out
> like a candle" at death, while at the same time he will tell you that his grandfather
> visited the kraal yesterday in the form of a snake. Later he will tell you that all yester-
> day his dead grandfather was living below the ground in a splendid world of enjoy-
> ment. This grandfather's spirit can be both material and immaterial, and it can exist
> and not exist at the same moment. When you point out how contradictory these
> statements are, the Kafir will re-examine the question, and his answer will turn on the
> mood he happens to be in. Opposing statements of fact vignette off in his mind into
> one another, apparently without passing through any region of conscious untruth or
> mental incompatibility.[11]

W. H. R. Rivers reports:

> During the course of the work of the Percy Sladen Trust Expedition to the Solomon
> Islands, we obtained in the island of Eddystone a long account of the destination of
> man after death. We were told that he stays in the neighbourhood of the place where
> he died for a certain time, when spirits arrive in their canoes from a distant island
> inhabited by the dead to fetch the ghost to his new home. On one occasion we were
> present in a house packed tightly with people who heard the swish of the paddles of
> the ghostly visitors and the sound of their footsteps as they landed on the beach, while

for several hours the house was filled with strange whistling sounds, which all around us firmly believed to be the voices of the ghostly visitors come to fetch the man who had lately died. . . . . Later, after visiting a cave at the summit of the island, we were given a circumstantial account of its ghostly inhabitants, and we learnt that after death the people of the island inhabit this cave. Here the natives possess two beliefs which seem to us incompatible with one another: if the spirits of the dead go to a distant island, they cannot, according to our logic, at the same time live in a cave on the island where they died. Of course the natural interpretation is that the ghosts live in a cave in the interval between death and the setting out for the distant island, or that, while some go to the distant island, others take up their abode in the cave. It was clear, however, that the contradiction was not to be explained in these simple ways, but that the people held the two beliefs that the dead go to a distant island, and yet remain on the island where they died.[12]

Primitive man's rational desire for cognition is weakly developed;[13] and, wherever it does show itself, it is inseparably connected with, even fundamentally influenced by, the emotional-normative tendency. This tendency dominates his inner world. "Not contemplation but rather action is the center from which radiates man's interpretation of reality," remarks Cassirer;[14] and he points out that in the first stages of mythical-religious consciousness "things exist for the ego only by becoming emotionally effective, that is, by causing emotions of hope or fear, of desire or fright, of satisfaction or disappointment. Nature, too, is presented to man in this way long before it can become the object of perception, or even the object of cognition."[15]

2. LACK OF CAUSAL THINKING

The idea that events are determined by laws of nature, the concept of the principle of causality—a fundamental basis of scientific thought which develops slowly and with difficulty in men's minds—is entirely beyond the grasp of primitive man.[16] One can speak of "causal thinking" only if the regularity perceived in any succession of events is also considered necessary. But precisely this regular chain of events, by which primitive man's behavior actually is guided and upon which he relies in his actions and omissions, gives him no cause for meditation: like a child, he accepts the chain of events without thinking about it. Indeed, one must be a Newton in order to discover the law of gravitation simply by observing that an apple loosened from the tree always falls to earth. Conscious reflection, from which alone can emerge the law of causality, occurs in the mental processes of primitive man only if extraordinary things happen through which the normal succession of events is unexpectedly interrupted—and, above all, if strong emotions are aroused.[17] For this reason a concept of causality or a tendency to causal thinking is out of the question for primitive man. If some ethnologists attribute causal thinking to him,[18] they impute our concept of causality to certain ideas which he has about the connection of events. Such an imputation can easily be induced, inasmuch as the modern law of causality originated, as we shall show, in the course of a gradual change of meaning, in primitive notions about certain social relationships according to which primitive man interprets nature. But neither this fact nor the fact that primitive man may actually utilize causal connections in his practical life—connections, that is, which civilized people interpret as causal—entitles anyone to attribute causal thought, or a tendency to causal thinking, to him. For, like an animal, he uses these connections without being aware of their nature and without ever reflecting about them.[19]

Above all, one must not identify, as is often done, a need for explanation with the tendency to causal thinking. True, primitive man has a certain need for explanation, but only in a limited degree; this need is less pronounced than any other he may have and is subject to his desires and fears. If extraordinary events which, really or imaginarily, touch upon his vital interests attract the attention of primitive man, his immediate response will be not rational explanation but emotional reaction.[20] His entirely secondary desire for explanation, however, is satisfied when he can interpret the facts in question according to his social order which also comprises nature; for instance, he is satisfied when the facts requiring explanation can be interpreted as reward or punishment or their condition. An example of this is the interpretation which primitive man gives to a death which would be wholly natural to us but in his opinion is a punishment inflicted by a superhuman authority or a delict committed by magic,[21] which consequently entails an act of revenge, justified by such an interpretation. Even though a warrior is killed in action and the cause of his death is obvious, the vengeance of his relatives is sometimes directed not against the killer but against a supposed faraway sorcerer, whom they try to discover by means of a strange ritual. On him retribution is exercised. Prejudiced in his belief in magic, primitive man does not assume a false or "mystic" cause. What interests him is, not the fact which is the cause of the death of his relative, but the individual responsible for it. Therefore, he need not go into an inquiry after the cause but can hold someone responsible for the death; that is, he can accuse some individual of the murder although, according to the modern view, there is absolutely no causal connection between the person held responsible and the death. The thinking of primitive man is dominated by this idea of retribution and not by the law of causality. It never occurs to him to find out the real causal connection, i.e., to attribute the result to some fact which alone can be considered the cause.

Schultze,[22] who concedes causal thinking to savages, gives the following example as proof of his assumption: "A Kaffir, who broke off a piece from the anchor of a stranded ship, died soon afterwards. Since then the Kaffirs have ascribed divine character to the anchor, and when passing, honored it with greetings in order to avoid its wrath." Schultze believes that "two events are subjectively brought into causal connection which have objectively no such relation, namely, the breaking off of a piece of the anchor and the death of the Negro." But there is no causal connection in this case, for the simple reason that the assumed connection in the interpretation of Schultze is limited to two quite concrete events. The Kaffirs, interpreting this incident, do not suppose that damage to an anchor generally causes death to the injurer. If they see in this event any application of a general law, then it is that of retribution and not that of causality. The anchor, imagined as a personal being, has taken vengeance on the injurer, just as men, because of injuries done to them, take and are entitled, if not obliged, to take vengeance. Such an interpretation is also an "explanation," although not according to the law of causality. It is an explanation merely in the sense of a normative justification legitimatizing personal behavior.

Phillips writes of the natives of the Lower Congo:

> In intellect we find the same stunted development as with the emotions; the relation of cause and effect, in all but the most patent and mechanical of cases, being beyond their grasp. Here again custom rules; just as many a school boy performs operations with fractions thus and thus because he has been told to do so, and believes the answer will be right because it is the rule, so the natives attribute known effects to the most inadequate causes, inadequate both quantitatively and qualitatively. Let us take a case. Some years ago, the chigoes, or burrowing fleas, were imported from Brazil; let us ask a Kabinda what is said as to their origin. He will probably say they have come because the King of Kabinda is not yet buried (a man who died forty or fifty years ago), and nothing will persuade him to the contrary. You may point out that in Loango, where the king is still alive, the chigoes are just as bad, or that they are as troublesome in Ambriz, where the Portuguese hold the land; nothing will alter his belief.[23]

This is a very characteristic example. The natives did not attribute an effect to an "inadequate cause," as Phillips assumes; they interpreted a natural event not according to the law of causality but according to the principle of retribution: the chigoes have come to Kabinda as a punishment for a sin committed in that country. Hence, the fact that in Loango and Ambriz the chigoes are just as bad as in Kabinda is no counterevidence at all.

One can assume a tendency to causal thinking only if, distinct from emotional drives, an inclination to pure cognition has been developed, or if, independent of desire and fear, a wish has become manifest to comprehend the objective connection of the phenomena of nature.[24] As a connection of phenomena independent of desires and fears, nature does not exist for primitive man any more than, in this sense, it exists for the child. The primitive man interprets those facts which in the scientific cognition of civilized man form the system of nature according to the same principles that determine his society.

3. LACK OF EGO-CONSCIOUSNESS

Hand in hand with the predominance of the emotional over the rational tendency in the soul of primitive man goes a remarkable lack of ego-consciousness, a lack of any developed experience of his self. Kidd says of the Kaffirs: "They are but dimly conscious of large tracts of their own individuality, which lie below the level of full consciousness. . . . . The subliminal self is enormously greater than that portion of it which rises to full self-consciousness."[25] This is typical as regards the condition of primitive mentality. This lack of ego-consciousness is, however, the reverse of fear of his environment, which dominates the whole life of primitive man; he sees the world which surrounds him as full of powerful spirits, particularly of the deceased, to which he ascribes superhuman powers. When questioned about the belief of his people, an Eskimo answered the explorer Rasmussen: "We do not believe, we fear. We fear everything unfamiliar. We fear what we see about us, and we fear all the invisible things that are likewise about us, all that we have heard of in our forefathers' stories and myths. Therefore we have our customs. . . . ."[26] Fear of the souls of the dead, that is, fear of vengeance which they may take on those who offend the social order, as well as hope for protection and support in the case of orderly behavior—in short, belief in the retributory function of the souls of the dead is the basis for the widespread ancestor-worship among primitive peoples. The dead forefathers are everything and have made everything. The living are nothing. Ethnologists agree in their reports that primitive man, in contradistinction to civilized man, does not consider himself as Lord of Creation, superior to animals, plants, and inanimate objects, but as equal, if not sometimes even inferior, treating these other beings and objects with respect and awe.

This attitude corresponds with the actual situation of the savage, who finds himself in a bitter struggle with the dangers of nature, which threaten him from all sides, and particularly with the frequently much stronger animals. It is easy to understand that he sees superhuman forces in this threatening world; and it is also possible to comprehend that under such circumstances there could not arise that proud ego-consciousness which separates civilized man from nature, technically overpowered by him, and particularly from animals, entirely subordinate to him. What Nieuwenhuis said about the native of central Borneo may be considered typical:

Indeed, the position which the inhabitants of central Borneo ascribe to themselves in the kingdom of Nature is very modest. For they regard themselves as not essentially, but only in degree, different from the animals, plants and stones of their environment. Characteristically, the Bahau ascribe not only to themselves, but also to all animate and inanimate beings the possession of souls (bruwa). According to their opinion, the soul of a tree, a dog, or a rock, reacts in the same way as the soul of man and is moved by the same feelings of pleasure and pain. The Bahau try, therefore, to allay by sacrifice the angry souls of animals, plants, and stones which they are compelled to damage or to destroy. . . . .[27]

Widespread is the belief that game animals cannot be killed against their will and that the animals or the spirits residing in them make the success of hunting dependent upon a certain behavior of the hunters.[28] An analogous idea toward the plant world can also be found. If, for instance, a tree is to be felled among the tribes of the Kattourie (India), the same rites are observed as hunters perform when they intend to kill an animal. The tree is asked to bless the undertaking and to permit the felling,[29] just as with other tribes the animal is requested to agree to being killed. Reports about the Dschagga in Africa are similar.[30] Even in the nineteenth century, lumbermen in the German Upper Palatinate begged the healthy tree's pardon before they "dispatched its life."[31] The Fiji Islanders ask the coconut tree's permission before they pluck a nut.[32] Among the Bakaonde of Northern Rhodesia the smith does not trace his work to his own skill. He believes that his father's death soul accomplishes what his own hands produce. He prays:

Oh! Spirit of my father: who worked iron here of yore,
Listen to me, and hear my prayer.
To-morrow I, too, will work at the iron.
I pray thee, help me, and guide my work, that it may prosper.[33]

Indeed, even toward the tools which he has manufactured with great skill and care, primitive man assumes a submissive attitude. Thus, in Togo, the smith directs a prayer to his hammer and tongs;[34] so also, the Baganda sacrifice to the bark in which they go out fishing.[35] Certain tribes in Indonesia offer food to the implements with which they work, and elsewhere people make sacrifices to the harpoons with which they kill the dugong.[36] The Tlingit (Tlinkit) Indian addresses his angling hook and line for his halibut-fishing as personages of respect, namely, as brother-in-law and father-in-law; and the Arapao at the sun dance directs his prayer to his digging tool. The Pangwe in Spanish Guinea regard their utensils as animate and hence as persons.[37] S. R. Riggs writes:[38]

> The Dakotas viewed every object known to them as having a spirit capable of helping or hurting them, and consequently a proper object of worship. . . . . Besides these, they pray to the sun, the earth, the moon, lakes, rivers, trees, plants, snakes and all kinds of animals and vegetables—many of them say to everything, for they pray to their guns, arrows—to any object, artificial as well as natural, for they suppose every object, artificial as well as natural, has a spirit which may hurt or help, and so is a proper object of worship.

The missionary Brebeuf reports of the Hurons:

> Every year they marry their nets or seines to two little girls, who must be only from six to seven years of age, for fear they may have lost their virginity, which is a very rare quality among them. The ceremony of these espousals takes place at a fine feast, where the seine is placed between the two virgins; this is to render them fortunate in catching fish.[39]

Preuss is right when he says: "Primitive man is a being who does not rely upon himself."[40] He considers his instrument a god, whereas civilized man sometimes goes so far as to recognize that even God is only an instrument of man.

4. Soul Belief and Experience of the Ego

How far the attitude of primitive man toward nonhuman beings and inanimate objects is determined by the idea that in them are incorporated human beings, namely, the souls of dead ancestors and the like, can be left aside here, as well as the question of the relationship between animal and human soul.[41] Decisive is the status which primitive man attributes to nonhuman beings in relation to himself. And this shows how small is his self-evaluation. Belief in the soul is of the utmost importance to him. This is especially true inasmuch as the savage does not consider himself capable of producing his own offspring, because, originally at least, he had no idea of the connection between the sex act and pregnancy. He sometimes interprets the birth of the child as an act of an ancestor whose soul has penetrated the woman's body in order to be reborn and thus to assure the continuity of his group.[42] From the idea of the reincarnation of an ancestral soul in the newborn child originates presumably the extraordinarily widespread and originally general belief of primitive man in the existence of two souls:[43] one which gives life and guarantees its most important functions, and another, entirely different one, which continues a man's existence after his death. The fact that the life soul of a man is the reincarnated death soul of an ancestor explains the peculiarity that primitive man by no means identifies himself with his life soul but sees in it a guardian spirit to whom he prays and sacrifices,[44] and who can, in his opinion, even reside outside the body, during sleep, for example, and under certain other circumstances.[45] In this nonidentification with his life soul presumably lie the deeper causes which explain why primitive man sometimes does not relate his spiritual activity to his inner center, to his ego. Of the Kaffirs, Kidd writes:

> When he feels qualms of conscience, they usually seem to him to come as unreasoned checks, almost *ab extra*. It is as if he suffered from some alternation of personality, or as if some faculties of his soul had suddenly arisen out of the strange hidden depths of his own personality, and made themselves felt in his consciousness. Frequently it seems to him as if a voice were arresting him, somewhat in the style of the Demon of Socrates, and, as in his case, it warns him what not to do, and does not urge him to positive duty.[46]

This is particularly characteristic of the fact that primitive man does not have any ego-experience, which probably is possible only if this dualism of souls is overcome and the life and death soul are combined into a unified concept of soul.[47]

The idea that the soul of a venerated ancestor lives in the body of a child may—at least in some cases—explain the fact that some primitive peoples in no way assume authority over children, that they treat them, despite their own actual superiority, respectfully, and that they do not dare to punish them or even to scold them. So, for instance, Stefánsson,[48] one of the best observers of the Eskimos, explains the respect shown by the parents to their children directly by their belief that the soul of a dead person is reincarnated in the child.[49]

Many ethnologists stress the extraordinary politeness shown by primitive peoples not only toward whites but also to one another. Kidd[50] describes the behavior of the Kaffir as follows:

B

He always begins with Yes, even when the next word is No; he always raises himself in the saddle when he points to the goal; he always declares the end of the journey is just over the rise. This he does out of natural politeness, for he is not troubled with our Western conception of truth. Politeness is far more important in his eyes than truthfulness; he consequently tells you the thing he thinks you would like to hear. An old author describes how he had been asking the natives about strange animals, and among other things he had made inquiries about a unicorn. The natives, wishing to agree with the white man, assured him there was a unicorn some way off. At considerable difficulty this traveller went out of his way for a day, and saw this wonderful unicorn. It turned out to be an old he-goat which had lost one of its horns. The natives did not mean to deceive. They meant to please.

And: "The man will tell you just what he thinks you wish to hear, and then he will give a grunt of satisfaction, as much as to say, 'There: that is nicely settled now.' " This is not the result of any special education, but the reflection of that inner weakness which arises from the lack of a solid center of personality. Lévy-Bruhl rightly says:

The primitive who has a successful hunting expedition, or reaps an abundant harvest, or triumphs over his enemy in war, debits this favourable result not (as the European in a similar case would do) to the excellence of his instruments or weapons, nor to his own ingenuity and efforts, but to the indispensable assistance of the unseen powers.[51]

In a report of Father Allouez of 1672–73 we read that the Indians (Outagamis)

do not attribute the victory either to the strength or bravery of their soldiers, or to the strategy of their captains, but to fate, or to the manitou, who gives one tribe to be eaten by another when it pleases Him. That is why they fast, for they hope that the manitou will speak and show himself to them at night, and will say to them: "I give thee some of thy enemies to eat; go and seek them." That is why, they said, the captain of one of those bands would infallibly kill some foes, because, they said, the manitou speaks to him. I explained to them that he would kill some enemies because he was valiant, brave, a good leader, etc.[52]

Since primitive man attributes his fortune to the influence of these dangerous unseen powers, he feels uneasy in his successes. A game haul which is too big and a harvest which is too good make him ill at ease.[53] Fear of the "envy of the gods" is a characteristic symptom of an ego-consciousness diminished by belief in the existence of superhuman powers.

It is comprehensible that primitive man makes every conceivable effort to secure for himself the favor of these invisible forces. The most direct way is by identification with those powers. Primitive man attains this identification by various means, but, above all, by the already mentioned belief that the soul of a mighty ancestor is reincarnated in the newborn child. The attempt to identify one's self with one's ancestor appears also in other forms—for example, in certain ceremonies which are performed by the Australian Arunta in honor of their ancestors. The participants fall into a sort of trance, believing they have become one with their mythical forefathers.[54] The identification with the superhuman authority is the counterpoise of an ego-consciousness abased by permanent pressure. Primitive man, however, identifies himself not only with the superhuman authority but also with other beings. This identifying thinking, so characteristic of primitive man,[55] has as its basis his weak ego-consciousness. Only because primitive man cannot distinguish clearly between his ego, the tu, and the id, and because he does not feel himself to be a subject clearly contrasted with the object,[56] can he so easily identify himself with other beings. That is the reason for his often observed capacity to understand instinctively other beings and for his striking ability to imitate men and animals.[57] From this weak ego-consciousness also arises his lack of self-confidence, which manifests itself clearly in the magic which occupies a central position among all primitive peoples.[58]

5. COLLECTIVE CONSCIOUSNESS AND TENDENCY TO SUBSTANTIALIZE

Lack of ego-consciousness is only the negative side of a mentality completely determined by social life. It is a well-known fact that young children, when they speak of themselves, do not use the first person. Primitive languages are characterized by the fact that the "possibilities of expression in the first person are comparatively undeveloped."[59] Ungnad writes that "in the original Semitic language there exists no expression for the 'Ego.' "[60] The "original Semit" does not say: "I kill," but: "Here killing." "Only gradually there developed what we mean by saying 'I kill.' " If the Maori speaks in the first person, he does not necessarily speak of himself but of his group, with which he naturally identifies himself. He says "I" have done this or that and means thereby, "my tribe has done it." "My" soil means the land of the tribe.[61]

A particularly striking symptom of the individual's complete solidarity with the group is the custom, observed among certain tribes, according to which, in case of illness, not only the sick person but also all the members of his family must undergo treatment.[62] Of the Kaffirs, Kidd writes:

A native will also sometimes take medicine by proxy. Thus, a man once came to me and complained of a long list of symptoms, and said he badly wanted some medicine. For a *placebo* I gave him some jalap and a dose of salts. As he was licking up the last few grains of Epsom salts with his tongue—how they love to have ill-flavoured medicine, and to eat it slowly!—he thanked me for the dose, and said that he hoped the medicine he had just taken would do his wife good, for the pains were hers and not his.[63]

If among the Guaranis, an Indian tribe in South America, a child falls ill, all the relatives have to refrain from eating the things which are considered to be harmful to the child.[64] Karsten says of the Jibaro Indians:

The conception of individual personality and consequently of individual responsibility does not exist among the primitive Indians in the same sense as among civilized peoples. The individual forms an inseparable part of a whole, namely, of the family or tribe to which he belongs. Especially the members of the same family are regarded as, so to speak, organically coherent with each other, so that one part stands for all and all for one. What happens to one member of that social unit happens to all, and for the deed of one member the rest are held equally responsible. How the Jibaros conceive this connection appears from certain of their social customs. For instance, custom requires that after a child is born the parents shall fast and observe other rules of abstinence for a couple of years, or until the child is named. This is due to the idea that something of the souls or essence of the parents inheres in the child so that all three in one way form a single organism, a single personality. But this mystic connection between the parents and the child also subsists after the child has grown up, although perhaps less intimately. Similarly the tie which unites brothers and sisters in a family is so intimate that they may be said together to form one organic whole. Among the Jibaros and the Canelos Indians, when one member of the family is sick the rest have to diet in the same way as the patient himself, for if they eat unsuitable food it would be the same as if the patient ate that food, and his condition would grow worse. From the same point of view we have to explain the custom prevailing among the Jibaros that when a man dies his brother must marry the widow. The departed husband, who is still jealous of the wife he left behind, does not cede her to any other man than his brother, who with himself forms one personality and represents him in the most real sense of the word. When a younger Jibaro is murdered by his enemies the duty of revenging his death is also first of all incumbent on his brothers.[65]

If primitive peoples censure homicide as a crime, they consider it rather as an injury inflicted upon the group, which has been deprived of a useful member, than as a wrong done to the person slain.[66] If a man has been killed, it is the blood of the group that has been shed. Among the Arabs, according to Robertson Smith,[67]

the ultimate kindred group is that which always acts together in every case of blood-revenge. And in Arabia this group was not the family or household, not the relatives of the slayer and the slain within certain degrees of kinship, as we reckon kinship, but a definite unity marked off from all other groups by the possession of a common group name. Such a group the Arabs commonly call a *hayy*, and the fellow-members of a man's *hayy* are called his *ahl* or his *caum*. To determine whether a man is or is not involved in a blood-feud it is not necessary to ask more than whether he bears the same group-name with the slayer or the slain. The common formula applied to man-slaughter is that the blood of such a *hayy* has been shed and must be avenged. The tribesmen do not say that the blood of M or N has been spilt, naming the man; they say "our blood has been spilt." .... No man who is within the group can escape responsibility merely because he is not a close relation of the slayer or the slain. If there is blood between Liḥyān and ꝰAdī there is war between every man of Liḥyān and every man of ꝰAdī till the blood is atoned for. And conversely if a man of Kinda sheds the blood of another man of Kinda it makes no difference whether he can actually count kin with his victim on our way of reckoning descents: "he has shed the blood of his people" and must die or be cut off from the name and place of his tribe.

Since the individual is nothing but a member of his group, he can be replaced by another one. Lafitau[68] reports of the North American Indians: "The loss [by death] of a single individual is a great loss but a loss that has to be repaired necessarily by replacing the missing individual by one or several other individuals according to the greater or smaller importance of the person who has to be replaced." Hence the institution of adoption, widespread among primitive peoples, especially Indians. Its function is to replace the deceased member of the group by a living individual.

Primitive man is induced to this collectivistic attitude not only by his lack of ego-consciousness but also by a peculiarity of thinking which may be termed a "substantializing tendency." He does not distinguish, as we do, between the body and its conditions, its qualities, the forces which move it, or the relation in which it stands to other bodies; he rather imagines these qualities, conditions, forces, and relations as substances. Inasmuch as he fears certain qualities or conditions or wishes to obtain them, he considers the thing feared or desired as somehow infectious, or as an emanating substance, contagious through touch. Thence the widespread method among primitive peoples of curing illnesses by sucking or tapping blood. So the Pawumwa Indians of Brazil, like many other primitive peoples,

wear a small short stick in the nasal septum, the ends protruding into the nostrils. This peculiar custom is associated with a primitive idea of medicine. They claim that disease is something solid and travels in a straight line like an arrow, while air is like nothing and can bend corners. Hence, when they breathe the disease strikes the end of the stick and falls out of their nostrils, while the purified air passes into their lungs.[69]

This also explains the fact that illness is regarded as a collective evil which befalls not only a single individual but also those who live in common with him, so that they, as well as the sick person, have to take the prescribed medicine even if the latter is only wounded.[70] Accordingly, primitive man also regards death as a contagious substance, which has its seat in the dead; hence his aversion to touch a corpse for fear of "pollution." Even pain is frequently considered a substance; from this originates the practice, still existent in certain parts of northern Europe, of getting rid of toothache by touching the aching tooth with a small stick, which is then driven into a tree, thereby transferring the evil.[71] The transfer of an illness from a human being to a tree among the natives of Lobi, a territory on the Upper Volta (West Africa), is described by Henri Labouret as follows:

> In this case the patient is at night carried by his parents to a junction of foot-paths in the bush. In this place, a priest waits for them, very near a big tree. The ill man is made to lean against the trunk and ointed with a special medicine, then the priest "catches the tree's breath," puts it beside him, then takes the man's breath and inserts it into the tree, whilst he makes the tree's breath pass into the body of the ill man. After this, the parents who have brought the patient may take him home. But he will have to beware of ever resting in the shadow of the tree which has been thus treated, and whose branches must not be cut to make a fire with, for if he inhaled its smoke he would die immediately. When the tree dries out and dies, the ill man is sure to recover, but if the trunk remains strong and full of life, the man is doomed to die.[72]

That primitive man cannot conceive of such an abstract concept as time is not to be wondered at. It is significant, however, that he considers time as a substance to be renewed perpetually.[73]

For the view that bodily qualities are transferable through touching there is an abundance of examples: among certain Papua tribes the back and limbs are rubbed against a rock in order to make them as strong as the latter;[74] should a Kaffir girl eat the protrusive underlip of an animal, she becomes ugly, for then she also acquires such a lip;[75] among the polar Eskimos, whenever parents wish their children to become strong, they sew the skin of a bear's throat into the child's hood. A favorite amulet is a piece of old hearthstone, for "fire is the strongest thing known; the old hearthstone has withstood the fire throughout many generations and must therefore be stronger than the latter. The man who carries it as an amulet, will live long and be strong in misfortune."[76] Cannibalism, especially corpse-eating, is frequently connected with the belief in the possibility of acquiring the strength and powers of the devoured. It has occasionally been observed in China that children had little pieces of their flesh cut out to be given to their sick fathers as medicine; this practice involves a transfer of the strength of youth, which is considered a substance.[77]

It is of the utmost importance for the collectivistic thinking of primitive man that not only bodily but also mental and especially moral qualities, such as good and evil, and even morally qualified acts, such as a committed sin, are regarded as substances, which in some way stick to, or are inherent in, the body of the evildoer. Upon this idea rest the purification ceremonies so characteristic of primitive morality and religion, especially the widespread custom of freeing one's self from a committed wrong by loss of blood, by spitting or vomiting. Confession of sins has the same sense; as widely observed among savages, it consists in speaking out the wrong one has done, frequently accompanied by actual vomiting.[78] On this same basis is founded the well-known practice of transferring the evil of which one feels guilty to an animal which is to be sacrificed or chased away—the scapegoat.[79]

The fact that primitive man imagines the values resulting from his social order as substances has given rise to the false idea that he is morally indifferent. This interpretation is quite wrong, for it is contradicted by the indubitable fact that primitive man, much more than civilized man, is socially bound and that his social bonds are much more efficient than those of modern man. Morality, however, is social order; and one is not entitled to speak of morality unless the spiritualization and intensification characteristic of modern morality have been reached. That the difference between the morality of primitive man and civilized man is only quantitative and not qualitative is clearly proved by the confession of sins—an institution common to both. If for modern man consciousness of a committed wrong had nothing "substantial" in it, then the feeling of relief which confession entails could hardly be understood.

The idea that moral and legal qualities are substances leads to the belief that evil, like illness, is contagious. Hence, the wrong committed by an individual assumes collective character because it necessarily spreads to those who live with the perpetrator or are in close social relationship to him. That is the reason for the collective liability which is so highly significant for a primitive legal order. It is self-evident for primitive man that retribution is exercised on the whole group, although the delict has been committed by a single member only; and it is entirely justifiable that children and children's children expiate the sins of their fathers. For, like illness, sin is a substance, and therefore contagious and heritable. Indeed, even the collectivum, the group, is considered a substance. A man belongs to one and the same group if he shares with others the same group-substance: the blood is preferably regarded as the seat of this substance. Blood community, blood brotherhood, the entire blood myth, still effective today, are ideas based upon this primitive tendency of substantialization—a tendency which is not yet entirely overcome in the scientific thinking of civilized man and which plays a fateful part in the social theory of our time, particularly in the doctrine of the state.[80]

Just as primitive man substantializes the social group as such, so does he substantialize every concrete social relationship—as, for instance, property.[80a] In conformity with a lack of ego-consciousness is the fact that at the beginning of social development individual property is unknown. As soon as it does appear, however, it is accompanied by an ideology based upon the already mentioned substantializing tendency. One regards certain objects, especially those of daily use, as belonging to a certain individual because they are connected with him by the transference to them of the substance of his personality;[81] for the personality of an individual, his specific "essence," is regarded as a transferable, radiating substance. Hence arises that peculiarity of primitive thinking which accepts the part for the whole. A fingernail loosed from the body, a cut tuft of hair, a man's excrements, contain his personality. Needless to say, this idea plays a significant part in the magic of savages.[82]

The substance which connects an individual to his group, the substance of the group or the social substance, manifests itself by far the strongest in primitive thought. In primitive consciousness, therefore, there is no possibility of any distinction between individual and community; thus the idea of an individual independent of the community cannot exist. What W. C. Willoughby says of the Bantu is typical: "In studying Bantu institutions it is necessary at the outset to eliminate our idea of the individual . . . . the individual does not exist in Bantu society. . . . . The unit of Bantu society is the family."[83] Elsdon Best asserts practically the same thing about the Maori: "In Maori society the individual could scarcely be termed a social unit; he was lost in the *whanau*, or family group, which may be termed the social unit of Maori life."[84] Occasionally this collectivistic attitude leads to highly paradoxical consequences. If a man meets with an accident which renders him incapable of working, he is pillaged by his group because he has damaged the whole community. Even the death of an individual may cause the group to despoil his relatives, who are considered guilty for not having prevented the demise. A man whose wife elopes suffers the same fate; he should have prevented her from running away. In this connection Elsdon Best remarks:

> Thus it was that the Maori obtained damages when he considered that the welfare of the community had suffered, or a wrong act committed. Now should one of us have the misfortune to break a leg, or meet with some other serious accident, the act of fining him for the offence would be considered a most improper procedure; yet it was a Maori custom. Their point of view is as follows—that man is not an independent unit, the individual does not exist, he is a part of a tribe and he has injured the tribe by being laid up and so rendering himself incapable of working or fighting—clearly he should be punished.[85]

About the Tlingit Indians, Oberg reports:[86] "Theoretically, crime against an individual did not exist. The loss of an individual by murder, the loss of property by theft, or shame brought to a member of a clan, were clan losses and the clan demanded an equivalent in revenge." In this connection the social positions of the perpetrator and the victim play a decisive part. "That is to say, if a man of low rank killed a man of high rank in another clan, the murderer often went free while one of his more important kinsmen suffered death in his stead." Unconditional submission to the community is especially significant:

> The man selected as compensation prepared to die willingly. He was given much time to prepare himself through fasting and praying. The execution took place before his house.—On the day set for the execution, the man put on all his ceremonial robes and displayed all his crests and emblems. He came out of his house, stood at the doorway, and related his history, stressing the deeds that he and his ancestors had performed. All the villagers were gathered around for this solemn occasion. He then looked across to the clan whom his death was to satisfy to observe the man who had been selected to kill him. If this man was great and honorable he would step forth gladly; but if the man was of low rank he would return to the house and wait until a man of his own rank or higher was selected to kill him. When this was done he stepped forth boldly with his spear in his hand, singing a girl's puberty song. He feigned attack but permitted himself to be killed. To die thus for the honor of one's clan was considered an act of great bravery and the body was laid out in state as that of a great warrior.

Such a custom is possible only as long as the average individual does not realize that he is a personality different from the group.

6. AUTOCRATISM, CONSERVATISM, AND TRADITIONALISM

Durkheim has remarked the fact that in primitive society, in which division of labor does not differentiate individuals according to their social function, no idea of an individual personality is yet formed.[87]

Corresponding to the circumstance that man does not regard himself as a separate individual, but only as a member of a collectivum, is the autocratic character which the social organization shows as soon as chieftaindom appears.[88] The chieftain represents the whole group, and the solidarity of the group is demonstrated by the individual's unconditional submission to the chieftain.

In his interesting study on Kaffir socialism, Dudley Kidd writes that the Kaffirs "are not obsessed with the European idea of personal liberty, but believe strongly that individuals belong to the chief, and that they are his property. They find their self-realisation in their constituted head, for the tribe comes to self-consciousness in the person of the chief."[89] There is no individual, only a collective consciousness, and consequently no private property:

Amongst the Kafirs, the person of the individual belongs in theory to the chief: he is not his own, for he is the chief's man. It is extremely difficult for us, with our advanced conception of the inviolability of the rights of the individual, to appreciate the bearing of this fact. . . . . The relation of the individual to the chief can be understood from the following statement made by a Zulu, who was describing to a white man the custom of the Festival of First Fruits. He said: "The Zulus, if the mealies are ripe, are not permitted by themselves to eat them. The king must always give them permission before they do so. If somebody is eating new mealies, before the king has given his permission, he will be killed entirely. The white men are wondering about it, and say: 'Is a man not allowed to go into his own garden for harvesting food, which he planted himself, and to eat it?' But the Zulus are not wondering about that, saying: 'We are all the king's men: our bodies, our power, our food, and all that we have, is the king's property. It is quite right that we do not commence to eat new mealies unless the king has permitted it.' "[90]

In theory, the entire property of all the members of the tribe belongs to the chief. When bargaining with the Kafirs for such things as assegais, and even snuff-boxes, the native, when reluctant to sell, has said that he had no right to part with the property of his chief.[91]

The Kafirs, however, only allow people to hold private property and cattle when this does not conflict with the good of the community; they make short work of the man who grows too rich and who neglects the interest of the clan. Such a man is sure to be accused of amassing wealth by using sorcery, and is consequently "eaten up" by the chief.[92]

All the land owned by the tribe is vested in the chief, who allows every man to use as much ground as his wives can till. No land can be sold, entailed, or devised, and yet a man knows that his gardens will never be taken from him so long as he cultivates them. All unallotted land that is not required for gardens, together with all wood and water, is regarded as common property for the grazing of cattle or for the needs of all the members of the clan. The nationalization of land is therefore absolute.—It is important to note that it was the sense of the solidarity of the clan that led to the tribalisation of the land. It is easy to imagine the institution of a carefully thought-out plan of land-tenure devised so as to prevent scandalous selfishness and neglect of the good of the people, and also so as to produce and foster a spirit of camaraderie and social unions: but this is not what happened amongst the Kafirs; for in their case the system of land-tenure is the effect and not the cause of their communism. In their case individual self-consciousness is not fully developed, though the clan-consciousness is amazingly strong. The individual amongst the Kafirs to a large extent confuses (we might say fuses) himself with his clan, and therefore has not that strong sense of personal property and "rights" that obtains amongst people who have become acutely conscious of their own individuality.[93]

This collectivistic attitude of the Kaffirs is essentially connected with the autocratic character of their political system.

When we come to speak of the sense of justice, this saying of the Zulu will be found of value in showing how a Kafir differs from a European in his conception of justice and of "rights." But in this place it is merely given to show how entirely the rights of the clan supersede those of the individual. So fully does the individual belong to the head of the tribe, that a chief, named Shiluvane, issued the decree: "I do not allow of anybody dying in my country except on account of old age." This command was given with a view to the checking of the use of sorcery and witchcraft to murder people; for the chief imagined that old age was the natural cause of death, and that none of his warriors could die in the prime of life unless they were bewitched by some private enemy. But the very expression, "I allow no one to die," shows how completely the people were regarded as the property of their chief. The very existence of the tribe depends upon the existence and maintenance of a great number of mature and ablebodied human beings: and in this sense the people themselves may be regarded as a means of production, for it is they who create and protect the tribe. For this reason, the individuals with all their personal rights must be socialised and brought into subjection to the recognised head of the tribe.[94]

Since the bodies of all the members of the tribe belong to the chief, any damage done to the person of the individual is regarded as a criminal offence, and restitution has to be made, not to the person injured, but to the chief. Thus if A breaks B's leg, or knocks out his eye, he has to pay damages, not to B, but to the chief. When a white magistrate reverses this procedure, the natives think he is doing the tribe an injury, for he is putting a premium on antisocial selfishness. The action of the white man is therefore regarded as an immoral one. Thus the tables are turned, and instead of Glaucon's objection, "'Tis a city of pigs, Socrates," applying to the socialistic state, it would be used by a Kafir as a remark applicable to our individualistic régime.[95]

We are prepared now to see that the Kafir does not regard justice as an abstract thing in the way we do in Europe: to him it is essentially a personal thing, and he cannot abide our Western idea of cold, impersonal, and abstract justice. He likes it to be hot, personal, and concrete. It is the chief alone who can give it to him, for justice is a thing that scarcely exists apart from the chief who creates it. As English children believe—or used to believe, in the good old days—in the necessary justness of all that their fathers do, and consider such decisions to be necessarily final, even so the Kafir, before he is educated, has a passionate faith in the essential rightness of the decision of his chief. It never occurs to him to question the word of his chief, for the verdict instantly inhibits all other action of his judgment. The man does not want abstract justice, but the personal opinion of his chief: and the last thing a Kafir would like to do would be to call in a white man to examine, and possibly to reverse, the decision of his chief, even when such decision had been given against him.[96]

Nationalism and political absolutism go together at all times. Inasmuch as the authority of the group, represented by its leader, absorbs all the individuality of its members, they lose every impulse to develop personal feelings of responsibility; this circumstance also leads to the already mentioned collective liability, peculiar to primitive morality, that is, to the idea, self-evident to primitive man but repugnant to civilized man, that a right or wrong act of a member is to be attributed to the group and that therefore not only the member but the whole group must bear the consequences.[97] Kidd writes:

> Perhaps the very central conception of Kafir law—a conception in intimate correlation with the whole idea at the base of the Clan-System—is that of collective, or corporate, responsibility. It is a conception most admirably suited to a race that is in a backward condition, for it is a great deterrent from crime in all immature societies.[98]

This complete submission of the individual to the group manifests itself also in a traditionalism peculiar to primitive mentality, in the customary character of the formation of law, in the exaggeratedly scrupulous observation of customs and usages inherited from, and watched over by, the ancestors, and in the fact that breaches of the social order occur less often in primitive than in civilized society;[99] thence can be explained the striking lack of any socially organized sanction against certain crimes—for instance, murder if committed within the group itself—whereas social reaction in the form of a blood feud appears clearly if the perpetrator belongs to another group. In one's own group the transcendental sanction, inflicted by superhuman authorities, i.e., the ancestral souls, is sufficient.[100] The fear of this transcendental power is, indeed, so great that it may even bring about the death of a person conscious of guilt.[101]

> The Let-htas . . . . have no laws or rulers, and the Karens say they do not require any, as the Let-htas never commit any evil among themselves or against any other people. The sense of shame amongst this tribe is so acute, that on being accused of any evil act by several of the community, the person so accused retires to a desolate spot, digs his grave and strangles himself.[102]

Labouret reports of the natives of Lobi:

> Though suicide is not frequent in this region one can find some cases of hanging or inflicting wounds by poisoned arrows. Generally it is believed that the deceased had

been driven to despair through a grave wrong which had irritated the gods. Consequently, he cannot have a funeral.[103]

A weak ego-consciousness connected with a strong collectivistic consciousness leads to an increased sensitiveness as far as the judgment of society is concerned, particularly to an increased fear of public disapproval. F. Nansen writes of the Eskimo: "It now and then happens that someone or other, wounded, perhaps, by a single word from one of his kinsfolk, runs away to the mountains, and is lost for several days."[104] D. Crantz reported: "Nothing so effectually restrains a Greenlander from vice, as the dread of public disgrace. And this pleasant way of revenge even prevents many from wreaking their malice in acts of violence or bloodshed."[105] With this is connected the frequently observed fear of being ridiculous. Gilbertson writes:

A remarkable and effective method of putting offenders to shame is the "drumdance" or singing combat, described by many writers on Greenland. . . . . The procedure was briefly as follows: If a person (women as well as men could carry on the contest) felt himself aggrieved by another, he challenged the offender to meet him at a certain time and place to hold a singing combat. Each of the parties then prepared satirical songs about his opponent. At the appointed time, before the assembled people, the contestants, by turns, attacked each other by these satires until one or the other had exhausted his resources.[106]

The obvious aim of this deal is to make the adversary appear ridiculous. This is his punishment.[107]

This collectivistic attitude manifests itself finally in a rigid conservatism, which may be ultimately increased into a strongly marked misoneism.[108] The dead rule over the living; therefore the past is considered sacred. Only what the forefathers have done must be done; and, in order to achieve success or to avert misfortune, it must be done in the same way.[109] The connection between an act, carried out according to tradition, and the success which primitive man expects from it consists in the belief that the ancestors are offended and punish with failure if their descendants do not act as they themselves acted, but reward with success if they do. For success and failure originate from the dead, but nonetheless living, ancestors. What has been described by various observers as the highly developed sense of justice of primitive man[110] is nothing more than the fact that the order which governs his community sticks far more securely in his heart than law and morality in the heart of civilized man, who considers himself an individual more or less independent of the group. In this connection the main significance of initiation rituals, common among primitive peoples, is to bring the boys into rapport with the spirits of the ancestors, who guarantee the social order, and to induce initiated man, by ceremonies which produce fear and awe of the superhuman authorities, to obey the tribal customs.[111]

The traditionalism which arises from this collectivistic sense of primitive man leads to a concept of truth entirely foreign to modern thinking. For primitive man a statement is not true because it conforms with the empirical reality perceived by his senses and confirmed by reason—such a reality does not exist for him—but because it has come down to him from his ancestors, who considered it true. Rasmussen[112] tried to discover from the Eskimos the reasons why they believe in traditional rules transmitted from their forefathers and why they follow them so strictly.

> For several evenings we had discussed rules of life and taboo customs without getting beyond a long and circumstantial statement of all that was permitted and all that was forbidden. Everyone knew precisely what had to be done in any given situation; but whenever I put in my query: "Why?" they could give no answer. They regarded it, and very rightly, as unreasonable that I should require not only an account, but also a justification, of their religious principles.

Finally, a particularly intelligent shaman said to Rasmussen:

> Therefore it is that our fathers have inherited from their fathers all the old rules of life which are based on the experience and wisdom of generations. We do not know how, we cannot say why, but we keep those rules in order that we may live untroubled. And so ignorant are we in spite of all our shamans, that we fear everything unfamiliar. . . . . Therefore we have our customs.

The sense of this answer is: We observe the order of life transmitted to us by our forefathers because we fear the consequences if we transgress it; and we believe in the terrible consequences of transgression because our forefathers, too, believed in them and taught us to do likewise. Primitive man does not dream of examining this doctrine or of comparing it with his own experiences. He regards the statement concerning the necessary connection between breach of norm and misfortune as true and thus considers the norm binding; and he bases this view on the authority of his ancestors, not on his reason. Melland writes that it frequently occurs among the Bakaonde that a man confesses to have committed a sin, though he is evidently innocent, "because he has been convicted in a manner sanctioned by custom."[113] He believes he has committed the sin not because he actually committed it but because he believes in the authority of an old rule which determines the procedure of evidence.

In primitive mythical thinking, governed by emotions, the logical and the moral-social values, the reason of true cognition and the reason of right volition, coincide. For primitive man truth is identical with the binding force of his social order. Just as the latter is valid because it is handed down from the forefathers and is enjoined upon the descendants, so what the ancestors taught to be true, that is, what they commanded their descendants to believe in, is true. In accordance with primitive traditionalism, social authority is the source of truth. This is only another form of the primacy of the emotional over the rational sphere of consciousness, and in this sense there exists an interrelation between the weak impulse to cognition and the curtailed ego-consciousness of primitive man.

CHAPTER II

THE SOCIAL INTERPRETATION OF NATURE

7. ANIMISM AS PERSONALISTIC APPERCEPTION OF NATURE

SINCE Tylor's famous investigations into primitive culture, one is accustomed to term primitive man's interpretation of nature as "animism," because early men imagine nature as inhabited by "spirits," as "animated."

One is in the habit of characterizing the animistic view as anthropomorphic; and one sees in this belief the tendency to personify, which is rightly considered one of the oldest elements of the human mind.[1] It is not quite correct, however, to speak of "personification" in connection with primitive man, for the personification of an object presupposes that the object is first perceived as such, i.e., as a thing and not as a person, and that the thing is only later personified.[2] Primitive man, it should be noted, comprehends reality immediately in the personal category. Shortland says of the Maori: "The Maori has a very limited notion of the abstract. All his ideas naturally take a concrete form. This inaptitude to conceive any abstract notions was, it is believed, the early mental condition of man. Hence the Powers of Nature were regarded by him as concrete objects, and were consequently designated as persons."[3] Crawley succinctly remarks: "Primitive man has only one mode of thought, one mode of expression, one part of speech, the personal."[4] It is proper, therefore, to speak of a personalistic view, or of personalistic thinking, but not of personification. Further, if one regards the personification of nature in the animistic view as a process by which primitive man projects his own personality upon the external world,[5] it is wrong to state that he interprets the events of nature according to an ego-analogy. Such a point of view presupposes a highly developed ego-consciousness in primitive man. And, indeed, one connects the "anthropomorphic" view of nature of early man with his alleged "egocentric" attitude.[6]

Possibly this conception of personification as the "projection of the ego" may have entailed the idea of "egocentricity" of primitive man, which but little consonants with the facts. The savage cannot project his ego upon the external world because he has not yet discovered his ego. He still lacks any real ego-consciousness, or any consciousness of

24

his own individuality as an entity, independent of his group. If, for instance, a primitive believes in the existence of ghosts, it is not necessarily his own soul continuing his existence after death of which he is thinking: it is rather the death soul of others. His own life after death is to him something unreal;[7] he simply does not imagine his own life after death. The Indians of Guiana believe, according to E. F. im Thurn, that

a person may pass his spirit into a body not his own. Yet a reservation must be here made. No Indian, unless, possibly, a *peaiman* [magician], believes that he himself is able at will thus to pass his spirit into another body, but he does believe that other men have this power. The transmission of the spirit seems to him something uncanny, something only to be done voluntarily. . . . . The Indian is never himself conscious of sending his spirit into another body—though, by the way, such cases of self-deception have been noted from other parts of the world—and he therefore believes that he has not the power; but on the other hand he sees certain animals which he has reason to believe are men in disguise, and therefore, knowing how loosely spirits are attached to bodies, he supposes that other men know how to acquire the power, denied to him, of transmitting their spirits into what bodies they will.[8]

It is hardly possible, therefore, that primitive man should interpret the phenomena of nature according to the analogy of the ego. Certainly he projects phenomena of his psychic life upon the external world: he regards dreams as real occurrences; and he does not relate his emotions to himself but imagines a different being than himself as their subject. He does so because he has as yet no ego-consciousness. Therefore, it is not his ego which he projects upon nature when he interprets it personalistically.[9]

8. PRIMITIVE MAN'S CAPACITY OF DIFFERENTIATION

This personalistic interpretation of nature, which represents the nucleus of what is called "animism,"[10] rests upon a fact which, observed by Westermann among the Kpelle, is typical of primitive man.

Men, living or dead, demons, animals, plants, and inanimate objects are, in the opinion of the Kpelle, essentially the same, and exist under similar conditions; they can in the same way influence man towards good and evil. For all of them he entertains similar feelings of cautious timidity and defends himself against them by the same means.

This distinguished observer says that it would be

a transfer of European ideas, should one impute to the Kpelle the belief that all these phenomena from man down to a piece of wood are "animated," or have even a "soul substance." Not even man has a soul. The question of what makes an object live never arises in a Kpelle's mind. He is satisfied in knowing simply that objects exist, he judges them according to their effect upon himself, and this has convinced him that essentially they are all the same, because all can be either harmful or useful to him; on the other hand he can influence them because they are all similar to him.[11]

E. F. im Thurn, describing the mentality of the Indians in Guiana, comes to a similar result. He points out that the Indian does not see

any sharp line of distinction, such as we see, between man and other animals, between one kind of animal and another, or between animals—man included—and inanimate objects. On the contrary, to the Indian, all objects, animate and inanimate, seem exactly of the same nature except that they differ in the accident of bodily form. . . . . It is, therefore, most important to realise both how comparatively small really is the difference between men in a state of savagery and other animals, and how completely even such difference as exists escapes the notice of savage men.[12]

The decisive point of these comments is that primitive man regards all things which arouse his attention as homogeneous; unlike civilized man, he does not differentiate them according to various points of view.[13] To be exact, the primitive individual does not regard these objects of his cognition as homogeneous with himself, for which he lacks the necessary ego-consciousness, but he does consider them homogeneous with his kinsmen. Primitive man regards animals, plants, and inanimate objects, in so far as they are in some way important to him, as essentially similar to the men with whom he lives and whom he knows from direct experience. Since primitive man does not discern an essential difference between man and animal, it is not as surprising as it might appear that Australian natives, when they first saw white men riding horseback, believed that the horses were the mothers of the men, inasmuch as among them children are carried on their mothers' backs; nor is it astonishing that they considered the pack buffaloes as white men's wives, because with them luggage is carried by their wives.[14] In the report of his voyage along the African shore in 1455 Aluise de Cada Mosto[15] relates that the natives considered the first bagpipe which they saw to be an animal. They also regarded the ship as a living being; the two loopholes in the stern were interpreted as its eyes, by which it found its way on the sea.

According to a report of the Portuguese major Monteiro,[16] the Muembas, a South African tribe, took the major's donkey, an animal they had never before seen, to be a being endowed with reason and the capacity of speaking. They invited the animal's opinions, and everything it did was interpreted in the light of human behavior. "The Cuna Indians," says E. Nordenskiöld, "do not believe in the Christian distinction between men and animals. . . . . They never say an animal has been transmuted into a man, for the animal is already a man in a beast's shape."[17]

Edwin James describes a hunting of bison among the Omaha Indians as follows: "On coming in sight of the herd, the hunters talk kindly to their horses, applying to them the endearing names of father, brother, uncle etc.; they petition them not to fear the bisons, but to run well, and keep close to them, but at the same time to avoid being gored."[18]

The missionary John Heckewelder writes:

I have often reflected on the curious connexion which appears to subsist in the mind of an Indian between man and the brute creation, and found much matter in it for curious observation. Although they consider themselves superior to all other animals and are very proud of that superiority; although they believe that the beasts of the forest, the birds of the air, and the fishes of the waters, were created by the Almighty Being for the use of man; yet it seems as if they ascribe the difference between themselves and the brute kind, and the dominion which they have over them, more to their superior bodily strength and dexterity than to their immortal souls. All beings endowed by the Creator with the power of volition and self-motion, they view in a manner as a great society of which they are the head, whom they are appointed, indeed, to govern, but between whom and themselves intimate ties of connexion and relationship may exist, or at least, did exist in the beginning of time. They are, in fact, according to their opinions, only the first among equals, the legitimate hereditary sovereigns of the whole animated race, of which they are themselves a constituent part. Hence, in their languages, those inflections of their nouns which we call *genders*, are not, as with us, descriptive of the *masculine* and *feminine* species, but of the *animate* and *inanimate* kinds. Indeed, they go so far as to include trees and plants within the first of these descriptions. All animated nature, in whatever degree, is in their eyes a great whole, from which they have not yet ventured to separate themselves. They do not exclude other animals from their world of spirits, the place to which they expect to go after death. . . . .

I have already observed that the Indian includes all savage beasts within the number of his *enemies*. This is by no means a metaphorical or figurative expression, but is used in a literal sense, as will appear from what I am going to relate.—A Delaware hunter once shot a huge bear and broke its back bone. The animal fell and set up a most plaintive cry, something like that of the panther when he is hungry. The hunter, instead of giving him another shot, stood up close to him, and addressed him in these words: "Hark ye! bear; you are a coward, and no warrior as you pretend to be. Were you a warrior, you would shew it by your firmness and not cry and whimper like an old woman. You know, bear, that our tribes are at war with each other, and that yours was the aggressor. You have found the Indians too powerful for you, and you have gone sneaking about in the woods, stealing their hogs; perhaps at this time you have hog's flesh in your belly. Had you conquered me, I would have borne it with courage and died like a brave warrior; but you, bear, sit here and cry, and disgrace your tribe by your cowardly conduct." I was present at the delivery of this curious invective; when the hunter had despatched the bear, I asked him how he thought that poor animal could understand what he said to it? "Oh!" said he in answer, "the bear understood me very well; did you not observe how *ashamed* he looked while I was upbraiding him?"—Another time I witnessed a similar scene between the falls of the Ohio and the river Wabash. A young white man, named *William Wells*, who had been when a boy taken prisoner by a tribe of the Wabash Indians, by whom he was brought up, and had imbibed all their notions, had so wounded a large bear that he could not move from the spot, and the animal cried piteously like the one I have just mentioned. The young man went up to him, and with seemingly great earnestness, addressed him in the Wabash language, now and then giving him a slight stroke on the nose with his ram-rod. I asked him, when he had done, what he had been saying to this bear? "I have," said he, "upbraided him for acting the part of a coward; I told him that he knew the fortune of war, that one or the other of us must have fallen; that it was his fate to be conquered, and he ought to die like a man, like a hero, and not like an old woman; that if the case had been reversed, and I had fallen into the power of my *enemy*, I would not have disgraced my nation as he did, but would have died with firmness and courage, as becomes a true warrior."[19]

The idea of the homogeneity of man and animals, plants, and other natural objects is particularly supported by the belief, which exists among the Marind-anim for instance, that men, like everything else in the world, were created by the mythical ancestors, the *dema*. Especially did the *dema* transform themselves into phenomena perceptible by the senses. Thus all things—men, animals, plants, animated objects, even implements made by men—are not only related to each other through the same descent but are more or less images of the *dema* which are perceived in human shape and are regarded not only as the creators but also as the prototypes of all reality. "Like animals and plants, tools also trace their origin to the ancestors, i.e., they were formerly human beings. Therefore human form, or parts of the human face can still be recognized in them." So, for example, the three seed holes of the coconut are the eyes and mouth of the *dema*.[20] Since the Marind-anim perceives in things the prototype of their creator, he decorates his tools with eye and nose ornaments and even with whole faces. The Maori believes that not only men but also animals, plants, and objects, which in our opinion are inanimate, have souls; for all things derive from a common source, the parental pair, Rangi and Papa. For the Maori, therefore, all things are homogeneous.

All things possess a *wairua* (soul or spirit), each after the manner of its kind. There is but one parent of all things, one god of all things, one lord of all things, one soul of all things. . . . . Therefore all things are one. . . . . The Maori personified all things, he believed all things to be related to each other, to be offspring of the same parents.[21]

Therefore the Maori regards a forest as a community of relatives, because the trees are beings of similar origin.

When the Maori entered a forest he felt that he was among his own kindred, for had not trees and man a common origin, both being the offspring of Tane [the son of the parental pair]? . . . . Thus, when the Maori wished to fell a tree wherefrom to fashion a canoe or house timbers, for two reasons he was compelled to perform a placatory rite ere he could slay one of the offspring of Tane. He saw in the majestic trees living creatures of an elder branch of the great family.[22]

And he considers mountains in the same way. In order to secure peace between two tribes, the daughter of one chieftain was married to the son of the other; at the same time, two mountains, selected as representatives of the tribes, were also married.

The Maori folk tell of weird happenings on the mist-laden days of long ago, when mountains were endowed with powers of speech and locomotion. Thus we hear of the great company of mountains that formerly stood in the Taupo district, and of the dissensions that arose among them, whereby they became separated, some moving to other parts. Sexual jealousy seems to have been the cause of the quarrel, which resulted in a dispersal of the mountain folk, some of whom . . . . remained at the old home.[23]

According to Gusinde,[24] the Selknam believe that their ancestors are not dead but are transformed into objects of nature. Therefore, nature seems to them inhabited by their ancestors.[25] "A group of hills is regarded as family, the highest elevation being its head." A certain mountain range is said

formerly to have been a woman who lived there with her three sons. The smaller natural object is considered the child or the younger relative of a larger object of the same kind. The same is said of two neighboring stars. . . . . The changes of wind and weather are the restless struggles of two eternal foes; sun and moon (regarded as husband and wife who had a quarrel) go on pursuing one another and the changes of the moon-woman are caused by her irreconcilable hatred of the inhabitants of the earth.[26]

The notion of the universal animation of nature is here apparently no more than primitive man's belief that nature is inhabited by personal beings, namely, his ancestors.

9. Tu-Analogy, Not Ego-Analogy, the Basis of Primitive Man's View of the World

Since primitive man considers animals, plants, and inanimate objects homogeneous with his tribesmen, he behaves in the same manner toward the things of nature as toward his fellow-men. Believing that both act according to identical principles, he thinks he must treat them as the rules of social behavior prescribe. He assumes on their part the same understanding of his utterances which his kinsmen possess; therefore he believes himself in a position to make himself understood by them as by his fellows, since they react to his behavior just as he reacts to theirs.[27] Not according to the analogy of his ego, but according to the analogy of the tu, which he has experienced earlier, does primitive man, like the child, conceive the world. Long before he tries to perceive nature as such, he becomes more or less aware, at first through his relation to his mother, then to his father, chieftain, mates, and enemies, of the principles of social behavior and of the social relations which directly affect him. Consequently, he interprets his environment in terms of social categories; for civilized man, however, the environment has assumed a nonsocial character; he makes a distinction between nature and society.

If social relations, such as kinship, are based on physiological facts, primitive man does not see the "natural" but only the social element of the phenomenon. Hartland characterizes the primitive idea of kinship as follows: "Kinship is a sociological term. It is not synonymous with blood-relationship; it does not express a physiological fact."[28] And Gomme writes with reference to some primitive tribes:

> The neglect of maternal and paternal kinship respectively in these two cases is obvious. . . . . Physical motherhood or fatherhood is nothing to these people, and one must learn to understand that there is wide difference between the mere physical fact of having a mother and father, and the political fact of using this kinship for social organization. Savages who have not learnt the political significance have but the scantiest appreciation of the physical fact. The Australians, for instance, have no term to express the relationship between mother and child. This is because the physical fact is of no significance, and not because of the meagreness of the language.[29]

Hence the fact that adoption is very frequent among primitive peoples and that adopted children are treated by their foster-parents in exactly the same way as their own children.[30] With reference to adoption among the Andaman Islanders, E. H. Man writes:

> It is said to be of rare occurrence to find any child above six or seven years of age residing with its parents, and this because it is considered a compliment and also a mark of friendship for a married man, after paying a visit, to ask his hosts to allow him to adopt one of their children.[31]

The "natural" relationship is out of consideration.

Since kinship is a social, not a "natural," relation, it cannot only be artificially established—by adoption, for example—but can also be artificially annulled. This is the meaning of so-called "cutting ekar," a custom observed among the Fanti of the Gold Coast. Sarbah writes:

> Cutting Ekar is a particular mode of disowning any one's blood relation. When a man desires to disown a blood relative, he brings him before the elders of his town or village, and in their presence, as well as in the presence of the other members of his family, an ekar is cut in twain, and saying clearly, "We are now divided," he takes

one-half and the disowned the other half. As soon as this ceremony is completed, the two persons have no more share or portion in the property of each other. Where a man is disowned, it affects him alone; but in the case of a woman, her issue is included, for the saying is, the children follow the mother's condition.[31a]

10. Actual Behavior of Early Man toward Objects of Nature

Primitive man's interpretation of nature in terms of social categories manifests itself by the way he actually behaves toward the objects and events of nature. Referring to the Kpelle (Liberia), Westermann writes:

In order to get rid of a devastating locust swarm they seize a few locusts and try by kind words to persuade them to go away. They say to them: "Now return to your homes, remember us to your people, and leave us alone for there is nothing more for you to eat here." . . . . Just as an encouraging and parrying word has its effect on men and animals, so it also affects things. Before a war they request their arrows and spears not to miss their mark. When burning bush-wood they address the fire with words and corresponding gestures: "Forward, fire, come on, blaze fiercely!" Under their totem plants they place cotton for clothing. Just like men and animals, objects are also "killed." A path not used for a long time, does not become overgrown but "dies."[32]

Labouret[33] writes that, if among the natives of Lobi a woman finds a grain of gold, she carries it home in a lump of clay made into a small vase.

Her relatives take the metal out, put it into another receiver, pour some indigenous liquid salt into it, go behind the house, collect some damp earth which they use in order to stop it up . . . . , dig a hole near the dunghill, put the pot inside and close up the hole. They say that this gold is a living thing; it must be made to die, and this is why they urine on it. At the end of a year, the gold is dead.

The gold may not be sold and the compensation not used before great sacrifices have been offered. "This gold is a living being; if a person takes hold of it and does not do what is due, e.g., sells it or uses the amount realized from it, it kills the man."

Le Roy relates:

Each time the Negrillos establish a new encampment, after clearing the place, they begin by making a fire on which each one puts a branch. If everything passes without incident, it means that the encampment is good; but if, in this first fire, a twig doubles up, it means that the earth protests and that it is futile to camp there: the place is at once abandoned and they go further on.[34]

Nature talks to men and warns them, and they act accordingly. Whenever the Sakai go out in search of the valuable camphor wood, "they must not state," writes Schebesta, "what their intention is, rather they say: We are going to the forest in order to play." The Jakudes even use a secret language the times they go to find camphor. Schebesta says: "Only through cunning may one get hold of camphor."[35] The Maori also believe that, before catching an animal or finding a plant, one may not utter its name, since the object thus sought may discover one's intention and withdraw.[36] If a Toradja (Celebes) wishes to top a tree, in order to acquire palm oil, he behaves toward the tree like a suitor. He speaks to the tree, asks for its hand, and embraces it violently.[37] Among various peoples the custom has been observed of a person—man or woman—marrying a tree.[38] Whether this is done merely for show or for magical purposes, it shows, nevertheless, the complete social attitude of primitive man toward things of nature.

In this respect R. F. Fortune's reports about the natives of Dobu are rather remarkable.[39] They regard the yam plants which are important for nourishment as human beings; they see in them their transformed ancestors. Accordingly, they deal with the yams, planted by them, as with men. They address them with incantations, which are simply requests expressing the desire that the plants may flourish. Fortune writes of these incantations: "In its particular application it is most strongly believed that yams will not grow, however well the soil is prepared and cared for, without the due performance of the long drawn-out ritual of gardening incantations." The natives believe that the yams are able at night to leave the gardens in which they are planted. In such incantations they ask the plants not to do this. Fortune says:

If then we come upon a ritual addressed to seed yams, let it not be supposed that a man is muttering a form of words to yams merely. He is addressing a Personal Being as truly as we are when we address God. For the yams are personal beings in metamorphized form. If we come upon a ritual addressed to a canoe-lashing creeper let it not be thought that a man is muttering a form of words to a bush creeper merely. The bush creeper is a personal being in metamorphized form.

These spells are murmured to the plants in a low voice. This is the native's explanation:

The yams hear. They say among themselves "this is our language—not loud like everyday talk." You must understand that yams are persons. . . . . If we call aloud the yams say "how is this—are they fighting among themselves." But when we charm softly they listen to our speech attentively. They grow big for our calling on them.

Fortune wanted to put the natives to a test to see whether they really believed the yams were personal beings; thereupon he received the following firm reply from one of them: "Yams are persons, with ears. If we charm they hear." And Fortune adds:

Next day he showed me the ears, organs of hearing, the several tendril buds about the growing point of the vine. The growing point buds are no more ears than an ear of corn is an organ of hearing. In Dobu the ears of the vine are most literally organs of hearing, however.

Fortune then goes on: "At a rite with burning green leaves and so producing a cloud of smoke, the charmer's husband said: 'The yams see it. They snuff it in to get its odour. They forsake the *kebudi* (stick for the climbing tendrils), climb over it, and trail down again.' " Between yam plants and men there exists a relationship comparable to that between a lord and his retainers. To a certain descendant of a man belongs a certain descendant of a yam plant.

Each *susu* family line [*susu*—the unit of a man, his sister, and his sister's children] has its own line of seed. It is pictured that one human family line has its one seed family line that will grow for it. But that seed line will not grow for a stranger family line; just as if the retainers of one house will work for the descendants of the blood of that house, but not for another house, the retainers and their descendants after them. Seed yams are not inherited outside the *susu* or given away outside the *susu*—this fact assumes in native expression an aspect of a human line of descent that is served and can be served only by one certain yam line of descent—the faithful retainers of the human line, faithless to other family lines.

Especially characteristic in this respect are the following statements:

The word *tomot* . . . . is the only word that covers man, woman, and child, irrespective of age or sex. It also connotes native as opposed to belonging to the white man when used adjectivally. This latter usage contains the prevalent idea that the white man is "another kind," not really a human person in the native sense, but a being with different qualities from the native. The Dobuan will class yams with his own people as personal beings, but he excludes white men.

Of the Selknam, who, as already mentioned, see in their natural surroundings their transformed ancestors, Gusinde writes:

Their idea of the universal animation of nature manifests itself by the increased awe which is rendered to all ancestors in their present forms. The negative side of this awe appears in the avoidance of depreciative judgments and contemptuous speech. Near those rocks or lagoons, which are known to them as ancestors, no one would dare say anything detrimental or even make conversational reference to them. . . . . These ancestors repay the impertinent babbler onerously with bad weather, or storm, with rain or snow. . . . . It is considered improper to talk in the presence of a visitor detrimentally about the weather of that visitor's country. For every one reckons himself one of the family of the ancestors of this or that region, and thus believes himself related to the wind and weather, rain and clouds, fog and thunderstorms which assemble around the mountains of his own country. Hence the visitor would be offended by contemptuous reference to his fore-fathers (the weather of his home-land), and would warn of their speedy revenge.[40]

Swanton[41] reports of the Tlingit Indians that they try to influence all objects of nature, such as the sun, moon, wind, lakes, mountains, glaciers, hot springs, the trees which they fell, etc., by addressing them as reasonable beings and asking them for good fortune. Eating certain mussels makes one ill; but, if one asks the mussels properly, one may avoid the bad effect. The Bushmen regard rain as a human being. They distinguish between a female, mild rain, and a male, heavy rain. So they believe they must treat rain like they treat man. One can arouse its anger, appease it, frighten it away, allure it—all these things can be accomplished by the same means with which an analogous behavior on the part of a man is induced.[42] In the *Jesuit Relations* of 1637 we read: "Father Buteux asked a savage (Montagnet Indian) why they fixed their javelins point upward. He replied that, as the thunder had intelligence, it would, upon seeing these naked javelins, turn aside and would be very careful not to come near their cabins."[43] Hollis reports in his book on the Nandi: "During a heavy thunderstorm, the Toiyoi seize an axe, and having rubbed it in the ashes of the fire, throw it outside the hut, exclaiming at the same time: Toiyoi *or* thunder, be silent in our town.[44] Nieuwenhuis writes:

Not knowing the real cause of thunder, lightning, rain, and wind, the Bahau regard them as expressions of beings or spirits, which, although more powerful than themselves, nevertheless feel pleasure and pain in the same way as man. Thus the spirits may be favorably impressed by presents and sacrifices of living or dead objects of value; but they can also be frightened away by those same things which arouse abhorrence and fear in man. I observed several times how the son of Kwing Irang, the chieftain of the Mahakam Kajan, rushed out of the house in the midst of a heavy storm. In order strongly to impress, and at the same time appease the spirits, he killed with his sword the first animal that crossed his path, once a pig, another time a chicken. I also saw how a man, holding in one hand a drawn sword and in the other a skull, dashed out of his house in order to put the storm spirit to flight. By shouting the Bahau also try to chase away wind and rain spirits; if this does not work, they place a skull as a deterrent in front of their houses. Once on a journey with the Mendalam Kajan, when we were caught by a violent thunderstorm and heavy claps of thunder frightened us, the Kajan drew their swords half from the sheaths in order to drive away the powerful spirits.[45]

Aelian writes of the Celts that "many of them await the overflowing sea, some throwing themselves armed into the waves and receiving their onset with drawn swords and threatening spears, just as if they could scare back or wound them."[46] Hartland, who quotes this passage, remarks rightly: "The sea and the waves were looked upon as personal beings with whom it was possible literally to fight, and who

might even be overcome."[47] It is a striking example of social interpretation of nature.

Karsten found the same attitude among the Jibaro Indians: "During violent thunderstorms, the Jibaro Indians are seen brandishing
their lances against the sky, springing in the air, shouting and challeng-
ing their invisible supernatural assailants with the same words as they
use in defying their natural enemies: 'Come on, we are ready to receive you!' "[48] Of the Abipones, Dobrizhoffer[49] reports: "When a
whirlwind drives the dust round in a circle, the women throw ashes in
its way, that it may be satisfied with that food, and may turn in some
other direction. But if the wind rushes into any house with that im-
petuous whirling, they are certain that one of the inhabitants will die
soon." Further: ". . . . to defend their dear planet from those aerial
mastiffs [dogs with which the air abounds], they send a shower of
arrows up into the sky, amid loud vociferations, at the time of the
eclipse."

Molina writes, in his *History of Chili*, of the aborigines of this country:

Not a storm happens upon the Andes or the ocean, which they do not ascribe to
a battle between the souls of their fellow countrymen and those of the Spaniards; they
say that the roaring of the wind is the trampling of their horses, the noise of the
thunder that of their drums, and the flashes of lightning the fire of the artillery. If the
storm takes its course towards the Spanish territory, they affirm that their spirits have
put to flight those of the Spaniards, and exclaim, triumphantly, *Inavimen, inavimen,
puen, laguvimen!* Pursue them, friends, pursue them, kill them! If the contrary happens, they are greatly afflicted, and call out in consternation, *?avulumen, puen, namuntu-
men!* Courage, friends, be firm![50]

"In Sumatra," records Tylor, "we have the comparatively scientific notion that an eclipse has to do with the action of the Sun and
Moon on one another, and, accordingly, they make a loud noise with
sounding instruments to prevent the one from devouring the other."[51]
Termer reports:

During earthquakes the Guaimi-Indians observe a peculiar custom which was
observed by Adrian de Santo Tomas. About midnight an earthquake disquieted, and
even angered, the Indians accompanying the padre. They immediately seized their
weapons and aimed them heavenwards. Upon the padre's inquiry into the meaning
of their action, the natives replied that the god Noncomala wanted to kill the earth and
therefore they came to their mother's rescue. Indeed, she would have been destroyed
long ago, if they had not always protected her on such occasions.[52]

Similarly, Wallace writes of the Uaupes Indians: "When it thunders
they say the 'Yurupari' [Great Spirit] is angry, and their idea of nat-

ural death is that the 'Yurupari' kills them. At an eclipse they believe that this bad spirit is killing the moon, and they make all the noise they can to frighten him away."[53] Grubb points out with respect to the Lenguan Indians: "On a cloudy day, when the sun has been obscured for some time, an old man is sometimes seen to take a firebrand and hold it up to the sun, apparently with the intention of encouraging the luminary to show his face again."[54]

The Kurnai, an Australian tribe, regard the South Pole light as a fire that has been lighted by a god in heaven. Therefore, as soon as they see it, they fear it may leap over to the earth and spread here. To prevent this they seek to drive away the fire by using the dried-up hand of a dead person, in which they suppose there is great strength. At the same time they shout: "Send it away, do not let it burn us up."[55] If it lightens, the Bushman glares at the lightning, thereby hoping to keep it at a distance. Meinhof interprets this action thus: "The Bushman believes the power of his glance is so great that the lightning shrinks back."[56] This same "look of strength" the Bushman in his daily life occasionally directs at his fellows; hence he knows its effectiveness. Bushmen beg the stars, especially the brightly shining Canopus, for power to wander without hunger and to reach their goal as safely as the stars.

To demonstrate that "physical nature," as we call it, is also known to primitive man, Marett writes:

What we call "physical nature" may very well be "nature" also to the savage in most of its normal aspects; yet its more startling manifestations, thunderstorms, eclipses, eruptions, and the like, are eminently calculated to awake in him an awe that I believe to be specifically religious both in its essence and in its fruits, whether animism have, or have not, succeeded in imposing its distinctive colour upon it. Thus, when a thunderstorm is seen approaching in South Africa, a Kaffir village, led by its medicine-man, will rush to the nearest hill and yell at the hurricane to divert it from its course.[57]

This example, however, illustrates the contrary of what Marett wants to prove. The Kaffirs treat the thunderstorm not as a natural phenomenon but as a social event, i.e., as a person socially related to other persons. They attempt to exert influence upon his will in the very manner which has proved effective in their social life. The storm, or rather the personal being which they see in it, stands in the same relation to them as any single member of their society. Even more significant is another example cited by Marett:

When a glacier in Alaska threatened to swallow up a valuable fishing stream, two slaves were killed in order to bring it to a standstill. Here the advanced character of the propitiatory rite probably presumes acquaintance with some form of the animistic theory. It may very well be, however, that sacrifice is here resorted to as a general religious panacea, without involving any distinct recognition of a particular glacier spirit.[58]

That the natives believe in a special "spirit" of a glacier is perhaps not sure, although highly probable. But undoubtedly they believe that the glacier is either a personal being itself or at least under the control of a personal being; this being understands their sacrifices and acts, therefore, just as a man who lives in a society with other men and finds himself induced by the conduct of others, for some reason agreeable to him, to act favorably toward them. Obviously, it is the law of retribution which determines the behavior of men toward the glacier. Unimportant in this connection is the meaning of the sacrifice, especially whether it is to be interpreted as a kind of substitutive punishment through which the conduct of the glacier, regarded as the primary punishment, is to be averted. The social character of the interpretation of nature, however, is beyond doubt.

11. Primitive Magic

A great part of what ethnologists call "magic" consists in nothing but this social interpretation of nature. Skeat writes in his work *Malay Magic:*

When the wind fails and the sails of a boat are flapping . . . . a Selangor magician would not unfrequently summon the wind in the following terms:

Come hither, Sir, come hither, my Lord,
Let down your locks so long and flowing.

And if the wind is contrary, he would say:

Veer round, Wind, a needle or twain (of the compass),
A needle to (let me fetch) *Kapar.*
. . . .
Let me repair to *Klang* for the morning meal
And *Langat* for the evening bathe.[59]

("Kapar," "Klang," and "Langat" are the names of some places.) The magician considers the wind simply as a personal being and consequently treats him as such.

As weather-magic are classified the efforts of the Takelma Indians to effect a cessation of snowing; they address the snow as follows: "Hitherwards drive the elks, the black-necked ones, that dwell back of the mountain, in dark places under the trees!"[60] Inasmuch as the Takelmas believe the snow is hostile to man, they request it to go on falling, thereby chasing the stags from the mountains, and thus aiding man more than inconveniencing him. Consequently, they expect the snow, their enemy who reasons as they do, to stop falling. Because primitive man regards natural events as the actions of personal beings, he thinks himself able, even though they are more powerful than he, to deceive them, just as he can deceive his fellow-men. In this whole procedure, then, from his viewpoint there is nothing "magic" or "supernatural." Nor is the behavior of the Selknam, which is termed "weather-charm," actually that at all; Gusinde[61] pictures their conduct in this manner: When the natives have too long been prevented by rain from going hunting or continuing their festivities, they take glowing logs, wave them about in the air, "as if fighting," and shout furiously to the bad weather:

When will you finally go away, bad rain?—Do, at last, go away, wicked rain!—Go to another place, impudent rain!—When will good weather come?—You, good weather, why do you put up with the rain so long?—When will you finally come, good weather?—Be ashamed of yourself, bad rain, and at last go away!

Just as the so-called "weather-charm" of the Selknam is not "magical," so the behavior of the rain-maker among the natives of Loango has no "magic" character. Pechuel-Lösche describes his manipulations as follows:

He [the rain-maker] jumps . . . . towards the approaching clouds and repels them with a compelling gesture, stretching out his arms, and swinging them with outspread fingers; he tramples with his feet and stirs up dust to the clouds, or even throws it with his hands, murmuring or hissing all the while.[62]

The same author mentions the poison test, customary among these natives as well as among many other peoples, through which the guilt of a person accused of a crime, especially of witchcraft, may be proved. The natives imagine the effect of the poison in the following way: In the *Ndodschi* [the witch or the wizard] there is evil. The poison looks for the evil, destroys it, and kills thereby the *Ndodschi*. Where there is no evil, poison has no effect.[63] Poison thus acts like an intelligent human being. Only it knows more than men, for it knows the culprit. A poison test made on a sorcerer among natives of the Congo is outlined by Nassau: "The decoction itself is supposed to have almost sentience—an ability to follow, in the various organs of the body, like a policeman, and detect and destroy the witch-spirit supposed to be lurking about."[64] Among the East African Safwa, if a person has to undergo a poison test to defend himself against the charge of sorcery, he says to the poison which he has taken and which he must vomit out

to prove his innocence: "*Mwamfi*"—that is the poisoned potion—
"come out so that I may emerge really white and purified."[65]

So-called "harm-magic" consists frequently in the fact that a substance, especially poison, is induced to kill a certain person, and only
that person. According to A. L. Kitching,[66] the chieftain Awin of
Patiko (Anglo-Egyptian Sudan) died after a meal which he shared
with several others. It was believed an enemy had killed him with a
poisoned chicken. But the others had also eaten the same chicken
without sustaining any ill effects. The "magician," it appears, had requested the poison to kill only the chieftain Awin; and, indeed, the
poison complied with his request. What is commonly termed "death-
magic" operates in much the same way: poison is strewn upon the
threshold of the enemy's house and is requested to kill only the enemy
himself when he should step across his doorstep; all others are im-
mune. C. R. Lagae, who reports such a procedure among the Azande,
states: "The drug does not at all act according to its chemical propensities. The action is purely magical, affecting only the individual
against whom it is directed."[67] The "magical" element of this procedure, however, consists only in the fact that the drug behaves, according to primitive man's belief, like a human being who uses his capacities as he or others may wish.

The Ekoi believe in trees with "magical" powers; at least that is
how R. H. Lowie[68] interprets their customs. If an Ekoi wishes to take
revenge on an enemy, he addresses a prayer to such a tree, gives it a
present, and calls out the name of the victim. The tree then complies
with the request by seizing the enemy's child and inclosing it within its
trunk. This behavior is a direct consequence of the social interpretation of nature. The natural object—in this case a tree—is regarded as
a manlike being, but endowed with superhuman powers, with whom—
and this is decisive—one can enter into social relations corresponding
to the status of the superior being.

If primitive man sees in the natural object, or behind it, a superhuman being, he frequently expresses the wish, which he expects to be
fulfilled by that being, not in everyday language but in a special sign-
language corresponding to the particular character of the superhuman
being. He demonstrates mimically, graphically, or otherwise visibly
what he requests from the superhuman authority. Hunting dances,
cave paintings, activities such as piercing or burning a doll representing the enemy, and especially the characteristic rites of so-called "rain-
making," as well as other procedures labeled "magic," are nothing

but requests to superhuman authorities in sign-language, a behavior
which in primitive man's opinion is neither "magical" nor "mystical,"
i.e., not supernatural but the "natural" consequence of his social interpretation of nature.[69]

12. SIGNIFICANCE OF THE SOUL BELIEF FOR PRIMITIVE MAN'S INTERPRETATION OF NATURE

The actual behavior of primitive man toward nature is of primary
importance if one wishes to "understand" his view of the world; of less
importance are the ideas which he himself forms of nature, his own
"theory," which, considering the weakness of the rational component
of his mind, must always be vague and contradictory. It is especially
of no importance whether primitive man is himself conscious of interpreting nature personalistically or whether he would say he personifies
nature. The distinction between person and thing is still foreign to
him. Therefore, it makes no difference whether or not primitive man
believes that nature is "animated."

The modern concept of soul and its presupposition, namely, the distinction between material and spiritual substance, becomes familiar to
man only after he has "personified" nature for some time. Nonetheless, we may term primitive man's view of the world "animistic." For
his interpretation of nature, which results from his actual behavior toward it and which is personalistical in our sense, is an essential pre-
requisite to the idea of the "animation" of nature. At first, primitive
man, because of the poverty of his reason, may interpret his environment in analogy with his earliest and most impressive experience,
namely, the relationship to his fellow-man; and he may even consider
animals, plants, and inanimate objects, which are of use or harm as
friends or enemies within the group, equally with them. But gradually, by means of his sharp senses, he must discover the external difference between men and other beings, especially inanimate objects. If
he then sticks to his original personalistic apperception, it is because a
powerful ideology urges him in that direction. An animal, a tree, a
river, etc., is obviously no human being. If these things behave as human beings, then an invisible man must reside in them. This is presumably the point where the originally sociomorphic (not anthropomorphic) interpretation of nature concurs with the belief in the existence of a death soul, which may assume any form; consequently, anything is or may be the dead. Inasmuch as natural events are considered as actions of personal beings, superior to men, inasmuch as super-

human authorities are feared and respected in nature, and inasmuch as, for instance in "magic," their help is invoked in order to effect what exceeds man's strength, then one may assume that, at least originally, these beings were the souls of the dead, imagined by primitive man as endowed with superhuman powers. As to the question of the origin of the primitive view of nature, one is naturally confined to hypotheses, the most plausible of which is still that one which brings animism, the personalistic-social interpretation of nature, into relationship with belief in the soul of the dead; indeed, this hypothesis is more compatible with the material given than any other.

13. No Idea of "Impersonal Forces"

Thus, on the one hand, it is incorrect to regard the personification, upon which the animistic view of nature rests, as an ego-projection of primitive man and hence to declare him "egocentric," i.e., attribute to him an ego-consciousness which, in fact, he lacks; and so, on the other hand, it is an almost inconceivable error to identify this lack of ego-consciousness of primitive man with the lack of any category of personality in primitive thinking. Granted that in the initial stages of mental development man lacks ego-consciousness; on that basis, however, it is wrong either to suppose that he is unable to comprehend harmful and useful events of nature as actions of personal beings or to believe that he regards such events merely as manifestations of objective impersonal forces. For the concept of impersonal force, a specific element in causal thinking and one of the latest achievements of scientific abstraction, presupposes a much higher stage of mental development than that in which the consciousness of one's own ego has not even been achieved.[70]

Just this lack of ego-consciousness and the all-pervading social character of his thinking and feeling are the reasons why primitive man interprets nature not like civilized man, according to the law of causality, as a mechanism of objective, impersonal "forces," but according to social categories, as a manifestation of subjective, personal "powers." He conceives natural events, even those which he himself brings about, as actions and reactions analogous to those within human society. It is not—as is sometimes suggested—the idea of "personal causality"[71] which influences primitive man in his interpretation of nature; it is something entirely different from causality. Certainly primitive thinking includes concepts of creation and production; myths deal frequently with the problems of creation. These concepts, however, have nothing to do with the idea of causality as an objective connection between phenomena determined by laws of nature. The notion which primitive man has about the mythical creator, writes Brinton,[72]

is that of the moulder or manufacturer, as the potter makes his pots, the shoemaker his shoes. This is the conception which underlies many myths of the Creator, as is shown by the names he bears. Thus the Australians called him *Baiame*, "the cutter out," as one who cuts out a sandal from a skin, or a figure from bark. The Maya Indians used the term *Patol*, from the verb *pat*, to mould, as a potter his clay, *Bitol*, which has the same meaning, and *Tzacol*, the builder, as of a house. With the Dayaks of Borneo, the Creator is *Tupa*, the forger, as one forges a spearblade and so on.

Another form in which primitive man imagines creation—and one which plays an important part in myths—is sexual procreation. This idea, too, is unrelated to the concept of causality; rather, it has a social character.

14. PERSONALISTIC AND CAUSAL THINKING

The law of causality is essentially characterized by the fact that it connects the effect with the cause. The cause is an objective event homogeneous to the effect and, like it, occurring in nature; being of the same kind as the effect, it is therefore itself the effect of a cause. Thence follows the endless chain of cause and effect, inconceivable to primitive man, which is an essential element in the scientific conception of causality. Personalistic and causal thinking exclude one another.[73] Primitive man traces events, which he wishes to understand, not to elements of the same kind but to elements of a different kind, not to an object but to a subject, not to a thing but to a person. If something must be explained, primitive man does not, like the scientifically educated civilized man, ask "How did it happen?" but "Who did it?" Meinhof[74] reports of African Negroes that they do not demand, if rain fails to come, "What prevents it?" but "Who prevents it?" "Because they suppose an evil intention, a person must be the cause." (More correctly, a person is guilty, i.e., responsible.)

Whenever primitive man wishes to explain a new event, unknown to him before, he does so by tracing it to a personal being or, if such is not visible, to a "spirit," or, more correctly, he imputes the events to that personal being. When a phonograph was exhibited to the Korjaks, they believed that an invisible person was inclosed in the box who could imitate human voices; they called it the "old one." The Lenguan Indians were convinced that the blue needle of a compass, pointing always to the north, was a blue spirit shut up in the little container. Schultze[75] reports a case of primitive men who, upon being shown a magnetic needle, saw in it a being which, abducted from its fatherland, "longed passionately for that desired region."

The attribution of phenomena to a fictitious person cuts short all research into causes.[76] That causal and personalistic thinking are in contrast to each other can be clearly shown by the fact that the former absolutely excludes the idea, observed again and again among savages, of being able to deceive nature; but such an intention is the direct consequence of a personalistic interpretation. Since desired, as well as feared, events are actions of personal beings, it must be possible to bring about or prevent such actions by deceiving the acting persons, even though they are more powerful than man. Innumerable customs of primitive peoples prove this attitude of theirs toward nature. And if "magic" seems incompatible with a scientific view of life, it is because it is based essentially on the idea that behind the events of nature stand personal demiurges whose help can be secured for good or evil.[77] Observers have occasionally been struck by the strange fact that some aborigines distinguish clearly between voluntary and involuntary loss of blood. They regard the former, even if it is considerable, as not dangerous; they themselves bring it about for various purposes. Of the involuntary loss of blood, even if it is negligible, they are afraid. This would be absolutely inconceivable if they imagined in blood an objective, impersonal power.[78] Their view is rather: If my blood flows without my wishing it, someone else, an evil spirit, must wish it. This personalistic manner of thinking explains why primitive man is afraid of an involuntary loss of blood while he is prepared, without the slightest concern, voluntarily to give up great quantities of the precious liquid. Nothing is more characteristic of this mental attitude than the previously mentioned belief that natural death does not exist, that every death is "artificial," that it is brought about by a personal being, such as a death soul, a magician, or a deity. Of a similar nature is the widespread notion that illness is an evil spirit or has been inflicted by an evil spirit and can be chased away only by another, more powerful spirit.[79] Disease is not for primitive man an objective situation which can be removed or altered by another objective, impersonal force but is represented as a conflict between two persons. The concept of a spirit or soul is again a specific instance of the use of personal categories.

15. "Imputation" to the Person and Normative Thinking

Primitive man does not investigate beyond the real or imaginary person to whom the event to be explained is attributed; his weak need for explanation is thus satisfied.[80] He imputes to these personal beings, to whom he traces all the pleasant and unpleasant events of nature, the same motives which determine his own behavior; he frequently ascribes to them, however, superhuman powers in addition. Consequently, he regards them as authorities toward whom he must behave respectfully, as he does toward the individuals in whom his group authority resides. This behavior is determined by the fact that sanctions are instituted by the superhuman authorities; these sanctions guarantee the social order and thus establish the social duties of individuals. So the personal beings imagined in the events of nature really represent the social authority. Natural order and social order consequently are identical. If the latter is violated, the former is also shaken.[81]

The relationship of primitive man to nature is based not upon the idea of an objective connection between facts, i.e., upon the assumption of a causal-nexus brought about by impersonal forces, but upon the idea of a connection between two persons, i.e., upon the assumption of a social relationship.[82] It has a marked normative character. Since the laws of nature are social norms, they can be violated. That is the reason for the conception, mentioned in various mythologies, of guardians who are instituted to watch over nature and to make sure that things happen according to prescribed rules. Typical is a myth of the Maori which tells, according to Elsdon Best, of "the appointment of certain supernormal beings as guardians of the different realms of the universe. . . . . Their duties were to regulate all things, forces, activities, realms and beings."[83] Of Tane and two other superhuman beings who were instituted as inspectors over all the other guardians of nature, it is said that their duty was "to preserve peace and harmony among them and among all other things in all realms. Thus was harmony preserved, not only among living creatures, but also among all things deemed inanimate by us, as the heavenly bodies, trees, stones."

For these reasons "nature," in the sense of an objective connection between facts, determined by the law of causality, is unknown to primitive man. "Nature" for him is not, as for civilized man, a sphere different from society. Such a dualism does not exist for primitive man. Still less does he conceive society, as do modern sociologists, as a part of nature; rather, nature for him is a part of society.

16. "Nature" as Part of Society

Primitive man sees social occurrences and relationships in cosmic situations and events. That heaven as man lies over earth as woman, that the universe is a single act of copulation, that Uranos and Gaia are the parent-pair, are among the earliest ideas of mankind.[84] Le Roy writes about the Fans of Gabon that they believe "the sun and moon were married: the stars are their children."[85] The Andamanese, too, regard the sun as the wife of the moon, and the stars as their children. They believe that the moon man becomes furious should there be a fire or any bright light after sunset.[86] The natives of Peru regard the sun and moon as brother and sister and at the same time as husband and wife; thus they justify brother-sister marriage, customary among the Incas.[87] According to the Pelauans, also, sun and moon are brother and sister,

destined to wander together. The moon, however, did not obey immediately but amused himself and consequently came too late, so that the brilliant sun undertakes her day-journey alone; the pleasure-seeking moon, however, pursues her by night. Therefore, work is done in the day-time. Moon nights on the other hand are devoted to pleasure and useless enjoyment.[88]

The Aztecs interpret the rebirth of the sun after the winter solstice as a dramatic struggle in which the sun defeats the stars and strikes off the moon's head.[89] Among South Australian natives the idea prevails that the sun is the bad wife of the good moon; at each new moon the bad wife kills the good husband.[90] The Narrinyeri interpret the waning of the moon, regarded as a woman, by the explanation that she grows lean because of excessive sexual intercourse.[91] Among the Yamana (Indians of the Terra del Fuego) the moon phases are explained as the different stages of pregnancy of the moon woman, called Hanuxa.

First when *Hanuxa* is very thin and lean (crescent moon) does she conceive a daughter. This child grows slowly in her womb and she finally becomes big (full moon). Then the child is born. Afterwards the moon woman grows leaner again and becomes sicker and weaker (waning moon). Finally she dies and cannot be seen again. Meanwhile the new-born daughter grows. She in turn, conceives, and the whole procedure repeats itself.[92]

To the Greenlanders, Anninga, the moon, is the brother of the sun, Malina, and in love with her; he pursues her without ever being able to catch her and, because of persistent yearning, grows lean.[93] Ehren-reich[94] remarks that among many peoples the first appearance of the menses is regarded as a defloration by the moon, who, as ancestor and forefather of the human race, is considered the first dead man. The fact that the moon is surrounded by stars and the sun not, is interpreted by the natives of Dahomey as the abundance and lack of children of these two, regarded as brother and sister. Originally, so these natives say, both had children, and then both made a pact to drown the children. The moon, however, betrayed the sun by throwing a sack of pebbles into the water, whereas the sun carried out the agreement. Thence follows the enmity between the two.[95] The northwestern Bushmen believe that the moon eclipse is caused by lions so that they may thereby easily prowl into the huts of men.[96] The Batak of Sumatra regard sun and moon as living persons fighting one another.[97] In the opinion of the Aranda (Arunta) the sun is a tall woman, endowed with divine powers; her rays are her pubic hair.[98] Whenever the Safwa see a halo around the moon, they say: "A chieftain has all his people assembled around him to discuss war against another country."[99] The Bahau of Borneo believe that fire and water fight each other as living beings and that wind and rain come to water's rescue.[100] In a South Sea fable it is said that once there has been no night, until it was bought by a man.[101] A story of the Maori reports that their ancestor, the hero Maui, tried to catch with a noose the speedily wandering sun, in order to slow down her course.

At last the sun came rising up out of his place, like a fire spreading far and wide over the mountains and forests; he rises up, his head passes through the noose, and it takes in more and more of his body, until his forepaws pass through; then are pulled tight the ropes, and the monster began to struggle and roll himself about, whilst the snare jerked backwards and forwards as he struggled. Ah, was not he held fast in the ropes of his enemies!—Then forth rushed that bold hero, Maui-tiki-tiki-o-Taranga, with his enchanted weapon. Alas! The sun screams aloud; he roars; Maui strikes him fiercely with many blows; they hold him for a long time, at last they let him go, and then weak from wounds the sun crept slowly along its course. Then was learnt by men the second name of the sun, for in its agony the sun screamed out: "Why am I thus smitten by you! Oh, man! do you know what you are doing? Why should you wish to kill Tama-nui-te-Ra?" Thus was learnt his second name. At last they let him go. Oh, then, Tama-nui-te-Ra went very slowly and feebly on his course.[102]

In the creation of fire by means of a fire-borer the Marind-anim see a sexual act.[103] The same idea exists among African peoples, especially in Loango, where, on the occasion of the boring of new state fires, coitus acts are in fact carried out. Baumann reports that among the Tschodwe whom he visited the furnace is regarded as a woman and breasts are molded on it. "The creation of fire in the smithy is, at least within the sphere of Rhodesian culture, considered as coition." In

Mashonaland, bellows are regarded as the man, smelting as copulation.[104] In short, whenever it is asserted that the thinking of primitive man is sexual thinking,[105] it means that primitive man interprets the events of nature according to the analogy of one social relationship, the relation between the sexes.

The social interpretation of nature becomes especially obvious in societies where totemism reigns;[106] here the social organization is transferred to nature. Representing a social organization, the totemic system includes not only men and animals but also plants, stars—in short, the whole universe. Everything in animate or inanimate nature belongs to a certain totem, which means to a certain social group. According to the much cited treatise of Cushing,[107] the tribe of the Zuñi Indians (New Mexico), as well as the village inhabited by them, is divided into seven parts. Accordingly, the Zuñi distinguish seven directions: north, south, east, west, above, below, and middle. Indeed, everything that exists or happens is classified in one of these seven categories. This seven-fold social organization is the scheme of interpretation for the whole cosmos. Similarly, among the Miwok Indians all nature is divided into those two parts into which the tribe itself is divided in accordance with their totemic organization. "Nature is divided," says Kroeber,[108] "into a water and a land or dry half, which are thought to correspond to the *Kikua* and *Tunuka* moieties among the people. . . . . The native concept is that everything in the world belongs to one or the other side." Corresponding reports come from various Australian tribes. W. Lloyd Warner writes of the Murngin:

> We found that there is a general idea which surrounds natural phenomena, and that nature is seen as a unity, as an alternation of the dry and rainy season. . . . . The natural phenomena are all organized in this dichotomy. We saw that the seasonal variations are given social categories by the identification of the rainy season with the male principle and the dry period with the female principle. This classification is mechanically accomplished in Murngin thinking by giving the seasons and the age-grade dichotomy the same symbols. . . . . The general activity of nature, that is, the alternation of the seasons, is the effect of man's uncleanliness in the mythologic past and in the present . . . . the identification, in the totemic concept, of the male and female principles with the seasonal cycles gives the adult men's group the necessary power to enforce its sanctions; the providing world of nature will not function if the rules of society are flouted and man's uncleanliness contaminates nature. Hence everyone must obey.[109]

Likewise, the idea, widespread among primitive peoples, may be recalled that the right side is regarded as good and the left as evil. This is an entirely subjective organization of the universe because it varies in accord with the actual position and view of the subject; nevertheless, it is a complete organization of the universe based on a concept of value which presupposes the moral and thus the social order. Such order alone makes possible a differentiation between good and evil.

For these reasons the customary characterization of primitive man as a "man in a state of nature" or a "natural man" is inept. Nothing appears "natural" to him because everything, as soon as he seeks to explain it, is "artificial" or "made," not necessarily by himself but by his fellow-men or even by superhuman beings;[110] a typical example of this is his already mentioned interpretation of death either as murder or as punishment. Primitive man is not a "natural man" because he is a "social man" in the strictest sense of the word. Therefore, one must not term the personal beings, to whom he traces the events of nature, as supernatural but rather as superhuman beings. Since he knows no nature, he cannot imagine a supernature. The dualism of a "natural" and a "supernatural," a "physical" and a "metaphysical," realm is not possible so long as there does not exist the dualism which alone constitutes the concept "nature," namely, that of nature and society.

CHAPTER III

THE INTERPRETATION OF NATURE ACCORDING TO THE PRINCIPLE OF RETRIBUTION

17. PRINCIPLE OF RETRIBUTION AND VENGEANCE

THE fundamental principle which determines primitive man's behavior toward nature is the same as that which decides his conduct toward the members of his own and other groups—the social principle of retribution.

There is a tendency to regard the reaction termed "retribution" as a primary emotion of man and to trace it back to a natural instinct for vengeance which may be observed not only among primitives but also among children and even animals. This view, however, rests upon the fact that the behavior interpreted as retribution is not clearly distinguished from a mere defensive reaction which arises from a desire for self-preservation or, at least among higher beings, as a countertendency to the causation of pain.[1] It is proper to speak of "vengeance" only if the reaction in question is made with the intent not only to parry the evil but also to inflict an evil in turn, either on the "author" of the evil or on someone associated with him who is thus regarded as collectively responsible.

18. "DIRECTED" AND "NONDIRECTED" VENGEANCE

In his well-known book on the origin of punishment, Steinmetz[2] distinguishes between "directed" and "nondirected" acts of vengeance, i.e., directed or not directed against the "culprit." In his opinion, "direction" is not necessary for vengeance. "Psychologically vengeance at first consists in the fact that the unpleasant feelings of being injured are neutralized by the pleasant feelings of injuring." "Direction" is only added later. Without "direction against the culprit," however, one cannot correctly speak of "vengeance." This "direction against the culprit" is not a matter of course, even if one understands by "culprit" only the author of the evil which arouses the "instinctive" reaction and does not connect with the word "culprit" any judgment of value, which is not possible unless one supposes a social order. It is not easy to explain on the basis of mere animal instinct why a living being tries to neutralize a feeling of pain, inflicted by others, by a feeling of pleasure attained by inflicting pain on others, especially upon the one who caused the pain. Why should not the neutralization of one's feeling of pain, caused from the outside, be brought about quite differently? Even if one may presuppose a natural desire for aggression, the satisfaction of which causes pleasure, no necessary relationship exists between a feeling of pain, caused by an outside force, and its neutralization by an act of aggression. Such a relationship seems to be effected only if the aggression is directed against the author of the evil sustained or other individuals, identified with him. A "directed" reaction of this sort presupposes a social situation.

That the injured individual tries to inflict upon the injurer what he himself has sustained from the latter can be explained *subjectively* only by the feeling of inferiority which the evil sustained arouses in the injured toward the injurer; this feeling of inferiority can very well be neutralized by placing the injurer in the situation of the injured. Thus the injurer becomes humiliated; the injured, elevated and satisfied. This feeling of satisfaction is significant for the instinct of vengeance. Such a situation, however, is possible only if a relationship involving a sense of value exists between both parties, at least in the consciousness of the individual in whom the reaction for "vengeance" originates; this, in turn, is possible only in a society.

"Vengeance," i.e., more than instinctive defense, against the author of an evil can be explained *objectively* by its preventive effect, possible only in the relationship between individuals living together socially. Merely to be the immediate cause of a feeling of pain does not suffice to stimulate the reaction of the injured party. Apart from the fact that an idea of causality cannot be presumed among animals, the "causes" of a fact are always innumerable. The reaction of vengeance is directed against a link in the chain of causes, against that special link which, if struck by the reaction, becomes a less probable cause for repetition of the evil. The "revenging" individual need not necessarily aim at such an effect. But some experience must exist to direct the instinct to that suitable point. And this can be the experience only of a socially living being. Vengeance and hence retribution—in the narrower sense of the word indicating a qualified reaction—are possible only in society, not in nature.

The idea of retribution presupposes that the evil arousing the reaction has been unjustly inflicted. No sharp distinction can be drawn between the reaction termed "vengeance" and that termed "retribution"; for the direction against the author of the evil, which is a twist given by society to the original instinct of defense, implies the tendency to regard the evil sustained as a breach of norms, a violation of the social order which exists in the consciousness of the individuals between whom retribution is exercised.

19. VENGEANCE AMONG ANIMALS

The often reported cases of animal vengeance should be treated with all possible caution. They are to be taken into consideration only with socially living animals. In his work on sociology of animals Alverdes asserts that among gorillas "the father of the family has his mate and young pick and bring him fruits and he boxes their ears if they do not carry out his demands quickly and plentifully."[3] In another instance, a wounded old baboon was leaning on younger monkeys and boxed their ears "whenever a detail of his flight was not enacted according to his wishes."[4] In another monkey society a female "who was guilty of unfaithfulness was slapped in the face and otherwise roughly handled by the Pasha."[5] It is foolhardy to interpret animal behavior according to an unproved and unprovable analogy to human conduct. This is especially true in the case of an avenging baboon mentioned by Darwin, according to a report of the zoölogist Sir Andrew Smith:

At the Cape of Good Hope an officer had often plagued a certain baboon and the animal, seeing him approaching one Sunday for parade, poured water into a hole and hastily made some thick mud which he skillfully dashed over the officer as he passed by, to the amusement of many bystanders. For long afterwards the baboon rejoiced and triumphed whenever he saw his victim.[6]

Almost unbelievable is a case which Westermarck advances as proof of "animal revenge." He quotes from Palgrave's report of a journey through central and eastern Arabia:

One passion alone he [the camel] possesses, namely revenge, of which he furnishes many a hideous example, while in carrying it out he shows an unexpected degree of far-thoughted malice, united meanwhile with all the cold stupidity of his usual character. One instance of this I well remember. It occurred hard by a small town in the plain of Ba'albec, where I was at the time residing. A lad of about fourteen had conducted a large camel, laden with wood, from that very village to another at half an hour's distance or so. As the animal loitered or turned out of the way, its conductor struck it repeatedly, and harder than it seems to have thought he had a right to do. But not finding the occasion favourable for taking immediate quits, it "bode its time"; nor was that time long in coming. A few days later the same lad had to reconduct the beast, but unladen, to his own village. When they were about half-way on the road, and at some distance from any habitation, the camel suddenly stopped, looked deliberately round in every direction to assure itself that no one was within sight, and, finding the road far and near clear of passers-by, made a step forward, seized the unlucky boy's head in its monstrous mouth, and lifting him up in the air flung him down again on the earth with the upper part of his skull completely torn off, and his brains scattered on the ground. Having thus satisfied its revenge, the brute quietly resumed its pace towards the village as though nothing were the matter, till some men who had observed the whole, though unfortunately at too great a distance to be able to afford timely help, came up and killed it.[7]

One does not know whether to wonder more about the camel's sense of justice or about its clever cautiousness, despite its stupidity, in committing a crime without any eyewitnesses, or about the fact that the men who killed the camel—to punish it?—were so far away that they could not come to the boy's rescue but nevertheless could watch the strange behavior of the animal and especially observe exactly its motives and intentions.

20. VENGEANCE ON INANIMATE OBJECTS

In the desire for revenge—observed not only among men but perhaps even among gregarious animals—there may be involved an elementary defense reflex which is aroused by a feeling of pain. In order that this reflex become a more or less conscious action, such as vengeance when directed against the "author," the original instinct must undergo a modification possible only through social life.[8] In the desire for vengeance it is not the pure original instinct of self-preservation which manifests itself; vengeance is a socially determined behavior.[9] It is known that children, like primitive men, take revenge on inanimate objects by beating and destroying them, inasmuch as they regard them as the cause of their pain. This behavior cannot be considered "natural," as children probably copy what they have observed in adults. And among primitive men this remarkable behavior is the result of an animistic concept, which may, in a certain degree, be presupposed among children as well.[10] In this connection Tylor[11] reports some impressive examples: a savage tramples a stone against which he stumbles or breaks the arrow which wounded him; the relatives of a savage who fell from a tree are obliged to take revenge on the tree by felling and cutting it up; a chieftain puts a boat, which has not sailed well, into irons, like a criminal. It is remembered that Xerxes had the Hellespont beaten up and that even in historic times a court existed in Athens where inanimate objects, such as spears and axes, which caused death to a man, were tried and formally punished. Retribution is exercised by primitive man (as will be shown later), especially on animals and plants. This behavior, too, can be explained only on the basis of his animistic ideas. Animism, however, is that kind of interpretation of nature which takes for granted a social situation, for it is specifically social and essentially characterized by the fact that primitive man interprets all the events which interest him personalistically and according to the principles which determine his social relationship—primarily, according to the principle of retribution.

21. Significance of the Idea of Retribution for the Social Life of Primitive Man

In all accounts of primitive social life, the pre-eminent and all-pervading power of this principle of retribution appears again and again. The importance of socialization for primitive man, the objective function of society, consists apparently in the increased protection it provides for certain interests—above all, for life, which to primitive man is the most precious, if not perhaps the only, good. It must be admitted that sometimes cases are reported of savages who do not regard life as the most precious of all goods and do not seem to fear death;[12] under certain circumstances, they even voluntarily give up their lives. These, however, are exceptions which, if they are at all correctly observed, can be explained by special conditions.

The first missionaries who worked among the American Indians reported that the savages feared death very strongly; but they met it cold-bloodedly. This seems to be a contradiction. But it can be explained by the fact that the individual wishes to appear courageous. The customs of the tribes require such a behavior,[13] and the social order is sufficiently effective to prevent the individual from showing his instinctive fear.

No doubt, the soul belief as belief in survival after death also plays an important part here. Thus, among the natives of the New Hebrides, according to a report of Turner,[14] old people are buried alive at their own wish. The idea of a soul continuing life after death has the effect of allaying the fear of death and of creating a fear of the dead, who are believed capable of revenging themselves upon their murderers. The function of such a belief is evidently to secure life. It must, therefore, be considered an excess if the belief in the existence of death souls induces a human being to give up the very good which this belief should protect. If its normal effect were to make human beings indifferent to earthly life, the human race would have been exterminated long ago.[15] The social order of primitive man normally guarantees, with all the means actually at its disposal, the preservation of human life within the community. This is true even of the most primitive community. Tylor remarked that "no known tribe, however low and ferocious, has ever admitted that men may kill one another indiscriminately."[16] Supported by rich ethnographical material, Westermarck says with reference to this statement:

It is commonly maintained that the most sacred duty which we owe our fellow-creatures is to respect their lives. I venture to believe that this holds good not only among civilised nations, but among the lower races as well; and that, if a savage recognises that he has any moral obligations at all to his neighbours, he considers the taking of their lives to be a greater wrong than any other kind of injury inflicted upon them.[17]

How easily the behavior of primitive man can be misinterpreted by observers who are under the influence of civilized conceptions of law and morality is shown by a report on a Bechuana tribe, cited by Westermarck as a case of the supposedly low esteem of life held by primitive men. Among these natives, so it is reported, murder "excites little sensation, excepting in the family of the person who has been murdered; and brings, it is said, no disgrace upon him who has committed it; nor uneasiness, excepting the fear of their revenge."[18] But this fact corresponds to that stage of social development in which vendetta still exists. That murder arouses excitement only in the family of the murdered man is natural, since only the family is obliged to take revenge. And it can obviously arouse only fear of vengeance, since courts which prosecute and punish the murderer do not yet exist. The institution of blood revenge, which can be traced back to the beginnings of social development, indicates clearly that death is not only the oldest crime but also the oldest socially organized punishment. For Marett[19] the three basic conditions of primitive blood relationship are: no incest, no internal bloodshed, but blood revenge in the relations with others. Blood revenge applies the most ancient social norm; he who kills must be killed. It is the most obvious manifestation of the principle of retribution. It fundamentally determines the mutual behavior of the members of society so far as this behavior is regulated by the social system, which from the very beginning has the character of a legal and at the same time moral order.

22. Principle of Retribution and Morality

It would be entirely incorrect to characterize primitive man's mental outlook, oriented on the principle of retribution and perfectly social because determined by the social order, as amoral or even immoral. Such an evaluation of primitive behavior is based on the view that moral consciousness comes into existence only through individualistic ideas. This would mean the identification of a morality independent of, and possibly in opposition to, the prevailing legal order with morality itself. The development of an individual morality, more correctly of a special morality of groups within society, is the result of far-reaching social differentiations, particularly the formation of classes; and any system of morality opposed to the legal order always contradicts that other system of morality which is expressed in the legal order itself. No legal order presents itself as morally indifferent or immoral even if it only realizes the morality of a certain group within the legal community or of a certain era which is realized in the legal order and which may conflict more or less with the morality of other groups or of a younger era.

In a primitive and comparatively homogeneous society, law and morality coincide. In a civilized society a differentiation of law and morality takes place as a result of the differentiation of society. The law of civilized society is more or less in conformity with the ethical conviction of one or the other group within society. But every social order is virtually a moral order[20]—"moral" from the point of view of one or the other group, i.e., relatively, not absolutely, moral.

Inasmuch as retribution is possible only in a society, it consequently always represents in some degree a moral principle. It is, therefore, more than problematical to distinguish, as Westermarck does,[21] between a "nonmoral" and a "moral" retribution (for the former Westermarck uses the term "resentment") and to qualify only the first one as "revenge." For in the "direction" which is essential for revenge, the direction against the author of the evil, a social and thus a moral element is involved. The reaction to be interpreted as mere vengeance is always more or less accompanied by the feeling that it is approved or even demanded by the members of the group and that one's own injury is indirectly an injury to the other members of the group as well. It is always not only an individual but also a collective interest which is satisfied by vengeance in a primitive society. That is, indeed, just the point where the instinctive, natural reflex of defense, aroused by an external causation of pain, distinguishes itself from social vengeance: in the former there is nothing but a subjective motive, in the latter—by virtue of the direction against the injurer—there is an objective function, prevention. It stands to reason that man becomes conscious of this function only after achieving critical knowledge of the social connections. Where the custom exists of avenging one's self for an injury sustained, i.e., of reacting against a behavior disapproved by social consciousness, there the beginnings of morality are already evident. It is, therefore, contradictory to report of primitive tribes that they have no morality whatever, that they lack any sense of the distinction between good and evil, but at the same time to assert that among them the principle of vengeance prevails.

Even if one accepts Westermarck's opinion and considers vengeance a morally indifferent or even immoral behavior, as long as a selfish and merely personal motive is decisive, the oldest case of socially organized retribution and the most important one in primitive society, blood revenge, still could not be understood as "extra-moral" retribution. For, in the case of murder, personal reaction on the part of the injured individual is out of the question, since it is impossible after the evil has been inflicted. In this instance retribution is not exercised by the person immediately concerned who alone could be the subject of that instinctive reaction, which can also be observed among animals. It is the family of the murdered individual, i.e., the oldest society itself, which exercises retribution. Wherever death is avenged, social needs must be satisfied thereby, and emotions must be soothed which are, if not created, at least considerably modified by social life. Blood revenge can only be a social function and, as such, must be a specifically "moral" reaction.

William Ridley says: "The Australian Aborigines carry out the principle of retaliation, not only as a dictate of passion, but as an ancient and fixed law."[22] Richard F. Burton writes of the natives of Central Africa: "Revenge is a ruling passion, as the many rancorous fratricidal wars that have prevailed between kindred clans, even for a generation, prove. Retaliation and vengeance are, in fact, their great agents of moral control";[23] and Dudley Kidd speaks of the "intrinsic justice of retaliation"[24] in which the Kaffirs believe. E. F. im Thurn remarks in his work on the Indians of Guiana:

In all primitive societies where there are no written laws and no supreme authority to enforce justice, such vengeance has been held as a sacred duty; for, in the absence of laws enforced by society, the fear of this vengeance to be inflicted by the injured individual, or by those nearest of kin to him, alone deters individuals from crime. Outside America, at various times in the history of the world, a custom in every way similar to this Indian *kenaima* system has prevailed. The best known instances are the vendetta, the Israelitish law of retaliation which gave rise to the "cities of refuge," and the Saxon system which resulted in the law of blood-money or were-gild, which was money paid to buy off just vengeance. This custom of recognized retaliation yet exists among the Indian tribes of Guiana, and must continue to exist until some system for the administration of justice is established in the districts inhabited by them.[25]

Among the ancient Hebrews it was the duty of the *goel*, the nearest of kin of a murdered man, to pursue and slay the murderer. The *goel*, H. Clay Trumbull writes, is "the person who is authorized to obtain blood for blood as an act of justice in the east."[26] Trumbull speaks "of the prevailing error in the Western mind" of "confounding justice with punishment." He stresses that the significance of the term *goel* is not— as erroneously assumed—"avenger" or "revenger." "His mission was not vengeance, but equity. He was not an avenger but a redeemer, a restorer, a balancer." In other terms, blood revenge was a legal and moral institution.

The degree of progress from primitive vengeance to the higher social technique of retributive punishment is indeed great. It consists in the fact that the reaction against the delict no longer has solely the character of self-help; it must not be exercised any more by the individual directly or indirectly injured but by an impartial authority. Nevertheless, the difference between the essentially social reaction of primitive vengeance and the retributive punishment is purely a quantitative one, whereas the difference between vengeance and the instinctive reflex of defense is qualitative. One should not overlook the fact that even today a very important branch of law, namely, international law, still remains, for the most part, in the technically primitive state of self-help.[27]

Lack of insight into the thoroughly "moral" character of retribution has led to the view, shared by Tylor,[28] that primitive religions are morally indifferent. This cannot be true, for the simple reason that the principle of retribution plays a decisive part in these religions. What Elsdon Best says of the Polynesians is equally true of all primitive peoples: "Among the Polynesians, including our Maori folk of New Zealand, fear of divine punishment was the very strongest deterrent force, and the key of social discipline. It was the power that held society together, and curbed a naturally strong-minded and somewhat turbulent people."[29] The institution of taboo, so important for primitive society, has specifically a religious character and is based essentially on the principle of retribution. Again, what Elsdon Best says of the taboo of the Maori is equally applicable to the taboo of all primitive peoples:

It may be said that *tapu* means prohibition, a multiplication of "Thou shalt not." These may be termed the laws of the gods, and they must not be infringed. The penalty for neglect of these unspoken commands is the withdrawal of the protecting power of the gods. . . . . Let us now seek the cause or origin of this fear of the gods and of the dread *tapu* empowered by the gods. That cause can be given briefly: it was the fact that offences against the gods are punished in this world, not in the spirit world to come.[30]

Formulating it more generally, one may say that the norms of the social order termed "taboo" are effective because one believes that their violation entails the imposition of sanctions in the form of retribution emanating from a superhuman divine power and executed in this world.

23. Retribution and "Talio," Exchange, Reciprocity

The principle of retribution first appears to primitive man in its most drastic form, the *talio:* an eye for an eye, a tooth for a tooth, a death for a death. Typical is what Thomson says of the Maori: "The great principle of justice upon which the New Zealanders acted was an eye for an eye and a tooth for a tooth, and the object of all their punishments was to obtain compensation for injuries, not to prevent crimes."[31]

In a report of 1709 on the Hindus of the district of Madura (India) a Jesuit missionary writes:

These Indians observe the Law of Retaliation very strictly. If there happens to be a Quarrel, and one of the Parties pulls his own eye out, or is guilty of Suicide; the other Party must inflict the like punishment upon himself, or on some of his Relations. The Women carry this barbarous custom still farther: When any Affront is put upon 'em, or reproachful Word used, they will go and break their Head against the Door of the offending Person; who is obliged to inflict exactly the same Punishment upon herself. If one Woman poisons herself, by drinking the Juice of a venomous Herb or Plant, the other Female, who was the Cause of it, is obliged to do the same; and shou'd she fail in it, the rest wou'd set Fire to her House; run away with her Cattle; and be perpetually tormenting her till such Times as she had made full Satisfaction.—This cruelty extends to their own Children: Not long since, at a little Distance from the Church whence I write, two of these Barbarians happening to quarrel, one of 'em ran to his own House, snatched up one of his Children, about four Years old; and coming in Sight of his Enemy, beat out the Child's Brains between two Stones. The other, without discovering any Emotion, took up a Daughter of his, who was but nine Years old, and plunged his Dagger in her Breast: Your Child, says he afterwards, was but four Years old, and my Daughter was nine; give me therefore a Victim equal to mine. That I will, replied the other; when spying, at his Side, his eldest Son, whom he was giving to dispose of in Marriage, he gave him four or five Stabs with a Dagger; and not contented with having spilt the Blood of his two Sons, he also killed his Wife, that his Enemy might be forced to murther his also. This tragical Scene ended with the Murder of a little Girl, and a Child sucking at the Breast; so that, in one Day, seven Persons were sacrificed to the Vengeance of two Men who thursted after human Blood and were more cruel than the fiercest Beasts.[32]

In Adair's *History of the American Indians* we read:

There never was any set of people, who pursued the Mosaic law of *retaliation* with such a fixt eagerness as these Americans. They are so determined in this point, that formerly a little boy shooting birds in the high and thick corn-fields, unfortunately chanced slightly to wound another with his childish arrow; the young vindictive fox, was excited by custom to watch his ways with the utmost earnestness, till the wound was returned in as equal manner as could be expected. Then "all was straight," according to their phrase. Their hearts were at rest, by having executed that strong law of nature, and they sported together as before.[33]

Of the Jibaro Indians, Karsten[34] writes:

The Jibaro Indian is wholly penetrated by the idea of retaliation; his desire for revenge is an expression of his sense of justice. This principle is eye for eye, tooth for tooth, life for life. If one reprehends a Jibaro because he has killed an enemy, his answer is generally: "He has killed himself."

When a murder committed by an own tribesman is to be avenged, the social morals of the Jibaros require that the punishment shall be meted out with justice, in so far that for one life which has been taken only one life should be taken in retaliation. Thereupon the blood guilt is atoned (*tumashi akerkama*) and the offended family is satisfied. Consequently, if a Jibaro Indian wishes to revenge a murder of his brother, it may well happen that he, in case the slayer himself can not be caught and punished, will assassinate his brother or father instead of him, but he does not take the life of more than one member of the family, even if he has an opportunity of killing more.

The substantializing tendency of primitive thinking makes man— even civilized man—believe that the evil which one sustains and the evil which one must inflict according to the principle of retribution can and shall be "equal"—equal in both a quantitative and a qualitative sense.[35] It has been observed among various tribes that an expedition of vengeance will not be terminated before the enemy has suffered the same number of dead as the avenging side.

The Quianganes of Luzon, writes F. Blumentritt,

are themselves carefully in their guard against hurting the feelings of another, and demand that others shall do the same with them. Blood vengeance is a sacred law with the Quianganes. If one plebeian is killed by another, the matter is settled in a simple manner by killing the murderer or some one of his family who is likewise a plebeian. But if a prominent man or noble is killed by a plebeian, vengeance on the murderer, a mere plebeian, is not enough; the victim of the sin-offering must be an equivalent in rank. Another nobleman must fall for the murdered noble, for their doctrine is, What kind of an equivalent is it to kill some one who is no better than a dog? Hence the family of the slain noble looks around to see if it can not find a relative of the murderer to wreak vengeance upon, who is also a noble; while the murderer himself is ignored. If no noble can be found among his relatives, the family of the murdered man wait patiently till some one of them is received into the noble's estate; then the vendetta is prosecuted, although many years may have elapsed.[36]

Leenhardt reports of the natives of New Caledonia that peace concluded after a battle

> is only consolidated and completed when the old balance of life is reestablished be-
> tween victor and vanquished. Every life lost in the battle is replaced by Caledonian
> money representing the dead man. It is the indemnity paid by the enemy. The two
> parties count their dead and then proceed with the exchange of the length of money.[37]

Of the natives of British New Guinea, C. G. Seligmann writes:

> .... that prisoners taken in warfare were brought alive to the hamlet-group,
> where they would be tortured before being killed and eaten. This apparently occurred
> only when a prisoner was to be killed in payment for the death of a member of the
> captor's community, and in spite of the pleasure to be derived from a cannibal feast
> it was clear that commonly prisoners would only be tortured and killed in such num-
> bers that their deaths made the score even between their community and that of their
> captors.[38]

The idea of an equivalence between the wrong sustained and the
wrong to be inflicted is characteristic of the principle of retribution.[39]
This makes retribution appear a kind of exchange, although it is more
correct to consider exchange a special kind of retribution.[40] Among
the Orokaiva, blood revenge is described by a word which means
"exchange of death-souls."[41]

The principle of retribution has, according to its idea, a double
character. It means not only that a disadvantage sustained by someone else has to be requited with the same disadvantage but also that an
advantage received has to be requited with the same advantage. Retribution does not only **mean** punishment but also reward. But in the
foreground of primitive consciousness we find the reaction against the
wrong. What Junod says of the Thonga is typical of all primitive
peoples: "There are more words applicable to the negative side of the
idea and signifying *bad*, than to the positive, signifying *good;* a phenomenon which may be observed in most primitive languages, even in
our French patois."[42] Where people believe in the existence of good
and evil spirits, the latter play a much greater role than the former.
J. L. Wilson writes of the natives of northern Guinea (West Africa):

> They are more particular about the religious worship they offer to the evil spirits
> than to the other, which is to be accounted for from the fact that their sense of guilt,
> and dread of punishment, is a much stronger feeling in their minds, than any emotions
> of love, or gratitude for favors received.[43]

This, too, is typical.

It seems that of the two functions of the principle of retribution—
punishment and reward—the latter became only gradually more im-

portant. At any rate, the principle in question gives its peculiar character not only to criminal law but also to other aspects of social life. One obtains a wife by ceding to the family of the girl some economic good in exchange for her; or one trades his sister for the girl whom one wishes to take to wife. When a child dies among the natives of New Pomerania, where the social organization exhibits elements of mother-right, its father must give a present to the maternal uncle in order to repair the loss which the family has suffered. Among the Kaffirs, should a member of the group die, the relatives must pay compensation to the chieftain.[44] According to Malinowski, the relationship between man, wife, and child of the Trobrianders is as follows: "He (the man) cohabits with her (the wife), he possesses her, she does for him all that a wife must do for a man. Whatever he does for a child is a payment (*mapula*) for what he has received from her."[45] To these natives the physiological connection between father and child is unknown: the sole bonds that exist between them are the rights and duties laid down by the principle of retribution. The great importance of this principle in the sexual life of primitive man has been pointed out by Thurnwald.[46] It is a matter of course that it is likewise decisive in their economic life. It is this principle of retribution which certain ethnologists have in mind when they emphasize that the functioning of primitive society is characterized by an element of "reciprocity." Thus Malinowski refers to "the reciprocal nature of all social co-operation," and rightly sees in it one of the most effective guaranties for the observation of social duties.[47] It consists in the fact that primitive man regards every performance which he expects from another individual or from the group as dependent upon a counterperformance by himself; above all, he imagines every omission of a performance imposed upon him by society as connected with a social disadvantage to himself. In this general sense the whole social system has a retributive character.

Of the Orokaiva, Williams writes:

For his liberality a man receives a reward of honour, but beyond that—and this should not be thought to disqualify it entirely as a virtue—he constantly looks for an equal return in kind. This is one of the striking features of primitive economics—the return of gift for gift, the maintaining of a balance. The return may be made long subsequently, but it may be called a matter of honour to equal or exceed the original gift; just as it is a matter of disgrace and lowered self-esteem to fail.[48]

Brown reports of the Andaman Islanders:

The giving of presents is a common method of expressing friendship in the Andamans. Thus when two friends meet after separation, the first thing they do after having embraced and wept together, is to give one another presents. In most instances the giving is reciprocal, and is therefore really an exchange. If a present be given as a sign of good-will the giver expects to receive a present of about equal value in return. The reason for this is obvious; the one has expressed his good-will towards the other, and if the feeling is reciprocated, a return present must be given in order to express it. So also it would be an insult to refuse a present offered, for to do so would be equivalent to rejecting the good-will it represents.[48a]

W. Koppers reports of the Yamana:

It is customary that for every present of that kind [food, articles for everyday use, trinkets] an equivalent present be given in return. To bestow gifts upon each other in this way is customary, especially when two people meet again after long separation. However, a present of somewhat higher value is not always welcome since it is sometimes very hard to requite it with an equivalent gift.[48b]

Krause says of the Tlingit Indians:

Whenever a Tlinkit gives a present, he expects some compensation. Therefore he is suspicious when he receives a gift. Either he believes he has a right to the present or he sees in it an intention on the part of the giver to obtain something from him. Thus Belcher says of the Jakutats, that they receive presents as debts rather than as gifts and that they adhere to the principle of "nothing for nothing."[49]

In the "Havamal," a poem of the *Edda*, the idea that every gift necessarily demands a gift in return appears in manifold expression. Thus it is said:

> Friends shall gladden each other with arms and garments
> As each for himself can see;   41
> Gift-givers' friendships are longest found
> If fair their fates may be.

> To his friend a man a friend shall prove,
> And gifts with gifts requite;   42
> But men shall mocking with mockery answer,
> And fraud with falsehood meet.

> If a friend thou hast whom thou fully wilt trust,
> And good from him wouldst get,   44
> Thy thoughts with his mingle, and gifts shalt thou make,
> And fare to find him oft.

> If another thou hast whom thou hardly wilt trust,
> Yet good from him wouldst get,   45
> Thou shalt speak him fair, but falsely think,
> And fraud with falsehood requite.

> So is it with him whom thou hardly wilt trust,
> And whose mind thou mayst not know;   46
> Laugh with him mayst thou, but speak not thy mind,
> Like to gifts his shalt thou give.

Better no prayer than too big an offering,
By thy getting measure thy gift;   146
Better is none than too big a sacrifice,
So Thund of old wrote ere man's race began.[50]

The old Nordic poem expresses an idea widespread among primitive societies. When Marcel Mauss,[51] who has made some interesting
investigations into this problem, raises the question, "What is the rule
of right and interest which, in societies of backward or archaic types,
makes it obligatory that a present be repaid?" the answer is this: the
idea of retribution, dominating primitive consciousness. It is this idea
that, because of the economic conditions of primitive society, bars the
emergence of the legal institution of gift in the modern sense of a transfer of property without consideration. The principle of retribution
manifests itself not only in the rule that every gift must be reciprocated
but also in the idea that violation of this rule causes trouble. Where
animistic ideas exist, punishment for the failure to compensate a performance by a counterperformance may arise from the object of the
unreturned performance itself, i.e., from the spirit living in the object.
Elsdon Best reports a characteristic example observed among the
Maori. His informant said to him:

Suppose that you possess a certain article, and you give that article to me, without
price. We make no bargain over it. Now, I give that article to a third person, who,
after some time has elapsed, decides to make some return (utu) for it [the word utu
means also retribution, exercised by the blood avenger];[52] and so he makes me a present
of some article. Now, that article that he gives to me is the hau of the article I first
received from you and then gave to him. The goods that I received for that item I
must hand over to you. It would not be right for me to keep such goods for myself
whether they be desirable items or otherwise. I must hand them over to you because
they are a hau of the article you gave me. Were I to keep such equivalent for myself,
then some serious evil would befall me, even death. Such is the hau, the hau of personal property, or the forest hau.[53]

Eskimos use amulets the magic effect of which consists in the fact
that the soul of the animal from whose body the amulet is made brings
about a desired result. The amulet may be given by the original owner
to someone else but, as Rasmussen writes,

the magic power can only be conveyed to the new owner if he gives something in
return. Unless this is done, the power of the amulet is not transferred to the new
owner, even though he may carry it about on his person. Hence it is quite possible to
lose an amulet and yet retain its virtue.[54]

From the omnipresence of this principle of retribution may be explained the fact—often observed with astonishment—that primitive

man lacks feelings of gratitude. Of the Maori, for instance, it is reported: "Gratitude is unknown, and no word expressive of this feeling is found in their language. . . . . Revenge is their strongest passion, and this feeling is kept alive for generations. . . . . They are liberal in giving presents, but presents are merely modes of trade, as returns are always expected.[55] Of the Marind-anim of New Guinea it is said: "Gratitude in our sense is unknown. There is no expression for thanking. One accepts a gift without a word." And the observer adds this remark: "Something is always given in return for a gift, be it sooner or later, even if it is only for some betelnuts."[56]

David Boyle[57] writes of the civilized Iroquois of Ontario: "Agreeably to the totemic idea thankfulness is out of place, or rather has no existence in any of life's conditions. For primitive man in his tribal relations, individualism has but a hazy meaning, if any at all." But he adds: "He gives as freely as he takes, neither expecting nor giving thanks, but his associations with us have taught him to comply with form at least, and thus in some measure to remove from himself the reproach of the white man respecting Indian 'ingratitude.' "

Certain writers[58] report that the Eskimos do not know the feeling of gratitude. But Rasmussen mentions the following saying of an Eskimo: "A gift always opens the door of an Eskimo heart. . . . . Thou gavest; see, I give too."[59] Only when a performance need not be repaid by an equivalent action in return does the obligation to have a feeling of gratitude and to express it by words and gestures appear, and then as a substitute for the real counterperformance.

24. Primitive Man's Sense of Justice

The dominance which this idea of retribution exerts over the consciousness of primitive man is closely connected with the social character of his mentality. In this respect it must be observed that the social bond becomes stronger the smaller the group is to which one belongs. It has earlier been mentioned that many observers have been struck by the highly developed sense of justice among savages;[60] and it has been said that this can only mean that the social order binds primitive man much more intensely than civilized man. The consequence is that primitive man, unshaken by any critical doubt, is firmly convinced about the inviolability of the basic principle of his social order; this basic principle is the principle of retribution. Therefore, he never forgets any injury and considers revenge justifiable under all circumstances. W. McCulloch writes that among the Koupouees (India) "the greatest misconduct is the forgiveness of an injury, the first virtue, revenge."[61] Of the Maori, Elsdon Best says: "To avenge insults, wrongs, etc., was considered to be one of the most important duties of man."[62] This is true of most primitive peoples. From the point of view of Christian morality, which commands one to love one's enemy and to forgive one's injurer, primitive man appears—wrongly—as immoral. Adair writes:

I have known the Indians to go a thousand miles, for the purpose of revenge, in pathless woods; over hills and mountains; through large cane swamps, full of grape-vines and briars; over broad lakes, rapid rivers, and deep creeks; and all the way endangered by poisonous snakes, if not with the rambling and lurking enemy, while at the same time they were exposed to the extremities of heat and cold, the vicissitudes of the seasons; to hunger and thirst, both by chance, and their religious scanty method of living when at war, to fatigues, and other difficulties. Such is their over-boiling, revengeful temper, that they utterly contemn all those things as imaginary trifles, if they are so happy as to get the scalp of the murderer, or enemy, to satisfy the supposed craving ghosts of their deceased relations. Though they imagine the report of guns will send off the ghosts of their kindred that died at home, to their quiet place, yet they firmly believe, that the spirits of those who are killed by the enemy, without equal revenge of blood, find no rest, and at night haunt the houses of the tribe to which they belonged: but, when that kindred duty of retaliation is justly executed, they immediately get ease and power to fly away: This opinion, and their method of burying and mourning for the dead . . . . occasion them to retaliate in so earnest and fierce a manner.[63]

25. RETRIBUTION IN RELATION TO THE DEITY

Primitive man acts according to the principle of retribution in all cases in which he experiences good or evil or inflicts such upon others, and it does not make any difference whether his behavior refers to a member of his own or a foreign group, to a human being or an animal, to a plant, an inanimate object, or a deity. Primitive man's relationship to the deity—despite all his fear—is essentially characterized by the principle of *do ut des*.[64] Brinton writes:

The Indian deposits tobacco on the rocks of a rapid, that the spirit of the swift waters may not swallow his canoe; in a storm he throws overboard a dog to appease the siren of the angry waves. He used to tear the hearts from his captives to gain the favor of the god of war.[65]

The missionary, Father Brebeuf, once heard among the Hurons the following prayer, directed to a local god: "Oki, thou who livest in this spot, I offer thee tobacco. Help us, save us from shipwreck, defend us from our enemies, give us a good trade, and bring us back safe and sound to our villages."[66]

Another missionary, Father Allouez, in 1670 was the first white man ever to come to a certain Algonquin settlement. The natives, terrified by his fair complexion and his long black robe, took him for a god. They invited him into their council hut, approached him with a handful of tobacco, and addressed him with the following prayer:

This, indeed, is well, Blackrobe, that thou dost visit us. Have mercy upon us. Thou art a Manito. We give thee to smoke.—The Naudowessies and Iroquois are devouring us. Have mercy upon us.—We are often sick; our children die; we are hungry. Have mercy upon us. Hear me, O Manito, I give thee to smoke. Let the earth yield us corn; the rivers give us fish; sickness not slay us; nor hunger so torment us. Hear us, O Manito, we give thee to smoke.[67]

Radin has recorded the ensuing address which a Winnebago medicine man directed to his auxiliary spirits when treating a sick person:

Spirits, a person is sick and he offers me tobacco. I am on earth to accept it and to try to cure him. . . . . Haho! Here is the tobacco, Fire. You promised me that if I offered you tobacco you would grant me whatever request I made. Now I am placing tobacco on your head as you told me to when I fasted for four days and you blessed me. I am sending you the plea of a human being who is ill. He wishes to live. This tobacco is for you and I pray that the one who is ill be restored to health within four days.[68]

The sacrifice ceremony of the Babali, a Negro tribe on the Ituri (Belgian Congo), Schebesta describes as follows: "Kolanuts are pounded in hot water and the mash is poured out in a circle on a previously cleaned spot. A black or white fowl is placed in the middle of the circle; then one leaves the spot saying: Kunshi [deity] here is what is yours, please give me what is mine!"[69]

The attitude expressed by these petitions to a superhuman authority is not amoral—as one would suppose from the point of view of Christian ethics—but entirely moral, for it rests upon the principle of retribution, the basic norm of primitive society. Therefore, it is not to be interpreted as a debasement of religious feeling if in a Vedic sacrificial formula the sacrificer says to the deity: "Give me; I give you. Put it there for me; I put it there for you. Make an oblation to me; I make an oblation to you." Such has been since time immemorial the basic idea of the sacrifice.[71]

The idea of retribution is so self-evident to primitive man that when his sacrifices fail he occasionally turns against the superhuman authorities who are the supreme administrators and guardians of the principle. Wiedemann writes of the ancient Egyptians:

The Egyptian was certainly not so consciously reverent as to subordinate his wishes to the will of his gods—nay rather, he sought to force his own views upon them. If the sacred beasts [which were considered to be the incarnations of a deity] could not or would not help in emergency, they were beaten; and if this measure failed to prove efficacious, then the creatures were punished by death. Similar superstitious practices are to be found among the lower classes of widely alien races. When Heaven does not fulfil the desires of the people, the offence is visited by them upon idols or statues of the saints, according to nationality. But in the valley of the Nile such ideas were not cherished by the people alone; it was particularly among the upper classes that these low conceptions of deity prevailed, and it was the priests themselves who condemned and executed the sacred animal. Afterwards, indeed, they sought to secure its immortality by the embalmment of the body, thereby hoping to appease the wrath of the god, lest he should avenge the killing of the creature in which he had been incarnate.[72]

M. Friedrich reports:

When a chief dies in the district of Ibouzo, on the Niger, without leaving a son, his *Ikengua*, or domestic wooden idol of the god of riches, is cut in two and flung away into the bush, because it has procured no male descendant for its worshipper.[78]

The relationship of primitive man to his "fetish" is described by Schultze as follows:

The fetish provides protection. Service, however, demands counter-service and hence protection is granted to the suppliant only if he scrupulously offers a service in return. . . . . If the savage has rendered all necessary reverence to his fetish he obstinately requests from the gods a corresponding compensation; should that compensation not be granted then the savage treats the fetish as he would under similar circumstances deal with his fellow man: he tries to compel the fetish by means of chastisement and punishment. . . . . If the Ostjak has not success in hunting he beats his fetish thoroughly. . . . . The inhabitants of Kakongo threw all their fetishes into the fire when the fetishes, despite supplications, did not rescue them from an epidemic.[74]

L. M. Turner reports of the Eskimo of the Ungava District (Hudson Bay Territory):

When an individual fails to overcome the obstacles in his path the misfortune is attributed to the evil wrought by his attending spirit, whose good will must be invoked. If the spirit prove stubborn and reluctant to grant the needed assistance the person sometimes becomes angry with it and inflicts a serious chastisement upon it, deprives it of food, or strips it of its garments, until after a time it proves less refractory and yields obedience to its master.[75]

During a thunderstorm, which is regarded as the manifestation of a powerful demon, the Sakai (Malaya) shoot poisoned arrows at the sky, while the women throw burning embers into the air, pound the earth with bamboo rods, and shout into the storm: "Go away and leave us alone! We have not done you any harm, therefore do not harm us."[76] Kidd reports similar actions of the Bushmen, who believe that lightning is caused by a hostile spirit: "Thus the Bushmen will throw stones or shoot poisoned arrows at the lightning, hoping to drive it away."[77]

"In time of drought or sickness, or great trouble," Kidd[78] writes of the Kaffirs, they sacrifice to the angry ancestors.

If the trouble does not vanish after this ceremony the people get angry and say to the spirits, "When have we ceased to kill cattle for you, and when have we ever refused to praise you by your praise-names? Why, then, do you treat us so shabbily? If you do not behave better we shall utterly forget your names, and then what will you do when there is no one to praise you? You will have to go and live on grasshoppers. If you do not mend your ways we shall forget you. What use is it that we kill oxen for you and praise you? You do not give us rain or crops, or cause our cattle to bear well; you show no gratitude in return for all we do for you. We shall utterly disown you. We shall tell the people that, as for us, we have no ancestral spirits, and this will be to your shame. We are disgusted with you."

And Kidd adds: "Shelley's Prometheus could not speak more disdainfully to Zeus."

Junod noted among the South African Thonga that the prayers which were addressed to the gods in the event of a great misfortune contained insulting remarks. "There are two words used to designate this curious part of the prayer: *holobela*, or *holobisa*, to scold the gods, or *rukatela*, the actual word for 'to insult.' "[79] As an example he mentions a prayer which is spoken when a child is ill:

You, our gods, and you so and so, here is our *mhamba* (offering)! Bless this child, and make him live and grow; make him rich, so that when we visit him, he may be able to kill an ox for us. . . . . You are useless, you gods; you only give us trouble! For, although we give you offerings, you do not listen to us! We are deprived of everything! You, so and so (naming the god, to whom the offering must be addressed in accordance with the decree pronounced by the bones, i.e., the god who was angry, and who induced the other gods to come and do harm to the village, by making the child ill), you are full of hatred! You do not enrich us! All those who succeed, do so by the help of their gods!—Now we have made you this gift! Call your ancestors so and so; call also the gods of this sick boy's father, because his father's people did not steal his mother: these people, of such and such a clan, came in the daylight (to *lobola* the mother). So come here to the altar! Eat and distribute amongst yourselves our ox (the hen!) according to your wisdom.[80]

The illness of the child is regarded as a violation of the principle of retribution, for the misfortune occurred although the prescribed sacrifices had been offered to the gods. The "insult" of the gods consists in nothing else but in the fact that they are reminded of their duty to observe the principle of retribution.

A shaman of the Chukchee said to W. Bogoras with reference to the evil spirits: "We are surrounded by enemies. 'Spirits' always walk about invisibly with gaping mouths. We are always cringing, and distributing gifts on all sides, asking protection of one, giving ransom to another, and unable to obtain anything gratuitously."[81]

According to C. K. Meek,[82] the Hona, a tribe of the Adamawa
Province in Northern Nigeria, venerate certain stones which are symbols of the dead forefathers. They address these symbols. Among others
they say: "For we care for you; do you also care for us." If they have
a bad harvest or no luck in hunting, no cult is undertaken, and they
say to the symbol: "This year I will give you nothing, as you have
hindered us. We did well by you, but you have done ill by us." Meek
writes of the Jukun in Nigeria: "The relations between the Jukun and
the gods are based on the idea of reciprocity, and if the former carry
out their part of the contract the latter are expected to act likewise. A
Jukun will give up a cult from which he has consistently derived no
advantage."[83] Particularly significant are the statements of R. F. Fortune[84] on the religion of the Manus. The Manus expect from their
god, the Sir Ghost, that he protects them against death. But, if someone dies in the house of a native, the latter hold Sir Ghost responsible
for this death:

> Then the personal guardian has failed to guard. The sins have all been shriven and
> expiated, the moral government has been honored and appeased, but the death has
> occurred nevertheless. So out with Sir Ghost! His skull may be battered to powder,
> and the powder thrown into flames, or it may merely be hurled into the sea. Sir
> Ghost becomes a vague lurking danger of the middle seas, not very seriously regarded
> —then a sea-slug. But the system goes on. A new skull is bleached from the corpse of
> the recently dead. It is installed in the house front with the women wailing at the
> reminder of the death. Long live Sir Ghost—but no longer than his son and heir
> whom he protects.

This phenomenon can be explained from the fact that the Manus
consider the relationship to his Sir Ghost to be a contract. Fortune
characterizes this as follows:

> A better way to describe the yoked relationship between an individual mortal and
> his own individual Sir Ghost is to state that the two are close relatives who preserve a
> compact between them for their mutual advantage. In this sense they own each other
> and one of them by breaking the terms of the compact can cause the other to disown
> him. . . . . The terms of the compact between ward and Sir Ghost include first that
> ward take part in the rites over the mortal remains which Sir Ghost left behind him.
> It may seem at first that this action might be prompted by sufficiently natural motives
> of familial piety and sorrow. So it is, but that does not prevent it from being ration-
> alized later as being a part of a compact. It is a common feeling in Melanesia that a
> mourner deserves payment.

One of the duties to Sir Ghost is the observation of all prescriptions of
the social order. As compensation Sir Ghost is obliged to protect his
protégé against misfortune, particularly death. Fortune adds to this
the following detail:

On occasion the ward speaks to Sir Ghost pointing out that he is giving Sir Ghost shelter and house room from the ills of the weather, food and warmth, an honoured place in the front of the house, and his own deep respect. In return Sir Ghost will give him and his household good health, or good luck in fishing, or a fair wind for a canoe voyage; the request varies according to the most urgent need at the moment. If at any time Sir Ghost appears not to be giving what had been asked of him, his ward will easily be fired to anger. He will then threaten Sir Ghost with a final breaking of their compact. Does Sir Ghost wish to be thrown out of the house into the open, "to be washed by all rains, scorched by all suns," to have his name called upon by no or ?, to be homeless and forgotten? If Sir Ghost continues to withhold good fortune from him, then out Sir Ghost must go. . . . .

On the other hand, the respect which primitive man has for the retribution emanating from superhuman authority is so great that he does not dare come to the rescue of a man injured in an accident if he considers the accident a punishment imposed by the deity. A thunderclap is essentially interpreted as just such a punishment. When once lightning struck a Bassuto hut in which several children were inclosed, no one, not even their parents, dared go to their aid. The law of divine retribution must take its course.[85]

26. The Idea of Retribution and Magic

The principle of retribution plays an important part not only in religion but also in magic—in so far as one can separate the two. The social character of magic in general has been mentioned in another connection. Primitive man's relationship to the superhuman authority whose help he requests in his magical operations is determined by social rules. There are two sociologically different methods by which a fellow-man can be induced to a certain behavior: the direct or the indirect influence upon his will. The first consists in the expression of a wish by one individual to another; if both are equals, then it is a request; if one is superior to the other, it is a command. The second method is to make a promise or grant an advantage in the event the desired behavior takes place or to threaten an evil in the event of the opposite behavior. It is the principle of retribution which functions here. These also are the two ways in which magical procedures are undertaken. All these expressions of wishes directed to a superhuman authority are really spoken, sung, or mimically performed prayers. Any effort to distinguish them from religious prayers is in vain. Wherever they have the character of commands which the magician directs toward the superhuman authority, or wherever he seems or pretends to exercise compulsion upon the transcendental powers by his magical operations, the circumstances are special, and certainly not typical. Such requests are characterized by the fact that the magician identifies himself with the superhuman authority, a phenomenon which is generally observed only among professional magicians, i.e., in a social organization in which a special class or caste of magicians exists. Identification with the superhuman authority, however, occurs also in that sphere in which one speaks of religion and priests and no longer of magic and magicians.[86]

Some magical operations have the character of acts of retribution. They not only serve to show the superhuman authority what one expects from it, but they also give it something in order to obtain an analogous return. The snake dance of the Hopi, which has the character of rain-magic, may be cited as an example.[87] One of the essential elements of the nine-day-long ceremonies in August which are supposed to bring about rain is the capture of some rattlesnakes, as well as snakes of other kinds. Immediately before the snake hunt the following prayer is uttered: "Now, you emerge! All you clouds come out arrayed. And having come out and thus letting your rain water meander through our crops, they will sprout and our children will (have something to) eat. Thus our fathers have sent us. Therefore, you come out quickly."[88] It is most significant that on the ninth day, on which the dance takes place, the snakes are plunged into a bowl of medicine water and dropped down on the sand field. "The snakes were now passed in handfuls to the Kalehtaka [snake priest] who plunged them into the water and cast them upon the sand field." Afterward the main ceremony, a dance, is performed in which the snakes are held in the mouths of the dancer—sometimes even two snakes in the mouth of one dancer.[89] The snakes are called "our fathers."[90] Possibly the souls of ancestors are believed to reside in the snakes.[91] Not only by the whole very clearly expressed aim of the festivity but also by the address to the capturers of the snakes, it becomes evident that the snakes are regarded as capable of bringing rain: "You must pray that the clouds from the four world quarters have pity on us and rain for us. And if you find a rattle snake you must pray to him and it will rain."[92] Another very characteristic feature of the ceremony is the repeated sprinkling of corn meal. Water and meal are shown and given to the superhuman authority in order to get back rain and hence a good crop.

When drought lasts too long in the interior of Celebes, the Toradja resort to the grave of a famous chieftain, whom they entreat for rain. There they hang a bamboo rod, filled with water, over the grave.

From a hole in the bottom of the rod, water constantly drips onto the grave. The container is periodically refilled until it rains.[93] Of the natives of New Caledonia, Turner reports:

There was a rain-making class of priests. They blackened themselves all over, ex-humed a dead body, took the bones to a cave, jointed them, and suspended the skeleton over some taro leaves. Water was poured on the skeleton to run down on the leaves. They supposed that the soul of the departed took up the water, made rain of it, and showered it down again. . . . . If there was too much rain, and they wanted fair weather, they went through a similar process, only they kindled a fire under the skeleton and burned it up.[94]

When the Moqui dip snakes, which embody the death souls of their ancestors, into water, when the Toradja have water drip onto their chieftain's grave, when the natives of New Caledonia sprinkle a skeleton with water, it means that they give water to the superhuman authority in order to receive rain in return. Many similar procedures of so-called "rain-magic" can be observed in which the object representing the superhuman power, such as a fetish in human shape or a twig of a tree in which a deity resides, is brought into connection with water. All these practices of employing the very substance which one expects to obtain in return illustrate the principle of retribution at work.[95]

In magic, whenever the expression of the wish is combined with the principle of retribution, the act of magic becomes a sacrifice. Rain-sacrifice and rain-magic are one and the same. In the Vedic epoch in India, sacrifices had the character of imitation or analogy-magic; they consisted in an artificial reproduction (created by priests) of natural phenomena.[96] It must be remarked in this connection that the sacrifice, originally based on the principle *do ut des*, is itself an expression of a wish and that no sharp line of distinction can be drawn between the two functions of the magic act, namely, to show to the superhuman authority what one wishes to obtain from it and to give to the superhuman authority what one wishes to regain—not exactly in the same, but in an analogous, substance. Especially if the wish is expressed in certain objects, the latter are often regarded as sacrifices offered to superhuman beings. An example is the so-called *faditra* of the natives of Madagascar. It is a case of imitation-magic, which a missionary once described as expiatory sacrifice, "piaculum":

To expel death, offer something of death, as a victim: for example, a quarter of beef will preserve a sick person. To avoid sudden distress, offer some earth upon which lightning has fallen (for lightning strikes suddenly). In the same fashion, illness is driven away by presenting wood from an unhealthy tree. To keep off an unexpected misfortune (death, enslavement, etc.), tender a grasshopper from which the wings and feet have been removed (because for the insect this is a calamity sudden and complete). To escape being cast off, disinherited, or disowned (by parent, etc.), sacrifice a piece of a nail or a little money.[97]

27. RETRIBUTION IN RELATION TO ANIMALS

Especially toward those phenomena of nature which affect his daily life, namely, animals and plants, does primitive man behave according to the principle of retribution. This is indicated by the belief that animals may be killed only when they agree. The missionary Le Jeune writes in his report on North American Indians:

> As I was laughing at them, and telling them that Beavers do not know what is done with their bones, they answered me, "Thou dost not know how to take Beavers, and thou wishest to talk about it." Before the Beaver was entirely dead, they told me, its soul comes to make the round of the Cabin of him who has killed it, and looks very carefully to see what is done with its bones; if they are given to the dogs, the other Beavers would be apprised of it and therefore they would make themselves hard to capture. But they are very glad to have their bones thrown into the fire, or into a river; especially the trap which has caught them is very glad of this.[98]

In an article on the "superstitions" of the Ten'a (Dene) Indians in the middle part of the Yukon Valley (Alaska), Father Julius Jetté[99] reports: "Many animals have a *yega* (a kind of guardian spirit), but not all." It seems that it is particularly the animals which are hunted and fished that have a *yega*. Jetté says: "As most of these animals [which have a *yega*] are killed either for their flesh or for their fur, the *yega* cannot be expected to avenge their death. . . . . What the *yega* prosecutes, is the irreverent disposal of the bones or carcasses, the stealing of an animal caught in another man's trap, or similar prejudicial actions." Such "prejudicial actions" are, in relation to the beaver—and "beaver hunt is a familiar pursuit of our Ten'a"—that the wife of the hunter, at the time when her husband is hunting, does not fulfil her "duty to keep actively engaged in work during the whole day. She is allowed no idle moments, but must fill the intervals between her usual occupations by some extraordinary labor. Cutting wood and carrying water are especially recommended. This because the beaver is a very industrious animal." What is the punishment? "Consequently the animals will go to the traps of those who imitate this industry, and will keep away from the others. . . . . The *yega* keeps them aloof from the lazy ones . . . . the *yega* can provide the hunter with his game as well as deprive him of it." Thus the *yega*'s function is determined by the principle of retribution. But the *yega* of the beaver does not only pun-

D

ish laziness of the women; it punishes also adultery. If, during the time the husband is hunting, "the wife should be unfaithful to her husband and have intercourse with another man, this one shall be forthwith afflicted with orchitis and the husband will be informed of his wife's misbehavior by the fact that the dying beaver will dung, or urinate, or in some noticeable way move its reproductive organs. If he notices a motion of this sort, the injured husband has it in his power to cause the guilty woman's death, by smashing the beaver into a pulp, between two rocks. This will arouse the *yega's* fury against the woman who is the cause of this disgraceful treatment, and she shall die."

Other animals, such as the caribou, the mink, the marten (*Mustela Americana*), punish the hunter who steals such an animal from another hunter by inflicting different diseases upon him or his children. The bear, the wolf, and the wolverine are animals which are regarded with particular respect. The head of the wolverine is tabooed for all except the owner of the trap in which it was caught. "Death, and a sudden one at that, is the unavoidable consequence of the breaking of this taboo." The thief cannot escape its fate. Not only the animals, but also the traps, snares, nets, etc., have their *yega;* that is to say that the punishment which the act of stealing from a snare or trap entails, the disease of the thief or his children, is attributed not only to the *yega* of the stolen animal but also to that of the trap. "A fish-trap must not be abandoned. When a Ten'a has no more use for it, he takes it out and lays it aside in the bushes . . . . because he fears the chastisement of the *yega* which is attached to it."

Since in the life of the Ten'a tobacco plays an important part, tobacco also has its *yega*, "which is in charge of punishing those who steal it." It seems, also, that playing cards and whiskey are considered as having some connection with a *yega*. For "the Ten'a are always ready to pay for these in cash without asking for the credit which seems to be a necessary condition of all their purchases."

It is obvious that the belief in the *yega* of the animals guarantees the most important norms of the social order of this hunting people. Theft and adultery are under the sanctions attributed to the *yega:* incurable disease, death, and—what Jetté calls—the "aloofness" of the animals, the fact that the animals "keep away from the prevaricating hunter and his traps." The behavior of these animals endowed with a *yega* is interpreted according to the principle of retribution.

According to P. E. Goddard, the Hupa Indians believe in the existence of certain divinities who dwell in some mountain, near some rock, or in the river at some riffle. Chief among these are the Tans, the deer-tending gods. Each has his definite abode; one lives near Mud Springs, eight miles east of the valley, another has his home on Bald Hill, and others on the principal ridges. They tend the deer on their special ranges. They are inclined to be stingy and hostile to strangers. When they wish they confine the deer inside the hills. When one of them sees a campfire on his territory he sends messengers to see who it may be and whether they are friends or strangers. A spider that comes down on a web and then goes back is thought to be the spy of a Tan. Small birds circling about are also his servants. To gain his favor, it is customary to spend the first night of a hunting-expedition singing songs and making prayers to him. If he is pleased he will send out deer which will stand still to be shot. Should he take a dislike to a man, he will not only withhold the game, but he will cause the hunter to become lost or even destroy him. He watches carefully to see that the deer he does permit to be killed are properly treated. It is believed that the deer's ghost tells his master that at such a house he was well treated and that he would like to go back again. This good treatment consists in the observance of all the many laws concerning the dressing, serving, and eating of the deer and also the disposal of the bones.[100]

Stefánsson writes of the belief of the Eskimo:

The seals and whales live in the salt water, and are therefore continually thirsty. They have no means of getting fresh water, except to come to men for it. A seal will therefore allow himself to be killed by the hunter who will give him a drink of water in return; that is why a dipperful of water is always poured into the mouth of a seal when he is brought ashore. If a hunter neglect to do this, all the other seals know about it, and no other seal will ever allow himself to be killed by that hunter.[101]

An explorer asked an Eskimo medicine man why there were no bears to hunt. The answer was: "No bears have come because there is no ice, and there is no ice because there is too much wind, and there is too much wind because we mortals have offended the powers."[102]

In the myths of the Pawnee Indians the behavior of animals is interpreted as the fulfilment of a tacit agreement with men: the hunters make the flesh of the buffaloes "holy," and in exchange the animals allow the hunters to kill them. There is a tale that a boy in a miraculous way—by marrying a buffalo cow—got into a buffalo village, whence he brought several buffaloes home. Here they were killed, but their flesh was made "holy." Thereupon the souls of the buffaloes returned with the news to the buffalo village.[103] This fable is always told at a buffalo ceremony in order that the animals should come and allow themselves to be killed. That the hunters make the flesh of the buffaloes "holy" means that a part of the flesh of the killed animal is offered in sacrifice ceremonies to the spirits of the buffaloes. In another Pawnee tale a girl goes to a buffalo village. Her brothers search for her and find her playing with the animals. They take her home.

Since that time the buffaloes have allowed themselves to be killed. But every year a young girl must be sacrificed to them.[104] Through their sacrifices men recompense the favorable behavior of ânimals.

The idea that animals become subject to men by means of a contract which obligates men to a counterservice is widespread in myths[105] and is significant for the way in which primitive man interprets nature in accordance with the normative scheme of retribution. Even in the Middle Ages it happened that magistrates concluded preventive treaties with harmful animals, e.g., with locusts, and that proceedings were instituted and animals punished for having violated their part of the agreement.[106]

A motive widespread in myths is gratitude which animals render men for favors bestowed. Plutarch relates this story: "Coeranus, a Parian by birth," once bought in Byzantium

a draught of dolphins caught in a net . . . . and in danger of slaughter, ... and put them into the sea again. It happened not long after that Coeranus took a voyage in a vessel of fifty oars, carrying, as the story goes, several pirates. But between Naxos and the Bay of Paros he suffered shipwreck, and when all the rest were drowned, he alone was taken up by a dolphin that hastened to his succor, and carried to Sicynthus, and set ashore near the cave which to this day bears the name of Coeraneum. . . . . Some years after Coeranus' dying, his relations burnt his body near the seaside; at what time several dolphins appeared near the shore, as if they had come to his funeral; nor would they stir till the funeral was over.[107]

An Eskimo story tells: "Many months ago, a woman obtained a polar bear cub but two or three days old. Having long desired just such a pet, she gave it her closest attention, as though it were a son, nursing it, making for it a soft warm bed alongside her own, and talking to it as a mother does to her child. She had no living relative and she and the bear occupied the house alone. Kunikdjuaq, as he grew up, proved that the woman had not taught him in vain, for he early began to hunt seals and salmon bringing them to his mother." This, however, excited her neighbors' envy, "and, after long years of faithful service, his death was resolved upon. . . . . Upon this . . . . the woman had a long talk with her son . . . . telling him . . . . that the only way to save his life and hers was for him to go off and not return." Thereupon the bear said: " 'Good mother, Kunikdjuaq will always be on the lookout for you and serve you as best as he can.' Saying this, he took her advice and departed." The woman, however, went often to the sea to meet the bear, the latter "always serving her and receiving the same unbroken love of his youth."[108]

A Servian story runs as follows:

A poor youth three times set free a gold-fish which he had three times caught. Later he was cast out of his father's house and sent into the world. He was joined by a man, who swore friendship with him on a sword, and accompanied him to a city where many men had been mysteriously slain while undertaking to pass a night with the king's daughter. The hero undertook the adventure, and was saved by his companion, who cut off the head of a serpent that came from the princess's mouth. In the morning the youth was married to the lady, and divided all his property with his helper. On their way home the latter demanded half of the bride, and, while she was held by two servants, swung a sword above her. With a shriek she cast first two sections, and finally the tail of a serpent from her mouth. Thereupon the friend leaped into the sea, for he was the gold-fish.[109]

On the other hand, man also believes himself obligated toward animals. Thus, West African myths base the respect which the natives have for certain animals upon gratitude for favors received.

A certain myth tells that in a time of great danger, an animal came to the rescue of the ancestor or chief of the clan, and saved him. He was fleeing, it seemed, pursued by enemies who were trying to seize him, and he was halted by a river, until a helpful crocodile appeared, took him on its back, and carried him safe and sound to the other side. Hence the respect and attentions which the members of this clan evidence towards crocodiles.[110]

28. SOCIAL SIGNIFICANCE OF THE ANIMAL SOUL

From the point of view of primitive man, society is not confined to human beings alone, for he also ascribes souls to animals. He regards animals as part of society and considers himself associated with them through the same norm—retribution—which binds him to his fellowmen. The idea widespread among various peoples that animals—more correctly, certain animals—have souls which survive after death is revealed by the fact that these animal souls, like the death souls of human beings, are feared and respected as punishing and rewarding powers. This belief in the death souls of animals is most apparent in the case of game animals. Success and failure in hunting are always interpreted according to the principle of retribution; and the ideology of retribution assumes, here as elsewhere, the form of belief in the soul. Accordingly, man attributes death souls executing retribution not only to those animals on which his food depends but also to those animals which are most dangerous, such as snakes, lions, tigers, crocodiles.[111]

What is feared of the death soul of an animal is primarily vengeance for having killed it. Lichtenstein[112] writes in his *Travels in South Africa:*

If an elephant is killed after a very long and wearisome chase, as is commonly the case, they seek to exculpate themselves towards the dead animal, by declaring to him solemnly, that the thing happened entirely by accident, not by design. To atone for the offence more completely, or to make his power of no avail, the trunk is cut off and solemnly interred, they pronouncing repeatedly: "The elephant is a great lord, and the trunk is his hand."

In case of manslaughter a purification rite is performed.

If any one kills a man he is considered as unclean. He must then roast his meat upon a fire made of a particular sort of wood, which gives it a bitter taste, and having eaten it, must rub his face over with the cooled embers till it is quite black. After a certain time he may wash himself, rinse his mouth with milk, and dye himself brown anew. From that time he is clean.

But an analogous purification rite is necessary in case a man has killed a lion.

Does a lion come into the neighbourhood of a kraal, the people go out in a considerable number, armed with hassagais, kirris, and shields. The lion is surrounded, and enclosed in a narrow circle. They then tease him with their lances till he springs out from the bush, and attacks one of the hunters; the latter falls upon the ground, covering himself with his shield, when the rest attack the animal with their spears, and dispatch him: sometimes, however, some of them are wounded, or even lose their lives in the conflict. The first who receives a wound is considered as a hero, though he is made unclean by it for a time. When the hunting-party return to the kraal, the hero is raised by his companions upon their shields, and held up to the view of the people. One of them steps forward with strange gestures, and makes a speech in praise of the warrior; the rest continue somewhat behind, singing a sort of hymn, and striking with their kirris upon their shields. Some others, in the meantime, hastily build up a small mean hut at a little distance from the general dwelling-place, and here the hero is shut up apart from all the rest for four complete days; he is then purified, and brought in solemn form by a life-guard of the Chief, back to the kraal. In conclusion, a calf is slain, which all his companions partake with him, as a proof that he is again clean.

Also, the Ila-speaking peoples of Northern Rhodesia observe certain ceremonies when they kill an elephant. Smith and Dale give the following account:

The motive underlying the rites is to prevent the ghost of the deceased elephant from taking vengeance upon the hunters, and to induce it to assist them in bringing the same fate upon other elephants. When the elephant is dead the hunter runs off and is chased in mock resentment by his companions. Then he comes back and climbs upon the carcase, bearing "medicine" which, after chewing, he ejects into the wound and anus; in doing this he crawls about over the body. He then stands up and executes a dance upon the carcase, his companions surrounding the elephant and clapping their hands in greeting and congratulation. They then proceed to cut up the carcase. A beginning is made by cutting out the fat in the hollows of the temples: from its quantity and quality they judge the condition of the animal. They then open the abdomen and remove the intestines. The linings of the cavity are carefully separated and spread out to dry; they are called *ingubo* ("blankets"), and are intended for presentation to the *bodi*, the ladies of the community. They then cut through the diaphragm: through the opening the hunter puts his head, seizes the heart in his mouth, and drags it out. He does not eat it, but the biting is to give him strength in future hunting. Having removed the contents of the thorax, they attack the head. There is some special significance attached to the nerve of the tusk, called *kamwale* ("the maiden"). It is carefully abstracted and buried under the site of the camp-fire. It is not to be looked upon by the tiros in hunting—they are called *bana* ("children"); all the time it is being handled they must turn their heads, for were they to see it they would meet with misfortune. Having now completed their work, they return to the village, beating their axes together and singing. The people on hearing the noise flock to meet them, and a great feast, with plenty of beer, is made. But first an offering is made to Leza ("The Supreme Being"), to the *mizhimo* ("the ancestral spirits"), and to the ghost (*muzhimo*) of the deceased elephant which has accompanied them to the village. Addressing this last they say: "O spirit, have you no brothers and fathers who will come to be killed? Go and fetch them!" The ghost of the elephant then returns and joins the herd as the guardian of the elephant who has "eaten its name." Observe that they regard the elephants as acting as men act: one dies and another inherits his position, "eats his name," as they say.[113]

We have described the ceremonies following the death of an elephant. When a man kills an eland he must also go through certain rites to avert the retaliating power in the animal. After killing an eland the hunter chews leaves of a Mukono or Munto bush, together with a piece of *kaumbuswa* (ant-heap), holding meanwhile a lump of the latter under his foot. Some of the chewed leaves he rubs on his forehead and some on the eland's forehead. Having done this he throws at the eland's head the piece of ant-heap that was under his foot. He also cuts and splits a stick and jumps through the cleft, as the killer of a man does. He then goes off to the village to get people to help him in carrying home the meat. On their arrival at the eland he sits apart while they open the carcass. He must not join them at first, but once it is opened he may help them to skin and cut up the animal. Were these rites omitted, the eland would trouble him—would come at night and horn him, or in any case cause his death.[114]

Of the Jukun (Sudan), Meek writes:

Certain animals are regarded as having a powerful soul-substance or *bwi*, and if a hunter kills any of these animals he must protect himself by special rites. If the rites for allaying the pursuing ghost are not performed the hunter will be pursued by the ghost and killed.[115]

Among the Safwa (East Africa) the hunter who has killed an elephant has to take a medicine which protects him from the revenge of the animal. Roots, dug on the spot where the elephant fell, are used to stop up the elephant's nose and anus, for these are the places where the animal's soul escapes. Then the natives dance around the slain elephant and sing in chorus: "I want to stopper well, I, the elephant eater, I want to stopper well." There follows a typical identification ritual: the spear, with which the hunter killed the elephant, is washed in water, and the hunter drinks the water. "If the hunter has swallowed the water the soul of the elephant cannot kill him."[116]

The Lango, a Nilotic tribe, believe, according to Driberg,[117] that animals have a *winyo*, a kind of guardian spirit. If the hunter does not carry out certain procedures on the killed animal, "the guardian spirit would die with the animal and the slayer would not again be able to kill an animal of that species; but having been released in this way, it is attracted to the animal's slayer by the succeeding ceremonial." Driberg says: "Thus in the case of an animal which has been killed its guardian spirit is inverted by the above procedure, i.e. the direction of its influence is altered." Certain, though not all, animals have a *tipo*, a kind of soul. If such an animal is killed, the *tipo* must be placated by different ceremonies, since otherwise the *tipo* would take revenge on the murderer. Regarding this, Driberg says: "As in the case of the souls of humans, their *tipo* . . . . are very vengeful and dangerous."[118]

An Eskimo said to Rasmussen:

All the creatures that we have to kill and eat, all those that we have to strike down and destroy to make clothes for ourselves, have souls, like we have, souls that do not perish with the body, and which must therefore be propitiated lest they should revenge themselves on us for taking away their bodies.[119]

Primitive man frequently regards the killing of an animal in the same way as the murder of a man. Since the exigencies of life compel him to kill animals, he tries as best he can to avoid the menacing retribution. In the works of Tylor,[120] Frazer,[121] and Lévy-Bruhl[122] many examples can be found which show hunters begging the animal's pardon or trying in every possible way to placate the animal. After a hunting expedition, the participants, as after war against another tribe, undergo purification and expiation ceremonies. Those parts of the slain animals which have not been eaten are buried like a human body, and the same mourning ensues as for a deceased relative.

A myth of the Cherokee Indians clearly shows how strongly the principle of retribution dominates the relationship between man and animal. That part of the fable dealing with this particular aspect relates how in ancient times animals, birds, fish, insects, and plants were all able to speak and lived with man in peace and friendship. Human population, however, increased so rapidly that the animals felt constrained. Finally men began to kill the larger animals because of their meat and skins, and even to squash the smaller beings, such as frogs and worms, merely because of carelessness or love of mischief. Thereupon the Deer

held a council under their chief, the Little Deer, and after some talk decided to send rheumatism to every hunter who should kill one of them unless he took care to ask their pardon for the offense. They sent notice of their decision to the nearest settlement of Indians and told them at the same time what to do when necessity forced them to kill one of the Deer tribe. Now, whenever a hunter shoots a Deer, the Little Deer, who is swift as the wind and can not be wounded, runs quickly up to the spot and, bending over the blood-stains, asks the spirit of the Deer if it has heard the prayer of the hunter for pardon. If the reply be "Yes," all is well, and the Little Deer goes on his way; but if the reply be "No," he follows on the trail of the hunter, guided by the drops of blood on the ground, until he arrives at his cabin in the settlement, when the Little Deer enters invisibly and strikes the hunter with rheumatism, so that he becomes at once a helpless cripple. No hunter who has regard for his health ever fails to ask pardon of a Deer for killing it, although some hunters who have not learned the prayer may try to turn aside the Little Deer from his pursuit by building a fire behind them in the trail. . . . . Next came the Fishes and Reptiles, who had their own complaints against Man. They held their council together and determined to make their victims dream of snakes twining about them in slimy folds and blowing foul breath in their faces, or to make them dream of eating raw or decaying fish, so that they would lose appetite, sicken, and die. This is why people dream about snakes and fish. . . . . Finally the Birds, Insects, and smaller animals came together for the same purpose, and the Grubworm was chief of the council. It was decided that each in turn should give an opinion, and then they would vote on the question as to whether or not **Man** was guilty. Seven votes should be enough to condemn him. One after another denounced Man's cruelty and injustice toward the other animals and voted in favor of his death. The Frog spoke first, saying: "We must do something to check the increase of the race, or people will become so numerous that we shall be crowded from off the earth. See how they have kicked me about because I'm ugly, as they say, until my back is covered with sores"; and here he showed the spots on his skin. Next came the Bird—no one remembers now which one it was—who condemned Man "because he burns my feet off," meaning the way in which the hunter barbecues birds by impaling them on a stick set over the fire, so that their feathers and tender feet are singed off. Others followed in the same strain. The Ground-squirrel alone ventured to say a good word for Man, who seldom hurt him because he was so small, but this made the others so angry that they fell upon the Ground-squirrel and tore him with their claws, **and** the stripes are on his back to this day. . . . . They began then to devise and name so many new diseases, one after another, that had not their invention at last failed them, no one of the human race would have been able to survive. The Grubworm grew constantly more pleased as the name of each disease was called off, until at last they reached the end of the list, when some one proposed to make menstruation sometimes fatal to women. On this he rose up in his place and cried "*Wadan!* (Thanks!). I'm glad some more of them will die, for they are getting so thick that they tread on me." The thought fairly made him shake with joy, so that he fell over backward and could not get on his feet again, but had to wriggle off on his back, as the Grubworm has done ever since. . . . . When the Plants, who were friendly to Man, heard what had been done by the animals, they determined to defeat the latters' evil designs. Each Tree, Shrub, and Herb, down even to the Grasses and Mosses, agreed to furnish a cure for some one of the diseases named, and each said: "I shall appear to help Man when he calls upon me in his need." Thus came medicine; and the Plants, every one of which has its use if we only knew it, furnish the remedy to counteract the evil wrought by the revengeful animals. Even weeds were made for some good purpose which we must find out for ourselves.[123]

Since the killing of an animal is regarded by natives of the Congo as equal to the murder of man, the slaying of an elephant entails a sham prosecution of the successful hunter.[124] In order to protect the killer against the vengeance of the slain beast, the usual identification rites are observed which are customary in relation to murdered enemies. Should a Bergdama kill a lion, he lets some blood drop from the heart of the animal into an incision which he cuts for that purpose in his arm.[125] And, just as among certain Papua tribes the slain enemy must not be eaten by the murderer, so it is the custom among certain natives of New Guinea that the hunter who has dispatched a kangaroo must neither carry nor eat it. He therefore exchanges it for a kangaroo killed by someone else.[126] As one must anticipate blood revenge on the part of relatives of an assassinated human being, so one believes that the slaying of an animal arouses the vengeance of its fellow-animals.

L. W. Benedict writes of the Bagobo (Philippine Islands):

The killing of a snake, though perhaps not carrying a direct prohibition, is regarded as unwise, in view of the attitude which the snake community might assume toward the offender. My mountain guide, Ayoba, on catching sight of a poisonous black viper on the trail, uttered a startled exclamation, then cut a stick, picked up the reptile carefully and tossed it into the jungle. They told me at Bungoyan's home that if the snake had been put to death all its relatives and its friends might have come to bite us.[127]

In a Hindu love story a beautiful girl kills a snake in order to take possession of a gem. But Wásuki, the king of the snakes, "heard of the slaughter of his subject, and he was wroth, and determined to punish the criminal. So he assumed the form of a man" and married the girl. On the day after the marriage she was found dead in her bed. On her bosom were two small marks. No bridegroom was to be seen. But a black cobra crept out of the bed and disappeared through a hole in the wall.[128]

E. F. im Thurn reports of the Indians of Guiana:

Before leaving a temporary camp in the forest, where they have killed a tapir and dried the meat on a babracot, Indians invariably destroy this babracot, saying that should a tapir, passing that way, find traces of the slaughter of one of his kind, he would come by night on the next occasion when Indians slept at that place and, taking a man, would babracot him in revenge.[129]

Heckewelder writes:

I found also that the Indians, for a similar reason, paid great respect to the rattlesnake, whom they called their *grandfather*, and would on no account destroy him. One day, as I was walking with an elderly Indian on the banks of the Muskingum, I saw a large rattlesnake lying across the path, which I was going to kill. The Indian immediately forbade my doing so; for, said he, the rattlesnake is grandfather to the Indians, and is placed here on purpose to guard us, and to give us notice of impending danger by his rattle, which is the same as if he were to tell us "look about!" Now, added he, if we were to kill one of those, the others would soon know it, and the whole race would rise upon us and bite us. I observed to him that the white people were not afraid of this; for they killed all the rattlesnakes that they met with. On this he enquired whether any white man had been bitten by those animals, and of course I answered in the affirmative. "No wonder, then"; replied he, "you have to blame yourselves for that! you did as much as declaring war against them, and you will find them in *your* country, where they will not fail to make frequent incursions. They are a very dangerous enemy; take care you do not irritate them in *our* country; they and their grandchildren are on good terms, and neither will hurt the other."[130]

Since it is believed that the slain animal may take vengeance, the behavior of the living beast is also sometimes interpreted according to the principle of retribution. Hence the death of a human being caused by elephants, lions, tigers, or bears is often regarded as an act of vengeance of the animal or its kind. Indeed, it is a widespread primitive inclination to interpret a human death inflicted by an animal as an act of vengeance for some committed wrong. In Tonga (Polynesia) it is believed, according to W. Mariner, that sharks do not eat innocent people.

If a man be guilty of theft, or any crime whatsoever, he is said to have broken the taboo; and as all such persons are particularly supposed liable to be bitten by sharks, an awkward mode of discovering a thief is founded upon this notion, by making all the suspected persons go into the water, where sharks frequent, and he who is bitten or devoured is looked upon as the guilty person. [131]

On the other hand, the killing of certain animals is permitted only under the title of retribution for a wrong committed by the animal or its relatives. Charles Hose and W. McDougall report:

Like all the other races of Sarawak, the Kenyahs regard the crocodiles that infest their rivers as more or less friendly creatures. They fear the crocodile and do not like to mention it by name, especially if one be in sight, and refer to it as "the old grandfather." But the fear is rather a superstitious fear than the fear of being seized by the beast. They regard those of their own neighbourhood as more especially friendly, in spite of the fact that members of their households are occasionally taken by crocodiles, either while standing incautiously on the bank of the river or while floating quietly at evening time in a small canoe. When this happens it is believed either that the person taken has in some way offended or injured one or all of the crocodiles, or that he has been taken by a stranger crocodile that has come from a distant part of the river and therefore did not share in the friendly understanding usually subsisting between the people and the local crocodiles. But in any case it is considered that the crocodiles have committed an unjustifiable aggression and set up a blood-feud which can only be abolished by the slaying of one or more of the aggressors. Now it is the habit of the crocodile to hold the body of his victim for several days before devouring it, and to drag it for this purpose into some muddy creek opening into the main river. A party is therefore organized to search all the neighbouring creeks, and the first measure taken is to prevent the guilty crocodile escaping to some other part of the river. To achieve this they take long poles, frayed with many cuts, and set them up on the river bank at some distance above and below the scene of the crime and at the mouths of all the neighbouring creeks and streamlets; and they kill fowls and pray that the guilty crocodile may be prevented from passing the spots thus marked. They then search the creeks, and if they find the criminal with the body of his victim they kill him, and the feud is at an end. But, if they fail to find him thus, they go out on the part of the river included between their charmed poles, and, with their spears tied to long poles, prod all the bed of this part of the river, and thus generally succeed in killing one or more crocodiles. They then usually search its entrails for the bones and hair of the victim so as to make sure that they have caught the offending beast. But even if they do not obtain conclusive evidence of this kind they seem to feel that justice is satisfied and that the beast killed is probably the guilty one.—Except in the meting out of just vengeance in this way, no Kenyah will kill a crocodile, and they will not eat its flesh under any circumstances. But there is no evidence to show that they regard themselves as related by blood or descent to the crocodiles or that their ancestors ever did so.[132]

The Kayan's attitude towards the crocodile is practically the same as the Kenyah's. We append the following notes of a conversation with a young Kayan chief, Usong, and his cousin Wan:—There are but very few Kayans who will kill a crocodile except in revenge. But if one of their people has been taken by a crocodile, they go out together to kill the criminal, and they begin by saying, "Don't run away, you've got to be killed, why don't you come to the surface? You won't come out on the land because you have done wrong and are afraid." After this he will perhaps come to the land, and if he does not he will at least float to the surface of the water and is then killed with spears.[133]

The Dayak of Borneo kill an alligator only if the latter has killed a man. In this connection J. Perham reports:

For why, say they, should they commit an act of aggression, when he and his kindred can so easily repay them? But should the alligator take a human life, revenge becomes a sacred duty of the living relatives, who will trap the man eater in the spirit of an officer of justice pursuing a criminal. Others, even then, hang back, reluctant to embroil themselves in a quarrel which does not concern them. The man-eating alligator is supposed to be pursued by a righteous Nemesis; and whenever one is caught they have a profound conviction that it must be the guilty one, or his accomplice.[134]

A similar relationship exists between the natives of Madagascar and the crocodiles. They never kill such an animal "except in retaliation for one of their friends who has been destroyed by a crocodile. They believe that the wanton destruction of one of these reptiles will be followed by the loss of human life, in accordance with the principle of *lex talionis.*"[135] Here the killing of an animal which is guilty of murder of a human being is carried out in the form of a criminal procedure.[136] "The Cinghalese are persuaded that the souls of men pass into domestic buffaloes rather than into other animals. Accordingly they will not kill these creatures lest they kill or injure their relations or friends."[137] The Batak of Sumatra regulate their behavior toward tigers according to the principle of retribution, which they formulate as follows: "He who owes gold must pay in gold: he who owes breath (that is, life) must pay with breath."[138] John Macrae writes of the Kookies:

> The Kookies are a race of people, that live among the mountains to the north east of the *Chittagong* province. . . . . The Kookies, like all savage people, are of a most vindictive disposition; blood must always be shed for blood; if a tiger even kills any of them, near a *Parah*, the whole tribe is up in arms, and goes in pursuit of the animal; when if he is killed, the family of the deceased gives a feast of his flesh, in revenge of his having killed their relation. And should the tribe fail to destroy the tiger, in this first general pursuit of him, the family of the deceased must still continue the chase; for until they have killed either this, or some other tiger, and have given a feast of his flesh, they are in disgrace in the *Parah*, and not associated with, by the rest of the inhabitants. In like manner, if a tiger destroys one of a hunting party, or of a party of warriors, on an hostile excursion, neither the one nor the other (whatever their success may have been) can return to the *Parah*, without being disgraced unless they kill the tiger.[139]

29. GUARANTEEING OF THE SOCIAL ORDER THROUGH THE RETRIBUTORY FUNCTION OF THE ANIMAL SOUL

Of great importance is the fact that primitive men believe that retribution may not only be exercised by animals when they are killed but also operates when the social order, or at least some norms, especially certain sex regulations, are violated. Such violations are under the sanction of punishment, the author and executor of which are animals, or their death souls, or some other deities who rule over animals and obviously present themselves as personifications of these animals. In his report on the Selknam Indians, Gusinde writes:

> If a hunter was especially lucky in killing several guanacos but left behind a whole animal or part of its flesh to rot and thus to become unusable, the rest of the guanacos grow furious at the hunter and cry out: "We shall play a trick on him which he will long remember." Even though he is an excellent sharpshooter he will be unable to bring anything home for months. Thus the remaining guanacos take revenge on him for allowing so much meat to spoil.[140]

The observance of the commandment not to waste the flesh of game animals is guaranteed by the animals themselves.

This extension of the function of retribution of animals, animal souls, or animal deities seems to have some connection with the frequently mentioned idea that animals cannot be killed against their will but that they give themselves up and allow themselves to be killed at their own choice and in exchange for certain counterservices in order to provide man with food. Consequently, the slaying of an animal cannot be regarded as a delict demanding retribution; the punishment which threatens from the animal must then refer to another wrong. Sometimes even the idea that the animal was killed with its own consent does not render reconciliation of the animal by the hunter superfluous. If the Giljaks kill a bear, they believe that this happened only because the bear allowed it; nevertheless, after the killing, they observe a ceremony which is directed at placation of the slain beast.[141] Such an act, however, may be only an expression of the respect which one feels for the power whose concern is maintenance of the social order. The missionary Petitot reports of the Dene, neighbors of the Eskimos: "For a long time our trapper Le Noir came to the mission only to sigh and complain that since he had been baptized the animals were making fun of him. 'There are elks about,' he said, 'I see them and I track them, but they will not let themselves be killed. . . . . They laugh at me.' "[142] Misfortune in hunting is interpreted as punishment for some committed wrong.

The punishment, however, consists not only in misfortune in hunting but also in other evils which befall the hunter or his family, such as illness or death. This is quite obvious in an account given by Boas of the Eskimos of Baffinland and Hudson Bay. They worship a goddess Sedna.

This woman, the mother of the sea-mammals, may be considered as the principal deity of the Central-Eskimo. She has supreme sway over the destinies of mankind, and almost all the observances of these tribes are for the purpose of retaining her good will. or of propitiating her if she has been offended. She is believed to live in a lower world, in a house built of stone and whale-ribs. . . . . She cannot walk, but slides along, one leg bent under, the other stretched forward. . . . . The souls of seals, ground seals, and whales are believed to proceed from her house. After one of these animals has been killed, its soul stays with the body for three days. Then it goes back to Sedna's abode, to be sent forth again by her. If, during the three days that the soul stays with the body, any taboo or proscribed custom is violated, the violation (*pitsse'te*) becomes attached to the animal's soul, and causes it pain. The soul strives in vain to free itself from these attachments, but is compelled to take them down to Sedna. The attachments, in some manner not explained, make her hands sore, and she punishes the people who are the cause of her pains by sending to them sickness, bad weather, and starvation. If, on the other hand, all taboo have been observed, the sea animals will allow themselves to be caught: They will even come to meet the hunter.[143]

Animals are endowed with superhuman powers. They have the ability to perceive whether a man has violated a taboo.[144] This belief apparently has some connection with the idea that violations of taboo must be confessed in order to avoid evil consequences.

The transgressor of a custom is distasteful to Sedna and to the animals, and those who abide with him become equally distasteful through contact with him. For this reason it has come to be an act required by custom and morals to confess any and every transgression of a tabu, in order to protect the community from the evil influence of contact with the evil-doer. The descriptions of Eskimo life given by many observers contain records of starvation, which according to the belief of the natives, was brought about by some one transgressing a law and not announcing what he had done.[145]

Eskimos believe that a sin can be expiated by such a confession. The gods who punish by means of misfortune in hunting, illness, starvation, and death and who reward with prosperity are the death souls of sea animals acting as agents of the goddess Sedna, who personifies the whole sea-animal world. Her essential function is to guarantee the social order of the Eskimo.

The most important object of the religious ceremonies of the Eskimo is to appease the wrath of Sedna, of the souls of animals, or of the souls of the dead that have been offended by the transgressions of taboos. This is accomplished by the help of the guardian spirits of the angakut.

The meaning of the ceremonies is that the souls of the angakut ("magicians") go to Sedna.

They ask her if they are to have plenty of food and good health. Then Sedna reproaches them for all the transgressions that they have made in previous times but promises them that if they will keep her laws, she will send them plenty of food and good health. Finally the souls of the angakut return, and they report the instructions and promises of Sedna.[146]

The natives of Bengal, according to many reports, believe that violations of sex taboos are punished by animals. When a village is afflicted by epidemics or devastations through wild beasts, they explain the calamities as punishment for certain sexual delicts. In the same way the Orang Glai, a tribe in the mountains of Annam, think that as punishment for prohibited sexual intercourse the culprit will be devoured by tigers.[147] It is reported that the Greenlanders interpret the migrations of whales, musk oxen, and reindeer as penalties for adultery; for the same reason an open channel is supposed to have remained icebound.[148] Frequently, retribution exercised by animals guarantees women's marital fidelity while their husbands are hunting. Thus elephant-hunters in East Africa believe that adultery committed by their wives in their absence entails their being wounded or even killed by animals. Similarly, the Moxos Indians in eastern Bolivia deem that a hunter whose wife is unfaithful during his absence will be bitten by a snake or a jaguar.[149]

30. Significance of Rites as Preparation for the Hunt

In line with the pre-eminent significance which the principle of retribution has for the relationship of primitive man to animals, especially game animals, and in close connection with the fact that his conduct during and after the killing of an animal is determined by the desire to avoid the threatening consequences of retribution from the animal are certain ceremonies observed among various peoples relative to good luck in hunting. In this way may be interpreted some specific expiation and purification rites among which temporary chastity, fasting, and other self-tormentings play a decisive part.

Especially widespread is the custom of desisting from sexual intercourse, which is regarded as an essential condition for success in hunting. "This practice of observing strict chastity as a condition of success in hunting and fishing is very common among rude races," writes Frazer,[150] who mentions several examples of the custom. And undoubtedly he is right when he denies that the practice has hygienic reasons, such as the intention of the hunter not to weaken himself before the exacting enterprise. For other customs which likewise pertain to preparation for the hunt, such as fasting for several days, have, in fact, just that effect which is mistakenly supposed to be avoided by chastity. But, on the other hand, one cannot agree with Frazer in his declaration that the custom is merely "superstition." "Superstition" offers no adequate explanation. However, he does give one: "In general it appears to be supposed that the evil effect of incontinence is not so much that it weakens him, as that, for some reason or other, it offends the animals, who in consequence will not suffer themselves to be caught." Yet there would seem to be scarcely any reason why animals should be offended by the sexual intercourse of the hunter. Such a belief, furthermore, is hardly compatible with the views which primitive peoples have about sexual life and with the extraordinary importance they attach to sexuality as one of their main enjoyments. It would mean to impute to primitive man Christian ideas of morality should one ascribe to him the conviction that sexual intercourse, especially the legal one between husband and wife, would be a sin and would offend the authority inflicting retribution. A more plausible explanation is that desistance from sexual intercourse—since it is essentially abstinence from pleasure, a self-tormenting similar to fasting and other expiation rites—is an anticipatory self-punishment. This idea is very familiar to primitive man. It can be explained by the predominance which the principle of retribution has among primitive men. He inflicts evils upon himself in order to punish wrongs committed. The substantializing tendency which dominates his thinking makes him believe that the wrong is thereby physically paralyzed, or rather expelled by the self-imposed penalty.[151] Absolved of sin, he will be able to evade that much worse punishment, namely, that the animals will not allow themselves to be caught, which awaits him should he go hunting burdened with sins. This would mean hunger not for himself alone but for the whole tribe. If bad luck in hunting is regarded as punishment for committed wrongs, then nothing is more natural than the attempt to avoid by self-torture the threatening penalty inflicted by animals.

No other meaning can satisfactorily account for the preparations of American Indians for a bear hunt with long fasts and purification ceremonies. They even offer new sacrifices to the death souls of animals slain in previous hunts and beg them to favor the hunters again.[152] Undoubtedly, fasting has the same significance as sacrifice and prayers. But why should the fasting of hunters be agreeable to the dead and especially to the still living bear when it is believed that animals agree to their being killed in order to provide men with food? By seeing in it a "mystical" or "magical" connection nothing is clarified; an explanation has actually been avoided. An explanation, however, can be found in the principle of retribution which determines primitive man's relationship to the game animals. Fasting, too, is an attempt to evade by self-punishment a much worse evil, which threatens from the superhuman authority for certain delicts.

31. Animal Soul and Human Soul as Retributory Authority

Thus the soul of an animal has the same function as the death soul of a man, namely, retribution. It is, therefore, to be assumed a priori that there is a certain connection between the idea of the death souls of men and the souls of animals. And, indeed, that is so. Primitive man, as already pointed out, does not, like civilized man, perceive an essential difference between himself and an animal. Savages regard animals as equal; frequently as superior to men in physical and psychic powers; sometimes even as divine beings. Just

in this relationship to animals the lack of ego-consciousness so characteristic of primitive man becomes apparent. Frazer is right in
saying: "The savage is not so proud; he commonly believes that animals are endowed with feelings and intelligence like those of men, and
that, like men, they possess souls which survive the death of their bodies either to wander about as disembodied spirits or to be born again
in animal form."[153] But primitive man does not only—perhaps not
even very much—believe that animal souls are reincarnated in
animal bodies; he also believes—and this shows convincingly the lack
of a feeling of difference between himself and the animal—that the
death souls of human beings may be reincarnated in animal bodies.

In this idea that the dead, and especially the dead ancestors, survive
in animal bodies, whence, as animal souls, they penetrate women's
bodies in order to be reborn as human beings—an idea which belongs
to the oldest elements of the belief in the souls of the dead—the origin
of totemism can be assumed.[154] Inasmuch as the animal is regarded as
embodying a human death soul, the difference between men and animals, self-evident for civilized man, has no meaning at all for primitive
man. Indeed, the living animal is considered the reincarnated man.
With this in mind, it is erroneous to assert that primitive men attribute
to animals a soul which survives after death. On the contrary, the
death souls of animals are the death souls of men. It is the human
death soul which performs that decisive function which causes the animal or its soul to be feared and respected as an authority of retribution. Cases illustrating this fact are more numerous than one would at
first be inclined to believe. Koch-Grünberg says of South American
Indians:

Whereas among the Bororo the souls of ordinary human beings penetrate into red
araras, the medicine men, in easily understandable extension, at death become other
animals than birds. . . . . Should such animals, in which medicine men are embodied,
unfortunately or foolishly be killed, then they avenge themselves by carrying off the
living. A Bororo once killed a huge Dourado and died soon afterwards. Thereupon
his kinsmen said: You see, the Dourado was a medicine man and killed him. The
death of one of their tribesmen is, therefore, regarded as an act of vengeance on the
part of a slain man.[155]

A tale of the Eskimos of Cumberland Sound relates that a woman,
after her death, entered into the body of a polar bear in order to avenge
herself for the injustices she had suffered during her lifetime.[156]

That the soul of a killed animal is a human death soul whose vengeance one fears and therefore tries to reconcile becomes apparent in the
ceremonies which the western Equatorial pigmies undertake when

killing an elephant. If a male elephant is killed, they cut off his penis and the chief wreathes his neck, as well as the elephant's tusks, with liana blossoms, with which a bride is attired before her wedding. The elephant is thought to be deceived by the rites which represent his death and emasculation as marriage. The chieftain sings a song in which the animal is addressed as "Father Elephant" and is assured that no one wanted to kill him. "The warrior did not take your life; your hour had come." The elephant is requested, like the soul of a deceased human being, not to return and not to be angry. "Your life will be better from now on, your life in the realm of the spirits. Our fathers will renew the bond with you."[157] It is decisive that the elephant is referred to as "father." This is certainly no mere manifestation of respect, but the expression of a conviction that in the beast lives the death soul of a powerful ancestor. That deceased chieftains survive in elephants is an idea familiar to these primitive people.[158]

The Kai of New Guinea believe that the death souls of human beings assume the form of a certain animal, the cuscus, which lives in those regions haunted by the souls of the dead. It is not prohibited to kill and eat these animals; this is allowed under certain restrictions, the most important of which is the duty to reconcile the slain animal. The hunter must not butcher the animal immediately

but must let it lie for some time, perhaps for a whole night, and must spread on its body the sacrifices which he offers to pacify the injured spirit. If the latter accepts the spiritual substance of these valuables the animal may be eaten. The sacrifice is accompanied by these words: "Take the presents and leave us what has become a wild animal that we may eat it."

This reconciliation ceremony is obviously intended to evade retribution from the slain animal. In fact, once when a house with all its inhabitants was buried in a landslide, the tragedy was interpreted as punishment "for the unexpiated killing of a serpent living in a place where spirits dwell."[159] Vendetta, which primitive man fears to arouse when he kills an animal, is frequently the vengeance of the ancestors who survive in animals. J. O. Dorsey reports of the Teton Indians:

The Tetons pray to gray spiders and to those with yellow legs. When a person goes on a journey and a spider passes, one does not kill it in silence. For should one let it go or kill it without prayer, bad consequences must ensue. In the latter case another spider would avenge the death of his relation. When the spider is met the person must say to it: "Ikto'mi . . . . O Grandfather Spider, the Thunderers kill you!" The spider is crushed at once and his spirit believes what has been told him. His spirit probably tells this to the other spiders, but they cannot harm the Thunderers. If one prays thus to a spider as he kills it, he will never be bitten by other spiders.[160]

The feared spider to which the Teton directs his prayers, is considered to be his "grandfather."

Especially in those cases in which certain animals guarantee the maintenance of the social order do those creatures appear as the abodes of human death souls, particularly ancestral spirits. The Batak call the tiger *ompu*, that is, "grandfather." They do not like to kill him, since the soul of an ancestor may reside in him. Should killing become inevitable, however, the slain beast must be reconciled by sacrifices. "The priest addresses the spirit of 'Mr. Grandfather,' begs his pardon, and explains why the killing was necessary."[161] Warneck reports that

some tigers are regarded as the temporary seat of a *sombaon* [ancestral soul of high rank]. If a tiger is slain, it is brought into the village and everyone brings his rice measure to show that he has not falsified the scales, for the tiger is regarded as the executor of punishment inflicted by ancestors and deities. Whoever is killed by a tiger must have committed a grave violation of custom.[162]

The Kenias and other tribes of Borneo presume souls of the dead in crocodiles. They call these animals "old grandfathers." The souls

watch over human beings and avenge all serious violations of traditions. If a villager is attacked and killed by a crocodile it is punishment for the infringement of an old practice, for example marriage to a Kayan girl which transgresses the law of tribal endogamy.[163]

On the Key Islands [Indonesia] it is said that in earlier times the spirits of the deceased entered the bodies of crocodiles, snakes, whales, and other animals; consequently even today the figures of these creatures are set up in fields to keep thieves away. Every family, as far as it knows its pedigree, chooses the corresponding animal as its *matakau* [that is, "red eye"]. "Should a field which is under the protection of such a *matakau* be robbed, the thief is not held liable by his fellowmen but his punishment is left to the *matakau*.[164]

Indonesians quite generally, says Kruijt, regard tigers, crocodiles, and elephants as reincarnations of their ancestors and therefore see in the killing of a human being by such an animal punishment for the violation of an *adat* provision. Otherwise primitive man, who has a vivid sense of justice, could not explain why such an animal should kill a man without provocation.[165] If a wrong is committed by a beast which may possibly be inhabited by the soul of an ancestor, one may react against the animal but only to punish it. This is the case in Java and Sumatra, where the crocodile is regarded as a "grandfather."[166]

The Canelos Indians of Ecuador believe that deceased men are reborn in jaguars. This does not prevent them from killing these animals; they do it, however, only to exercise lawful retribution for injustices perpetrated by the jaguars.[167]

To exercise retribution on an animal presupposes that it is considered as a human being, i.e., a member of one's own society. This is sociologically the sense of the idea that a deceased man is reincarnated in animal form. Natives of Cham (Indo-China) trace their illnesses to the displeasure of squirrels. These rodents, according to their belief, embody the souls of dead children.[168] The Pangwe (West Africa) are of the opinion, says Tessmann, that there are both "good" and "bad" souls. It seems, however, that the latter are not so "bad" in themselves as they are dangerous to bad men. For, "angered over the wickedness of their fellow men, they can transform themselves into animals, especially man-killing beasts like leopards, elephants, buffaloes, etc."[169] As such, they can take revenge on the village folk who provoked their indignation.

A close connection also exists between the prohibition of eating meat of certain animals, a taboo the violation of which entails illness or death, and the retributory function of human death souls. This is true of the South American Indians, about whom Karsten writes:

Since the souls of dead Indians—especially the souls of the *baris* [medicine men]—are reincarnated in the birds, fishes and animals, these are taboo and cannot be eaten. The death or sickness of the person who eats of their flesh is interpreted as an act of revenge on the part of the animal killed, or rather of the spirit incarnated in it. This is in fact the most common kind of taboo in all South America.[170]

Among these primitive peoples belief in the reincarnation of human death souls in animals is so prevalent that Karsten notes: "Thus there is hardly an animal being, however insignificant, which may not serve as the temporary abode of a human soul."[171] The idea that all animal beings were once human beings, or vice versa,[172] is probably a consequence of this belief in reincarnation. Wherever such credence exists, one may presume that the souls attributed to animals are human souls, namely, the souls of the deceased which continue their existence in animals; this is especially true if retribution is thought to be exercised by living or dead animals.[173]

32. RETRIBUTION IN RELATION TO PLANTS

Just as the relationship of primitive man to animals, so his relationship to plants—especially to trees, at least to those trees important to him—is determined by the principle of retribution. Should one "kill" them, that is cut them down, because they are necessary for the satisfaction of one's needs, then one must expect retribution. Therefore one has to conciliate them. The Kayan of Borneo consider plants animated; hence the latter take revenge if they are not well treated.

"After building a house these natives do penance for a whole year for having thereby ill-treated several trees; that is, a period follows in which many things are prohibited (lali)."[174] When the Kattourie (India) fell certain trees, they observe rites similar to those performed by hunters in respect to the animals they wish to kill. The intention of these ceremonies is to assuage the anger of the soul which they presume in the tree.[175]

The same precautions are taken by the Dschagga[176] (East Africa) when they cut down those trees which provide wood for their beehives or in which the hives themselves are located. The leader of the woodsmen addresses the tree, before it is felled, as follows: "Msedi, you who are so large, I bring to you the longori (axe), the mixer. Poverty makes me come to you, a need for children, goats, and cattle."[177] Especially significant is the behavior toward a tree called mringa, which the Dschagga also fell for their bee-keeping. "The owner must not participate in the felling. All measures to make use of the tree are represented to him as preparations for a wedding." The tree is referred to as a girl who is to be married and thus released from her father's or brother's, i.e., the owner's, house. On the day before the hewing, the owner approaches the tree and offers various sacrifices, such as milk, beer, honey, beans, etc.

First he puts some of the beans into his own mouth, chews, and spits them at the trunk of the tree with the words: "Mana mfu," that is, departing child, my sister, "I give you a husband. He shall marry you, my daughter. You must go now to your husband. . . . . Do not think that I force you to go, but you are grown up now and have reached maturity like other children. . . . ." On the next day the owner leaves home before the acquirers come in order not to be witness to the felling. His place is taken by a rite assistant, the mngari. The latter is instructed by the owner to hand over the tree to the acquirers, just as a girl is given away when she marries. Among the customary ceremonies the acquirers present the mngari with a calabash full of beer and ask him for his sister. After drinking it, the mngari pours the rest on the tree and says: "My departing child, I have drunk the child-parting beer and accepted my delivery present—I deliver you to your husband today as you were told by your father yesterday. . . . . Good luck, my child! Your face should beam; it should be coveted by all bees; they ought to come and ask for you." Then the mngari departs and the men begin to work. When they lay on the longori (axe) the foreman says: "Departing child of a human being, we do not fell you but we marry you. And we do not marry you by force but with gentleness and kindness."

After the tree is felled and the woodsmen are occupied with it,

the owner approaches as if by chance. He collapses when he sees the felled tree and laments as he would over an outrage which he could not prevent because he came too late. "You robbed my sister, you have taken my child!" With these and many other words he shows the tree his anger. The others try their utmost to soothe him and to make him believe that everything will turn out much better for his sister; they attempt to convince him that they will make life more agreeable for her so that he, too, will have more joy of her than before. At the same time they extend their folded hands until he finally grasps them, comforted, and agrees to an amicable settlement.[178]

This is a characteristic example of the fact that primitive man, even though he fears the superhuman authority because of the retribution emanating from it, nevertheless attempts to deceive it.

When a native builds a beehive, he does not, as is customary, anoint his body with butter.

For God might take him for rich and might deny him the bees. A similar practice is indulged by a ditch digger while he is digging a pit-fall. He does not wash himself but goes to bed covered with dirt because he wishes to appear to God and his ancestors as a very poor man who must anoint himself with earth.[179]

That the souls imagined in the trees are ancestral souls or at least are connected with them is expressly attested by the baobab tree, which provides the bast necessary for beekeeping. The Dschagga address this tree as "father." Before they detach the bast from the tree, they offer drink-sacrifices. From the bast they manufacture rope. This rope, too, receives an offering and "is by that legally introduced to the community of the family and the clan."[180] The tree *mrie*, to which beehives are attached, has to be notched. They address the tree as follows: "*Mrie*, you chieftain, be of good luck to us. . . . . *Mrie*, I notch you, but you who are a chieftain do not think I do it because I consider myself powerful. It is poverty which makes me come to you, etc." The natives fear that the tree may take revenge for the injury; therefore they request:

When a man climbs you do not let him fall. . . . . Do not let the swarm of bees fall because of a broken twig, *mrie*, strengthen the twigs. And when we leave you after having asked you for the privilege of fixing bee-hives on you, please remain kindly disposed so that no thorn will prick us, that no rhinocerous strike us, that we need not say: it is a tree which destroys.[181]

Rattray reports that the Ashanti, before felling a tree, offer a sacrifice to it and say the following prayer: "I am coming to cut you down and carve you, receive this egg and eat . . . . do not let the iron cut me, do not let me suffer in health."[182] A. and G. Grandidier write of the natives of Madagascar: "Almost every tree, every rock, every well, every field has, according to the idea of the Betsimisaraka, who are essentially animistic, its soul, its spirit which punishes the wrongs inflicted upon them exercising its power to do evil rather than good deeds."[183] The Ilokanes (Luzon) believe that *anitos*, death souls, reside in big trees. "Therefore the natives beg the tree's pardon before felling it."[184] It is supposed "on the Isle of Seram (Indonesia) that the *nitu*, the souls of the dead, dwell everywhere, especially in the larger trees. Whoever cuts down such a tree will be punished with illness by the outraged *nitu*."[185]

In northern Schleswig no one dared top off the branches of an elder without having first bended knees and, with uncovered head, said the following prayer: "Mrs. Elder, give me some of your wood, then I shall give you also some of mine when it grows in the forest." Mann-hardt,[186] who reports this, has collected much material to illustrate the belief that the souls of the dead live in trees. "When the Mandans," an Indian tribe of Dakota, writes Brinton, "cut a pole for their tents, they swathe it in bandages so that its pain may be allayed."[187] Of the South American Indians Karsten[188] reports:

> The Jibaros speak to the plants as if they were endowed with human thought and feelings, and when intoxicated by the narcotic drinks prepared from certain vines and herbs, the Jibaro Indian professes to see the spirits of these plants in a definite human form, namely, as remote ancestors of his. Even sex is attributed to each kind of tree or plant: some are supposed to be men, i.e., to have a man's *wakani* or soul; others, again, are said to be women, i.e., to have a woman's soul.
>
> That not only a human spirit, but even a sex, is ascribed to trees, also appears from the belief of the Cavinas in North Bolivia. To them the demon of the *kautschuk*-tree is a woman. A myth of the Cavinas tells of a man who, in a dream, had intercourse with this demon, and died shortly afterwards. If the tree is beaten with a stick the spirit gets angry and will take revenge. But when the Indians tap the rubber-tree the spirit does them no harm, for the whites have obliged them to do it.

In his work on the origin of religion the same author remarks: "When the Tagalogs of the Philippines . . . . have to cut down a tree they beg pardon of the genius of the tree and excuse themselves by saying that it was the priest who bade them fell it."[189] Another passage from the same book tells us how "the Wanika of Eastern Africa honour especially the spirits of coco-nut palms in return for the many benefits conferred upon them by the trees. To cut down a coco-nut palm is an inexpiable offence, equivalent to matricide. Sacrifices to the trees are made on many occasions."[190]

Of the East Semang (Pangan) on the Malayan Peninsula, Skeat and Blagden[191] report: "Whenever an East Semang (Pangan) dies, his birth-tree dies soon after." A "birth-tree" is one sympathetically con-nected with the life of a man. The idea is widespread among various peoples. "If the tree dies first, this is a sign that the owner's death will follow. Hence, big and strong trees are selected as birth-trees. And when one Semang kills another, except in war, he avoids the other's birth-tree, for fear it will fall on him." The tree is evidently considered the abode of the avenging soul of the murdered man.[192] To the plants and plant souls which exercise retribution the same assumption applies as for animals and animal souls fulfilling identical functions: the real authority of retribution is the human death soul which is reincarnated in the plant.

Just as the animal, so the plant, according to the idea of primitive man, is not only the subject but also the object of retribution; a tree may not only take revenge, but revenge may also be taken on it if it commits a wrong.

Of the Kookies who kill tigers to revenge the death of a kinsman killed by this animal, Macrae reports:

A more striking instance still, of this revengeful spirit of retaliation is, that if a man should happen to be killed, by an accidental fall from a tree, all his relations assemble, and cut it down; and however large it may be, they reduce it to chips, which they scatter in the winds, for having, as they say, been the cause of the death of their brother.[193]

Spieth relates of the Ewe that they treat in a special way the corpse of anyone who has met with a fatal accident.

After they have bathed the dead body, they carry it to the road where they lay it out on a bier and spread white ocher over it. They destroy his house. On his behalf, the whole village is sprinkled with holy water. Shooting and beating the drums are forbidden. But vengeance has to be taken for his death. Hence men go to the place where he met with the accident: where a snake bit him or a tree fell on him. When they reach the spot, one of the men cries out the name of the deceased and says: "We come to take vengeance for you and to bring you home." If the dead was bitten by a snake, the men kill as many snakes as possible in the bush; if his death was caused by a flint, they dig up the ground where the accident occurred, fill a pot with the earth, bind it up with white cloth, and carry it home; if a branch killed the deceased, they fell the tree and place a bough on his grave.[194]

33. Interpretation of Illness and Death According to the Principle of Retribution

Primitive man also interprets according to the principle of retribution those happenings which directly affect him, such as illness, accidents, and death. Further, he includes such striking and terrifying cosmic phenomena as thunder, lightning, volcanic eruptions, tempests —above all, the longed-for rain—and finally the sun, moon, and stars. These are phenomena which induce him to think—that means, to connect the phenomena mentally. Rasmussen[195] writes of the Eskimos:

They know only powers or personifications of natural forces, acting upon human life in various ways, and affecting all that lives through fair and foul weather, disease and perils of all kinds. These powers are not evil in themselves, they do not wreak harm of evil intent, but they are nevertheless dangerous owing to their unmerciful severity where men fail to live in accordance with the wise rules of life decreed by their forefathers.

Nature itself punishes any violation of that social order transmitted by the ancestors.

When any transgression takes place in regard to these [rules of the taboo system] which are expressly laid down as essential to success in hunting, the spirit of the sea intervenes. The moon spirit helps her to see that the rules of life are duly observed, and comes hurrying down to earth to punish any instance of neglect. And both sea spirit and moon spirit employ Sila to execute all punishments in any way connected with the weather.

Primitive thinking characteristically connects the elements as follows: natural phenomena are related to social events, especially to violations of the social order, and are interpreted either as punishment for not complying or, less frequently, as reward for complying with certain important norms. The idea of retribution is likewise maintained if the natural phenomenon to be explained is qualified as wrong and thus connected with some future fact as its penalty.[196] "In native belief," writes Elsdon Best,[197] "illness is a condition brought about by such supernormal powers, either as a punishment for wrong committed, such as a transgression of *tapu*, or such beings were the agents employed by a magician who wished to afflict or destroy him." Illness may be a punishment, or it may be a wrong committed by means of magic. To the examples already given in another connection the following particularly characteristic ones may be added.

The Bakairi in central Brazil trace all evil, especially illness and death, back to the magic influence of the members of other tribes. The contrast between good and evil coincides for them, as for other primitive peoples, with membership in their own or a foreign group. In their language "*kura* means: we, we all, our, and at the same time, good (our people); *kurapa*, on the other hand, means: not we, not our, as well as bad, sordid, unhealthy."[198] Since these savages do not, like civilized man, perceive illness and death scientifically as physiological processes, but from a moral-social point of view, they see in these occurrences something evil and therefore the deeds of foreigners, i.e., enemies. Among other central Brazilian Indians, the Bororo interpret illness and death as retribution exercised by slain animals on hunters.[199] Martius reports of the Macusis, Indians in the upper regions of the Rio

Branco (Brazil), that they relate sickness and death to acts of vengeance of an enemy; and he says in this connection: "This superstition thus connects the fate of each man with the wicked hostility of another man."[200] This "superstition" is nothing else but the social interpretation of the facts in question.

W. C. Farabee writes of the Waspisianas in British Guinea:

All sickness, disease and death are due to the evil influence of a medicine man of another tribe in another village. Men ought to live forever and would do so but for evil spirits under the influence of hostile medicine men. Hence it is necessary to have one medicine man to counteract the evil done by another.[201]

Man never dies a natural death and would live forever if it were not for the *kenaima*, or evil spirits which kill him.[202]

The Indians, indicates Koch-Gruenberg, have gradually come to the point

where they attribute all trouble and misfortune which occurs without apparent reasons, as well as illness and death, to a cause which they call by the general term, *kanaima*. Consequently, those evil spirits which walk abroad by night and which kill men in terrible and mysterious ways are *kanaimas*, that is, avengers for injuries which one has inflicted upon living or dead; for the natives always understand these evil spirits as the souls of the dead.[203]

The death souls to which illness or death is directly or indirectly (through magic) traced are the spirits of vengeance; they exercise retribution. Thus can be explained—partly at least—the fear which South American Indians have of sick people and why they treat them so badly.[204]

Bolinder[205] says of the Ijca Indians that illnesses, since they are believed to proceed from the spirits, are cured by the medicine man by finding out why the spirits are displeased with the ill person. To this end the native practitioner asks the sick individual to confess the wrong which he may have committed. This confession is essential for the healing.

In September when the rainy season started and epidemics used to appear, the old Peruvians were accustomed to celebrate their purification ceremonies. Of these Karsten writes:

Before the feast began, all strangers, all those whose ears were broken, all deformed persons, were sent two leagues out of the city. They were said to be in a state of punishment for some fault and so could not take part. Unfortunate people should not be present because their ill-luck might drive away some piece of good fortune.[206]

Karsten goes on:

According to a primitive idea, which in South America anyhow is quite common, sickness and deformity of any kind in newborn children is the result of supernatural influence. Persons suffering from any congenital.disease are consequently regarded as "marked" by evil spirits. In the more advanced religious dogma of the Incas this idea had developed into the belief that such an unlucky state was not purely accidental, but was due to the transgression of certain moral precepts. But the way in which, among the ancient Peruvians, old savage taboos were transformed into ethical rules of religious sanction, can be studied with more detail in an Inca institution of singular interest, the rite of confession, with which I shall deal later.[207]

Inasmuch as the idea of retribution appears as one of the oldest elements in the development of the human mind, it is not correct to assume that only in advanced religion the belief is developed that illnesses or other bodily harms are not mere coincidences but punishments for a violation of norms. It is not correct to speak of a transformation of primitive taboos into ethical norms, since the most primitive taboo is already a social norm, i.e., a prohibition which has a social and therefore a moral or legal character. These two qualities cannot be separated in early social development. Whatever entails evil consequences is considered prohibited by primitive man. And it is significant for his normative attitude toward nature that he interprets according to the principle of retribution everything that he experiences as evil as a consequence of a violation of norm. This normative interpretation corresponds to the prevalence of the emotional element in his consciousness. It is not, as Karsten thinks, that primitive man at first believes that certain evils are actions of a superhuman authority and only later begins to realize that it is prohibited to do those things which entail these evil consequences. Rather, a logical and temporal correlation exists between these two ideas.

North American Indians frequently interpret illness and death as punishment by a superhuman authority, or as vengeance accomplished through magical means, or as a crime which has to be avenged.[208] Philander Prescott writes of the Dacota Indians:

If an Indian has bad luck in hunting, he says it is caused by the misconduct of some of his family, or by some enemy; that is, his family have not properly adhered to the laws of honoring the spirits of the dead, or some one owes him a spite, and by supernatural powers has caused his bad success and misery, for which he will take revenge on the person he suspects the first time an opportunity offers.[209]

Aginsky reports of the Pomo Indians:

The Pomo Indians of Northern California cannot comprehend suicide as we know it. To them, every death and misfortune was the result of indirect or direct retaliation either from (1) the "supernaturals" or (2) from some individual.[210]

The supernaturals retaliated either for the infringement of a taboo or for the calling upon them for too much power. . . . . . Retaliation from a "supernatural" for the breaking of a taboo resulted in sickness which was followed by death unless remedial measures were set in motion.[211]

As far as death due to retaliation from an individual is concerned, every Pomo individual was constantly apprehensive that.he was being the object of sorcery by the traditional enemies of members of his family and by the enemies he had made during his own life. The retaliation, and frequently it was only a fancied wrong that brought it about, was very drastic. Death, with but a few minor exceptions, was always the objective, and the objective was always attained unless the relatives of the stricken man called in a "doctor" to cure the ill person.[212]

Particularly characteristic is the fact that the Pomo do not know any "accident." "What we call accident they call retribution from the 'supernaturals.' They explain a great many accidents as being due to the failure to observe some rule concerning their own or some relative's bundle." Aginsky writes:

During my field trips I continually endeavoured to find a case of "pure accident" which had befallen a Pomo. A few times I thought I had come upon a case, but eventually found that the individual had broken some taboo or accumulated too much power. Thus what we consider accident is explained by them as retaliation due to failure to comply with their religious precepts.[213]

Krause reports of the Tlingits:

Every deviation of traditional customs, every oddness is called *chlakass* and regarded as the most common cause for all misfortunes, for tempests, illness, bad luck in hunting and war. Thus the Tschilkat believed that long lasting bad weather in the first months of 1881 originated in the fact that in the preceding autumn at the persuasion of a missionary two children were buried instead of cremated. Then again they sought the cause in their failure to seclude a girl during her first period of puberty.[214]

The fact that the Kenay of Alaska were afflicted with a great increase in mortality was interpreted by the old men of the tribe as the result of not having strictly observed the totemistic rule of exogamy.[215]

·If a child becomes ill among the central Eskimo the medicine man, above all, questions the mother whether she has violated any taboo regulation. As soon as the mother confesses a wrong, the child's health will be restored.[216] Rasmussen[217] has drawn a picture of the treatment of a sick Eskimo woman by a medicine man. At the beginning of the procedure the medicine man directs a question to his auxiliary spirits as to which taboo violation has caused the illness. Then to the queries of the medicine man the patient makes the following confessions: "The sickness is due to my own fault. I have but ill fulfilled my duties. My thoughts have been bad and my actions evil." Then: "Oh, I did comb my hair once when, after giving birth to a child, I ought not to have

combed my hair; and I hid away the combings that none might see."
Finally: "Alas, yes, I did borrow the lamp of one dead. I have used a
lamp that had belonged to a dead person." The report concludes by
stating that the natives who were present at the treatment left the
house convinced "that all the sins and offences now confessed had
taken the sting out of her illness, so that she would now soon be well
again."[218]

W. Schmidt[219] says of the religion of the whole arctic cultural region
that the superhuman authority—"the highest being" in this ethnolo-
gist's opinion—inflicts inconvenience and pain upon men only as punishment for wrongs. "These punishments consist mainly in deprivation of food, in illness and death." The Chukchee believe that a natural death is caused by evil spirits, and therefore they regard it as
shameful to allow their parents to die such a death. Death through
violence, however, is considered an honor.[220] This idea may be a relic
of the belief that "natural" death is a punishment for a committed
delict.[221]

Sometimes even the killing of an enemy is not justified as vengeance
on the part of the killer but as punishment for some wrong committed
by the victim. Kruijt[222] reports of the Toradja (Celebes) that, in order
to protect themselves against the vengeance of the slain enemy, they
say to the skull which they have cut off from the victim's body: "We
killed you, but do not be angry. You died because you committed a
sin. Otherwise we could not have killed you." Elsewhere the same
author writes: "Among the tribes of the Indonesian archipelago with
which I came in contact it is said of anyone killed through violence
that he was guilty."[223] If a woman on the Timorlao and Tamembar
Islands dies in childbirth, it is supposed that she has committed incest
or adultery and is being punished for it.[224] The Batak of Sumatra trace
all illnesses to the fact that a *begu*, or death soul, holds fast to the *tondi*,
or life soul of a human being, which has left him; "as long as the *tondi*
is absent from the body the man is ill and must die if the *tondi* does not
return."[225] It is the *begu* which inflicts illness as well as other evils upon
men if the latter neglect to pay due homage to the *begu* or if they are
guilty of other violations of the prevailing order.[226] Healing consists in
inducing the *begu* to release the *tondi* of the sick man. Here, again, the
principle of retribution is applied: in return for releasing the *tondi*, the
begu must be compensated. What is offered is only a *parsili*, a human
image, which is artificially supplied with a *tondi*.[227] Thus the Batak
substitute a mere picture for the real human being as the object of

punishment. They think thereby to deceive the superhuman authority; deception of this kind is frequently resorted to by primitive peoples.[228]

The principle of retribution as the idea which underlies a cure for illnesses interpreted as punishment becomes even more apparent when close relatives inflict evils upon themselves in order to save the sick man; these injuries seem to have the character of a substitutive penalty. Children in the Fiji Islands sacrifice a finger joint if one of their parents is ill, convinced that they have thereby satisfied the desire for retribution of the superhuman authority who sent the illness as punishment.[229] If a wrong has been committed, expiation must take place. But, according to the idea of primitive man, it is not necessary that the "culprit" himself suffer the punishment. The inviolability of the principle of retribution is maintained if anyone sustains grief or pain. That is the reason for the belief in the possibility of vicarious suffering.[230]

Mallat tells that the Negritos in the Philippines blame every death among them on the evil magic of the Malayans, their sworn enemies.

When a member of their group dies one of their warriors presents himself to the mourning friends and relatives with a quiver on his back and bow and arrow in hand; then he declares that he intends to leave and swears not to return unless he kills one or more Indians [Malayans] as revenge for the death of their friend which he attributes to the evil influence of their rivals.[231]

Of the Negritos of Zambales, Reed writes:

Disease is usually considered a punishment for wrongdoing, the more serious diseases coming from the supreme *anito* [spirit], the lesser ones from the lesser *anitos*. If smallpox visits a rancheria it is because someone has cut down a tree or killed an animal belonging to a spirit which has invoked the aid of the supreme spirit in inflicting a more severe punishment than it can do alone.[232]

According to Percival, the natives of Ceylon believe that "every disease or trouble that assails them is produced by the immediate agency of the demons sent to punish them; while on the other hand every blessing or success comes directly from the hands of the beneficent and supreme God."[233]

Kubary[234] reports of the Palauans that they believe the cause of illness to be the wrath of a deity; therefore, healing is possible only if the deity is conciliated by sacrifice. "In the case of sickness there is always the presumption that some spirit has been offended," writes Codrington of native belief in the Banks Islands.[235] "Throughout Polynesia no one was believed to die a natural death; there was always some special offence against the gods."[236]

In Tahiti, according to Ellis,

every disease was supposed to be the effect of direct supernatural agency, and to be inflicted by the gods for some crime against the tabu, of which the sufferers have been guilty, or in consequence of some offering made by an enemy to procure their destruction. Hence, it is probable, in a great measure, resulted their neglect and cruel treatment of their sick. The same ideas prevailed with regard to death, every instance of which they imagined was caused by the direct influence of the gods.[237]

Among the Trobriand Islanders, according to Malinowski,[238]

the belief in sorcery is deeply rooted and every serious sickness and death is attributed to black magic. . . . . An interesting denouement, illustrating the legal aspect of sorcery, is furnished by the custom of finding out the reasons for which a man has been killed by witchcraft. This is achieved by the correct interpretation of certain marks or symptoms to be seen on the exhumed body.

Certain delicts have typical marks; for example,

if the body shows scratches, especially similar to *kimali*, the erotic scratches impressed during sexual dalliance, this means that the deceased has been guilty of adultery. . . . . Swellings like the beams of a rich yam-house signify that the dead one indulged in too ambitious decorations of his hut or store, and thus aroused the chief's resentment.

Thus, if the death appears as legal retribution upon a law breaker, "the survivors are relieved of the burdensome duty of vendetta."

Fortune writes of the Manus (Admiralty Islands):

The Manus are not aware that modern Christianity challenges their most fundamental postulate—that unexpiated sin causes death. They are not aware of any secular attitude towards the health or the illness of the body. They suffer much from malaria and have supplies of quinine given them by the Government. Yet, in cases of malaria, they always have recourse to their oracles to shrive them of their sins, never to the quinine. The Government quinine supply is poured into the sea, and application put in for more on occasion in order to please the Government . . . . there is no secular attitude towards the life and death of the body or towards the body's ills. Death is regarded as punishment of sin. It is not accepted as unpersonal. From this fact flows the Manus pragmatism in belief.[239]

Turner reports of the natives of Fakaofo (Bentwich Island):

After death the friends of the deceased were anxious to know the cause of his death. They went with a present to the priest, and begged him to get the dead man to speak, and confess the sins which caused his death. The priest might be distant from the dead body, but he pretended to summon the spirit, and to have it within him. He spoke in his usual tone, and told him to say before them all what he did to cause his death. Then he (the priest) whined out, in a weak, faltering voice, a reply, as if from the spirit of the departed, confessing that he stole cocoanuts from such a place, or that he fished at some particular spot forbidden by the king, or that he ate the fish which was the incarnation of his family god. As the priest whined out something of this sort he managed to squeeze out some tears, and sob and cry over it. The friends of the departed felt relieved to know the cause, got up, and went home.[240]

Among the inhabitants of the coast of the Gazelle Peninsula (New Pomerania) there is, according to P. Joseph Meier,[241] a story that sunstroke is a punishment for a delict directed against the sun. Once a man hated the sun [presumably because it burned too hot]. He therefore placed a noose on the spot where the sun used to rise.

As soon as he saw it rising, he tightened the noose about the sun's feet and pulled it down. In vain were the sun's supplications: "Brother! Why have you seized my feet in the noose? Must I be killed?" Thereupon the man answered: "Yes, you must die!" Then the sun retorted: "If you kill me now another sun will avenge me. Where will you take refuge?"

The man, however, was not deterred and killed the sun. "Another sun appeared, and, searching for the culprit, set all the trees on fire. The soil, too, glowed." Finally the new sun shone so fiercely on the head of the murderer that his skull was burned up and he died.

If a person falls ill among the Cook Islanders, they consult a priest in order to find out the nature of the sin which aroused the wrath of the deity or the enmity of the magician.[242] Similar practices are reported of the natives of the Society[243] and Hawaiian Islands.[244] Also, on the Tonga Islands every illness is regarded as punishment for some delict. William Wilson reports:

Besides these [deities], they imagine every individual to be under the power and control of a spirit peculiar to himself, which they call odooa, who interests himself in all their concerns, but, like Calla Filatonga [a deity of wind], is little regarded till angry, when they think he inflicts upon them all the deadly disorders to which they are subject; and then, to appease him, the relations and other connections of the afflicted person, especially if he be a chief, run into all the inhuman practices of cutting off their little fingers, beating their faces, and tabooing themselves from certain kinds of food.[245]

An account from Tahiti is of special interest in this connection. A white man spent a night in a cave in which an old hermit lived. Since his guest felt cold, the hermit gave him a coat which he himself had received as a present from another native. When the white man learned the latter's name, he was frightened, because he knew that this man was sick with leprosy. The hermit, however, tried to calm the white man by ridiculing the idea of contagiousness, taught by modern science, as stupid superstition. He offered, instead, the native belief that lepers communicate their disease only to those who have wronged them. Whoever behaves well toward a leper need have no fear of the malady. He himself, who was a friend of the sick man, had worn the coat next to his skin for a long time without becoming ill. Of course, it would have been different had he been unfriendly to the sick man. As proof of his theory he related the story of two other leprous patients.

E

One was treated with all possible care by his family. He died without having infected his relatives, although they were constantly in the closest contact with him. The other patient, however, was left alone by his relatives when the first symptoms of the disease began to appear. They all fell ill with leprosy.[246] Whether, according to this view, the will of the sick man or the will of a superhuman authority directs the illness, in either case the will is exerted according to the principle of retribution.

Elsdon Best[247] says of the Maori:

> The native treatment of disease was empirical with a vengeance. Even herbal remedies were not used by the Maori practitioner, for he was the village priest, the shaman, and so taught that all forms of sickness and disease emanated from the gods. Such afflictions were held to be punishments inflicted by the gods for offences, as against the laws of *tapu*, or were the results of black magic. Even in the latter case the powers of the magic that caused the affliction came from the gods.

If the death is not the consequence of a wrong, but a wrong itself, then retribution must ensue.

> Should it be thought that a person has been slain by magic arts, then one would procure a fern-stalk (stipe of bracken) and strike the body with it, saying: "Here is your weapon by which to avenge your death." This is meant to incite the *wairua* [spirit or soul] to avenge the destruction of its physical basis.

Also in Australia the idea can be found that death is either a delict brought about by magic or a punishment inflicted by a superhuman authority for the violation of a norm.[248] Of aborigines of western Australia, George Grey reports:

> The natives do not allow that there is such a thing as a death from natural causes; they believe, that were it not for murderers or the malignity of sorcerers, they might live for ever: hence, when a native dies from the effect of an accident, or from some natural cause, they use a variety of superstitious ceremonies, to ascertain in what direction the sorcerer lives, whose evil practices have brought about the death of their relative; this point being satisfactorily settled by friendly sorcerers, they then attach the crime to some individual, and the funeral obsequies are scarcely concluded, ere they start to avenge their supposed wrongs.[249]

According to Robert Brough Smyth,

> the natives of the Melbourne district say that *Myndie* is a great snake—very long, very thick in the body, and very powerful. He is under the dominion of PUND-JEL [a deity]. When PUND-JEL commands him, *Myndie* will destroy black people—young or old. He can do nothing of himself. PUND-JEL must first order him. He is known to all tribes, and all tribes are known to him; and when any tribe is very wicked, or when any tribe fails to overtake and kill wild blackfellows, then PUND-JEL makes *Myndie* give them diseases, or kills them, as he thinks fit. . . . . *Myndie* has several little creatures of his own kind, which he sends out from time to time to carry diseases and afflictions

into tribes which have not acted well in war or in peace. These little ones are very troublesome, but their visits are not so much dreaded as the visits of *Myndie* himself, who is very large, very powerful, and from whom no one can escape. All plagues are caused by *Myndie* or his little ones.[250]

Strehlow reports of the Aranda that every dead man is avenged, since all deaths are attributed to a foreign tribe and hence demand retribution. After the funeral ceremony the brother of the deceased addresses the assembled men: "Tonight each of you will bring to the meeting a *gururkna* [a necklace or belt made from hairs of the dead] because tomorrow we shall go out to avenge his death."[251] Thereupon they undertake an expedition of vengeance against some far-off settlement.

In his work on the natives of Australia, Curr asks why the blacks obey so strictly the rules which regulate their life; and he finds:

My reply is . . . . that the Black is educated from infancy in the belief that departure from the customs of his tribe is inevitably followed by one at least of many evils, such as becoming early grey, ophthalmia, skin eruptions, or sickness; but above all, that it exposes the offender to the danger of death from sorcery.[252]

Spencer and Gillen report an interesting case in which a man's death is interpreted among the Warramunga (central Australia) both as a punishment for a delict committed by the deceased and as a crime committed on him. They write: "It must be remembered that, though the man was declared by the old doctors to have died because he had violated tribal custom, yet at the same time he had of course been killed by some one, though by whom they could not yet exactly determine."[253]

On the basis of his experiences in Africa, Le Roy illustrates the attitude of savages toward nature by the following example:

Here, for example, is a tree covered with fruit. He tries one, finds it good, eats it, and encouraged by the experience, he takes others; it is a permitted fruit. The day after, he perceives another tree; made confident by the repast of the preceding day, he takes some; but this fruit has not the same taste and makes him wretchedly sick; it was evidently a forbidden fruit. He will remember and, to save his children from the same experience, perhaps the same misfortune in relation to the hidden Master of creation, he will interdict that tree for them: "My children, that fruit is a forbidden fruit for us; do not touch it!"[254]

This example illustrates plainly the thoroughly normative attitude of primitive man toward nature. The damaging effect of the fruit simply means that it is prohibited and that the harm it inflicts is the punishment for the violated norm. In this same connection Le Roy reports an incident which he experienced personally. An explorer who accompanied him on his journeys once killed a wild boar. The native carriers refused to eat the boar's meat because it was prohibited. As a protest against this superstition the white man ate particularly of the meat. When he fell ill during the night, the Negroes were, of course, convinced that this was the punishment for violation of the taboo. They sang in chorus: "It's the pig, It's the pig, It's the pig that revolts!" Then came the solo: "O pig! Come out if you wish. But do no evil to our white man, For he ate you by mistake!"

Among the Fan a sick person is requested by the fetish priest to confess his sins publicly in the presence of all the villagers in order to be healed in his illness.

> The sanction of morality is . . . . assured by the action of that higher, invisible world from which nothing escapes. If any one has a misfortune, an illness, or other trouble, his neighbors and those of his own household will consider it a just punishment for faults committed by him. He will attempt an expiation by making an offering or a sacrifice to the spirits or the manes.[255]

Commenting on the religion of the Bantu, E. W. Smith says that, in general, every illness is regarded as a penalty inflicted by a deity for some disrespect on the part of a man. In this connection the social organization plays an important part.

> The children belong to the father; the mother's divinities, while they may assist the father's in guarding the children, have no right to sicken them. It is within their right to make the wife ill, as the father's divinities have the right to make him and his children ill; but they must not trespass on each other's prerogatives.[256]

Gottschling describes the belief of the Bavenda, a Bantu tribe, as follows: "Any fortune that comes to the Bavenda is sent as a reward from Ralowimba, and every misfortune that befalls them is a punishment sent by him."[257] Among the Kaffirs, according to Kidd's report,[258] the idea prevails that illness, as well as drought and famine, is to be traced to the wrath or discontent of the death souls, who are accustomed to revenge negligence in these ways. Illnesses, however, can also be brought about through magic. If neither of these causes can be assumed, then a natural explanation is accepted.

> Sickness which is due to the interference of ancestral spirits . . . . is treated with a very marked ceremonial. . . . . A priest or doctor selects an ox which is killed in the cattle kraal. . . . . The theory is that the spirits send sickness to show their displeasure with the people of the kraal. This is one of their ways of calling attention to the fact that the people have neglected to offer sufficient sacrifices of late; or it may be a way of informing the people that some of the ancient customs have been neglected, or broken. It is a common saying, that if the ancient customs are not kept up the people will find their teeth falling out. In that case even an American dentist could not help

them. A diviner would be called in to find out the culprit, and some one would be accused of sorcery, for the hypothesis is that no one could wish to break old tribal customs unless he wished to gain power over others through magic. Thus custom is most tenacious of life; it has managed to get the diviners on its side. This conception of the cause of sickness is of very ancient date, and has existed ever since the first glimmerings of historical record. In Chaka's days the Zulus said that most sickness was caused by *Vagino*, or evil spirits, who made people ill out of revenge, or because some enemies had bought over these *Vagino* by offerings and sacrifices. These spirits were supposed to come and dwell in the bodies of the sick, and cause all their pains and aches. Relics of this theory are still extant in Swaziland, where the people consider certain forms of epilepsy to be caused by enraged ancestral spirits, who stab people from within, thus causing the convulsions. It also happens that the Kafirs sometimes think sickness to be due to the spirits of ancestors of fabulous monsters living in the rivers. In such cases cure is sought by throwing oxen into the river to appease the spirits.[259]

Cayzac writes of the Kikuyu, a Bantu tribe in East Africa: "The punishment and effect of 'sin' is illness, death, and every possible hardship; and the ordinary cause of illness, death, and every possible hardship is 'sin.' "[260]

The Akposso in Togo have a myth which says:

God created fire, which was illness, and coldness, the relief. He commanded a man: if you are cold, do not approach the fire! Since the man transgressed this commandment God let a rusty brown bird ascend from the fire. This bird struck the culprit with its wings and thus caused leprosy. This is the origin of illness.[261]

Of the natives of Sierra Leone it is reported that they

conceive that no death is natural or accidental, but that the disease or the accident by which it is immediately caused, is the effect of supernatural agency. In some cases it is imagined that death is brought about by the malign agency of some individual, who employs witchcraft for that purpose; in other cases it is supposed that death is inflicted by the tutelar demon of some one on whom the deceased, when discovered and punished by the avenging hand of griffee [guardian spirit], was practising incantations. It is most usual to assign the former cause for the sickness and death of chiefs, and other people of consequence, and their connections; and the latter for any of those of the lower class.[262]

Among the natives of Loango, illnesses, accidents, and apparently unnatural deaths are traced, according to Pechuel-Loesche,[263] to hostile acts of powerful human beings, achieved by means of magic, or to the influence of superhuman authorities, as consequences of transgressions of norms. They are, therefore, interpreted, either as delicts or as punishments. The following example shows the peculiar confusion of both elements: One method of magicians to harm man, even to kill him, consists in "making him violate his *Tschina* (a taboo prohibition). One need mix only a little prohibited food into his meal. As a result of this he most certainly dies even though he is not conscious of having violated a taboo."[264] Here the "magician" only puts into operation the commonly effective mechanism of delict and punishment.

The Bubi of Fernando Poo trace illness and death to "evil" souls. These souls, Tessmann explains, are the death souls of those men who behaved evilly on earth and are therefore not allowed, like the souls of good men, to proceed to the realm of God. They are condemned to return to earth and to perpetuate their evil. Tessmann says of this "bad" soul:

> Bad as this soul is and furious at not being allowed to proceed to God, its only aim is to harm its former fellow men. On them it lays the real blame for its wicked deeds on earth, for they gave it cause for envy and anger and thereby led it to evil. Above all does this soul persecute its former mate; on the one hand, it supposes that its mate may have poisoned it, on the other hand, it is particularly annoyed that its mate is still alive whereas it had to die. Every human being whose mate—I wish to avoid the term "friend" since a negro does not know real friendship or faithfulness—or whose relative of the same age has died believes in the existence of a special soul which persecutes and vexes him and which is called *elopa*. I translate *elopa* as vexing-soul. Every indisposition, every illness is blamed on *elopa*. *Elopa* will finally bring about death, for its envy and vindictiveness is greater than the love and care of one's guardian soul.[265]

This "guardian soul" is the death soul of a good human being which is allowed to enter the realm of God and which "purchases" there an unborn soul, takes it down to earth, and puts it, unseen, into the embryo of a pregnant woman. This death soul thenceforth functions as the guardian of the human being whom it procured by "purchasing."[266] This dualism in which there is a death soul functioning as a guardian and another soul, "purchased" by it, functioning as a life soul is obviously the result of a disintegration of the death soul.

Originally the death soul, reincarnated in the embryo, played the two roles simultaneously, inasmuch as it was both the life soul and the guardian spirit of the newborn human being. The modification of the soul belief among the Bubi has seemingly come about through external influence. These influences are evident in the description of the activity of the death soul which Tessmann labels "bad." Originally it was not the death soul, the *elopa*, which laid the blame on its fellow-men for its evil deeds on earth. Probably these fellow-men or Christian interpreters of their belief qualified the death soul as "bad" because it persecutes the living. In the beginning the death soul harassed the living because the latter inflicted some wrong upon the former. From the sentences "The death soul supposes it may have been poisoned by a living human being" and "Its vindictiveness is greater than the love of the guardian soul" the original belief can be restored. This concept has been misinterpreted or modified under the influence of Christian ideas about retribution in the other world. The natives themselves, like other primitive peoples, conceive, or did so originally, illness and death as punishment for their sins in general; they feel themselves responsible for the death of a fellow-man and imagine, therefore, his death soul as a revengeful spirit. For every death, if not a penalty, is murder and thus cause for retribution by the deceased. Tessmann refers to these "bad" souls as "hell souls" and thus reveals where the scheme of interpretation originated according to which he or some native influenced by Christian religion represents the soul belief of these primitive people.[267]

Of the Ekoi in Cameron and South Nigeria, Lowie writes:

When several well-known men have died in succession in an Ekoi village, suspicion is naturally aroused that they are the victims of black magic, and some friendless woman may be pounced upon as the probable culprit. Illness, when not traceable to the anger of offended spirits, is likewise derived from the practices of witch or wizard.[268]

Among the South-Bambala in the Congo the death of children is regarded as punishment for adultery. A woman who becomes pregnant must confess to her husband all her former love affairs;[269] if she conceals one, her child will die.

Like many other tribes, the Bergdama, according to a report by Vedder, do not believe in natural death. For them every demise is brought about either by Gamab, a deity, or by the gamagu, the death souls of their ancestors. From a prayer formula for a gravely ill person it appears clearly that illness is regarded as punishment:

You fathers, hear me! Soothe your anger! Think mildly, you, there above! Aren't these your children whom you left on earth when you went hence: What have they done or greedily denied you that you make them sick? You have ceased to bless them. Death carries them off. You consume your children's goods. Why do you punish them? Soothe your anger! Think mildly, you, there above![270]

The Agui Negroes of the Ivory Coast are sure that perjurers are killed by the death souls of ancestors or by the spirits by whom they swore. The natives of Togo believe that the god Uwoluwu punishes perjurers with death. Only a transcendental sanction exists for such a delict.[271] Godfrey Wilson writes of the Nyakyusa of the Rungiol District of South Tanganyika:

Whenever a man or his wife, child, or beast falls sick or dies, when his crops fail, or his cows go dry, he usually goes at once to the diviner (ondagosi) to confess all his remembered sins and to find out whether any of them is responsible for the misfortune or not.[272]

.... these beliefs interpret the unhappiness and misfortune of his [the native's] life in a necessary connexion with his sin; that unhappiness and those misfortunes which his best effort and skill are unable to avoid, and which his mind cannot see to be the effects of the ordinary actions of nature or his fellows, they explain as the effect of supernatural causes acting morally. The religion of the Nyakyusa uses sickness, death, hunger and misfortune as instruments for his education in right behaviour, within the society to which he belongs; and in this also compares exactly with other faiths, which in like manner, connect misfortune supernaturally with sin.[273]

Among the Jukun (Nigeria), different rites are observed after a man's death. One of them is described by Meek[274] as follows: A person presenting the dead (or his death soul) turns to the surviving women; he

begins calling out in a muffled voice the name of an immediate female relative of the deceased, saying: "I am so-and-so (giving the name of the deceased), and I have come to tell you why I left you." .... The woman replies: "I know not why you left us. And it is in order to hear the reason that I and all the other women are assembled here." The ghost may then inform them that the reason of his death was either (a) that he had set aside corn or a chicken for sacrifice but had used it for his private consumption, and so had been killed by Akwa; or (b) that he had sold property belonging to some cult; or (c) that he had made some error while offering rites, such as failing to sweep the ground round the symbols before depositing the sacrificial foods. Or (d) that he had come into contact with a menstruous woman and had failed to purify himself; or (e) that it was a punishment for showing disrespect to senior men; or (f) that a certain man or woman (a wizard or witch) had met him and captured his soul. If he had died of snake bite he may say that a woman had turned herself into a snake and bitten him. It is to be noted that immediately after a man's death the reason for his death is discovered by the divining apparatus, and that the reason given by the divining apparatus is that which is publicly announced later by the man personating the ghost of the deceased.

Thus death is interpreted as either punishment or crime.

After this any woman, who may have a request to make, hands a cloth to the interpreter (the Kuku) and may say: "I am not well and would like to know the reason." The ghost may reply that it is because she has not been quite faithful to her husband. .... Another woman may state that she is suffering from an illness. Her husband, present within the enclosure, may then whisper to the man personating the ghost that his wife had polluted the compound during some period of menstruation, and had failed to have her offence purged by sacrifice. The ghost thereupon informs the woman that Akwa had brought illness upon her because she had polluted the compound and had made no atonement.

Meek notes:

It might appear at first sight that in some of their features the Aku-ahwâ rites are nothing but an imposture on the women who are disciplined and mulcted by fraudulent means. It must be remembered, however, that the male members of the community themselves live under the perpetual discipline of their cults, and are constantly required to incur heavy expenditure.[275]

When among the northern tribes of Nigeria a man dies, an investigation is sometimes made in order to determine the cause of his death. "Among the Angas the investigation is postponed until the fourth day after burial, and the verdict of the diviner usually is that the dead man's death was due to his own neglect—he had failed to appease with libations and sacrifices the spirits of his dead forefathers."[276] Meek writes of the Ibo-speaking peoples of southeastern Nigeria:

In some communities [e.g., at Ache] the labouring woman may be invited to make a confession of any act of unfaithfulness to her husband, with the warning that failure to confess may cause her death. She may then mention the name of a lover, or say: "If I have ever had sexual relations with any other man than my husband may I die in giving birth." At Ache the lover mentioned has to pay a fine of two fowls to the husband's family.[277]

Similar customs are reported of the Ashanti[278] and of the natives of Lobi.[279]

The idea that illnesses can be brought about by natural causes becomes only gradually known. An example for the fact that illnesses are partly traced to natural causes and partly interpreted as punishment or crime can be found in Smith and Dale's monograph on the Ila-speaking peoples.[280] They write:

It will be noticed that disease is regarded as something almost material which can be passed from one person to another and got rid of by washing or other means. Some diseases come through contact, more or less intimate, with certain dangerous things: things dangerous because of some maleficent quality inherent in them. In some cases there is no actual contact, rather *actio in distans*. Such things are: (a) animals, e.g., the Chinao and Chikambwe; (b) dirt; (c) menstruous women; (d) a foetus. Disease is caused also by witchcraft. There need not be any direct contact: the warlock can harm his victim from a distance. Other disease is caused by breaking a taboo. It is as if the act, e.g., of eating something forbidden, releases some maleficent energy which afflicts the culprit. This applies not only to actions that are specifically *tonda* ("taboo"), but also to such things as jealousy, false swearing, trespassing, discontent. The bad action has material consequences. Other diseases are put down to such natural causes as exposure to the sun.

Of particular importance are the illnesses and deaths which are traced to the influence of death souls: ". . . . many sicknesses and deaths are ascribed to the direct action of the ancestral spirits who are offended by neglect."

34. INTERPRETATION OF ALL KINDS OF MISFORTUNE ACCORDING TO THE PRINCIPLE OF RETRIBUTION

In another connection various examples have been given which show that primitive men generally regard death caused by animals as an act either of punishment or vengeance. Here are some more. The Jakuns of the Malayan Peninsula believe that the tiger that attacks a human being is itself a human being who changed himself into a tiger in order better to exercise retribution.[281] In Madagascar the idea prevails that a certain deity uses snakes as instruments to avenge itself for any injury.[282] The Indonesians, too, believe, according to Kruijt,[283] that the superhuman authority employs animals to warn and punish men. It is their firm conviction that no harm can befall a man except as retribution for a wrong committed by him. Insufficient produce from plants or dryness, according to the same writer, are connected with a special crime, incest.[284] This delict, in the opinion of the Indonesians, may also be committed by animals, especially by dogs and pigs. Hence these animals must be punished[285] in order that the community may not be afflicted by an evil intended as retribution.

We have already referred to the widespread idea that bad luck in hunting and fishing is usually considered as punishment for some violation of the social order. Here are a few more examples. Rasmussen[286] reports the following incident among the polar Eskimos. Once, when hunting was unsuccessful, the shaman undertook to determine the cause by necromancy. On the basis of his findings he established that his daughter-in-law had had a miscarriage but had concealed it in order to evade the punishment. Thereupon the woman was chastised by being frozen to death in a snow hut. It has already been mentioned that the Tlingit Indians, according to Krause, traced a severe storm which made hunting and fishing impossible to the fact that, shortly before, the corpse of a child had been buried rather than cremated.[287] Castren relates that the Samojedes believe in a deity called Num.

Num knows and sees all the happenings on earth. If he sees men doing good deeds, he rewards them with good livelihood, gives them reindeers, and a good haul, and grants them long life, etc. If, however, men commit sins, Num plunges them into ruin and misery and makes them die soon. Lacking a clear perception of future life the Samojedes believe that retribution takes place in this world. This conviction keeps them continually in horror of sin (*haebea*) and wicked deeds, particularly murder, theft, perjury and adultery. . . . . As far as the special penalties are concerned with which Num afflicts the sinners I was told that murder and perjury are punished with death, theft with poverty, unchastity with miscarriage, etc.[288]

In the works of Lévy-Bruhl[289] many examples are cited in which taboo violations entail some misfortune, especially bad luck in hunting. In all these cases primitive man perceives a connection between the event regarded as evil and the social fact qualified as a breach of norms. This way of connecting elements—so different from causality —presents itself as retribution. The point is that primitive man relates

misfortune to a breach of norm; that is, he interprets the fact norma-
tively[290] and does not regard misfortune—as is sometimes suggested—
as an automatic or causal effect of a violation of taboo. The idea of an
"automatic" effect is thoroughly modern and scientific, even if the supposedly automatic reaction is qualified as "magical."

35. Interpretation of the Weather According to the Principle of Retribution

Among various peoples the idea prevails that rain falls in the wet
season only if the chieftain behaves properly. Should the rain not
come, it is considered a punishment for the chieftain's improper conduct, and consequently he is frequently held responsible. This is so not
only with the absence of rain but also, for example, in the whole of
Polynesia, with other calamities, such as storms, bad harvests, illnesses, and the like.[291] According to A. R. Brown,[292] the Andaman
Islanders believe that Biliku or Puluga, a higher deity, punishes with
bad weather the infringement of such rules as burning or melting
beeswax, killing a grasshopper, making noise while the cicada chirps,
or eating certain foodstuffs. E. H. Man[293] maintains that the anger of
this deity is aroused not only through transgression of ritual norms but
also through murder, theft, adultery, etc. This is denied by Brown.
Among the Bavili of Loango certain totemistic marriage prohibitions
prevail, one of which is that a man may not marry a woman who belongs to the same totem group as the family of his mother. Of these
norms Dennett says: "As in the case of the Hebrews, so in that of the
Bavili contravention of these laws is believed to be punished by God, by
His withholding the rains in due season."[294] Among the Kaffirs confession of sins, according to Kidd,[295] is regarded as a means of bringing
about rain. The Yahgans (Tierra del Fuego) believe that they are
punished by an evil spirit with wind, hail, and snow for having committed sins.[296] Among the Greenland Eskimos it is customary to say:
"The air is angered, the air is annoyed." By this they mean that the
air, or its personification (the "air spirit"), is displeased with certain
delicts of human beings and intends to punish them for their conduct.[297] Parkinson[298] reports that the Sulka (New Pomerania) saw in
the destruction of the village Pahalum by a landslide the act of vengeance of a spirit, or, more specifically, punishment for having killed a
snake which was the abode of this spirit.

Frequently the undesired event of nature is not punishment but a
delict which will be followed by the punishment. If, among the Durru

(Cameroon mountain land), rain is not forthcoming for an unusually long period and thus grave peril threatens the harvest, the people go to the fortuneteller and ask him about the causes. He seeks the oracle and finds that some wicked man is holding the rain back. Thereupon the people run to the smith, to whom they ascribe magic powers and who, therefore, is able to discover the guilty person. This is done as follows: Everyone goes to a water hole near by. Then the smith requests each one to take some water in his hand, to drink it, and to say: "If I held the rain back, the water should kill me." Whoever refuses to act accordingly must, so they believe, die a terrible death, for he is recognized as the culprit. They kill him by cutting off his head.[299]

36. Interpretation of Thunder, Lightning, etc., According to the Principle of Retribution

The belief that thunder and lightning are instruments in the service of retribution is widespread. Kidd writes of the Kaffirs:

Natives sometimes say that thunder is caused by thieves, who eat thunderbolts (or attract them). When the thunder begins they say: "We do not eat the wealth of others." They spit on the ground and assure one another: "We do not eat the wealth of others." The sin of the thief is supposed to attract the thunder.[300]

More or less clearly the idea persists that thunder and lightning are connected somehow with the souls of the ancestors. The Waniaturu, a Bantu tribe, interpret the lightning that kills a man as punishment for the man's having been a sorcerer.[301] The same idea prevails among the Safwa (East Africa).[302] Should lightning strike the chieftain of one of their clans, the pygmies of Equatorial Africa regard it as an infallible sign of the wrath of the deity.[303] According to the view of the Bacwa-Pygmoides, the deity exercises retribution in this world by making evildoers ill or by killing them by means of lightning, falling trees, or wild animals.[304] The Efe-Pygmies explain why men need not be afraid of lightning by the following story. Lightning is a powerful man whom the pygmies once rendered a good service by killing an elephant that had devastated his plantations. Lightning was very pleased and loaded the pygmies with presents. He escorted them to earth as far as their camps. From that circumstance originates the friendship between the Efe and the lightning. They are not afraid of him. He does not harm them. He is their friend.[305]

The Semang of Malaya interpret thunder as reaction to a "sin" committed by someone. One can evade the threatening punishment of Karei, a deity, only by offering a blood-sacrifice. The culprit scratches his leg, pours some of the blood on the earth, and throws the rest toward the sky. Neglect of this blood offering would cause a natural catastrophe. If a murder has been perpetrated and thunder is heard, all the inhabitants of the settlement must proffer blood-sacrifices. "If Kaiei (Karei) does not desist but goes on thundering then the murderer has to be killed. They slit open his body and throw his blood towards the sky. At that Kaiei will certainly cease thundering." Certain delicts, however, cannot be expiated by blood. In such cases Karei inflicts punishment in the form of illness or even by death. When a tiger kills a human being, this is also considered punishment by the deity.[306] Among the Bahau of Borneo thunder spirits (to belare) function as authorities of retribution. They punish "laughing-at-animals," which is considered a crime, by wringing the culprit's neck.[307] According to Parkinson, the tribesmen of central New Pomerania regard lightning as "the infallible avenger of various crimes."[308] Laplanders once believed that thunder was a human being who had his abode in the clouds. If anyone spoke evilly about him or insulted him in any way, this thunder being could be expected to punish the slanderer with lightning.[309]

Fire is also, like lightning, frequently considered an authority of retribution. Among the Bergdama (Southwest Africa) "the holy fire" is the center of all their religious beliefs. It is called socha-ais. Vedder[310] writes about it: "Socha is for the Bergdama every object withdrawn from daily use by religious custom. It possesses the inexplicable power of bringing good luck to the obedient observer of customs, but it plunges into disaster the voluntary or involuntary transgressor." Fire is blown up by the twig of a bush which has the significant name gous; gous means "good behavior." Vedder thinks that "through this custom a kind greeting may be voiced. Not without selfishness, one greets the new fire and vows to treat it well according to the good old custom of their forefathers." There are likewise certain rules which govern the conduct of people assembled around a fire. Especially when the food is distributed must one not express any dissatisfaction with his allotted portion.

The grumbling of the insatiable is harmful to the fire and will be avenged by it. At the distribution of meat it cannot be avoided that one gets a larger share than another—all the more so as squinting eyes never see well. One must take care, however, not to complain audibly; but even hidden envy and anger are observed by the fire. As a consequence it may deprive the whole assembly of its meat-bestowing blessing. . . . . For the Bergdama the holy fire is an animated being capable of hearing, seeing, feeling, and wishing, and possessing the power either to bless or to punish deeds.

If the Aleutian Islanders believe that the moon drops stones upon an insulting person,[311] it means that they interpret the falling of meteoric stones as punishment. And if the Apache Indian, pointing toward heaven, says, "Do you not believe that God, this sun, sees what we do and punishes us when it is evil?"[312] it proves that he perceives in the celestial light not so much a natural but a social function essential to man, namely, the function of retribution. The Indians of Peru, Dobrizhoffer reports, used to believe that "when the sun is obscured, he is angry, and turns away his face from them, on account of certain crimes which they have committed."[313] The Euahlayi (Australia) interpret the eclipse as follows: The sun is a voluptuous woman whose advances the moon, a man, refuses. The sun wishes to avenge herself and attacks the moon, intending to kill him. Her desire is finally frustrated by the spirits, however.[314]

37. The Idea of Retribution in the Myths of Primitive Peoples

The decisive part played by the principle of retribution in primitive man's interpretation of nature appears especially in his myths. It would be an error to regard the myth as a causal explanation of reality.[315] In mythical thinking the primacy of the emotional over the rational, and thus the precedence of the normative over the causal, element emerges quite distinctly. The questions which mythical thinking seeks to answer are not: What is really happening; why does it have to happen that way; why can it not happen otherwise; and what are the objective causes of this event? These are the questions of natural science. The myth rather attempts to find out what ought to happen and whether things do happen as they ought. In other words, does the actual happening correspond to or contradict the normative order which primitive man assumes to be valid? The myth must confirm that all ought to be as it is; further, the myth must justify and thus secure the social reality which includes all of nature.[316] Therefore, mythology likes to go back into the past. For the past is the period of the ancestors, who, for primitive men, are the authorities par excellence.[317] Thus the mythical past offers the correct standards for the present, the manner of existence of the authority, and hence a sphere which—just like the Platonic idea (this philosophical transfiguration of primitive myth)—in relation to reality presents the prototype and the ideal. So little is the myth a causal explanation of reality that its recitation has frequently the character of a magical action through which the present right state of the social and thus also of the natural, socially inter-preted, world is to be preserved.[318] Consequently, the myth presents itself as the direct opposite of rational cognition; it is a genuinely con-servative ideology, arising from emotional consciousness.

The justifying function of the myth manifests itself unequivocally in the frequently appearing retribution motive. Mythological research, however, has not sufficiently recognized the importance of this theme. In Wundt's fundamental work, for instance, which examines myths from many aspects, the motive of retribution is rarely touched upon. This motive, it is true, cannot always be found on the surface and therefore can easily be missed, as, for example, in the following Aus-tralian fairy tale. The magpie was a wicked old woman who gathered much grass seed. Once upon a time a neighboring tribe came along and camped near where she was. One day, when the men had gone out hunting, the magpie went to the encampment and persuaded the women to go out in search for honey and fruit. She promised to watch the children in the meantime and to give them grass seed to eat. While the women were away, the magpie gathered the children into her home, which was built in a hollow tree. Then she locked it up. The returning women heard the cries of the children but never were able to find them.[319] The loss of the children in the fable is apparently intended as punishment for negligent care.

Many such myths in which re-examination reveals the motive of retribution are presented by Wundt in entirely different aspects. Thus some stories are pictured merely as adventure tales, in which a moral is supposed to play no part. The following Kaffir story is cited as an example. The hero, Sikulume, evades the pursuit of several cannibals by daubing a stone with fat; the cannibals smell the fat and quarrel for the stone; one of them swallows it, whereupon the others eat their companion. This is repeated several times, until the cannibals break their teeth in biting the stone, which they regard, by virtue of magic, as something special, and desist from their pursuit of Sikulume. It is obvious that cannibalism, already morally condemned, is punished here.

The continuation of the story reveals even more clearly the motive of retribution. Sikulume comes to a village the inhabitants of which have been swallowed by a water monster. The hero jumps into the water and allows himself also to be swallowed; then he bores a hole from the inside, so that the monster dies and the whole village, men and animals, reappear. Finally, the daughter of a wicked sorcerer falls in love with the hero. He elopes with her and returns with her to his own village, where he becomes a great chieftain.[320] It is clear that the evil monster is punished with death, whereas the noble hero receives his deserved reward. Wundt, therefore, is wrong when he says of this so-called "adventure tale": "The only condition is that the hero comes off victorious from all his fights."[321] For the hero ordinarily struggles against evil, and his victory is victory of the good—all of which is retribution.[322] It is this motive of retribution which produces the satisfying effect of the tale. Consequently, it is hardly possible to distinguish clearly, as Wundt does, between these "genuine adventure tales" and the "fortune tales," in which the motive of retribution, of vengeance for evils sustained, or of reward for favors received are connected with the vicissitudes of fortune itself.[323] The difference consists, in the main, in that the motive of retribution appears more distinctly in the one than in the other.

Those myths, characterized as "riddle myths," in which he who is unable to solve the enigma has to die or is punished in some other way, whereas he who solves it receives a prize, are, in truth, also retribution myths. For prudence is regarded as virtue deserving reward, just as its opposite deserves punishment. This is especially true of the so-called "wager tales," among which those about races are of particular importance. The manifold variations in which the story of the race between the hare and the tortoise is told among different peoples are typical. The hare jeers at the slow pace and at the legs of the tortoise, and so the latter challenges him to a race. The hare relies on his speed and goes to sleep during the race. The tortoise, on the other hand, conscious of his own slowness, proceeds without interruption and overtakes his sleeping rival.[324] Victory is the reward for persistence. The hare's defeat is punishment for his carelessness, as well as for his arrogance and derision of the insignificant-looking animal which has been treated unkindly by nature. The feeling aroused by all these stories—and this is essential—is that the vanquished deserved the defeat, according to the principle of retribution.

How often relatively subordinate circumstances are considered the characteristic elements of myths, whereas the main motive, retribution, remains completely unnoticed, is shown by the stories which Wundt labels "devouring tales" because in them men are swallowed by animals or monsters.[325] A Melanesian story can be cited as an example: Once upon a time there lived a cannibal who was as tall as a tree and who had a mouth large enough to swallow a house with its inhabitants. Finally a whole native village fled from him with the exception of one woman, who remained hidden in a cave, where she gave birth to a son. When the boy reached twenty years of age, he determined to kill the monster. He built a house in the top of a huge tree and waited for the cannibal's arrival. When the monster came, the lad threw stones and rocks at him and pierced his eye with a spear. Then he tossed a burning log into the giant's mouth. Thereupon the cannibal died. When the people heard this good news, they returned to their abandoned village. The young man married the giant's daughter and became a great chieftain.[326]

That the mythical event takes place in heaven, whither the hero goes by means of an arrow ladder, is essential for certain myths represented as "heaven tales."[327] From a sociological point of view, the motive of retribution also appears to be decisive in them. This is so in the following Indian fable, the content of which is abbreviated as follows: Once upon a time there lived in heaven a chieftain whose name was Sunman. He had two beautiful daughters but did not want them to marry. Therefore he killed all their suitors. At the same time a chieftain dwelled on earth named Fairweather. He had two sons who were idlers. Once the father became annoyed and shouted: Why do you spend your time in indolence? You should rather go and woo the daughters of Sunman! Thereupon the sons started to shoot at heaven with arrows until a ladder was formed which reached from earth to heaven. Then they climbed up to heaven. After various adventures, and especially after they had passed difficult tests imposed upon them by the wicked Sunman, they succeeded in killing him with the aid of animals obedient to them. According to another version, only one of the brothers reached heaven on the arrow ladder, served there as a slave to Sunman, and secretly wooed his younger daughter. As revenge for the bad treatment he had to endure from his father-in-law, he killed him.[328] In both variants of this myth the retribution motive is obvious.

Myths which have utterly moral tendencies—they praise virtues such as gratitude, and condemn vices, like unfaithfulness—show decisive traces of the influence of the principle of retribution. But even these myths are ordinarily not classified from this point of view. And so, for instance, the following Pawnee Indian tale is listed by Wundt[329] in the section: "Marriage between Human and Animal Beings and Their Descendants." This fairy tale tells of a boy who left his village because of disappointment in love. "Grieving, boy sets out . . . . and

enters Prairie Dog town where he marries young Prairie Dog. . . . ."
Upon the request of his mother, "boy returns home, followed by his
Prairie Dog wife, who is pregnant. She rolls herself in dust and becomes woman. . . . . He becomes great man." But when he met his
former love, the dog-wife and her child left him. "From that time on
boy has bad luck and dies broken-hearted."[330] Wundt remarks that
here the marriage between human and animal beings appears as the
"specific motive." But, since the dog becomes a human being at the
very moment when the man appears with her in the village, the decisive part of the story does not deal with marriage between human and
animal beings. The important thing is that the man was punished for
unfaithfulness and ingratitude.

In many so-called "animal tales" it is entirely immaterial that the
actors are animals—for example, in those fables in which curious animals are punished.[331] If the myth tells of an evildoer upon whom the
deserved penalty is finally imposed, as in the well-known German tale
of the wolf and the seven kids, then it is relatively unimportant that the
scamp is a wolf and that his crime consists in swallowing young kids.
The "swallow-motive"[332] here is, compared with the main theme of
retribution, only of minor importance. That the fable actually refers
to human beings and not to animals is borne out by the fact that the
youngest kid which reports everything to the returning mother saved
itself only by hiding in the "clock case." Similarly, if in various tales
innocence, modesty, and true virtue are rewarded, whereas spite and
boastful arrogance are punished, it matters little that the question of
the relationship between brothers and sisters arises, that a good sister
confronts a wicked sister, or that two hostile brothers, of whom one is
good and the other bad, are in conflict with one another. Considered
only with respect to more or less subordinate elements, they are
"brother and sister tales";[333] but, according to their very nature, they
are retribution myths.

The fact that the principle of retribution serves not only to guarantee
the social order by rewarding good and punishing evil but also to
justify institutions of positive law is born out by a characteristic story
of the Ashanti. Among them, succession is regulated according to
mother-right principles; the father is not succeeded by his own offspring but by his sister's children. The story which explains this custom is as follows:

There lived in former times a king of Adanse who had a "linguist" named Abu.
This Abu incurred the king's anger and was heavily fined. Now, at that time children

used to inherit from their father. Abu asked his children to assist him to pay the fine imposed by the king, but they refused and all went off to their mother's relatives. But Abu's sister's children rendered him assistance to pay off his debts, and Abu, therefore, when he died left all his belongings to them. Other people then copied him and willed their property to the sister's children.³³⁴

38. The Motive of Retribution in the Culture Myths

The principle of retribution is intrinsic to the so-called "culture myths." A classic example is the legend of Prometheus, who brought fire, withheld by the gods from human beings, from heaven to earth and, as punishment, was chained to a cliff, where each day an eagle tore to pieces his liver, which revived every night. Thus the possession of fire, evidently considered a crime even though a specific cultural good, rests upon a violation of law for which the bringer of culture, considered the representative of humanity, was punished.

That this thought is not confined to the Greeks is shown by an Indian fable of Yelth, the raven. Yelth was not always a blackbird; once upon a time he was a handsome man who was changed into a bird by the magic of his enemies. The daughter of his uncle, the eagle, was in love with him. This uncle, a powerful chieftain, an enemy of men, was the guardian of fire, sun, moon, stars, and fresh water. Yelth stole all these things from his uncle and escaped with them through the smoke hole of the tent. He put the sun, moon, and stars in their proper places and let water fall down to earth, so that then there were lakes and rivers and men had water to drink. He continued his journey, however, with the fire. But soon the whole stick was on fire, and the smoke blackened his body and his beak; thereupon he had to drop the fire, and it fell to earth.³³⁵ Here, too, the possession of fire rests upon theft. And the thief, to whom humanity owes this good, is punished with the loss of his beauty.

A tale of the Smith River Indians (California) tells of a flood in which all the Indians were drowned, except one couple. From that forlorn hope all the Indians of present day descend as well as all the animals. There was no fire, however, on the earth. So the spider-Indians and the snake-Indians decided to steal fire from the moon. Indeed, the spider-Indians succeeded in outwitting the moon-Indians, so that the snake-Indians were able to descend to earth with the fire. Out of revenge, the moon held the spider-Indians in captivity for a long time. When they were released and returned to earth, they expected to be greeted as benefactors. The ungrateful men, however, killed them to prevent the moon-Indians from taking further revenge for the fraud.³³⁶

In another Indian tale the principle of retribution appears in the form of exchange. Originally, so the fable tells, the souls of the dead possessed the fire: K'ak'eiq, the mink, goes to steal the fire. When he approaches the houses of the spirits, he hears a child cry in the home of the chieftain. He steals it and takes it home with him. The spirits who wish to regain the child propose an exchange to him. He, however, declines everything they offer him, such as the woven cloths in which the dead are wrapped or hides that have been given to them. When they suggest the fire-borer, he accepts and returns the stolen child.[337]

A myth of the Ekoi, an African tribe, tells of their mythical hero, the "Lame Boy." As a benefit to Etim'Ne, the first human being, he stole the fire from Obassi Osaw, the god of heaven, by carrying it off under his loincloth from the house of the wives of the god, where he was a guest. As a consequence, the god condemned him to limp.[338]

A myth of the Kwottos of Toto District (northern Nigeria) relates how the god Hinegba

gave to each [animal] some firewood and commanded them all to go and kindle fire in order that they might obtain the warmth necessary to their existence. They accordingly did so, but all, except the dog, after they had kindled their fire, swallowed it; which accounts for the fact that they are able to live at the present time by means of fire inside them without having recourse to artificial fire such as man finds it necessary to use. The dog, however, brought his wood to man and offered to share it with him, saying that when he required warmth, he would come and share man's fire. And this is how man first obtained wood and why the Kwottos habitually allow a dog to share their fire with them. It is the reason also why the Kwottos do not eat dogs . . . . whom they regard as their friends, and why, if a dog dies, they will attend to its burial.[339]

In this instance the fire-bringer is rewarded rather than punished.

A peculiar reversal of the usual incidents occurs in a myth of the Zande. In this tale, too, the animals originally possess fire, whereas the first human beings must eat their food uncooked. One of them robs the animals of the fire. Thereupon the animals send out the hen and the bitch to fetch back the fire. The two envoys, however, accept food from men and are thereby captured. So they become the first domestic animals.[340] From the point of view of the wild animals, this domestication means punishment for desertion. The motive of retribution is obviously shifted here.

Still another fire myth is told by the Andaman Islanders. The descendants of the first human being aroused the anger of the creator, Puluga.

He sent a great flood which covered the whole land and destroyed all living. Four persons (two men . . . . and two women . . . .) who happened to be in a canoe when the catastrophe occurred, were able to effect an escape. When the waters subsided they . . . . discovered that every living thing on earth had perished; but Puluga re-created the animals, birds, etc. In spite of this, however, they suffered severely in consequence of all their fires having been extinguished. . . . . At this juncture one of their recently deceased friends [that is, a death soul] appeared in their midst in the form of a bird . . . . seeing their distress he flew up to . . . . the sky . . . . and attempted to carry away in his beak a burning log, but . . . . the blazing brand fell on Puluga, who, incensed with pain, hurled it at the intruder; happily . . . . the missile missed its mark and fell near the very spot where the four survivors were deploring their condition.[341]

So an attempt was made to punish the fire thief, but it did not succeed; this is the more remarkable inasmuch as it was inflicted by the creator himself.

The principle of retribution appears in a somewhat weaker form in an Australian tale. As far as it is of interest in this connection, the story is as follows:

The tribe [Kurnai] being engaged fishing, Bulun, Baukan, and their son Buluntut coming to the camp, took away all the fire, and began to ascend to the sky by way of . . . . a cord. . . . . Wagulan, the Crow, had observed the robbery . . . . and went in haste to tell the Brown Hawk . . . . he hereupon swooped on them [the thieves], and striking violently with his wings caused Baukan to let fall the fire. This falling to the ground was seen by Bembrin (the Robin), who carefully blew it into a flame, and smearing some of the fire over his breast, has remained thus marked to this day. In this manner the Kurnai regained their fire.[342]

Also in those myths which deal with the origin of various economic systems does the motive of retribution appear. Thus, in some African tales, hunting—apparently because it is more enervating and dangerous than cattle-breeding and agriculture—is regarded "as punishment for certain delicts committed in ancient times."[343] According to a fairy tale of the Bassonge, the Batua (pygmies) became hunters for the following reasons: To four men who came to visit in heaven, God gave four baskets and commanded that they should not be opened before the men regained the earth. Two of the men, however, opened their baskets earlier, and wild beasts jumped out. The other two opened theirs only when they arrived in the village; goats, sheep, and chickens emerged. The former two, as punishment for their disobedience, had to hunt the wild animals with bows given them by God.[344] They were the Batua.[345]

The Ba-Kaonde accept the existence of wild animals as punishment for the disobedience of the honey bird, Mayimba, into whose care God intrusted three gourds, and who opened them in defiance of God's command. Death, sickness, and all manner of carnivores and death-bringing reptiles sprang out of the third gourd.[346]

Agriculture, since it is more toilsome than cattle-breeding, is, in relation to the latter, interpreted as punishment. The agricultural inhabitants of Irangi tell the following story:

Once upon a time God made a large pit and in it he put some oxen. Nearby stood Moassai (Massai), Mgogo, and Mrangi, the ancestors of the three peoples of these names. God promised the greatest wealth to him who dared to jump into the pit. And Moassai jumped into the pit. Thereupon God said: "You are the most courageous; you will be a great warrior" and he gave him two oxen. Then Mgogo jumped into the pit and God said: "You are not so courageous and less of a warrior, therefore you get only one ox, and, in order that you may live you will have to cultivate the fields." Mrangi was the last jumper. Therefore he obtained the worst ox. And God said to him: "You have the least courage and you will be the worst warrior. Your ox is bad and not valuable; you will have to work strenuously on your field in order to obtain food."[347]

Many culture myths of the Yamana[348] justify the toil of life by stating that man must deserve the advantages of culture through labor. In one of these stories, "the elder Yoalox [culture hero] once obtained from his sister a remarkable harpoon. . . . . Never did this weapon miss its mark so that he always got his booty. Each time he threw the harpoon it came back to his hand." Once, however, the harpoon broke. Thereupon the elder Yoalox said to his brother:

How agreeable would it be to have a harpoon which would neither go astray nor break! Indeed it should be this way: on the first throw the sea-lion should be killed and immediately thereafter the harpoon should return to the hand of the hunter. This would spare much work and toil to us as well as to other men. Then we would not even have to manufacture the harpoons. Bacon and meat of the sea-lion would be secured for all. Nowadays it requires toil and cunning to kill a sea-lion! The younger Yoalox listened carefully to all his words. When his elder brother had finished, he contradicted him angrily and energetically: "Never may it be as you plan. It is good for men to work and toil, and it is socially useful that everyone make his own harpoon. Man would lose all these advantages if he were given such a harpoon as you propose. It is also just that a clumsy and careless hunter break or lose his harpoon. If an awkward man throws the harpoon badly, it is in order that the animal may escape; for everyone must strive and toil!"

A very interesting myth of the Waraus (Guiana), reported by Brett, justifies their inferiority in relation to the Caribs. The country in which the ancestors of the Waraus lived was

abundantly supplied with game, but water was scarce. The Great Spirit, in reply to their supplications, created the Essequibo and other streams. Moreover, he formed for the Waraus, his dear though erring children, a small lake of delicious water, charging them "only to drink of it, but not to bathe therein, or evil would ensue." This was the test of obedience, and all the men religiously observed it.—Near that pleasant spot there dwelt a family of note among the Waraus, consisting of four brothers, named

respectively, Kororoma, Kororomāna, Kororomātu and Kororomatitu, with their
sisters Korobōna and Korobonāko. The latter, two beautiful but wilful maidens, disregarded the injunction, and in an evil hour ventured into the forbidden water. In
the centre there was planted a pole, which, while it remained untouched, was their
safeguard. This excited their curiosity. There was a secret which they must find out.
The boldest of the two at last ventured to shake it, and thereby broke the charm which
had bound the spirit of the pool . . . . and he immediately took possession of the
maiden as his lawful prize.—Great was the indignation of her brothers when, after
a time, their sister became a mother. But as the babe was in all respects like one of
their own children, they, after long consultation, allowed it to live and grow up with
them, and the mother's offence was forgiven.—She could not, however, forget the
pleasant pool and its mysterious inhabitant, and after a while repeated her transgression. Then came the threatened woe! The offspring of the second offence only resembled the human race in the head and upper parts, which were those of a beautiful
boy . . . . the other extremity resembling that of the variegated python or camudi of
the rivers and swamps of Guiana.—Though terrified at the appearance of her offspring, Korobōna yet cherished it secretly in the depth of the forest where she had
brought it forth. Her brothers at length discovered her secret, and transfixed the
serpent-child with their arrows, leaving it for dead. But under the mother's nursing it
revived, and soon grew to a formidable size. The suspicion of her brothers having
been again aroused by her frequent visits to the forest, they followed her, and from a
distance beheld her conversing with it, themselves remaining unseen.—Fearing
that they would themselves be eventually overpowered by a creature so terrible,
which, after what had happened, must naturally look upon them as foes, they resolved
on an onslaught with all the power at their command. Accordingly, they made many
arrows and put their other weapons in order. Their sister, asking the purpose of those
preparations, received an evasive answer. On this she fled to give warning, and they
pursued. Attacking the mysterious being, which sought refuge in its mother's embrace, they disabled it from a distance with showers of arrows, and to make all sure,
cut it in pieces before her eyes.—The unhappy Korobōna carefully collected the
remains into a heap, which she kept continually covered with fresh leaves and guarded
with tender assiduity.—After long watching, her patience was rewarded. The
vegetable covering began to heave, and show signs of life. From it there slowly arose
an Indian warrior of majestic and terrible appearance. His brow was of a brilliant red,
he held bow and arrows in his hand, and was otherwise equipped for instant battle.
—That warrior was the first CARIB—the great father of a powerful race.—He forthwith commenced the task of revenge for the wrongs suffered in his former existence.
Neither his uncles, nor the whole Warau race whom they summoned, could stand
before him. He drove them hither and thither like deer—took possession of such
of their women as pleased him, and by them became the father of brave and terrible warriors like himself. From their presence the unhappy Waraus retired, till
they reached the swampy shores of the Atlantic, forsaking those pleasant hunting-
grounds which they had occupied on their first descent from heaven.[349]

The superiority of the white race is also explained according to the
principle of retribution. This is aptly pictured by Kidd in a myth of
the Kaffirs taken over from the Hottentots.

Teco, or Tixo, made three kinds of men, namely, Hottentots, Kafirs, and white men. A day was fixed for these men to appear before Tixo. As they were gathering together, a honey-bird, which leads people to the place where honey is to be found, came flying about in great excitement. With the Hottentots it is almost a religion to leave any important work unfinished and immediately to follow the honey-bird. So the Hottentots at once ran after it. Tixo was very cross with this action of the Hottentots and declared that they should be a vagrant race, living on honey, beer, and wild roots. After this, vast herds of cattle appeared, and the Kafirs were so excited that they began to squabble, one claiming this beast and another claiming that. One wanted this red cow, another wanted that black bull, and so they went on wrangling. Tixo was very cross, and said that they should be a restless people whose chief possessions should consist in cattle. The white men waited patiently, and Tixo was so pleased that he gave them cattle, horses, sheep, and many kinds of useful things; and that is why the white man is so superior to the Kafir. He gained all his useful knowledge by waiting.[350]

It is decisive that the superiority of the white race is regarded as a reward judged from the standard of the principle of retribution.

39. The Motive of Retribution in the Deity-, Hero-, Ancestor-, and Death-Soul Myths

The extraordinary importance of the motive of retribution—be it in the barbarous form of personal vengeance or in the morally refined forms of victory (thus a reward) of good or of defeat (thus a punishment) of evil—in the myths of such peoples as the Greeks and Germans, who have attained higher stages of culture, is so obvious that further proofs are unnecessary.[351] It is, however, not superfluous to point out that the same theme appears constantly and importantly in myths of still primitive peoples which deal with ancestors appearing as gods or heroes and with death souls endowed with superhuman powers. For instance, the Eskimos of Baffin Land tell of a man who killed his son-in-law, an ice gull, in order to avenge the injustices which the latter had inflicted upon his daughter, the sea gull Sedna. The ice gulls, however, take revenge by provoking a terrific storm which compells the father to sacrifice his daughter to the vindictive birds. In turn, Sedna avenges herself on her father by inciting the dogs to gnaw on his hands and feet while he sleeps.[352]

The myth which the Brazilian Bakairi recount of their ancestors is essentially a retribution myth. Keri and Kame, the two legendary ancestors, kill their foster-father, Oka, a jaguar, and his mother, Mero, a snake, to avenge their mother, who was killed by Mero and eaten by Oka.[353]

During the Inca period the Peruvians venerated the god Ataguju,

who, in their belief, created earth and heaven and ruled over the firmament. Their legend reports, according to Brinton, that

from him proceeded the first of mortals, the man Guamansuri, who descended to the
earth and there seduced the sister of certain Guachemines, rayless ones, or Darklings,
who then possessed it. For this crime they destroyed him, but their sister proved
pregnant, and died in her labor, giving birth to two eggs. From these emerged the
twin brothers, Apocatequil and Piguerao. The former was the more powerful. By
touching the corpse of his mother he brought her to life, he drove off and slew the
Guachemines, and, directed by Ataguju, released the race of Indians from the soil by
turning it up with a spade of gold. For this reason they adored him as their maker.[354]

Two heroes, Hunahpu and Xbalanque, are the principal characters
in a myth of the Quiché Indians. They are two brothers begotten in a
miraculous way: The evil gods of the underworld had killed two
brothers and hidden the head of one in a pole. The pole became a
fruit tree. A girl, while trying to pick a fruit from the tree, became
pregnant and later gave birth to the two heroes, who obviously are the
reincarnations of the murdered brothers. In order to avenge the death
of their ancestors, the two heroes killed the underworld gods and then
the one became the sun and the other the moon.[355]

A myth of the Aztecs accounts for the birth of the sun-god as follows:

Couatlicue was impregnated by a shuttlecock which fell upon her and which she
hid under her petticoat. Her other children, the daughter, Coyolxauh, and the four-
hundred sons, the Uitznaua, were enraged over this disgrace and wanted to kill her.
The child in her womb, however, comforted and encouraged her, and it was born at
the very moment when the attackers were near. It immediately struck off the sister's
head and destroyed or dispersed the four-hundred Uitznaua.[356]

In the creation story of the Apapocuva one of the chief motives is
vengeance, which the hero takes for the murder of his mother. On the
other hand, he grants the opossum, in gratitude for its having nursed
his twin brother after his mother's death, the capacity of bringing forth
its young without pain.[357]

In the myths of the Uitoto, collected by Preuss,[358] the pre-eminent
importance of the principle of retribution is clearly shown. It appears
in the form of a vendetta of sons on the murderers of their father, of a
father on the slayer of his son, of a tribe on the murderers of one of its
members, of a woman on the killers of her sister. Also, the owner of an
animal which is valuable to him avenges its death. And the animal
takes revenge for the death of its master.

Retribution is not only exercised as blood revenge. Thus a suitor
takes revenge on the girl who refuses him. And a girl is punished who
refuses all her suitors. A father eagle wishes to eat his daughters be-

cause they have devoured his eggs. A man desires to kill another man with his blowpipe because the latter has committed adultery with his wife; by mistake, however, he hits his wife; she is then avenged by her brothers, who bewitch the husband with a head illness; in turn, a third man rescues the husband from this affliction and is supposed to obtain a reward, etc. Through his auxiliary spirits a man kills a rival who has committed adultery with his wife. A wife leaves her husband for another man, for whom she plants yuka; out of revenge the former destroys the field by means of his auxiliary spirits, who act as mice. Because she burns a magic implement of her husband, a woman is punished by losing her capacity of transformation. A female moth calls bats "ugly"; in retaliation they eat her and all of her family.[358a] "Before the sun yet existed, Hitiruni (the dark) crushed . . . . a fly, a Rigama, which had stung him. Thereupon it dawned and another Rigama conferred with his tribesmen about the punishment for this murder."[358b] Trees, too, take revenge. And so Rigama, with the aid of auxiliary spirits acting as capricorn beetles, gnaws off the branches of a tree but later fears the tree's revenge. Nofuyetoma creates a tree the leaves of which furnish a means of finding game animals by night. Out of revenge on its creator the tree produces evil spirits in the form of toads, which then kill Nofuyetoma's wife.[358c]

Myths often deal with the revenge imposed by death souls. Preuss expressly states that the soul "appears in myths only after a violent death in order to take revenge." Many examples can be cited to prove this statement. Hedo, through Sibunaforo's guilt, falls from a tree and dies; "Now his soul will return since Hedo is a powerful magician," says Sibunaforo. The soul arrives running, climbs to the roof because the door is closed, asks for a spear, and receives one from Sibunaforo. With it the soul makes several thrusts at the trough which Sibunaforo has put into the hammock in place of himself. Thereupon the soul proceeds into the underworld, believing it has killed its enemy. The soul of Doboseiroke lives in a nut and every night vexes the wife of his adversary (at whose instigation he was bitten by a poisonous snake) by stretching out her *nymphae*. The nut is finally crushed, and the soul is killed. The soul of the devoured Kudi-Buneima, called *matina*, appears in the poisoned leg wound of one of his enemies as a worm. Amenakuduma was burned to death in sleep; afterward his soul takes revenge by throwing a maggot into the pigments with which the son of Nofugireima, his adversary, painted himself. When the latter could not sleep during the night and was cooling his wound in the draft from an open door, the soul appeared as a giant with one leg in the door of one hut and the other in the door of another dwelling, so that his knees rose above the top of the huts. Shaking his head, he announces death to the inhabitants. Those who sleep, dream all this. Therefore the soul is called Nikairama from *nikai*, which means "to dream." One night the inhabitants tied a long rope around each of the giant's legs, so that, when it went away in the morning, they were able to follow and kill it after felling the hollow Cumare palm in which it took refuge. Then they ate the soul. But the soul reappears as an endless procession of maggots, which the villagers collect and eat. But they have to vomit them out; wallowing in the dust, they finally become wild boars.[358d]

Higireima was eaten by the Himue, the men of Himuege, and his soul went to his old fishing place to eat fish. His brother Nubadyamui watched one night to find out who stole his fish, and saw at dawn that someone pulled up the net. It was the soul of his devoured brother which he grasped. The soul bitterly reproached the living brother for not having avenged his death although preparations were already completed for the festivity, *bai*.[359*]

The skull of a dead woman, whose husband was to blame for her death, perches on his shoulder and, in order to take revenge, eats all his food. And then the digested stuff runs down his body in a black substance. The skull of a murdered man requests his sons to avenge him.[359a]

Casalis[360] reports a legend of the Basuto in which is told how a young man murdered his brother and afterward was persecuted by the death soul in the shape of a bird who cried out: "I am the heart of Maciloniane. Macilo killed me. My corpse lies near a well in the desert." Casalis calls this story "one of the best I have ever heard. The existence of the soul, its immortality, and the vengeance which persecutes the murderer wherever he is, are clearly indicated."

Among the legends of the Kaffirs reported by Kidd, several contain the retribution theme—for instance, the story of Unyengebule, who killed his wife because she did not bring him honey. The *Isala*, a feather decoration worn by his wife, changes itself into a bird and sings: "I am the little *Isala* of Unyengebule's wife. I was murdered." Thereupon Unyengebule also kills the bird, but it returns again and again to chant its accusation, until finally the people kill the murderer.[361] A Maori myth tells of two brothers, Tuteamoamo and Waihuka. The younger, Waihuka, has a beautiful wife and therefore is envied by the older. When both go out fishing, Tuteamoamo wishes to drown his younger brother. The latter, however, is rescued by a whale, his ancestor. Thereupon Waihuka kills his elder brother.[362]

40. The Motive of Retribution in the Creation Myths

Of great interest for this investigation is the application of the principle of retribution in the so-called "nature myths," which really are society myths, inasmuch as they interpret, as has been shown, phenomena of nature according to an essentially social scheme. This appears strikingly in the "creation myths" where, as in Genesis, the universe is not perceived as the product of an objective process of the elements but is traced to the command of a personal being, a specifically social act. Consequently, the origin of the various parts of the world seems to be the carrying-out of an imperative directed at the objects to be created. "And God said, Let there be light: and there was light. . . . . And God said, Let there be a firmament in the midst of the waters. . . . . And God said, Let the earth bring forth grass, the herb yielding seed. . . . ." Between the personal creator and the things not yet existent the same relationship is assumed which exists between the chieftain and the members of the tribe obliged to obedience. Nature is thus created in compliance with a norm issued by the competent authority.

The motive of retribution becomes remarkably noticeable in the Babylonian cosmogenesis upon which the biblical creation story is probably based.[363] In the beginning, so the Babylonian legend relates, there existed neither heaven nor earth, but only the Father Apsu (Ocean) and the Mother Tiamat. Then the gods were created, both those of the nether world and those of the upper world. The myth further tells how Tiamat, the "mother of the gods," revolts together with the powers of the nether world against the "upper gods." In the ensuing struggle Tiamat and her followers are confronted by the other gods under the leadership of Marduk. He is expressly called the "avenger" of the gods. To his father, who calls upon him to fight, he says:

> If I, your avenger,
> Bind Tiamat and keep you alive,
> Convene the assembly. . . . .[364]

His condition is that the gods transfer dominion to him. The gods are satisfied and say:

> Thou Marduk art our avenger.
> We have given thee kingship of universal power over the
> totality of all things.[365]

Marduk then overcomes Tiamat and her followers. His victory is represented as punishment for the evil deeds of his enemies. Before the battle, it is said of Tiamat:

> Unto Tiamat who raged he thus addressed her:
> "As for thee thou art become great, thou hast been lifted
> up on high.
> Thy heart has prompted thee to summon to conflict.
> . . . . their fathers . . . .
> . . . . their thou hast cursed. . . . .
> Thou hast exalted Kingu unto marriage.
> Thou hast made his decree greater than the decree of Anu.
> Evil deeds thou seekest and
> Against the gods my fathers thou hast established thy
> wickedness.
> Let thy host be equipped and let thy weapons be girded on.
> Stand thou by and let us, me and thee, make battle."[366]

Marduk captures Tiamat in a net and kills her. Her followers are also captured. Of them the poem tells:

> Into a net were they thrown and in the snare they sat down.
> They stood in secret chambers, being filled with lamentation.
> They bore his punishment being bound in prison.[367]

The "Gods, his fathers," reward the victor with presents for his deed. Marduk is appeased and begins to create the world: "to create ingenious works." He cuts Tiamat's body in two parts. Out of one part he makes the firmament; he bolts and bars its doors; he places guards so that the water may not flow over it. Then he creates sun, moon, and stars. Obviously, this myth intends not so much, as Gunkel[368] says in his excellent book, "to describe the cause of a given fact," to explain causally the existing situation, as to justify the world as it is and to picture it as the result of a just fight between the power of good and order (Marduk) and the powers of evil and chaos (Tiamat). "The characteristic function of the myth" is not, as Gunkel[369] believes, to answer "by a story" the questions which man asks when he perceives the world but to interpret reality according to the principle of retribution, which can be realized only in a social process. That this process is represented in a story is of minor importance.

The idea of retribution is also presented as a struggle between the principles of good and evil in those myths in which the creation of the world is traced to the action of two personalities, who, as representatives of the two principles, fight one another. The one creates good things and beings, those which are useful to men; the other, wishing to destroy the work of the former, creates evil things, those which are harmful to men. The most genuine of these dualistic myths[370] can be found in the Iranian religion, in the center of which are Ormuzd and Ahriman. Both exist from the beginning. Ormuzd, who is omniscient, shows Ahriman the inevitable end: victory of the good and defeat of the evil. This arouses in Ahriman such consternation that Ormuzd is able, in the following three thousand years, to create without obstruction these worldly things: heaven, water, earth, plants, animals, and finally human beings. When the first world period comes to an end, Ahriman begins the fight against Ormuzd—a fight which lasts for nine thousand years. He creates evil spirits and also such harmful things as flies and worms which destroy trees,[371] or mountains,[372] which make trouble for men. In Ahriman, above all, originate illness and death.[373] His intention is to ruin the pure things created by Ormuzd. Finally, however, Ormuzd conquers and destroys all evil. This victory of Ormuzd over Ahriman culminates in a last judgment at the end of time. This is the "great decision," which is made according to those very laws which Ormuzd gave at the beginning, the just law of retribution. "I first perceived you as holy, Mazda Ahura [Ormuzd], when I saw you creating good things, and predetermining the reward for word and deed: evil to the evil man, good to the good man, through your power on the last day."[374] On this last day all mountains will melt and overflow the earth as a river of liquid metal. [In the realm of pure good and perfect justice the world will be flat.] All human beings must pass through this river. For the righteous man it will be warm milk; for the unrighteous, however, destroying fire. Finally, Ahriman and all his evil spirits are to be thrown into this glowing river.[375] Such will be their punishment. Then the world will be perfectly pure again; only then will the creation of the good god be completed.

The principle of retribution appears less abstractly and much more naïvely in the creation stories of primitive peoples, such as the Indians. A legend of the Hurons tells[376] of twin brothers as creators of the world. One is good; the other evil.

The bad brother made fierce and monstrous creatures proper to terrify and destroy mankind—serpents, panthers, wolves, bears, all of enormous size, and huge mosquitoes. . . . . In the mean time the good brother, in his province, was creating the innocent and useful animals. Among the rest he made the partridge. . . . .

Thereupon the good brother went to the land of the evil brother. There "he did not destroy the evil animals . . . . but he reduced them in size, so that men would be able to master them." A fight between the brothers ensues, in which the good brother kills the evil. "But the slain combatant was not utterly destroyed. He reappeared after death to his brother and told him that he had gone to the far west, and that thenceforth all the races of men after death would go to the west, like him."

In a creation myth of the Sioux Indians,[377] "Bladder and the Monster were twins and the sons of the Turtle. Bladder hunted his brother all over the world to slay him, because his body was of stone and caused his mother's death."

According to a myth of the natives of Loango reported by Pechuel-Loesche, Nsambi, a Supreme Being, created everything, also man. But

men were not better than they are today. They quarreled as before and fought each other and committed wrongs. Nsambi did not like this and he prohibited many things. There were good and bad men. The bad men did not abide to the prohibitions. Thereupon drought came upon the land; and together with it, hunger and illnesses were ordered by Nsambi; and many people died, the good ones as well, since they did not watch over their bad brethren. Again and again men cried for Nsambi to help them. And when he finally came, everybody shouted and accused the others. They made bad palavers. Everyone wanted him and cried out his requests and petitions, and there was a great noise. This went on for a time, until Nsambi became annoyed: he went away and did never return.[378]

Since then, Nsambi does not care for the human beings.

As a deity he appears to be completely beyond their conduct of life. They fear the evil which threatens them on earth, and not him. And because he does not mind that evil things occur on earth, and men help themselves against them by other means, they do no longer need him. This practical people expects reciprocity. Nsambi is too big, too far away; he is little concerned with the welfare of his beings. Since he shows no interest in them, they do not care about him.[379]

This indifference of the Supreme Being toward men is interpreted by the latter as punishment.

In those myths which represent creation as the sexual act of the parent-pair, the principle of retribution also appears. The classical form of this myth is the one of Uranos and Gaia. In Hesiod's *Theogony*[380] the injustice which father Uranos inflicts on mother Gaia by restraining their children in her womb and not allowing them to see the light of the world is avenged by their son, Cronos. Gaia calls upon the children:

My children, gotten of a sinful father, if you will obey me, we should punish the vile outrage of your father; for he first thought of doing shameful things! So she said; but fear seized them all, and none of them uttered a word. But great Cronos the wily took courage and answered his dear mother: "Mother, I will undertake to do this deed, for I reverence not our father of evil name, for he first thought of doing shameful things." So he said: and vast Earth [Gaia] rejoiced greatly in spirit, and set and hid him in an ambush, and put in his hands a jagged sickle, and revealed to him the whole plot. And Heaven [Uranos] came, bringing on night and longing for love, and he lay about earth spreading himself full upon her. Then the son from his ambush stretched forth his left hand and in his right took the great long sickle with jagged teeth, and swiftly lopped off his own father's members. . . . .

From the blood drops which fell from Uranos onto Gaia the Erinyes, the vengeance spirits of Greek religion, arose. And just as Uranos outraged Gaia and their children, so did Cronos affront his wife-Rhea by devouring their children because he feared that one of them might sometime seize dominion from him. This had been prophesied to him, apparently as retribution for the crime committed upon his own father. When Rhea was about to give birth to Zeus, she prayed to her parents, Gaia and Uranos, "to devise some plan with her that the birth of her dear child might be concealed, and that retribution might overtake great, crafty Cronos for his own father and also for the children whom he had swallowed down."³⁸¹ This vengeance is carried out. Cronos is duped by a trick: instead of the infant Zeus, he swallows a stone wrapped in a napkin. Later he is in turn overthrown by his son, Zeus. Retribution is thus the leading motive of Hesiod's *Theogony*.

The hate and vengeance motive in the love story of Heaven and Earth also appears in the fable of the Maoris about Rangi, Father Heaven, and Papa, Mother Earth, well known because of its striking resemblance to the Uranos-Gaia myth.

Darkness then rested upon the heaven and upon the earth, and they still both clave together, for they had not yet been rent apart; and the children they had begotten were ever thinking among themselves what might be the difference between darkness and light. . . . . At last the beings who had been begotten by Heaven and Earth, worn out by the continued darkness, consulted among themselves, saying, "Let us now determine what we should do with Rangi and Papa, whether it would be better to slay them or to rend them apart. . . . ." Tane-mahuta, the father of forests, says to his five brothers: "It is better to rend them apart, and to let the heaven stand far above us, and the earth lie beneath our feet. Let the sky become as a stranger to us but the earth remain close to us as a nursing mother."

And, indeed, Tane-mahuta succeeds in separating the groaning parents. But "in the breast of Tawhiri-ma-tea, the god and father of winds and storms" arose

a fierce desire to wage war with his brothers, because they had rent apart their common parents. He from the first had refused to consent to his mother being torn from her lord and children; it was his brothers alone that wished for this separation, and desired that Papa-tu-a-nuku,.or the Earth alone, should be left as a parent to them. . . . . So he rises, follows his father to the realm above [and makes war on his brothers].

After having broken and torn to pieces Tane-mahuta and his offspring and after Tangaroa and his children had fled to the depths of the ocean or the recesses of the shore, he

rushed on to attack his brothers Rongo-ma-tane and Haumia-tikitiki, the gods and progenitors of cultivated and uncultivated food; but Papa, to save these for her other children, caught them up, and hid them in a place of safety; and so well were these children of hers concealed by their mother Earth, that Tawhiri-ma-tea sought for them in vain. Tawhiri-ma-tea having thus vanquished all his other brothers next rushed against Tu-matauenga, to try his strength against his; he exerted all his force against him, but he could neither shake him nor prevail against him. . . . . Tu-matauenga, or man, still stood erect and unshaken upon the breast of his mother Earth . . . . fierce man . . . . next took thought how he could turn upon his brothers and slay them, because they had not assisted him or fought bravely when Tawhiri-ma-tea had attacked them to avenge the separation of their parents, and because they had left him alone to show his prowess in the fight. . . . . Thus Tu-matauenga devoured all his brothers, and consumed the whole of them, in revenge for their having deserted him and left him to fight alone against Tawhiri-ma-tea and Rangi. . . . . Four of his brothers were entirely deposed by him, and became his food; but one of them, Tawhiri-ma-tea, he could not vanquish or make common, by eating him for food, so he, the last born child of Heaven and Earth, was left as an enemy for man. . . . .[382]

Such is the essential content of the Maori myth. The idea of retribution is obvious. The mother-right elements, as in the Greek fable, are likewise manifest. Finally there is even an indication of a contrast in value between heaven and earth: heaven is the evil, and earth the good, principle. It may be that this form of the Maori legend is of recent date, but the essential content seems to be very old. This is further borne out by the similarity to the ancient Greek account as well as to the old Egyptian fable of Nut, the (female) heaven, and Keb, the (male) earth. According to the version handed down to us,[383] Nut and Keb also had to be separated. Above all, it is the principle of retribution which represents the original element in the Maori myth, for it can be found in other nature myths, especially those which go back to the most primitive stages.

41. THE MOTIVE OF RETRIBUTION IN THE MYTHS OF NATURE

The relationship between heaven and earth is paralleled in many myths by the affinity supposed between the sun and moon. Both situations are equally illustrative of the principle of retribution. The west-

F

ern Equatorial pygmies tell a story in which the sun, a man, is angry
with his wife, the moon, because she has been unfaithful. The pygmies
say:

> Moon went away to the village of her mother and Sun has never agreed to see her
> since. You never see Sun at night. But Moon wanted to return to her husband.
> Therefore you often see her on the sky run after him in the evening when Sun has not
> yet gone to sleep, or in the morning when Sun is already up; but he never wants to see
> her again.[384]

Earlier the West African Negro myth has been mentioned which
explains the supposed enmity between the sun and moon by the fact
that both once agreed to drown their children; but the moon deceived
the sun and is surrounded by its star-children, while the sun is childless. A similar story can be found among the Mintira (Mantra) of the
Malayan Peninsula; in this case the idea of retribution is even more
apparent. Tylor[385] writes:

> The Moon is a woman, and the Sun also: the Stars are the Moon's children, and
> the Sun had in old times as many. Fearing, however, that mankind could not bear so
> much brightness and heat, they agreed each to devour her children; but the Moon,
> instead of eating up her Stars, hid them from the Sun's sight, who, believing them all
> devoured, ate up her own; no sooner had she done it, than the Moon brought her
> family out of their hiding-place. When the Sun saw them, filled with rage she chased
> the Moon to kill her; the chase has lasted ever since, and sometimes the Sun even
> comes near enought to bite the Moon, and that is an eclipse; the Sun, as men may still
> see, devours his Stars at dawn, and the Moon hides hers all day while the Sun is near,
> and only brings them out at night, when her pursuer is far away.

Tylor adds:

> Now among a tribe of North East India, the Ho of Chota-Nagpore, the myth re-
> appears, obviously from the same source, but with a varied ending; the Sun cleft the
> Moon in twain for her deceit, and thus cloven and growing whole again, she remains,
> and her daughters with her which are the Stars.

Just as the form of the moon is interpreted according to the principle
of retribution, so also is the human face imagined in the moon; the
lunar spots are likewise viewed in the same light. Elsdon Best reports
of the Maori: "Rona is the woman in the moon, translated thereto
from earth in punishment for having insulted that useful orb by applying an offensive expression to it."[386]

A North American Indian fable contains an interesting explanation
of the lunar spots. After the death of his parents, a boy flies to heaven
in the skin of an eagle. There he comes first of all to the house of the
sun, where he finds six girls. Three are the daughters of the sun, and
they are beautiful; the three others are the daughters of the moon, and

they are ugly and humpbacked. He marries one of the daughters of the sun. Thereupon the moon becomes annoyed and persecutes the young man in many ways. The young man's grandmothers manufacture from a few logs of wood and from their combs, which are transformed into paws, two bears. He casts them against the moon, whose face the animals scratch. Afterward the moon leaves the Indian boy alone.[387]

In the myths of the South American aborigines the relationship between sun and moon is imagined as that between husband and wife, or between brother and sister, or as both at the same time. The Ona have a legend which accounts for the lunar spots by explaining that the sun, the husband, hit his wife, the moon, in the face because she divulged certain secret rites. According to a myth of the Guarayo, the sun pursues the moon because the latter has committed incest; in anger, the sun scratches the moon's face. A similar idea is incorporated in an Eskimo story.[388] "The Khasias of the Himalaya say the Moon falls monthly in love with his mother-in-law, who throws ashes in his face, whence his spots."[389] The Ndonga-Ambo, a tribe of the western Bantu territory, have the following myth: One day the sun gave the moon two livers to roast, one for the moon and one for men. The moon put them in two pots. When the fire began to die out, the moon fetched new logs of wood, and the liver for the human beings started to burn; the pot of the moon, however, was still filled with water. When the moon recounted these hardships to the angered sun, the latter said: "Although you were present you let the pot burn in which was the liver for your relatives! You did it intentionally! Bring me the other liver." The moon replied: "Nothing is left, everything is burnt." Thereupon the sun grew even more enraged. "You failed in your duty," she screamed, "You seem to wish your relatives might die and never rise from death. Well, you alone shall rise from death." And with these words she burnt the moon's face. Thus these natives explain the moon's sears.[390] An old Lithuanian poem contains the following account. "The moon embraced his wife, the sun, and from this embrace the stars arose. Once the moon fell in love with the morning star; thereupon the angered god Perkun slashed the face of the moon with his sword."[391]

The Yamana[392] regard the sun, Lem, as a man and the son of an older sun-man named Taruwalem. This is apparently their explanation of the origin of the sun. Taruwalem is pictured as evil, whereas Lem is good and friendly disposed toward human beings. The old sun-man was extremely strong and displayed great might. Once he became angry and caused everything within reach to be burnt. Then he was much nearer to the earth than to-day. He made all the water of the sea boil in the terrific heat. And all the forests burned down; since then the tops of all mountains are treeless. All this happened be-cause of the heat which he produced in his great anger. From the beginning no one had liked Taruwalem. But afterwards everyone hated him. Not only he but also his relatives were despised. His whole family was shunned by everyone, for each member of this family behaved maliciously and tried to hurt others. Only Lem, the son of old Taruwalem, was a remarkable exception. He was kind to all. He was an excellent hunter and clever in everything. He treated everyone pleasantly and was always help-ful. The women, who in these mythical times had the dominance, meditated secretly for a long time. Finally they agreed to kill malevolent old Taruwalem. One day they all attacked and tried to strangle him. But inasmuch as he was very strong he suc-ceeded in extricating himself. He immediately rushed out into the canopy of heaven. There he still stands as a bright star. But he has lost his former strength.

Today's sun is Lem. And his son is the planet Venus, called Yexalem; "this son infallibly follows his father at his elbow, but is not as strong as his father." The form of the rainbow is also explained according to the principle of retribution by the Yamana in the following legend: Akainix, the rainbow, was an exceedingly handsome man. He took revenge on some men who dared make love to his wife and sister by killing them. Thereupon the relatives of these men desired retaliation on Akainix. They

seized him with all their strength but were unable to kill him. For some time they tried to strangle him. Because he was a powerful *yekamus* (magician), they did not succeed despite all their efforts. They were successful, however, in bending his neck and his long back so that since then he has been unable to stand upright.[393]

There is a widespread inclination among primitive peoples to inter-pret the eclipse either of the sun or the moon as an act of vengeance or a punishment imposed by a deity which is angered because of a delict. "In the South Sea Islands," writes Tylor, "some supposed the Sun and Moon to be swallowed by an offended deity, whom they therefore in-duced, by liberal offerings, to eject the luminaries from his stom-ach."[394] The reason for the continual heavenly wanderings of the moon is explained in an Australian legend which "says that Mityan, the Moon, was a native cat, who fell in love with some one else's wife, and was driven away to wander ever since."[395]

Not only punishment but also, although more seldom, reward ap-pears as explanatory justification of certain natural phenomena. In this way, in a myth of the Australian Narrinyeri the color of the sun is explained. They picture the sun as a woman who, after she sets, walks through the land of the dead. For a service which she renders to some of the dead she receives the skin of a red kangaroo. In this red robe she is dressed when she rises in the morning.[396] In a sun myth of the Marind-anim the girls of the tribe, in the name of all, speak thus to the anthropomorphically perceived sun: "Sun, care for us always; be gracious to us, and we shall also be good to you."[397]

A tale of the Eskimos reports that the raven once put the sun in a bag because of men's wickedness. Moved by rich presents of food and fur offered to him, "he let them have the light for a short time. . . . . After this a long time would pass and it required many offerings before he would let them have light again. This was repeated many times." Finally the brother of the raven succeeds, through a trick, in putting "the sun in its place again. . . . . He remembered that his father had called to him not to keep it always dark, but to make it partly dark and partly light. Thinking of this, he caused the sky to revolve so that it moved around the earth, carrying the sun and stars with it, thus making day and night."[398] In other sun fables, especially those which explain how men obtained the sun and which are reminiscent of the fire-theft myths, the principle of retribution also occurs.

A tale of the central Brazilian Indians is just such an account. Keri and Kame are requested by their aunt, Ewaki, to fetch the sun, which is in the possession of the red king vulture, Urubu. After various experiences Keri grasps the vulture so violently that the latter is almost killed.

Only if he surrenders the sun, may he remain alive. Thereupon the king vulture dispatches his brother, the white vulture, to fetch the sun. At first, however, he brings only the aurora. "Is this right?" Kame asks Keri who still holds the royal vulture. 'No, not the aurora," answers Keri. Thereupon the white Urubu brings the moon. Again Kame asks: "Is this right?" "No," replies Keri. Only then does the white vulture bring the sun. And when Kame asks: "Is this right?" Keri answers: "Now it is." Without delay he releases the red Urubu who was very angry.[399]

Here retribution appears as exchange: the royal vulture delivers the sun and therefore retains his life.

In a tale of the Pomo Indians there is told how it happened that the sun hangs in the middle of the firmament. Various birds try to fix it there but without success; finally the Crow brothers succeed. "The people of the village rejoiced greatly that they had the sun and had it hung up in the proper place so that it could give them light. They brought out all kinds of beads, baskets, blankets, and food as presents to the Crows for the service they had rendered."[400] The raven, in a fable of the Chukchee, wins the sun by inducing the young daughter of its possessor Kele to tease her parents for the sun-ball . . . . but her father gives her the ball of the stars instead. She plays with it, and, when she throws it to the Raven, he contrives to toss it upward with such strength that it bursts, and the stars fly out and stick to the sky. In a similar way he succeeds in freeing the moon, and finally the sun. After that the father becomes angry with his daughter, and he takes her and hangs her, head down-ward, from a steep cliff. At last the line snaps. She drops into the water, and turns into a walrus, whose tusks are formed of the mucus that ran from her nose when she was weeping.[401]

There is an Indian tale from British Columbia which is pertinent because of its similarity to the Greek myth of Phaethon, the son of Helios and Clymene, who, in order to prove his origin, asks his father for permission to drive the sun-chariot for one day but is unable to rein the horses and sets everything on fire, whereupon he is killed by Zeus with a flash of lightning.

A boy with name Gyalasta'kome lived alone with his mother. Once he asked her whether he had a father. She replied that his father was far away. At this the boy began to weep and cry: "I want to find my father. . . . ." He met Hantle'k (the marksman) who gave him a bow and some arrows. Gyalasta'kome shot one arrow towards heaven where it remained stuck. He shot another one which stuck fast in the notch of the first. And so he continued until a chain was formed between heaven and earth. . . . . He made his way up this arrow ladder and came to the door of heaven where his step-mother sat in the doorway. . . . . When the sun, his father, returned home in the evening, he was happy to see his son and requested him to take his place and carry the daylight. . . . . He gave the boy his clothing and jewelry and warned him not to walk too fast. . . . . The son, however, paid little attention to his father's words. He soon grew impatient and began to run faster and faster. On earth it be-came so hot that the rocks burst into pieces, the sea began to dry up, and the mussels were burnt black. The father became furious at his son's behavior, seized the boy and threw him down to earth, saying: "You are of no use whatsoever; become a mink so that men will hunt you henceforth."[402]

A myth of the Arekuna Indians runs as follows (abridged): The youth Akalapizeima, an ancestor, tried to catch the frog Waloma, but was prevented from doing it by the frog's father, Waloma-podole, who drew the youth into the sea and took him to an island where the car-rion kites soiled him with their excrements. Akalapizeima asked in vain the morning star and the moon to help him. Both refused to as-sist him, with the words: "You never gave me maniok cakes. Wei [the sun] will help you, since you gave him some." And, indeed, Wei saved the youth from the carrion kites. In return Wei demanded that Aka-lapizeima should marry his two daughters. The youth, however, made love to the daughters of carrion kite, whereupon Wei punished Akalapizeima by removing him again to the island of the carrion kites.

Then Wei himself slept with his daughters and transformed them into stars in order to light the Milky Way, the road of the dead.[403]

Scarcity of water in one region and abundance in another is interpreted in a myth reported by Parkinson.

Many, many years ago the island Lou (St. George Island) was inhabited by a great flock of Tjaukas (*Philemon coquerelli*). When the Lou people were at work one day, a man tried to rape a woman; but a Tjauka who saw this cried out: A Lou is committing evil! And when the man realized he was discovered, he desisted from his attempt and went home annoyed. In order to take revenge he offered betelnuts as a reward for the extirpation of all the Tjaukas. The Lou people captured the Tjaukas in nets. Only one succeeded in hiding. He sucked up all of the water on Lou in his beak and carried it to Lomondrol, the main island. Since then water is scarce in Lou, whereas Lomondrol has an abundance of water.[404]

A typical myth theme is the transformation of men into rocks. In a story of the Yamana[405] two stones are regarded as murderers metamorphosed as punishment for their crime. Two brothers, the Wasenim, fell in love with the beautiful wife of old Ketela and pursued her with immoral proposals. One day, when the young woman was alone in her hut, the two Wasenim prowled along; and, when the woman refused to gratify their desire, they became infuriated. One "seized the young woman, threw her on the floor, forced her legs apart, and held her in that position." Meanwhile the other Wasenim grasped with tongs a small longish stone which had been heated in the fire "et lapidem in vaginam eius introduxit, sicuti membrum virile fuisset." Thus the Wasenim took revenge. The young woman died immediately. Besides, they jeered at her sarcastically: "Since you did not agree to our proposals you shall not be the wife of Ketela either!" The two criminals, however, did not escape retribution. The furious relatives and friends of the murdered woman pursued the killers, intending to kill them with stones; but they could not hit them. So they called for little Omora, an excellent stone-thrower. They told him

why they were in mourning and furious at the same time, for the two murderers, the Wasenim, could not be struck by any of them. Upon hearing this, Omora also became infuriated. He had only three stones near him. He put one in the sling and shot it; it passed close to the heads of the Wasenim. Then Omora took the second stone and shot it; it hit the breast of one of the brothers so that he fell and did not move any more. Quickly Omora threw the third stone; it struck the second brother so that he fell dead to earth. Everyone was amazed at Omora's strength and skill. And all were happy that the two murderers had received their deserved punishment. Everyone returned home, but the two killers were turned into stone and remained on the spot where little Omora killed them. There they can still be seen today.

In the myths of the South American aborigines, according to Ehren-reich, this same motive frequently appears; for example, "the sun hero transforms his enemies and those who disobey him into stone."[406] Karsten, speaking of the natives of Peru, states that there "individual persons, and even whole nations, were supposed to have been con-verted into stones by the creator, as it is generally stated, in 'punish-ment' for some sin committed."[407]

Smyth reports:

About two miles east of Narneian or Brushy Creek (a tributary of the River Yarra) [in Australia], and adjacent to a small outlier of dense hard black basalt, there occurs in the Upper Silurian rocks a stratum of limestone rich in fossils. It crops out about half-way between the Brushy Creek and the Running Creek. Receiving the storm-waters which fall on the basaltic ridge, it has undergone decomposition, and the waters, percolating the limestone, have carried away some parts of the rock, and formed a cave or deep chasm about 120 feet or more in depth. The occurrence of limestone in the Silurian rocks of Victoria is not common, and still less common are caves or pits such as this near Narneian. The Aborigines have a legend relating to this natural opening. They call it *Buk-ker-til-lible*. They say that it has no bottom. They throw stones into it; the stones give forth a hollow, dull sound as they strike against and rebound from the sides of the chasm, and the blacks fail to catch the last dull thud as the stones fall on the bottom. If you tell them that the bottom can be found at a great depth, they say that there is a small hole not easily found which leads to greater depths—depths without end. PUND-JEL, they say, made this deep hole. He was once very angry with the Yarra blacks. They had committed deeds not pleasing to him, and he caused a star to fall from the heavens and to strike a great many blacks; and to kill them; and the star fell deep into the earth, and made the chasm which is to be seen near Narneian.[408]

42. THE MOTIVE OF RETRIBUTION IN ANIMAL MYTHS

The motive of retribution is especially prevalent in tales dealing with the form, color, individuality, and habits of animals. From the abundant material a few examples may be cited.[409] A Bantu legend runs as follows:

The crocodile "has no tongue," nothing but jaws and teeth; and this is how levia-than is condemned to go tongue-less: When it and the iguana, a species of land lizard measuring three to four feet when full grown, and with a long forked tongue, were made, two tongues were made and placed at a distance from them. They were then told to run a race, and the first to arrive was to have both. The iguana won, and his larger and more savage rival had to be content "with a stump in its throat."[410]

In a tale of the Fang, Nzame pursues Bingo. Bingo is aided in his flight by the spider, Ndanabo, and the chameleon, but is betrayed by Vière, the snake. After his rescue Bingo emerges from the cave in which he took refuge.

Chameleon, he says, you have acted nobly. Here is your reward: from now on you will be able to change your color whenever you wish. Thus you will escape your enemies. Then Bingo turned to the spider: Ndanabo, you also have acted honorably; what can I do for you? Nothing, replied Ndanabo, my heart is satisfied. May your presence bring good fortune, said Bingo and went away. On the way he met Vière and crushed the serpent's head.[411]

A fable of the Bornu explains the fact that the hole-Piri, a blackbird about as large as a pigeon, may put its eggs in hidden holes so that no one can steal them; this right it received as a reward for having once saved the life of the toad.[412]

The Cherokee Indians relate that

the buzzard used to have a fine topknot, of which he was so proud that he refused to eat carrion, and while the other birds were pecking at the body of a deer or other animal which they had found he would strut around and say: "You may have it all, it is not good enough for me." They resolved to punish him, and with the help of the buffalo carried out a plot by which the buzzard lost not his topknot alone, but nearly all the other feathers on his head. He lost his pride at the same time, so that he is willing enough now to eat carrion for a living.[413]

Another bird, the bull bat, according to a fable of the Blackfoot Indians, obtained its pretty and queer-looking beak as a reward for having saved the life of the old Na'pi.[414] A myth of the Chane Indians explains the special form of the flea, of the tick, and of the sheathed ant by stating that they were trampled on as punishment for a theft.[415]

In a tale of the central Brazilian Indians it is told how the culture hero "Keri raced against the Seriema" (a bird related to the South American ostrich).

The Seriema stopped for a moment, so that Keri overtook the bird. Thereupon Keri challenged the Seriema who soon took the lead. Keri became very much annoyed. He brought leaves of the Uakuma palm, seized the ostrich and punished it so that the bird lost all its beautiful feathers; today it has only small and ugly plumage.[416]

The Eskimo of the Bering Strait have a story about reindeer which begins with an account of how these animals once attacked the native huts.

The villagers covered the third house with a mixture of deer fat and berries. When the reindeer tried to destroy this house, they filled their mouths with the fat and sour berries, which caused them to run off, shaking their heads so violently that all their long, sharp teeth fell out. Afterwards small teeth, such as reindeer now have, grew in their places, and these animals became harmless.[417]

A fable of the Burjats tells: "The striped chipmunk (tamias striatus) always collected nuts. One time the bear asked it for some of the nuts, with which request the chipmunk complied. In appreciation, the bear stroked the chipmunk, thereby causing it to be striped."[418]

The Ainu relate:

The river otter was sent down by the Creator in order to make clothing for the foxes. He was told to clothe them in red. But the otter had such a very bad memory that, before he could accomplish his task, he quite forgot what color it should have been, and so made their skins white. Hence foxes were, when first discovered by the Ainu, of a white color, and not red as now seen. The fox was exceedingly angry at this piece of forgetfulness, and upbraided the otter finely for his carelessness and neglect of duty. White was too imposing a color to suit Reynard's tastes. In order, therefore, to remedy the mistake, the otter went to a stream, and, after catching a salmon, took out its roe. He then invited the fox to lie down, and, after mashing the fish-roe into a liquid, proceeded to rub it over its skin, and in that way changed its color from white to red. Hence it is that foxes are now red and not white as formerly. The fox was very much pleased with the change, and, in order to return the compliment for this good act, procured some bark of the Shikerebeni [*Phellodendron arnurense*], boiled it, and dyed the otter's skin with the liquor, making it the beautiful dark brown color we now find it to be.[419]

A Japanese tale explains why the jellyfish has no shell. There was once a sick sea-princess who could be healed only by eating the liver of a monkey. The shrewd turtle was requested to fetch a living monkey. But the jellyfish intervened and told the captured monkey the whole story. Forthwith the monkey fled, and the other monkeys punished the turtle by tearing off his breast scutum (shield).

The princess became angry at this and as punishment she took away the jelly-fish's shell. From it she made a new breast piece for the turtle. So it happened that the jelly-fish must carry its tender body around in the water without any protection. Had it not been presumptuous and babbled so, the jelly-fish would have retained its shell like all the others of its kind.[420]

In Formosa they tell:

A bulong snake fell in love with a young girl, to whom he appeared as a handsome young suitor . . . . she gave birth to a child, which, to the astonishment of all, was human only to the waist, underneath that it took the shape of a serpent. The parents, knowing she had no lover among the young men of the village, naturally suspected something supernatural, and their thoughts reverted to the fact that they had often observed a snake crawl across the yard . . . . they kept watch, and, when the snake appeared, killed it . . . . the act roused such a spirit of revenge among the serpents that they all swore an eternal enmity towards mankind . . . . ever since . . . . the bite of the bulong has proved fatal, and that of many other snakes causes great suffering.[421]

The Maoris have a fable which recounts an adventure of the hero Maui:

Maui requested some birds to go and fetch water for him. He directed the *ti-eke* (*Creadion carunculatus*) to go and fetch some water for him; but the bird would not obey: so he threw it into the water. He next requested the *hihi* to go for water; but it would not obey: so he threw it into the fire, and its feathers were burnt. He asked the *toto-ara* to fetch some water for him: it did so; and he rewarded it by making the feathers of the fore-part of its head white. He asked the *kokako;* and it went and filled its ears full of water, and took it to Maui, who drank it, and pulled the bird's legs long in payment for its act of kindness to him.[422]

A story of the Woiworung (Australia) runs as follows:

The Bat is the brother of all the men. A long time ago, the whole country was covered with long grass so that people could not walk over it. Bunjil said to the Bat: 'Come and be with us on our side." But he replied: "No, yours is a very dry ground, you ought to come over to me." Bunjil said, "Very well! then I will leave you alone."

And he allowed the land of the Bat to burn up. "The Bat and all his children were scorched. That is why he is so black and has such a grinning face."[423]

Two myths of the Aborigines of Victoria (Australia) are as follows:

Mirram (the Kangaroo) and *Warreen* (the Wombat) were once men, and they dwelt in the same place; but *Warreen* had a good camp (*willum*) made of bark, but *Mirram* had none. *Mirram* lived day and night in the open air. This was very good for *Mirram* when the weather was fine, and very good for *Warreen*, too, who often slept in the open air with *Mirram*. They were very good friends. At length a great rain fell. *Warreen* went to his *willum*, made a good fire, and lay down comfortably in front of it, well sheltered by his covering of bark. The rain fell so heavily that *Mirram's* fire was put out, and he became wet and very cold. He sat a long time, the cold rain falling upon him, thinking that *Warreen* would ask him to go into the *willum*, but this *Warreen* did not do. At last, quite overcome with the wet and the cold, and when he could no longer bear the suffering, he went to the *willum*, and asked *Warreen* to allow him to go in and sit down in a vacant corner. *Warreen* said, "I want that corner for my head"; and he turned over and laid his head there. *Mirram* said, "Never mind, this place (pointing to an unoccupied spot) will do." *Warreen* moved and laid his feet over that spot, and said, "I want that place for my feet." *Mirram* spoke again: "This place will do," pointing to the spot where *Warreen's* feet had been. *Warreen* answered, I cannot give you that place; I want to lie this way," and he raised himself and lay down in front of the fire. *Mirram* grew very angry. He could bear such treatment no longer, and he went away and got a stone, and came back quietly and struck *Warreen* on the forehead with the stone, and made his forehead quite flat. *Mirram*, when he had done this, said, "Now, your forehead will always be flat, and you shall remain in a dark hole." Ever since poor *Warreen* has had to live in a dark hole in the ground; and his forehead is flat at this day, as it was made flat when *Mirram* struck his head with the stone. But *Warreen* was at length in a position to retaliate. One day he took his spear and threw it at *Mirram*. It hit him, and stuck fast at the lower end of his back-bone. 'Now," says *Warreen*, "that will always stick there, and will be a tail (*Moo-ee-bee*) for you, and you will have to use it when you run, and never shall you have *willum*." This is how *Mirram* came to have *Moo-ee-bee*, and why he has always to use it when jumping and running, and why he has to sleep in the open air.[424]

The Murray blacks say that the Crow killed the son of the Eagle. This deed made the Eagle very angry; and, to be revenged, he dug a large hole, and made a trap, and carefully covered it up, so as, if possible, to catch his enemy. Attaching a string to his trap, he retired to a distance and waited. At length the Crow approached the trap, and entered it; the string was pulled, and he was caught. The Eagle killed the Crow. After a time the Crow came to life again and disappeared. The Gippsland people say that the Eagle left his son in charge of the Mopoke while he with his wives went to hunt kangaroos. The Mopoke put the young one in a bag, and sewed up the bag and left him. The Eagle during his hunting excursion became uneasy about his son, and finally returned to ascertain how he had been treated. When he came to know what had been done, he grew very angry. He at once made a search for the Mopoke, and found him, after some trouble, sitting in a tree. The Eagle, when he saw his enemy, used guile. He exhibited no anger. He spoke gently. He determined to kill him by subtlety. He slyly requested the Mopoke to go into a hole in the tree to look for an opossum. The Mopoke obeyed, but returned without any. He was told to go again, and he obeyed; and as soon as he was in the hole, the Eagle closed the hole, and made the Mopoke a prisoner. The Mopoke cried aloud when he found himself fastened up, and he used these words: *Wun-no nat jel-lowen gnong-ona wok-kuk* (When I cut a hole Mopoke), which means, "When will the Mopoke cut a hole?" He was determined to get out, and, finding all means fail him, he at length, in great sorrow, broke his leg and took out one of the bones, and very patiently bored a hole sufficiently large to creep through. He got free. Again the Eagle met him, and they spoke together, and the Eagle and the Mopoke made a solemn agreement and a treaty of peace. . . . . The conditions were as follows: The Eagle was to have the privilege of going up into the topmost boughs of the trees, so that he might from so great a height see better where kangaroos were feeding; and the Mopoke was to have the right to occupy the holes of trees. Thus ended the disputes between the Eagle and the Mopoke.[425]

The tales which deal with the origin of the noxious insects illustrate the principle of retribution in different versions. Occasionally the vermin appear as created by the evil principle, or again they are presented as punishment for wicked deeds. In a fable of the Kootenay Indians mosquitoes are pictured as originating from the cremated corpse of a bad woman who was killed as a penalty for having captured and eaten small children.[426] According to a tale of the Dene, a woman became unfaithful to her husband by having immoral relations with a snake. Her husband surprised and killed her. He smashed her head to pieces, but it continued to follow him. With a stroke of an ax the man made dust out of it, but this dust only created flies and mosquitoes. They buzzed round the murderer during his whole life.[427] Here the vermin are apparently avenging spirits of the death soul of the murdered wife.

Many tales represent the various characteristics of animals as the result of a distribution whereby the Creator punished discontent, obstinacy, arrogance, negligence, and forgetfulness.[428] The principle of retribution is also expressed in fables which explain a distinctive feature of an animal by the fact that it was obtained from another animal in an exchange. This is so in a Cherokee story:

> The Grouse used to have a fine voice. . . . . The Turkey had not a good voice, so he asked the Grouse to give him lessons. The Grouse agreed to teach him, but wanted pay for his trouble, and the Turkey promised to give him some feathers to make himself a collar. That is how the Grouse got his collar of turkey feathers.

The cause for the turkey's gobbling lies in the fact that he was so excited at the first lesson "that he could not raise his voice for a shout, but only gobbled."[429]

It is the principle of retribution which determines the nature of the tales which protest against dishonesty in an exchange. Such a story is told in New Pomerania (Gazelle Peninsula).

> In olden times the Kau (*Philemon cockerelli Kl.*) had the gay colored plumage of the Mallip (*Lorius hypoenochrous H.R.Gr.*, a kind of parrot) and the latter had the grey feathers of the former. One day the Kau went bathing and placed his attire carefully on the bank. The Mallip, too, went bathing and took off his grey attire before entering the water. He perceived the gayly colored plumage of the Kau and walked nearer to admire the marvellous decoration. Unobserved, he dressed himself in the iridescent feathers and when he was fully clothed, he shouted to the Kau: "Look how beautiful I am!" The Kau was very angry and requested him to take off his robe. The Mallip, however, flew away. Thereupon the Kau became infuriated and threw a lump of earth at the Mallip. The clod hit the Mallip's head and since then he has a great black spot on his gorgeous red head. The Kau had to wear the costume of the insignificant looking Mallip. Until today he has been continually unsuccessful in regaining his former attire.[430]

According to a Mongolian tale, the camel originally had

> the horns of the reindeer. He struck men with his horns and bit them with his teeth. The camel destroyed many nations, until a khan who was then Guigen (Buddhist high priest) placed in his nose a wooden stick, and fastened to it a rein . . . . subdued him . . . . then the camel began to carry argal, and men began to lead him by the nose to drink. Once, when the camel was browsing on grass, the reindeer (*Cervus elephas*) came to him. . . . . The reindeer said, "Give me thy horns: to-day is the marriage of the lion and the tiger. To-morrow, when thou comest to the drinking-place, I will return them to thee." The camel gave his horns. On the morrow he went to the drinking place, but there was no reindeer; so the camel was left without horns, for the reindeer had tricked him. That is why the camel now, when he drinks water, looks about to right and left, and lifts his head high—he is trying to see where the reindeer is. The reindeer also sheds his horns every year, because they do not belong to him.[431]

The reason for an animal's habitat—whether it lives on land or in the water, whether it lives gregariously or alone—is frequently expounded according to the principle of retribution. An Indian tale may serve as an example: Once upon a time a raven married a seadog who already had one son. When the boy accompanied his stepfather on a hunting expedition, he was killed and devoured by the latter. At home the raven told his wife that her son had fallen into the water and drowned. She, however, saw through his deceit. As punishment she left her husband and jumped into the sea. Since then, seadogs have lived in water.[432]

Of the myths which refer to the various foods of animals Daehnhardt says:

> The fables explain this peculiarity partly by certain commandments which God gave to the animals, and partly by agreements through which the animals obligated each other. It was God's wish that the wolf should rob and that the bee should shun the red trefoil; and it is an acquired right of the gadfly's to suck the blood of the ox.[433]

The social character of the interpretation of nature could not be more obvious.

The principle of retribution is also apparent in these myths, as, for example, in this tale of the Ainu: "Each time the sun rises in the end of the world (i.e., in the east), a devil comes to swallow it. But someone throws two or three crows or foxes into the devil's gullet so that the sun may rise meanwhile. . . . . As reward for this service, crows and foxes may eat whatever men eat."[434] An Estonian fable reports that in early times the wolf did not eat sheep but guarded them like the most faithful sheep dog. In return every night he received warm bread from the landlady. One evening, however, she threw a glowing stone into the wolf's throat instead of the bread. The heat burned the animal's gullet black, which it is to this day. And since then the wolf tears sheep to pieces to take revenge on all landladies.[435]

In those myths which attempt to explain friendship and enmity among animals the principle of retribution also plays an important part. A fable of the Bogos (North Abyssinia) tells:

> Since the time of their creation, cows have always belonged to the hyena. The hyena, however, hired man as cowherd. Man, after having stood guard for the whole day, returned home each evening with a load of wood to make fire. But the hyena always ran away. After a short while, however, it came back. The cowherd considered this and thought to himself: "I shall drive the hyena away and take the cows for myself." He loaded wood and went home. The hyena fled and the cowherd pursued it. Thereupon the hyena said to itself: "My vengeance will come upon you because you drove me away; from now on I shall eat the udder and back of the cow."[436]

Finally, the motive of retribution also appears in those tales which deal with the transformation of animals. According to an Indian fable, the unfaithful wife of Hoots, the bear, was changed into a grouse as punishment for her infidelity. "Now she sits in the forest and mourns all the time because of her bad deeds."[437] In another Indian story Quaw-te-aht, the changer, on a journey met a man sharpening the edge of a stone knife. He said to him:

"Why do you make the knife sharp?" "To cut meat," answered the man. "That is double talk, you make sharp the edge of Opitsah, the knife, that you may kill me, for I know your mind and can see your thoughts. Give me the knife," said Quaw-te-aht, and started towards the man. Now the man knew that Quaw-te-aht saw his thoughts and so he was very much frightened and started to run away. In his great haste he dropped his knife and then Quaw-te-aht picked it up and threw it at the man and it struck him in the heel. When the knife stuck in his heel, the man began to jump about and ran into the woods. Quaw-te-aht, to punish him for his evil thoughts, said, "Go and be Mowitch, the deer, and jump about in the woods always," and so by the great magic of Quaw-te-aht, the changer, this wicked man became the first deer, and still jumps about in the woods with the knife in his heel, for you may see the handle of it sticking out just above the foot of the deer, where he has another toe, and his feet are split in two because the knife split the foot of the evil man.[438]

A fable of the Yamana[439] explains the hoot of the owl as follows: A fatherless boy who lived with his mother in the house of his uncle was badly treated by the latter, as well as by others. Above all, he was given little food and that not good, so that he became weak and miserable. One day his mother suggested that he himself should go hunting. And—what wonder!—the weak little boy proved to be an excellent hunter who brought home the biggest guanacos. People did not believe that the frail boy succeeded in what was impossible even for strong men. So the boy invited them to accompany him to his hunting place to see with their own eyes. There they found the guanacos shot the day before.

These animals were really freshly killed, not even the entrails had been removed. Consequently the men could no longer doubt that the little lad had actually shot all these animals. Then the boy shouldered a large guanaco and went home. Each of the men picked up a guanaco, too. But soon each one felt his burden becoming heavier and heavier. Again and again they had to rest and could walk only slowly. The boy, however, apparently did not feel the weight and soon was far ahead of the others. These men were furious that this lad walked so quickly while they were tired and had to rest every moment. But whenever they tried to overtake the boy they had to give up and rest. They strained themselves so much and got so tired that they became *kuhurux* (owls). Only the boy returned to the village a short time later. When the other people of the camp saw him come home with a guanaco, they begged him for meat. He, however, said: "I cannot give you any of my guanaco. Wait a little while until the return of the other men, your relatives, who went out with me this morning. You have never given me anything to eat before. Now you must wait for your relatives!" And so they waited a long time. Only late at night did the owls arrive. But they did not bring anything. They approached the huts in which they had lived and which their relatives still inhabited, but they did not enter them. They also came to the hut where the little boy lived with his mother. They could see how the two ate. But the owls received nothing. They only cried: *kuhurux, kuhurux* . . . . , and withdrew into the forest.

In other myths of the Yamana the transformation of a human being into an animal is represented as punishment for incest. This is so in the following story:

"Little Detehurux was very young but nevertheless he was in love—with his own mother. She took her little son with her wherever she went. She made a special sack from pieces of hide into which she put Detehurux and always carried him on her back. Never did she take him out of the bag. Whenever she left her hut she shouldered the sack. Thus the boy was never away from his mother. Often the woman went into the forest. To others she explained: "I like the *esef* so much that I often go to the forest to pick many of these mushrooms." Regularly she went out alone with the sack on her back. As soon as she would discover a hidden spot in the forest she would halt. Immediately the boy left the sack in which he rested and became a grown-up man. Without delay he would climb the trees to collect *esef*. He threw them down and the women gathered them together. After a while he said to his mother: "Humi accumbe et distende crura quam maxime, malo jacere esef in vaginam tuam!" Mulier statim summa voluptate humi accubuit et cruribus distensis vaginam latissime aperuit. Filius ab arbore jactis *esef* vaginam matris attinguit, quod utrique maximo oblectamento fuit. Hisce ludis tempore sat longo protracto filius ab arbore descendit. Tunc matri incubuit eique commiscuit cum voluptate, quia membrum ejus pergrande fuit. After some time they finally got up. The son crawled back into the bag, became smaller and smaller until at length he became a baby again. Then the mother hurried back to her hut. As usual she brought a great quantity of *esef* with her. She distributed them among the other women; all ate much and were greatly pleased. Mother and son, however, went often to the forest and they always repeated the same evil play." Finally their criminal behavior was discovered by the other women; and the husband was told of it. He took a sharpened knife and when his wife came home, he cut the sack from her back. The bag fell down with the boy so that he came to lie on his back with his legs spread apart. Tunc pater eius observare potuit membrum magnum filii sui, nam vestitus non erat. Now he knew enough! Beside himself with disgust, he grasped the sharp knife, et amputavit membrum filii sui magnum. Much blood gushed forth but the raving man did not care. The little boy, however, was transformed into a bird. Ever since he has stayed in the forest, never returning to the hut of his parents. This is the little Detehurux (woodpecker) which still today has a strong beak in which sticks his long, red tongue.[440]

There are many other similar myths which refer to the woodpecker, such as the "Story of the Woodpecker Pair."

A brother fell in love with his sister and tried in every possible way to meet her alone in order to sleep with her. His sister had early noticed his intention so she always avoided him for she did not want to have prohibited intercourse with him. She was half-willing, however. The brother meditated by what pretext he could allure her from the house. One day he discovered some big berries in an open place in the forest. A shrewd idea came into his mind. He said to himself: 'I shall tell my sister what I have seen. Certainly she will come to pick the berries!'' Thereupon he ran to the hut and said to his sister: ' I have discovered some big berries in a certain place in the forest. You ought to go and fetch some of them.'' The girl took her basket and ran into the woods. Without being observed the brother quickly followed her. At a place which she had to pass he hid. When she came near enough, he embraced her. Then they lay down and enjoyed themselves. When they wanted to get up from their evil doings, they saw they had been transformed into birds. Both were totally black. The brother had in addition a light red head. This came from the big red berries about which he told his sister in order to commit incest with her.[441]

It is well known that in Greek mythology men were metamorphosed by the gods into animals and plants as punishment for evil deeds. Within the compass of the belief in metempsychosis the transformation of men into animals always has the character of retribution.

43. The Myths of the Origin of Death

How far the mythical thinking of primitive man is dominated by the principle of retribution is shown by the decisive part which this concept plays in the most important myths of humanity: in the myth of death and, connected with it, in the myth of the lost paradise, as well as in catastrophe—especially flood—fables.

Stories of various peoples dealing with the origin of death are all based on the common primitive idea that man does not die by "nature" but could live forever if death as a specific social event, as delict or punishment, did not intervene. The necessity of death is ordinarily justified by the myth as a punishment for a delict. But what man loses by his crime is not the possibility of an eternal individual life; such an idea is beyond the experience of primitive man. In some myths it is only the ability to rise from the dead which man is forced to relinquish as punishment for some wrong; this capability man is supposed originally to have possessed, like the moon, the ancestor. But death itself existed from the outset; it was, however, nothing final, merely a transitional stage, lasting a short time. Thus the Masai believe that

one day Naiteru-kop told Le-eyo that if a child were to die he was to say when he threw away the body: "Man, die, and come back again; moon, die, and remain away." A child died soon afterwards, but it was not one of Le-eyo's, and when he was told to throw it away, he picked it up and said to himself: "This child is not mine; when I throw it away I shall say, 'Man, die, and remain away; moon, die, and return.' " He threw it away and spoke these words, after which he returned home. One of his own children died next, and when he threw it away, he said: "Man, die, and return; moon, die, and remain away." Naiteru-kop said to him: "It is of no use now, for you spoiled matters with the other child." This is how it came about that when a man dies he does not return, whilst when the moon is finished, it comes back again and is always visible to us.[442]

Yīmantūwiñyai, the chief divinity of the Hupa Indians,

had two wives who had each borne him a child, one a boy and the other a girl. After a time he went to the end of the world toward the south. There he became enamored of a beautiful maiden. He remained with her and had a son born from her. His wives at Leldiñ became jealous and buried his children alive. They came out again and were again buried until they remained in the ground. This was the first case of death. Before this time people had grown old, but had renewed their youth by sleeping in the sweat-house. The people were frightened and fled down the river to avoid the contamination. Yīmantūwiñyai came back with his latest born in his pocket, punished his jealous wives, and followed his people.[443]

In a legend of the Fiji Islands it is said: "There was a dispute between two gods as to how man should die: Ra Vula (the Moon) contended that man should be like himself—disappear awhile and then live again. Ra Kalavo (the Rat) would not listen to this kind proposal, but said: 'Let man die as a rat dies.' And he prevailed."[444] The rat is a typical death-soul animal, and the idea that death comes from the dead is one of the oldest concepts of mankind. Belief in the reincarnation of the death soul of an ancestor—which at first survives in animal form—in a newborn member of the living generation is concerned in a lesser degree with this same idea of resurrection.

The Pomo Indians in California have the following myth:

The moon and the coyote wrought together in creating all things that exist. The moon was good, but the coyote was bad. In making men and women the moon wished so to fashion their souls that when they died they should return to the earth after two or three days, as he himself does when he dies. But the coyote was evil disposed, and he said that this should not be, but that when men died their friends should burn their bodies, and once a year make a great mourning for them. And the coyote prevailed. So, presently when a deer died, they burned his body, as the coyote had decreed, and after a year they made a great mourning for him. But the moon created the rattlesnake, and caused it to bite the coyote's son, so that he died. Now, though the coyote had been willing to burn the deer's relations, he refused to burn his own son. Then the moon said unto him: "This is your own rule. You would have it so, and now your own son shall be burned like the others." So he was burned, and after a year the coyote mourned for him. Thus the law was established over the coyote also, and, as he had dominion over men, it prevailed over men likewise.[445]

The guilt which is the reason for which death is inflicted upon mankind does not necessarily have to be the guilt of the men who are thus punished. For, just as it is self-evident for the primitive sense of justice that the whole group is responsible for a wrong committed by a single member, and inasmuch as primitive man sees in such collective responsibility the unlimited effect of the principle of retribution, so we must recognize the justifying function of this principle in any myth which traces the necessity-to-die of human beings back to an "evil" act of a superhuman being. This is the case in the Maori myth in which the fire-procuring motive is connected with the idea of the necessity of death. The hero Maui, not a fire-bringer, but a fire-destroyer, kills four of the five children of Mahuika, a female personification of the fire, intended for mankind. The sister of the offended fire-goddess, Hine, who is a personification of death, punishes Maui with death. Thus death comes into the world.[446] Frequently the evil deeds of animals cause death as punishment to mankind. The extension of the circle of subjects for whose behavior the individual may be held responsible is due to the nature of the primitive concept of collective responsibility. And it must be remembered that the animal or the superhuman being for whose delict mankind—i.e., the social group which identifies itself with mankind—is punished actually represents some ancestor and is thus a member of the group.[447]

The wrong which occasions the punishment is usually some kind of disobedience to a commandment or prohibition, the superhuman origin of which is not always clear and the importance of which is not always discernible. For instance, the natives of the Gazelle Peninsula (New Pomerania) tell this story:

A good old woman died and then dug herself out of the grave. She asked a child: "Bring me some fire so that I may warm myself!" The child, however, refused to go and did not obey the good old woman who admonished in vain. Consequently the old woman died again. If the child had carried out her requests, human beings would never have had to die. We would have been buried, but could have dug ourselves out again and have returned to life by warming ourselves at fire. But since the child did not obey the old woman, human beings may not return to life but die once for all.[448]

It is probably only another version of this same myth which Parkinson reports from the northern part of the Gazelle Peninsula: One day the god To Kabanana, who had created the world well and beautifully, sent a boy off

to fetch fire for the workers. The boy did not want to go and so To Kabanana asked him: "why don't you want to go?" But the boy did not reply. Thereupon the snake [the death soul animal par excellence] said: "All right then, I shall go and bring the fire." And the snake glided away and procured for To Kabanana the desired fire. Thereupon the god spoke to the snake: "Snake you shall live forever; but you people of the coast, you will die."[449]

The widespread idea that the snake need not die goes back to its peculiarity of sloughing its skin from time to time. C. E. Fox found the following myth among the natives of San Cristoval (Solomon Islands):

Agunna [the serpent ghost] created men. He created a woman who, when she became old, went one day to change her skin in the stream, for that was then the custom. She had a daughter whom she left in the village. When the old woman had changed her skin she came back, looking young and lovely once more, but her daughter said, "This is not my mother, this is a strange woman," and would have nothing to do with her. So the old woman went back to the stream . . . . she put on the old skin and returned to her daughter. "Now I know you," said her daughter, "you are my mother." And so death came into the world, because the child cried and did not know her mother. Otherwise men would always have changed their skins when they grew old.[450]

Death is punishment for the fact that the daughter does not recognize her mother, or rather does not want to recognize her because of jealousy. The motive, that the younger generation desires the death of the older one, is the half-conscious motive of the myth. Everyone has to die since the young people begrudge the old ones their life.

Kidd reports a legend of the Bushmen relative to the origin of death:

Urezhwa created men, and then took to himself a wife. The wife fell sick, and so Urezhwa shut her in a cave and went away on a long journey to fetch medicines. He told the people who watched her on no account to bury his wife if she died in his absence. However, she died soon after he left, and the people were so disgusted with the dead body that they buried it. When the creator came back, he found what they had done and in anger said that if they had only obeyed him he would have raised her up to life, and would have given them power to become alive again after death. Now they must suffer for their disobedience. He then went above into the heavens.[451]

According to R. P. Colle, a legend of the Baluba, a tribe in the Congo Valley, runs as follows: In the beginning, the earth was without any men. Then Kabezya-Mpungu created a man, Kyomba, and two women. The favorite wife bore a boy to the man; later, both wives had more children.

One day, the older son's mother faints, and falls into a deep lethargy. . . . . The father alone knows what it means. He carries the poor woman away, without telling anybody, and disappears in the wood.—There, he starts to build a cabin, a spacious house; in the middle, a well sheltered and warm room; around it, walls, not less than ten. When all is ready, he deposits his companion in the central room, firmly closes all doors, and goes home, as if nothing had happened.—Nevertheless, Kyomba watches over his shut-in wife. Every day he goes to her, carrying a little meal and a certain medicine (it is not known what it consisted of). The oldest son, having been told about it, accompanies his father; but he has been strictly forbidden to tell his second mother, being threatened of the most terrible punishment if he did. Kyomba, by the way, fears that his second wife could believe her rival would never more return, and profit to show herself arrogant.—The days follow one another, without bringing any change to this order of things.

One day, Kyomba said: "I am leaving for a journey," and goes away. Before starting, he says to his son: "If your mother goes towards the hidden dwelling-place, tell her I oppose myself to it; that it is dangerous, that to disobey me would have, for all of us, disastrous consequences."—Meanwhile, two days pass, and Kyomba does not come back. His wife then gives the boy a pot pierced in three places, and tells him: "Go, my son, go to fetch water from the river." The child obeys. He has not left long before the woman cries out: "My husband has gone for a walk, so will I too." And she leaves towards the wood. Suddenly, she sees a little trodden path, follows it, and reaches the dwelling built by Kyomba.—Unhappily, the son is not with her to prohibit her going inside. She opens a door,—then a second, and a third one. The more she approaches, the more her curiosity is awakened. Finally, she has crossed the ninth door and is ready to open the tenth. But, hush, a voice is heard from the interior: "Do not enter! Do not enter!" "And why not?, I want to."—"Please, do not open the door, if you come in, I have to die immediately, and you, too, will die." "I do not believe a word of it; it is a humbug, you are lying." And she pushes the door wide open. She sees a beautiful young girl, all white, all fresh, you would say she had just been born. She looks and falls down, dead. Her inquisitive companion falls at her side.

Meanwhile, Kyomba comes back from his trip. Not seeing his wife, he asks the oldest son where she is. "I do not know," he answers; "she sent me to fetch water in a pot pierced with holes. I stayed at the river a long time, vainly trying to fill it. Finally, tired and impatient, I came back, and did not find our mother. I have been waiting for her for a long while."—Kyomba goes deep into the wood, calling his wife in all directions; the echo alone answers him. At last, fearing a misfortune, he goes towards the secret dwelling-place, finds all its doors open, and in the middle two corpses. Seeing this, he is overcome by a great pain. He returns to his home and says: "Children, a great catastrophe has befallen us. Your first mother had fallen into a deep sleep. I carried her to the very middle of the wood; there, she was to remain for some time; then she should waken up; and in this moment, she was to undergo a transformation and become young and beautiful again. But nobody was to have a look at her, before everything was completely finished. Only I, your father, could do it. Your second mother, driven by her curiosity, overcame all obstacles and saw her, and instantly death has stricken both. They are now dead, my children, they will speak no more, will not come to us ever again. We, too, are condemned likewise to die. If your first mother could have achieved her transformation, she would have obtained immortality for all of us, we should all have had the advantage of eternally rejuvenating, but now we must all die like her."[452]

The Lambas of Northern Rhodesia have the following fable:

Long ago the chief on earth used to travel from place to place, but eventually he desired to settle down; he therefore sent some of his people to God to fetch seeds, that he might sow them and have his own gardens. When his messengers reached God they were given some little bundles tied up, and instructed not to undo a certain one of the

bundles, but to deliver them to their chief . . . . they undid the forbidden package—
the package of death . . . . they went to their chief and confessed to him that one of
their number had opened the little package and let death escape. And the chief . . . .
said: "let us kill him." . . . . And death entered the world.[453]

A myth of the Ba-Kaonde (Northern Rhodesia) is as follows: God
gives to "Mayimba," the honey-guide bird, three gourds in order that
it may bring them to the two first men; and he commanded that only
two of the gourds may be opened, which contained seeds of various
plants. The third gourd must not be. opened. But the curious bird
opens also the third gourd, from which death, illness, dangerous beasts
and reptiles emerge. For this disobedience of the honey-guide bird
men have to suffer. God says to them:

> Mayimba is a great sinner. I told him that on no account was the third gourd to be
> opened until I came: but he disobeyed me. Thereby he has brought you much trou-
> ble, sickness, death; and the risks from lions, leopards, snakes and other evil animals
> and reptiles. This I cannot help now, for these things have escaped and cannot be
> caught. So you must build yourselves huts and shelters to live in for protection from
> them.[454]

In Le Jeune's reports on North American Indians we read that a
savage related

> to Father Brebœuf that his people believed that a certain Savage had received from
> Messou the gift of immortality in a little package, with a strict injunction not to open
> it; while he kept it closed he was immortal, but his wife, being curious and incredulous,
> wished to see what was inside this present; and having opened it, it all flew away, and
> since then the Savages have been subject to death.[455]

The Pomo Indians (California) have the following myth: Kó-do-
yam-peh, the world-maker,

> sent on the earth the man whom he had created to gather food from the face of it.
> Now, before this all the game and all the fish, the grasshoppers, the birds of the air,
> and the insects of the earth had been tame, so that a man had only to reach forth his
> hand among them and take whatever he wished for his food. Also the soil had been
> prolific up to this time, yielding all products, acorns, manzanita berries, pine-nuts, and
> many kinds of rich grass-seed for the sustenance of man.. So when Kodoyampeh sent
> forth the man whom he had made he told him to take freely of all that he saw and
> desired—of the game and the fish and the birds and the nuts, seeds and berries—for
> all these things he had created for him. One injunction only he laid upon him, and
> that was that he should bring home to his house whatever he wished to cook, and not
> kindle a fire in the woods.—So the man went out to catch game, but the devil saw
> him and told him to cook in the woods whatever he wished. And he did so. Therefore
> all the game and the fish, all the grasshoppers, the birds, and the insects, when they
> saw the smoke in the woods, became wild, as they are to-day. More than that, the
> ground was changed, so that the oaks yielded no more acorns, and the manzanita no
> more berries, nor was there anything left for the food of man on the face of the earth,

save only roots, clover, and earth-worms. These three things were all that men had to eat.—Also Kodoyampeh changed the air so that it was no longer always the same the year round, but now there was frost, and rain, and fog, and wind, and heat, and drought, together with the pleasant days. As a recompense he gave them fire to warm themselves, whereas before they had only stones to press against their bodies. He established the seasons—Kum'-men-ni (the rain seasons); Yo'-ho-men-ni (the leaf seasons); I'-hi-lak-ki (the dry seasons); Mat'-men-ni (the falling-leaf seasons). He also instituted the sacred *ku'-meh*, the assembly-hall, and gave the Konkau songs to sing, but he did not yet give them any dances. Before this time they had had no diseases and no deaths, but after they cooked and ate in the woods they became subject to fever and pestilences, and many died.[456]

Disobedience is also the decisive reason for death inflicted as punishment in the legends in which the necessity to die or the release from death supplies the content of the message sent to men by the superhuman authority. This is so in the frequently cited story of the Zulus (and in similar tales of other Bantu tribes), according to which Unkulunkulu sends first a chameleon to men with the order to inform them that they need not die. The lazy chameleon, however, does not hurry to deliver the message but actually stops on the way. Thereupon Ukulunkulu dispatches the speedy lizard (also a typical death-soul animal) with the contrary message for men. The lizard arrives before the chameleon, and hence men must die.[457] Among the Namaqua (South Africa) the myth about the death message formulates the element of default even more clearly: Once upon a time the moon sent the hare to men with the following message: "Like as I die and rise to life again, so you also shall die and rise to life again." But the hare said to men: "Like as I die and do not rise to life again, so you also shall die and not rise to life again." Then the hare returned and told the moon what he had said. Whereupon the moon hit the hare with an ax and cut his lip, which is the reason why hares still have, as punishment, a split lip. According to a different version, the hare fled and is still fleeing today. In any event, the Namaqua never eat hare meat.[458]

Of the Margi of Nigeria, Meek reports the following myth:

When death first entered the world, men sent a chameleon to God to ascertain the cause. God told the chameleon to let men know that if they threw baked porridge over a corpse it would be restored to life. But as the chameleon was slow in returning, and death was rampant in their midst, men sent a second messenger—a lizard this time. The lizard reached the abode of God soon after the chameleon had left, and God, being angered at the second message, told the lizard that men must dig a hole in the ground and bury their corpses there. The lizard reached home before the chameleon, and when the chameleon arrived the corpses had already been buried. And thus, owing to the impatience of men, or the deceit of the lizard, the ghosts of the dead are forced to hover round their graves until they are released by the final funeral rites to a realm from which they may be reborn.[459]

In another group of African myths men lose the immortality intended for them by sleeping. The essential content of these legends is: "Men sleep when God wishes to call to them the word of immortal life and thus incur the fate of having to die forever."[460]

Sometimes the wrong punished with death consists only of a simple mistake or merely a false choice. The Poso-Todjo-Toradja of Celebes have a myth which tells that in ancient times heaven was very near earth. On earth lived a man and woman who were the first human beings created by Lamoa. One day

Lamoa lowered from heaven a stone attached to a rope. But the man and woman did not accept it; they called to Lamoa: "What shall we do with this stone? Give us something else!" Thereupon the stone was pulled up and loosened from the rope. And instead Lamoa attached a "comb" of *pisang* (bananas). As soon as he had lowered this to earth the *tau piamo* (the first human beings) rushed to the bananas and took them. Thereupon Lamoa said: "Ha, you human beings! Because you have chosen the bananas, your life shall be like theirs. When the banana-tree produces offspring the parent trunk dies; so you will die and your children shall take your place. If you had taken the stone, your life would have been like the stone's life: unchangeable (immortal)."[461]

Among the Bakongo pygmies Schebesta found the following myth:

In the beginning men did not die. Muri-muri (Supreme Being) gave a pot to a toad and commanded to watch lest the pot break; for in it death was enclosed. Should the pot break to pieces everybody would have to die. On its way the toad met a gaily hopping frog who offered to carry the pot. But the toad had doubts and hesitated. Finally, however, since the pot was too heavy, it gave the pot to the frog but exhorted it to be careful. The frog hopped away and the pot broke to pieces. Thus, death emerged and came upon mankind.[462]

It is said among the Birhors (India) that

in olden days death meant only a temporary separation of the soul or rather souls from the body. It was only by a trick of a *lindum* (a species of centipede) that Death came to mean a permanent severance of the soul from the body. The traditional Birhor story of the origin of Death is as follows: A Birhor, who was dead, revived as usual, and, after having bathed in a stream, was returning home, when on his way he met a *lindum*. The crafty *lindum* barred his way and told him, "Count my 'legs' first, and then you will go home." The man agreed and began to count the legs of the *lindum* when it moved a few steps forward and the man had to begin counting the legs over again. And again before he had finished counting, the *lindum* moved a few steps backwards, and the man had to begin counting once more. This trick the *lindum* went on repeating so that the man could never finish his task and walk back home. Since then the dead do not return to life.[463]

In the best-known death myth, the story of the fall of man in the first book of Moses, the wrong consists in the violation of a food prohibition.[464] But the eating of the forbidden fruit implies clearly, although the original meaning is slightly obliterated in the biblical account, a prohibited sexual act.[465] This is a typical element of primitive symbolism. P. Joseph Meier reports that among the Gunantuna natives of the Bismarck Archipelago, the prohibition of eating one's totem simply means that one may not have sexual intercourse within his totem group, "since sexual intercourse is comprehended by the image of eating."[466] In a myth of the Pangwe, related by Tessmann,[467] the sexual significance of the food prohibition is clearly understood: The god Essamnyamaböge leaves his son Mode and his son's wife alone for a moment and says when going away: "I will be back soon so you must not eat the fruit *ebon*." The word *ebon*, however, also means "female sexual organ." After having departed, the god recollects that he forgot to leave his son the crops and the fire. He therefore sends another son, Otöng, the snake, back with these things. Instead of giving them to Mode, the snake says to him: "You must eat the fruit *ebon*." The phallic and at the same time death-bringing character of the snake obviously plays an important part here. Thereupon God casts off the snake and returns to Mode and his wife. When they see him come, they hide themselves. He asks Mode: "Why did you transgress my commandment when I expressly told you I would set the time myself." To Mode's wife, he says: "You will give birth to human beings. Half of them will die but the other half will live." This means: death and birth. Then he speaks further to Mode: "I tell you this so that you alone will know it, that I shall no longer remain here. If you try to find me it will be in vain, for remember that I shall have gone over the seas. Do not search for me there, for I shall have gone to heaven. Your children will not know this." Whether and to what extent this story is influenced by Christianity may be left aside here, since the nucleus of the myth is not specifically Jewish-Christian but is a general idea of mankind which appears in different aspects among various peoples—thus, for instance, among the Chagga (Dschagga). They have, according to Ch. Dundas,[468] the following myth: Ruwa (the Supreme Being) said to men:

"I give you leave to eat all the fruit of the bananas, also all the potatoes in the banana grove. Eat all the bananas and potatoes, you and your people. But the yam which is called Ula or Ukaho, truly you shall not eat it. Neither you nor your people may eat it, and if any man eats it, his bones shall break and at last he shall die." Then

Ruwa left the people and went his ways. And every morning and evening he came to greet the elder and his people. Now one day a stranger came and greeted the elder and begged for food. The elder said to the stranger: "Go into the banana grove to eat bananas and potatoes there, but the potato Ula do not eat at all. For Ruwa directed me and my people that we should not eat it, therefore do you not eat it." The stranger said: "It is now noon, this morning early Ruwa bade me tell you to give me a cooking-pot that I might cook this Ula, to eat it with you and your people that we may rejoice." The elder, hearing that Ruwa had sent this stranger, gave him a cooking-pot. And the stranger took a digging-stick and dug up the Ula and put it in the pot. The elder and the stranger cooked the Ula yams, and they started to eat.

As they were eating, Ruwa's Minister smelt the odour of cooking like to the odour of Ula. At once he came running and asked them: "What do you? What are you eating?" So the elder and the stranger were astonished and greatly afraid, they could find nothing to reply. Then the Minister of Ruwa took the pot with the yams and carried it to Ruwa. When Ruwa saw them he was very angry and sent his Minister a second time. And he went and spoke to the elder and his people: "Because you were deceived by a stranger and ate my Ula, I shall break (your bones) and burst your eyes, and at last you shall die." So the Minister returned to Ruwa. Since that day they have not seen him again, and Ruwa has not sent word to them again, and people commenced to be broken, and their eyes to be closed, and afterwards they died. Thus the old men of the Wachagga tell and know.

When the Minister had gone to Ruwa, at once the people and their elder commenced to sicken in their bones and eyes. So the elder prayed to Ruwa for honey and milk. And Ruwa hearkened to him, and he sent his Minister again to tell the elder, "Now I will have mercy on you and your people. Know henceforth that you shall grow to a great age, and when you die you shall cast your skin as a snake does, and afterwards you shall become as a youth again. But not one of your people may see you when you cast your skin, you must be alone at such time. And if your child or grandchild see you, in that hour you shall die altogether and not be saved again."

So they lived until the elder became very aged. His children seeing this gave him his granddaughter to care for him, that he might not fall into the hearth and be burnt. Now the old man knew that the day was come for him to cast his skin as Ruwa had sent word to him by his Minister. And he considered how to be rid of the granddaughter to give him opportunity (to change his skin). And he said to the granddaughter: "Bring a gourd and fetch me water here." And the granddaughter brought a gourd. The old man took a large needle and made small holes in the bottom of the gourd and gave it to the girl and instructed her to bring water. The old man knew she would not return quickly for the gourd was pierced with many holes. The granddaughter went quickly to draw water. But when the bowl was filled she saw that all the water leaked out because the gourd was pierced with many holes. And she made effort to plug the holes. When she had finished plugging the holes she filled the gourd. And she placed the gourd on her head and hastened home to her grandfather. As she entered the house she was startled, for the old man had cast half his skin. The old man stared at her in great amazement, and cried out aloud: "So be it, I have died, all of you will die, I have died, all of you shall die. For you, granddaughter, entered while I cast my skin. Woe is me, woe is you." So the old man slowly wrapped himself up in his skin and died. And his children came with his grandchildren and they buried him. And that bad grandchild they drove away, and she went into the forest. And she became a wife and bore children, but not human children, she gave birth only to children with four legs and a tail. And these indeed are the baboons, and monkeys, and apes, and colobus monkeys. Thus the baboons and these others are the children of her who offended against her grandfather. For this reason the baboons and their like are called "People of the Forest" or "Children of the Curse."[469]

The natives of old Calabar, who are culturally closely related to the Pangwe, have a myth which states that the god-pair Abassi and Atai sent the first human beings to earth.

Since god was afraid of the numerous descendants of man he ordered the man and woman to lie on different mats and warned them not to cohabit. He also forbad them to work; instead, they had to fetch food from heaven. But a friend suggested to the woman to cultivate a field in order to save the journey to heaven. Later the man slept with the woman despite the prohibition. She became pregnant and so he had to go alone to god. Questioned about his wife, the man confessed his guilt. Thereupon god sent death.[470]

Among the Australian aborigines of the river Murray this myth takes the following form:

The first created man and woman were told not to go near a certain tree in which a Bat (*Bon-nel-ya*) lived. The Bat was not to be disturbed. One day, however, the woman (*Nonga*) was gathering firewood, and she went near the tree in which the Bat lived. The Bat flew away, and after that came death. Many amongst the Aborigines died after that.[471]

Preuss[472] assumes that the idea of a connection between the sexual act and death has led to the belief widespread among primitive peoples that "procreation is an extremely dangerous act during which one may die if one does not observe all possible precautionary measures." This concept has, to a great extent, contributed to the origin of certain initiation rites "which are usually held at the age of puberty. During these ceremonies, fixed rites are administered to the sexual organs (circumcision, etc.) and other rites are performed the meaning of which is death and resurrection. By anticipating the death feared in the sexual act, it is magically averted." In this connection, Preuss refers to a myth of the Selknam which states that the first ancestor, Kenos, procreated men by forming out of humid earth male and female sexual organs, which copulated. These first men, the ancestors, did not die. When they grew old and weak, they lay down, wrapped themselves in a coat, in order to rise lively and youthfully after a deathlike sleep. Kenos had only to wash the cadaverous smell off them each time.

When men later had sexual intercourse and lost their immortality, the festivities of the secret societies were instituted to serve as initiation and instruction for all young people. First they were washed just as Kenos had cleansed the bodies after rejuvenescence; then, it is alleged, they were familiarized with copulation by the female spirit Chalpen who bore a child to one of them. At this time they were also killed by spirits and resuscitated. All these acts have the obvious meaning to protect men against death during future sexual intercourse.[473]

This idea of the connection between the sexual act and death—perhaps only the generalization of a concrete incest prohibition threatening death as punishment—is based on the notion of retribution, in so far as the latter aims at equality or equilibrium. The greatest pleasure finds its counterpart in the greatest pain. One compares the disadvantages which man experiences by nature with the advantages which nature offers him and finds that they equal each other. Nature is thus justified by the principle of retribution; nature is just. Rasmussen[474] relates of the Eskimos that they believe that the first human beings did not suffer death, but neither did they have daylight. "Let us be without day if we may be without death," said one group; but others cried out: "No, we want light and death!" And so it happened. "And with death there came sun, moon, and stars." Just as in the belief of other primitive peoples sexual enjoyment, so in the Eskimo's mythical interpretation of nature, light is requited by death.

The fact that men have to die is the compensation for an advantage attained by mankind. This idea appears also in the following myth of the Wakuluwe:

Ngulwe [Supreme Being] had told the man that he was not to look for medicines among plants, nor on the ground, nor anywhere else, but that if any illness occurred he would cure it, and that man and his offspring should never die. One day one of the children was ill, but, remembering Ngulwe's instructions, the man did not seek any medicine. The following day, however, seeing that the child was not better, he went out into the bush and secured some herbs, which he gave to the child and cured it; but Ngulwe was angry, and told the man that since he preferred to find remedies for himself he could do so, but that his immunity from mortal diseases would be removed and that he and his descendants would die.[475]

Improper behavior toward a higher being is the cause for the fact that death came upon mankind. In a myth of the Roro-speaking tribes of British New Guinea, Oa Rove Marai, "a spiritual being of greater power than others," brought men to kill each other as punishment for their having ill-treated him.

Then Oa Rove called together all the inhabitants of the Roro and Mekeo villages in the plain of the St. Joseph River, and told them that the Arabure people had treated him badly, but that if they had treated him well, everyone would have been happy and always have had plenty of food. Then he gave them spears and black palm-wood clubs, and he sent battle, theft, and adultery among them, and sorcerers who kill people. Thus death came to these villages.[476]

A special reason of retribution may be found in the fact that man lends an ear to the personified evil principle—i.e., to the opponent of God as the good principle—and allows himself to be seduced by the "devil," as the Christian myth puts it. Among the Wintun and Maidu Indians it is the creator Olelbis who is confronted by the evil coyote. Olelbis wishes that men should not die and that children should be born without sexual procreation. For old people a fountain of youth must be built, and children will emerge half-grown from a thing which their parents place between them during the night. But the coyote frustrates the plans of Olelbis by telling men working on the fountain of youth how monotonous and unsupportable life will be under such circumstances. Consequently, they relinquish their building activities.[477] The principle of retribution is also applied, inasmuch as the messenger, usually the opponent of God, who is directly responsible for the loss of immortality, is individually punished. Such is the fate of the hare in the myth of the South African Namaqua, and of the beings hostile to the Creator in the tales of the western Algonquin, Shoshones, and northwestern Selish Indians.[478]

In all these death myths there are interspersed more or less pronounced elements of a good-evil speculation which has its origin in the antagonism of life and death. These speculations become apparent not only in the enmity between a life-granting and a death-bringing superhuman authority (which in the early stages of religious evolution manifests itself in the dualism of the life and the death soul and which finally is represented by such figures as Ormuzd and Ahriman, God and the devil) but also in other details; thus, for instance, in the African myths, the messenger of life is a sun-animal while the messenger of death is a moon-animal.[479]

44. The Myths of Painful Parturition, the Necessity of Work, and the Lost Paradise

Also, other advantages than eternal life are lost through guilt; or, more correctly, other misfortunes besides death and deprivation of other goods than immortality are justified in myths according to the principle of retribution. A legend of the Caribs, for instance, deals with the question of "how pain, misery, and death came into the world." In olden times, so the story runs, there were no quarrels, ev-

eryone was happy, and no one became ill or died. All this suddenly
changed one day when the Caribs committed a great wrong. They
killed the child of a Yurokon woman (bush spirit) who had come to
visit them. When she discovered the crime, the woman said:

> "Why have you punished me in this way? I have never had a bad mind against any
> of you, but now I will make you pay me. In future your children shall all die, and this
> will make you weep as I am weeping. And when children are born to you, you shall
> suffer pain and trouble at their birth. Furthermore, with regard to you men I
> will give you great trouble when you go out to catch fish. . . . ." And so she did, because
> in those days we Caribs only had to go to the waterside, bail the water out with our
> calabashes, and picking up the fish that were left exposed at the bottom of the stream,
> just put the water back again to breed fish once more. Yurokon altered all this and
> made us go to the trouble, annoyance, and inconvenience of poisoning the pools with
> various roots.[480]

The Yamana[481] regard menstruation as punishment for woman's
concupiscence. Yoalox, their culture-hero, who is considered the husband of every woman, causes the flow of blood by a sexual act. One
myth tells of an extremely beautiful woman, Makuxipa, who lived
with the two brothers Yoalox. She preferred the younger one. One
day, believing the older brother was away, she laid on the bed with the
younger Yoalox and whispered to him:

> Membrum tuum mihi summopere placet. Tantum est quantum repleat vaginam
> meam. Rubrum est sicut *maku* (a red blossom). Frater tuus membrum minutum
> habet, quod me non ita irritat. Ecce, multo magis membrum magnum tuum mihi
> placet quam fratris tui. Tecum tempus diuturnum concumbere malo.

The younger Yoalox was pleased at her words. His brother, however,
who was outside leaning against the hut, understood perfectly well
what had been whispered.

> Thereupon he called to Makuxipa: "All right I will make you feel tamen mem-
> brum meum magnum atque tumidum esse!" He approached the bed where she lay
> and his brother moved away. Then he began to caress and embrace Makuxipa.
> Postea mulieri incubuit et immisit membrum suum in vaginam eius. Membrum suum
> ita intumuit, ut laceret mulieris vaginam. Statim copia sanguinis sat magna effluxit.
> Yoalox eam interrogavit: "Desiderasne utrum membrum meum adhuc succrescat,
> necne? Satisfacta es?" Makuxipa did not reply.

This was the first menstruation. Since then every woman must endure
it.

Labor pains attendant upon childbirth are especially regarded as
evils explainable only as punishment. Myths which interpret these
throes as consequences of the fall of man can be found not only in the
Bible but also in other places where biblical influence need not neces-

sarily be supposed. Among the Ashanti the fable exists that the spider, the Creator, forbade the cohabitation of the sexes. As punishment for the transgression of this prohibition the spider commanded that men must work and must pay bridal money for obtaining their wives, whereas women must endure pains when giving birth to a child.[482] The Luba tell that God punished men with toil and death because they ate forbidden bananas.[483] The Wakuluwe have the following myth:

> The first woman used to take a single grain of millet (about the size of an ordinary pinhead), and put it in a pot covered by a flat basket, and it was turned into sufficient porridge for her needs and her husband's. When her daughter grew up, the mother told her to take a single grain, and, having ground it, place it under the basket, but the daughter, not knowing that her mother had done this for a long time, thought she must be mad to imagine that one grain could produce the required quantity of food, so she set to work and ground a whole basket of millet. The mother discovered this and cursed her, saying that for the future they would always be obliged to work hard and grind all their flour.[484]

A myth of the Kavirondo (Bantu, near Lake Victoria), is as follows:

> The first man and woman came from heaven. Their names, however, are un-known. In some localities, they give their firstborn the name of *Lwan'ga*, the father of *Pondi*, whose son was called *Kwambo*. The first man from whom all on earth were born, lived in perfect happiness, and so did his wife. The earth brought forth all they wanted. They only had to put the hoe in the ground where they wanted their food to grow.—All this was communicated by the husband to his wife. All went all right for some time. But one day the woman put her hoe in the ground where she wanted her millet to grow. Nothing happened for some days. At last the woman doubted the power and goodness of *Were* [god] and started cultivating herself. *Were* appeared to her husband and said: "From henceforth the earth will not bring forth any food, unless you cultivate and constantly weed because you doubted my word."—After that the first pair begot children and men multiplied on earth and were subject to all kinds of misery, but death had not yet taken away any of them. One day a cameleon said to one of them: "Bring me a pot of beer." The cameleon slowly crept up the beer-pot and dipped himself in the beer. After he had taken his bath, he ordered the man to drink it. His natural abhorrence for the cameleon, thinking him to be poisonous even to the mere touching of his skin, made him refuse. On his refusal the cameleon said: "From henceforth you all will die." Whilst he was saying this, a snake came along and the cameleon ordered the snake to sip of the beer. The snake obeyed the order and sipped of the beer. Hence men die and the snake not, because they think the snake to be reborn every time he sheds his skin.[485]

A myth of the Ba-Kaonde is as follows: Lesa created the two first human beings, Mulonga and Mwinambuzhi. They had neither genital organs nor an anus. In order to ameliorate his creation Lesa gave two parcels to Mulonga, one for himself and the other for his female companion. At night Mulonga placed the one, as Lesa had commanded, between his legs, and in the morning he awoke as a man; but because of its bad smell he threw away the parcel for Mwinambuzhi. Lesa gave her a new one through the use of which she became a woman. As punishment for Mulonga's disobedience he, as well as all other men, had to pay a marriage-gift ever after.[486]

The function of bearing children is also regarded as punishment in a myth of the Caribs. To understand this legend it first must be explained that among certain South American Indians the idea exists that the office of the male in procreation is to place the·sperm, the "egg," into the woman during the sexual act. She then broods the egg which has been placed inside her. W. E. Roth recounts the myth as follows:

Uraima [the culture-hero] once had in his possession a bird's egg which he kept in a calabash; he took great care of it until it should hatch out. He met two girls on the road: they saw the egg and asked him to let them have it. "No!" he said, "I cannot." They worried and even followed him, but he still refused. So they seized the egg, and in the course of the scuffle broke it. Uraima then spoke to the women as follows: "Since you have done this, trouble will follow you from now onward. Up to the present, the egg has belonged to man. For the future it will belong to woman, and she will have to hatch it." It is only the female that lays eggs nowadays.[487]

In a story of the western Equatorial pygmies the scene of the fall of man is shifted to the animal world (which, however, in the view of the primitive man is not different from the human world). The guilt consists in eating the fruits of a prohibited tree. The punishment is the loss of human speech, of which the animals were masters until that time.[488] Thus, the most striking difference between man and animal is interpreted according to the principle of retribution.

According to Frobenius, the Watji (Africa) tell:

Once when their ancestors stood on a mountain, they heard lovely tunes in heaven. Thereupon a chain was lowered from heaven to the mountain top. Heavenly beings descended who told beautiful things about the agreeable place whence they came. But they also spoke to the ancestors about their intention to remain with them should peace and unity reign. They hated war and disunion for they were children of peace. At that the ancestors told the heavenly spirits they.would not like it down here for peace is rare among men. When the celestial beings heard that they bade the ancestors goodbye and returned to heaven on the chain. The ancestors were very sad to see them go. And ever since they have been vainly waiting for their return.[489]

As punishment for their dissensions, men may not achieve paradise.

A myth of the Mian Balantak says that, whenever the first human pair needed anything, the man had to climb up a rotang to heaven, where the Lord supplied him with all necessities. But, as time passed, men began to plant one thing and another; and, when they were able to feed themselves, this connection with heaven was abandoned. God, the creator of the world and of men, was furious at this arbitrary behavior of his children and therefore effected a complete separation of heaven from earth, of God from man.[490]

The Waraus, an Indian tribe of Guiana, have the following myth:

The original abode of the Waraus was not on this lower earth at all, but in a pleasant region above the sky. In that region they were happy, there being neither wicked men nor noxious animals to make them afraid. Beautiful birds abounded, and were the game of their young hunters. One of these, named Okono rote, having wandered far in pursuit of a choice bird, discharged an arrow at it, which missed its mark and disappeared. While searching for the arrow he found a hole through which it had fallen, and on looking through it he saw this lower world stretched out beneath, with herds of bush-hogs, numerous deer, and other animals, feeding and roaming undisturbed through its green forests and savannahs. Finding that the aperture would allow him to pass through, he resolved to make a rope or ladder of cotton (of which there seems to have been abundance above) and descend. Assisted by his friends, he at length completed the rope,—descended by it, and again with infinite labour returned to the upper regions:—to report the wondrous things he had seen (and eaten) below, and to counsel a migration thither.—The Warau race listened to this tale of unlimited animal food till their desires and appetites could no longer be controlled, and without regarding, as it seems, the will of the Great Spirit, they unanimously resolved on a descent to the terrestrial hunting-grounds. They accordingly descended by the same means, followed by their children and their wives, all except the last—an unfortunate person who, being too stout to squeeze through, remained fixed in the narrow aperture, completely filling it. No effectual assistance could be given from below: and as none were left above to render aid, all communication with the regions above the sky was closed by her sad mishap, and return rendered impossible. The Waraus were thus of necessity confined to this earth, without even a glimpse of their former abode.[491]

Karsten writes:

One of the most beautiful myths of the Jibaros tells us how once, in primeval times, the goddess [Nungüi, the Earth-deity] appeared to the Jibaro women and taught them the cultivation of the different fruits which still make their chief vegetable food. At that time the goddess herself lived amidst her people. But since her children proved ungrateful, she one day suddenly disappeared in a dense smoke in the interior of the earth.[492]

45. THE FLOOD AND CATASTROPHE MYTHS

More than any others, the flood myths clearly illustrate the similarity between the mental beginnings of different peoples and show how even the most civilized groups in the infancy of their thinking betray the same characteristics as the most primitive societies. Among the common elements of flood and catastrophe tales the principle of ret-

G

ribution is so manifest that one must consider it, if only for that reason, as one of the oldest ideas of humanity.

That retribution is the chief motive in the biblical account of the Flood, as well as in the story of the sulphur and fire rain over Sodom and Gomorrah, are not conclusive proofs, since these stories may be later versions. But, also, the Babylonian record of a great flood handed down in the *Gilgamesh Epic*, to which the biblical story can be traced, contains the idea of retribution. The gods—foremost among them, Bel—agree to inflict punishment upon men for their sins; this punishment will assume the form of an immense flood to destroy all human beings. One god, Ea, however, chooses a certain man whom he wishes to save, Utnapishtim (the meaning of the name is "he found life"), of the town of Shurippak.[493] He had the nickname Atrachasis, which means "the very intelligent."[494] His devoutness is stressed in the poem. Ea tells Utnapishtim of the decision of the gods and commands him to build a boat and take into it living beings of all kinds. Thus the pious Utnapishtim is saved. Bel, the real author of the flood, is furious at first when he sees Utnapishtim and his people saved. But at Ea's suggestion that in the future he should punish the sins of men with famine, pestilence, and wild beasts, rather than by floods causing general destruction, Bel is finally reconciled to the rescue of Utnapishtim. He even grants the man and his wife divine nature and removes them far away, to the mouth of the rivers, to lead a life of immortality.[495] Piety receives its greatest reward. The words spoken by Ea to Bel to calm his wrath at the saving of Utnapishtim are important for the significance which the poems give to the flood:

> Thou mighty among the gods, warrior,
> Thus, thus rashly hast thou caused the deluge.
> May the sinner bear his sin's reward, and the wicked his
>   wickedness.
> Be lenient, let not (all) be crushed; be merciful, let
>   not (everything) be destroyed.
> Instead of causing a flood, lions might have come and
>   diminished mankind.[496]

The idea of retribution is obvious.[497] The Babylonian flood fable is probably of Sumerian origin. Even in its oldest form the motive of retribution is apparent: Ziugiddu, or rather Ziudsuddu, at once king and a priest of the god Enki, the Sumerian deity who was the equivalent of the Semitic Ea, is warned by Enki, as reward for his piety, of the coming flood and thus escapes certain death in a boat.[498]

The destruction of sinful mankind, executed at the order of the highest god, Ra, by the vengeance-goddess, Hathor, is the content of in-
scriptions which decorate the tomb of Pharaoh Seti I (about 1350
B.C.).[499] Zeus destroyed the bronze race, as punishment for its crimes,
by means of a flood which overflowed the whole of Greece. Only the
two just people, Deucalion and Pyrrha, were spared. Because Zeus
and Hermes were denied hospitality by all human beings except two
old people, Philemon and Baucis, the gods transformed the inhos-
pitable country into a lake; only the friendly old couple were allowed
to survive in their little cottage.[500] In the *Mahabharata* the flood appears as the expiatory washing of the earth.[501] The "Brahmana of
the hundred paths" (*Satapatha-Brahmana*) reports that once, when
Manu, the first human being, was washing himself, he suddenly found
a small fish which asked to be spared and requested protection from
the big fishes which devour the smaller ones. In return the fish promised Manu to save him from an imminent flood. And, indeed, events
happened as the fish had predicted they would.[502] Here, too, the principle of retribution serves as justification not so much of the catastrophe
as of the rescue; the element of reward, and not that of punishment, is
in the foreground.

In the *Bundahis* of the Persians there is a story of the angel Tistar,
who in his fight against the Evil Spirit produced rain until "all noxious
creatures, the breed of the Evil Spirit, were drowned." This is the reason why the sea is salty today.[503] The catastrophe employed as a factor
in the victorious contest of the good principle against the evil is only a
more abstract treatment of the principle of retribution as it appears in
the ordinary flood fables. In the *Younger Edda* the giants—obvious representatives of evil—who are hostile to the gods, drown in a sea of
blood which springs up from the killing of the giant Ymir by the sons
of the god Bör.[504]

The Australian natives have a legend which tells how Bahlu, the
moon, let it rain until everything was inundated by the water and
Murego was drowned in the flood as a penalty for not having lent one
of his boomerangs and opossum bags to Bahlu.[505]

The aborigines of Victoria have the following myth:

There was a time when men and women were numerous. In some parts of the
earth they were very numerous, and they were wicked; and PUND-JEL became angry.
PUND-JEL became very sulky (*Nar-eit*), when he saw that men and women were many
and very bad. He caused storms to arise, and fierce winds to blow often. In the flat
lands there arose suddenly whirlwinds of great force, and on the mountains the big
trees were shaken with strong winds. PUND-JEL came down to see the men and women.

He spoke to no one. He carried with him his big knife. With his knife he went into the encampments, and he cut with his knife. He cut this way and that way, and men, women, and children he cut into very small pieces. But the pieces into which he had cut the men, women, and children did not die. Each piece moved as the worm (*Tur-ror*) moves. *Bullito, bullito, koor-reen, pit-ker-reen* (great, great storms and whirlwinds) came and carried away the pieces that moved like worms, and the pieces became like flakes of snow (*Kabbing*). They were carried into the clouds. The clouds carried the pieces hither and thither over all the earth; and PUND-JEL caused the pieces to drop in such places as he pleased. Thus were men and women scattered over the earth. Of the good men and good women PUND-JEL made stars. The stars are still in the heavens, and the sorcerers can tell which amongst the stars were once good men and good women.[506]

Another version tells how Bundjel became angry at the blacks be-cause they had behaved evilly. He punished them by urinating until all were drowned in the urine except the good ones, whom he fished out and placed as stars in the firmament.[507]

A kind of flood myth is this tale of the Aranda reported by Streh-low.[508] Originally the earth was covered with water; only a few moun-tains emerged. In heaven a godly being, Altjira, reigned. On the mountains lived other godly beings, the *altjirangamitjina* (or *inkara*), who were the totem gods of men. Since they were unable to find any food on earth, they repeatedly had recourse to heaven, where they hunted in Altjira's realm and returned with booty. Later on, Altjira forbade the *altjirangamitjina* to hunt in his realm. Then one of these totem gods grasped a stick and beat the water, commanding it to go away. Thereupon the sea withdrew to the north, and the continent appeared. Disobeying Altjira's order, several *inkara*, the *wetoppetoppa* (the slender ones), went up to heaven to hunt. Whereupon, at the command of Altjira, the tall mountain Eralera submerged, cutting off the retreat of the *wetoppetoppa*. They were forced to remain in heaven, where they now live as stars.

The Narrinyeri (South Australia) relate that a man whose two wives deserted him brought about by magic a great flood in which both women were drowned.[509]

In the Kabadi district of New Guinea the natives have a tradition that

once on a time a certain man Lohero and his younger brother were angry with the people about them, and they put a human bone into a small stream. Soon the great waters came forth, forming a sea, flooding all the low land, and driving the people back to the mountains, till step by step they had to escape to the tops of the highest peaks. There they lived till the sea receded, when some of them descended to the low-lands, while others remained on the ridges and there built houses and formed planta-tions.[510]

The Valmans on the northern coast of New Guinea have a myth about a flood sent as punishment for the fact that the people, despite the warnings of a good man, killed and ate a certain large fish. Everyone was drowned except the good man and his family.[511]

The Fijians speak of a deluge which, according to some of their accounts, was partial, but in others is stated to have been universal. The cause of this great flood was the killing of Turukawa—a favourite bird belonging to Ndengei—by two mischievous lads, the grandsons of the god. These, instead of apologizing for their offence, added insolent language to the outrage, and, fortifying, with the assistance of their friends, the town in which they lived, defied Ndengei to do his worst. It is said that, although the angry god took three months to collect his forces, he was unable to subdue the rebels, and, disbanding his army, resolved on more efficient revenge. At his command the dark clouds gathered and burst, pouring streams on the devoted earth. Towns, hills, mountains were successively submerged; but the rebels, secure in the superior height of their own dwelling-place, looked on without concern. But when, at last, the terrible surges invaded their fortress, they cried for direction to a god, who, according to one account, instructed them to form a float of the fruit of the shaddock; according to another, sent two canoes for their use; or, says a third, taught them how to build a canoe, and thus secure their own safety. All agree that the highest places were covered, and the remnant of the human race saved in some kind of vessel, which was at last left by the subsiding waters on Mbengga: hence the Mbenggans draw their claim to stand first in Fijian rank. The number saved—eight—exactly accords with the "few" of the Scripture record. By this flood, it is said, two tribes of the human family became extinct. One consisted entirely of women, and the other were distinguished by the appendage of a tail like that of a dog.[512]

An interesting "nature" myth of the Palau Islands is reported by Kubary.[513] The story refers to a god, Obakad. The name hints a relation to man; for *oba* means "possess" and *kad* means "man." Therefore the name of the deity in question seems to imply a lord or creator of man. And this is borne out by the contents of the fable which Kubary calls "the most important of all the tales dealing with Obakad."

In times of yore before the present race of human beings existed, the inhabitants of the Palau Islands were all Kaliths (deities); they were strong and achieved wonders. One of these Kaliths, whose name was Athndokl, who was one of the Obakads [this implies that there were several Obakads, perhaps a family of gods of that name], came to Ngarekobukl, which today is in Eyrray, and was killed by the inhabitants there. Seven friendly gods went out to search for him and came to the same village, the residents of which were known as malicious and presumptuous. The gods were received everywhere unkindly with the exception of one woman, Milathk, who welcomed them to her house and told them of the death of Athndokl. Grieved and infuriated, the gods resolved on vengeance. In order to repay the woman's kindness, however, they agreed to spare her and suggested to her that she prepare a raft and fasten it to a tree by a rope. At the time of the full moon a terrific flood came upon Palau which covered the whole village.

Milathk also perished but was recalled to life by the oldest Obakad, who even wanted to make her immortal. This, however, was prevented by another god, Tariit, who was in turn punished by the angry Obakad. Milathk became the mother of mankind. Anyone reading this nature myth without prejudice must be impressed by the fact that its essential content is the idea of retribution, especially the punishment for the murder. The Kaliths, who apparently are the ancestors elevated to gods, are regarded as the authors and guarantors of this fundamental principle of human society.

Of the flood fables of Polynesia, W. Ellis writes:

> Traditions of the deluge . . . . have been found to exist among the natives of the South Sea Islands, from the earliest periods of their history. . . . . The principal facts are the same in the traditions prevailing among the inhabitants of the different groups, although they differ in several minor particulars. In one group the accounts state, that in ancient times Taaroa, the principal god (according to their mythology, the creator of the world) being angry with men on account of their disobedience to his will, overturned the world into the sea, when the earth sank in the waters, excepting a few *aurus* or projecting points.[514]

The natives of the Leeward Islands tell the following: A fisherman angled in a prohibited place; his line became entangled in the hair of a resting deity. The god, infuriated at the violation of the taboo, wanted to destroy the whole sinful country but was placated by the pleas of the penitent fisherman and gave him a chance to save himself from the great flood which he nevertheless loosened upon the land.[515] On the Hervey Islands there is the following legend of a deluge: "A king named Taoiau (peace-bearer) was on one occasion greatly incensed against his people for not bringing him the sacred turtle. The irate chief 'awakened' all the mighty seagods . . . . who . . . . rose up in anger . . . . and the ocean swept over the entire island."[516]

In a tale of the Maoris of New Zealand the deluge came upon men because "the worship of Tane was neglected and his doctrines openly denied." Two teachers, cursed by men, called forth the deluge by prayers so that it "would convince men of the power of Tane."[517] Another Maori fable reports that the hero Tawhaki, having been murdered by his brother-in-law but revived by his wife, asked the gods to avenge him. Thereupon they sent a flood called "the overwhelming of the Mataaho," by which all human beings perished.[518]

A legend of the Batak of Sumatra connects the great flood with the fight of the good principle against the bad. According to the idea of these people, the earth rests on the head of a giant snake, Naga-Padoha. One day the reptile became weary of supporting its burden;

so it shook off the earth into the water. But the god, Batara-Guru, caused a mountain to fall into the water in order that he might provide a place of residence for his daughter, Puti-orla-bulan. She had three sons and daughters from whom the new human race was derived. Later the earth was replaced on the head of the snake. From that time there has been a continual struggle between the evil reptile which wishes to rid itself of the burden and the deity who wants to avoid that disaster.[519]

The natives of Nias, an island to the west of Sumatra, say that

in days of old there was a strife between the mountains of their country as to which of them was the highest. The strife vexed their great ancestor Baluga Luomewona, and in his vexation he . . . . said: "Ye mountains, I will cover you all." . . . . The ocean rose higher and higher till only the tops of two or three mountains in Nias still stood above the heaving billows . . . . and the strife is proverbial among his descendants to the present day.

They interpret the catastrophe as punishment for arrogance and disunion.[520]

A myth of the Dayak of Borneo intimates that the flood was sent as punishment for the killing of a snake.[521] In a story of the Toradja of Central Celebes the principle of retribution, as in other flood myths, becomes apparent after the catastrophe. "Nobody escaped the flood except a pregnant woman and a pregnant mouse." The mouse procured a little rice for the woman. "But . . . . the mouse stipulated that as a recompense for her services mice should henceforth have the right to eat up part of the harvest."[522] The Andamanesian tale of a flood inflicted upon men by Puluga, the Creator, as punishment for their disobedience has been mentioned in another connection.[523]

The Bahnars, a primitive tribe in Cochin China, tell how "once on a time the kite quarrelled with the crab, and pecked the crab's skull so hard that he made a hole in it, which may be seen down to this very day. To avenge this injury to his skull, the crab caused the sea and the rivers to swell."[524] The Lolos (in the mountains of Yunnan) have a legend of the deluge which says "that people were wicked and Tse-gu-dzih to try them sent a messenger to earth, asking for some blood and flesh from a mortal. All refused but Du-mu. Tse-gu-dzih then locked the rain-gates and the waters mounted to the sky. Du-mu was saved with his four sons."[525] A tale of the Hos or Lurka Kolse in southwestern Bengal relates that god once destroyed mankind "because people became incestuous (some say he destroyed it with water, some say with fire)."[526] The flood which appears in the tales of the Singphos[527] and the

Ahoms of Assam[528] is mentioned as punishment for the omission of pre-scribed sacrifices.

In Africa flood fables are comparatively scarce. In those which do exist, however, the principle of retribution appears prominently. So when the natives of Unyoro say that "God, infuriated at the arrogance of human beings, threw the firmament to earth and thus completely destroyed the first human race,"[529] they have in mind the idea of retri-bution—and of a flood. The Herero label an extraordinary rainfall with the words, "heaven breaks down," because they believe that the rain clouds (heaven as a substance) fall to earth.[530] Hence the expres-sion "God threw heaven to earth" in the fable of the Unyoros prob-ably also signifies rainfall.

In the myths of the Edo or Bini there is a story according to which the god Ogiwu intended to punish men for the death of his son by letting heaven fall down on earth. But the Edo had a great king, the hero Ewuare, who frustrated Ogiwu's intention.[531]

The Yoruba tell of a god Ifa who

became tired of living in the world, and accordingly went to dwell in the firmament, with Obatala. After his departure, mankind, deprived of his assistant, was unable to properly interpret the desires of the gods, most of whom became in consequence an-noyed. Olokun was the most angry, and in a fit of rage he destroyed nearly all the inhabitants of the world in a great flood."[532]

A tale of the Basonge relates how the leopard, buffalo, elephant, and zebra woo Ngolle Kakesse, the granddaughter of God. Only the zebra, whose name is also Ngólle, is accepted as a son-in-law. The zebra, however, breaks its promise not to allow Ngolle Kakesse to work. From her stretched-out legs runs water which floods the whole land. And Ngolle herself drowns.[533]

The Mandingo and Mossi (hinterland of the Ivory Coast) have a story of a charitable man who distributed all his possessions among the animals. As a consequence his wife and children deserted him. But he nevertheless gave Ouende, a celestial god who wandered unrecognized on earth, the last meal he had. Since he had no more grain, Ouende gave him three handfuls of flour in a basket. When he sowed the three handfuls of flour, they perpetually renewed themselves in the basket; finally they became gourds, which God asked him to cut. From the sliced fruits great quantities of cowry, millet, gold, and even girls, etc., emerged. Then Ouende suggested to the man that he should depart from that place with all his goods, inasmuch as the god desired to pun-ish the selfish relatives of the man. Thereupon Ouende caused it to

rain for six months. Everything perished. But the new descendants of
the rich man spread and formed the present human race."[534]

The formation of Lake Dilolo is the subject matter of the following
account: "A female chief, called Moéne Monenga . . . . asked for a
supply of food . . . . and was refused. . . . . In order to show what she
could do, she began a song; in slow time, and uttered her own name,
Monenga-woo. As she prolonged the last note, the village, people,
fowls, and dogs sank into the space now called Dilolo."[535] Myths of
this kind, according to Baumann,[536] are frequently found in Africa.

As in the case of the other continents, the Americas also produced
flood tales in which the motive of retribution appears more or less
decidedly. A myth of the Yamana relates[537] that

once upon a time at the approach of spring a man looked up and saw a Bandurria
(female ibis) fly over his hut. He was extremely happy about this and called out to his
neighbors: "A Bandurria is flying over my hut. Look there!" When the others heard
this news, they ran out of their houses and cried: "Spring is here. The ibis are already
flying!" They leaped with joy and noisily amused themselves. The Lexuwa [the ibis
woman], however, is very sensitive and needs to be treated gently. When these men,
women, and children shrieked so loudly and for such a long time, she heard the noise
and became excited. In her annoyance and anger, she loosened a thick snow storm
accompanied by cold and much ice.

The whole earth was covered with snow and ice; and many people
died. When the snowfall ceased,

a hot sun burned down so fiercely that all the snow and ice, which covered the earth
up to the mountain tops, melted. Great quantities of water flowed into the rivers and
the sea. Indeed the sun shone so strongly that the mountain tops burned and have
consequently remained treeless until today. The ice which covered both the broad
and narrow streams also dissolved so that people were able to get to the coasts and to
enter their canoes in order to look for food. On the mountain slopes and in the deep
valleys the thick ice has remained until today. . . . . Since then the Yamana treat
every Bandurria with great respect. When the bird approaches their huts people remain silent and calm the children so they do not cry.

In one of the myths of the Uitoto, Nofuyeni causes an earthquake
and a flood because Meni has stolen the ax-shaped parrot.[538] In another story Dyaere lets it rain incessantly because Nadyerekudu mu-
tilated a red parrot.[539] According to a legend of the Carayas (Brazil),
the great flood was caused by a demoniacal being called Anatiua, who
became furious because men did not understand him and wanted to
run away.[540] In a myth of the Tupinamba, Monan, in order to punish
men for ingratitude, effects a natural catastrophe.[541] Ehrenreich[542]

points out that generally the crimes of men against the culture-hero are the causes of cataclysms in the myths of South American aborigines.

The Ipurina (on the Purus River, an affluent of the Upper Amazon) regard the sloth as their ancestor. They have a myth in which Mayuruberu, the chief of the storks and the creator of all birds, produced a great flood by making a kettle of water boiling in the sun overflow.

Mankind indeed survived, but of the vegetable world nothing escaped but the cassia. . . . . Next the sloth begged Mayuruberu to give him seeds of useful fruits. So Mayuruberu appeared with a great basket full of plants, and the Ipurina began to till their fields. He who would not work was eaten by Mayuruberu. Every day Mayuruberu received a man to devour.[543]

Punishment for laziness is the chief theme of this story. But the connection between this motive and the flood itself is not clear.

In a tale of the Murato Indians (a branch of the Jibaros in Ecuador) the deluge appears as the vengeance of a crocodile—the mother of crocodiles in general—for the murder of her child.[544]

According to a fable of the Acawoios (British Guiana), the flood was caused by the lazy and mischievous monkey who opened a basket in which the swelling water was inclosed. He, "whose dishonest propensities caused the flood, remained uncured of his idleness, love of mischief and pilfering, and transmitted those qualities unimpaired to his children."[545]

The Arawaks in British Guiana "believe that since the Creation the world has been twice destroyed; first, by a flame of fire sent to sweep over it, and afterwards by a flood of water. Each of those destructions was on account of the evil doings of men and specially threatened by Aiomun Kondi, the great 'Dweller on High.'"[546] The motive of retribution is varied in a peculiar way in a myth of the Muyscas, natives of the plateau of Cundinamarca (Colombia).[547] Here the flood is not punishment but itself a wrong which must be avenged; this idea is similar to the primitive concept of death as either punishment or a crime, caused by magic:

In olden times before the moon existed, the tableland of Cundinamarca was shut off and the pass of Tequendama was not yet open. The Muyscas still lived as savages without government or agriculture when there came to them a bearded old man who had the following names: Botschika, Nemquetheba, Zuhe. He taught them to cultivate the land, manufacture clothes, venerate the gods, and form states. His wife also had three names: Huythaca, Chia, and Yubecayguya. She was beautiful but malicious and wanted to destroy all the good works of her husband. And indeed by means of magic she caused the river Funza, now the Rio Bogota, to swell so that the whole plateau was flooded. Only a few of the inhabitants could flee to the mountain tops.

Botschika became furious and banished the wicked woman from the earth, changing her into the moon. In order to redress the disaster on earth Botschika opened the pass and the water poured down in the majestic waterfall of Tequendama. The country dried out and was cultivated by the remaining human beings.

According to another tale of these Indians, the flood was sent by the god Chibchachum as punishment for the insults heaped upon him by their ancestors. But the great god Bochica saved mankind and punished Chibchachum by condemning him "to bear on his shoulders the whole weight of the earth. . . . . When the weary giant tries to get a little ease by shifting his burden from one shoulder to another, he causes an earthquake."[548]

Farabee reports the following myth of the Jivaran Indians, an Arawakan tribe.

A great feast was to be held, and two boys were sent away into the forest to get game. They made a camp under a tree, and went out to hunt. They secured much game, dressed it, and hung it up at the camp. The second day when they returned heavily laden with game, they were surprised to find that their first day's catch had been stolen. When they returned on the third day, they again found the meat had been stolen. On the next day, one remained in hiding to discover the thief. He found it was a great snake that lived in the hollow of the tree under which they had camped. To destroy the snake they built a fire in the tree, and the snake fell into the fire. The boys were hungry, and one of them ate some of the roasted flesh of the snake. He soon became thirsty, drank all of the water they had at the camp, then went to the spring, and from there to the lake. He was soon transformed into a frog, next into a lizard, and finally into a snake, which began to grow very rapidly. His brother was frightened, and tried to pull him out of the water, but the lake began to overflow. The snake then told his brother that the lake would continue to grow until the whole world would be covered, and that the people would perish unless he returned and told them to make their escape. He told his brother to put a calabash in his pocket, to go on top of the highest mountain, and when the water came, to climb the highest palm tree. The brother returned, and told his people what had happened, but they refused to believe him, accusing him of destroying his brother; so he fled to the top of the mountain, and when the water came, climbed the palm tree. After many days the water began to subside, and he came down to the ground. From the top of the mountain he could see the vultures eating the dead people in the valley, so he went back to the lake where he found his brother, and carried him away in his calabash.[549]

The motive of retribution appears several times here. First, the killing of the snake is vengeance for the theft. The transformation of the one of the brothers into a frog, lizard, and a snake is punishment for the fact that the snake was killed and that its flesh was eaten. The flood, too, is punishment for this delict. Finally, men drown as punishment for not having believed in the warning and for having falsely accused the other brother.

A tale of the Quiché Indians (Guatemala) recorded in the *Popol Vuh* (popular book) which was discovered at the beginning of the eighteenth century, justifies the catastrophe by pointing out the inadequacy of the first beings created by the gods.[550] The fact that they are not guilty, according to modern concepts of justice, should not be a hindrance to our seeing here, too, an application of the principle of retribution which in the sense of primitive thinking also comprises absolute liability.

According to the Popol Vuh the gods, having created animals were dissatisfied with them because the beasts could neither talk nor venerate the deities. Therefore the gods created men out of clay; but these were also imperfect. They could not move their heads and although they could speak they were unable to hear. Thereupon the gods destroyed these defective creations by a flood. A second creation of men followed; this time man was composed of wood and woman of resin. This second race of humans was better than its predecessor but the people still had an animal demeanor. They could speak only indistinctly and they were not at all grateful to the gods. Hurakan, the "Heart of Heaven," let burning resin fall to earth and then sent an earthquake in which nearly all the human beings perished. Those who survived, however, became monkeys.[551] At last the gods formed human beings out of yellow and white maize. They were so perfect that the gods were frightened; therefore they took some of the qualities away. Thus they became men to whom the Quiche trace their descent.

An interesting shift of the motive of retribution may be found in a tale of the Papagos:[552] The godly king Montezuma saved himself from the flood, the cause of which is not divulged. When the world was again repeopled, the care and government of the new race had been allotted to Montezuma;

but puffed up with pride and self-importance, he neglected the most important duties of his onerous position, and suffered the most disgraceful wickedness to pass unnoticed among the people. In vain the Great Spirit came down to earth and remonstrated with his vicegerent, who only scorned his laws and advice, and ended at last by breaking out into open rebellion. Then indeed the Great Spirit was filled with anger, and he returned to heaven, pushing back the Sun on his way, to that remote part of the sky he now occupies. But Montezuma . . . . set about building a house that should reach up to heaven itself. Already it had attained a great height . . . . when the Great Spirit launched his thunder and laid its glory in ruins. Still Montezuma hardened himself . . . . he ordered the temple-houses to be desecrated. . . . . Then the Great Spirit prepared his supreme punishment. He sent an insect flying away towards the east, towards an unknown land, to bring the Spaniards. When these came, they made war upon Montezuma and destroyed him, and utterly dissipated the idea of his divinity.

Presumably the motive of retribution was transferred from the flood tale itself to the fate of the survivor, since his downfall had to be explained. The biblical-Christian influence on Montezuma's tower is obvious.

The retribution theme appears among the Maya (Yucatan) in the form of a prophecy relative to the end of the world. Brinton[553] records this document as follows:

> At the close of the ages, it hath been decreed,
> Shall perish and vanish each weak god of men,
> And the world shall be purged with a ravening fire.
> Happy the man in that terrible day,
> Who bewails with contrition the sins of his life,
> And meets without flinching the fiery ordeal.

The Caribs (Antilles) report "that the Master of Spirits, being angry with their forefathers for not presenting to him the offerings which were his due, caused such a heavy rain to fall . . . . that nearly all the people were drowned."[554] In a tale of the Tarahumares (Mexico) the deluge is interpreted as punishment for internal dissension.[555]

Of the flood myths of the North American Indians the following may be mentioned: A tale of the Wiyot (central California) tells of a deity who sent a flood which destroyed everything because men were wicked.[556] The existence of the motive of retribution can be deduced indirectly from a tale of the Zuñi Indians (western New Mexico). Here the flood is removed by a human sacrifice: "A youth and a maiden, son and daughter of two priests, were thrown into this ocean."[557] Through the sacrifice it is intended that the ire of the water-god be allayed. The wrath of the deity, however, generally means that a norm proclaimed by it, issued in its interest, or guaranteed by it, has been violated. The idea that in return for the offering the deity takes the flood away is a direct application of the principle of retribution. This concept is clearly expressed by the Mandan Indians in their tale of a great flood. Here the story of the deluge is the basis of certain yearly rites which include sacrifices to the water spirit. The Mandan believe "that the omission of this annual ceremony, with its sacrifices made to the waters, would bring upon them a repetition of the calamity which their traditions say once befell them, destroying the whole human race."[558] In a story of the Acagchemem Indians (California) the deluge is an act of vengeance.[559]

A myth of the Potawatomi is reminiscent of the tale of the Quiché Indians.

> Kčemnito first created the world and filled it with a race of beings that did not look like men. They were perverse, ungrateful, and malicious dogs which never raised their eyes to heaven to beg for the assistance of the great spirit. Such ingratitude aroused his anger and so he submerged the whole world in a great lake.[560]

The Navajo Indians have the following myth:

The world in which we now live is the fifth world. Our fathers dwelt in four worlds before reaching this. In the first world there dwelt three; the first man, the first woman and the coyote. It was dark there and the world was small, so they ascended to the second world. On the second world they found two other men; the Sun and the Moon. There was then no sun or moon in the firmament; but these people are so called because they afterwards became the sun and the moon (or the sun and the moon gods). Yet there was light in the second world. In the east there was a great darkness; it was not a cloud, but it was like a cloud. In the south there was blue light; in the west a yellow light and in the north a white light. At times the darkness would rise in the east until it overspread the whole sky and made the night. Then the darkness would sink down, the blue light would rise gradually in the south, the yellow light in the west and the white light in the north, until they met in the zenith, and made the day. . . . .

But the land into which they came was not empty; another race of people dwelt in the mountains, and they called the people of the mountains into council and said to them: "We have come to this land to stay a long time and we desire to live at peace with you." And they of the mountains said: "It is well; the land is wide enough for us all, and we seek not war; but there lives in the great water beyond the eastern mountains, a monster named, Tìèholtsòdi (he who seizes you in the sea), whom we warn you not to approach or harm." The Navajos promised to heed this warning and the council broke up. But the coyote listened to no one, and he went where he chose, none controlled him. So, in time he strayed to the great water beyond the eastern mountain, stole two of the children of the ocean monster, brought them back into camp unperceived and hid them in his blankets.—When Tìèholtsòdi missed his young he went in search of them. He sought in the great waters at the four corners of the earth, but found them not, so he, at length, came to the conclusion that they must be in the possession of the strangers who had recently come from the lower world. Then he caused the waters that were in the east, the south, the west, and the north to rise and flow over the land; so that at the end of the second day there was but little dry land left for the people to stand on. They all became greatly alarmed and held a council. They knew they must have done some wrong; but what the crime or who the culprit, they could not discover.—Then they took soil from all of the four corner mountains of the world, and placed it on top of the mountain that stood in the north, and thither they all went including the people of the mountains, the salt-woman, and such animals as then dwelt on the third world. When the soil was laid on the mountain the latter began to grow higher and higher, but the waters continued to rise and the people climbed upwards to escape the flood. At length the mountain ceased to grow and they planted on the summit a great reed, into the hollow of which they all entered. The reed grew every night but it did not grow in the daytime; and this is the reason why the reed grows in joints to this day—the hollow internodes shows where it grew by night, and the solid nodes shows where it rested by day. Thus the waters gained on them in the daytime. The turkey was the last to take refuge in the reed and, therefore, he was at the bottom. When the waters rose high enough to wet the turkey they all knew that danger was near. Often did the waves wash the end of his tail; and it is for this reason that the tips of the turkey's tail-feathers are, to this day, lighter than the rest of his plumage. At the end of the fourth night from the time it was planted, the reed had grown up to the floor of the fourth world, and here they found a hold through which they passed to the surface. . . . .

But all this time the coyote had still kept hidden the young of the sea-monster, Tïèholtsòdi, and the latter having searched for them in vain in all the seas of the fourth world, caused the waters to rise as before. Again was the council held, again was soil taken from the four mountains; . . . . once more the reed sheltered the fugitives and bore them upwards out of danger. In short all the circumstances that attended their flight from the third world was repeated until they reached the floor of the present world, when an appalling difference was observed. Instead of finding a hole through which they could pass, as on the former occasion, all above them, as far as they could see, was solid earth, like the roof of a great cavern. . . . .

On the fifth day the sun arose, climbed as usual to the zenith and stopped. The day grew hot and all longed for the night to come, but the sun moved not. Then the wise coyote said: "The sun stops because he has not been paid for his work; he demands a human life for every day that he labors; he will not move again till some one dies." At length a woman, the wife of a great chief, ceased to breathe and grew cold, and while they all drew around in wonder, the sun was observed to move again, and he travelled down the sky and passed behind the western mountain. As we now never see him stop on his way we know that every day some one must die. . . . .

That night the moon stopped in the zenith, as the sun had done during the day; and the coyote told the people that the moon also demanded pay and would not move until it was given. He had scarcely spoken, when the man who had seen the departed woman in the nether world died, and the moon, satisfied, journeyed to the west. Thus it is that some one must die every night, or the moon would not move across the sky.[561]

In the biblical story of the fall of man the first human beings, with their moral inadequacy, are created by an omnipotent authority who, angered at his own creatures, punishes them. Consequently, those primitive religions in which the punishing deity is at the same time the author of the moral evil for which men are punished are not so very remote from the Jewish-Christian myth which considers the justice of God as compatible with his omnipotence, because it still maintains the primitive idea of absolute liability. In this connection a flood tale of the Algonquin Indians is significant. A serpent (one may not be wrong in suspecting in it an ancestral soul) is the "foe" and "great evil" which brings sin to men and then punishes them cruelly. This is the form in which the myth has been handed down to us:

Long ago came the powerful serpent (*Maskanako*) when men had become evil. The strong serpent was the foe of the beings, and they became embroiled, hating each other. Then they fought and despoiled each other, and were not peaceful. And the small men (*Mattapewi*) fought with the keeper of the dead (*Nihanlowit*). Then the Strong Serpent resolved all men and beings to destroy immediately. The Black Serpent, monster, brought the snake-water rushing, the wide waters rushing, wide to the hills, everywhere spreading, everywhere destroying. . . . . Then the waters ran off, it was dry on mountain and plain, and the great evil went elsewhere by the path of the cave.[562]

The genuine old Algonquin legend of the flood seems, according to Frazer,[563] to be the following, which was found among the Chippeway Indians:[564] The medicine man Wis-kay-tchach, while hunting, loses a young wolf, his "nephew," who is then killed by some water lynxes. In order to avenge the wolf, Wis tries to kill one of these beasts but succeeds only in wounding it. The creatures rush to a river, which overflows its banks and floods the whole country. This same tale can be found in various versions among other tribes. All show the same motives: vengeance for the killing of the wolf and countervengeance in the form of a flood.

According to a fable of the Tinneh Indians, the flood was foreseen by an old man who warned his fellows, but all in vain. They were all drowned.[565] In another fable of the same tribe the flood comes as an act of vengeance.[566] The Loucheux Indians explain the flood as punishment for the killing of a raven.[567] A tale of the Tlingit Indians also describes the flood as punishment for the attempted murder of Jelch, the raven.[568] In a tale of the Tsimshian Indians the flood is said to have been sent by heaven as a punishment for the ill-behavior of man.[569] According to a fable of the Kootenay Indians,[570] the flood was produced because a small gray bird, despite the prohibition of her husband, the chicken hawk, bathed in a certain lake. "Suddenly the water rises, and a giant . . . . comes forth, who seizes the woman[571] and ravishes her." Her husband is very angry when he learns of this, and, going to the lake, shoots the monster, who swallows up all the water, so there is none for the Indians to drink. The woman "pulls the arrow out of the giant's breast, whereupon the water rushes forth in torrents, and a flood is the result. . . . . In a variant of this legend the 'giant' is a 'big fish' . . . . it is the blood of the fish that causes the deluge. . . . . In another variant the 'giant' is a 'lake animal.' " The Twanas, an Indian tribe of the state of Washington, have a tradition of a deluge, from which only good Indians were saved.[572] In another tribe the flood is supposed to have been caused by the fact that a beaver, whose wife left him to marry a panther, cried for five days until the whole country was flooded with his tears.[573] Obviously, this is to be interpreted not only as an expression of pain but also as an act of vengeance.

It cannot be denied that many flood tales do not contain any trace of a motive of retribution.[574] This may be partly accounted for because in the texts handed down to us no reasons for the floods are given; this, in turn, is quite often due to the fact that the problem under consideration concerns the violation of a religious taboo. And primitive man, who is restrained on this point, may be inclined, when questioned by an explorer, to omit those parts of the tale which violate his self-consciousness because they reflect discredit on his ancestors. Another reason for the incompleteness of the material may be that explorers have not paid much attention to finding out the causes of the flood. This may be particularly true if some act which modern morality would not consider a "sin" seems to have been the cause. It must also be borne in mind that a motive of retribution which existed originally may have faded into insignificance or even have disappeared altogether. Considering the decisive importance which the principle of retribution has in the interpretation of nature of even the least civilized peoples and considering that primitive man is inclined to interpret those facts which directly affect him and which arouse his fear, such as illness, death, lightning, and earthquake, according to the principle of retribution, one may assume that, originally at least, this principle also appeared in many of those flood tales where it is no longer apparent today.[575]

PART II

GREEK RELIGION AND PHILOSOPHY

CHAPTER IV

THE IDEA OF RETRIBUTION IN GREEK RELIGION

46. THE IDEA OF RETRIBUTION IN THE SOUL BELIEF

THE close relationship between primitive man's belief in the soul and the idea of retribution has already been demonstrated. This soul belief, the nucleus of all religion and religious metaphysics, is in truth an ideology of retribution. It is obvious that in such highly developed religions as the Egyptian and Christian, the concept of a soul surviving after death serves the idea of retribution in so far as the soul is punished for the evil and rewarded for the good which man did in this world. Less often, however, has it been noted that belief in the soul, even in the most primitive religions, has essentially the same social function—only here the soul appears not as the object but as the subject of retribution. The soul does not represent a human being which, although dead, nevertheless survives in transcendental form and is to be rewarded or punished by a deity; rather, in primitive religions the soul is itself a punishing or a rewarding superhuman authority: it is itself a deity. Originally it exercises retribution upon the survivors solely on the basis of their behavior toward itself. Later on, however, it guarantees the social order by its specific reactions toward the lawful or unlawful conduct of the members of the group.

It is, however, not within the scope of the present study to describe in greater detail this oldest religious idea or to prove that the two basic forms which the principle of retribution assumes in the soul belief—the soul as object and the soul as subject of retribution—are only two typical stages in the development of this belief among many peoples.[1] Only the religion of the ancient Greeks is of interest here, not only because the two main stages of the soul belief become especially apparent and because the idea of retribution plays a decisive part, but, above all, because in the religious speculations of the Greeks lies the origin of their philosophy of nature in which the metamorphosis of the principle of retribution into the law of causality has been accomplished.

47. The Supposedly Amoral Character of Greek Religion

When one speaks of Greek religion, one usually refers to the Homeric religion of the Olympic gods, for this was the dominant religion from the time it was shaped in the two immortal epics until the decline of Greek culture.[2] This relatively rational and aesthetically oriented faith in the Olympic gods, sustained by the national consciousness, was the belief of the ruling class. But underneath this religious stratum, in the lower class of the population, another religion survived which originated in the pre-Homeric, even pre-Hellenic, times but which continued its religious traditions, including worship of the dead and belief in demons.[3] It is true that the Olympic Zeus religion, as an upper-class creed,[4] had overcome the spirits, demons, and chthonian deities of the older religion; but it never succeeded in wholly suppressing this belief.[5] It was probably this belief surging up from a lower religious layer which strongly influenced the mystical doctrines of the Orphics and Pythagoreans, which appear in the seventh and sixth centuries, as well as the Eleusinian mysteries.[6]

An examination of the sociological function of the Greek religion and of the importance which it has as an ideology for Greek society leads one first to analyze the official religion of the ruling group. This religion is so utterly different from what used to be regarded in Christianity as religion that it is often asserted that the Greeks had no "true," no "real," religion. Such a judgment is correct only if one considers Christianity as *the* religion par excellence, a view which can hardly be maintained. Despite the difference between the Greek and Christian concepts of God—the Greek deity is neither the cause nor the creator of the world; he is not omnipotent, and he cannot, although himself immortal, avert death from human beings—and, despite the fact that the Greeks attributed many human characteristics to their gods, in one point there is a striking similarity: the Greek deity, like the Christian, is a just deity. Believing people never had any doubt of his justice. The idea of an unjust deity is, not only for the pious Christian but also for the pious Greek, a *contradictio in adjecto*.[7] It is a deep-rooted conviction that the gods rule the world justly. Justice is such an essential quality of the gods that "one would begin to doubt the very existence of the gods and thus of all worship if it could not actually make itself manifest."[8] If the gods are not just, then they do not exist;

but, as certainly as they do exist, they are just. Inasmuch as the Greek spirit is based on religion, it is filled with this conviction. And in the opinion of the Greeks, justice—as in all religious views of life—is the principle of retribution. To the Sybarites, who at a feast murdered a poet before the altar of Hera, the Delphic Oracle uttered these words:

> Go from my tripods, for thy hands profane
> Distilling blood my sacred pavements stain:
> From me expect no answer, who didst slay
> The Muses son; thou for his death must pay.
> None that transgresseth, vengeance can decline,
> Not though descended from Jove's mighty line
> He and his children, and their children must
> Expect due vengeance for that act unjust.[9]

Belief in divine retribution is expressed in Homer when the aged Laertes, hearing that the insolent suitors have been killed, exclaims: "Father Zeus, verily ye gods yet hold sway on high Olympus, if indeed the wooers have paid the price of their wanton insolence."[10] Or when it is said in the *Oinomaos* of Euripides: "When I see the evildoers perish then I believe in the existence of gods."[11] This tragic poet touches the deepest roots of the national religion when divine justice is doubted in his tragedies.

48. The Idea of Divine Retribution in the Homeric Religion

Admittedly, the idea of divine justice is not as strikingly expressed in the religious system represented in the Homeric epics as it is in Hesiod, who, because of his passion for justice, has frequently been compared with the old Jewish prophets.[12] The gods, under whose dominion the world is imagined, have to be just not so much in the religion of the ruling aristocracy, whose bard was Homer, as in the belief of the governed peasants, whose bard was Hesiod. But, also, among the upper classes of Homeric society there existed relationships involving superiority and inferiority, rights and duties, property and family matters; and, also, the positive order of these relationships has to be conceived of as just. Therefore, here, too, the government was considered to be instituted by God. In particular, the conviction existed that the king has obtained his power from Zeus. The *Iliad*, as well as the *Odyssey*, emphasizes the theory of the divine right of kings and the divine origin of the order issued by them. The scepter of Agamemnon, the symbol of his royal power, was manufactured by Hephaistus himself; Zeus gave it to Hermes, and he in turn to Pelops, from whom Agamemnon inherited it.[13]   The kings are always referred to as διοτρεφής ("cherished by Zeus");[14] their τιμή, i.e., their competence,[15] "is from Zeus, and Zeus, god of counsel, loveth them."[16] Not only the scepter but also the laws (θέμιστες) which the king is authorized to issue and administer come from Zeus. Nestor addresses Agamemnon as follows: "Most glorious son of Atreus, Agamemnon, king of men, with thee will I begin and with thee make an end, for that thou art king over many hosts, and to thee Zeus hath vouchsafed the sceptre and judgments [better: laws], that thou mayest take counsel for thy people."[17] Equally famous are these words: "No good thing is a multitude of lords; let there be one lord, one king, to whom the son of crooked-counselling Cronos hath vouchsafed the sceptre and judgments [laws], that he may take counsel for his people."[18]

The dominion over Ithaca is also represented in the *Odyssey* as a fee invested by Zeus.[19] Since the king has acquired his power from god, he is obligated to exercise it justly.   It is emphasized in the *Iliad* that Sarpedon guarded "Lycia by his justice [δίκῃσι] and his might;"[20] and Odysseus says to Agamemnon, exhorting him to a reconciliation with Achilles: "Towards others also shalt thou be more righteous [δικαιό-τερος] hereafter; for in no wise is it blame for a king to make amends to another, if so be he wax wroth without a cause."[21] In the *Odyssey* it is said: "A sceptred king must heed righteousness in his heart."[22]

Nestor is praised as he "who beyond all others knows judgments and wisdom and . . . . like unto an immortal he seems to me to look upon."[23] Of Odysseus it is said: "He wrought no wrong in deed or word to any man in the land, as the wont is of divine kings—one man they hate and another they love. Yet he never wrought iniquity at all to any man."[24] And Odysseus himself chants the glory of

the fame of some blameless king, who with the fear of the gods in his heart, is lord over many mighty men, upholding justice; and the black earth bears wheat and barley, and the trees are laden with fruit, the flocks bring forth young unceasingly, and the sea yields fish, all from his good leading; and the people prosper under him.[25]

Fertility is apparently the reward of the gods for the justice of the king who exercises dominion in their name.

There are several illegalities because of which human beings must expect retribution from the gods; as expressly stated in the *Iliad*, these include such sins as delicts against the gods, parents, and suppliants, injury of one's host, breach of contract, and, above all, perjury. The last is an especially grave crime because in the oath divine retribution is invoked. Without the idea of retribution the oath has no meaning. Also, a dishonest judgment is a delict to be punished by the gods.[26] Much cited are the words of the *Iliad* which picture how Zeus punishes with a tempest the crimes of men, who "by violence give crooked judgments in the place of gathering, and drive justice out, recking not of the vengeance of the gods."[27] For not only kings but also judges carry scepters; they, too, it is said in the *Iliad*, "guard the dooms by ordinance of Zeus."[28] There cannot be the least doubt that Homer represented the given social order as divinely willed. Consequently, it is comprehensible that the basic principle of this order—retribution—proceeded from the gods and that this was their most important function.

This divine retribution is the chief motive of both epic poems.

49. THE *Iliad*

The *Iliad* represents the fight against Troy and its destruction as just retribution for the crime which Paris, and therefore Troy, committed against Menelaus, and hence against the Greeks. To the Trojans, Menelaus says: "Wherewith ye have done despite unto me, ye evil dogs, and had no fear at heart of the grievous wrath of Zeus, that thundereth aloud, the god of hospitality, who shall some day destroy your high city."[29]

The downfall of the city of Troy is an act of retribution for still another crime—the breach of the solemnly concluded treaty whereby the warring parties swore to settle the war by a duel between Paris and Menelaus. Before the fight Homer relates how the Achaeans and Trojans prayed: "Father Zeus, that rulest from Ida, most glorious, most great, whichsoever of the twain it be that brought these troubles upon both peoples, grant that he may die and enter the house of Hades, whereas to us there may come friendship and oaths of faith."[30] And before the duel Menelaus himself beseeches: "Zeus, our king, grant that I may avenge me on him that was first to do me wrong, even on goodly Alexander, and subdue thou him beneath my hands; that many a one even of men yet to be may shudder to work evil to his host, that hath shown him friendship."[31]

The fight is thus presented as a judgment of God through which the wrongdoer may be punished. When the Trojan Pandarus, Lycaon's son, breaking the sworn treaty, injures Menelaus by a bowshot, Agamemnon says to his brother:

The Trojans have thus smitten thee, and trodden under foot the oaths of faith. Yet in no wise is an oath of none effect and the blood of lambs and drink-offerings of unmixed wine and the hand-clasps, wherein we put our trust. For even if for the moment the Olympian vouchsafeth not fulfilment, yet late and at length doth he fulfil them, and with a heavy price do men make atonement, even with their own heads and their wives and their children. For of a surety know I this in heart and soul: the day shall come when sacred Ilios shall be laid low, and Priam, and the people of Priam, with goodly spear of ash; and Zeus, son of Cronos, throned on high, that dwelleth in the heaven, shall himself shake over them all his dark aegis in wrath for this deceit. These things verily shall not fail of fulfilment.[32]

This is the expression of an unflinching belief in divine justice which is retribution; it is an inviolable law which, if not experienced immediately, most certainly is executed later. Therefore, it is undoubtedly not without reference to the idea of retribution that Homer, in the *Iliad*, represents Zeus, the "counsellor most high,"[33] with golden scales in his hand weighing out the fates to the two warring peoples:

The Father lifted on high his golden scales, and set therein two fates of grievous death, one for the horse-taming Trojans, and one for the brazen-coated Achaeans; then he grasped the balance by the midst and raised it, and down sank the day of doom of the Achaeans. So the Achaeans' fates settled down upon the bounteous earth and those of the Trojans were raised aloft toward wide heaven.[34]

The balance is the specific symbol of retributory justice. Since the fate of the Achaeans is judged too heavy, it is fitting that, for a time at least, they are deserted by the fortunes of war. It is significant that, in order to explain the misfortune of the Achaeans, the poet uses precisely this symbol and that he sees in the fate-weighing balance an essential attribute of Zeus. The lord of heaven consults by means of a balance the fate which, already here, is considered a general law above his influence. This general law is undoubtedly the law of retribution. This is clearly manifested in that peculiar episode in which is pictured how the "Erinyes checked the voice" of the horse Xanthus, which suddenly could speak and prophesied to Achilles his imminent death. The law of nature which denies animals the capacity of speech and which prevents human beings from seeing into the future is threatened with violation. Thereupon the Erinyes, goddesses of vengeance, intervene. The fact that it is their function to guarantee the order of nature proves that Homer considered it a legal order.[35]

The statement that justice is an essential quality of the Homeric gods and especially of Zeus seems to be incompatible[36] with the fact that obvious injustices are also traced to them. Thus it is Zeus himself who induces the Trojans to break the sworn treaty. Yielding to

Hera's urging, he says to Athene: "Haste thee with all speed unto the host into the midst of Trojans and Achaeans, and contrive how that the Trojans may be first in defiance of their oaths to work evil upon the Achaeans that exult in their triumph."[37]

The notion that an injustice committed by human beings is caused by the gods is the inevitable consequence of belief in the power of the deity which here, as in every religion, comes into conflict with the concept of the justice of the deity. Particularly in the *Iliad* is stress laid on the idea of the might of the gods and on the conviction that all human events are directed by the gods.[38] Therefore, the opinion that evil, too, can be traced to the gods is expressed by a poet, Aeschylus, whose belief in the justice of the deities is beyond doubt. Since he, with his deep religiosity, sees man only as the instrument of a powerful deity, he has to attribute not only good but also evil deeds to a divine will. Also the evildoer is directed by the deity: ". . . . when man hasteneth to his own undoing, God too taketh part with him";[39] "God planteth in mortal men the cause of sin whensoever he wills utterly to destroy a house."[40]

Nothing is more characteristic of this imputation of evil to the deity in a thoroughly religious-moral system than the figure of the vengeance-demon Alastor in Aeschylus. Alastor's specific function is to punish crimes—in other words, to execute retribution. But he always does it by involving the criminal in new crimes.[41] Also, the pious Sophocles writes:

> For none is wise save him to whom God pays honour;
> But he who looks towards heaven, even though it bid him
> Overstep right, must set himself to obey;
> For nought is shameful, when prescribed by heaven.[42]

The wrong caused by the deity is for the believer right—right in a higher sense, which he may not comprehend but which he nevertheless humbly accepts. Consistency, and the consequent lack of contradiction, does not belong to the equipment of a religious ideology.

How little the idea that the evil deeds of men are caused by the gods disturbs Homer's belief in the inviolability of the principle of retribution is illustrated by the fact that Zeus himself obviously presupposes this principle in the course of the discussion which leads to the command to Athene to induce the Trojans to break the oath. For he reproaches Hera for her persecution of the Trojans, inasmuch as they had committed no wrong. "Then stirred to hot anger, spake to her Zeus, the cloud-gatherer: 'Strange queen, wherein do Priam and the sons of Priam work thee ills so many, that thou ragest unceasingly to lay waste the well-built citadel of Ilios?'"[43] Then Zeus says to Hera, who wishes to destroy Troy:

> Do as thy pleasure is; let not this quarrel in time to come be to thee and me a grievous cause of strife between us twain. And another thing will I tell thee, and do thou lay it to heart. When it shall be that I, vehemently eager to lay waste a city, choose one wherein dwell men that are dear to thee, seek thou in no wise to hinder my anger, but suffer me.[44]

And Hera replies: "Not in their defence do I stand forth, nor account them too greatly. For even though I grudge thee, and am fain to thwart their overthrow. . . . .[45]

It is this same idea of retribution which Thetis accepts as a matter of course when she asks Zeus to avenge the wrong inflicted upon her son Achilles and in this connection refers to the many good deeds which she has rendered to the lord of heaven: "Father Zeus, if ever amid the immortals I gave thee aid by word or deed, fulfil thou me this prayer: do honour to my son, who is doomed to a speedy death beyond all men beside. . . . . But do thou show him honour, Olympian Zeus, lord of counsel."[46]

Retribution is regarded—always and everywhere—as a kind of trade in which good is exchanged for good and bad for bad. Thus it is said at the beginning of the *Iliad:* "Whoso obeys the gods, to him do they gladly give ear."[47]

In order to penetrate Homer's world, one has to consider that the poet represents the relationships between the gods according to the analogy of human relations—which is almost inevitable in a polytheistic system—and that the human element in the relationship between god and god does not prejudice primitive man in his concept of the relationship between god and·man. Particularly the conversation between Zeus and Hera is not to be understood as a critical representation of cruel and unjust gods who turn over to one another the cities of men. There was no intent on the poet's part to carry the religious ideology *ad absurdum*, as there was in Euripides, in whose *Hippolytus* the goddess Artemis explains why she does not defend her protégé against his enemy, Aphrodite:

> . . . . And this the Gods' wont is:—
> None doth presume to thwart the fixed design
> Willed by his fellow: still aloof we stand.[48]

The same thought which in Euripides is to be understood as an expression of ironic skepticism has in Homer the meaning of pious naïveté.

How can a primitive man explain that a city, although it has a power-ful guardian-god, is nevertheless destroyed? By all possible means ex-cept by questioning the authority of this guardian-god and thus divine justice.

50. THE *Odyssey*

Since the gods, according to primitive belief, rule over the world like an autocrat over the people, the question about their "moral-ity" has, from the viewpoint of the believer, no greater importance than the question about the "morality" of the monarch. Just as the latter, so the deity, since in his private relationships he does not appear as the ruler of the world, is not bound to abide by the norms which he has instituted for human conduct. Like an absolute monarch, the deity is above and beyond the law. Everything that would be a sin or a crime if committed by a man is not and cannot be such if it is com-mitted by a deity. In this respect Zeus is an absolute monarch, who, without having personally to be moral, guarantees the morality of man-kind by administering the principle of retribution. Much of what ap-pears to us as the "immorality" of the Greek gods is to be traced back to the fact that Homeric theology had not yet solved the problem of theodicy in the way the dualistic religions have, namely, by dividing the deity into two beings—a god and a countergod, Ormuzd and Ahri-man—and by imputing to the former the good, to the latter the evil.

The fact that the Greek deity has also to play the role of the devil is more a technical than a moral defect of this religious system. Besides in Homer a tendency can be found to supply a devil theology, an attempt to insert, with respect to the evil committed by man, an intermediate being between the evildoer and the deity: Ate. The latter's function is to "blind," i.e., to take away someone's brain, after which evil may be presented to that person as good and good as evil.[49] Nevertheless, the human being, even though misguided by the evil spirit, remains re-sponsible for his behavior and liable to retribution. Indeed, the *Odys-sey* expressly rejects the imputation of evil to the gods and defends the modern thesis that the imputation of evil must not go beyond the re-sponsible human being. With reference to the crime of Aegisthus, Zeus says:

Look you now, how ready mortals are to blame the gods. It is from us, they say, that evils come, but they even of themselves, through their own blind folly, have sor-rows beyond that which is ordained. Even as now Aegisthus, beyond that which was ordained, took to himself the wedded wife of the son of Atreus, and slew him on his return, though well he knew of sheer destruction, seeing that we spake to him before.[50]

Whoever commits a wrong acts "beyond that which was ordained," i.e., he acts against that destiny which is divine retribution.

Belief in this principle pervades the epic poem, which culminates in the judgment inflicted by Zeus through Odysseus upon the insolent suitors. Thus Pallas Athene speaks to Telemachus: "Out on it! Thou hast of a truth sore need of Odysseus that is gone, that he might put forth his hands upon the shameless wooers";[51] and: "Yet these things verily lie on the knees of the gods, whether he shall return and wreak vengeance in his halls, or whether he shall not."[52]

The idea of a just god appears even more distinctly and clearly in the *Odyssey* than in the *Iliad*, where too much stress is laid on the heroic element and thus on the power of Zeus. Consequently, in the *Iliad* the idea of justice has to recede into the background. In the *Odyssey*, however, there are frequent references in which the notion of divine justice is expressed. And it is always the principle of retribution in which the poet sees the idea of justice. In the first book Telemachus says to the malicious suitors: "But I will call upon the gods that are forever, if haply Zeus may grant that deeds of requital may be wrought. Without atonement, then, should ye perish within my halls."[53] This idea of divine retribution—ever a chief motive of the epic—reappears as soon as Odysseus arrives back in his homeland. Since he does not immediately recognize the land but thinks himself betrayed by the Phaeacians who had promised to conduct him to Ithaca, he exclaims: "May Zeus, the suppliant's god, requite them, who watches over all men, and punishes him that sins."[54] With reference to the malicious suitors Eumaeus says to Odysseus:

Verily the blessed gods love not reckless deeds, but they honour justice and the righteous deeds of men. Even cruel foemen that set foot on the land of others, and Zeus gives them booty, and they fill their ships and depart for home—even on the hearts of these falls great fear of the wrath of the gods.[55]

And of the king of the Egyptians who prevented his soldiers from killing Odysseus, the latter says: "But he warded them off, and had regard for the wrath of Zeus, the stranger's god, who above all others, hath indignation of evil deeds."[56] When Menelaus is retained in Egypt, he regards his delay as punishment for a committed wrong.[57] Athene appears to Penelope in a dream and consoles her: Telemachus will return home, for he has not committed any sins against the gods.[58] Since the gods exercise retribution, they must know the good and evil

of men. Therefore to Antinous, who treated Odysseus, disguised as
a beggar, in a cruel fashion, the suitors say:

> Antinous, thou didst not well to strike the wretched wanderer. Doomed man that
> thou art, what if haply he be some god come down from heaven! Aye, and the gods
> in the guise of strangers from afar put on all manner of shapes, and visit the cities,
> beholding the violence and the righteousness of men.[59]

And when Odysseus says to the supplicating Medon, who had dealt
kindly and well with Telemachus, "Be of good cheer, for he has delivered thee and saved thee, that thou mayest know in thy heart and
tell also to another, how far better is the doing of good deeds than of
evil,"[60] it sounds as if the poet intended his hero to utter the moral
principle of the poem. The *Odyssey*, too, is an epic of divine justice.

This view of the Homeric poems, especially of the *Iliad*, is at vari-
ance with the more recent interpretations which, in contradistinction
to the older viewpoint, deny any ethical content to the Homeric poems,
especially to the *Iliad*.[61] That the older interpretation is correct is substantiated by what has been said so far. It is generally accepted that
later Greek works of poetry, history, and philosophy show belief in
divine justice. Therefore, only the most essential references are mentioned to illustrate the decisive importance of the idea of retribution
in the religiously oriented literature of the centuries following Homer.

51. The Idea of Divine Retribution in the Post-Homeric Period

The poems sung by the peasant Hesiod, the shepherd of Ascra, do
not come from the heights of mankind, like the epics of Homer, but
from the lower, although not from the lowest, sections of society. More
passionately and more strongly, therefore, than the *Iliad* and the *Odyssey* does the *Works and Days* profess a belief in divine justice. Inasmuch
as the experience of an injured right forms the basis for this poem, the
conviction of its sacredness appears all the more clearly. Because men
break the law, Zeus must protect it; this law is Dike, "the daughter
of Zeus."[62] Despite all defeats, she must be victorious in the end.
Hesiod calls to his brother Perses, to whom he lost in a hereditary dispute because of the partiality of the judges:

> But you, Perses, listen to right and do not foster violence; for violence is bad for
> a poor man. Even the prosperous cannot easily bear its burden. . . . . The better
> path is to go by on the other side towards justice; for Justice beats Outrage when she
> comes at length to the end of the race.[63]

Breach of law must entail disaster; compliance with law, however, brings salvation.

> And she [Justice], wrapped in mist, follows to the city and haunts of the people, weeping, and bringing mischief to men, even to such as have driven her forth in that they did not deal straightly with her.—But they who give straight judgements to strangers and to the men of the land, and go not aside from what is just, their city flourishes, and the people prosper in it: Peace, the nurse of children, is abroad in their land, and all-seeing Zeus never decrees cruel war against them. Neither famine nor disaster ever haunt men who do true justice.—But for those who practice violence and cruel deeds far-seeing Zeus, the son of Cronos, ordains a punishment.[64]

Certainly there is much injustice in this world—almost more than one can bear[65]—and often the lawbreakers are able to maintain the power. But eventually Zeus punishes the wrongdoer: "the son of Cronos lays great trouble upon the people, famine and plague together, so that the men perish away, and their women do not bear children, and their houses become few, through the contriving of Olympian Zeus."[66] Divine retribution is certain, especially since no wrong can remain hidden from the gods: ". . . . for the deathless gods are near among men and mark all those who oppress their fellows with crooked judgment and reck not the anger of the gods."[67] Further: "The eye of Zeus, seeing all and understanding all, beholds these things too, if so he will, and fails not to mark what sort of justice is this that the city keeps within it."[68]

In order to guarantee the most important condition of divine justice, namely, knowledge of the committed wrong, Hesiod introduces certain intermediate beings between Zeus and men, whose task it is to watch over the doings of human beings. In his account of the various ages he reports that the men of the golden age were changed by Zeus into angels, who "are kindly, delivering from harm, and guardians of mortal men; for they roam everywhere over the earth, clothed in mist and keep watch on judgements and cruel deeds, givers of wealth; for this royal right also they received."[69] Later, following the assurance that these immortals watch for "crooked judgements" in order to exercise retribution, it is said: "For upon the bounteous earth Zeus has thrice ten thousand spirits, watchers of mortal men, and these keep watch on judgements and deeds of wrong as they roam, clothed in mist, all over the earth."[70] An unwavering belief in just retribution completely fills the imagination of this poet.

When Hesiod speaks of law, he means the law prevailing among men—we would say the "positive law"—which is for him at the same time divine justice, represented as a deity living on Olympus. Law is a specifically human institution, unknown to animals. "For the son of Cronos has ordained this law for men, that fishes and beasts and winged fowls should devour one another, for right is not in them; but to mankind he gave right which proves for the best."[71]

This typical human good, however, "is virgin Justice [Δίκη], the daughter of Zeus, who is honoured and reverenced among the gods who dwell on Olympus."[72] Since she lives also among men, she may also be insulted by them. "Whenever anyone hurts her with lying slander, she sits beside her father, Zeus the son of Cronos, and tells him of men's wicked heart, until the people pay for the mad folly of their princes who, evilly minded, pervert judgement and give sentence crookedly."[73]

The people, the mass of the powerless, pay for the wrongs of their powerful rulers. Resentment against the ruling class is obviously at the basis of Hesiod's concept of justice. Therefore one finds in his work a retribution formula which is typical of the indignation of the weak against the strong, the poor against the rich—that principle according to which justice is simply a reversal of the existing situation, since the existing situation is unjust. Thus Jesus preached that "that which is highly esteemed among men is abomination in the sight of God"[74] and that "many that are first shall be last; and the last first."[75] Enunciating a similar doctrine, Hesiod glorified Zeus as the god "through whom mortal men are famed or unfamed, sung or unsung alike, as great Zeus wills. For easily he makes strong, and easily he brings the strong man low; easily he humbles the proud and raises the obscure, and easily he straightens the crooked and blasts the proud."[76]

It is particularly interesting when a legislator like Solon appears as poet, for the lawmaker is the competent ideologist of divine justice. In the preserved fragments of his poems is repeatedly the unbending conviction expressed that divine justice must necessarily come true in life because retribution exists on this earth. Thus it is said in the poem which is directed against the avarice of the state's rulers: "Nor have [they] heed of the awful foundation of Justice, who is so well aware in her silence of what is and what hath been, and soon or late cometh alway to avenge."[77] Similarly in another fragment the poet proclaims:

For the works of man's wanton violence endure not for long, but Zeus surveyeth the end of every matter, and suddenly, even as the clouds in Spring are quickly scattered by a wind that stirreth the depths of the billowy unharvested sea, layeth waste the fair fields o'er the wheat-bearing land, and reaching even to the high heaven where the Gods sit, maketh the sky clear again to view, till the strength of the Sun shineth fair over the fat land, and no cloud is to be seen any more,—even such is the vengeance of Zeus. He is not quick to wrath, like us, over each and every thing, yet of him that hath a wicked heart is He aware alway unceasing, and such an one surely cometh out plain at the last. Aye, one payeth to-day, another to-morrow; and those who themselves flee and escape the pursuing destiny of Heaven, to them vengeance cometh alway again, for the price of their deeds is paid by their innocent chil-. dren or else by their seed after them.[78]

An unjust good brings no blessing. This lesson is also taught by Theognis. Treasure unlawfully acquired "at the first him seemeth to get him gain, but in the end it becometh bad likewise, and the mind of the Gods overcometh him."[79] But, whereas Solon advocates the viewpoint of hereditary liability and regards as a matter of course that sons are punished for their fathers' sins, Theognis protests energetically against such views.

Father Zeus, I would it were the Gods' pleasure that wanton outrage should delight the wicked if so they choose, but that whosoever did acts abominable and of intent, disdainfully, with no regard for the Gods, should thereafter pay penalty himself, and the ill-doing of the father become no misfortune unto the children after him; and that such children of an unrighteous sire as act with righteous intent, standing in awe of thy wrath, O Son of Cronus, and from the beginning have loved the right among their fellow-townsmen, these should not pay requital for the transgression of a parent. I say, would that this were the Gods' pleasure; but alas, the doer escapeth and another beareth the misfortune afterward.[80]

Despite his obviously displayed piety, the poet now and then seems to have doubts about the system of divine justice. He queries: "How then is it, Son of Cronus, that Thy mind can bear to hold the wicked and the righteous in the same esteem . . . . ?"[81] And so, following the earlier cited reference in which the poet advocated individual liability rather than hereditary liability, it is said:

Yet how can it be rightful, O King of the Immortals, that a man that hath no part in unrighteous deeds, committing no transgression nor any perjury, but is a righteous man, should not fare aright? What other man living, or in what spirit, seeing this man, would thereafter stand in awe of the Immortals, when one unrighteous and wicked that avoideth not the wrath of God or man, indulgeth wanton outrage in the fulness of his wealth, whereas the righteous be worn and wasted with grievous Penury?[82]

The poem nevertheless ends with a request to avoid sins. Occasionally it is doubted that justice comes true on earth; but there is no doubt that this justice consists in retribution. The desire to complete the Homeric religion in order somehow to maintain the idea that the happenings of the world correspond with the concept of justice becomes obvious here.

52. The Idea of Divine Retribution in Greek Tragedy

The problems of justice and law play an important part in the Greek tragedies.[83] They are the center of most of the dramas of Aeschylus and Sophocles, the tragic element of which consists mainly in a conflict between the individual and the prevailing social order. The dramas glorify the sacredness of the social order and the fact that it is divinely willed. Thus the religious character of the tragedies of Aeschylus and Sophocles culminates in the demand·for humble submission to the authority which represents itself as divine but which cannot be separated from the authority of the state invested in human beings.

It is the authority of the divine law. In Sophocles' *Oedipus the King* the chorus sings:

> My lot be still to lead
> The life of innocence and fly
> Irreverence in word or deed,
> To follow still those laws ordained on high
> Whose birthplace is the bright ethereal sky.
> No mortal birth they own,
> Olympus their progenitor alone:
> Never shall they slumber in oblivion cold,
> The god in them is strong and grows not old.[84]

Just as Sophocles declares that the laws reside in heaven, so does Aeschylus declare that the maintenance of the law is indispensable for a god-fearing government. In the tragedy *The Persians*, the chorus says of the prosperous rule of Darius, "a monarch like a God" (which is contrasted with the insolence of Xerxes, who dared to defy the gods):

> For first we showed the world our noble hosts;
>   And laws of tower-like strength
> Directed all things. . . . .[85]

The gods guard and watch over the maintenance of the laws. Thus in Aeschylus' tragedy, *The Suppliant Maidens*, the chorus of Danaides, who fled to Argos, prays: "But, ye gods of our race, hearken unto me, and regard with favour the cause of righteousness; if ye grant not unto youth to have fulfilment of its unholy desires, but eagerly abhor wantonness, ye would be altogether righteous toward marriage."[86] And to the king the suppliant chorus says: "Take Justice as thy ally, and render judgment for the cause approved righteous by the gods."[87]

The law which comes from Zeus is, in Aeschylus and Sophocles, as in Hesiod, personified as the goddess Justice (Dike). She is the most frequently mentioned deity in Greek tragedy; her importance to the older drama is tremendous. In *The Libation-bearers* of Aeschylus, it is said of her, the goddess of punishment: "And he hath come whose part is the crafty vengeance of stealthy attack; and in the battle his hand was guided by her who is in very truth daughter of Zeus, breathing wrath to the death upon her foes. Justice we mortals call her name, hitting well the mark."[88] And in *Agamemnon:*

But Righteousness [Dike] shineth in smoke-begrimed dwellings and holdeth in esteem him that is virtuous. From gold-bespangled mansions, where men's hands are defiled, she departeth with averted eyes and taketh her way to pure homes; she worships not the power of wealth stamped counterfeit by the praise of men, and she guideth all things to their proper end.[89]

The Dike of the tragic poets is an avenging goddess, who appears in closest connection with the Erinyes.[90] According to the older tragedy, the essence of law and justice is the principle of retribution arising out of blood revenge. In the *Agamemnon* of Aeschylus, Clytemnestra justifies the murder of her husband as an act of retribution for the sacrifice of her daughter Iphigenia. She swears: "This too thou hearest, this the righteous sanction of my oath: By Justice [Dike], exacted for my child, by Ate, by the Avenging Spirit [Erinys], unto whom I sacrificed yon man . . . ."[91] After the crime Aegisthus says:

Hail gracious light of the day of retribution! At last the hour is come when I can say that the gods who avenge mortal men look down from on high upon the crimes of earth—now that, to my joy, I behold this man lying here in a robe spun by the Avenging Spirits and making full payment for the deeds contrived in craft by his father's hand.[92]

Atreus, Agamemnon's father, killed Aegisthus' brothers when they were infants and offered them to Thyestes, Aegisthus' father, as food. "But grown to manhood, justice has brought me back again. . . . . So even death were sweet to me now that I behold him in the toils of justice."[93]

Just as Aegisthus regards his vengeance on Agamemnon as an act of justice, so the chorus in *The Libation-bearers* interprets the murder of Aegisthus and Clytemnestra, desired by Electra and committed by Orestes, as an act of justice. In the introductory dialogue between Electra and the chorus, held at the tomb of Agamemnon, Electra asks how she should pray and especially what she should request for the murderers of her father.

ELECTRA: What shall I pray? Instruct my inexperience, prescribe the form.
CHORUS: That upon them there may come some one or god or mortal—
ELECTRA: As judge or as avenger, meanest thou?
CHORUS: Say in plain speech "one who shall take life for life."
ELECTRA: And is this a righteous thing for me to ask of Heaven?
CHORUS: Righteous? How not? To requite an enemy evil for evil![94]

H

Accordingly, Electra prays to the gods that "there appear one who will avenge thee, father, and that thy slayers may be slain in just retribution ('Tis thus I interrupt my prayer for good, for them uttering this prayer for evil). But to us be thou a bringer of blessings to the upper world by favour of the gods and Earth and Justice [Dike] crowned with victory."[95]

For Orestes she requests aid in his bloody crime:

> May Might and Justice, with Zeus the third,
> Supreme over all, lend thee their aid![96]

Since Orestes commits the crime at the order of Phoebus, he regards it as an act of justice.

> After injustice 'tis justice I demand as of my right.
> Hearken, O Earth, and ye honoured powers below![97]

And he prays to his dead father: "Either send Justice [Dike] to battle for those dear to thee, or grant us in turn to get like grip of them, if indeed after defeat thou wouldst in turn win victory."[98] The chorus announces the crime of Orestes in these words:

> But the keen and bitter sword is nigh the breast and driveth home its blow at the bidding of Justice. For verily the unrighteousness of him who hath unrighteously transgressed the sovereign majesty of Zeus lieth on the ground trampled under foot. The anvil of Justice is planted firm. Destiny [Aisa] fashioneth her arms and forgeth her sword betimes; and the famed and deep-brooding Spirit of Vengeance is bringing the son into the house, to requite at last the pollution of blood shed of old.[99]

After the crime has been committed, the chorus sings: "As unto Priam and his sons justice came at last in crushing retribution, so unto Agamemnon's house came a twofold lion, twofold slaughter. Unto the uttermost hath the exile, the suppliant of Pytho's god, fulfilled his course, urged justly on by counsels from above."[100] Orestes himself, after the murder has been committed, calls to Helios that he "in the day of judgment may be present as my witness that with just cause I pursued this death."[101]

In the *Electra* of Sophocles, which deals with the same subject, the crime of Orestes is also interpreted as execution of a divine command and judgment. Orestes relates:

> Know then that when I left thee to consult
> The Pythian oracle and learn how best
> To execute just vengeance for my sire
> On those that slew him, Phoebus answered thus:
> Trust not to shields or armed hosts, but steal
> The chance thyself the avenging blow to deal.[102]

Foreboding the deed, the chorus sings:

> Count me a prophet false, a witless wight,
> If Justice, who inspires my prophecy,
> Comes not, my child, to vindicate the right.
> She comes and that right speedily.[103]

And when the heroine in Sophocles' *Antigone*, in order to justify having buried the corpse of her traiterous brother, Polyneices, against the order of King Creon, calls upon "the immutable unwritten laws of Heaven," she is, of course, thinking of the law of retribution:

> They were not born to-day nor yesterday;
> They die not; and none knoweth whence they sprang.
> I was not like, who feared no mortal's frown,
> To disobey these laws and so provoke
> The wrath of Heaven. . . . .[104]

The principle of retribution, personified by the goddess Dike, is formulated in various ways. Thus in Aeschylus: "The spoiler is spoiled, the slayer maketh atonement. Yet, while Zeus abideth on his throne, it abideth that to him who doeth it shall be done—for it is an ordinance."[105] Or:

Ye mightly Fates, through the power of Zeus vouchsafe fulfilment thus even as Justice now turneth! "For word of hate let word of hate be said," crieth Justice aloud as she exacteth the debt, "and for murderous stroke let murderous stroke be paid." "To him that doeth, it shall be done by," so saith a precept thrice-aged.[106]

And in Sophocles:

> But the proud sinner, or in word or deed,
> That will not Justice heed,
> Nor reverence the shrine
> Of images divine,
> Perdition seize his vain imaginings,
> If, urged by greed profane,
> He grasps at ill-got gain,
> And lays an impious hand on holiest things.[107]

Or:

> Heaven's Justice never smites
> Him who ill with ill requites.
> But if guile with guile contend,
> Bane, not blessing, is the end.[108]

53. The Retribution Dramas of Aeschylus and Sophocles

Several tragedies of Aeschylus and Sophocles are entirely dominated by this principle of retribution as the idea of divine justice, especially

the *Oresteia*. The passages already quoted show that the murder of the
returning Agamemnon, perpetrated by Clytemnestra and Aegisthus,
is interpreted as retribution. And the killing of these two guilty lovers
by Orestes is explained in the same way. The end of the second tragedy deals with the retribution on Orestes. The Erinyes appear to him
and begin his persecution. The third tragedy, the *Eumenides*, brings
the solution by terminating the chain of retribution which, according
to the older idea of justice, is endless: Orestes is released by Apollo
and Pallas Athene from the fury of the Erinyes, who, calmed by the
two gods, become worshiped in Athens as Eumenides. The actual solution of the dramatic knot is handled as follows: In order to decide
whether Orestes is guilty and whether there is need for the Erinyes to
exercise retribution, Pallas Athene, who has herself been called upon
for a judgment, institutes a tribunal. Thus it is apparent in this drama
how the idea of retribution, exercised by a court as an impartial authority, detaches itself from the more primitive principle of blood revenge.

In his drama *The Persians*, Aeschylus represents the Greek victory
as the just retribution of the gods. "The outcome of the battle showed
that the gods rule justly."[109] In the tragedy the spirit of Darius says
that

heaps of dead shall make known, even to the third generation, a voiceless record for
the eyes of men that mortal man needs must not vaunt him overmuch. For presumptuous pride, when it has burgeoned, bears as its fruit a crop of calamity, whence it
reaps a plenteous harvest of tears.—Mark that such are the penalties for deeds like
these and hold Athens and Hellas in your memory. Let no one of you, through dis-
dain of present fortune and lust for more, squander his abundant wealth. Zeus, of a
truth, is a chastiser of overweening pride and corrects with heavy hand.[110]

The *Electra* of Sophocles is also a tragedy of retribution; it deals
with the same subject as *The Libation-bearers* of Aeschylus, but it is
noteworthy that in Sophocles' tragedy the Erinyes do not appear to
Orestes on the stage after he has murdered his mother. The tragedies *Oedipus the King* and *Oedipus at Colonus*, both by Sophocles, are also
dominated by the concept of retribution. In the second tragedy, however, an important modification of this principle may be distinguished.
A more refined sense of justice rejects the notion of absolute liability,
according to which the perpetrator is responsible even though the result of his act was achieved involuntarily and unforeseen. Since Oedipus did not know that the man whom he had killed was his father and
that the woman whom he had married was his mother, the retribu-

tion exercised on him according to the old tale is no longer acceptable. A new idea appears: only for a result brought about intentionally is the perpetrator to be held responsible. In that sense Oedipus suffered innocently. Sophocles expresses this in a particularly striking way. Oedipus settles in a prohibited place consecrated to the Erinyes, the goddesses who, above all, avenge murders committed on relatives. This is a place which, according to the traditional notion of retribution, nobody should fear more than Oedipus himself. But, just as Aeschylus' Orestes evades the vengeance of the Erinyes because blood revenge is replaced by the jurisdiction of courts, so the Erinyes remain well disposed toward Oedipus because absolute liability, liability for the result, is supplanted by culpability, by liability for the intent. Despite warning, Oedipus remains in the prohibited place and there finds a peaceful end after a suffering life. He does not, like other people, die feeling the pains of death. The gods—it is not known whether those of heaven or earth—take him away.[111] His tomb afterward affords protection to the country. The characters of Orestes and Oedipus, the tragedies of Aeschylus and Sophocles, mark two important, perhaps even the two most important, stages in the development of the idea of retribution, which for those times coincided with the idea of law.

The whole development is accomplished within the compass of the principle of retribution. This principle is and remains for both Greek dramatists identical with justice. Despite the refinement which the principle of retribution achieved through its detachment from blood revenge and the abandonment of absolute liability, justice still has not, as for modern people, the serene connotation of liberation from evil, the character of redemption. Justice is represented rather as inexorable destiny gloomily hanging over man.[112] In *Oedipus the King* of Sophocles the hero announces solemnly at the beginning of the play that he intends to avenge the murder of Laius in order to free his country from disaster. He ends his speech as follows:

> My loyal subjects who approve my acts,
> May Justice [Dike], our ally, and all the gods
> Be gracious and attend you evermore.[113]

It is Justice from whom salvation is expected. But what does she bring? New disaster for him who seeks her. Only the wisdom and knowledge of Teiresias can put Oedipus on the trail of the murderer. But the seer whom Oedipus seeks at first refuses to disclose the truth and thus to allow justice to take its course. Scolded by the king, he sighs: "Well, it will come what will, though I be mute."[114] The inexorable destiny, foreseen by the soothsayer, is the justice sought by the king.

Justice is the goddess Dike bearing the executioner's sword, forged by Aisa, goddess of destiny; thus Aeschylus pictures her in *The Libation-bearers*. In Sophocles' *Oedipus* this character of Justice as destiny becomes clearly apparent. The poet evidently intends to picture the hero as innocent; nevertheless, he does not regard the destiny decreed by the gods as unjust, inasmuch as it conforms with the old idea of retribution. Therefore, even in this relatively advanced stage of the development of morality these dramatic poets cling to an idea which is to be regarded as the real gain of the belief in divine justice, namely, the unconditional submission to the natural and social order which is established by gods and which manifests itself even in a mysterious fate.

And so beside the dramas of retribution stands the drama of obedience, the *Prometheus Bound* of Aeschylus. It preaches obedience to the prevailing authority, represented by Zeus; and, more than any other drama, it shows Destiny or Fate as a power superior even to the king of the gods. In this work, too, the motive of retribution plays a decisive role. Prometheus is punished because he disobeyed Zeus. But he consoles himself with the thought that Zeus' dominion will not be eternal. He constantly refers to this hope: "The Prince of the Blessed shall have need of me to reveal the new design and by whom he shall be stripped of his sceptre and his dignities."[115] Zeus is not absolutely the highest authority. Destiny is superior to him. At the beginning of the tragedy Prometheus says: "My allotted doom I needs must bear as lightly as I may, knowing that the might of Necessity brooketh no resistance."[116] That Fate is superior to Zeus is particularly stressed by the poet in a dialogue between Prometheus and the leader of the chorus:

PROMETHEUS: Not thus, nor yet, is fulfilling Fate destined to bring this end to pass. When I have been bent by pangs and tortures infinite, thus only am I to escape my bondage. Art is feebler far than Necessity.

CHORUS: Who then is the steersman of Necessity?

PROMETHEUS: The triform Fates and mindful Furies.

CHORUS: Can it be that Zeus hath lesser power than they?

PROMETHEUS: Aye, in that at least he cannot escape what is foredoomed.

CHORUS: Why, what is foredoomed for Zeus save to hold eternal sway?

PROMETHEUS: This thou must not learn as yet: be not importunate.

CHORUS: 'Tis some solemn secret, surely, that thou dost enshroud in mystery.

PROMETHEUS: Bethink ye of some other theme, for 'tis in no wise meet time to discourse of this.[117]

Zeus overthrew the dominion of his father Cronus; therefore his sway will also be overcome. Nevertheless, one must not refuse to obey his commands; thus it is just that Prometheus be punished. Zeus's dominion and the whole universe with it are under the same law, according to which the world of men is ruled by the Olympian gods, under Necessity, the helm of which is guided by the Erinyes. This universal law, too, is that of retribution.

54. EURIPIDES

With Euripides, Greek tragedy turns from a religious to a national ideology. But the law suffers no loss of authority, although it is divested of the glory of religion. The idea that the social order is divinely willed is somewhat shaken; however, this has no consequences for the validity of the social order itself. Despite strong doubt in the gods—indeed, even in spite of unconcealed denial of their very existence—the tragedies of Euripides manifest a deep awe of Dike, and an unreserved glorification of the Nomos.[118] In the *Suppliants* Theseus makes this more than skeptical assertion:

> O fools, learn ye the real ills of men:—
> Our life is conflict all: of mortals some
> : Succeed ere long, some late, and straightway some;
> While fortune sits a queen: worship and honour
> The unblest gives her, so to see good days;
> The prosperous extols her, lest her breeze
> Fail him one day. . . . .[119]

But the chorus joins in with the following words:

> Fear not: while thou upholdest Justice' light,
> Thou shalt not fear what men can say of thee.[120]

In Euripides' *Cyclops*, Polyphemus reviles the gods as the alleged givers of human laws:

> Eat plenty and drink plenty every day,
> And never worry—*that* is, so I say,
> The Zeus that suits a level-headed man;
> But as for those who framed an artful plan
> Of laws, to puzzle plain men's lives with these—
> I snap my thumb at them. . . . [121]

Nevertheless, the whole drama is a derision of the cultureless and therefore lawless anarchy of the Cyclops.

In *Electra* skeptical doubts are expressed with respect to the myth of the Golden Lamb:

It is told of the singers—scant credence such story,
Touching secrets of Gods, of my spirit hath won—
That the Sun from that vision turned backward the glory
Of the gold of the face of his flaming throne,
With the scourge of his wrath in affliction repaying
Mortals for deeds in their mad feuds done.
Yet it may be the tale liveth, soul-affraying,
To bow us to Godward in lowly obeying.[121a]

But Electra says:

Let none dream, though at starting he run well,
That he outrunneth Justice, ere he touch
The very goal and reach the bourn of life.[122]

And the chorus sings: "Great is Justice' might."[123] Euripides' Justice (Dike), as it has rightly been asserted, is the poet's deity κατ' ἐξοχήν; it is retribution.

In *Helen* it is said:

None prospered ever by unrighteousness:
In righteousness all hope of safety dwells.[124]

And in *Hecuba:*

For wherever it cometh to pass that the rightful demand
Of justice's claim and the laws of the Gods be at one,
Then in ruinous bane for the sinner, O ruinous bane![125]

Elsewhere in this play the poet writes:

Foul deeds thou didst and awful penalty
A God hath laid on thee with heavy hand.[126]

A fragment of *Archelaus* reads: "Do you believe that Dike lives far from the mortals? No, she is very near and, unseen herself, she sees and knows everybody who deserves punishment. Never does one know whether she will quickly destroy the evil-doer."[127] And from a fragment of *Antiope:*

Tho' Justice, ere she come, be late,
Conceal'd by the behests of fate,
She menaces each villain's head.[128]

Similarly one reads in *Phrixus*, another work of which only parts have survived:

Whoever thinks, tho' daily he offend,
That he shall 'scape th' observance of the Gods,
Judges amiss, and finds himself entangled
In his own craft: for soon as Justice finds
An hour for retribution, he endures
The punishment his foul misdeeds deserve.[129]

That the Dike of Euripides is not the goddess of justice of the Zeus religion—in which case the poet would have had to have accepted the whole Olympian world and thus the polytheistic religion which he so violently opposed—is borne out by the following fragment from the drama *Melanippe:*

> How think you? Are they separate winged things,
> The sins of men; and rise each on his wings
> Up to the throne, where in a folded book
> Some angel writes, that God some day may look
> And utter judgment due? Not all God's sky
> Were wide enough to hold that registry;
> Not God's own eye see clear to deal each sin
> Its far-off justice. She is here, within,
> Not distant nor hereafter; with each deed
> Its judgment fellow-born, would ye but heed.[130]

This can only mean that Dike is not, as commonly believed, with Zeus. Dike is among us; we have only to open our eyes. Divine justice, it is true, does not exist, but there is a human justice. Law prevails even without religious ideology. One must have a sincere desire to see the facts and must not cloud one's views with ideologies. Euripides' Dike is not a transcendental goddess; she is the principle of earthly justice, immanent to the events.[131]

This idea of the immanence of justice is reinforced by the fact that Euripides often pictures justice as a function of time, so that justice and time are almost identical.[132] In a fragment of *Antiope*, Justice is called "Time's Daughter."[133] And in the remains of *Bellerophontes* it is said:

> The prosperous fortunes, and the haughty wealth
> Of an unrighteous man, we never ought
> To deem establish'd on a solid base,
> Or that the children of th' unjust can prosper:
> For Time, who from no Father springs, applies
> His levell'd line, and shews man's foul misdeeds.[134]

In *The Madness of Hercules* the chorus sings: "For no one ventures to contemplate the vicissitudes of time, having transgressed law, and given joy to lawlessness; and he breaks the dark chariot of wealth."[135] In a fragment of the first *Hippolytus* it is written: "Time, in its course, reveals everything."[136]

Dike is identified with Chronos (Time), and retribution is recognized as a function of time and thus as a general world law immanent to the events. This idea we will find again in the older philosophy of nature. There, as well as in Euripides, who is the poet of Greek rationalism, a tendency to replace the inviolable will of the deity by the

necessity of an impersonal fate may be perceived. In the tragedies of
Aeschylus and particularly of Sophocles it can be seen how the deity
coincides with fate. Indeed, for these two older dramatic poets fate
itself is still a deity, a deity mysterious to man but, nonetheless, just
and one which it is a moral duty to obey. However, in the tragedies of
Euripides, Dike, identified with fate, becomes almost an impersonal
principle, approximating the law of causality. This principle is endowed by the poet with various names, such as μοῖρα, τύχη, ἀνάγκη,
δαίμων, sometimes φύσις, or simply θεός. In the *Iphigeneia in Taurica*,
Athene says to King Thoas: "'Tis well: for thee, for Gods, is Fate too
strong."[137] No one, either man or god, can evade it. This idea is frequently expressed by the poet. Thus in *Alcestis* it is said:

> I have searched all truth with mine eyes;
> But naught more strong
> Than Fate [Necessity] have I found.[138]

And in *Bellerophontes:* "Powerless is everything against Necessity."[139]
In *The Madness of Hercules:*

> Whoso with eager struggling would writhe out
> From Fate's net, folly is his eagerness.
> For doom's decree shall no man disannul.[140]

This power, which one vainly tries to obstruct, is occasionally conceived even as Nature; thus a fragment of *Phoenix* reads:

> Still Nature her pre-eminence maintains:
> For by the aid of virtuous Education
> Can no man ever make what's evil, good.[141]

And a fragment of *Chrysippus:*

> None of thy wholesome counsels have escap'd me,
> But nature's force subdues my better reason.[142]

That this deity, transformed into an absolute necessity of fate or nature,
lies in the eternal, morally indifferent change of things is obvious from
the words with which the deity is characterized in *Helen:*

> Daughter, how manifold God's counsels are,
> His ways past finding out! Lightly he turns
> And sways us to and fro: sore travaileth one;
> One long unvexed is wretchedly destroyed,
> Having no surety still of each day's lot.[143]

The identification of the deity with fate as nature is also a means of
denying the former's existence and of negating the specific significance
which religion gives it.

55. Theodicy in Greek Theology

The law of divine retribution according to the popular belief of the Greeks is an eternal principle of world order guaranteed by Zeus himself.[144] An idea of equality is expressed in this principle of justice; equal is compensated by equal, evil by evil, and good by good. Accordingly, divine justice has a dual character: it is both punishing and rewarding. But emphasis is laid on the punishing aspect; this is proved by the fact that one considers the concept of justice maintained and not suspended even when the good man has to suffer with the bad man because he is connected with him by some relationship,[145] even though he may not be at all responsible for this connection. It is more important that the guilty person be punished than that the innocent individual remain free from punishment; this is symptomatic of the fact that the idea of justice is an ideology of the state, of the positive social order which is a coercive order—an order of punishment and not of reward.[146]

In order to maintain the notion that the divine government of the world is just, that divine justice is realized in human society, ancient Greek theology developed, as all theologies have done, a specific system of ideas to solve the awkward problem of theodicy. These ideas serve not so much to prove that in reality good is rewarded but rather that evil is punished. Such proof is possible only if one concedes that punishment is inflicted not upon the bad man alone but upon the good man as well—indeed, sometimes only upon the latter. For the fundamental problem which constantly threatens to shake the belief in divine justice, and hence in the existence of the gods, is that daily experience shows the criminal unpunished—frequently even blessed with fortune. At this point emerges the doctrine, widespread in the ancient world, that divine retribution is realized slowly and hesitatingly but all the more certainly.[147] The mills of the Greek gods, too, grind slow, but sure. Since in many cases this notion does not suffice, Greek theology, as every other theology, resorts to the doctrine of vicarious retribution. In order that equilibrium be maintained in the world system, it is necessary that the evil of a crime be balanced by the evil of an ensuing punishment. This punishment, however, need not necessarily be inflicted upon the individual who himself committed the crime. Justice is satisfied if children suffer for their parents[148] or if a whole community, a people, a city, suffer for one of its members, particularly for a representative member such as a king.[149] It is possible not only that all suffer for one but also that one suffers for all. The sacrificial death which a hero or heroine undergoes in order to avert the wrath of the gods aroused by a whole city is a frequent motive in tragic poetry.[150]

56. THE BELIEF IN A RETRIBUTION IN THE HEREAFTER

Finally, retribution which failed to materialize in this world is removed to the other world. It is easy to understand why the idea of punishment and reward occurring after a man's death originally was remote from Greek belief. Indeed, in the Homeric epic poems almost no traces can be found.[151] If we do find two references in the *Iliad*[152] to the idea that perjurers are punished in the underworld after their death, we may safely assume that these are elements of a much older belief in death souls and demons, relics of which still survived in Homer's world. The punishing powers which originally operated against perjurers in the upper world of the living are removed by Homer to the under world, the realm of the dead, because there is no more room for them in the upper world, the sphere of life, which is ruled by the gods of heaven.[153] In the *Odyssey* we find a similar reference in Odysseus' report of his voyage through the underworld. In this connection the hero tells how in the realm of Hades he had seen Tityus, Tantalus, and Sisyphus, all of whom had to suffer punishment for crimes committed during their lifetime.[154] But this passage is a later interpolation, perhaps of Orphic origin.[155] Belief in retribution exercised in the other world is unknown to Homer; indeed, such a belief is incompatible with Homer's picture of Hades, where "dwell the unheeding dead, the phantoms of men outworn,"[156] and with his conviction of the unreality and unsubstantiality of the souls of the dead.[157] These unfeeling and unconscious shades are not suitable objects of a retributory justice. This is all the more so since the soul of the dead, ψυχή, begins its existence only when the individual dies. It can, therefore, hardly be held responsible for the good or evil deeds that man performed during his lifetime. The life soul which exists in a living man is called by Homer ϑυμός; but it also appears under the name of certain organs in which it is thought to be localized, such as κραδίη, κῆρ, ῆτορ, φρένες.[158] The Homeric concept of soul, like that of most primitive peoples, is intrinsically dualistic or even pluralistic. The idea of a retribution exercised on the soul of a dead person becomes possible only if the death soul is united with the life soul into a single, uniform entity.

In Solon's[159] and Theognis'[160] writings we still find essentially the Homeric concept of soul and therefore also the conviction of Homeric society that divine justice is exercised in this world and not in the other world, and that the prevailing social order, the positive law, which comes directly or indirectly from the gods, is the will of Zeus. This observation also holds true for the Orators of the fifth and fourth centuries and for the great tragic poets. The belief of Aeschylus and Sophocles is the same as that of Homer: all guilt is avenged in this world.[161] Only slowly do criticism, finally recognizing the human origin of the social order, and a more refined sense of justice, no longer satisfied with the concepts of collective and hereditary responsibility and absolute liability, press metaphysical speculation to the illusion of a posthumous retribution. The function of this new idea is to console the believer about unjust reality and to satisfy both his feeling of individual responsibility and his desire for personal reward. Belief in a posthumous retribution is necessarily connected with a change in the Homeric concept of soul.[162] One may assume that this change is enforced by ethical-political necessities. The soul of the dead must be such that it is capable of being rewarded as well as punished. Even detached from the body, the soul must attain real life; it becomes immortal. This is exactly the concept of the soul developed by the Orphics and Pythagoreans.

57. THE SOUL BELIEF IN PRE-HOMERIC RELIGION

The Homeric psyche of the dead, however, is not only different from the idea of an immortal soul as developed by the Orphics and Pythagoreans but there is also an essential difference between the Homeric psyche and the pre-Homeric concept of the soul of the dead. It is especially noteworthy that the pre-Homeric concept of soul resembles the post-Homeric concept more closely than it resembles Homer's idea of the soul of the dead as a powerless and unreal shade. For the death souls of pre-Homeric times are powerful spirits, which display all the distinctive symptoms of real life; thus they have the one characteristic which distinguishes the immortal soul from the dead body—life, a superempiric, transcendental life. Whereas the Homeric death souls have no influence, either useful or harmful, upon the living, and can in no way interfere with their fate, the pre-Homeric death souls are powerful demons. This concept of soul manifests itself in a highly developed worship of the dead, of which we have many proofs of pre-Homeric times;[163] even the *Iliad* retains some traces in the funeral ceremonies which Achilles arranges for Patroclus.

Supposedly, the soul belief as belief in the power of a soul surviving after death as a demon played a decisive part in pre-Homeric religion. This pre-Homeric religion was a religion of the chthonian powers. It was probably the religion of the aborigines which was suppressed by the Zeus religion of the tribes who invaded the Greek Peninsula. The religion of the subdued peoples, which influenced the beliefs of the victors, may have originated in the idea of the death soul.[164] In any case, it retained a belief in the souls of the dead together with a belief in higher deities, divine powers of earth, especially Mother Earth. The pre-Homeric worship of the dead, confirmed by abundant materials, shows all the essential elements of the same belief that can be observed among contemporary primitive peoples; they feared the souls of the dead, which were considered to be endowed with superhuman powers, and they attempted to soothe them by certain rites; sacrifices were offered to the death souls, and gifts were given to the dead in the graves. Among these gifts Charon's penny is especially characteristic; it is a coin pressed between the dead man's teeth. That the coin was supposed to be the fare for Charon, who rowed the soul over the Styx into Hades, is certainly a later interpretation. Probably this custom originally had the same sense as similar usages among other peoples.[165]   Thus, in the Harz Mountains (Germany) the dead is given a coin and addressed as follows: "I am giving you money for provisions but now leave me money for food." In Bohemia one or two kreutzers are placed in the coffin of the dead man by the heir, who says: "Here you have what is yours, leave me what is mine." In Masuria one presses a coin in the dead man's hand and says: "Here you have your wages, hence you may not return." The meaning of all these rites is that, according to the principle of retribution, the dead is paid for something, obviously for his right to his property to which his soul always wishes to return; it is just this return which is feared, and therefore the attempt is made to prevent it.

58. The Fear of the Death Soul and Its Retributory Function

But why does the living person fear the dead one; why does he "double" him by adding to the dead corpse a living soul to which he traces various evils which he has already endured or fears to endure, such as illness and death? And why does he regard this "soul" as angry with him, as wishing him evil, even as threatening him with death? The explanation suggests itself that primitive man has an elementary fear of death and transfers this fear to a concrete object, to the dead. Thus the fear of death becomes a fear of the dead. This fear of the dead, therefore, is not an instinctive reaction but the result of some reflection. This is proved by the fact that animals which show fear, and especially fear of death, lack any fear of the dead. Why should man fear the dead when every experience teaches him that the dead can do no harm; when, relying on his experience, he kills the being he fears in order that the latter can no longer inflict any harm—above all, death—upon him? The fear of the dead is particularly strange inasmuch as primitive man begins to fear only at the moment when that situation occurs which otherwise he himself brings about in order to deprive the feared object of its fear-arousing qualities. Equally strange is his fear of his dead father, mother, relatives, and, under certain circumstances, his own child—people whom he had loved when they were alive.

Indeed, it is just this fear of the dead ancestor which represents the nucleus of the belief in the soul of the dead. But a more careful investigation of the material reveals that primitive man does not transfer his fear of death to all beings whose death he observes. Primitive man does not always transfer his fear of death to the dead in the same way, and particularly in the same degree, as would be the case if the transfer mechanism functioned instinctively, uninfluenced by other factors. The process in which fear of death is transformed into fear of the dead is differentiated whether a dead man or a dead animal is involved; further, it is different with regard to different groups of men. Close study shows that social facts determine this differentiation. One may assume, therefore, that in primitive man's fear of the dead, in this reaction upon which his religion and thus his whole culture is founded, in this attitude which distinguishes him from the animal which he otherwise resembles so much, a very important social ideology is working.

The answer to the question why primitive man fears the dead is partly given by primitive man himself. He often says that the dead is angry because he has been offended either by slander, through violation of the old rule that one may speak only kindly of the dead, or by nonobservance of the usual death rites, such as leaving the corpse unburied or not offering death sacrifices. The wrath of the dead means vengeance, retribution. Fear of the dead is fear of its vengeance. The dead punishes the violation of norms obligating the living to a certain behavior toward the dead. But what is the origin of these norms concerning the cult of the dead? It is obviously the fear of the dead which

creates these norms. Hence their violation cannot be the only, and
especially not the first, cause for the wrath of the dead. Certainly the
dead person is angry with the living because of a wrong which the living has inflicted upon him. But this need not—and cannot—be only a
wrong inflicted upon the already dead; it must also be a wrong inflicted while the dead person was still living, a wrong which was not
avenged during his lifetime. The most feared souls are everywhere the
ones of murdered people, who themselves take revenge on the murderer or cause the surviving relatives to do so. Even in Homer's epics,
where the souls of the dead fade into unreal shades, we still find traces
of the fear of the avenging soul of the dead. One of these traces is the
belief that the death soul can enter Hades and find peace there only if
the corpse is properly buried. The duty to bury one's relatives, friends,
and countrymen is considered sacred in Homeric society;[166] and the
burial of the dead has, here as elsewhere, its origin not in hygienic reasons but in the intention to prevent the feared return of the dead. In
the *Iliad*,[167] after Achilles has killed Eëtion, it is said: "Yet he despoiled
him not, for his soul had awe of that; but he burnt him in his armour,
richly dight." And the hero of the *Odyssey*[168] warns Eurycleia, who is
rejoicing over the death of the suitors: "In thine own heart rejoice, old
dame, but refrain thyself and cry not out aloud: an unholy thing is it to
boast over slain men." Although belief in the vengeance of the death
soul had already disappeared from Homeric religion, yet fear of such
vengeance obviously prevented anyone from taking up the weapons of
a dead foe or from rejoicing over his death.[169]

For the idea of an avenging death soul proofs from post-Homeric
times are much more convincing. In *The Libation-bearers* of Aeschylus
the chorus, inciting Orestes to avenge his murdered father, sings as
follows: "My child, the consciousness of the dead is not quelled by
fire's ravening jaw; but he bewrayeth thereafter what stirreth him.
The slain man hath his dirge, the guilty man is revealed. Lament for
fathers and for parents that hath just cause, when raised full loud and
strong, maketh search on every hand."[170] And in the *Electra* of Sophocles the chorus says at the death of Clytemnestra:

> The curses work; the buried live again,
> And blood for blood, the slayer's blood they drain,
> The ghosts of victims long since slain.[171]

Xenophon[172] lets Cyrus on his deathbed speak thus to his sons:

For assuredly, this one thing, so it seems to me, you do not know clearly, that I
shall have no further being when I have finished this earthly life; for not even in this

life have you seen my soul, but you have detected its existence by what it accomplished. Have you never yet observed what terror the souls of those who have been foully dealt with strike into the hearts of those who have shed their blood, and what avenging deities they send upon the track of the wicked? And do you think that the honours paid to the dead would continue if their souls had no part in any of them?

Herodotus'[173] report tells that the Tyrrhenians, after a sea battle against the Phocaeans, had in violation of international law stoned many prisoners of war near the town of Agylla.

But after this all from Agylla, whether sheep or beasts of burden or men, that passed the place where the stoned Phocaeans lay, became distorted and crippled and palsied. The Agyllaens sent to Delphi, desiring to heal their offence; and the Pythian priestess bade them do what the people of Agylla to this day perform: for they pay great honours to the Phocaeans, with religious rites and games, and horse-races.

A similar story can be found in Pausanias:[174] On his wanderings after the fall of Troy, Odysseus landed in Temesa, where one of his sailors was stoned by the natives. Disregarding this loss, Odysseus sailed on.

But the ghost of the stoned man never ceased killing without distinction the people of Temesa, attacking both old and young, until, when the inhabitants had resolved to flee from Italy for good, the Pythian priestess forbad them to leave Temesa, and ordered them to propitiate the Hero, setting him a sanctuary apart and building a temple, and to give him every year as wife the fairest maiden in Temesa. So they performed the commands of the god and suffered no more terrors from the ghost.

Here the death-soul demon is called "hero." And this story is typical of the worship of heroes widespread in post-Homeric times. Such a practice of making the death soul a hero is often the means of calming its anger.[175] For the close connection between this form of death-soul belief and the idea of retribution still another story of Herodotus[176] is characteristic. It shows that the hero may be angered not only by a wrong inflicted upon him but also by a wrong inflicted upon others. At the same time the report offers important evidence for the existence of an interstate law in ancient times. The hero Talthybius, the Homeric herald, was venerated as ancestor and guardian spirit of a Spartan family in which the honorary post of envoys of their country was hereditary. Once when the Spartans, in violation of international law, killed the envoys of the king of the Persians, the hero Talthybius was angry with his people until Sperthias and Bulis, two members of a noble family, offered their lives as retribution to the Persian king. They then went to Xerxes, but he did not accept their offer. He told them that ·

he would not imitate the Lacedaemonians; "for you," said he, "made havoc of all human law by slaying heralds; but I will not do that which I blame in you, nor by

putting you in turn to death set the Lacedaemonians free from this guilt." Thus by
this deed of the Spartans the wrath of Talthybius was appeased for the nonce, though
Sperthias and Bulis returned to Sparta. But long after that it awoke to life again in
the war between the Peloponnesians and Athenians, as the Lacedaemonians say.

For they sent the son of Bulis, Nicolas, and the son of Sperthias, Aner-
istus, as envoys to Asia, where they were betrayed, captured, sent
to Attica, and killed by the Athenians. Herodotus interprets this as
"heaven's doing by reason of Talthybius' anger."

In pre-Homeric religion, as in other primitive religions, in addition
to fear of the soul which takes revenge and punishes may be added
the desire for protection and help from it. If the soul has the power to
inflict harm, why should it not use its power for the protection of the
survivors? The attitude toward the death soul is ambivalent throughout. Characteristic of this are the customs which were exercised in
Athens even in post-Homeric times at the annual festivities, celebrated
in honor of the dead, the Anthesteria. On the last day of the festival,
according to the belief of the people, the souls of the dead come to the
upper world.

Therefore the temples were closed so that they might not be polluted by the dead;
in one's own house, too, protection was sought against their harmful influence; the
doors were besmeared with pitch which according to popular belief kept the spirits
away, leaves of hawthorn were chewed as that plant was also regarded as a deterrent
to demons. At the same time sacrifices were offered to the souls and their guide,
Hermes; everyone entertained the souls. But at the end of the festivities they were
driven from the houses with these words: Get out, you souls, the Anthesteria are
over.[177]

Worship of the dead is in Greece, as elsewhere, in connection with
the worship of Mother Earth, into which the dead are deposited. In
a chthonian religion not only fear of a bad harvest, as punishment
for sins, but also hope for a good harvest, the desire for fertility, plays
an important role.[178] The second element, however, appears to have
had in the Greek cult of the dead, just as among all other primitive
peoples, only a secondary character. Of primary importance was the
calming of the feeling of guilt, the fear of punishment rather than the
expectation of reward.

For this reason all the ideas which deal with belief in the soul and
worship of the dead are most clearly manifested in the institutions of
blood revenge and atonement for murder. The blood relatives owe it
to the soul of the murdered man to take revenge on the perpetrator.
The claim of the soul is satisfied by the revenge.[179]

At Athens even in the fourth and fifth centuries the belief still survived in un-
diminished vigour that the soul of one violently done to death, until the wrong done

to him was avenged upon the doer of it, would wander about finding no rest, full of rage at the violent act, and wrathful, too, against the relatives who should have avenged him, if they did not fulfill their duty.[180]

The soul itself becomes a spirit of vengeance.

When blood revenge was later replaced by the judgment of state courts, the duty of the relatives to the soul of the murdered man was confined to the accusation of the murderer. If the latter, however, succeeded in fleeing across the state boundary, he was safe not only from punishment by the state, the legal power of which came to an end at the boundary, but also from the soul of the slain man. Its power, too, ceases, as Rohde[181] pointed out, "at the boundaries of the country." This is the clearest evidence for the close relationship between the concept of soul and the idea of law. The purification rites performed by the murderer also show this connection. The purification priest lets the blood of an animal, which was sacrificed instead of the murderer, run over the hands of the polluted man; this signifies "that by blood-stain blood-stain I may cleanse"[182]—in other words, that "murder is driven out by murder."[183] The pollution which is washed away by the blood of the sacrificed animal is, according to Rohde, the anger of the soul of the murdered man. According to the idea of the ancient Greeks, it is the soul which sets the principle of retribution in motion.

59. THE ERINYES

The close connection between the concept of soul and the idea of retribution is proved by the Erinyes, which are of great importance in Greek mythology. They belong to the oldest deities of law; in pre-Homeric times they were the executors of vengeance on murderers. Since the oldest legal community was the family, they appeared as Erinyes of the murdered mother, less often as Erinyes of the murdered father. Not Clytemnestra, who killed her husband, but Orestes, who murdered his mother, is a victim of the Erinyes.[184] The connection between the Erinyes and the family law is also shown by the relationship between these demons and the vengeance of the insulted father or the offended mother in Homer's epic poems. Particularly significant in this connection is the fate of Phoenix. Incited by his mother, he sleeps with his father's concubine. The father calls for vengeance upon the Erinyes, who punish the criminal by depriving him of the ability to procreate children.[185] A pendant to this is the peculiar story of Altheia, who called for the vengeance of the Erinyes against her own son Meleager, who had killed her brother.[186] In the *Iliad* the divine messenger,

Iris, expressly states that the Erinyes protect the right of the older generation against the younger.[187]

The Erinyes appear also as avengers of perjury. When Agamemnon makes an oath, he calls upon Zeus and Helios, as well as upon the very old earth-goddess Ge and the Erinyes "that under earth take vengeance on men, whosoever hath sworn a false oath."[188] The legal function of these catachthonian powers is clearly manifested. But it is significant that, although he calls upon them, Agamemnon does not, in case he commits perjury, expect punishment from them but from the Olympic gods. He ends his oath with these words: "And if aught of this oath be false, may the gods give me woes full many, even all that they are wont to give to him whoso sinneth against them in his swearing."[189]

How the function of retribution is passed on from the old chthonian powers, especially from the Erinyes, to the Olympic gods is magnificently presented by Aeschylus in the tragedy *Eumenides*. The Erinyes who persecute Orestes for the murder of his mother appear here as older deities and executors of the blood revenge of the clan; thus they are strongly contrasted with the younger gods, Apollo and Pallas Athene, who represent the superior legal principle of Zeus, the jurisdiction of the state court. Consequently Orestes is not exposed to the vengeance of the Erinyes. They say: "Such are the doings of the younger gods, who rule, altogether beyond the right. . . . . [190] The enmity between the younger generation of gods, such as Zeus, Apollo, Pallas Athene, to which group Dike also belongs, and the old Erinyes is emphasized over and over again. Thus the chorus of Erinyes sings: "At our birth this office was ratified unto us; but the Deathless Ones may not lay hand upon us, nor doth any of them share our feasts in common with us; and in festal robes of pure white I have nor lot nor portion . . . .";[191] or: "For Zeus hath deemed unworthy of his converse this our hateful and blood-streaming band."[192] Again: ". . . . pursuing our appointed office dishonoured, despised, separated from the gods by a light not of the sun."[193] The attempt of Apollo and Pallas Athene to withdraw Orestes from the vengeance of the Erinyes through a judgment of the court makes them angry: "Now is the end of all things wrought by new ordinances, if the wrongful cause of this slayer of his mother is to triumph."[194] And they call to Apollo: "Thou it was in truth who didst beguile with wine those ancient goddesses and thus abolish the dispensations of eld."[195] After Orestes' acquittal by the court they groan: "Shame! Ye younger gods, ye have ridden down the ancient laws and have wrested them from my grasp";[196] and complain:

> I to be treated thus, oh shame! I, sage in ancient wisdom, to dwell beneath the earth a thing dishonoured (oh shame!) and detested! My spirit pants with fury and utter rage. Oh, oh, the shame of it! What anguish steals into my breast! O mother Night, give ear to the cry of my passion! The gods, holding me a thing of naught, have reft me of mine immemorial honours by their resistless craft.[197]

In post-Homeric times the Erinyes play an important part as avengers of murder. Under their auspices murder trials at the state courts were held.[198] On the Areopagus, the hill of the Erinyes "over the sacred chasm in which they themselves, the 'Venerable Ones,' have their dwelling," the Athenian criminal court held its sessions. "At the commencement of the proceedings both parties take an oath in the name of the Erinyes," so that, in case the court punishes the innocent party, the guilty one, as perjurer, is exposed to the spirits of vengeance. It was more important that the criminal be punished than that the innocent be saved. The dark side of retribution is here, too, thrown into the foreground. Later the Erinyes became the protectors of the entire legal order, the "handmaids of Justice [Dike]," as they are called in a fragment of Heraclitus.[199]

The Erinyes, who play such a decisive part in the legal ideology of Greek religion, originate, in all probability, in the death-soul belief. This is made evident by the fact that there is a plurality of Erinyes. Since there is not one, but many, death souls, so there is not one, but many, Erinyes.[200] The ambivalence which is so characteristic for the functioning of the death soul is clearly manifested by the double nature of the Erinyes, who not only may be evil deities but, as Eumenides, are also good, protecting, and blessing deities. That they are connected somehow with the dead is apparent from the fact that they emit a cadaverous odor.[201] Above all, it must be remarked that the snake, a typical death-soul animal, is associated with them.[202] They themselves frequently appear as snakes, or they carry snakes in their hair or hands. An ancient Greek vase pictures the murder of Eriphyle by her son Alkmeon.[203] Behind the fatally wounded woman "a big snake rises up and hisses at the murderer. This is the soul of the mother and her Erinys in one being." Rohde[204] is right, therefore, when he says "that the Erinys was nothing else but the soul itself of the murdered man, indignant at its fate and seizing its revenge for itself—till later ages substituted for this the conception of the ghost from hell taking over to itself the rage of the dead man's soul."

60. The Transfer of the Retributory Function
to the Olympic Gods

The decisive fact of this metamorphosis is that the retributory function of the death soul is transferred to central deities corresponding to
a more progressive process of social integration, originally to the goddess of earth, Mother Earth, who in pre-Homeric religion had certainly the character of a goddess of law.[205] The Erinyes function as connecting links; they become the servants and executors of the retribution which now proceeds from a superior deity. With the conquest
of the aborigines by the Greeks immigrating from the north and with
the victory of their Zeus religion over the belief of the subdued population in the chthonian powers,[206] the legal function of retribution
passed to the Olympic gods—above all, to Zeus, the king of the gods.
These new gods were the religious correlatives of a strong monarchic-
aristocratic state power. This power is based, in great measure, on a
belief in the divine origin of the rulers and the prevailing law. Consequently, this law is considered the divine justice realized on earth. It
is no longer only the soul of the dead which takes revenge for a wrong
committed against itself; now it is an Olympic deity, it is Zeus, who
punishes every wrong and whom the Erinyes serve as subordinate
auxiliary gods.

When Odysseus came to Hades, he encountered the soul of his companion Elpenor, who had met with a fatal accident in Circe's house
and whose corpse was left unburied there. This soul, however, is not
angry and does not threaten to take revenge for the delict committed
upon it; it only requests: "Leave me not behind thee unwept and unburied as thou goest thence, and turn not away from me, lest haply I
bring the wrath of the gods upon thee."[207] The pre-Homeric demon
would itself have taken revenge. The Homeric death soul is dependent
upon the vengeance of the gods. This attenuation of the belief in the
soul of the dead is the real reason for the fact that in Homer's epic
poems blood revenge no longer appears as a religious duty, and relatives obliged to take revenge may accept the wergild instead. Thus
Ajax says to the angered Achilles: "Lo, a man accepteth recompense
from the slayer of his brother, or for his dead son; and the slayer abideth in his own land for the paying of a great price, and the kinsman's
heart and proud spirit are restrained by the taking of recompense."[208]

The fact that in the martial heroic atmosphere of the Homeric world
the wergild may relieve blood revenge proves that the latter is based
not so much on primitive instincts as on a certain social ideology,

namely, belief in the death soul which either takes revenge itself or coerces the relatives to execute vengeance. The Homeric wergild, however, also represents a transitional stage between the unredeemable vendetta of the pre-Homeric society and the criminal courts of the post-Homeric state.[209] The fact that in the two epics the dead are still regarded as something, be they only unreal shades, indicates that formerly they had played a more decisive part. During the pre-Homeric period in the cult of the dead, and to a large extent also in the religion of the chthonian deities, they were the very bearers of the principle of retribution. Since the function of retribution was taken over by the Olympic deities, the Homeric religion lacked one of the chief motives for the belief in a real survival of the soul. The unreal shades of the dead in Homer's epics are the "souls" of the dead which have lost their essential social function and thus became mere "phantoms"; they are demons which, with regard to the sole authority of the Olympic gods, were almost completely divested of their demoniacal character. Only the Olympic gods—above all, Zeus—are to be feared.[210]

61. The Soul-Belief in the Post-Homeric Religion Orphics and Pythagoreans

Soul belief, however, survived beneath the surface of Homeric religion and continued to be, although in quite a different sense, an instrument of the idea of justice. Originally the avenging soul of the dead had been the subject of retribution; it was conceived as a demon with the character of a punishing deity. Later, during the social revolutions in the seventh and sixth centuries,[211] belief in justice realizing itself in this world was shaken, and desire for a compensatory justice in the other world became stronger and stronger. In the course of this social and religious movement the idea of the soul was subject to a radical change. The soul became the object of retribution; it prolonged the individual's existence after death, not to punish or reward others, but to be itself punished or rewarded, either in another world or, after being reborn, during a second life in this world.

As the soul was changed from the subject to the object of retribution, from a punishing and rewarding authority to a subject to be punished and rewarded, the quality of immortality became more and more prominent. The assumption suggests itself that belief in divine justice entirely realized in this world decreased in the same degree in which belief in the divine origin of law as a result of social upheavals became shaken; law was finally recognized as human work. If the

deity is only the remote cause for human law, or perhaps not a cause
at all, then it becomes necessary to supplement the imperfect legal
order of the state, the empirical law, by the supernatural retribution of
a transcendental order; then the religious ideology has to procure a
suitable object upon which this transcendental retribution can be
executed.

This concept of a transcendental retribution is the center of the post-
Homeric belief in immortality. With its ideas of a judgment of the
dead and the transmigration of the soul, this belief is entirely different
from the pre-Homeric religion because it is based upon another soul
concept. The beginnings of this belief go back into the sixth and perhaps even as far as the seventh century.[212] It forms the nucleus of
Orphic, as well as of Pythagorean, doctrine.[213] The fundamental character of both is ethical-religious; their chief motive is the idea of retribution. This is clearly apparent in the Dionysus myth, which is the
basis of the Orphic religion. Dionysus, the son of Zeus and Persephone, is left the dominion of the world by his father. But he is killed
by the Titans, who tear his body to pieces and devour it. Only his
heart is brought to Zeus by Athene; Zeus eats it in order to procreate
with Semele the "new Dionysus." As punishment for their murder
the Titans are killed with lightning by Zeus. From their ashes, and
therefore also from the ashes of Dionysus devoured by them, human
beings arise. Thus the origin of mankind is here, too, involved with
crime and punishment. Just like the substance from which they are
formed, the nature of human beings is also half Titanic, half Dionysiac: the body is Titanic, the soul Dionysiac. Thus the Orphics, as well
as the Pythagoreans, teach that the immortal soul is confined like a
prisoner in the mortal body, that the dominion of the body has to be
restricted by asceticism, and that after the death of the body the soul
comes to the underworld in order to be tried and punished for the
wrongs with which it polluted itself during life.

The idea of the judgment of the dead, which was especially developed among the Orphics, is connected, not quite organically and not
without some contradiction, with the idea of a transmigration of the
soul. The soul does not remain in the underworld. After the punishment suffered there, the soul must return to the upper world in order to
commit in new reincarnation new sins and thus suffer also new punishments. The soul becomes a prisoner of the body as punishment for the
sins committed in an earlier life. The evil deeds of its former life are
retributed in its next life; all that man inflicted upon others then, he

must suffer now. Thus he atones fully for old guilt. This is the meaning of the Orphic philosophy; it is nothing but the idea of retribution.
According to the doctrine of the Pythagoreans, who also share the belief in metempsychosis, the nature of justice, of the δίκαιον is τὸ
ἀντιπεπονθός, that means, ἅ τις ἐποίησε ταῦτ' ἀντιπαθεῖν.[214] It is the
principle of *talio:* pain for pain. According to Rohde, the doctrine of
metempsychosis is used by the Orphic theologians—and the same must
be true for the Pythagoreans, who agree with them on this point—to
express emphatically "the conception of the inevitable connection between guilt and penance."

The ultimate goal of Orphics and Pythagoreans is the establishment
of a theodicy, to prove the justice of human destiny. The achievement
of this goal is confronted with two obstacles: the guiltless suffering and
the impunity of the evil. Belief in the judgment of the dead removes
the latter; the doctrine of metempsychosis, however, removes both.
The suffering visible in this world is punishment for the unknown guilt
of a former life which has vanished from our consciousness; on the
other hand, guilt which is visible but not atoned in this world is bound
to be punished in a later life. How strong must be the desire for retribution if it can drive imagination so far beyond the limit of all experience controlled by reason! The Orphic, as well as the Pythagorean, doctrine is a grandiose attempt to regard the world, in the center
of which is human life, as just by interpreting it as the realization of
the principle of retribution.

62. The Idea of Retribution in the Eleusinian Mysteries

The principle of retribution seems also to have dominated those
religious ideas in the center of which were the Eleusinian mysteries.
Probably existing from pre-Hellenistic times, these mysteries were a
form of worship of the earth-goddess Demeter.[215] The cult was originally practiced secretly, for it was the religion of a conquered people
who had to hide their faith, suppressed by the religion of the victors.
As worship of an earth-deity, the Eleusinian mysteries were from the
earliest times closely connected with the worship of the dead and the
old death-soul belief. In Attica, in fact, the dead were called "De-
metrioi," i.e., appertaining to Demeter, the Earth Mother.[216] A representation of the initiation into the mysteries on a Roman cinerary
urn shows a snake,[217] the typical death-soul animal, in the lap of the
sitting Demeter. The so-called "fifth Homeric Hymn" to Demeter,
which was written in the middle of the seventh century, at a time

when the Eleusinia received new impulse in connection with the social movements and the religious renaissance, deals with the founding of the mysteries. The myth begins with the rape of Persephone, the daughter of Demeter, by Hades. This is a breach of law the criminal character of which is emphasized by the fact that Demeter is an old deity of law, older even than Zeus, and that the rape is carried out with the approval of Zeus, the younger deity of law. Enraged, Demeter shuns Olympus, takes on human shape, and, disguised as a poor old woman, goes to Eleusis, where she is well received in the house of Keleus, who asks her to care for his youngest child. When Demeter declares herself a goddess, a temple is established for her. There she holds herself apart from all the other gods. As punishment for the unlawful rape of her child, she holds the crops back in the earth. Not only men are discomforted thereby, but the gods also, for her action renders impossible the offering of the due sacrifices. So Hades is compelled to allow Persephone to return to earth at least for part of the year. As soon as Demeter sees her daughter again, she takes the infertility from the earth. Grateful to men for their kind reception, she teaches them, among other things, the holy rites. Thus the myth interprets the existence of the mysteries according to the principle of retribution; they are the reward for the fulfilment of one of the most sacred duties—hospitality. Even the little we know of the mysteries themselves makes it certain that the dominant idea was the realization of justice and that this justice was retribution.

The process by which one was admitted into the Eleusinian secret was divided into two stages: the preparation of the neophyte and the actual consecration. Preparations consisted mainly of purification rites, such as fasting, chastity, and sea bathing. The already mentioned representation of the initiation into the mysteries shows the purification rite that has to be performed before the initiation. The neophyte, who stands before the priest, is covered by a hide, apparently the hide of an animal sacrificed in his stead. This is a typical means of identifying one's self with a sacrificed animal; such an identification is necessary inasmuch as the offering of the animal has the character of a substitutive punishment; through it, the wrong from which the human being is to be purified seems to be atoned for.[218] The purification and atonement rites have here the same character as among all other primitive peoples: purification aims at the removal of the evil of sins, imagined as substance which adheres to, or exists in, the body and can

therefore be washed off or expelled; the atonement is effected by anticipatory self-torment (fasting, chastity, etc.) or by killing the substitutive object (human or animal) with which the atoning individual identifies himself. Thus the feared punishment is anticipated.[219]

One is accustomed to call the "purity" thus achieved a mere "ritual" purity and to contrast it with "moral" purity.[220] But this "ritual"
purity corresponds to an older, more primitive form of morality, one
which is characterized by the substantializing and identifying thinking
of primitive man, a kind of thinking which makes possible the idea of
vicarious suffering. In the preparatory rites the neophyte frees himself
from all his sins in order to avoid the punishment which, according to
the Eleusinian belief, threatens him. In addition, the mysteries ex-
hibit an even higher degree of morality, since in the times about which
we have information they excluded anyone polluted with murder. Yet
slaves were freely admitted.

We are confined to mere conjectures as to what happened at the
main initiation rites. One thing is certain: the neophytes were not
lectured on the doctrine but were shown holy objects, such as the
mother's lap of the goddess, religious performances, etc. The intention
of the initiation was to portray the death and rebirth of the neophyte.
This is borne out by their formula, "I have gone down into the lap of
the queen of the underworld,"[221] and the call of the Hierophant, "The
venerable goddess gave birth to a blessed one, the strong one gave
birth to a strong one."[222] The neophyte dies and, as a snake, penetrates the body of the goddess in order to be reborn by her. This process corresponds to the old widespread belief in the reincarnation of the
soul. The snake on the lap of Demeter in the previously mentioned
representation supports such an interpretation.[223] The man standing
before the goddess touches the head of the snake with his hand, thus
indicating his relationship with the reptile. The emphasis of the whole
procedure was laid upon what one saw and experienced during the
time between death and rebirth. The fate of the soul after death seems
to have entailed pleasures for "good men" and pains for "bad men."
Through the initiation anyone becomes a "good man." Happiness
awaits him in the other world by virtue of his having experienced the
initiation in Eleusis. In the Demeter Hymn it is said: "Happy is he
among men upon earth who has seen these mysteries; but he who is
uninitiate and who has no part in them, never has lot of like good
things once he is dead, down in the darkness and gloom."[224] This is

why the cynic Diogenes derided the mysteries: "What! Do you mean to say that Pataecion, the robber, will have a better portion after death than Epaminondas, just because he is initiate?"[225]

But, even if the Eleusinian religion reserves rewards in the other world only for its own believers and leaves the uninitiated ones to the torments of hell, the idea of retribution in the other world cannot be doubted. That religious ethics identifies "good" and "bad" with "true belief" and "unbelief" is self-evident. Even a religion with such high moral standards as the Christian ascribes to baptism an importance which is not too different from that which the Eleusinian religion attributes to its initiation. In this connection, it must not be overlooked that during the time decisive for the development of the Eleusinian mysteries, the seventh and sixth centuries before Christ, religious feeling was characterized by a moral pessimism which manifested itself in the so-called Kathartic practices[226] appearing in those times of social revolutions, in an increased conscience of guilt, in a morbid fear of pollution, and in an exaggerated urge for purification. That everyone is sinful and that he who does not secure salvation for himself by participation in a certain cult will be condemned in the other world are ideas which could be defended by the priests of the cult without remaining far behind the average moral notions of a later, more enlightened world.

The climax of the initiation procedure was probably a representation of the fate of the soul in the other world. Probably the neophyte himself played some part in this performance.[227] He experiences his future life in the underworld by being persecuted by the Erinyes and put to trial. If this is true,[228] then participation in the mysteries implied a symbolic anticipation of the retribution feared in the other world. Since symbol and reality are not clearly distinguished in religious-mythical thinking and since in primitive belief the symbol not only represents but actually is the reality, the accomplished initiation means that the initiated man has already endured what the uninitiated has still to expect—punishment in the other world. Therefore, he can calmly await his real death. Purified in the preparatory rites, symbolically punished and reborn in the main initiation, he need no longer fear the other world. He has already fulfilled the law of retribution.

63. THE IDEA OF RETRIBUTION IN PINDAR

The relationship between the Orphics and the Eleusinian mysteries[229] must be left undecided here. In any case, Pindar's ideas of the soul, of metempsychosis, and of a judgment in the other world are to be traced to Orphic and Pythagorean influences.[230] Of the judgment in the other world it is said in the second Olympian Ode: "But if, in very deed, when he hath that wealth [of virtue], he knoweth of the future, that immediately after death, on earth, it is the lawless spirits that suffer punishment,—and the sins committed in this realm of Zeus are judged by One who passeth sentence stern and inevitable." Here the good ones are rewarded, the bad ones punished.

While the good, having the sun shining forevermore, for equal nights and equal days, receive the boon of a life of lightened toil, not vexing the soil with the strength of their hands, no, nor the water of the sea, to gain a scanty livelihood; but, in the presence of the honoured gods, all who were wont to rejoice in keeping their oaths, share a life that knoweth no tears, while the others endure labour that none can look upon.

Of metempsychosis the poet says:

But, whosoever, while dwelling in either world, have thrice been courageous in keeping their souls pure from all deeds of wrong, pass by the highway of Zeus unto the tower of Cronus, where the ocean-breezes blow around the Islands of the Blest, and flowers of gold are blazing, some on the shore from radiant trees, while others the water fostereth; and with chaplets thereof they entwine their hands, and with crowns, according to the righteous councils of Rhadamanthys, who shareth forevermore the judgment-seat of the mighty Father, even the Lord of Rhea with her throne exalted beyond all beside.[231]

Aeschylus, born in Eleusis and initiated into the mysteries, mentions the Orphic retribution in the other world, although this notion does not at all affect his concept of justice. Thus it is said in *The Suppliant Maidens*: "There also, so men tell, among the dead another Zeus holds a last judgment upon misdeeds."[232] And in the *Eumenides*:

> There thou shalt see if any other man
> Has sinned in not revering God or guest,
> Or parents dear, that each receiveth there
> The recompense of sin that Justice claims
> For Hades is a mighty arbiter
> Of those that dwell below, and with a mind
> That writes true record all man's deeds surveys.[233]

64. THE IDEA OF RETRIBUTION IN PLATO

Orphic-Pythagorean metaphysics has influenced the philosophy of Plato, which is the main source for the modern doctrine of the immortality of the soul. Plato's writings in his post-Socratic period have an essentially religious-theological character. His ethical-political ideas show a metaphysical tendency. And ethical-political motives prompt him to accept the dogma of the immortality of the soul in his philosophical system.

The dualism of soul and body appears clearly as a contrast between good and evil.[234] If Plato in his *Phaedo* describes the soul, as the Orphics and Pythagoreans describe it, namely, as imprisoned in the body alien to and polluting it, he obviously intends to interpret the struggle between soul and body as a conflict between good and evil. The soul for Plato is the good element in man and thus enables man to perceive the absolute good, the deity. The soul mirrors the ideas, though its reflection is often blurred by the body. Thus the soul is, above all, a kind of reproduction of the central idea, the idea of the absolute good. The doctrine of the immortality of the soul nowhere so directly and essentially serves the idea of justice as in Plato's writings. Three of his most important dialogues—*Gorgias, Phaedo,* and *The Republic*—end with accounts which bring the belief in immortality into the closest connection with the realization of retributory justice. At the end of the dialogue devoted wholly to the question of the immortality of the soul, the *Phaedo,* a picture is drawn of the other world, where the soul goes after the death of the body. No one can fail to recognize that the whole soul doctrine of Plato culminates in this concept of the other world taken from Orphic-Pythagorean sources.[235] Its only meaning is that, after judgment upon the souls, some of them are punished for the wrongs committed during lifetime, whereas the others are rewarded for their justice. One has to be just in this world to insure a happy fate for the soul in the other world.

Wherefore . . . . seeing all these things [in the other life], what ought not we to do that we may obtain virtue and wisdom in this life? Fair is the prize, and the hope great![236]

Wherefore, I say, let a man be of good cheer about his soul, who having cast away the pleasures and ornaments of the body . . . . has arrayed the soul in her own proper jewels, temperance, and justice, and courage, and nobility, and truth—in these adorned she is ready to go on her journey to the world below, when her hour comes.[237]

And the *Gorgias* ends: "For no man who is not an utter fool and coward is afraid of death itself, but he is afraid of doing wrong."[238] For death is nothing more than the immortal soul freeing itself from the body in order to appear before the judges of the underworld. Consequently, the soul must endeavor to appear as healthy, and that means as just as possible before the tribunal of the dead which adjudges punishment and reward by sending the unjust souls to the hell of Tartarus and the just souls to heaven, to the Islands of the Blessed.

Just as Plato's dialogue dealing with the immortality of the soul, the *Phaedo*, ends with justice, so his great dialogue dealing with justice, *The Republic*, ends with the immortality of the soul. After having proved that "the soul of man is immortal"[239] and that the soul finds her highest good in justice,[240] Plato concludes his work by "enumerating how many and how great are the rewards which justice and the other virtues procure to the soul from gods and men, both in life and after death."[241]

In the following account the emphasis is laid not so much on the proof of justice in this world as on the description of retribution in the other world. For, in order to achieve the latter, life must continue after death; consequently, there must exist a bearer of this life after death, namely, the dead but still living human being, the human being as soul detached from the body. "And yet, I said, all these things are as nothing either in number or greatness in comparison with those other recompenses which await both just and unjust after death."[242] This passage is followed by a visionary description of the other world in which the idea of retribution is pre-eminent. Judges sit on the threshold of this other world. They direct the souls of the just to a path on their right which leads up to happiness, and the souls of the unjust to a path on their left which leads down to bitter suffering. The last words of *The Republic* reveal, as clearly as possible, the ethical-political sense of the Platonic "soul" and its immortality:

Wherefore my counsel is, that we hold fast to the heavenly way and follow after justice and virtue always, considering that the soul is immortal and able to endure every sort of good and every sort of evil. Thus shall we live dear to one another and to the gods, both while remaining here and when, like conquerors in the games who go round to gather gifts, we receive our reward. And it shall be well with us both in this life and in the pilgrimage of a thousand years which we have been reciting.[243]

A will, like that of Plato, directed with such elementary force to the idea of justice, not only sets imagination in motion in order to build up, beside this inadequate world, another world satisfying the demand for justice but also essentially influences the cognition of this world. Thus Plato has taken over from the Orphics and Pythagoreans more than their soul belief with all its machinery of retribution; he has also accepted their ethical-political interpretation of nature. In *The Republic* it is said that the cognition of good is the highest science; in connection with the doctrine of immortality and retribution in the other world, the priority of ethics as the cognition of good and evil over all other sciences—indeed, its exclusive value—is proclaimed.[244] His doctrines of the soul and of ideas Plato consciously opposes to the philosophy of nature of his time, which becomes more and more a science based on the principles of causality. The interpretation of reality according to Plato's doctrine of ideas, however, has a purely normative, i.e., moral, character. It is in the dialogue *Phaedo* that Socrates, and through him Plato, expresses his deep disappointment with natural science, which he had highly appreciated in his youth. In the famous polemic against the philosophy of Anaxagoras he declares that mere insight into the relation between cause and effect is absolutely inadequate to understand the meaning of the world. Cognition must be directed not to natural reality perceived by delusive senses but to ideas, to values known by reason, to the highest good. It is this good that holds things together. Only in ideas, the center of which is the idea of good, may the true nature of things be perceived.[245] Plato's doctrine of ideas presents itself as the most consistent attempt to replace the scientific explanation of the world, oriented to the law of causality, with an interpretation according to a normative principle and a system of values. It is a view of the world the center of which is not nature but society, i.e., man in his relationship with his fellow-men; it is a philosophy the main problem of which is justice; therefore it is a metaphysics the central dogma of which is the immortality of the soul. For this dogma has necessarily to be presupposed in order to accept the principle of retribution as the fundamental law of the world.[246]

The contrast between Plato's normative religious, essentially Orphic-Pythagorean, interpretation of the world and the causal scientific concept of reality in the Greek philosophy of nature was originally not great. For its fundamental scheme: the law of causality, which this philosophy developed for the first time in the history of the human mind, arose from the norm of retribution and detached itself only gradually from this all-dominating principle of mythical-religious thinking. This process is to be examined in the next chapter.

CHAPTER V

THE LAW OF CAUSALITY AND THE PRINCIPLE OF RETRIBUTION IN THE GREEK PHILOSOPHY OF NATURE

65. Origin of the Philosophy of Nature in Mythical-Religious Thinking

THE Greek philosophy of nature arose from the mythical-religious thinking of ages past. Hence its speculation had originally a normative character. This first great attempt at a scientific comprehension of reality was affected by the conception of values derived from the social sphere. The social categories were accepted without question and were considered to be such an incontestable part of human knowledge that they were taken as a starting-point for the first scientific endeavor to grasp reality. In early Greek philosophy, as in the mythical thinking of primitive man, nature was explained by analogy with society.

The authoritarian community, the state, furnishes the pattern of the order according to which this philosophy tries to comprehend the universe. Man had become accustomed to regard the state as order itself and, owing to much older theological speculation, as an absolute value. But the analogy between nature and society constantly weakens as a result of progressive observations. The idea of a universal law of nature, which was at first only the projection of the law of the state onto the cosmos, is thus visibly freed from its prototype and given a fully independent meaning. The law of the state, the norm, on the one hand, and the law of nature, the law of causality, on the other, become two totally different principles. Joël[1] is not quite right when he says that science began with a "nationalization [*Verstaatlichung*] of the view of the world." For this "nationalization," or rather socialization, of nature had already been achieved in myths. The new science of nature began where the myth ended; but from the beginning this science tended to separate φύσις from νόμος, nature from society, to contrast science with politics, or at least to establish a dualism of both which was entirely alien to primitive thinking.[2]

I

66. Thales, Anaximander, and Anaximenes

If Thales of Miletus, with whom Greek philosophy begins, if Anaximander and Anaximenes, seek a fundamental principle, ἀρχή, by which the universe may be uniformly explained, they are thinking of something that rules the world like a monarch. If Thales finds this something in water—still very similar to the Homeric myth which declares the god Oceanus as the origin of all things[3]—Anaximander in the unlimited, ἄπειρον, Anaximenes in the air, then all three have construed the cosmos as monarchy. The law of the ἀρχή establishes here a μον-αρχία and means not only "beginning" but also "government" or "rule"; and, as Heraclitus says, ". . . . it is law [νόμος], too, to obey the counsel of one."[4] It is certainly not accidental that this philosophy of nature flourished at a time when the influence of oriental despotism became more and more apparent in Greece.[5] Anaximander expressly states, according to Aristotle, that the basic principle, the ἄπειρον, is regarded as "embracing and governing [κυβερνᾶν] all."[6] And in a fragment of Anaximenes, who considered air the basic principle, it is said: "Just as our soul, being air, holds us together [συγκρατεῖ], so do breath and air encompass the whole world."[7] When Anaximenes declares the soul to be an aeriform being,[8] it must be noted that "he held that air is god [aera deum statuit]"[9]—hence a being endowed with reason and will. In this sense, air as the basic principle "rules" the world. Joël believes that Anaximenes saw air as the soul of the world. The question about the origin of the world had for the old philosophers of nature the implication of seeking not "a principle of substantiality, but of mobility."[10] Aristotle[11] says of Thales that the latter seemed to have "conceived soul as a cause of motion, if it be true that he affirmed the loadstone to possess soul, because it attracts iron." The cause, as the mover, is still thought of in an animistic, or rather personalistic, way; it intentionally sets something in motion, it governs something, it attracts something as a magnet attracts iron. Such an idea is, even today, not entirely foreign to the popular concept of causality. We can understand the idea that the "soul" is the cause of motion, and thus the cause itself, if we do not overlook the fact that the concept of soul arose from that of the death soul and that its original function—its first "effect," so to say—was vengeance.

This idea of causation reminds one in other respects, too, of the primitive concept of retribution; the cause attracts the effect just as the wrong, or, more exactly, the man by his wrongful act, attracts punishment. The fact that the idea of retribution plays a decisive role in the notion of ἀρχή, the fundamental principle, is shown chiefly in the doctrine that things, since they affect one another, must originate from the same source. A fragment of Diogenes of Apollonia[12] runs as follows:

My view is, to sum it all up, that all things are differentiations of the same thing, and are the same thing. And this is obvious; for, if the things which are now in this world—earth and water, and air and fire, and the other things which we see existing in this world—if any one of these things, I say, were different from any other, different, that is, by having a substance peculiar to itself; and if it were not the same thing that is often changed and differentiated, then things could not in any way mix with one another, nor could they do one another good or harm. Neither could a plant grow out of the earth, nor any animal nor anything else come into being unless things were composed in such a way as to be the same. But all these things arise from the same thing; they are differentiated and take different forms at different times, and return again to the same thing.

Aristotle[13] said: "Unless all things were derived from one, reciprocal action and passion could not have occurred." Only when things originate from the same source do they have the same nature, and only like things can react on one another; that is, only things alike in a specific sense can help or injure one another. That like things can influence only like things is an idea which can be found in different variations throughout the Greek philosophy of nature. Thus Empedocles teaches that equal can be attracted only by equal: "So sweet lays hold of sweet, and bitter rushes to bitter; acid comes to acid, and warm couples with warm."[14] Especially famous is his doctrine, taken over by Plato and also by Goethe, that equal can be understood only by equal. "For it is with earth that we see Earth, and Water with water; by air we see bright Air, by fire destroying Fire. By love do we see Love, and Hate by grievous hate."[15]

The idea that only like things can affect like things may still be found among the atomists, who detached the principle of causality from its mythological origins. This thesis that only like can affect like, that the cause must be equal to the effect (in which form this idea subsisted in nineteenth-century physics), clearly had its origin in the principle of retribution. Here is its proper sense, here alone there is a maintainable meaning: that between punishment and wrong, between reward and merit, exists a sort of equality. This equality is primarily qualitative, since evil entails evil, and good entails good, since the evil of wrong is connected with the evil of punishment and the good of merit with the good of reward. Within the religious ideology of retribution there already existed the idea that evil begets, or "gives birth" to, evil and that the equality of wrong and punishment is of the same kind as that whereby children equal their procreators. In his play *Agamemnon* Aeschylus expresses the thought that the traditional belief that too much good fortune brings bad luck is erroneous. It is rather sin which brings misfortune, and the misfortune consists in the commission of another sin, for one ill deed creates another, as parents produce children similar to themselves.[16] The "equality" of wrong and punishment becomes the identity of both, since punishment consists in a new wrong. But the likeness of wrong and punishment, merit and reward, is not only qualitative but also quantitative. The greater the wrong, the greater must be the punishment; the greater the merit, the greater must be the reward. A fragment of Heraclitus says: "Greater deaths win greater portions [rewards]."[17]

If the relationship of things is to be that of cause and effect, then the things must be "equal" in nature, as are wrong and punishment, merit and reward. For this reason they must originate in the same primary element, water or air. It is not a mere figure of speech when Diogenes of Apollonia[18] expresses the fact that one thing influences another in these words: "One thing does 'good' or 'harm' to another thing." For "good" is merit and reward; "harm," however, is wrong and punishment.

The idea of similarity contained in the notion of ἀρχή appears, in another aspect, as the idea of equilibrium, in so far as this idea has the meaning of justice. This equilibrium is the specific function of retribution which balances punishment against wrong and reward against merit, as on scales. Thales taught that water was the primary element. Since the transformation of this substance into things other than water was not easily explainable, Anaximander began with the ἄπειρον, that is, with the infinite—an eternal, imperishable substance, out of which came the opposites: wet and dry, hot and cold. Finite things are always in conflict with one another: hot fire with cold air, dry earth with the wet sea. The preponderance of one element over the other is unjust; their equilibrium is just. Heat creates injustice in summer, cold in winter. In order to attain equilibrium, they must revert to their common base, to their ἀρχή.[19] If fire should gradually dry up all the water, the "injustice" of the situation would ultimately lead to the destruction of the world. Mixed with water, however, fire loses its special nature and becomes the primary substance; its function, then, is to produce equilibrium in the sense of retributive justice.[20] Only in this sense of universal justification does it provide a universal explanation of the world. If one assumes that this is the fundamental idea of Anaximander, one can understand the following fragment: "And into that from which things take their rise, they pass away once more, as is meet, for they make reparation and satisfaction to one another for their injustice according to the ordering of time."[21] Here, for the first time in the thinking of mankind, the notion of an immanent law governing the whole universe is comprehended.[22] It is the earliest statement of the law of causality. But, even though generalized, it is still essentially the law of retribution.[23] Chronologically, the cause, as the wrong, must precede the effect, as the punishment. Just as necessity (τὸ χρεών) is the compulsion of the legal rule of retribution, so is the chronological order, the earlier and the later, the sequence of wrong and punishment. In this dynamism of retribution, scientific thought for the first time realizes the time category (τοῦ χρόνου τάξις).[24]   The reason why modern science still characterizes the relationship of cause and effect as asymmetrical and still maintains that the cause must precede the effect in time is that the cause was originally the wrong and the effect was the punishment.

67. HERACLITUS

Like Anaximander, Heraclitus saw in nature a tension of opposites and interpreted it by means of a purely social explanation, namely, that of πόλεμος, war. Diogenes Laertius reports that Heraclitus said: "All things come into being by conflict of opposites";[25] and: "things are brought into harmony by the clash of opposing currents."[26] Equally well known and much cited is Heraclitus' saying: "War is the father of all and the king of all."[27] But whereas Anaximander saw injustice in this strife, Heraclitus taught: "We must know that war is common to all and strife is justice [δίκη] and that all things come into being and pass away through strife."[28] In this war which the elements wage with one another, he recognized a universal law of life. This universal law, the "central concept of his whole philosophy," was "the idea of the *logos*, which means the same as eternal, transcendental, universal reason governing all things."[29] Of this universal law (λόγος), which is eternal, he said: "Men are as unable to understand it when they hear it for the first time as before they have heard it at all. For, though all things come to pass in accordance with this Word [law], men seem as if they had no experience of them."[30] Obviously, by the "logos," according to which all things come to pass, the law of causality is meant.

In this manner the law of nature was identified with destiny or fate (εἱμαρμένη). According to Diogenes Laertius,[31] Heraclitus taught that "all things come about by destiny"; and, according to Aetius,[32] he said: "Fate is the universal law [logos] which, as the result of the opposite up and down, forms all things." He also said: "Everything occurs according to fate and fate is identical with necessity." Further, Heraclitus explained fate as "the logos which penetrates the whole universe." The necessity of events, this essential function of causality, was for Heraclitus the inviolable will of a deity which presented itself as personification of reason. It is the expression of the absolute validity of the order in which the will of the deity is manifested; as absoluteness, inviolability can appear only as a quality of a transcendental authority that is assumed to exist beyond all experience. This necessity, the fate, is expressed by the word εἱμαρμένη. The verb μείρομαι means "to get a share"; etymologically it comes from σμέριομαι, the root of which is smer, "to allot"; the corresponding term in Latin is mereo, "I merit."[33] Possibly the word expressing causal necessity originally meant "merited allotment." One's fate is whatever is allotted to him as reward or as punishment. Presumably the idea of retribution leads to the concept of fate or destiny. Fate, then, is one's allotment according to merit or wrong, through the inexorable will of a requiting deity. Indeed, for Heraclitus the εἱμαρμένη is the inviolability of the legal rule, and the legal rule is undoubtedly that of retribution.

The thoroughly normative character of the universal law of Heraclitus, the norm that ought to be obeyed but which through folly is occasionally not obeyed, becomes evident in several of his fragments. "So we must follow the common; yet though my Word [logos = the law] is common, the many live as if they had a wisdom of their own."[34] Again, "those who speak with understanding must hold fast to what is common to all as a city holds fast to its law [νόμος] and even more strongly. For all human laws are fed [i.e. are valid] by the one divine law. It prevails as much as it will, and suffices for all things, with something to spare."[35] If human laws derive their validity from the divine universal law, it is because the divine universal law, the inviolable law of causality, is only a projection of the human law, i.e., the legal rule, onto the cosmos. And this legal rule projected onto the cosmos is inviolable because it is regarded as the absolute will of a deity. It is the fundamental idea of all natural law in the sense of a natural legal order that is formulated here.

That this legal rule is the law of retribution is clearly expressed in that famous fragment which may be called the counterpart of that of

Anaximander. "The sun will not overstep his measures [i.e., the pre-scribed path]; if he does, the Erinyes, the handmaids of Justice [Dike], will find him out."[36] The Erinyes are the well-known demons of venge-ance of the Greek religion. Dike, as she appears in the following frag-ment, is the goddess of retribution: "The most esteemed of them knows but fancies, and holds fast to them, yet of a truth justice [Dike] shall overtake the artificers of lies and the false witnesses."[37] Dike is called "inexorable" by the Orphics[38] and "the punisher of those who fall short of the divine law."[39] The significance which the saying of Heraclitus has for the history of scientific thought lies in the fact that the inviolability of the law of causality because of which the sun fol-lows its path is the compulsion of the goddess Justice [Dike]—an obli-gation imposed by a legal rule, a normative necessity.[40] The invio-lability of the universal law does not consist in the fact that it is always observed—the possibility of the sun going beyond its measure is not excluded. The inviolability consists rather in the fact that violation of the law is always and without exception punished. For the universal law, as a legal rule, is a norm laying down sanctions; this norm is, according to its tenor, a law of retribution and, as such, the unshakable will of a deity. The logos of Heraclitus is Dike, the goddess of inescap-able revenge.[41] The inviolability of the causal law, so contested in modern natural science, the absoluteness of its validity, originated in the inviolability which myth and the philosophy of nature evolving from it attributed to the principle of retribution as the substance of a divine and thus absolutely binding will. From this principle of retribu-tion the earliest natural science worked out its law of nature.[42]

That the principle of retribution is the basis for Heraclitus' universal law is also shown by his doctrine of world fire. According to this the-ory, the original cause of the world was fire, from which all things came and to which all things return.[43] A fragment reads: "All things are an exchange for Fire, and Fire for all things, even as wares for gold and gold for wares."[44] The universal process of transformation of fire into things, and vice versa, is represented as barter, which is only a special form of retribution. The effect follows the cause just as gold is given for wares. The causal nexus is not merely compared with the tie which the principle of retribution establishes between its two elements but is considered an application of this principle. The Christian bishop Hippolytus, therefore, did not much alter the Heraclitian theory of Ekpyrosis when he represented it by saying that "a judgment of the world and all things in it takes place by fire, expressing himself thus:

'Now, thunder pilots all things,' that is, directs (them), meaning by the thunder everlasting fire. But he also asserts that this fire is endued with intelligence, and a cause of the management of the Universe and he denominates it craving ·and satiety. Now craving is, according to him the arrangement (of the world), whereas satiety its destruction. 'For,' says he, 'the fire coming upon (the earth), will judge and seize all things.' "[45]

68. PARMENIDES

The notion that the necessity which holds the cosmos together is the absolute obligation of a divine legal norm and that this norm, the law of nature, as the law of eternal being, is retribution appears no less clearly in Parmenides than in his great antagonist, Heraclitus. In order to arrive at the knowledge of this law, he set out upon the imaginary journey described in his theoretical poem. This journey led him to $\Delta i\kappa\eta$ $\pi o\lambda \acute{v}\pi o\iota\nu os$, to the "goddess of retribution."[46] She holds the key to the gate through which leads the road to light, to true knowledge. Dike, the goddess of justice, is also the goddess of truth. For in this thoroughly ethical-juridical view of the world, truth is identical with justice, whose inexorableness appears here as "the unshakable heart [$\dot{a}\tau\rho\epsilon\mu\grave{\epsilon}s$ $\mathring{\eta}\tau o\rho$] of the well-rounded truth."[47]

The fundamental thesis of the Parmenidian ontology, namely, that coming into being and passing away are mere illusions, and that, by virtue of necessity, there is only eternal, unchangeable being, is expressed as follows: "Wherefore, Justice [Dike] doth not loose her fetters and let anything come into being or pass away, but holds it fast."[48] That is $\Delta i\kappa\eta$ $\pi o\lambda \acute{v}\pi o\iota\nu os$, the goddess of retribution. The same idea is repeated later: "Moreover, it [the being] is immovable in the bonds of mighty chains, without beginning and without end; since coming into being and passing away have been driven afar, and true belief has cast them away . . . . for hard necessity ['$A\nu\acute{a}\gamma\kappa\eta$] keeps it in the bonds of the limit that holds it fast on every side."[49] And Parmenides further writes: "Fate [$\mu o\hat{\iota}\rho a$] has chained it so as to be whole and immovable."[50] The "hard necessity" and "Fate" are identical with Dike, the goddess of retribution. The determination of the law of nature, the inviolable rule of existence (being) is the compulsion of an absolute legal norm. The inviolability of the universal law, "the unshakable heart of the truth," is the iron will of the deity of justice, the inescapability of retribution. This same idea was expressed by the poet Aeschylus in his *Prometheus Bound*, where necessity is a power even above Zeus. The leader of the chorus asks: "Who then is the steersman of Necessity?" To which Prometheus replies: "The triform Fates and mindful Furies."[51]

69. EMPEDOCLES

Retribution is also a concept—if not the fundamental concept—of the philosophy of Empedocles, which was influenced by Orphic and Pythagorean elements. At the center of this philosophy lies the idea of the transmigration of the soul,[52] according to which the thinker of Akragas, who was more prophet than philosopher, interprets his own fate. Here, as everywhere, the doctrine of the transmigration of the soul is a specific ideology of retribution.

There is an oracle of Necessity ['Aνάγκη], an ancient ordinance of the gods, eternal and sealed fast by broad oaths, that whenever one of the daemons, whose portion is length of days, has sinfully polluted his hands with blood, or followed strife and forsworn himself, he must wander thrice ten thousand seasons from the abodes of the blessed, being born throughout the time in all manners of mortal forms, changing one toilsome path of life for another. For the mighty Air drives him into the Sea, and the Sea spews him forth on the dry Earth; Earth tosses him into the beams of the blazing Sun, and he flings him back to the eddies of Air. One takes him from the other, and all reject him. One of these I now am, an exile and a wanderer from the gods, for that I put my trust in insensate strife.[53]

It is nature itself, the four elements of which, according to the doctrine of Empedocles, are air, water, earth, and fire, that punishes the evildoer. Thus it is nature itself whose function is recognized to be retribution.

The wrong which incurs the retributive reaction is by no means merely a social evil, an injury inflicted by one individual upon another in human society. The notion that the human soul can be embodied in other beings, in animals or plants, leads here, as also in totemistic systems, to the idea of a society embracing not only men but all other beings as well. This society is constituted by an order which subjects all beings to the same law and, especially, guarantees to all beings the same right to live. The fundamental norm of this order is the prohibition of killing. In this way nature obviously becomes a part of society; consequently, the law of retribution becomes the law of nature. Diogenes Laertius[54] reported of Empedocles that "he says . . . . the soul . . . . assumes all the various forms of animals and plants." In this same connection Aristotle[55] said: "In fact, there is a general idea of just and unjust in accordance with nature, as all men in a manner divine, even if there is neither communication nor agreement between them. . . . . And as Empedocles says in regard to not killing that which has life, for this is not right for some and wrong for others." In Cicero[56] these words are found: "Pythagoras and Empedocles declare that the same principles of justice apply to all living creatures (unam omnium animantium condicionem iuris), and insist that inevitable penalties threaten those who injure an animal." A statement of Empedocles which has been handed down verbally runs: "Will ye not cease from this ill-sounding slaughter? See ye not that ye are devouring one another in the thoughtlessness of your hearts?"[57] Another statement explains:

And the father lifts up his own son in a changed form and slays him with a prayer. Infatuated fool! And they run up to the sacrificers, begging mercy, while he, deaf to their cries, slaughters them in his halls and gets ready the evil feast. In like manner does the son seize his father, and children their mother, tear out their life and eat the kindred flesh.[58]

It seems that Empedocles considered this law of life governing men, animals, and plants which was sanctioned by retribution—by "inevitable penalties"—to be a special case of a still more general law dominating the whole universe. He characterized this law in these words: "(This is not lawful for some and unlawful for others;) but the law for all extends everywhere, through the wide-ruling air and the infinite light of heaven."[59] This universal law is in his view a law of retribution.[60]

This universal law manifests itself in the philosophy of Empedocles as the eternal and necessary interchange of two fundamental forces: one principle binding the elements together and mixing them, the other separating and isolating them. He calls them "Love" ($\varphi\iota\lambda\iota\alpha$, 'Αφροδίτη) and "Strife" (νεῖκος). By no means does he use these conceptions metaphorically; undoubtedly, he has in mind the social categories of association and dissociation, though still in a mytho-sociological sense. For Love and Strife appear to him not only as conditions or objective phenomena within the elements of nature but as personal beings, as deities or demons who fight one another with the victory going now to one, now to the other.

I shall tell thee a two-fold tale. At one time it grew to be one only out of many; at another, it divided up to be many instead of one. There is a double becoming of perishable things and a double passing away. The coming together of all things brings one generation into being and destroys it; the other grows up and is scattered as things become divided. And these things never cease continually changing places, at one time all uniting in one through Love, at another each borne in different directions by the repulsion of Strife. Thus, as far as it is their nature to grow into one out of many, and to become many once more when the one is parted asunder, so far they come into being and their life abides not. But, inasmuch as they never cease changing their places continually, so far they are ever immovable as they go round the circle of existence.[61]

That in Love and Strife there is involved not only a mechanical attraction and repulsion but also the social relations implied under those names is borne out by the fact that Empedocles speaks in his speculation devoted to the mere interpretation of nature of the "soft, immortal stream of blameless Love"[62] and of "cruel Strife."[63] One of the fragments contains these words:

For all of these—sun, earth, sky, and sea—are at one with all their parts that are cast far and wide from them in mortal things. And even so all things that are more adapted for mixture are like to one another and united in love by Aphrodite. Those things, again, that differ most in origin, mixture and the forms imprinted on each, are most hostile, being altogether unaccustomed to unite and very sorry by the bidding of Strife, since it hath wrought their birth.[64]

The eternal cycle of the world process, governed now by Love, now by Strife, began with a period when Love ruled alone—a state of harmony, happiness, and peace. All things form one whole, the round "Sphairos" about which Empedocles said: "There [in the sphere] are distinguished neither the swift limbs of the sun, no, nor the shaggy earth in its might, nor the sea,—so fast was the god bound in the close covering of Harmony, spherical and round, rejoicing in his circular solitude."[65] In addition, the philosopher pointed out that "there is no discord and no unseemly strife in his limbs."[66] Later Strife came in, and the process of disharmony and isolation began. The original condition of the universe is strikingly parallel to the original state of society which Empedocles pictures as a kind of golden age, of peace and happiness.[67] "And just so far as they grow to be different, so far do different thoughts ever present themselves to their minds (in dreams)";[68] and: "For all things were tame and gentle to man, both beasts and birds, and friendly feelings were kindled everywhere."[69] This golden age, it may be safely conjectured, ended with the outbreak of Strife. And it may be supposed that with his cosmology Empedocles projected his sociophilosophical ideas onto the universe.[70]

That φιλία and νεῖκος in the cosmos are only the projections of human Love and Strife is borne out by the previously mentioned principle, according to which like things can be recognized only by like things. For, when it is said that only by our love (the love within us) can we perceive Love (in the cosmos) and Hate (νεῖκος) by grievous hate, this is not to be understood in a biological sense; it is not because of the elements of love and hate contained in our blood that we are enabled to recognize cosmic Love and cosmic Hate.[71] Rather, we must understand that these cosmic processes are equal to the social phenomena which we experience as love and hate, and thus are recognizable to us. Just as these phenomena are deities in the myths, they appear also as such in the cosmology of Empedocles. So one fragment runs: "But, as divinity was mingled still further with divinity" [i.e., Love with Strife].[72] And another: "But when Strife was grown great in the limbs of the god and sprang forth to claim his prerogatives, in the fulness of the alternate time set for them by the mighty oath."[73] Aristotle pointed out that "Empedocles seems to imply that the alternating power of attraction (love) and repulsion (strife) effectively to move things was always there of necessity and the periods of rest between."[74] Indeed, Aristotle was right when he interpreted the fight between the two hostile, alternately victorious forces in Empedocles' writings as the antagonism between good and evil.[75] This consideration of the world process as a struggle between good and evil inevitably presupposes the idea of retribution, for it is essentially the reaction against the evildoer which suggests the idea of a "fight" against "the evil."

Through careful examination of the available fragments one gains the impression that in Empedocles the law of eternal and necessary change between Love and Strife has the meaning of retribution. Strife is the evil. It is the wrong of those who resort to strife. At the same time it is their punishment.[76] In Greek mythology it is often the same deity who seduces one to do evil and then punishes the evildoer. In a fragment in which the retributive character of the transmigration of the soul is expressed together with the self-confession of Empedocles, we read:[77] ". . . . whenever one of the daemons . . . . has . . . . followed strife . . . . he must wander thrice ten thousand seasons. . . . . I now am an exile and a wanderer from the gods, for that I put my trust in insensate strife." Hippolytus interprets this passage as follows: "This is the punishment which the Demiurge [Strife] inflicts. . . . ."[78]

The Strife through which one is seduced and becomes involved in wrong inflicts punishment upon the evildoer. Such retribution is not only exercised upon the sinful man—sinful because engaged in strife— but also on the separating elements themselves. In the previously cited fragment which deals with things "united in love by Aphrodite" and things "that differ most in origin, mixture and the forms imprinted on each," the latter are characterized by the words: "[They] are most hostile, being altogether unaccustomed to unite and very sorry by the bidding of Strife."[79] It is the will of Strife, obviously punishing and exercising retribution, which makes things "unaccustomed to unite and very sorry." The interpretation of Hippolytus receives full confirmation here. When things pass from the state of love, which is a condition of good and therefore of peace and happiness, into a state of strife, which is a condition of evil, they become at the same time inflicted by misfortune, i.e., punishment. The eternal law governing this change is the law of retribution. Its inviolability has, therefore, a specifically normative character. The "oracle of Necessity" which decrees this law, this "ancient ordinance of the gods," is "eternal and sealed fast by broad oaths." As a consequence this norm is as firm as a promise sealed by oath. The oath is a specific guaranty of law. In Empedocles, too, Ananke is identical with Dike, and the inviolability of the law of nature is the absoluteness of a normative bond.

70. THE ATOMISTS

The modern concept of causality was in principle established in the writings of the atomists Leucippus and Democritus. These founders of pure natural science achieved almost complete separation of the law of causality from the principle of retribution by consistently eliminating all theological elements from their interpretation of nature and by strictly rejecting causes which are simultaneously ends. As long as the world order is conceived as the expression of a more or less personal, rational, and therefore purposefully functioning will, the law of nature must have the character of a norm, which by analogy with the social norm, the rule of law, guarantees the normal state of things by means of sanctions. The universal law must be the law of retribution. Any deviation of events from this law is considered the condition of a reaction proceding from a divine will and tending to restore the balance in nature. We find the same idea in modern jurisprudence. Here the delict is the condition of the sanction; and the sanction, especially the punishment, the reaction against the delict, is considered the re-establishment of the law. Consequently, the inviolability of the law of nature, its absolute necessity, refers not so much to the fact that nature without exception obeys the law to which it is subject as to the fact that the reaction against possible disobedience, the punishment of Dike, goddess of justice, is inevitable. The sun must keep to its lawful path; but, if it should once deviate from its way, it would unresistingly be corrected by the punishment demons of the goddess of retribution. Heraclitus still considered the law of nature in that way. But for the atomists it ceased to be a norm, i.e., the expression of a divine will. It became the manifestation of an impersonal objective necessity.[80]

"Democritus," Aristotle[81] says, "neglecting the final cause, reduces to necessity [εἰς ἀνάγκην] all the operations of Nature." Democritus did not consider the universe to have been constructed by some personal being. "Democritus assumes," writes Pseudoplutarch,[82] "the all to be infinite because it was never created by anyone. . . . . The causes of that which now occurs had no commencement; all that has happened, now is, or will be has existed from all eternity and is already in the lap of necessity." Nothing is more characteristic of the truly scientific spirit of the atomists, based entirely upon a mechanical conception of the world, than the sentence ascribed to Democritus "that he would rather discover one single law of causation than receive the kingdom of Persia."[83]

The freeing of the interpretation of nature from the principle of retribution in the philosophy of the atomists is exactly parallel to the analogous emancipation of the social theory in the philosophy of the sophists. Protagoras, the contemporary of Leucippus, taught that the specific technique of the state order, which reacts to a socially harmful deed with a coercive act directed against the wrongdoer, is not justifiable by the religious idea of retribution but by the rational intent of prevention. Punishment is inflicted not because of some obscure reason but for a clear purpose.

No one punishes the evil-doer under the notion, or for the reason, that he has done wrong,—only the unreasonable fury of a beast acts in that manner. But he who desires to inflict rational punishment does not retaliate for a past wrong which cannot be undone; he has regard to the future, and is desirous that the man who is punished, and he who sees him punished, may be deterred from doing wrong again. He punishes for the sake of prevention.[84]

In this manner the law of the state, like the law of nature, was freed from the myth of retribution.

The causal principle, however, even in the purified form which it assumed in the writings of the atomists, cannot entirely deny its origin. According to Aetius,[85] Leucippus states that everything happens of necessity (κατ' ἀνάγκην), which is identical with fate (εἱμαρμένη). "Naught happens for nothing, but everything from a ground and of necessity [ἐκ λόγου τε καὶ ὑπ' ἀνάγκης]." The concept of cause is here expressed by λόγος. This is the λόγος of Heraclitus, whose doctrine has strongly influenced the atomists. The λόγος, in accordance to which, in Heraclitus, "all things come to pass [γινομένων γὰρ πάντων κατὰ τὸν λόγον],"[86] is in Leucippus' doctrine transformed into the mechanical cause. If the latter works here with absolute necessity (ἀνάγκη), it has taken over this quality from the inviolable will of the deity, which is the λόγος of Heraclitus.

The origin of the idea of strict causality is still clearer in Democritus. According to Aetius, he seems to have understood by necessity (ἀνάγκη) the blows and counterblows of the atoms which clash against one another.[87] In order to understand this formulation of physical causality, one must realize that, according to Democritus, change is only the collision and separation of atoms; nothing exists but atoms, which "are in disaccord with one another" and crash against one another in empty space. In this manner things appear and disappear. Diogenes Laertius[88] presents the theory of Leucippus as follows:

The world comes into being thus. There were borne along by "abscision from the infinite" many bodies of all sorts of figures "into a mighty void," and they being gathered together produce a single vortex. In it, as they came into collision with one another and were whirled round in all manner of ways, those which were alike were separated apart and came to their likes.

The decisive facts are the collision and separation, the blows and counterblows, of the atoms. It is in these facts that ἀνάγκη, the necessity which we call "causality," manifests itself. This signifies that the atomists saw causality in a phenomenon the scheme of which is action and reaction. This idea is similar to the principle of retribution, which connects an action with its specific reaction, the wrong with the punishment, the merit with the reward. The atoms strike against one another "in disaccord"—just as in Heraclitus things are constantly "at war"—and "are brought into harmony by the clash of opposing currents."[89] The elements connected by the principle of retribution are opposite with respect to the direction of their action but not with respect to their nature, since it is like which is requited with like. Thus, according to Democritus' law of causality, among atoms which are "in disaccord" only like can affect like. In the Hibeh Papyri[90] is found the following passage: ".... he [Democritus] says that in a wet substance like is (drawn) to like as in the whole creation, and thus the sea was created and all else that is .... through the combination of homogenous atoms." Likewise in a fragment of Democritus one reads:

Animals associate with the same kind of animals—doves with doves, cranes with cranes, and the remaining animals similarly. The same is true for lifeless things as one can see in the case of grains of seed sifted promiscuously and in the case of pebbles in the surf. For in the former instance, a whirling motion of the sieve effects a separation so that lentils go to lentils, barleycorn to barleycorn, grains of wheat to grains of wheat. In the latter, the longish pebbles are driven to the longish ones, the round ones to the round by the swell of the surf as if the similarity peculiar to things created a power of attraction between them.[91]

And Aristotle says:[92]

Most thinkers are unanimous in maintaining (a) that "like" is always unaffected by "like," because (as they argue) neither of two "likes" is more apt than the other either to act or to suffer action, since all the properties which belong to the one belong identically and in the same degree to the other, and (b) that "unlikes," i.e. "differents," are by nature such as to act and suffer action reciprocally. For even when the smaller fire is destroyed by the greater, it suffers the effect (they say) owing to its "contrariety"—since the great is contrary to the small. But Demokritos dissented from all the other thinkers and maintained a theory peculiar to himself. He asserts that agent and patient are identical, i.e. "like." It is not possible (he says) that "others," i.e. "differents," should suffer action from one another: on the contrary, even if two things, being "others," do act in some way on one another, this happens to them not qua "others" but qua possessing an identical property.

It is because "like is drawn to like" that the magnet attracts the iron. "With this supposition," said Alexander Aphrodisiensis,[93] "he [Democritus] assumes that the magnet and the iron consist of the same kind of atoms." So wrong attracts punishment which is essentially similar to it; for example, murder attracts murder (as blood revenge or death penalty); merit attracts reward because they are essentially similar. Thus the magnet attracts iron because the latter is "like" the former. When Democritus described the fact that a cause has an effect on a thing by the words, the thing "suffers" the effect, the idea of "suffering" punishment was in the background.

71. The Significance of αἰτία

Pliny's assertion[94] that Democritus recognized only two deities, *Poenam et Beneficium* (Punishment and Reward), is quite understandable. When Aristotle[95] pictured the atomistic law of causality in these words, ". . . . that nothing happens casually, but that everything we speak of in that way has really a definite cause" (τι αἴτιον), and when, in Democritus[96] as well as elsewhere in the old philosophy of nature, "cause" meant αἰτία, then one must not forget that this word's original meaning was "guilt."[97] The cause is "responsible" for the effect. This is the internal connection between the two elements of the law of causality; and the idea of such an internal connection between cause and effect has not yet entirely disappeared from the thinking of modern natural science.

PART III

MODERN SCIENCE

CHAPTER VI

THE LAW OF CAUSALITY IN MODERN
NATURAL SCIENCE

72. HUME'S CRITIQUE OF THE CONCEPT OF CAUSALITY

ORIGINALLY developed in the doctrines of the atomists, the principle of absolutely valid causality, which as a natural law admitted no exceptions, was subsequently taken over by Epicurus and his followers. After the triumph of Christianity, however, this idea was in danger of being lost again in the theological view of the world that prevailed in the Middle Ages. But the new natural science founded by Bacon, Galileo, and Kepler resuscitated and revised the principle of causality so that it remained the sole scheme for the interpretation of nature until quite recently, when in certain spheres of modern physics it was questioned, if not completely denied. If one speaks today, whether rightly or wrongly, of a crisis in this principle, one must not forget that this crisis began with Hume's famous critique of the belief in causality. Hume's objections are directed mainly against the idea, still prevalent in his time, that there exists an objective connection between cause and effect, a connection inherent in the things themselves—an inner bond such that the cause somehow brings about the effect; the cause does something in inducing the effect. Hence, the cause is conceived of as an agent, a substance emitting force.[1] Such an idea seems to have been supported by the experience of the operation of the will of man, who considered his ego or his "soul" (a concept similar to that of force) as the "cause" of his actions. The decisive turn which Hume gave to the problem of causality was the transfer of the connection between cause and effect from the sphere of the objective to that of the subjective, thus making an epistemological problem out of an ontological one. To put it more correctly, he split the problem of causality into ontological and epistemological components·

by asserting that in nature there is no causality in the sense of a necessary connection but only a regular succession of events. The idea of a
general law of causality, according to which similar causes necessarily
produce similar effects, is merely a habit of thought which, originating
from the observation of regular successions of events, becomes a firm
conviction.[2] Starting from this point and carrying on in the direction
Hume had indicated, Kant arrived at his own doctrine. He declared
that mere observation of reality could not establish the necessity of a
connection between two facts, such as cause and effect; consequently,
he pointed out, the concept of causality is an inborn notion, an a priori
category, an inevitable and necessary form of cognition by means of
which we mentally co-ordinate the empirical material of sensuous perception.

73. The Idea of the Objective Necessity of the Causal Connection

Whence, then, comes the idea that the necessity of the connection
between cause and effect is objective and, therefore, inherent in the
events? What is the basis for the belief that the cause brings about or
entails the effect? And, finally, why is it that there exists not only a
post hoc but also a *propter hoc* between cause and effect? Hume's explanation is not sufficient. He only says: "Having found, in many instances, that any two kinds of objects—flame and heat, snow and cold
—have always been conjoined together; if flame or snow be presented
anew to the senses, the mind is carried by custom to expect heat or
cold, and to *believe* that such a quality does exist, and will discover itself upon a nearer approach."[2a] Our mind is led by custom to expect
that a certain phenomenon will always be followed in the future by the
same phenomenon which has regularly followed it in the past. However, our mind is not led by custom to believe that an exception is absolutely excluded. Hume's theory is obviously influenced by the idea
of customary law prevailing in England in his time. In this connection
he expressly states: "Custom . . . . is the great guide of human life."
But even custom does not constitute rules without exceptions. The
idea that the connection between cause and effect has the character of
absolute necessity cannot be the result of a custom or habit of thought.
Probably, as the development of ancient Greek philosophy has shown,
it arises from the principle of retribution.

This principle is the expression of a transcendental will, independent
of the human beings subjected to it, of a specifically objective au-

thority which connects punishment with wrong and reward with merit by allotting punishment "on account of" the wrong, and reward "on account of" the merit. As long as the idea of a transcendental authority endowed with reason and will exists, there can be no distinction between the connection of wrong and punishment or merit and reward, on the one hand, and cause and effect, on the other. For in each case this connection must be effected by the will of the authority. Thus one cannot differentiate between the law of morality and the law of nature so long as both are considered to be the will of the deity. As long as there is a belief in the existence of a transcendental authority ruling over human society as well as nature, the will of this authority is the objective bond which holds cause and effect together even though the law of causality has separated itself from the principle of retribution.

The attempt to eliminate the idea of a transcendental will from the interpretation of nature has not always had complete success. The transcendental will has simply been metamorphosed into the metaphysical cause. It is the cause which "wills" the effect. And the result is the same if the relationship between cause and effect is conceived by analogy with the connection which is assumed between the soul of man—i.e., the deity within man—and the actions of man "caused" by his soul. Already in mythical thinking the connection between wrong and punishment brought about by the will of the deity had been projected to the connected facts; the punishing will of the deity was imagined as having its seat somehow in the substantially conceived wrong. In the Bible the shed blood cries out for vengeance, for in it is the avenging soul of the murdered man. Thus, also, in the Greek myth the Erinyes originate from the blood of Uranus, criminally castrated by his son Cronus. The objective bond imagined between cause and effect is the transcendental will projected onto nature. In transforming causality from an objectively necessary connection of cause and effect, immanent to nature, into a subjective principle of human thinking, Hume and Kant merely freed the law of causality from an element which it inherited as a successor to the principle of retribution.

74. THE EQUIVALENCE OF CAUSE AND EFFECT (THE PRINCIPLE OF EQUIVALENCE)

Another element of the concept of causality with which modern physics takes issue is the thesis that the effect must be equal to the cause: *causa aequat effectum*. Mach has already shown this proposition,

which Robert Mayer,[3] the discoverer of the principle of the conservation of energy, frequently used, to be completely "empty."[4] And
Philipp Frank[5] is of the opinion that

it is a main feature of the popular concept of causality that cause and effect must
somehow be equal or at least proportional. The stronger the cause the stronger the
effect. Yet a suitable method of measuring all possible causes and effects was wanting,
a method to ascertain when a certain portion of a cause was equal to a certain
portion of the effect. Anyway one believed to have a certain feeling for it. Finally, in
the physical principle that any system of bodies can increase in energy only in the extent that it takes energy from surrounding bodies, did there appear the equivalent
concrete formulation of the fact that the effect must be equal to the cause. Driesch
explicitly states: "Energy is the measure of causality."

Frank, however, after calling attention to the problematical character
of the conception of energy,[6] maintains that from the point of view of
physics it is impossible simply "to consider energy as a general measure
of causality."[7]

But, even if one assumes that the principle, "The cause must be
equal to the effect," has led to the physically true principle of the conservation of energy, one cannot declare, as is sometimes done, that the
principle of causality is identical with the principle of energy or that
the former is the "logical equivalent" of the latter.[8] The principle that
through the disappearance of a certain amount of energy of one kind a
certain amount of energy of another kind comes into existence has a
completely different meaning from the principle that the cause must
be equal to the effect.[9] Only through a radical change of significance
could it lead to the principle of the equivalence of energies. In an
earlier chapter on the ancient philosophy of nature it has already been
pointed out that this element of the theory of causality likewise originated in the doctrine of retribution—in the principle that like must be
given for like.[10] Here it may be observed that the idea of an objective
measure of both facts, connected with one another in the principle of
retribution, as well as the resulting demand that the greater the wrong
the greater must be the punishment, and the greater the merit the
greater the reward, is founded on the substantializing tendency of
primitive thinking. This tendency renders all qualities, conditions, and
forces, also "good" and "evil," in quantitatively determinable substances. Thus guilt, wrong, and sin, considered as substances and attached to the wrongdoer, are washed off in purification rites; or, in
other cases, they are considered substances residing within the wrongdoer and are either spit out, vomited, or spoken "out" in confession.
Only when the evil of wrong and the evil of punishment are quanti-

tatively determinable substances can they be counterbalanced in retribution. In criminal law, if the ideology of retribution, and thus the idea that wrong and punishment are substances, is abandoned and, in place of retribution, prevention as the purpose of punishment is accepted, then the equivalence of wrong and punishment loses its sense. For punishment under these conditions would no longer be inflicted "on account of" the wrong committed but in order to prevent future wrong. Neither wrong nor punishment are objectively measurable quantities. Nevertheless, something like equivalence of wrong and punishment seems to be imaginable. The more harmful a fact, qualified as wrong, is regarded, the more must be feared the evil threatened to prevent it and the more "severe" must be the punishment. The problematical character of this proportion is borne out by the fact that the measurements of the two elements have no objective character but represent merely subjective evaluation. For the theory of prevention the equivalence of wrong and punishment has—in so far as it can be maintained at all—a totally different significance from that which it has for the theory of retribution; and just so, the principle of the equivalence of energies, interpreted as quantitative proportionality—if such an interpretation is at all possible—has a totally different significance from the principle of the equality of cause and effect in the older theory of causality. In physics the energetics seems to constitute the same kind of progress as the theory of prevention in juristic thinking; both signify a triumph over the principle of retribution.

75. The Bipartite Character of the Law of Causality

The problematical character of the statement that the cause must be equal to the effect, and vice versa, is also discernible in the related idea that a cause has only one effect and that an effect is traceable to only one cause. The principle of causality, according to its popular conception, has an essentially bipartite character. Since, however, each cause must itself be considered in turn as the effect of another cause and each effect as the cause of further effects, each point to be determined causally lies in an endless chain of causality which has the character of a *continuum*. The phenomena described as "cause and effect" constitute a direct, though not always immediately perceptible, connection of events. The so-called "cause" changes imperceptibly into the so-called "effect."[11] Cause and effect are, in the words of Goethe, "an indivisible phenomenon." That we nevertheless separate them from one another, even oppose them to one another, that we intentionally isolate from the continuous chain of innumerable elements two alone as *the* cause and *the* effect which is imputed to this cause alone, is due to the age-old habit of interpreting nature according to the principle of retribution. The latter connects a particular event, characterized as wrong, with the punishment, likewise a precisely determined event clearly separated chronologically from the first. The possibility of isolating these two facts from a continuous stream of events is due to the fact that both are "arbitrarily" determined and linked together by either divine or human will expressed through the norm of retribution. This method of isolating phenomena, derived from normative thinking, does not prevent the attainment of useful theoretical, as well as practical, results in the field of natural science.

But these results must be corrected by the realization that each effect has an infinite number of causes and each cause an infinite number of effects. Such a correction is all the more necessary since a realistic analysis shows that each effect is not only the end of a chain of causes but also the beginning of a new chain and, at the same time, the point of intersection of an infinite number of chains. No event is dependent upon one cause alone. Starting with this fact, certain philosophers have completely abandoned the concept of cause as useless and have replaced it by that of "conditions" or "components" of the event.[12] Similarly, the concept of effect had to be replaced by that of "resultants." However, it was deemed necessary to indicate one of the conditions or components of an event as the "decisive" one. Thus a distinction was made between the "cause" as the collective conception of all the conditions of an effect taken together and the "cause" in the narrower sense of an "immediate" condition, or the "decisive variation"[13] of one of the conditioning circumstances. Hence, the notion of causality was not really abandoned but only modified. What was given up was simply one element, namely, the idea that causality is a connection between two facts only, that the principle of causality is bipartite, a notion which originated in the sphere of retribution. Here, and here alone, is this idea incontestably appropriate: one delict, one punishment. The postulation that one ought not to be punished more than once for the same delict, that the law of retribution should be exhausted by a single reaction to one fact and thus literally is bipartite, is expressed by the maxim: "Ne bis in idem." Criticism of the law of causality, made by what has been termed "conditionism,"[14] aims only at its separation from the principle of retribution.

76. The Temporal Sequence of Cause and Effect

According to the principle of retribution, the two parts are connected in the sense that one must chronologically precede the other: first the crime and then the punishment; first the merit and then the reward. But the two divisions are not interchangeable. And the simultaneity of the two parts is inconceivable. The law of causality is, or was originally, considered in this light—namely, by analogy to the principle of retribution, the two parts of which are linked in an irreversible chronological sequence. In this form of an asymmetrical principle the law of causality was conceived as the fundamental form of the law of nature. As soon as it became necessary to relinquish the assumption of the immanent connection of cause and effect and to replace it with the concept of a purely functional dependency, this idea was no longer maintainable. The chronological sequence of phenomena is consequently not an essential element of a law of nature. Functional dependency may exist between even simultaneous events. But if simultaneous events display functional dependency, then they are also reversible. Indeed, modern natural science knows of many connections where no temporal difference appears between the connected elements.[15] Thus there are laws of nature which do not correspond to the original scheme of causality. To be sure, these connections are still frequently represented "causally," i.e., as relationships of a chronologically preceding cause to a chronologically succeeding effect. But in reality, from the point of view of physical knowledge, functional connections do exist between simultaneous phenomena. Thus the fact that a thrown body, under the influence of the force of gravity, follows a parabolic orbit is explained by saying that gravity is the cause which has as its effect the parabolic orbit of the body. The decisive relationship, however, is the one between position, velocity, and acceleration, which are simultaneously existing elements.[16] Boyle's law, for example, sets up a connection between the pressure and the volume of a gas, which are simultaneous elements,[17] although it is customary to say that increased or diminished pressure is the cause for the increase or the diminution of the volume. According to Kepler's third law, a certain period of rotation is associated with a certain distance of a planet from the sun; but one can also put it the other way round and say that a certain distance from the sun is associated with a certain period of rotation.[18] In the law of Kirchhoff, absorption and emission are connected functionally with one another. Both are simultaneously exist-

4

ing coefficients.[19] Thus, neither may be called the "cause" or the "effect" of the other.

This means that causality—using the term in its original sense—has lost its significance. The modern view of the law of nature as a concept of functional dependency has been emancipated from the older notion of causality as the concatenation of two events immanently connected with one another in an irreversible chronological order. The choice is now between two possibilities: either, to cease to identify any longer this enlarged concept of the natural law with that of the causal law, since it is not desirable to speak of causality in the case of simultaneously existing events,[20] and thus to assume laws of nature which are not laws of causality, or, in accordance with historical development, to see in the modern law of nature, which comprehends the functional dependency of simultaneous events, a modification of the law of causality. If the latter choice is made, the law of causality might be formulated as follows: generally speaking, a specific event—the effect—occurs when another specific event—the cause—has previously occurred or occurs simultaneously.[21] Thus the law of causality, even in a modified sense, remains the fundamental form of all natural law. This modification in the meaning of the law of causality also signifies its emancipation from the essentially asymmetrical principle of retribution.[22]

77. ABSOLUTE NECESSITY OR STATISTICAL PROBABILITY

It is generally accepted that the main blow at the law of causality was struck by the recently developed quantum mechanics, the mechanics of subatomic particles. The assumption, based on the law of causality, that mechanical phenomena can be predetermined in their prescribed course by knowledge of the initial state of motion has proved to be useless, since in the sphere of atomic physics the initial state of motion can never be fully determined. Of the two variables which constitute the initial state of motion—for example, position and velocity, or time and energy—only one can be measured with comparative accuracy, for the inaccuracy of the value of one variant increases in proportion to the degree of accuracy attained in measuring the other. If one variable is determined with absolute accuracy, the other variable remains absolutely indeterminate. This is the "principle of indeterminacy," discovered and formulated by Heisenberg.[23] If one assumes predictability as the criterion of causality,[24] as is done in the modern philosophy of nature, and declares an event to be causally determined when it can be safely predicted, then there is, according to the general interpretation, no causality in the sphere of quantum mechanics, or at least causality cannot be proved even where it is "objectively" given. But it is said that the causal determination of subatomic processes is unnecessary for arriving at physical laws for macroscopic phenomena. To be sure, such laws would not express absolute necessity but merely statistical probability.

Reichenbach[25] interprets the crisis in modern physics not as an issue involving the replacement of causality by statistical laws but, more correctly, as a modification of the concept of causality. It is a modification in the direction of a transition from absolute certainty to mere probability, a development which began, however, in classical physics. "Every assertion of causality applied to the prediction of a natural event has the form of an assertion of probability." The concept of probability which is used here is that of statistics, and it is "not a disturbing intruder but a necessary part of every description of reality through which alone the principle of causality achieves any conceivable sense." Bergmann[26] formulates the result of the criticism of modern physics as follows: "Instead of presupposing the absolute necessity of an individual event, one has to be satisfied to assume the postulate that whatever possesses the greater mathematical probability occurs proportionally more often in nature." Here "probability" replaces the "necessity" in the previous formulation of the law of causality. The assumption that a necessary connection exists between cause and effect is replaced by the assumption that the connection is only a probable one.[27]

Sometimes, however, philosophers deny that the results of the quantum mechanics force us to replace the assumption of causality in the sense of an absolutely necessary connection between cause and effect with a weaker assumption of the law of nature, namely, the assumption of mere probability.[28] This supposition relies essentially on the fact that quantum mechanics itself presupposes the strict principle of causality as an epistemological postulate. But, even if that is true, the above-mentioned formula of Reichenbach would not be affected. For the latter apparently views causality as a law of nature describing reality, whereas the advocates of the theory of strict causality comprehend it as an epistemological postulate. As such, it could very well have the form of an inviolable norm. It is the norm which demands that a cause be sought for every event. J. Loewenberg,[29] comparing Kant's causal category with his "categorical imperative," says: "Like the latter, which urges that duty is to do one's duty, the causal category is but a command to judge causally." That means that causality as category, in the sense of Kant's philosophy, is a norm directed to human thinking. This norm may be valid without exception, even though experience permits only approximate conformity with it and warrants a description of reality only in terms of statistical probability.

78. LAPLACE'S "ABSOLUTE INTELLIGENCE" AND PREDICTABILITY AS CRITERION OF CAUSALITY

Whether or not the replacement of absolute necessity by statistical probability in the concept of natural law is traceable to quantum mechanics with its principle of indeterminacy may be left undecided. If the law of causality was used to predict future events, even before Heisenberg's discovery, only a calculation of probability was possible.[30] In his *Essai philosophique sur les probabilités* Laplace[31] wrote:

> An intelligence which at a given moment knows all the forces that are effective in nature and the respective situation of the beings who compose it—an intelligence sufficiently vast to submit these data to analysis—would embrace in the same formula the movements of the greatest bodies of the universe and those of the lightest atoms. Nothing would be uncertain for it, the future, like the past, would be open to it. The human mind in the perfection which it has achieved in astronomy is a weak model of this intelligence. . . . . All its efforts in the quest for truth have the tendency incessantly to draw the human mind closer to the intelligence which we have just mentioned but from which it will always remain infinitely remote.

Since it is quite impossible for the human mind, which is always infinitely remote from Laplace's absolute intelligence, to know all forces at any given moment, the human mind can foresee the future only in terms of probability. Likewise it can explain the present by the past only with probability, inasmuch as the past, too, it knows but imperfectly. To be sure, to the question which role God plays in his system, Laplace answered that he does not need that hypothesis. But his omniscient intelligence is only a euphemistic circumscription for the notion of God, clothed in the disguise of an epistemological fiction.

In the infinite distance between God and man, theology has from time immemorial expressed the limitation of human beings, contrasted with the infinity of God. Only God can foresee the future with absolute certainty, since only God fully knows the present; and only God can fully comprehend the present, since only God fully knows the past. The strict idea of causality, the absolute necessity of the connection between cause and effect, is realized only in the unlimited knowledge of God, not in the limited knowledge of man;

and in this respect it makes no difference whether it is the question of determination of the future by the present or the present by the past. Transferred from the emotional to the rational sphere, this is merely the age-old idea that the law which governs the world is God's will, and therefore a norm. The norm determines what is to happen in the future. The law of nature, on the contrary, explains reality by seeking the cause of present events in the past. The laws of nature by which science describes a given reality in the most general and simplest way are the results of experience, and experience is drawn not from the future but from the past. Predictability is a criterion, though by no means the only criterion, of causality; but it is not causality itself. The presence of a causal nexus is proved not only by the fact that, as in an experiment, a predicted effect actually occurs, but also by the fact that the past existence of a fact assumed to be the cause of a given event can be demonstrated. The application of the law of causality to future events, an application which originated in practical necessity, is a secondary function resulting from the fact that cognition, although independent of volition and action, is placed at their service. Prophecy is no longer pure cognition, but knowledge applied to technique. The future can be surmised from the present only on the assumption that the past, by which the present is explained, repeats itself in the future. Whatever is grasped of the future by means of knowledge is, at bottom, merely the past. If one perceives the essence of the law of causality in the fact that it determines the future, even if only for a Laplacean intelligence, then one confirms, perhaps unconsciously, the normative origin of the law of causality.

79. The Law of Causality as Norm

Starting from the assumption that the laws of nature predict future events, T. H. Huxley[32] considered the rules of law as laws of nature, for the former predict how men will behave. The typical rule of law says, according to Huxley: "If a man steals, a judge will punish him." This is not correct. As norms, the rules of law express motor-affective, rather than cognitive, attitudes. Norms, especially legal norms, are not statements about future events; they are not even statements about reality. They cannot be true or false. They are norms which indicate what ought to happen; therefore they are good or bad, useful or harmful. Norms, however, do refer to future events; in a divine mind, but not in a human one, that which ought to happen is identical with that which will happen. We are inclined to ignore the difference between the rule of law and the law of nature because the law of nature was originally a rule of law expressing the will of God.

If its historical development is carefully followed, the amazing conclusion is reached that, in the Christian Era, at least until Hume, the idea of causality was considered merely as a norm, since it was felt to be the expression of the divine will. God is not only the absolute moral authority determining by his will the norms of social life; he is also the creator of the universe, its *prima causa;* and if natural events occur according to a definite rule, this rule is but a manifestation of his omnipotent will. In another connection we pointed to Genesis, chapter 1, where the creation is represented as obedience to commands God directs to things not yet existent. "And God said, Let there be light: and there was light." The effect obeys the cause. In Job 28:26 it is said: "God made a law for the rain and a way for the lightning and the thunder." E. Zilsel,[33] who quotes this passage in his interesting article on the origin of the concept of physical law, remarks:

> The Hebrew text uses the word *chok* [to express the idea of "law"]. This is derived from the verb *chokak*, meaning to engrave, and is the same term which is used for moral and ritual laws in the Old Testament. The Septuagint translates very freely "he numbered the rain ($\eta\rho\iota\vartheta\mu\eta\sigma\epsilon\nu$)," the Vulgate literally gives "ponebat legem."

In Job 38:11 we read that the Lord says to the sea: "Hitherto shalt thou come but not further; and here shall thy proud waves be stayed."

If we compare the concept of natural law (law of nature) in the Old Testament with that of Anaximander and Heraclitus, it strikes us that the former does not provide sanctions. This can be explained by the fact that in the Old Testament the idea of the omnipotence of God was so predominant that disobedience of nature seemed to be impossible, and sanctions against nature therefore superfluous. It stands to reason that, according to Augustin and Thomas Aquinas, the eternal law by which the universe is ruled is interpreted as God's will or providence. Copernicus compares the universe, with respect to the regularities observed in it, with a machine; he speaks of the "machine of the world founded by the best and most regular artificer";[34] and William Gilbert, when discussing the precession of the vernal point, of a "rule and norm of equality" that may be ascribed to complicated astronomical movements by some hypothesis.[35] Nature, according to Galileo, originates, just as the Holy Writ, in the Divine Word—the Writ as a dictation of the Holy Ghost, nature as "an executor of God's orders."[36] Gassendi accepts Epicurus' theory of atoms, but he states that God, who is the cause of all, has imparted the impulse to the atoms.[37] Kepler explains the regular course of the planets by the fact that God is "proceeding in a mathematical way"; he states that God ordered the universe according to the principle of "geometrical beauty."[38] Descartes used the principle of causality as proof of the existence of God and derived the laws of nature from his free will. He said of these laws that God has "put them into nature."[39] According to Newton, everything is in God; hence, also the laws of nature are established by his will.[40]

The theory of Malebranche may be mentioned as a particularly characteristic example. He taught that on the basis of our experience we can perceive no necessary connection between phenomena and no forces of causation. We can observe only regular successions. Considering the phenomenon of a moving ball striking against a stationary one and setting it in motion, he stated that men ought not to conclude

that a Bowl put into Motion, is the principal and true Cause of the shaking of another Bowl that it meets in the way, since the first had not the power of Motion in itself. They can only determine, that the meeting of two Bowls is an occasion to the Author of the Motion of Matter to execute the Decree of his Will, which is the universal Cause of all things. . . . .[41]

The conformity of the behavior of things to law is interpreted as the execution of a divine command. Malebranche transferred the causal relationship which he did not find in finite things to the transcendental sphere, to God—or, more accurately, to the will of God. This signifies that he conceived the law of causality as a norm; he characterized it directly as "Decree." In this Malebranche did not differ essentially from Spinoza, who reduces the finite causality of things to the infinite causality, that is, to the omnipotence of God,[42] and characterizes "the immutable and universal laws of nature" as "decrees of God";[43] or from Leibnitz, Locke, and Berkeley.[44] The latter says:

If therefore we consider the difference there is betwixt natural philosophers and other men, with regard to their knowledge of the phenomena, we shall find it consists not in an exacter knowledge of the efficient cause that produces them—for that can be no other than the will of a spirit—but only in a greater largeness of comprehension.[45]

Thomas Reid,[46] a contemporary of Hume, examines our belief that the future shall always be similar to the past, which is the fundamental presupposition of the predictability of events and, hence, according to some modern writers, of causality. Reid denies that this belief is based on experience; no man can see a necessary connection between two facts. "Experience informs us that they have been conjoined in time past; but no man ever had any experience of what is future: and this is the very question to be resolved, How we come to believe that the future will be like the past?" Our belief in causality, in the continuance of the course of nature, is "the effect of instinct, not of reason." It is God who guarantees this continuance by establishing the "present laws of nature."

He governs nature by fixed laws, so that we find innumerable connections of things which continue from age to age. Without this stability of the course of nature, there could be no experience. . . . . He hath implanted in human minds an original principle by which we believe and expect the continuance of the course of nature, and the continuance of those connections which we have observed in time past.

Causality exists but in God's will.

Hume's real achievement does not consist in pointing out that no necessary connection of cause and effect can be assumed on the basis of experience. That had already been ascertained before his time. It consisted rather in the fact that he gave up looking for the necessity of the causal nexus in the will of God and abandoned this idea together with the entire previous notion of causality. The law of causality ceased to be an expression of the divine will, a norm. The only element to which absolute necessity could be attached, the transcendental will which established the objective connection between cause and effect, was now put aside.[47] Only a norm can lay claim to inviolability, for a norm is not a statement about reality and therefore can never contradict it. Reality, however, as it now appears to human knowledge, does not admit an inviolable law as a scheme of interpretation.[48] The transformation of the notion of causality, the last step of which is the replacement of absolute necessity by simple statistical probability, is correctly considered "revolutionary" in scientific thinking. Its significance lies in the fact that the notion of causality was stripped of its most important element, with which it was still burdened as the heir of the principle of retribution: Ἀνάγκη. This is necessity with which Δίκη, the goddess of retribution, punishes evildoers and at the same time keeps nature in its prescribed course.

CHAPTER VII

NATURAL AND SOCIAL SCIENCE

80. The Emancipation of the Law of Causality from the Principle of Retribution

IN THE metamorphosis of the principle of retribution into the law of causality, two tendencies are of outstanding importance. The primitive's need of explanation is limited to those facts which directly affect his individual interests. These are the facts which he, with his collectively oriented consciousness, considers useful or harmful to his group. They alone press upon him for interpretation. Since the individual interprets the harmful facts as punishment and the useful facts as reward, by means of which the inviolable will of the superhuman authority reacts to human behavior which it likes or dislikes, he believes in a certain rigidity governing events—no punishment without wrong, no reward without merit. With the advancement of the rational components of individual consciousness at the expense of the emotional, the circle of facts to be interpreted broadened to include objects not immediately stimulating feelings of pleasure or pain. Man now tried to interpret all facts, even those which were of no direct importance to his or his fellow-men's physical life. Man's curiosity, his desire to understand the world which surrounds him, increases. Taste for inquiry and, hence, science as an independent human activity arises. Consequently, facts could no longer be conceived of as punishment or reward in the original and narrower sense. Punishment and reward became the "effect" and could no longer be connected with wrong and merit. Formerly the fundamental rule was, "No punishment without guilt" (the guilt of the wrongdoer). Afterward it was, "No event without guilt," the guilt meaning the cause. As has already been remarked, the Greek word αἰτία means both guilt and cause. The effect was still connected with the cause in the same way punishment was related to wrong and reward to merit. Since the effect, as a sort of punishment or reward, was connected with the cause, conceived as a sort of wrong or merit, the connection retained the character of absolute necessity, of Ananke.

Along with the generalization of the notion of law goes a certain objectivation, which consists in the fact that the egocentric, or more

exactly the sociocentric, standpoint is abandoned in the interpretation
of nature. When nature is interpreted according to the principle of
retribution, phenomena, in so far as they require explanation, are related to the individual or his group, since the group is collectively responsible. When the principle of retribution is generalized and assumes the meaning of causality, facts as effects are connected with
other facts as causes; under such circumstances these facts by no means
merely reflect the behavior of individuals contrary to, or in conformity
with, the norms of the social order. The law of causality no longer
links the natural event to the individual member of society, as did the
principle of retribution, but rather connects facts within nature, as it
were. The subject of cognition is thus separated from its object. Causality is not a central connection of facts, such as the principle of retribution; it is a peripheral association. The last remnant of the an-
thropocentric, i.e., sociocentric, interpretation of nature connected
with the principle of retribution, the Ptolemaic conception of the universe with the earth as the central point, vanished with the introduction of pure causal thinking into the astronomy of Copernicus and
Kepler.

81. The Separation of the Concept of Nature from the Concept of Society (Law of Causality and Norm)

Together with the emancipation of the law of causality from the
principle of retribution occurred the divorce of the notions of nature
and society. Nature appeared to be a part of society when it was interpreted according to the principle of retribution. After the extension of
the principle of retribution to the universal law, which was still considered a norm and the original model of all social laws, nature appeared to be the ideal society, since it was an absolutely just order, in
contrast to which the human society seemed an imperfect copy. The
idea of nature as the ideal society suggests itself especially in Christian
theology. Here the norms which as commands God addresses to nature—that means to animate and inanimate beings except man—need
not provide sanctions. God's omnipotence, in relation to nature, excludes any disobedience and therefore makes sanctions superfluous.
Nature is the perfectly obedient society. In this point a very characteristic difference exists between the Christian and the old Greek theology. According to the latter, the power of the divine authority manifests itself not in the fact that nature cannot violate the divine law pre-
scribing its course but in the fact that every violation, without excep-

tion, meets its punishment. Hence the universal law is formulated by Anaximander and Heraclitus as penal law. But the idea that it is impossible to disobey God's commands can be maintained by Christian theology only in relation to nature, not in relation to society, i.e., to human behavior. For here the possibility of violating the divine laws, the existence of the evil, the sin, is too evident. Here, and only here, not in relation to nature, the problem of theodicy rises. Therefore here, and only here, theology is forced to admit a limit of God's omnipotence. In order to explain the existence of evil, theology establishes the idea of freedom of will. Only man living in society has a free will; such a thing does not exist in nature. Hence only the divine laws which refer to society have the character of norms providing punishment and reward. The principle of retribution remains their basis, whereas it plays no part in the divine laws directed to nature.

Thus a certain dualism of nature and society arises within the theological view of the world. Man's free will signifies not only a limit of divine omnipotence, which theology, of course, tries to disguise, but also a restriction of the principle of causality, which theology emphasizes. The exceptional position conceded to man within nature constitutes an open contradiction in the theological system. In this contradiction the theological dualism of nature and society originates. It is an intrasystematic dualism. For it is still a dualism of natural law (in the sense of a natural legal order) and society, i.e., of natural law and positive law. The idea of "natural law" as a natural legal order is essentially bound up with the idea that nature is a creation of God, that its laws are an expression of God's will and are therefore norms; consequently, these laws are essentially similar to social, i.e., legal, laws whose true content results from the order of nature.

With the emancipation of causality from retribution and of the law of nature from the social norm, nature and society prove to be two entirely different systems. The idea of a system of norms regulating human behavior and constituting society as an order totally different from the laws of nature is possible without the fiction of freedom of will and therefore without contradiction to the principle of causality. From this point of view, society and nature are two different systems whose difference rests on the fact that the phenomena, and especially human behavior, are interpreted according to two essentially different kinds of "laws." The idea of a natural law (in the sense of a "natural" legal order), the law of a natural society whose order corresponds to that of nature, becomes impossible. It is incompatible with the presupposed

K

dualism of nature and society. The idea of natural law, as we have
seen, presumes a dualism within nature conceived as a universal society; the real, inadequate human society is contrasted with the ideal
cosmic society. It is the antagonism of man and God, of the empirical
and the transcendental. With the emancipation of the causal from the
normative interpretation of nature, i.e., nature as the creation of God
and under the rule of the divine will, the antagonism of the empirical
and the transcendental disappears from the sphere of science. Hence
there is no longer room for a natural behind or above a positive legal
order.

82. The Dualism of Nature and Society

The dualism of nature and society is by no means the last step in the
evolution of science. In the course of a critical analysis into the nature
of the norm, this dualism, too, becomes problematical. The claim of
the "ought" to a meaning completely different from the "is," that is to
say, the claim of the norm to be a law of society different from and independent of the law of causality as the law of nature, is characterized by
certain theorists as a mere "ideology" behind which most concrete
interests of individuals and groups are concealed. If these individuals
and groups come into power, they represent their interests as "norms."
The dualism of nature and society is replaced by that of reality and
ideology. For modern sociology a social event appears as part of reality, determined by the same laws as a natural event. No essential difference between natural and social laws, i.e., between the laws determining nature and the laws determining society, exists as soon as the
natural law itself relinquishes its claim to absolute necessity and satisfies itself with being an assertion of statistical probability. There is no
fundamental hindrance to prevent sociology's arriving at this kind of
laws in its own domain. In religious speculation nature was a part of
society ruled according to the law of retribution. After the complete
emancipation of causality from retribution in the modern notion of
law, society is—from the point of view of science—a part of nature.

NOTES

CHAPTER I

1. Wilhelm Wundt, *Voelkerpsychologie*, Vol. IV: *Mythus und Religion* (2d ed.; 1910), Part I, p. 60, points out that the motives of mythical, and therefore primitive, thinking are "not ideas but emotions which everywhere accompany ideas; by stimulating imagination they influence the formation of ideas. The emotions of fear and hope, of wish and desire, of love and hate, are widespread sources of myth."

2. Wilson D. Wallis, *Religion in Primitive Society* (1939), p. 316, says: "Man is not fundamentally rational or primarily rationalistic. He acts before he thinks; emotional attitudes precede logic. He behaves and subsequently becomes aware of his behaviour and its import.—Emotional attitudes are primary, cherished logical inductions are secondary and derivative. Reason is profoundly affected by preceding or concomitant emotional attitudes. It is guided by them; their character largely determines rationalized objective and emphasis. . . . ." P. 321: "If the savage is potentially a civilized man, the civilized man is potentially a savage."

3. Irving King, *The Development of Religion* (1910). pp. 44 f.: "The world does not present itself first of all to us as a mass of objective facts, with little or no relation to ourselves and the things we may be striving to do. It is rather as a world of values and interests that it is first apprehended; the world of cold fact is an abstraction from this earlier and more primitive aspect of things and events. That is to say, what we call, for want of a better term, the appreciative attitude is directly connected with man's active relation to his environment, both physical and social. The values which we recognize, the appreciations which we feel, are built up in us by the way we take hold of our world and deal with it. The things that interest us, the acts that we approve or disapprove, the ends, or goals, of action such as we come to regard as worth while, find their way into our conscious experience because we are most of the time striving to *do* something. It is in this way that they establish their relationship to us. At some later time these objects, acts, and ideals may become so familiar that they may be cognized, relatively at least, independently of our purposes or doings."

4. Leopold Ziegler, *Ueberlieferung* (1936), p. 18. The prevalence of the emotional over the rational component in primitive thinking is also stressed by R. R. Marett, *Faith, Hope, and Charity in Primitive Religion* (1932), p. 3.

5. Ziegler, p. 19: "Accordingly the wishes give way to excesses in the same degree in which the instruments and tools remain undeveloped and accomplish little for a purposeful satisfaction of desires. . . . ," P. 21: "Magic! Man as a 'Wunsch-Wesen' is the *homo magus*, the magician himself. In contradistinction to the man of will he relies less on technical instruments and mechanical tools than on magic when he tries to influence reality. Insofar as everything being the object of a wish . . . . signifies also a reality, a reality *sui generis*, a reality in *statu nascendi*, the fulfillment of which is to be performed by powers immanent to nature . . . . he turns confidently towards these powers in order to make them favorably disposed towards his wishes. This is the source of all magic."

6. Bernhard Ankermann, "Die Religion der Naturvoelker," in *Lehrbuch der Religionsgeschichte*, herausgegeben von Bertholet und Lehmann (4th ed.; 1925), p. 35, remarks: "We have no right to suppose that men of that early stage of development have a tendency to cognition; for, many people even today lack such a tendency." And Fritz Graebner, *Das Weltbild der Primitiven* (1924), p. 135: "From the historical point of view, practical reason is the *a priori* of theoretical reason."

7. See Ch. Letourneau, *La Psychologie ethnique* (1901), pp. 95, 156. Lucien Lévy-Bruhl, *Primitive Mentàlity*, authorized translation by Lilian A. Clare (1923), p. 59, speaks of "lack of curiosity."

Ladislaus Magyar, *Reisen in Suedafrika in den Jahren 1849–1857* (1859), I, 346, writes of the Kimbunda (South Africa): "They look at an eclipse of the sun or the moon with complete apathy. . . . . They are so indifferent with respect to the phenomena of nature that during the eight years of my residence among them I never have been asked the cause, for instance, of an eclipse."

8. Herbert Spencer, *The Principles of Sociology* (1897), Vol. I, par. 46, pp. 88 f., says of the mentality of primitive man: "Along with absence of surprise there goes absence of curiosity; and where there is least faculty of thought, even astonishment may be excited without causing inquiry."

Richard Cobden Phillips, "The Lower Congo," *Journal of the Anthropological Institute of Great Britain and Ireland*, XVII (1888), 221, writes: "The ideas are mostly of the simpler forms, seldom passing the concretes of actual experience, generalizations being, as a rule, beyond their power. Association of ideas though good as implied by good memory only takes place in the concrete form of contiguity in time and space as actually already perceived. . . . . The fundamental act of intelligence, the intuition of likeness and unlikeness, is very circumscribed; and high acts of intellect are thereby negatived. . . . . An accompanying trait is the absence of rational surprise; on seeing something new a vacant wonder is all that is observable, and this is very transient, and the new experience is classified as 'white man's fashion.' It almost follows as a matter of course that there is no curiosity, no wish to enquire into the cause of a novel experience; it never occurs to the native that there is a cause of the novelty or an explanation required. In like manner there is almost total absence of theorizing about natural phenomena."

Alexander Le Roy, *The Religion of the Primitives*, trans. by Newton Thompson (1922), p. 47: "Nothing surprises him, and the inquiry into primary causes is a matter of utter indifference to him."

9. Cf. Ernest Crawley, *The Mystic Rose* (new ed. by Theodore Bestermann, 1927), I, 23 f.

10. Fritz Schultze, *Psychologie der Naturvoelker* (1900), p. 251.

11. Dudley Kidd, *The Essential Kafir* (1904), p. 74.

12. W. H. R. Rivers, "The Primitive Conception of Death," *Hibbert Journal*, X (1911–12), 395–96.

13. L. Lévy-Bruhl, *The Soul of the Primitive*, authorized translation by Lilian A. Clare (1928), p. 110.

14. Ernst Cassirer, *Das Mythische Denken* ("Philosophie der symbolischen Formen," Part II [1925]), p. 193.

15. *Ibid.*, p. 247.

16. Cf., e.g., Spencer, Vol. II, par. 560, p. 599: "The primitive man has no idea of cause in the modern sense. The only agents included in his theory of things are living persons and the ghosts of dead persons."

Adolf Bastian, *Die Vorstellungen von der Seele* ("Sammlung gemeinverstaendlicher wissenschaftlicher Vortraege," herausgegeben von Rud. Virchow and Fr. von Holtzendorff, X. Ser., Heft 226 [1875]), p. 11: "His [primitive man's] sequence of ideas appear to be . . . . short and abruptly cut off and he is unable to cling to the thread of a causal connection. Thus he lacks the principle of causality which allows a deeper insight into the genesis of phenomena and their connection."

Wundt, *Mythus und Religion*, p. 62, writes: "Causality in our sense is entirely unknown to primitive man." Further, cf. Max Friedmann, "Ueber die Entwicklung des Urteils bei Naturvoelkern," in *Berichte des dritten Internationalen Kongresses fuer Psychologie in Muenchen* (1897), p. 333, and L. Lévy-Bruhl, *Primitives and the Supernatural*, authorized translation by Lilian A. Clare (1935), pp. 80 f.

Thomas Achelis, *Die Religion der Naturvoelker* (1919), p. 18, says: "The naïve mind of primitive man is not yet capable of thinking consistently and particularly not capable of comprehending the concept of a general law or of inevitable causality and necessity."

Max Moszkowski, *Auf neuen Wegen durch Sumatra* (1909), p. 90, speaks of the "extraordinarily weak tendency to causal thinking" of the Sakai and rightly says: "The beginning of all culture is the fact that man inquires with ever growing intensity into the causes of events, so that one may say that culture is a function of the etiological desire."

Aurel Krause, *Die Tlinkit-Indianer* (1885), p. 151, writes: "Their power of comprehension is limited. . . . . It is true, their tales about the origins of things manifest a vivid phantasy but at the same time they defy all reasonable interpretation and show scarcely any idea of the causal connection of events. Despite his constant intercourse with nature the Tlinkit is familiar with it only in the degree to which the most ordinary necessaries of life demand. He knows every suitable way for landing or fishing, every valley offering a path into the interior, and gives them special names; but the summits of mountains, even if they are distinguished by form and height, are scarcely noticed by him. Animals and plants are given names only if they are useful or harmful; —all others are included in such general concepts as 'little bird,' 'vegetable,' etc."

17. According to Wundt, pp. 262 ff., primitive man divides all events into two great spheres: "In the ordinary every day events which are accepted as a matter of course and in the unusual events which arouse his curiosity and above all his fear and astonishment." About everyday events he does not reflect at all. "Unusual events are illness and death, further, accidents of all kinds, peculiar dreams and visions, and finally, strange natural events, but not those which occur regularly, particularly those which arouse fear and anxiety, such as thunderstorms, or those which are longed for, such as the refreshing and reviving rain in the torrid zone."

18. E.g., Emile Durkheim, *The Elementary Forms of the Religious Life*, trans. by J. W. Swain (n.d.), p. 363. Graebner, pp. 20 ff., ascribes a certain importance to primitive man's "tendency to causality," a fact which does not conform with the primacy of practical over theoretical reason advocated by the same author. If primitive thinking, as Graebner believes, has an associative character, then the associations of primitive man are determined much more by emotional than by rational factors. Graebner admits that among primitive men "the suggestive firmness of the association . . . . is partly the result of a passionate desire or at least to a vivid wish." He says, p. 24, that the category of causality works much stronger in primitive thinking than the category of substance. This is hardly believable. We shall refer later to the extraordinary importance of the substantializing tendency in primitive thinking.

19. R. Thurnwald, "Im Bismarckarchipel und auf den Salomo Inseln, 1906–1909," *Zeitschrift fuer Ethnologie*, Jahrg. 42 (1910), p. 145, says of these natives: "Their knowledge of nature is . . . . very defective . . . . a recording of facts is the utmost they achieve. A deeper causal connection is lacking throughout and in principle. The lack of insight into the connections of events is the source of fear and superstition." But in his essay "Geistesverfassung der Naturvoelker," in K. Th. Preuss, *Lehrbuch der Voelkerkunde* (1937), p. 47, the same author states that "logic and causal connections" exist in the thinking of primitive peoples. For it is logical and shows insight into the causal connection if a hunter sets traps to capture animals. But this means only that the so-called "natural man" uses the objectively existent connection, which civilized man interprets as causal, but not that he is conscious of it in his thinking. The animal, too, uses it; thus a bird builds a nest or a bee collects honey just as hunting or food-collecting people do. Are we, therefore, entitled to assume that animals think logically and use the category of causality in their thinking? Is it not more correct to speak, like L. Lévy-Bruhl, in *Primitive Mentality* (authorized translation by Lilian A. Clare [1923]), p. 443, of an intuition which guides primitive man? "Rather is it that their hand has acquired its skill by a sort of intuition which is itself directed by acute observation of objects possessing peculiar interest for them. Such intuition would carry them far."

Martin Gusinde, *Die Feuerland-Indianer*, Vol. I: *Die Selknam* (1931), p. 1088, asserts that among the very primitive Selknam Indians "conscious causal thinking" can be observed. But what is his evidence for that assertion? He says that the Selknam Indian reflects "whether the means suffice for the aspired end, and which cause [*Anlass*] effects this or that event; he uses capable assistants and suitable tools because through them he increases his own capacities for achieving the desired." But this statement says only that the Selknam uses actual connections which we interpret as causal ones. That he puts the question, "Which fact 'effects' this or that event?" does not mean that he assumes a causal nexus between the events. Thus he believes that the "cause" of death and illness, which he regards as punishment inflicted by a superhuman authority, is a delict. Consequently, he does not connect the phenomena in question according to the law of causality but according to the principle of retribution. Gusinde goes on: "Whatever he manufactures himself or what he has earned or received is regarded by him as his property, as his private fortune, since he achieved it through his own efforts." This is no causal connection but a justification of private property according to catholic legal philosophy which Gusinde naïvely imputes to the Indians. "He [the Selknam] also finds an explanation that satisfies him for the Why of so many natural events, for the existence of mountains and rivers, of animal and human beings, for the movements of weather-powers and planets, even for the manifold shaping and allotment of his homeland to his people, for the dominant customs and the prevailing social order which are causally attributed to Temaukel, the highest being." That primitive man "seeks and finds an explanation that satisfies him" does not at all mean that it has to be a causal explanation; and that he refers his social order to a "highest being" does not mean that he sees in that being a *prima causa* but that he sees in it the highest authority. According to Gusinde's own version, Temaukel is not the "cause"—more correctly, not the creator—of the world. The world was created by the ancestors who transformed themselves into the things of nature. Cf. below, chap. ii, nn. 73 and 80.

The lack of an idea of causality in primitive thinking can also be explained by the fact that primitive man has a highly developed sense of space but only a weakly developed sense of time. Letourneau, p. 40: "For the child there is scarcely a past and a future. Like the savage, it lives almost exclusively in the present moment." Cf. Waldemar Bogoras, "Ideas of Space and Time in the Conception of Primitive Religion," *American Anthropologist*, N.S., XXVII (1925), 230 ff. Bogoras points to the fact that in the world of primitive man, as it is expressed in his religion or magical ideas, time has only a relative character. The ideas that time stops, that it shrinks, that it has no importance, are frequent.

Ziegler, p. 49, says: "If an event does not take place immediately in the present then it does not make much difference whether it occurred in the past or will occur in the future. There is no irreversible sequence of events in time." Therefore there is no causal thinking.

In his article, "Primitives Denken," in *Reallexikon der Vorgeschichte*, ed. Max Ebert, X (1927–28), 302 ff., R. Thurnwald asserts that any attempt to doubt the tendency to causal thinking of primitive peoples could only be made from the point of view of "exaggerated rationalism." But it is an exaggeration of the rationalistic interpretation of primitive man if causal thinking—rational thinking par excellence—is imputed to him. Any serious doubts about the "tendency to causal thinking" of primitive man arise mainly by the fact that a prevalence of the emotional over the rational elements in the mind of primitive man is assumed. Sometimes it is asserted that primitive man thinks causally but that his concept of causality is totally different from that of civilized man (cf., e.g., G. van der Leeuw, "La Structure de la mentalité primitive," *Revue d'histoire et de philosophie religieuses*, VIII [1928], 6). But this is an abuse of terminology. Causality is what science understands as such.

20. Edwin Sidney Hartland, *Transactions of the Third International Congress for the History of Religion* (Oxford, 1908), I, 31, strikingly remarks: "Action thus grew up in advance of speculation. In the prepotency of action I find the cause of the vivid development of the ritual in lower culture as contrasted with the feebleness of speculative thought."

21. Daniel G. Brinton, *Religions of Primitive Peoples* (1897), p. 68, says: "The savage knows not death as a natural occurrence. His language has no word meaning 'to die,' but only 'to be killed.' "

That death is an "unnatural" occurrence for primitive man has recently been denied (cf. John Koty, "Die Behandlung der Alten und Kranken bei den Naturvoelkern," *Forschungen zur Voelkerpsychologie und Soziologie*, ed. R. Thurnwald, XIII [1934], p. 233). It may be that among very primitive groups certain deaths—as, for instance, decease due to the weakness of old age—are not traced to the act of a superhuman authority. This need not imply that such a death is considered a "natural" event but can only mean that no "explanation" is sought, since one is accustomed to it and indeed expects it. The idea that death is caused by a superhuman authority is the first attempt at explanation of primitive man and therefore appears only in those cases which are unexpected and which hit the group hard, such as the death of young and strong men. If death is inflicted by the violent action of another man, the situation is totally different. Primitive man sees in this a social occurrence which is comprehensible to him; as such he interprets it and not as a "natural" or physiological-biological process. Only when the fact does not represent a social event is primitive man, by his socially oriented tendency to explanation, inclined to imagine the interference of a superhuman authority. To this authority primitive man ascribes the same motives as to his fellow-men. The most striking evidence to show that primitive man regards death as a social and not as a "natural" event is the myth, widespread among primitive peoples, which explains how death came to this world. This myth justifies death as punishment inflicted by a deity for a wrong committed by man. The biblical story of the fall of man, which has the consequence that man must die, whereas he would have lived eternally without it, is a fundamentally primitive idea (cf. Ziegler, p. 45).

Hermann Baumann, *Schoepfung und Urzeit des Menschen im Mythus der afrikanischen Voelker* (1936), p. 291 (following K. Th. Preuss, *Tod und Unsterblichkeit im Glauben \der Naturvoelker* [1930], pp. 3–16), declares that on the basis of his experience alone, primitive man cannot believe in the inevitability of death: "a belief in the command of a higher being was necessary in order to convince primitive man that all human beings must die." The inevitability of death is not the necessity of a causal law but the inviolability of a norm.

22. Schultze, pp. 43, 223 f. The example cited is taken from Henry Lichtenstein, *Travels in Southern Africa* (1812), I, 313: "At the mouth of the river Keissi, or Keisskamma, as it is called by the Hottentots, lies the anchor of a stranded ship. Chacháge, the grandfather of the present king, had a piece of it broken off, and it so happened that the person by whom this was done died soon after. The anchor was immediately considered as an enchanter, who had power over the sea, and was angry at the offence which had been given him; a name was in consequence conferred upon him, and he is saluted by it whenever any one passes the spot."

A similar case is reported by Elsdon Best, *The Maori* (1924), I, 229. The master of a ship had a watch which the natives regarded as a superhuman being. One day this watch fell overboard. After the departure of the ship an epidemic broke out among the natives, and this event was immediately related to the demonic watch. But how? Elsdon Best tells: "The natives vowed vengeance against the white skinned searovers. In such cases it is the next visitor who suffers." This means that the Maori interpreted the dropping of the watch as an attempted delict. The white man caused the illness of the natives with the help of the watch demon. Such a grave wrong permits the exercise of retribution on the white man, whoever he may be. The nature of the connection between the dropping of the watch and the epidemic is not decisive for the primitive interpretation of the event; the decisive factor is the question whether the epidemic is punishment for a wrong committed by the Maori or whether it is itself a wrong committed against them. If it is the latter, to whom is it to be ascribed? Of course, the white men are enemies and, as magicians, dispense the powers of the spirits. The watch in which such a spirit was imagined is remembered as a potential source of evil. The epidemic is therefore considered a crime which has to be avenged. The fact in question, the epidemic, is associated with a future action, and thus a connection is established which "explains" the fact in question.

For the specific "causality" of primitive man which is supposed to differ from our concept of causality, van der Leeuw, p. 5, reports the following example: "In the Congo a missionary killed a crocodile which attacked his pigs during the night. He opened the animal's body and found in its stomach two rings. Immediately these objects were recognized as having belonged to two women who had disappeared, on different dates, when they went to the river for water. Consequently we would say the fate of these poor women is evident. But the native does not share our opinion. The crocodile did not devour the women for crocodiles do not do that sort of thing." But what about the rings? Are they not palpable evidence that, in this case at least, the crocodile devoured the women? "No, the crocodile snatched them and then handed them over to the sorcerer whose accessory he was; as far as the rings are concerned, the crocodile took them for his salary." Van der Leeuw concludes: "Thus primitive man establishes a kind of causality, the laws of which absolutely contradict that which we consider reasonable, and even evident. Facts do not count; logic is lacking."

But this is not true. Primitive man simply considers facts other than we recognize as given. He believes in the power of the sorcerer; for him it is a fact, like gravity is for us. And he believes that crocodiles do not devour men, just as we consider bacteria the cause of certain illnesses. Perhaps in future times what we now consider fact will be regarded as error, just as we regard as errors the facts accepted by primitive peoples. But the essential difference between primitive man and ourselves is not that facts do not count for him but that he connects the facts, or what he regards as such, in a different way than we do. He sees the disappearance of the women as a social and not as a "natural" event. He ascribes it to a man, a sorcerer, who, as a more careful investigation of the event would undoubtedly show, snatched the two women from their families to take revenge. The crocodile merely carried out an order of the sorcerer and received the rings as reward. The principle connecting the disappearance of the women with the rings in the stomach of the animal is that of retribution.

Wundt, p. 62, also limits his assertion that primitive man is unaware of causality in our sense when he says: ". . . . not intellectual interest, but a desire to satisfy the emotions determines the connection of events in the mind of primitive as well as of superstitious men today." This is certainly right. Wundt continues: "It is true that one may also call this connection a causal one. But it is a magic causality, absolutely different from the logical causality of science, although it also connects certain events with one another. It is an individual causality which may change from case to case . . . . for it applies only to those restricted aspects of reality which lie within the sphere of human emotion. In all that, it differs entirely from the logical causality of science even though it may be that the idea of the connection of externally separated events, which dominates all causality, has its origin in this magic causality."

But it is misleading to call a mere individual connection of phenomena causality, even "magic" causality. Moreover, there exists in the thinking of primitive man a general principle, and thus a law, connecting these elements—the principle of retribution. But this kind of connection is still quite remote from a causal one. Only if one follows Schultze and Wundt and understands by "causality" every connection of phenomena in the broadest sense may one speak of causality among primitive men or, like Wundt, p. 264, of an "awakening of causal thinking" in relation to exceptional and unexpected events. Only this supposition makes Wundt's remark right. "In view of the ethnopsychological facts, David Hume's well-known theory of causality could be completely reversed. The origin of the idea of causality is not in the regular and customary sequence of events but, on the contrary, in the unexpected and the unusual, in everything that arouses fright, fear, surprise, or unusual emotions of happiness because it deviates from the regular course of events." With these events primitive man links other events which seemingly have no causal connection; but a connection does exist according to the principle of retribution, which is a social, and not at all mystic or magical, principle. From this principle of retribution the law of causality arose in a much later stage of the development of the human mind and after a thorough change of significance; and it arose not least because the principle in question was also applied to ordinary sequences of events, recognized as regular and evoking no special emotions.

23. Phillips, p. 220.

24. It is often asserted that the idea of natural laws is strange to primitive man (cf. Brinton, pp. 39, 48). E. S. Hartland, *Primitive Paternity* (1909–10), I, 3, says of the savage: "For him it is hardly too much to say the laws of nature do not exist; every thing depends on the volition and the might of beings conceived, whatever their outward form, in the terms of his own consciousness." See also Lévy-Bruhl, *Primitives and the Supernatural*, p. 20; Rafael Karsten, *The Origins of Religion* (1935), p. 133. In his book *The Civilization of the South American Indians* (1926), p. 295, Karsten writes: "Savages are not wont to work out their ideas in a logical way, and a problem which only has a theoretical interest would hardly present itself to their mind." K. Th. Preuss, *Die Nayarit Expedition* (1912), I, xlvii, points out: "Nature for the Cora is not a series of regularly occurring events. For him laws of nature do not exist because natural events reflect the activities of persons endowed with will and reason." Also, Paul Ehrenreich, *Die allgemeine Mythologie und ihre ethnologischen Grundlagen* ("Mythologische Bibliothek," Vol. IV, Part I [1910]), p. 56, asserts that savages do have a sense of causality, but he says that "savages lack any concept of a law of nature." Consequently, they cannot have a "sense of causality."

25. Kidd, p. 71.

26. Knud Rasmussen, *Intellectual Culture of the Iglulik Eskimo*, Vol. VII, No. 1, of the *Report of the Fifth Thule Expedition, 1921–24* (1929), p. 54.

27. A. W. Nieuwenhuis, *Quer durch Borneo* (1904), I, 96.

28. Cf. L. Lévy-Bruhl, *How Natives Think*, authorized translation by Lilian A. Clare (1925), p. 231. Charles Hill Tout, "Report on the Ethnology of the StlatlumH of British Columbia," *Journal of the Anthropological Institute of Great Britain and Ireland*, XXXV (1905), 136, reports: "Indeed, the Indian looked upon all his food, animal and vegetable, as gifts voluntarily bestowed upon him by the 'spirit' of the animal or vegetable, and regarded himself as absolutely dependent upon their goodwill for his daily sustenance. Hence his many curious customs and observances to propitiate the spirits and secure their favour and regard."

29. Lévy-Bruhl, *Primitives and the Supernatural*, pp. 103 f.; cf. also pp. 95 ff.

30. Cf. Bruno Gutmann, "Die Imkerei bei den Dschagga," *Archiv fuer Anthropologie*, N.F., XIX (1922), 10 ff. Cf. also above, pp. 94 f.

31. Wilhelm Mannhardt, *Wald- und Feldkulte* (2d ed., 1904), I, 10.

32. J. G. Frazer, *The Golden Bough* (1920), Part I, Vol. II, p. 13.

33. Frank H. Melland, *In Witch-bound Africa: An Account of the Primitive Kaonde Tribe; Their Beliefs* (1923), p. 137.

34. C. Meinhof, *Die Religionen der Afrikaner in ihrem Zusammenhang mit dem Wirtschaftsleben* (1926), p. 58.

35. Ernst Mosbacher, "Untersuchungen zum Suendenbegriff der Naturvoelker," *Baessler Archiv*, XVII, No. 1 (1934), 42.

36. Lévy-Bruhl, *Primitives and the Supernatural*, pp. 109 ff.

37. K. Th. Preuss, *Die geistige Kultur der Naturvoelker* (2d ed., 1923), p. 26. The worship of tools (apparently a remnant of primitive stages) can still be found in relatively advanced civilization. Spencer regards this phenomenon as fetishism and says of it (I, § 162): "And then, if we ask where fetishism has culminated, we are referred to a people whose civiliza-

tion, older in date than our own, has created vast cities, elaborate industries, a highly-structured language, great poems, subtle philosophies. In India, 'A woman adores the basket which serves to bring or to hold her necessaries, and offers sacrifices to it; as well as to the rice-mill, and other implements that assist her in her household labours. A carpenter does the like homage to his hatchet, his adze, and other tools; and likewise offers sacrifices to them. A Brahman does so to the style with which he is going to write; a soldier to the arms he is to use in the field; a mason to his trowel.' And this statement of Dubois, quoted by Sir John Lubbock, coincides with that of Mr. Lyall in his 'Religion of an Indian Province.' 'Not only,' he says, 'does the husbandman pray to his plough, the fisher to his net, the weaver to his loom; but the scribe adores his pen, and the banker his account-books.' "

38. S. R. Riggs, "Mythology of the Dakotas," *American Antiquarian*, V, No. 2 (1883), 148, 149.

39. *The Jesuit Relations and Allied Documents* (1636), X, 167.

40. Preuss, *Die geistige Kultur der Naturvoelker*, p. 27. In the same book, p. 2, he remarks that "the ego-consciousness of the individual was then [in times of primitive culture] much less developed than with us. . . . ."

41. James J. Jarves, *History of the Hawaiian or Sandwich Islands* (1843), p. 74: "The fishermen believed, to some extent, in transmigration, and frequently cast their dead into the sea to be devoured by sharks. Their souls were supposed ever after to animate those fishes, and incline them to respect the bodies of the living, should accident ever throw them into their power."

42. That in the earliest times the physical relationship between father and child was unknown has already been mentioned by E. S. Hartland, *The Legend of Perseus* (1894–96), I, 180 f.; II, 410. Cf. also J. von Reitzenstein, "Der Kausalzusammenhang zwischen Geschlechtsverkehr und Empfaengnis in Glaube und Brauch der Natur- und Kultur-voelker," *Zeitschrift fuer Ethnologie*, Jahrg. 41 (1909), pp. 644 ff. Reitzenstein says: "One may even call it a monstrous supposition to assume that primitive man knows of the connection between *cohabitatio* and *conceptio*." This conclusion is particularly based upon results of research among Australian natives. Cf. Baldwin Spencer and F. J. Gillen, *The Northern Tribes of Central Australia* (1904), pp. xi, 330; Arnold van Gennep, *Mythes et légendes d'Australie* (1905), p. xlviii; Hermann Klaatsch, *Die Anfaenge von Kunst und Religion in der Urmenschheit* (1913), p. 34. This view, however, has been frequently attacked, especially by those who oppose the doctrine of evolution and by the theologically oriented ethnologists—e.g., by P. Wilhelm Schmidt and his school. Malinowski's most recent researches among the Trobriand Islanders confirm the opinions of Hartland and Reitzenstein. Cf. Bronislaw Malinowski, *The Sexual Life of Savages, etc.* (1929), pp. 140 ff., especially pp. 153 ff., and "Baloma, the Spirits of the Dead in the Trobriand Islands," *Journal of the Royal Anthropological Institute of Great Britain and Ireland*, XLVI (1916), 403. Cf. also E. S. Hartland, *Primitive Society* (1921), pp. 18 ff.

W. Lloyd Warner, *A Black Civilization* (1937), pp. 23 f., reports of the Murngin, an Australian tribe: "During my first eight or nine months among them I was firmly convinced that the people had no understanding of physiological conception and believed in the spiritual impregnation of a woman by a totemic child spirit. All the fathers told me their children had come to them in dreams as totemic souls, or in some extra-mundane experience. The men had complied with the request of the children, who had entered the vaginas of the mothers. . . . The second time I entered the area . . . . I could inquire directly of certain old men just what the semen did when it entered the uterus of a woman. They all looked at me with much contempt for my ignorance and informed me that 'that was what made babies.' I had not been able to obtain this information earlier because the ordinary savage is far more interested in the child's spiritual conception, which determines his place in the social life of the people, than he is in the physiological mechanism of conception. He would far rather talk about the ritual and myth than about ordinary mundane affairs."

The fact that primitive people of today know of the connection in question but do not officially admit such knowledge because of religious or other reasons which prompt them to another explanation of pregnancy, particularly to the idea of the reincarnation of an ancestral soul, does not at all contradict the assumption of an original ignorance on their part. What is today a consciously preserved religious ideology must formerly have been a real belief. What else could have been the origin of this ideology? Wherever people believe in the reincarnation of the souls of dead in newborn children, there must have been originally no knowledge of the true cause of pregnancy.

John Roscoe, *The Baganda* (1911), p. 46, writes: "While the present generation know the cause of pregnancy, the people in the earlier times were uncertain as to its real cause, and thought that it was possible to conceive without any intercourse with the male sex. Hence their precautions, when passing places where either a suicide had been burnt, or a child born feet first had been buried. Women were careful to throw grass or sticks on such a spot, for by so doing they thought that they could prevent the ghost of the dead from entering into them, and being reborn. Women, who were found to be with child in circumstances in which they ought not to be with child, might deny any wrong doing on their own part; they might affirm that some flower falling from a plantain upon them, while they were digging, had caused them to become pregnant. If the reader considers what a close connection was thought to exist between the plantains and the ghosts of the after-birth, and also how the ghosts of ancestors were thought to reside amongst the plantains, he will readily understand that the conception was supposed to have taken place by the reincarnation of one of the ghosts." On p. 64 we read: "Each grandmother went to her grandchild and mentioned the names of first one, and then another, of her son's forefathers, beginning with the name of the deceased ancestor nearest to her son, but not mentioning any living person. As she rehearsed their names, each time going further back, she watched the child, and when it laughed it was a token to her that the ancestor just named was he whose ghost would be the child's guardian. If the child subsequently fell ill, or if it did not thrive, they changed its name and appointed another guardian, because the former was supposed to dislike the child." The idea that the ghost of an ancestor becomes a child's guardian spirit is probably but a later modification of the belief in reincarnation of the ancestor in the child. The life soul of a child as the reincarnated death soul of an ancestor and the child's guardian spirit are mostly closely connected and often identical.

43. The distinction made between life soul and death soul by the natives of the Indian Archipelago has been remarked by A. C. Kruijt, *Het Animisme in den Indischen Archipel* (1906). For the same distinction among African natives see Bernhard Ankermann's article, "Totenkult und Seelenglaube bei afrikanischen Voelkern," *Zeitschrift fuer Ethnologie,* Jahrg. 50 (1918), pp. 93 ff. Cf. also Ernst Arbman, "Untersuchungen zur primitiven Seelenvorstellung mit besonderer Ruecksicht auf Indien," *Le Monde oriental,* XX (1926); XXI (1927); and his "Seele und Mana," *Archiv fuer Religionswissenschaft,* XXIX (1931), 293 ff. Others who treat the subject are Wundt, pp. 78 ff., and M. P. Nilsson, "Existe-t-il une conception primitive de l'âme?" *Revue d'histoire et de philosophie religieuses,* X (1930), 113 f. That the life soul is frequently imagined as a tiny being, a kind of Tom Thumb (E. Crawley, *The Idea of the Soul* [1909], pp. 7, 200 ff., 230 ff.), is probably connected with the belief that only in this shape can it penetrate the body of the woman who is to give it birth.

44. Thus the Batak of Sumatra distinguish, according to J. Warneck, *Die Religion der Batak* ("Quellen der Religionsgeschichte," herausgegeben im Auftrage der religionsgeschichtlichen Kommission bei der Koeniglichen Gesellschaft der Wissenschaften zu Goettingen [1909]), pp. 8 ff., between the *tondi,* the life soul, and the *begu,* the death soul. "The *tondi* is a sort of man within man, but it does not coincide with the latter's personality and

is often even in conflict with his ego; it is a special being within man with a will and desires of its own which it knows how to accomplish often in a disagreeable fashion against the will of the man himself." The Batak constantly fears that his *tondi* will leave him. Therefore he is much more concerned with treating his *tondi* respectfully and with sacrificing to it than in venerating distant deities whom he neither fears nor loves. According to J. Warneck, "Der Batak'sche Ahnen- und Geister-Kult," *Allgemeine Missionszeitschrift*, XXXI (1904), 13, an ill man addressed the following prayer to his life soul: "Here you have a betel (which he places before it). I am telling you, my soul, that I have sinned against you. (Then he relates his sin which consists mainly in the fact that he has not given the soul any presents for a long time.) I swear to you that I shall do better and here I give you a betel as payment on account. As soon as I am well again I will bring you nice food, clothes, and jewelry, whatever I have, just as you wish. Have pity on me." It must be added here that the Batak believe in the reincarnation of an ancestral death soul in the newly born child.

45. That the life soul may leave the body during sleep and that dreams are its adventures, and not the adventures of the sleeping man, are frequently appearing ideas. Closely connected with these notions is the belief that the life soul, as the guardian spirit, lives outside the man whose life it guarantees—for instance, in an animal or plant. Between the individual and the guardian plant or animal in which his life soul resides there exists a sympathetic connection of such intimacy that the fate of the one is bound to the fate of the other. If the guardian animal or plant should fall ill or die, then the man must also fall ill or die. Cf. Crawley, *The Idea of the Soul*, pp. 7, 178 f., 227.

46. Kidd, p. 284.

47. Crawley, pp. 267, 277, points out that primitive man does not localize his thoughts in the brain. Frequently it has been observed that primitive man interprets various emotions and feelings as expressions of a being different from himself. Thus hunger, for example, is considered as the "gnawing" of a spirit within the body cavity. Schultze, p. 269, is right when he declares that in ego-consciousness the unity and simplicity of man's soul are manifested. The idea that man has only one soul is the result of a long evolution. If one may interpret certain spiritual conditions of psychopathics as regression to a primitive state of mentality, then the split personality appearing in schizophrenics, the fact that the sick man experiences certain ideas and even actions which he carries out as the ideas or actions of someone else, is perhaps related to the peculiarity of primitive man of not identifying himself with his life soul even to the point of regarding it as an externally living being. Into the same relation can be brought the well-known experience of the double, the fact that one sees one's self outside one's own body as someone else. Cf. van der Leeuw, pp. 8 ff.

48: Vilhjalmur Stefánsson, *My Life with the Eskimo* (1913), pp. 395 ff.: "One family of Eskimo were the servants of the expedition for its whole four years and I had known them also on a previous expedition. This family consists of the man Ilavinirk, his wife Mamayak, and their daughter Noashak. When I first knew Noashak I formed the opinion that she was the worst child I had ever known and I retained that opinion for over six years, or until she was a young woman of perhaps twelve years. (Some Eskimo girls are fully developed at the age of twelve or thirteen.) In spite of her badness Noashak was never punished.

"The two stock explanations of why Eskimo do not punish their children are: first, that the children themselves are so good that they do not need being punished (but that scarcely applied to Noashak's case); or that the Eskimo are so fond of their children that they cannot bear to punish them, which is not true, either, for they show in many ways that they are no fonder of their children than we are.

"I had noticed ever since I knew them that Mamayak in speaking to Noashak always addressed her as 'mother.' When one stops to think of it, it was of course a bit curious that a woman of twenty-five should address a girl of eight as 'mother.' I suppose, if I thought about the matter at all, I must have put this practice of theirs in the same category with that which we find among our own people, where we often hear a man addressing his wife as 'mother.'

"One day another Eskimo family came to visit us, and strangely enough, the woman of the family also spoke to Noashak and called her 'mother.' Then my curiosity was finally aroused, and I asked: 'Why do you two grown women call this child your mother?' Their answer was: 'Simply because she is our mother,' an answer which was for the moment more incomprehensible to me than the original problem. I saw, however, that I was on the track of something interesting, and both women were in a communicative mood, so it was not long until my questions brought out the facts, which (pieced together with what I already knew) make the following coherent explanation, which shows not only why these women called Noashak 'mother,' but shows also why it was that she must never under any circumstances be forbidden anything or punished.

"When a Mackenzie Eskimo dies, the body is taken out the same day as the death occurs to the top of some neighboring hill and covered with a pile of drift-logs, but the soul (*nappan*) remains in the house where the death occurred for four days if it is a man, and for five days if it is a woman. At the end of that time a ceremony is performed by means of which the spirit is induced to leave the house and to go up to the grave, where it remains with the body waiting for the next child in the community to be born.

"When a child is born, it comes into the world with a soul of its own (*nappan*), but this soul is as inexperienced, foolish, and feeble as a child is and looks. It is evident, therefore, that the child needs a more experienced and wiser soul than its own to do the thinking for it and take care of it. Accordingly the mother, so soon as she can after the birth of the child, pronounces a magic formula to summon from the grave the waiting soul of the dead to become the guardian soul of the new-born child, or its *atka* as they express it.

"Let us suppose that the dead person was an old wise man by the name of John. The mother then pronounces the formula which may be roughly translated as follows: 'Soul of John, come here, come here, be my child's guardian! Soul of John, come here, come here, be my child's guardian!' (Most magic formulae among the Eskimo must be repeated twice.)

"When the soul of John, waiting at the grave, hears the summons of the mother, it comes and enters the child. From that time on it becomes the business of this acquired soul not only to do the thinking for the child, but to help in every way to keep it strong and healthy: to assist it in teething, and in every way to look after its welfare, things which the child's own soul with which it was born could not possibly do for the child, on account of its weakness and inexperience.

"The spirit of John not only teaches the child to talk, but after the child learns to talk it is really the soul of John which talks to you and not the inborn soul of the child. The child, therefore, speaks with all the acquired wisdom which John accumulated in the long lifetime, plus the higher wisdom which only comes after death. Evidently, therefore, the child is the wisest person in the family or in the community, and its opinions should be listened to accordingly. What it says and does may seem foolish to you, but that is mere seeming and in reality the child is wise beyond your comprehension.

"The fact that the child possesses all the wisdom of the dead John is never forgotten by its parents. If it cries for a knife or a pair of scissors, it is not a foolish child that wants the knife, but the soul of the wise old man John that wants it, and it would be presumptuous of a young mother to suppose she knows better than John what is good for the child, and so she gives it the knife. If she refused the knife (and this is the main point), she would not only be preferring her own foolishness to the wisdom of John, but also she would thereby give offense to the spirit of John, and in his anger John would abandon the child. Upon the withdrawal of his protection the child would become the prey to disease and would probably die, and if it did not die, it would become stupid or hump-backed or otherwise deformed or unfortunate. John must, therefore, be propitiated at every cost, and to deliberately offend him would be in fact equivalent to desiring the child's misfortune or death and would be so construed by the community; so that a man is restrained from forbidding his child or punishing it, not only by his own interest in the child's welfare, but also by the fear of public opinion, because if he began to forbid his child or to punish it, he would at once become known to the community as a cruel and inhuman father, careless of the welfare of his child.

"We can see here how much there is in the point of view. On the basis of this explanation it is easy to understand how a man, tired and hungry and at the limit of his strength, would still haul his daughter on top of the sled rather than compel her to get off and walk, for to compel her to do so would have been equivalent to desiring to bring upon her serious misfortune, if not death, through giving offense to her guardian angel."

The fact that the child is addressed as "mother" (or "father") justifies the conjecture that originally the life soul of the child was the reincarnated soul of the dead person and that later on the latter assumed the character of a guardian spirit.

49. The fact that many primitive peoples do not punish their children may, of course, have different causes. Cf. S. R. Steinmetz, "Das Verhältnis zwischen Eltern und Kindern bei den Naturvölkern," *Zeitschrift für Sozialwissenschaft*, I. Jahrg. (1898), 607–31. Steinmetz explains the fact only by biological causes, but this is not sufficient. Civilized peoples, too, love their children but, nevertheless, do not hesitate to punish them.

In his *Journal of a Voyage to North America* (1761; ed. Louise Phelps Kellogg, 1923), François Xavier de Charlevoix stated (II, 114–15) that the Indians did not chastise their children. "Sometimes in order to correct their faults they employ tears and entreaties, but never threats; these would make no manner of impression on minds which have imbibed this prejudice, that no one whatever has a right to force them to any thing. . . . . Generally the greatest punishment which the Indians make use of in chastising their children, is by throwing a little water in their face." But Charlevoix added: "Notwithstanding, since they have had a more frequent commerce with the French, some of them begin to chastise their children, but this happens only among those that are Christians, or such as are settled in the colony." This is very significant. It is obviously a religious reason that prevented the Indians from punishing their children. On p. 153 Charlevoix writes: "There are others, who acknowledge two souls in men; to the one, they attribute every thing I have been just now speaking of, and pretend that the other never quits the body, unless it is to pass into some other, which however happens only, say they, to the souls of little children, which having enjoyed but a short term of life, obtain leave to begin a new one. It is for this reason that they bury children by the high-way sides, that the women who pass that way may collect their souls."

George Henry Loskiel, *History of the Mission of the United Brethren among the Indians in North America* (1794), p. 56, writes of the Delaware Indians: "They suppose that when the souls have been some time with God, they are at liberty to return into the world and to be born again." And, pp. 61–62: "Both parties [parents] are very desirous of gaining the love of their children, and this accounts for their conduct towards them. They never oppose their inclinations, that they may not lose their affection. Their education therefore is not much attended to. Their children have entirely their own will, and never do anything by compulsion. The parents are very careful not to beat or chastise them for any fault, fearing lest the children might remember it, and revenge themselves on some future occasion."

William H. Keating, *Narrative of an Expedition to the Source of St. Peter's River* (1825), I, 420–21: "The Dacotas appear to take but little pains in the education of their children; they follow no regular system. What the children learn, on the subject of their religious opinions and traditions, is collected gradually, and altogether in the course of unpremeditated conversations. The only attention which they receive is towards the development of those qualifications, both of mind and body, which shall enable them to make active hunters and dauntless warriors. To rise early, to be inured to fatigue, to hunt skilfully, to undergo hunger without repining, are the only points to which the Dacota thinks it important to attend to in the education of his children. Corrections are never resorted to; they are never flogged; indeed, with the exception of occasionally throwing cold water upon them to make them rise in a morning, they never resort to any authoritative measures, all which they consider as cruel and unnatural." And p. 421: "No event appears of more importance to a Dacota parent than the bestowing of a name upon his offspring; it is attended with much ceremony; a large feast or sacrifice is prepared; the relations and friends are invited. The name which is given is generally one derived from some visible object in the heavens or earth. The infant is made to support a pipe, the stem of which is directed towards the object from which the name is taken; a sacrifice is offered to the spirit which is supposed to reside in that object." It is quite possible that this custom had its origin in an old belief in reincarnation.

Krause, p. 160, writes of the Tlingit that one seldom hears loud outbursts of pleasure or pain from him, and "small children are treated by their parents with love, even with tenderness. We never saw them being beaten and only seldom did we hear a rough and reprimanding word." In another connection, Krause reports, pp. 217, 282, 310, that the Tlingit believes in the reincarnation of the dead in children.

Warneck, *Die Religion der Batak*, p. 11, reports: "Parents must treat their children gently and are afraid to punish them in order not to insult the *tondi* (the life soul functioning as the guardian spirit; it is the reincarnated ancestral death soul) of the dear one and thus make it run away. In this manner the whole education of the child is poisoned by the idea of the *tondi*."

According to F. Blumentritt, "Die Igorroten von Pangasinan: Nach den Mitteilungen des Missionars P. Fr. Mariano Rodriguez," *Mitteilungen der k. k. Geographischen Gesellschaft in Wien*, XLIII (1900), 96, the Igorrots of Luzon (Philippine Islands) use to name a newborn child after a deceased ancestor. If the child falls ill and neither family medicine nor exorcism have the desired effect, one assumes that the child has to be named after another ancestor "who has a better right to the child being named after him." The widespread practice of naming children after ancestors is undoubtedly in close connection with the belief in reincarnation (cf. Hartland, *Primitive Paternity*, I, 222). The name is or represents the soul of the dead reincarnated in the newborn child.

Blumentritt reports further: "The children enjoy a rather unlimited freedom; they never are beaten."

According to C. G. and Brenda Z. Seligman, *The Veddas* (1911), p. 90, the Veddas "are affectionate and indulgent parents, never refusing a small child anything it wants, and giving it always of the best. . . . . We saw a naked boy of about two and a half years strut proudly up and down . . . . with his father's axe hung on his shoulder; he was extremely happy and all went well, until he threatened one of the dogs with the axe. Then his mother was obliged to interfere and the child tried to hit her with it. The father seeing this got up and tried to coax the child into giving up the axe, but the boy was now excited, and would not give it up; at last he flung it at his father and hit his leg. The man was obviously annoyed and threw the axe from him into the jungle, but he did not attempt to scold or punish the child who was now howling with rage; indeed, after a little while some food was given him to pacify him." On p. 103 the Seligmans report: "Father and mother give the child its name, usually choosing that of an ancestor. . . . . Our informant gave his father's name to his second child, not to his first, because his father was alive when his first son was born. A woman's name is generally given to a grand-daughter born after her death."

A. R. Brown, *The Andaman Islanders* (1922), p. 77, writes: "The children are treated with extreme kindness and are never punished, and hardly ever scolded. Should the parents die, the children are adopted by friends or relatives, and such adopted children are treated by the foster-parents in exactly the same way as their own children." It is obviously not a physiological fact which constitutes the relationship between children and parents. "The baby is named some time before it is born, and from that time the parents are not addressed or spoken of by name. For example, if the name chosen be Rea, the father will be spoken of as Rea aka-mai (Rea's father) instead of by his own name. The mother may be referred to as Rea it-pet, from the word it-pet meaning 'belly' " (p. 89). The mother is evidently considered to be only the receptacle of a higher being, to which even the father's personality stands back. Among the Andaman Islanders, too, this attitude toward children is combined with belief in reincarnation. Brown reports, pp. 90 f.: "If a baby dies and within a year or two the mother again becomes pregnant, it is said that it is the same baby born again, and the name of the deceased child is given to it." "At a place called Tonmuket in the North Andaman there is a spot to which it is said that women may resort if they wish to become pregnant. On the reef at this spot there are a large number of stones which, according to the legend, were once little children. The woman who desires a child walks out onto the reef when the tide is low and stands upon these stones. It is believed that one of the baby souls will enter her body and become incarnate. In the North Andaman there is some sort of association between the unborn souls of babies, the green pigeon, and the Ficus laccifera tree. The same name, Reykos, is used to denote both, the green pigeon and also the Ficus laccifera of the fruit of which the pigeon is very fond. The belief of the natives is sometimes stated by saying that the souls of unborn children live in the ficus trees, and that if a baby dies before it has been weaned its soul goes back to the tree. Another statement of the natives is that it is when the green pigeon is calling that the soul of a baby goes into its mother. The Ficus is to a certain extent tabu." It is only those who die in infancy that are thus reincarnated. But this may be a later modification of a general belief in reincarnation.

The Ibo-speaking peoples in southeastern Nigeria believe in reincarnation. C. K. Meek, *Law and Authority in a Nigerian Tribe* (1937), p. 61, reports: "The belief in the power of the ancestors also influences the relations of parents and children, for many parents show an excessive indulgence towards their children on the ground that they will be dependent on their children for their nourishment and status in the next world. Moreover, as they may be reborn into the world by their own children they may expect harsh treatment if they had previously treated their children harshly. A son who ill-uses his father is often excused on the ground that his father had in a former life illtreated him. On the other hand, many parents are not afraid of dealing roughly with their children when necessary; for if after their [the parents] death, the children vindictively refuse to perform adequately the final funeral rites, the dead parents can retaliate by heaping misfortunes on their descendants."

Similar facts are reported of other primitive tribes. Cf. Lévy-Bruhl, *The Soul of the Primitive*, pp. 321 ff., 330; and Schultze, p. 184; H. Ploss, *Das Kind in Brauch und Sitte der Voelker* (2. Aufl.; 1884), II, 334; D. Macdonald, *Oceania* (1889), p. 195; J. Ignatius Molina, *The Geographical, Natural, and Civic History of Chili* (1808), II, 104; W. H. Brett, *The Indian Tribes of Guiana* (1868), p. 99; E. R. Smith, *The Araucanians* (1855), p. 201.

50. Kidd, pp. 8, 72. And L. K. Anantha Krishna Iyer, *The Cochin Tribes and Castes* (1909), I, 29, writes of the Malayans, a jungle tribe inhabiting Cochin forests: "Their command of language is poor, the defect of which is made up by gestures. Whenever an officer or member of a higher caste puts them a question, they invariably say 'yes,' with a nodding of the head, believing that a negative answer might displease him."

Lévy-Bruhl, *Primitive Mentality*, p. 403, says that the Fijian tries "to please his interlocutor by assenting to what he says."

J. Henry, *L'Ame d'un peuple africain: Les Bambara* ("Bibliothèque Anthropos," Tome I, fasc. 2 [1910]), p. 47, writes about the Bambara: "Knowing that the Mohammedan, the missionary and every European does not believe in fetishes and despises them, the Bambara accuses God before them of having caused the death of one of his kin. This way of behaving, with him, is only a courtesy, a devious way of respecting the belief of those to whom he speaks, whose life he shares and whom he fears."

51. Lévy-Bruhl, *Primitive Mentality*, p. 308.
52. *The Jesuit Relations and Allied Documents* (1672–73), LVIII, 54.
53. Lévy-Bruhl, *Primitives and the Supernatural*, p. 45.
54. *Ibid.*, pp. 30 f.; also p. xxxii.
55. Cf. Preuss, *Die geistige Kultur der Naturvoelker*, pp. 12 ff.
56. Lévy-Bruhl, *The Soul of the Primitive*, p. 15: "He refers the sensations, pleasures, pains he experiences to himself, just as he does the acts of which he knows himself to be the doer. But from this it does not follow that he apprehends himself as a 'subject,' nor especially that he is conscious that he apprehends himself as anything different from 'objects' not himself. . . . . In the vague idea which the primitive has of himself. . . . ." It has already been pointed out that primitive man frequently refers even facts of his own psychic life to another being than himself, to his life soul, which he regards as a kind of guardian spirit.

In order to avoid possible misunderstandings it may be expressly pointed out here that the lack of a clear ego-consciousness is psychologically compatible with a behavior which we call "egoism" and which consists of a desire to satisfy one's wishes without regard for others, especially without regard for the prevailing moral order. Egoism is characterized by a specific quality of the emotional function and not—as the lack of an ego-consciousness, which is ignorance of one's own ego, a missing distinction between the subject and object of cognition—by a weakness of the rational function. Primitive man is undoubtedly an egoist, for his desires are stronger than his thinking. But his egoistic tendencies become involved with the social order under the coercion of which he lives; thus they do not become fully developed. In regard to this point, a certain difference exists between primitive man and the child, who also has a weak ego-consciousness. The child is thoroughly egoistic, since the social order is not yet fully applied to it. On the lack of ego-consciousness of children see Jean Piaget, *La Représentation du monde chez l'enfant* (nouvelle éd.; 1938), pp. 110 ff. Piaget speaks of "a complete absence of ego-consciousness." He remarks, p. 159: ". . . . the child does not distinguish between the psychic and the physical world . . . . it does not observe precise limits between its ego and the external world."

Egoism, signifying only a moral qualification, has to be distinguished clearly from egocentrism, meaning a psychological and an epistemological attitude. The latter is a way of understanding the surrounding world by imagining one's own ego in the center and referring all things to it. Such a method of interpreting the world presupposes a clear distinction, even a contrast, between the ego and the non-ego, between the subject and the object of cognition, and is psychologically impossible without a clearly developed, hypertrophical ego-consciousness. It is, therefore, contradictory to ascribe either to primitive man or to the child—as, unfortunately, is done so often—egocentrism and at the same time a lack of ego-consciousness.

57. Spencer, Vol. I, par. 42, p. 83, states: "Among the partially-civilized inferior races, we find imitativeness a marked trait." See also the references mentioned there.

John H. Weeks, *Among Congo Cannibals* (1913), p. 177, says of the Bangala on the Upper Congo: "He has a wonderful power of imitation, but he lacks invention and initiative." Cf. Theodor Wilhelm Danzel, *Kultur und Religion des primitiven Menschen* (1924), pp. 12, 52, 78. Danzel thinks that primitive man lacks all consciousness of an ego separated by clear boundaries from the non-ego. "As seen from our point of view, the ego appears to be enormously extended." Danzel rightly perceives the great importance of primitive man's identifying thinking. Primitive man, he says, by identifying himself with many things in the external world, extends his ego to these things. Yet it is obviously more correct to interpret the phenomenon in question not as hypertrophy but, on the contrary, as weakness or lack of ego-consciousness.

58. R. H. Codrington, *The Melanesians* (1891), p. 120, reports: "If a man has been successful in fighting, it has not been his natural strength of arm, quickness of eye, or readi-

ness of resource that has won success; he has certainly got the *mana* [magic power] of a spirit or of some deceased warrior to empower him, conveyed in an amulet of a stone round his neck, or a tuft of leaves in his belt, in a tooth hung upon a finger of his bow hand, or in the form of words with which he brings supernatural assistance to his side. If a man's pigs multiply, and his gardens are productive, it is not because he is industrious and looks after his property, but because of the stones full of *mana* for pigs and yams that he possesses."

Melland, p. 129, writes of the belief of the Bakaonde: "The spirits are all-hearing, all-seeing, all-pervading, all-powerful. Nothing but spirits (and in some cases, prescribed payments) can counteract spirits: none but the witch-doctor can show how this is to be effected. Man himself is impotent."

Felix Speiser, *Ethnographische Materialien aus den Neuen Hebriden und den Banks-Inseln* (1923), pp. 300 f., remarks of the natives of New Hebrides: "The native knows just as well as we do that a blow of a club must entail death; but he also assumes that the successful blow not only rests upon the ability of the enemy but also upon a magical force guiding his hand. This belief is a touching expression of the helplessness of man towards nature. Just as the native seeks to secure magical assistance in all his doings as counterpoise for his own inability, so no misfortune inflicted upon him can be completely destructive without magic." This statement could very well be generalized.

59. Danzel, p. 52.

60. Arthur Ungnad, "Zur Geschichte des Ichbewusstseins," *Zeitschrift fuer Assyriologie*, XXXVI (1925), 269.

61. Best, I, 397, writes: "In studying the customs of the Maori, it is well to ever bear in mind that a native so thoroughly identifies himself with his tribe that he is ever employing the first personal pronoun. In mentioning a fight that occurred possibly ten generations ago he will say: 'I defeated the enemy there,' mentioning the name of the tribe. In like manner he will carelessly indicate ten thousand acres of land with a wave of his hand, and remark: 'This is my land.' He would not suspect that any person would take it that he was the sole owner of such land, nor would any one but a European make such an error. When Europeans arrived on these shores many troubles arose owing to the inability of the Maori to understand individual possession of land, and land selling."

62. Walter E. Roth, "An Inquiry into the Animism and Folk-Lore of the Guiana Indians," *30th Annual Report of the Bureau of American Ethnology* (1915), pp. 352 f.

63. Kidd, pp. 136 f.

64. Ploss, II, 193.

65. Rafael Karsten, *Blood Revenge, War, and Victory Feasts among the Jibaro Indians of Eastern Ecuador* (Bureau of American Ethnology, Bull. 79 [1923]), pp. 11 f.

66. Cf. Edward Westermarck, *The Origin and Development of the Moral Ideas* (2d ed.; 1912), I, 373.

67. W. Robertson Smith, *Kinship and Marriage in Early Arabia* (1903), pp. 26 f.

68. P. Lafitau, *Mœurs des sauvages américains comparées aux mœurs des premiers temps* (1724), II, 163.

69. J. D. Haseman, "The Pawumwa Indians of South America," *American Anthropologist*, N.S., XIV (1912), 342. Gusinde, p. 744, writes of the Selknam Indians: "Every bodily suffering and disagreeableness, real pains or over-sensitiveness, above all depression and despondency, fear and inner disquietude, generally the consequence of certain dreams, depend one and all upon the *kwake*. The latter is considered a substance, a small object, a foreign body which penetrates the body of a person and makes itself felt there." Accordingly, the medicine man heals the patient by extracting the foreign substance from his body through sucking.

70. Cf. van der Leeuw, p. 7.

71. Karsten, *The Origins of Religion*, p. 45

72. Henri Labouret, *Les Tribus du Rameau Lobi* (Université de Paris, "Travaux et mémoires de l'Institut d'Ethnologie," Vol. XV [1931]), p. 318.

73. Cf. van der Leeuw, p. 11.

74. Ch. Keysser, "Vom Sattelberg zum Markham," *Zeitschrift fuer Ethnologie*, Jahrg. 44 (1912), p. 561.

75. Kidd, p. 140. There are many more examples.

76. Knud Rasmussen, *Neue Menschen* (1907), pp. 166 ff.

77. Richard Karutz, "Der Emanismus," *Zeitschrift fuer Ethnologie*, 45. Jahrg. (1913), p. 585.

Of the natives of Madagascar, A. et G. Grandidier, *Ethnographie de Madagascar*, Tome III (*Histoire physique, naturelle et politique de Madagascar*, Vol. IV [1917]), 375, write: "Like the Hebrews, like the Hindus etc., the Malagasy believe that, as a body, however dirty it may be, is purified by a more or less prolonged bath, so the soul, may it be ever so much soiled, ever so criminal, cleans, purifies itself by external performances, by mechanical procedures, by water or fire or sacrifices."

78. Among the Aleutians the custom exists of wrapping one's self in grass so that it may absorb the sins; then the grass is burned. Cf. Marett, *Faith, Hope, and Charity in Primitive Religion*, p. 122.

According to Frank H. Melland and Edward H. Cholmeley, *Through the Heart of Africa* (1912), p. 23, illness is interpreted among the Wakuluwe as punishment for a crime. The sick seeks recovery through public confession. "The man about to confess stands at the doorway of his hut, facing west, with a basket in his hands, in which are placed some sand and a few pieces of dry grass. Having confessed his *mpondo* (crime) aloud, he throws the grass and sand into the air, and the wind carries away the pieces of grass while the sand falls back into the basket. The man then cries out, 'My *mpondo* are now gone like the blades of grass, my *tusinza* (petty offences or misdemeanours) are as numerous as the grains of sand in this basket, let them go too,' and, suiting the action to the word, throws out the sand. He then says, 'I have no more *mpondo*, and *Ngulwe* (the highest being) will cure my sickness. . . . .' "

George Brown, *Melanesians and Polynesians* (1910), pp. 229 f., writes of the natives of Samoa: "They attached great value to confession of wrong-doing in times of danger, but, so far as I know, there was no expression of repentance or amendment or any prayer for forgiveness made on such occasion." This is only the consequence of their idea of the substantial character of the crime. Brown goes on: "If, for instance, a sailing-boat or canoe were crossing the channel between Savaii and Upolu, and was in danger of being swamped, the steersman would head the boat to the wind and each man would make confession of any wrong-doing. One would say, 'Well, I stole a fowl at a certain village.' Another would acknowledge wrong-doing with some married woman at another village; another to some other fault or breach of conduct. Another man would perhaps say that he had done nothing, and he would be passed over. This would continue until every man had confessed or declared his innocence, when the boat would be put before the wind again with confidence that the crew would make the passage safely."

The Araucan (Chili) perform the following operation upon a young man considered morally objectionable. He is wounded near the heart, and the gushing blood is poured into a river. The native medicine man interprets this operation by saying that the evil is removed from the heart and thrown into the water in order that it may be carried away (Lévy-Bruhl, *Primitives and the Supernatural*, p. 91).

Kidd reports, p. 5: "A Kafir woman was very indignant that her son had renounced heathenism and embraced Christianity. She promptly administered a strong emetic and purgative to dispel the hated religion."

Especially significant is what P. P. Cayzac, "La Religion des Kikuyu (Afrique orientale)," *Anthropos*, V (1910), 310 ff., reports: "Among the Kikuyu . . . . sin is transmissible and remissible, whence the two phrases which one hears everywhere: *Kogwatis ne sahu*, 'to be seized by the sin of another'; and, *Kotahikio*, 'to be relieved of sin.' 'To be seized by the sin of another' means more exactly 'to undergo the consequences of another's sin.' For the *sahu* is the consequence of a *noki*, or 'forbidden act.' Above all, a woman frequently transmits her sin to her children; for example, a young girl commits a *noki* before her marriage, later her child will have *sahu* if he falls ill, and the illness will be attributed to the *noki* of the mother. . . . . Sin is essentially remissible: it suffices to avow it. Ordinarily this is accomplished through a 'sorcerer' who expels the sin by a ceremony the principle ritual of which is a simulated vomiting: *kotahikio*, derived from *tahika*, to vomit. . . . . The Kikuyu also recognize the scape goat, in the case of incest for example. The guilty party ought to die, but offers a sacrifice, a goat. They perform an ignoble ceremony intended to transfer the crime to the animal; then its throat is cut as punishment. The guilty one is thus redeemed. . . . . A little Christian girl died and I had ordered a pagan worker to dig a grave. He obstinately refused to commit this sin . . . . for him the digging of a grave was *noki* having *sahu* as punishment. In fact, being the father of a family, his children would become afflicted. If he were a single man, it would have been different; he could not have infected anyone."

Loskiel, p. 37, reports that the Indians believe that to get after death "a place among the good spirits . . . . they must be first thoroughly cleansed from their sins, and gave the poor people vomits, as the most expeditious mode of performing this purification."

D. G. Brinton, *The Myths of the New World* (1868), p. 127, writes of the Indians: "Avowedly to free themselves from this sense of guilt the Delawares used an emetic . . . . the Cherokees a potion cooked up by an order of female warriors . . . . the Takahlies of Washington Territory, the Aztecs, Mayas, and Peruvians, auricular confession." Cf. further Lévy-Bruhl, *Primitives and the Supernatural*, pp. 348 ff.; Le Roy, pp. 247 f.; Karsten, *The Origins of Religion*, pp. 242 ff.; Mosbacher, pp. 20 ff.

An interesting combination of sin confession with the scapegoat may be found in Kidd, p. 261. "When men are ill among the Kafirs, and the witchdoctors can do them no good, natives sometimes adopt the custom of taking a goat into the presence of a sick man, and confess the sins of the kraal over the animal. Sometimes a few drops of blood from the sick man are allowed to fall on the head of the goat, which is turned out into an uninhabited part of the veldt. The sickness is supposed to be transferred to the animal, and to become lost in the desert." Not only is the illness transferred to the animal, but also the sins of the members of the group who are considered responsible for the illness of the member.

79. Cf. L. R. Farnell, *The Evolution of Religion* (1905), pp. 65 ff., 118 ff.

80. The substantializing tendency of primitive thinking establishes the connection between religion and society, and even the identity which exists between primitive man's ideas about his community and his notions about the deity. He conceives the social community as a substance common to all members of the group. The substance which constitutes the community is the blood. "Kinship among the Arabs," writes Robertson Smith, p. 27, "means a share in the common blood which is taken to flow in the veins of every member of a tribe."

But the group may also be based on something different from common descent or blood community. It may be effected by eating and drinking with the stranger, by consuming with him the same substance. Equally, the community with the deity is either a blood community, because the deity is the common ancestor, or it is effected by a common sacrificial meal which the sacrificers consume together. The consumed object represents the deity itself whose substance they thus incorporate. Another idea which also prevails is that the sacrificers consume the sacrifice together with the deity. This particular significance of the sacrifice has been stressed by W. Robertson Smith, *Lectures on the Religion of the Semites* (1894), pp. 226 f.

80a. Individual property as a legal institution presupposes not only a certain economic but also a very definite psychologic condition, namely, a minimum of ego-consciousness. Primitive man, whose consciousness is completely socialized, does not fulfil the condition essential to the rise of individual property. His mentality presents the ideal condition for collective property. Under the influence of the evolutionary theory of the nineteenth century, ethnologists and historians were convinced that collective property was the original form of ownership. Sir Henry James Sumner Maine wrote in his famous work *Ancient Law* ("Everyman's Library," No. 734, pp. 152 f.): "Ancient law . . . . knows next to nothing of Individuals. It is concerned not with Individuals, but with Families, not with single human beings, but groups." "It is more than likely that joint-ownership, and not separate ownership, is the really archaic institution, and that the forms of property which will afford us instruction will be those which are associated with the rights of families and of groups of kindred." In the course of the increasing opposition against evolutionalism a different theory concerning the origin of property was set forth. For instance, Richard Hildebrand, *Recht und Sitte auf den primitiveren wirtschaftlichen Kulturstufen* (1907), maintains that among the most primitive peoples who obtain their sustenance by gathering fruits or by hunting, there is no property in land at all, since land is so abundant that, like the air, it has no economic value. Consequently, land cannot be the object of ownership. The land is *res nullius*. Out of this state of no ownership, individual property originated by occupation. This hypothesis cannot be correct, because, first, only fertile land and hunting grounds abounding in game become economically important—and such land is never so abundant as the air is; second, the hypothesis is based on a purely economic consideration, and economic considerations play no, or no decisive, part in primitive thinking and feeling. As a matter of fact, we find among primitive food-collectors, hunters, and stock-raisers, who all are still nomads, a very definite relationship between the group and the land occupied by the group. The relationship is characterized by the fact that any other group is excluded from the land —if necessary, by force. The claim to exclusive possession is the essential element of property. The members of the group consider the pastures where their herds graze, the grounds where they hunt, as "their" land. Indeed, it is the collective property of the group.

E. Sidney Hartland, *Primitive Law* (1924), pp. 92 f., writes: "A community of roving hunters seeking their food from game, or from wild fruits and seeds (and this is a stage that science does not enable us to get behind), rarely travels beyond the district with which its members are familiar, unless driven by want of supplies or some other special cause. That district may be wide; but, however wide, it has boundaries hardly recognizable to us but well known to the community. Within those boundaries it is looked upon by the community as its own territory. It resents the intrusion, without permission, of members of any other community upon it. At this stage, and for long afterwards, no individual is regarded as the exclusive owner of any part of it." Even Father Wilhelm Schmidt, who vigorously opposes the evolutionary doctrine of the origin of property, admits in his work *Das Eigentum auf den aeltesten Stufen der Menschheit*, Band I: *Das Eigentum in den Urkulturen* (1937), pp. 288 ff., that among the peoples whom he considers to be the most primitive, the peoples of the so-called "*Urkultur*," namely, the Pygmies and Pygmoids north and south of the Equator, some Indian tribes in California, the Salishan and Algonquin Indians, the Indians of Tierra del Fuego, the Reindeer Eskimo, the Bushmen, the Bergdama, and some tribes in southeastern Australia, the land is owned by groups, not by individuals. It is sometimes the *Gross-Familie* (the enlarged family), sometimes the village community, or the tribe that are the proprietors. Schmidt stresses, however, that among these peoples ownership in movable things, such as articles of food and clothing, tools and weapons, has the character of individual property. But these peoples, like many other very primitive tribes, show a decidedly communistic attitude in consuming and using these things. Fruits and game, even if the result of gathering or hunting by a single individual, are divided among the members of the group according to quite definite rules of customary law. Tools and weapons are not exclusively used by the "owner" but are more or less at the disposal of the other members of the group when they need them. It is usual to lend out personal belongings and to exchange gifts so that movable things permanently change their possessor.

Some examples may illustrate these customs. James Dawson, *Australian Aborigines* (1881), p. 22, reports of some tribes in the Western District of Victoria: "There are strict rules regulating the distribution of food. When a hunter brings game to the camp he gives up all claim to it, and must stand aside and allow the best portions to be given away, and content himself with the worst. If he has a brother present, the brother is treated in the same way, and helps the killer of the game to eat the poor pieces, which are thrown to them, such as the forequarters and ribs of the kangaroos, opossums, and small quadrupeds, and the backbones of birds. The narrator of this custom mentioned that when he was very young he used to grumble because his father gave away all the best pieces of birds and quadrupeds, and the finest eels, but he was told that it was a rule and must be observed."

Paul Schebesta, *Among the Forest Dwarfs of Malaya*, trans. by Arthur Chambers (n.d.), p. 83, writes: "Food is eaten by the family in common. Even when the women have brought in enough roots from the forest, or when each family has rice, meat or game, it is nevertheless divided among all. Each family contributes from its own food, already cooked and prepared to every other family. If one family on any particular day is unusually well supplied, they give generously to all kindred families, even if it leaves them with too little. If other families not belonging to the group are in the camp, they do not share or only to a very small extent, in the distribution. It is therefore quite justifiable to speak of a kind of communism among the Semang, but it is only family communism applied to food."

A. R. Brown, *The Andaman Islanders*, p. 43, reports that among the Andaman Islanders all food is private (individual) property and belongs to the man or woman who has obtained it by his or her own effort. But he adds: "Every one who has food, is expected, however, to give to those who have none. An older married man will reserve for himself sufficient for his family, and will then give the rest to his friends. A younger man is expected to give away the best of what he gets to the older men. This is particularly the case with the bachelors. Should a young unmarried man kill a pig he must be content to see it distributed by one of the older men, all the best parts going to the seniors, while he and his companions must be satisfied with the inferior parts. The result of this custom is that practically all the food obtained is evenly distributed through the whole camp, the only inequality being that the younger men do not fare so well as their elders. Generosity is esteemed by the Andaman Islanders one of the highest virtues and is unremittingly practised by the majority of them."

P. Schebesta, *Among Congo Pigmies*, trans. by Gerald Griffin (1933), pp. 124 f., reports of the Bambuti: "Everything is common property, even the ant-hill and any game that is captured or killed in the course of the day's hunting. . . . . The members of a family group are in constant touch with one another throughout the daily round; they form an entity which aims at the welfare of the group as a whole. The proceeds of the hunt and the fruits of the forest are common property. The day's game is cut up by the family group elder, and is divided among the individual families. The man who killed the animal has no say in the actual division. And even an outside family group, in the same camp, can come in for a share of the spoil if it has any claim on the grounds of kinship by marriage. Vegetables are rarely shared out in this fashion owing to the fact that all the women of the family group who set out together in quest of food, usually bring home approximately similar quantities. But when members of a family group, from whatsoever cause, have brought nothing home, the others come to their assistance."

According to B. von Zastrow, "Die Herero," in E. Schultz-Everth and L. Adam, *Das Eingeborenenrecht* (1930), II, 259, collectivistic ideas prevail among the Herero. Everybody believes himself to be entitled to take away from his fellowman what he wants if the other has plenty of it. They have a peculiar institution called *okuramberia*. If someone is hungry he has the right to take a head of cattle, for instance, or a sheep, from the flock of his neighbor, to kill it and eat it immediately. The "owner" reacts in no other way than by doing the same thing at the first opportunity.

J. Jetté, "On Ten'a Folk-Lore," *Journal of the Royal Anthropological Institute of Great Britain and Ireland*, XXXIX (1909), 483, reports of the Ten'a Indians in Alaska: "The Ten'a hunt is conducted on communistic principles: in a band of hunters it is never the one who killed a piece of large game who gets it; he generally receives but an insignificant share, or none at all. By common agreement it is distributed among the party, or given whole to one who then is expected to cook it and serve it as a banquet to the whole village."

As far as property in tools and weapons is concerned, the following example is instructive. Dawson, p. 24, reports of the above-mentioned Australian tribe in the Western District of Victoria: "The natives have few tools; the principal one is the stone axe, which resembles the stone celts found in Europe. . . . . The stone axe is so valuable and scarce that it is generally the property of the chief of the tribe. He lends it, however, for a consideration, to the best climbers, who use it to cut steps in the bark of trees, to enable them to climb in search of bears, opossums, birds, and nests, and also to cut wood and to strip bark for their dwellings." That means that the most important tool, the stone ax, is the collective property of the tribe and that the chief, as representative of the tribe, is competent to regulate the use of the ax by the members of the tribe.

A. R. Brown, p. 42, reports of the Andaman Islanders: "While all portable property is . . . . owned by individuals, the Andamanese have customs which result in an approach to communism. One of these is the custom of constantly exchanging presents with one another. . . . . It is considered a breach of good manners ever to refuse the request of another. Thus if a man be asked by another to give anything that he may possess, he will immediately do so. . . . . Almost every object that the Andamanese possess is thus constantly changing hands."

E. H. Man, "On the Aboriginal Inhabitants of the Andaman Islands," *Journal of the Royal Anthropological Institute of Great Britain and Ireland*, XII (1883), 340, writes: "The weapons, tools, and other property pertaining to one member of a family are regarded as available for the use of his or her relatives, but such articles as cooking-pot, canoe, or sounding-board, when not required by the owner, are looked upon somewhat in the light of public property by members of the same community; in short, the rights of private property are only so far recognized that no one would without permission appropriate or remove to a distance anything belonging to a friend or neighbor."

Among the Yamana Indians in Tierra del Fuego it is usual to exchange gifts. J. M. Cooper, *Analytical and Critical Bibliography of the Tribes of Tierra del Fuego and Adjacent Territory* (1917), p. 179, writes: "A gift was made, regardless often of the wishes of the recipient, who could not refuse it without affronting the giver and who was expected to give something in return." W. Koppers, "Die Eigentumsverhaeltnisse bei den Yamana auf Feuerland," in *Atti del XXII. Congresso degli Americanisti* (Roma, 1928), II, 192, reports: "The Yamana lend anything they are asked for. They wait patiently until the borrower returns it, and never urge or admonish him."

Robert H. Lowie, *Primitive Society* (1920), p. 209, remarks that many of the usages of the Arctic populations "really smack of communism." E. W. Nelson, "The Eskimo about Bering Strait," *18th Annual Report of the Bureau of American Ethnology* (1899), p. 294, writes: "The only feeling of conscience or moral duty that I noted among the Eskimo seemed to be an instinctive desire to do that which was most conducive to the general good of the community, as looked at from their point of view. . . . . if a man borrows from another and fails to return the article he is not held to account for it. This is done under the general feeling that if a person has enough property to enable him to lend some of it, he has more than he needs. The one who makes the loan under these circumstances does not even feel justified in asking a return of the article, and waits for it to be given back voluntarily." Valdemar Bogoras, "The Chukchee," *The Jesup North Pacific Expedition* ("Memoirs of the American Museum of Natural History," Vol. XI), VII, 630, reports of the Chukchee: "A man who has an extra boat often gives the use of it to some of his neighbors. It is contrary to the sense of justice of the natives to allow a good boat to lie idle on shore, when near by are hunters in need of one. In such a case a boat crew is also formed, under the direction of one who is considered to be the boat-master, and responsible for the boat. Nothing is paid for the use of the boat, even when the hunt has been exceedingly successful. . . . . To pay for such use is believed to endanger the hunting luck." Lowie, p. 210, says: "Arctic society recognizes two axioms, the altruistic sharing of food supplies and the necessity for effective use of extant means of economic production. Arctic communism thus centers in purely economic considerations. Apart from them there is room for the assertion of individualistic motives." Communism—not only primitive communism—always centers in economic considerations. But the same is true of the opposite system, economic individualism. The fact that primitive peoples incline more to the former than to the latter can be explained not only by economic reasons but also, and perhaps better, by the collectivistic character of their consciousness.

81. Karsten, *Blood Revenge, War, and Victory Feasts among the Jibaro Indians of Eastern Ecuador*, p. 12, writes: "The Jibaro can not even distinguish his own personality from his material belongings; at least not from things he has made himself. When he fabricates a shield, a drum, a blowpipe, or some other delicate object, he has to diet and observe abstinence in other ways; for, according to his own idea, he actually puts something of his own personality, his own soul into the object he is making. His own properties, both the essential and habitual ones and those occasionally acquired through eating a certain food, etc., will therefore be transferred to that object. The division of labor existing among the Indians depends on the same peculiar view. Thus, for instance, the Indian woman has to fabricate the clay vessels and manages these utensils, because the clay of which they are made, like the earth itself, is female—that is, has a woman's soul. She is connected with the fire and has to cook the food, because the fire has a female soul, etc."

Edwin W. Smith and Andrew Murray Dale, *The Ila-speaking Peoples of Northern Rhodesia* (1920), I, 347, speak of "a very close connection, amounting almost to identity, between a person and his possessions."

82. The substantializing tendency of primitive man is characterized by R. Kreglinger, "La Mentalité primitive et la signification première des rites," *Actes du Congrès International d'Histoire des Religions* (tenu à Paris en octobre, 1925) (Paris, 1925), I, 189 ff., as follows: "More than anything else, primitive man perceives the solid and weighty bodies which he can see or touch; he imagines all other things by analogy with them; everything seems to him to be extended in space, and consequently material; all feeling, all thought, all quality is for him an object, a substance, impregnating the beings who possess them, but remaining independent of them. In the moral life, vice is a miasma which seizes hold of a man and makes him evil and which moves and propagates through contagion; virtues are other powers, also clearly individualized, but contrary in their effects. A person is good or bad depending upon the good or evil substance with which he is charged. The intent is irrelevant; whoever is impregnated with vice will be punished. Vice, Aeschylus tells us, extends itself mechanically from the criminal to all those who are near him and the descendent inherits it from his ancestors. . . . . So the whole moral life confirms the material character of primitive thinking; even some profound theories of civilized peoples retain a trace; thus the Pauline doctrine of grace, and the Jewish belief in the identity of the punishment with the crime. The evil which inheres in the delinquent hurts him as much as the victims of his crime; he will be unhappy as well as wicked, and his distress which necessarily results from the presence in him of a deleterious miasma is thus sufficient proof of his guilt. . . . . Each individual, on the other hand, is made of a certain substance which marks his individuality and impregnates all his organs; its presence makes them its own, and its

persistence, even when they are detached, maintains an effective solidarity. . . . . One generally explains these facts by the principle of *pars pro toto*. What characterizes this kind of thinking is that the member continues to be a part of the whole from which it is separated. . . . ." Kreglinger goes on: "It has often been said that the life of a primitive bathes in a religious atmosphere, that religion plays in him a predominant role, and that history at bottom is only a gradual secularization of humanity. But this, it seems to me, is an absolute mistake." Of the primitive man's notion of the world, he writes: "His view of the world . . . . is not at all mystical. He does not believe more than we, but rather less than many of our contemporaries, in the intervention of superior beings; his physics is not ours but it is none the less positive and none the less logical; it is decidedly not 'supernatural.' "

It is undoubtedly true that a great many primitive ideas and practices which modern ethnology treats as "magic" or "religious" are only expressions of the substantializing tendency of primitive man and have nothing to do with the idea of superhuman (in this sense "mystical") powers, an idea essential for magic or religion. Besides there remains enough in the life of primitive man which may rightly be separated from the profane sphere as magic or religion, especially in so far as patterns of conduct are involved which presuppose a belief in the existence and power of superhuman beings. If Kreglinger thinks so little of the religious (or magical) factor in the primitive conception of the world, he overlooks the tremendous role which the belief in the soul of the dead plays in its various aspects; he takes no notice that in the view of primitive man the bearers of those substantially conceived forces, abilities, and qualities are, to a great extent, personal beings characterized as "souls" or as "spirits" and thus rightly incorporated in magic or religion. Probably these "spirits" were, originally, nothing else than souls of the dead. The thesis of Spencer, I, 305, that "the ghost is the primitive type of supernatural being," has not yet been refuted. And the assertion of Wundt, pp. 269 ff., that belief in magic originated in the belief in the soul, remains valid today despite all efforts to prove a pre-animistic magic; it has since been confirmed many times by later materials.

Proceeding from those facts in which the substantializing tendency of primitive man is expressed, Karutz, pp. 545 ff., labels as an essential element of primitive thinking the belief "that the substance radiates, emanates, and transfers to the surrounding world its qualities and that these emanations—of the physical qualities of inorganic bodies, of the physiological qualities of organic beings, of the psychic or intellectual qualities of men and animals— are transferred to other things and organisms." According to primitive man's belief, "every thing is the source of characteristic emanations through which it radiates its qualities and transfers them with specific effect to its surroundings" (p. 570). This characterization of the primitive way of thinking certainly hits upon one essential point, the transferability of qualities. But it overlooks that this transferability, the emanation, is only the consequence of the imagined substance nature of the qualities. Therefore, Karutz is mistaken when he assumes that, according to primitive man's belief, "the emanation" proceeds from a "force." "This force inheres alive in the natural qualities of things. This is neither magic nor inexplicable mystics, but the clear idea that the happening is the effect of concrete objects of the surrounding world" (p. 555). But this nonanimistic, because impersonal and thus modern scientific, concept of force is psychologically impossible in primitive mentality. Karutz probably became induced to make this assumption by the fact that he found certain similarities between the phenomena which he calls "emanism" and the hypothesis of modern radio activity from which he borrowed the expression. If primitive man knows "emanation," why should he not also know the modern physical concept of force? This would be a rash conclusion. Karutz, like Kreglinger, is right when he reproaches ethnology for exaggerating the magic theory. But he overlooks the fact that these "emanations" in many cases, especially those particularly important for primitive life, proceed not from natural objects but from invisible personal beings to whose superhuman power the "emanated" effect is traced.

83. W. C. Willoughby, *Race Problems in the New Africa* (1923), pp. 82 f. Cf. also van der Leeuw, p. 7.

84. Best, I, 341.

85. *Ibid.*, pp. 359 ff.

86. K. Oberg, "Crime and Punishment in Tlingit Society," *American Anthropologist*, N.S., XXXVI (1934), 146 ff.

Gusinde, p. 1143, believes that he has observed among the Selknam a "highly increased ego-consciousness." But more careful investigation reveals that it is, in fact, only a strongly developed tribe or group consciousness. His proof is the following utterance of an old Indian: "When I was a young man our group announced a race to which an old man brought a good friend of his who was known to be a good racer. He said to him: 'Do your utmost. Don't let yourself be overtaken!' Soon the race started. That young man ran very well and overtook the others; thus he was the first to come in and he continued running until the others came in. Immediately all the spectators followed the racers and the old man who had brought the runner exclaimed full of satisfaction: 'We won! Our men are excellent racers, like our ancestors. I brought this man and so we won. We had to surpass the other group!' All our people were glad and extremely satisfied." Gusinde adds: "Thus after scores of years Tenenusk repeated that event with the greatest enjoyment as if he had himself achieved a memorable and exceptional success. This is typical of the Selknam." Only if one identifies himself entirely with the group can "we won" mean "I won." But this signifies the lack of any real ego-consciousness; only such a lack makes Gusinde's following observation plausible. "The Selknam observes as a matter of course and without the slightest doubt the old customs and prevalent usages; should he be despised or condemned for violations he feels it bitterly. When he grants himself permissible privileges, like taking a second or even a third wife, he tries to balance the decrease of good reputation by increased skill or stronger emphasis on his personal values." In reality these "personal values" are the values which the individual has for the group. "No one thinks of grumbling over the old obligations and rules; in fact, everyone more or less tries to be a good and useful individual."

87. Emile Durkheim, *On the Division of Labor in Society*, trans. by George Simpson (1933), p. 194. Lévy-Bruhl, *The Soul of the Primitive*, p. 95, writes: "Since in these societies the true unit is the social group (clan, family or sib) of which individuals are merely the component elements, it is quite natural that these should not be sole arbiters of the most important actions of their lives. It is the group, or its chief, who will decide for the individuals."

88. H. A. Junod, *The Life of a South African Tribe* (2d ed.; 1927), I, 382, writes of the Thonga: " 'Royalty,' in the mind of the Native, is a venerable and sacred institution; respect for the Chief, and obedience to his commands are universal; his prestige is maintained, not by a great display of riches and of power, but by the mystical idea that, as the body lives by nourishment taken through its head, so the life of the nation is sustained through its chief.—The Thongas do not explain this in abstract words, but by images which are very striking. The chief is the Earth. . . . . He is the cock by which the country is sustained. . . . . He is the bull; without him the cows cannot bring forth. He is the husband; the country without him is like a woman without a husband. . . . . A clan without a chief has lost its reason (*hungukile*). It is dead. Because who will call the army together. . . . . The chief is our great warrior (*nhena*), he is our forest where we hide ourselves and from whom we ask for laws." Cf. also Lévy-Bruhl, *Primitive Mentality*, p. 401; in a report of a missionary quoted there, it is written: "The nation has but one mind, one will. The individual is annihilated, we have here the centralization principle pushed to its extreme limit or, to put it in another way, the death of all for the sake of one."

89. Dudley Kidd, *Kafir Socialism* (1908), p. 80.

90. *Ibid.*, pp. 6–7.

91. *Ibid.*, pp. 8–9.

92. *Ibid.*, p. 11.

93. *Ibid.*, p. 17.

94. *Ibid.*, p. 8.

95. *Ibid.*, p. 9.

96. *Ibid.*, p. 73.

97. Meek, p. 208, writes of the Ibo, a tribe in southeastern Nigeria: "To commit murder was an offence against Ala (Earth deity) and it was the concern of the whole community to see that the steps prescribed by custom were carried out." From the prescribed rites it follows that "the family of the murderer was considered as sharing in the responsibility of the crime, unless it took steps to dissociate itself from the murder. . . . . If the murderer did not immediately hang himself, but took refuge in flight, his family had also to fly, for the kin of the murdered man . . . . immediately made a raid on the compounds and property of the kin of the murderer."

R. F. Fortune, *Manus Religion* ("Memoirs of the American Philosophical Society," Vol. III [1935]), p. 28: "For if his ward's eldest son sins, Sir Ghost [the soul of an ancestor] does not necessarily take his ward's eldest son's soul stuff. Sir Ghost takes the soul stuff of the next person in that household to fall ill. By the laws of probability, sin is much more likely to hurt someone else than the sinner." Such a collective liability, or, more generally, such a substitutive liability of others for the perpetrator, is also a consequence of the system of transcendental sanctions. These transcendental sanctions are not sanctions executed rationally by society, i.e., by men themselves. They consist only in an interpretation of facts. Therefore, in order to maintain the connection between the wrong and the evil, interpreted as punishment, a scheme of interpretation must be accepted according to which the case that the actual evildoer remains free of the evil, whereas an innocent is subjected to it, may be regarded as an application of the principle of retribution. This is the idea of collective or substitutive liability.

98. Kidd, *Kafir Socialism*, p. 75.

99. Cf. Spencer, I, par. 36, p. 66; A. S. Diamond, *Primitive Law* (1935), p. 187.

100. A. W. Howitt, *The Native Tribes of South-East Australia* (1904), p. 296, writes of the efficacy of the social order among the natives of southeastern Australia: "It is quite true that many such laws or customs are obeyed without the dread of physical punishment being inflicted for their breach, by any tribal authority, individual or collective. But such laws or customs are obeyed because the native has been told, from his earliest childhood, that their infraction will be followed by some supernatural personal punishment."

W. Lloyd Warner, *A Black Civilization* (1937), p. 17, reports of the Australian Murngin: "Within this group [the clan] no violent conflict ever takes place, no matter how much cause is given. Members may quarrel, but for clansmen to fight one another would be considered an unnatural act in Murngin society and never occurs." P. 162: "Occasionally men are killed within the clan, but this is not a cause for war or retaliation by members of the clan or by near relatives from without the clan." From Warner's account it appears that, according to the belief of the Murngin, the ancestral souls punish their descendants for the delicts committed by them (cf. pp. 131, 163, 304). Blood revenge, however, directed from one group against another group, is a generally accepted principle among Australian tribes.

Charles Dundas, "The Organization and Laws of Some Bantu Tribes in East Africa," *Journal of the Royal Anthropological Institute of Great Britain and Ireland*, XLV (1915), 266, commenting on the fact that among certain Bantu tribes a delict committed within the inner family entails no or a much milder retribution than a delict committed upon a member of another family, writes: ". . . . among people with whom the family bond is so remarkably close we cannot assume that the slaying of a father or a son is regarded as a minor offence (in contradistinction to a delict committed by one who is not a member of the family). Indeed it is said that a parricide is doomed to die himself. An incident related to me as absolutely authentic, told of a man who, having speared his father, was cursed by the dying parent, and forbidden ever to drink water or eat food excepting from remote localities.

For some time the unhappy man lived on sugar cane juice, but one day, forgetting the curse, he drank water from the river, and being unable to swallow it, died of suffocation. Leprosy is believed to be one of the results of parricide." Delicts committed within the inner group entail a transcendental sanction and not a socially organized one like blood revenge, which is an action performed by one group against another group.

101. Cf. Crawley, *The Mystic Rose*, I, 176, where it is strikingly said: "Primitive man has some differences in his code of morals, but on the whole he is more moral in the social sense than is civilized man. . . . . Death often occurs from this moral fear."

102. Archibald Ross Colquhoun, *Amongst the Shans* (1885), p. 76.

103. Labouret, p. 325.

104. Fridtjof Nansen, *Eskimo Life* (1893), pp. 267 f.

105. David Crantz, *The History of Greenland* (1820), I, 165.

106. Albert Nicolay Gilbertson, "Some Ethical Phases of Eskimo Culture," *Journal of Religious Psychology*, VI (1913), 344. See also Henry Rink, *Tales and Traditions of the Eskimo* (1875), p. 34.

107. Paul Radin, *Primitive Man as Philosopher* (1927), pp. 30 ff., contradicts the view that the primitive has only a weakly developed ego-consciousness by saying that he has an "insatiable desire for prestige," or at least that this phenomenon can frequently be observed among primitive people. Certainly, primitive man, too, has a desire for prestige, and this desire becomes the greater the more he respects the social order. But this does not mean that he has ego-consciousness, that he regards himself as a being different from, and at least equivalent to, the group. For the desire for prestige can appear in two entirely different forms: either in the desire to be respected by the society as an obedient member, more correctly in the fear to be socially condemned, and therefore in the desire not to be the object of blame, reprimand, or punishment, or in the desire to be in opposition to society, to be above the social order, and to degrade it by a behavior violating and opposing it. In the former behavior there is expressed the "desire for prestige" of an individual with a weak ego-consciousness of an undeveloped personality. It is the type of the obedient man. In the second there is expressed the type of the revolutionary. Both have a "desire for prestige." For desire for prestige is an expression of the will to live, of the instinct of self-preservation. Thus it is characteristic of primitive man that he satisfies his "desire for prestige" by the consciousness to behave entirely in conformity with the social order, to have the approbation of his fellows and in no way to oppose the social order. He is the typical nonrevolutionary.

Radin himself confirms this by pointing to the important role which the fear of the ridicule plays in primitive man's life. P. 50: "Stated broadly, we may say that every mistake, every deviation from accepted opinion, every individual and purely personal interpretation, every peculiarity and eccentricity, may call for the ridicule. It is ridicule and not indignation and horror that assails a man who attempts to change a detail in a ceremony, to tell a story in some new and original manner, or who acts counter to some definitely accepted belief and custom, and it is the same fundamentally ill-natured laughter that greets him when he becomes unwittingly the victim of some untoward accident. To avoid it a man will go to any length. He may even commit suicide in consequence of it." "The fear of the ridicule is thus a great positive factor in the lives of primitive peoples. It is the preserver of the established order of things and more potent and tyrannous than the most restrictive and coercive of positive injunctions possibly could be."

The reaction of society which holds the violation of its norms up to ridicule is the expression of a malicious pleasure which the others have when the damage is inflicted upon the violator. Radin is right when he compares the ridicule which strikes the violator of the norm with the ridicule to which the victim of an accident is subjected. The ridicule of the victim is the effect of the malignity of society. But only he who has not enough ego-consciousness can be hurt by malignity and laughter. A man who is conscious of his value because he is conscious of his ego defies it; it cannot hurt him. From the fact that primitive man is afraid of ridicule we can conclude that he has no ego-consciousness. What Radin says of primitive man's fear of ridicule proves that tyrannic rule of society which Radin would like to deny.

108. Spencer, I, § 38, p. 71, writes: "The primitive man is conservative in an extreme degree." Cf. also Lévy-Bruhl, *Primitive Mentality*, p. 387.

109. Melland, p. 137, writes of the Bakaonde that they stubbornly refuse all technical improvements shown to them by Europeans: "They indeed admitted the superiority of the new model [of a bellow] and its simplicity, but they would not use it, as the innovation would have aroused the spirits to anger." And p. 171: "The immense force for conservatism will be noticed; the inevitable argument against an innovation is that what was good enough for our elders is good enough for us: in other words, there is fear lest the family '*akishi*' will be displeased and will withdraw their support." Cf. Lévy-Bruhl, *La Mythologie primitive* (1935), pp. 162 f. With reference to a remark of F. E. Williams ("Trading Voyages from the Gulf of Papua," *Oceania*, III, 157 f.), concerning the observation of tradition in the shipbuilding of primitive people, who strictly comply with the old rules handed down to them in myths, he says: "These precedents established by their mythical ancestors are imperative. It is absolutely necessary to comply with them. To behave oneself according to these 'models,' 'to imitate' these ancestors is the only way to conciliate their favor and at the same time to participate in their power."

110. F. E. Williams, *Orokaiva Society* (1930), p. 309, stresses the sense of morality and justice of the natives. Of the norms which govern their behavior he writes: "Selected by generations, they have been unconsciously designed to suit the narrow needs of family, clan, or tribal unit; they are essentially social norms, and they are meant to ensure the smooth running and happiness of social life. It is our first business then to formulate these standards—a work in which unfortunately we may look for little direct assistance from the native himself, who is not a preacher or a moralist. Now these standards, although there is no central authority to enforce them, are nevertheless observed with a large measure of fidelity; for the individual is so sunk in the social unit that he obeys its laws for the most part automatically."

Phillips, p. 220, says of the natives of the Lower Congo: "Although I have considered the emotional nature low, there is a remarkable exception, the sentiment of public justice. In any dealings with the natives, if a European suffer aggression and can clearly prove that such is the case, he is certainly adjudged to be in the right, and the offender condemned to a penalty which is assessed by the natives and the European; and further, if a chief promise such and such a fine shall be paid his word is in all cases sufficient. I have never known an instance where this statement fails."

For the sense of justice among the Papua see R. Neuhauss, *Deutsch Neu-Guinea* (1911), I, 181. Cf. also Junod, p. 436; Le Roy, p. 205; Kruijt, pp. 170, 389; Gusinde, p. 1143.

111. Graebner, p. 27, remarks: "Whereas primitive man learns by somewhat automatic imitation to satisfy the necessities of individual life, the laws of social life are stamped upon his mind through an impressive measure of education. In the so-called initiation rites through which the boy or lad is made a man, this purpose is not only achieved physically by various magical acts, but the mind, made susceptible to all impressions by staying awake and by fasting, is innoculated with the higher knowledge of the man-world, above all of the prescribed customs, particularly respect and obedience to the older men."

112. Rasmussen, *Intellectual Culture of the Iglulik Eskimos*, pp. 54 ff. Kidd, *The Essential Kafir*, pp. 95 ff., reports the following reply, which one constantly receives to the question why the Kafirs observe a custom which seems to be absolutely senseless: "We do it because it is our custom." And Kidd adds: "That answer, with a Kafir, is the end of all argument."

113. Melland, p. 130.

CHAPTER II

1. Karsten, *The Origins of Religion*, pp. 27, 33, shares Darwin's view that even the higher animal has the tendency "to personify inanimate things . . . . to endow even inanimate nature with a life similar to that in himself and his equals." But personification presupposes thought; and thinking, even among the higher animals, can be assumed only on the basis of highly problematical analogy interpretation. Prompted by the desire to prove the continuity of development from animal to man, Darwin was inclined to assume in animals certain mental qualities which even in men become apparent only in the higher stages of development. Thus he interpreted the acts of certain animals as acts of vengeance.

2. According to Klaatsch, *Die Anfaenge von Kunst und Religion in der Urmenschheit*, p. 52, "the personal as the oldest and most primitive" element appeared also in the concept of God; but many authors "perceived in it the highest laboriously attained stage of the cognition of God. The common, generally accepted view was and is that man created the gods from the various elements by personifying them, such as a thunder-god, a wind-god, etc. But this would presuppose complicated considerations and constructions, impossible among primitive people."

3. Edward Shortland, *Maori Religion and Mythology* (1882), p. 5.

4. Crawley, *The Idea of the Soul*, p. 43. He continues: "Conversely, as we have seen, he is not fully conscious of personality even his own; things and persons are objects, and he speaks originally of their relations only. We have no right to say, therefore, that he infers objects to have a personal life and will, because he has; he does not know he has; and he gets to know that he has from external persons." Crawley relies mainly upon E. J. Payne's *History of the New World Called America* (1899). There it is said, Vol. II, p. 146: "Primitive man finds personality everywhere, in all the forms of animal life, in whatever yields the sensation of sound, in whatever has perceptible motion; even inanimate objects, not excluding instruments made by human hands, are capable of producing personal impressions. Whatever fills a certain space in the consciousness tends to become personalized . . . . whatever speaks to his ear is a person." Payne points to the decisive role of language in the personalistic apperceptions of primitive man. He says, pp. 104 ff.: "Personality . . . . is a hidden attribute involved in all general terms; we shall identify the effort to express it as the hidden germ of language itself, the essential characteristic of its earliest stage, and the formative principle of the grammatical system which it ultimately creates." Cf. also Crawley, p. 41.

5. Karsten, *The Origins of Religion*, p. 28, writes: "The savage necessarily projects upon the objects and phenomena of the external world the innate and intrinsic consciousness of himself as a living subject, active, exercising a will of his own, capable of emotions and passions, thus transforming them into living deliberate subjects."

6. R. Thurnwald, "Im Bismarckarchipel und auf den Salomo Inseln, 1906–1909," p. 132.

7. E. Laetitia Moon Conard, "Les Idées des Indiens Algonquins relatives à la vie d'outre-tombe," *Revue de l'histoire des religions*, XLII (1900), 274: "If it is true that his own life after death is to the Indian something unreal, if he is living in the present time and for the present time only, his world of the present time comprises the visible as well as the invisible world. The souls of the dead are an intrinsic and a highly real part of this world in which he lives."

8. Everard Ferdinand im Thurn, *Among the Indians of Guiana* (1883), p. 349.

9. Psychoanalysis has discovered elements of primitive mentality in the state of mind of some neurotics. This method of analysis also recognizes primitive man's characteristic pro-

jection of the events of his inner life onto the outer world as analogous to narcissism. Leo Kaplan, *Das Problem der Magie und die Psychoanalyse* ("Die magische Bibliothek," Vol. II [1927]), p. 8, thinks that primitive man perceives nature "as though various objective events were only objectifications (projections) of his inner life." This may be true of the narcissistic neurotic, but it is just the contrary with primitive man. The latter does not regard external events as objectifications of his inner life, but he does consider certain events which are, according to our interpretation, phenomena of his inner life, as objective occurrences. That the narcissistic individual regards external events as objectifications of his inner life is, in fact, the result of the hypertrophy of his ego-consciousness. For primitive man, however, it is the lack of any ego-consciousness which forces him not to refer the events of his inner life to his ego but to transfer them to the exterior world rather than to the interior.

10. Edwin Sidney Hartland, *Ritual and Belief* (1914), p. 27, says: "Animism thus conceived is, it is obvious, too complex and elaborate to be really primitive. It appears to be itself derived from a simpler and earlier conception, whereby man attributes to all the objects of external nature life and personality. In other words, the external world is first interpreted by the savage thinker in the terms of his own consciousness; animism, or the distinction of soul and body, is a development necessitated by subsequent observation and the train of reasoning which that observation awakens." The statement that primitive man interprets the external world "in the terms of his own consciousness" is correct, provided that we recognize that his consciousness has a social character.

11. Diedrich Westermann, *Die Kpelle* ("Quellen der Religionsgeschichte," herausgegeben im Auftrag der Religionsgesch. Kommission bei der Gesellschaft der Wissenschaften zu Goettingen [1921]), p. 174.

12. Im Thurn, pp. 350–51.

13. Schultze, *Psychologie der Naturvoelker*, p. 217, says the thinking of primitive man is undeveloped and "wholly unable to discover and set so many differentiations as we do." Hence, "all of nature must appear to them more homogeneous than to us." This inability of primitive thinking to differentiate is in contrast with the extraordinary sharpness of primitive man's senses. Cf. Schultze, pp. 21 ff.

14. Gennep, *Mythes et légendes d'Australie*, p. civ.

15. *Reise des Aluise da Cada Mosto im Jahre 1455 laengs der afrikanischen Kueste bis Rio Grande, von ihm selbst beschrieben und aus dem Italienischen uebersetzt.* ("Allgemeine Historie der Reisen zu Wasser und zu Lande" [Leipzig, 1748], Vol. II), p. 89.

16. *Tagebuch der portugiesischen Expedition unter dem Commando des Majors Monteiro, ausgefuehrt in den Jahren 1831 und 1832, redigiert von dem Major Gamitto, zweiten Commandanten der Expedition.* Im Auszug mitgeteilt von W. Peters, *Zeitschrift fuer allgemeine Erdkunde* (1856), pp. 407 f.

17. Erland Nordenskiöld, "La Conception de l'âme chez les Indiens Cuna de l'isthme de Panama," *Journal de la Société des Américanistes*, N.S., XXIV (1932), 12.

18. Edwin James, *Account of an Expedition from Pittsburgh to the Rocky Mountains* (1823), I, 208.

19. John Heckewelder, "An Account of the History, Manners, and Customs of the Indian Nations Who Once Inhabited Pennsylvania and the Neighbouring States," *Transactions of the Historical and Literary Committee of the American Philosophical Society, 1819*, I, 247–49.

20. P. Wirz, *Die Marind-anim von Hollaendisch-Sued-Neu-Guinea* (Hamburgische Universitaet, "Abh. aus dem Gebiet der Auslandskunde," Vol. X [1922]), I, Part II, 1 ff.; (Vol. XVI [1925]), II, Part III, 104.

21. Elsdon Best, *The Maori*, I, 91, 129.

22. *Ibid.*, II, 452.

23. *Ibid.*, I, 203 f.

24. Gusinde, *Die Feuerland Indianer*, Vol. I: *Die Selknam*, p. 540.

296   SOCIETY AND NATURE

25. Elise Kootz-Kretschmer, *Die Safwa. Ein ostafrikanischer Volksstamm in seinem Leben und Denken* (1926–29), I, 236, relates the following statement of a native: "The ancestors are wherever they want to be. The ancestors sleep in great lakes, in great stones, in great trees. On the other hand, the small ancestral children who died when they were young sit at the cross-ways."

26. Gusinde, p. 687.

27. Hartland, *Transactions of the Third International Congress for the History of Religion*, I, 27 ff., says that the view of life of primitive man is determined by two elements: "the sense of personality and the sense of mystery." He believes "that early man surrounded by the unknown would be oppressed by awe and wonder and the feeling of power which lay behind external phenomena. Interpreting those phenomena in the terms of his own consciousness he would regard them as manifestations of personality." Also: "Man's relations with all nonhuman personalities are conceived as analogous with the relations of men among themselves. Beings more powerful than himself he must invoke and conciliate; others he may direct, control, subdue or even destroy. In either case his end is gained by acts and words; these are the expression of his will. . . . ."

28. Hartland, *Primitive Paternity*, p. 257. Lowie, *Primitive Society*, pp. 47 ff., writes of the Toda in southern India: "Most commonly, but not always, Toda polyandry is of the fraternal variety. That is, when a man marries a woman it is understood that she becomes the wife of his brothers, who normally live together. Even a brother subsequently born will be regarded as sharing his elder brothers' rights. In cases of fraternal polyandry no disputes ever arise among the husbands, and the very notion of such a possibility is flouted by the Toda mind. When the wife becomes pregnant, the eldest of her husbands performs a ceremony with a bow and arrow by which legal fatherhood is conventionally established in this tribe, but all the brothers are reckoned the child's fathers.—The situation becomes more complicated when a woman weds several men who are not brothers and who, as may happen, live in different villages. Then the wife usually lives for a month with each in turn, though there is no absolute rule. In such cases the determination of fatherhood in a legal sense is extremely interesting. For all social purposes that husband who performs the bow and arrow ceremony during the wife's pregnancy establishes his status as father not only of the first child but of any children born subsequently until one of the other husbands performs the requisite rite. Usually it is agreed that the first two or three children shall belong to the first husband, that at a later pregnancy another shall establish paternal rights, and so forth. Biological paternity is completely disregarded, for a man long dead is considered the father of a child provided no other man has performed the essential rite."

29. George Laurence Gomme, *Folklore as an Historical Science* (1908), p. 232. M. F. Ashley-Montagu, *Coming into Being among the Australian Aborigines* (1937), pp. 306 ff., says that "in Australia the concepts of 'motherhood' and 'fatherhood' are viewed as of an essential non-biological, exclusively social nature; that there is an absence of any concept of blood relationship between mother and child as well as between father and child—a fact which has been generally completely overlooked." Also: "I think that it is extremely likely that this absence of any recognition of blood relationship is one that was characteristic of that much abused creature, primeval man."

30. Cf., e.g., Brown, *The Andaman Islanders*, p. 77. C. E. Fox, "Social Organization in San Cristoval, Solomon Islands," *Journal of the Royal Anthropological Institute of Great Britain and Ireland*, XLIX (1919), 109 f., writes: "Adoption is very common and puts a person into the actual place, as it were, of those born in these relationships: a boy adopted is considered the real son of the man who adopts him, just as much as one born to him by his wife. The woman who cuts the umbilical cord, and who shaves the head of the baby, is the baby's mother henceforth. Children bought become the 'real children' of the man who buys them—again a difficult point of view for an Englishman, who insists that these are not 'real children' at all; but when a man is giving a pedigree he makes no distinction between adopted children and those born to him. Yet in using relationship terms he may think of

the relationship in which the boy stood before he was bought, and give that, or sometimes that and sometimes the new relationship. Moreover, people are not merely adopted as sons or daughters, but also as fathers, mothers, grandfathers, and grandmothers. A boy may be adopted to take the place of a man's father and keep his memory green; the father's name is given to him, and he takes his standing: he is classed as grandfather to boys of his own age or even older than himself. The unusual marriages, helped perhaps by this system of adoption, have made it now impossible to tell from a person's age in what generation he stands; one classed as your father may be of your own age, a brother may be as old as your father." On p. 119 we read: "Is the physical fact of fatherhood recognized? At the present day probably it is. If the reason be asked for the custom of burying alive the first-born child, who is called *ahubweu* or thick-head, the almost universal reply is that this is because the child is not likely to be the man's true child, but born to the woman by some other man. But there are certainly a number of facts on the other side; and the embryo (*hasiabu*) is said to be put in the womb of women by an *adaro* named *Hau-di-bwari*, who lives on a mountain in Marau Sound in Guadalcanar (Marau Sound is where the spirits of the dead go after death), or by *Kauraha*, a snake spirit."

31. E. H. Man, "On the Inhabitants of the Andaman Islands," *Journal of the Anthropological Institute of Great Britain and Ireland*, XII (1883), 125.

31a. John M. Sarbah, *Fanti Customary Laws: A Brief Introduction to the Principles of the Native Laws and Customs of the Fanti and Akan Districts of the Gold Coast* (1904), quoted by A. Kocourek and J. H. Wigmore, *Evolution of Law* (1915), I, 326.

32. Westermann, pp. 175, 203.

33. Labouret, *Les Tribus du Rameau Lobi*, pp. 81 f.

34. LeRoy, p. 58.

35. Paul Schebesta, *Orang-Utan: Bei den Urwaldmenschen Malayas und Sumatras* (1928), p. 77.

36. Best, I, 226.

37. Crawley, *The Idea of the Soul*, pp. 293 f. Compare with this the analogous behavior of the African Dschagga when they fell a tree.

38. Crawley, *The Mystic Rose*, II, 55 ff.

39. R. F. Fortune, *Sorcerers of Dobu: The Social Anthropology of the Dobu Islanders of the Western Pacific* (1932), pp. 94 ff., 97, 101 f., 107 ff.

40. Gusinde, p. 687.

41. John R. Swanton, "Social Conditions, Beliefs, and Linguistic Relationship of the Tlingit Indians," *26th Annual Report of the Bureau of American Ethnology* (1908), pp. 451 ff., 459.

42. Lévy-Bruhl, *La Mythologie primitive*, p. 102.

43. *The Jesuit Relations and Allied Documents* (1637), XII, 25.

44. A. C. Hollis, *The Nandi* (1909), p. 9.

45. Nieuwenhuis, *Quer durch Borneo*, I, 97.

46. Aelian *Variae historiae* xii. 23.

47. Hartland, *Ritual and Belief*, p. 161.

48. Karsten, *The Origins of Religion*, p. 204.

49. Martin Dobrizhoffer, *An Account of the Abipones* (1822), II, 84–85, 86.

50. Molina, *The Geographical, Natural, and Civic History of Chili*, II, 82.

51. E. B. Tylor, *Primitive Culture* (6th ed., 1920), I, 330.

52. F. Termer, "Ein Beitrag zum religioesen und kulturellen Leben der Guaimi-Indianer im XVI. Jahrhundert," *Korrespondenz-Blatt der Deutschen Gesellschaft fuer Anthropologie, Ethnologie und Urgeschichte*, L (1919), 55. The citation is based on a report of Padre Fray Adrian de Santo Thomas (late sixteenth, early seventeenth, century).

53. Alfred Russel Wallace, *A Narrative of Travels on the Amazon and Rio Negro* (1889), p. 348.

54. W. B. Grubb, *An Unknown People in an Unknown Land* (1911), p. 138.

L

55. A. W. Howitt, *The Native Tribes of South-East Australia* (1904), p. 430; cf. also p. 277.

56. Meinhof, *Die Religionen der Afrikaner in ihrem Zusammenhang mit dem Wirtschaftsleben,* p. 43.

57. R. R. Marett, *The Threshold of Religion* (2d ed., 1914), pp. 13 f.

58. *Ibid.*, pp. 14 f.

59. W. W. Skeat, *Malay Magic* (1900), p. 107.

60. Edward Sapir, "Religious Ideas of the Takelma Indians of Southwestern Oregon," *Journal of American Folk Lore,* XX (1907), 38.

61. Gusinde, pp. 683 f.

62. E. Pechuel-Loesche, *Die Loango-Expedition*, Dritte Abt., Zweite Haelfte (1907), p. 448.

63. Pechuel-Loesche, p. 423.

64. Robert Hamill Nassau, *Fetichism in West Africa* (1904), p. 244.

65. Kootz-Kretschmer, I, 199.

66. A. L. Kitching, *On the Backwaters of the Nile* (1912), pp. 242 ff.

67. C. R. Lagae, *Les Azande ou Niam-Niam*, p. 114, cited by L. Lévy-Bruhl in *Primitives and the Supernatural*, p. 85.

68. Robert H. Lowie, *Primitive Religion* (1925), p. 44.

69. Of the many kinds of conduct of primitive man resulting from his social interpretation of nature, one may stress as "magic" in a specific sense that particular kind which is characterized by the fact that man, in order to attain fulfilment of his wishes, turns to a superhuman authority. Only the relationship of primitive man to this superhuman authority furnishes a reliable criterion of this concept, which is so important to modern ethnology. Where there is no such relationship to a superhuman authority—where, for instance, the behavior of primitive man results only from his substantializing tendency, as in the case when an illness is cured by sucking—then there is no reason to distinguish such behavior from ordinary behavior by labeling it as "magical."

In so far as the superhuman authority is a "soul" or "ghost" or a "spirit"—in other terms, a superhuman personal being—magic has essentially an animistic character. In modern ethnology, however, a theory of "preanimistic magic" prevails. According to this theory, the magician does not appeal for assistance to superhuman personal beings but to supernatural impersonal forces. It is, however, a fact, that primitive man himself treats the "forces," the help of which he desires, as if they were personal beings. All the magical procedures, the spells, conjurations, symbolic acts, etc., presuppose that the "supernatural force" understands the magician and his performance and is willing to fulfil his wishes. The "supernatural force" is considered by the magician to be a being endowed with intelligence and will and with a power surpassing human powers. The theory of "preanimistic magic" stands and falls with primitive man's capacity to think in terms of impersonal forces. Cf. the following note.

70. The idea of impersonal forces is one of the characteristic achievements of modern science based on the principle of causality and wholly foreign to a primitive mind.

Crawley, *The Idea of the Soul*, p. 9, remarks: ".... the assumption that early man conceived the idea of an impersonal, abstract 'power,' and subsequently, whether from this or otherwise, evolved the idea of a personal concrete soul, is an argument from the abstract to the concrete. The psychological order is always the other way, from the concrete to the abstract." Wundt, *Mythus und Religion*, Part III, p. 38, is also right when he stresses the fact that mental development progresses from the concrete to the abstract rather than vice versa. This truth militates against the hypothesis of preanimism, which asserts that before the emergency of the animistic interpretation of nature primitive man believed in the existence of impersonal "magical" powers.

Karsten, a scholar who was not prejudiced by the preanimistic thesis, did not find among South American Indians any idea of impersonal powers. He writes, in *The Origins of*

Religion, p. 33: "I think, moreover, that it is hardly compatible with the psychology of primitive man." And on pp. 128–29: ". . . . that, in the evolution of religious thought, the impersonal magic 'power,' as found among certain higher peoples, represents a secondary notion in relation to the purely animistic idea of a spirit." The theory of preanimistic magic goes back to the representations which Codrington, in his well-known and already cited book, *The Melanesians*, has given of the *mana* of the Melanesians. This *mana* is the prototype of the impersonal force of preanimism. But an unprejudiced examination of the material presented by Codrington shows that it can hardly be an argument for the pre-animistic hypothesis. Karsten, *The Origins of Religion*, p. 32, rightly characterizes *mana* as "the most misused term in the modern science of religion." He calls the *mana* theory an unproved construction and says, p. 47: "A theory which would make religion begin with a belief in impersonal magical powers and explain, for instance, *mana* as 'that very living stuff out of which demons, gods, and souls have slowly gathered shape,' is founded on a psychological impossibility: it overlooks that strong and constant tendency to personify the object of the religious awe and reverence which is characteristic of primitive man."

If the hypothesis of the preanimists proves to be wrong, then Tylor's animism theory remains unshaken. The material added by recent ethnological research confirms Tylor's basic assumption.

71. E.g., Preuss, *Die geistige Kultur der Naturvoelker*, pp. 13, 22.

72. Brinton, *Religions of Primitive Peoples*, p. 123.

73. This is the reason why the following statement of J. G. Frazer, in *The Belief in Immortality and the Worship of the Dead* (1913), I, 18 ff., cannot be accepted: "The idea of cause is simply that of invariable sequence suggested by the observation of many particular cases of sequence"; and then: "All this is as true of the savage as of the civilized man." Thus Frazer believes that primitive man has the same concept of causality as civilized man. But he says that "when he [the savage] seeks to discover the causes of events in the external world, he should, arguing from experience, imagine that they are produced by the actions of invisible beings like himself, who behind the veil of nature pull the strings that set the vast machinery in motion . . . . in short he personifies the phenomena as powerful anthropomorphic spirits and believing himself to be more or less dependent on their good will he woos their favour by prayer and sacrifice." Cassirer, *Das Mythische Denken*, p. 58, also thinks that "the general category of 'cause' and 'effect' is not at all absent from mythical [i.e., primitive] thinking; in fact, it belongs in a certain sense to its fundamental character." This obviously does not conform with his statement, *Die Begriffsform im mythischen Denken* (p. 31), that "our modern, analytical-scientific concept of causality is not an original element of mind but one of its latest methodical achievements."

74. Meinhof, p. 67.

75. Schultze, p. 231, who understands fetishism in a very broad sense and comprehends in it the oldest form of the relationship of man to a superhuman authority, says that the result of fetishism is that primitive man has an immediate explanation for every event and therefore never reflects upon the real causes. Thus he never gains "a true perception of the natural connection of things." The fetish is the *prima causa* of everything. The decisive point in this "short circuit" of primitive thinking is that the "fetish" is imagined as a personal being, endowed with superhuman power. Any investigation into the causes is barred by this imputation to a person.

76. Lévy Bruhl, *The Soul of the Primitive*, from whom the first two of the three examples mentioned in the text have been taken, remarks, p. 112: "The primitive has no notion of a more or less complex concatenation of phenomena which condition themselves. He believes in the real and concrete presence of one or more complete little beings within the individual, and this idea exempts him from paying any attention to actual processes."

77. Consequently, Ziegler, *Ueberlieferung*, p. 32, is right when he believes that the magical period in the history of mankind was the "precausal" one. Primitive man's magic is no

symptom of a "prelogical" mentality, as Lévy-Bruhl asserts, but of a precausal, i.e., pre-scientific thinking. Vernon Brelsford, *Primitive Philosophy* (1935), p. 23, writes: "Reality in the western world has gone the way of attempting to master things; reality for the African is found in the region of the soul—not in the mastery of self or outer things, but in the acceptance of a life of acquiescence with beings and essences on a spiritual scale.—In this fashion only is the native a mystic. Not because of any pre-logical function of mind but merely because he is the possessor of a type of knowledge that teaches that reality consists in the relation not of men with things, but of men with other men, and of all men with spirits." P. 48: "The savage has a motive for conduct, he has a theory of life, he has a set of principles of life. They may be the principles of a pre-scientific age, but the savage has at least progressed so far upon the road to culture as to have developed a mode of life that is controlled and regulated by a theory of life."

Therefore, it is false to speak of a "magical" or "mystical" causality of primitive man, as is done by Charles Blondel, *La Mentalité primitive* (1926). On pp. 82 f. he says: "Our causality is a natural causality. . . . . On the other hand, for primitive men, natural causal-ity is of secondary importance. They neglect it. They do not apperceive it, or if they do, they see in it the external and accidental expression of the one causality that counts for them—that which concerns the actions of mystical spirits." This "mystical causality" is the reason why accident (*casus*) is unknown to primitive man. On p. 94 it is said: "In his mind there is no room for accident. A native of Tully River (Australia), a 'doctor,' throws a lance from a tree, but it rebounds and kills an old man. The relatives of the victim believe that the death is due to the sorcery of the doctor. Nothing can dissuade them. The fight begins and is not ended until the doctor is wounded. If a tree falls in New Guinea, however rotten it may be and however violent the wind may have blown, it is always a sorcerer who made it fall. In West Africa, a chief when hunting was horribly wounded by an elephant; before he died, he accused twelve of his wives and slaves of having bewitched his flint." These examples prove that primitive man does not inquire after the cause but after the responsi-bility, that he does not seek the cause but the person to whom he can impute the fact in question; this enables him to apply the principle of retribution. Primitive man does not find in the magic procedure the "cause" of the event that concerns him; the decisive thing is that he perceives in it the delict because of which retribution must be taken.

Blondel remarks, p. 97, that the "mystical cause" is not always determined accurately in itself except "when it is a question of the violation of a tabu or a religious interdiction. When a tabu is violated then misfortune is caused and when a misfortune occurs, then it is because a tabu has been violated. In Uganda, pregnant women must not eat salt; the health and the life of the child are at stake. If the newly born child falls ill, the husband accuses the wife of having eaten salt. In other cases, even though they recognize that the cause of the event is mystical, they do not know exactly which cause it is. Bad weather per-sists, dryness is prolonged, epidemics break out, hunting or fishing is unsuccessful—perhaps a tabu has been violated, but it is also possible that the ancestors are dissatisfied or that a sorcerer has played some tricks. Such is the problem which is to be solved in the interests of the community and its members. . . . ." But the problem to be solved is not to find a "cause" but a guilty person; it is not a question of causality but one of retribution. Blondel further points out, p. 95, that primitive man, "preoccupied by mystical and invisible causes and prejudiced by their existence does not see what would otherwise be obvious." It would be more correct to say that, preoccupied by the idea of retribution which dominates his consciousness, primitive man does not perceive the causal nexus even though the latter is obvious to civilized man.

78. Pointing to these facts, Lévy-Bruhl, *Primitives and the Supernatural*, p. 274, rightly asks: "How are we to account for this change in his attitude?" And he adds: "To him the greater or lesser amount of blood lost is not the thing that matters . . . . he has no concep-

tion of the physiological functions of the blood." But Lévy-Bruhl misses the essential fact when he says: "But he has a very vivid and, at times, very agonizing conception of its magic power." For why should the blood itself be that power? In that case the power would also be effective for a voluntary loss of blood. And why should the power have a "magical" character? The mystical element of the event apparently consists in the fact that primitive man fears a superhuman being who with hostile intent makes him lose his blood.

79. Cf. Mary Kingsley, *West African Studies* (2d ed., 1901), p. 153, and Codrington, *The Melanesians*, p. 196. Among certain West African tribes the idea prevails that the "spirit" of the remedy fights the "spirit" of the illness. Thus illness, created by a sorcerer with the help of an evil spirit, has to be fought by another stronger sorcerer with the aid of the spirit which is at his disposal. For the idea of illness as substance see pp. 13 f.

80. If theologically oriented ethnologists, like P. Wilhelm Schmidt in his well-known book, *Der Ursprung der Gottesidee*, Vol. I (1912), and Vol. VI (1935), assume causal thinking among primitive men, they follow the authority of Thomas Aquinas, who taught that every human being has a "natural" desire to perceive the causes of an event. This assumption does not rest upon empirical observation but upon the dogma that the God of the Bible revealed himself to the first man as the Creator of the universe, as *prima causa*, that is to say, as personal cause of the world.

The statements of W. Schmidt are characteristic of this belief. He says, I, 427, that primitive man has a "tendency to causality" but that it is mixed up with his desire for personification. In the first stages of development causal thinking is strongly influenced by the tendency to personify. The sequence of cause and effect seems to have the same character as the relation between the external actions of man and his acts of will and cognition. Since the concept of causality is drawn from this source, there is a tendency to assume for apparently homogeneous effects, namely, movements which do not appear to be caused from the outside, also a homogeneous cause, namely, will and cognition; and this is personification. According to W. Schmidt, one has to put the tendency to causal thinking into the earliest stages of human development; but the desire for personification, which is, according to W. Schmidt, inseparably connected with the tendency to causality, must also be placed in the same period. The desire for personification is indeed a characteristic element of primitive mentality; but it is not, as W. Schmidt thinks, "inseparatedly connected" with the tendency to causal thinking. First of all, it is not true that the concept of causality proceeds from an observation of the sequence between the psychic act and the bodily movement. This cannot be so, because the distinction between these two elements presupposes a high degree of mental development, or, in any case, an intensity of self-observation and thus an ego-consciousness which primitive man absolutely lacks. Primitive man's personification is by no means an ego-analogy. Above all, causal thinking tends to free itself from the desire for personification originating in the precausal period of human thinking; that is, it tends to perceive the cause as an impersonal objective fact similar to the effect and not as a person.

81. Lévy-Bruhl, *Primitives and the Supernatural*, p. 24, says of the idea which Eskimos have of nature (on the basis of a report by Rasmussen): "As if by a kind of tacit agreement, the unseen powers will maintain a state of affairs favourable to man, provided he faithfully follows these precepts positive as well as negative. [Lévy-Bruhl means the social norms laid down by the ancestors.] To this extent the natural order—a feeble one without any guiding principle of its own, according to the Eskimos—does in fact rest upon the observance of rules which we would call moral and social. If these be violated the natural order is upheaved, nature herself totters, and human life becomes impossible. . . . . Whoever violates these laws, either voluntarily or involuntarily, breaks the compact with the invisible powers, and consequently imperils the very existence of the social group. . . . ."

A Greek story relates that the crime of Thyestes—robbery of the golden lamb—resulted in a disturbance of the course of nature. Euripides pictures that catastrophe in his *Electra* (727 ff. [Loeb]):

"Then, then, in his anger arose Zeus, turning
    The stars' feet back on the fire-fretted way;
Yea, and the Sun's car splendour-burning,
    And the misty eyes of the morning grey.
    And with flash of his chariot-wheels back-flying
Flushed crimson the face of the fading day:
    To the north fled the clouds with their burden sighing;
    And for rains withheld, and for dews fast-drying
The dwellings of Ammon in faintness were yearning,
    For sweet showers crying to heavens denying.
It is told of the singers—scant credence such story,
    Touching secrets of Gods, of my spirit hath won—
That the Sun from that vision turned backward the glory
    Of the gold of the face of his flaming throne,
    With the scourge of his wrath in affliction repaying
Mortals for deeds in their mad feuds done."

82. Lévy-Bruhl, *How Natives Think*, pp. 129 ff., attempts to determine primitive man's interpretation of nature by the concept which he calls "participation." The "prelogical mind"—this is how he characterizes primitive mentality—"does not objectify nature thus. It lives it rather, by feeling itself participate in it, and feeling these participations everywhere; and it interprets this complexity of participations by social forms." Not the "participation" but rather the "social forms" are decisive. Consequently, Lévy-Bruhl is right when he says, p. 45: "But to the mentality of undeveloped peoples, there are no natural phenomena such as we understand by the term." The reasoning that one cannot speak of nature in our sense, since primitive people assume a mystical connection between things, is untenable. The true reason is that primitive people regard nature as a part of their society. The connection is not mystical but social.

83. Best, I, 104.

84. A myth of the Toradja (Celebes) relates: "In the beginning heaven said to earth: 'Spread yourself and I shall then spread myself over you.' 'No,' said earth, 'do not let us do this, for should I spread myself first, you will not be able to embrace me.' Heaven, how-ever, did not comprehend this and so earth agreed and spread herself. But when heaven wanted to extend himself over her, it became evident that he was too small; hence he re-quested earth to shrink. Thus mountains and valleys were created. This marrriage brought forth sun and moon; these two married in turn and brought forth the stars." (H. Th. Fischer, "Indonesische Paradiesmythen," *Zeitschrift fuer Ethnologie*, Jahrg. 64 [1932], p. 209.)

According to Melland, *In Witch-bound Africa*, p. 155, Lesa, the Supreme Being of the Kaonde, lives in heaven. He is married with Chandashi, who lives in the earth. Lesa manifests himself in lightning and thunder, whereas Chandashi manifests herself in earth-quakes.

Among the ancient Egyptians heaven, *pet*, was female and the earth, *to*, male. Heaven was imagined as a huge cow whose legs rest on earth or as a woman who leans with feet and hands on the earth. Nut, the goddess of heaven, is the wife of Keb, the god of earth. Typical is the representation, reproduced by Adolf Erman, *Die Religion der Aegypter* (1934), p. 62, of Nut lying over her husband Keb. An older personification of Mother Heaven is perhaps the goddess Isis and of Father Earth the god Osiris. Cf. Erman, pp. 32, 40. Originally, Osiris seems to have been "the god to whom the yearly circle of seasons was ascribed. If the inundation came, Osiris was the 'new water' which made the fields green. If the plants withered and died, it was said that Osiris had also died. But he was not completely dead, for the next year the herbs came forth again from his body and showed that he was alive. Every year Osiris is reborn and makes all the herbs grow and the earth fertile. That Osiris once had this character is born out by one of the Osiris festivals where the god's revival was represented by germinating plants." There also exists a representation of Osiris which shows the god lying on his back with plants sprouting from his body (Erman, p. 40). The latter have an obvious phallic character, just as did the symbol of Osiris, a pillar with a fourfold projection at its end. Similarly, the symbol of Isis can easily be interpreted as a female one. In the well-known myth, Isis, in the shape of a sparrow hawk, sits on the corpse of her husband, Osiris, and in this position is fecundated by him. A pyramid inscription (*Pyramidentexte*, ed. Sethe, par. 632) containing a speech of Isis to her husband-brother, Osiris, runs as follows: "Your sister Isis is coming to you, happy in your love. You placed her on your phallus and your sperm entered her body . . . ." (according to Hermann Kees, *Aegypten* ["Religionsgeschichtliches Lesebuch," herausgegeben von Alfred Bertholet, No. 10 (1928)], p. 29).

The male and female sex of heaven and earth in mythical thinking is related to different systems of economy, hunting, and agriculture, as well as to the organization of the family according to father-right or mother-right. Whether the idea of earth as man is the older concept cannot be asserted for certain. Neither is the temporal priority of patriarchal organization over matriarchal organization provable. The sequence of the different types of economy alone is not decisive. For the idea of the relationship between heaven and earth as the parent-pair among African peoples, see Baumann, *Schoepfung und Urzeit des Menschen im Mythus der afrikanischen Voelker*, pp. 167 f., 174 f. In a native tale of Nanumanga (Hudson's Island, in the South Pacific) the earth appears as a man who marries the female sea serpent and with her procreates the ancestors of men (in G. Turner, *Samoa, a Hundred Years Ago and Long Before* [1884], p. 288).

85. Le Roy, p. 51.

86. A. R. Brown, *The Andaman Islanders*, p. 141.

87. Tylor, *Primitive Culture*, I, 289. Cf., also, Wundt, *Mythus und Religion*, Part II, pp. 335 f.

88. J. Kubary, "Die Religion der Pelauer," in A. Bastian, *Allerlei aus Volks- und Menschenkunde* (1888), I, 56.

89. K. Th. Preuss, *Der religioese Gehalt der Mythen* ("Sammlung gemeinverstaendlicher Vortraege und Schriften aus dem Gebiete der Theologie und Religionsgeschichte," No. 162 [1933]), p. 15.

90. Schultze, p. 321.

91. Gennep, p. 43.

92. Martin Gusinde, *Die Feuerland Indianer*, Vol. II: *Die Yamana* (1937), p. 1153.

93. Schultze, p. 322, according to J. B. Friedreich, *Die Weltkoerper in ihrer mythisch-symbolischen Bedeutung* (1864), p. 264.

94. Paul Ehrenreich, *Die allgemeine Mythologie und ihre ethnologische Grundlage* (1910), p. 125.

95. Preuss, *Der religioese Gehalt der Mythen, etc.*, pp. 44 f.

96. W. Schmidt, *Der Ursprung der Gottesidee*, IV, 591.

97. Warneck, *Die Religion der Batak*, p. 6.

98. C. Strehlow, *Die Arandja- und Loritja-Staemme in Zentral-Australien* ("Veroeffentlich. aus dem Staedt. Voelker-Museum Frankfurt am Main" [1907–20], Vol. I), pp. 16 f. If primitive people perceive the stars as personal beings or the abodes of spirits, they do so because they regard the relationship of those beings with one another and with men as essentially social in character. This is especially obvious where these spirits are the death souls of ancestors. Karsten, *The Origins of Religion*, p. 137, writes: "The sun was not wor-

shiped by the Incas as such, i.e. as a heavenly body, but because it was looked upon as the abode of a spirit. On this point one of the best-known authorities on the modern Aimara culture states: 'It was not the orbs (sun and moon) to which a certain worship was offered, but to the spiritual beings that dwelt in them, the Achachilas or Pacarinas believed to reside both in the sun and the moon' (Adolph F. Bandelier, *The Islands of Titicaca and Koati* [1910], p. 150). 'Achachila' and 'Pacarina' were words used by the ancient Quichua and Aimara to denote their ancestors, worshiped at the sacred places called *huaca*."

As already mentioned in another connection, Karsten, p. 142, traces the personification of nature to the fact that primitive man projects his inner life onto the external world. "In its widest sense, therefore, nature-worship proves to be simply a part of the worship of man himself." Such self-worship is, however, psychologically incompatible with primitive man's lack of ego-consciousness. But it is correct to see in his veneration of nature a worship of society. The authority which primitive man perceives in natural phenomena is, in reality, the authority of his own society based on the fear of the death souls of the ancestors. The social relationship between natural phenomena and men manifests itself also in the widespread belief in omens and the like; nature warns men or predicts events to them in order to protect them. Thus, among the Kaffirs, for instance, an eclipse of the moon signifies that a great chieftain has died; the Namaquas believe "that a falling star is a sign that the cattle will get ill" (Kidd, pp. 108 f.).

99. Kootz-Kretschmer, I, 231.

100. Nieuwenhuis, I, 54.

101. Danzel, *Kultur und Religion des primitiven Menschen*, p. 52.

102. George Grey, *Polynesian Mythology and Ancient Traditional History of the New Zealanders* (1855), p. 37 f.

103. Wirz, I, Part II, 83.

104. Baumann, p. 358.

105. J. Winthuis, "Das Zweigeschlechterwesen," *Forschungen zur Voelkerpsychologie und Soziologie*, herausgegeben von R. Thurnwald, V (1928), 14. Karsten, *The Civilization of the South American Indians*, pp. 272, 306, reports that the Indians frequently ascribe male or female sex to animals, plants, and inanimate objects, independent of the sex they actually have; thus the roe deer is female, even if it is a male animal. And for the Cavina Indians of northern Bolivia the ule tree (*Siphonia elastica*) is a female. A story tells of a man who had sexual intercourse with such a tree and died soon after. The attribution of sex to nature originated in the fact that one perceived in animals, plants, and inanimate objects incarnations of human death souls. Whether the object in question is male or female depends on whether a man or a woman is incarnated in it. Here, the connection between the death-soul belief and animism as the social interpretation of nature is directly illustrated.

106. Lévy-Bruhl, *How Natives Think*, pp. 38 f., 128, 363 ff. S. Reinach, *Cultes, mythes, et religions* (1905), I, 17 ff., lays down the following principles as the "code of totemism": (1) certain animals are neither killed nor eaten but men breed specimens and give them special care; (2) animals that die accidentally are mourned and buried with the same rites as members of the group; (3) sometimes only certain parts of an animal must not be eaten; (4) when animals which ordinarily are not to be killed, are killed because of necessity, apologies are addressed to the animal, or attempts are made by various tricks to attenuate the violation of the taboo; . . . . (5) one mourns for the taboo animal even after its ritual killing; (6) men clothe themselves with the hides of certain animals, particularly at religious ceremonies; where totemism exists, these animals are the totems; (7) the clan and the individuals take animal names; where totemism exists, these animals are the totems; (8) many groups have pictures of animals painted on their insignia and weapons; many men paint such pictures on their bodies or impress them by tattooing; (9) dangerous totem animals are supposed to spare those members who belong to the totemistic clan by birth; (10) totem animals help and protect members of the totem group; (11) totem animals predict the future to

faithful members and serve as their guides; (12) members of the totem group often consider themselves related to the totem animals by bonds of common descent. Reinach consequently asserts (p. 10): "The fundamental character of animal totemism depends upon the existence of a pact, badly defined, but of a religious character, between certain groups of men and certain groups of animals." This pact signifies "the extension of the universal and primitive taboo: you must not kill." Further, Reinach believes that the idea of a contract between the two groups was later replaced by the idea of an affinity between them. The hypothesis of a social contract is not a very good formulation for the relationship which exists between man and animal in totemistic systems. Undoubtedly, the correct nucleus of the relationship is that totemistically organized primitive people interpret their relationship to the totem animal according to the principle of reciprocity: we do not kill you, in order that you will not kill us; or, more correctly, we respect you, in order that you adapt your behavior to our interests. This is the sense of the attitude which primitive man assumes toward nature which he interprets personalistically; it is also the meaning of his attitude toward the super-human authority, his gods. The principle of retribution dominates the totemistic system, especially in the idea of an affinity between man and animal. Through this affinity the principle of retribution, originally applied only to the relationship between men, is extended to cover the relationship between man and animal. It is, therefore, improbable that this idea of an affinity replaced the idea of a contract.

107. Frank Hamilton Cushing, "Outlines of Zuñi Creation Myths," *13th Annual Report of the Bureau of Ethnology* (1896), pp. 367 ff. Cushing speaks of "mytho-sociologic organization."

108. A. L. Kroeber, *Handbook of the Indians of California* (Bureau of American Ethnology Bull. 78 [1925]), p. 453.

109. Warner, *A Black Civilization*, p. 395.

110. The child, too, imagines nature as "made" by someone. Consequently, Jean Piaget, *La Représentation du monde chez l'enfant*, pp. 232, 255 ff., speaks of "infantile artificialism."

CHAPTER III

1. The instinct for vengeance is connected, in a certain sense, with man's original tendency of aggression. Herbert Spencer, *The Principles of Ethics* (1897), I, 361 ff., writes: "Aggression leads to counter-aggression. Where both creatures have powers of offence, they are likely both to use them; especially where their powers of offence are approximately equal, that is, where they are creatures of the same species: such creatures being also those commonly brought into competition. That results of this kind are inevitable, will be manifest on remembering that among members of the same species, those individuals which have not, in any considerable degree, resented aggressions, must have ever tended to disappear, and to have left behind those which have with some effect made counter-aggressions. Fights, therefore, not only of predatory animals with prey but of animals of the same kind with one another, have been unavoidable from the first and have continued to the last.— Every fight is a succession of retaliations—bite being given for bite, and blow for blow. Usually these follow one another in quick succession, but not always. There is a postponed retaliation; and a postponed retaliation is what we call revenge. It may be postponed for so short a time as to be merely a recommencement of the fight, or it may be postponed for days, or it may be postponed for years. And hence the retaliation which constitutes what we call revenge, diverges insensibly from the retaliations which characterize a conflict.— But the practice, alike of immediate revenge and of postponed revenge, establishes itself as in some measure a check upon aggression; since the motive to aggress is checked by the consciousness that a counter-aggression will come; if not at once then after a time."

2. S. R. Steinmetz, *Ethnologische Studien zur ersten Entwicklung der Strafe* (2d ed., 1928), I, 100.

3. Friedrich Alverdes, *Tiersoziologie* ("Forschungen zur Voelkerpsychologie und Soziologie," herausgegeben von Rich. Thurnwald, Vol. I [1925]), p. 32.

4. *Ibid.*, p. 76.

5. *Ibid.*, p. 38.

6. Charles Darwin, *The Descent of Man, and Selection in Relation to Sex* (2d ed., revised and augmented, 1888), I, 105.

7. William Gifford Palgrave, *Narrative of a Year's Journey through Central and Eastern Arabia (1862–63)* (1866), I, 40; Edward Westermarck, *The Origin and Development of the Moral Ideas* (1912), I, 37 f.

8. Determined by the same evolutionary hypothesis which influenced Darwin, Herbert Spencer, *Justice* (Part IV of the *Principles of Ethics* [1892]), pp. 3 ff., 8 ff., even goes so far as to speak of "animal-ethics." He assumes a "subhuman" justice and (pp. 277 ff.) observes among animals the phenomenon of conscience, especially among dogs a strong feeling of "ought." He thinks that "in inferior animals the consciousness of duty may be produced by the discipline of life." Letourneau, *La Psychologie ethnique*, pp. 12 and 22, believes that dogs may have remorse and a sense of duty. Franz Boas, *The Mind of Primitive Man* (1938), p. 161, says: "Among higher animals social duties belong to the leader of the herd, male or female, to scouts or watchers." But to conclude from the external behavior of animals—which alone is open to observation—the content of their consciousness is problematical. Haeckel's statement that we can already perceive the beginnings of morality among the protists (*Die Lebenswunder* [1904], p. 501) need not be discussed here (cf. Victor Cathrein, *Die Einheit des sittlichen Bewusstseins der Menschheit* [1914], I, 10 f.). Also, Wilson D. Wallis, *Religion in Primitive Society* (1939), p. 11, seems to go much too far by this statement: "Many species of beasts distinguish the natural and the supernatural"; which he proves by the fact that "a horse shies at an opened umbrella or a paper moving on the ground."

9. Steinmetz, I, 361, believes that primitive vengeance "only weakly tends to intimidate and prevent culprits from doing harm but rather strives to achieve satisfaction and to raise the spirit." This is not exactly true, since the direction of the emotion against the "culprit" cannot be explained by the mere tendency of self-preservation and self-assertion. Blood revenge, the most important form of revenge in primitive society, is more a conscious action, determined by social norms, than a reflex movement caused by strong feelings of pain. For blood revenge proceeds from individuals who are not directly affected by the murder, the deed to be avenged. It is more the fear of the revengeful soul of the dead than the thirst for revenge which urges the relatives to revenge. Steinmetz overestimates this thirst for revenge when he writes, p. 318: "If man's own thirst for revenge is weak, belief in the vindictiveness of the dead cannot make it strong. For man necessarily attributes to the souls of the deceased the same qualities as exist in his own soul." Steinmetz, however, adds restrictively that primitive man's idea of the souls of the dead is influenced by the "public opinion" of his society. Public opinion, a specific social fact, creates belief in the existence of a revengeful death soul which urges the relatives of a murdered man to revenge. Not the thirst for revenge of the individual obliged by public opinion to exercise retribution, but the fact of living together, creates the idea of obligatory retribution. It has frequently been attested that the thirst for revenge of primitive man is not at all so strong, and that the "savage" is not at all so savage, as one may assume. Of the Dayak of Borneo, who are "cruel" head-hunters, Nieuwenhuis, *Quer durch Borneo*, II, 454, says that they are by no means revengeful and bloodthirsty, as "may appear, but that only their deep-religious conviction and love for the deceased urges them to kill men." A. B. Ellis says the same of the Tshi-speaking tribes of the West-African Gold Coast (*The Tshi-speaking Peoples of the Gold Coast of West Africa* [1887], p. 159). And Steinmetz himself has to admit (I, 321) that the revengefulness of primitive man is impulsive, easily satisfied, and quickly vanishing. Thus, subjection to the principle of retribution, particularly to the institution of blood revenge, proceeds less from natural instinct than from social demands which create the ideology of a "revengeful" death soul. In his description of the life of the Kai people, Ch. Keysser ("Aus dem Leben der Kaileute," in R. Neuhauss, *Deutsch Neu-Guinea*, III, 61) writes: "From mere blood-thirstiness no Papua will ever murder an adult man, be he black or white." And he points out (p. 63) that the chieftains do not easily resolve to undertake an action of retribution. "If his fear of the vengeance of gruesome spirits were really not greater than his fear of men and his love for valuables, especially for pigs, then the Papua, certainly the Kai, would never undertake a warlike expedition." And wars are normally actions of retribution to avenge a death traced to witchcraft. The fact that the decisive motive of blood revenge is not so much an innate desire for vengeance as a duty imposed by the social order explains the frequently observed cases of sham vengeance. Here, primitive man by various means feigns to the superhuman authority which has urged him to vengeance against his inclinations and interests that he has fulfilled his obligations. Steinmetz himself cites various examples (I, 308).

A certain similarity exists between sham vengeance and substitutive vengeance; the latter consists in the fact that the action is directed against someone other than the culprit because the evildoer is either unknown or cannot be reached by the avenger. In this case, it seems, the desire for revenge, aroused by a grave violation of interests, is satisfied by some act of aggression. Steinmetz, I, 339, gives an example which he takes from George Grey's *Journals of Two Expeditions of Discovery in North-West and Western Australia during the Years 1837, 38, and 39* (1841), II, 241. Among the natives of Australia a murderer is pursued by the relatives of the victim. But "should he [the criminal] elude his pursuers, they wreak their vengeance on any native they meet." Steinmetz is inclined to qualify all such cases as "blind" revenge, revenge on the "innocent," as "nondirected" revenge, which he regards as the older and original form of revenge. But in the example cited the revenge is first directed against the "culprit" and is only diverted to someone who is innocent because it cannot be executed on the former. "Vengeance on the innocent" is obviously a secondary and not a primary phenomenon. As long as the action is not directed against a "culprit," we cannot speak of "vengeance." The other examples which Steinmetz lists as cases of "vengeance on the innocent" must also be interpreted as cases of substitutive vengeance, which can often be explained by the fact that countervengeance is feared.

The action which seems to be "vengeance on the innocent" is frequently simply human sacrifice offered as substitute for the murderer or for the feared punishment of those who make the sacrifice because they consider themselves guilty or fear to be considered guilty by the death soul. In this way can be explained the action of the Apayaos from the Philippines on the occasion of the death of a chieftain or some nobleman: they roam about in the forests in order to ambush and kill wanderers, to cut their heads off, and to place them around the chieftain's body in burial (Steinmetz, I, 347, according to F. Blumentritt, "Der Ahnenkultus und die religioesen Anschauungen der Malayen des Philippinen-Archipels," *Mitteilungen der geographischen Gesellschaft in Wien* [1882], pp. 155 f.). In the same category falls a case quoted by Steinmetz (I, 337) from F. Jagor, *Travels in the Philippines* (1875), p. 212: "If a man dies, his nearest kinsmen go out to requite his death by the death of some other individual taken at random. The rule is strictly enforced. For a dead man a man must be killed, for a woman a woman, for a child a child. Unless, indeed, it be a friend they encounter, the first victim that offers is killed." Men who are killed in connection with a death are not always victims of blood revenge; so, the Negritos of northern Luzon shoot with arrows all those who step on the grave of a relative (F. Blumentritt, *Versuch einer Ethnographie der Philippinen* [1882], p. 8). The "real motive" behind the killing of strangers on behalf of the deceased is not, as Steinmetz, I, 345, asserts, the fact that the revenge desired by the soul of the dead is imagined as "nondirected." For the vengeance which threatens from the death soul is feared only by the relatives, because, for various reasons, they believe it to be directed against themselves. Hence they torment themselves or kill others as substitute for the punishment threatening them. Or, they may believe that the dead, for some reason, wishes to be avenged on someone else, in which case they fear to arouse the wrath of the dead by violating their duty of revenge. Therefore, they kill anyone as substitute if they are unable to locate the culprit.

Speiser, *Ethnographische Materialien aus den Neuen Hebriden und den Banks-Inseln*, p. 341, says that the sense of justice of the natives of the New Hebrides and the Banks Islands is "based on the natural law that every wrong must be requited by a like wrong. Every stolen pig must be replaced by a like pig. Murder must be expiated by murder or a fine. Wars can end only when both sides have suffered the same amount of dead." Thus a strict principle of retribution prevails. "One can also find symptoms of that strange phenomenon that if a man is injured by another and cannot find the wrong-doer or considers himself too weak to take revenge, he inflicts the same wrong upon a third person. They believe that in this way either the public's attention will be aroused or that the third party will either find the culprit or inflict the same damage on a fourth; the latter, then, would take revenge on the culprit or on a fifth; in any case, the culprit will finally be punished." Whether this interpretation of "retribution on the innocent" is a true one, i.e., whether Speiser reproduced his own opinion or that of the natives, must be left undecided here.

10. On the animism of the child, cf. Piaget, *La Représentation du monde chez l'enfant*, pp. 159 ff.

11. Tylor, *Primitive Culture*, I, 286 ff.

12. E.g., the Fiji Islanders, according to James George Frazer, *The Belief in Immortality and the Worship of the Dead*, I (1913), 419 ff. But their defiance of death may partly be due to their warlike ideology. There is nothing peculiar in the fact that they die willingly, once they are old and weak. The idea of the fate of the soul after death is so disagreeable that Frazer's assumption that their readiness to die is a result of their belief in immortality is hardly plausible. The natives of the Marquesas Islands, too, are supposed to show no fear

of death. Frazer, II (1922), 352 f., reports that in former times a native, when feeling the nearness of death, ordered a coffin and put it up in his house. But according to the ideas of these people about life after death, this coffin is of the utmost importance as a vehicle to the other world. Concern for one's fate after death is compatible with love for life. Christians, too, while still alive, care for nicely kept graves and dignified funerals; but one cannot maintain, therefore, that death is a matter of indifference to them. The assertion that the natives of the Marquesas Islands do not fear death does not agree with other details of their customs, reported by Frazer, such as their mourning customs, which prove their fear of the death soul.

13. E. Laetitia Moon Conard, "Les Idées des Indiens Algonquins relatives à la vie d'outre-tombe," *Revue de l'histoire des religions*, XLII (1900), 272–73.

14. George Turner, *Samoa, a Hundred Years Ago and Long Before* (1884), pp. 335 f.: "The aged were buried alive and at their own request. It was even considered a disgrace to the family of an aged chief if he was not buried alive. When an old man felt sick and infirm, and thought he was dying, he deliberately told his children and friends to get all ready and bury him."

15. Westermarck, *The Origin and Development of the Moral Ideas*, II (1917), 535, contradicts the reports of those observers who refer to the indifference of certain primitive peoples toward death: "But it is a fact often noticed among ourselves, that a person on the verge of death may resign himself to his fate with the greatest calmness, although he has been afraid to die throughout his life. Moreover, the fear of death may be disguised by thoughtlessness, checked by excitement, or mitigated by dying in company. There are people who are conspicuous for their bravery, and yet have a great dread of death. Nobody is entirely free from this feeling, though it varies greatly in strength among different races and in different individuals. In many savages it is so strongly developed, that they cannot bear to hear death mentioned. And inseparably mingled with this fear of death is the fear of the dead."

16. E. B. Tylor, "Primitive Society," *Contemporary Review*, XXI (1873), 714; Westermarck, I, 331.

17. Westermarck, I, 328.

18. William J. Burchell, *Travels in the Interior of Southern Africa* (1824), II, 554; Westermarck, I, 329.

19. Marett, *Faith, Hope, and Charity in Primitive Religion*, p. 169.

20. Graebner, *Das Weltbild der Primitiven*, p. 27, remarks: "The God guarantees not only the physical but, above all, the social existence of man. . . . ." The social existence of primitive man is identical with his moral existence.

21. Westermarck, I, 38 ff.

22. William Ridley, *Kamilaroi, and Other Australian Languages* (2d ed., 1875), p. 159.

23. Richard Francis Burton, *The Lake Regions of Central Africa* (1860), II, 329.

24. Kidd, *Kafir Socialism*, p. 84.

25. Im Thurn, *Among the Indians of Guiana*, p. 330.

26. H. Clay Trumbull, *The Blood Covenant* (2d ed., 1893), pp. 259 ff.

27. Wundt, *Mythus und Religion*, Part III (1915), pp. 320 ff., distinguishes too sharply between vengeance and retribution as a form of justice.

28. Tylor, *Primitive Culture*, I, 427; II, 361.

29. Elsdon Best, *The Maori*, I, 358.

30. *Ibid.*, p. 251.

31. A. S. Thomson, *The Story of New Zealand* (1859), I, 98 f. Kootz-Kretschmer, *Die Safwa*, I, 203, gives the following account of a Safwa: "If one has injured another during a battle by hurting his eye, knocking out a tooth, breaking an arm or leg, then the injured individual says to himself: 'I, too, want to injure him just like he has injured me; we wish to be like one another; his body should be injured like mine; he has put out my eye, conse-

quently, I shall put out his.' " Spencer, *The Principles of Sociology*, Vol. II, par. 533, p. 528, writes: "The principle of requiring 'an eye for an eye and a tooth for a tooth,' embodies the primitive idea of justice everywhere."

32. John Lockman, *Travels of the Jesuits into Various Parts of the World: Compiled from Their Letters* (London, 1743), II, 410 f.

33. James Adair, *History of the American Indians, 1775*, ed. S. C. Williams (1930), p. 157.

34. Karsten, *Blood Revenge, War, and Victory Feasts among the Jibaro Indians of Eastern Ecuador*, pp. 10, 13. Of blood revenge among these Indians he says (p. 11): "But blood revenge among these Indians is not merely owing to moral or ethical, but also to religious reasons. The soul of the murdered Indian requires that his relatives shall avenge his death. The errant spirit, which gets no rest, visits his sons, his brothers, his father, in the dream, and, weeping, conjures them not to let the slayer escape but to wreak vengeance upon him for the life he has taken. If they omit to fulfil this duty the anger of the vengeful spirit may turn against themselves."

35. Lévy-Bruhl, *Primitives and the Supernatural*, pp. 390 ff., believes that the principle of *talio* has to be traced to the primitive idea that a bad influence can be stopped or neutralized by the opposition of an analogous influence: "to a given act, the same act, reversed, must be opposed; that what has been done must be done again, but in the contrary direction. The reaction, or rather, the counter-action, must be equal and contrary to the action," like the principle of homeopathy: *similia similibus curantur*. "This necessity for a counteraction which is equal and similar to the action is closely linked up with the law of compensation (*la loi du talion*) applied in so many cases in most primitive communities. It is not merely the expression of a harsh desire for vengeance, seeking satisfaction at all costs, by inflicting on the author of some injury or suffering exactly the same injury or suffering." The nature of *talio* consists in "a counter-action which is exactly proportioned to the action, and which 'cancels' it" (p. 392). But in the cases in which *talio* is exercised, the question is not to "cancel" an action by a counteraction; such a cancellation is a priori impossible. The significance of the counteraction is not to paralyze a bad influence or to prevent an evil effect but to react to an already existing violation of law which cannot be undone with an evil; that is the character of retribution. The importance of this principle in the life of primitive man is not sufficiently recognized by Lévy-Bruhl. Thus he asserts (p. 233) that the illness which befalls man after the violation of a taboo is not interpreted as punishment. "It does not attack the man because he has infringed the law, but occurs automatically. From the circumstance that the taboo has been violated, the man finds himself defenceless against the evil influence which threatened him in case of contact." But the "automatic" reaction of the violated taboo is simply the function of the principle of retribution.

Lévy-Bruhl overlooks the fact that the *talio* is only an application of this principle of retribution. He admits, however, that cases may occur in which the action cannot be canceled. He believes (p. 392) that, if one has put out the other's eye, "the deed cannot be undone, and as it is in this case impossible to reverse it, they must make provision for it in some other way, as nearly like it as possible. The man who has done the deed must submit to it in his turn and one of his eyes will be put out accordingly. . . . . In other words, where it is impossible to cancel the action by repeating it in a contrary sense, the natives have recourse to reciprocity." But "reciprocity" is essentially different from "reversion." In order to paralyze the bad influence which is exercised upon a man, in order to remove an evil which is threatening him or which has already been inflicted upon him, it is necessary to administer to this same man a counterinfluence, to neutralize the inherent poison by a counterpoison. In the case of *talio* this counteraction is directed against someone else. Its aim is not to remove an evil from the injured individual but to harm the injurer. That the evil or the wrong sustained is "repaired" or "cured" by the retributory punishment is a rather questionable figurative expression of modern juristic terminology.

36. F. Blumentritt, "The Quinganes of Luzon," *Popular Science Monthly* (New York), XXXIX (1891), 390.

37. Maurice Leenhardt, *Notes d'ethnologie Neo-Caledonienne* (Université de Paris, "Travaux et Mémoires de l'Institut d'Ethnologie," Vol. VIII [1930]), p. 46.

38. C. G. Seligmann, *The Melanesians of British New Guinea* (1910), pp. 569 f.

39. Edward Westermarck, *Early Beliefs and Their Social Influence* (1932), p. 95, speaks of "jus talionis, or rule of equivalence between injury and retaliation, which is characteristic of savage justice."

40. Cf. Lévy-Bruhl, *The Soul of the Primitive*, pp. 226 ff. He sees the nature of revenge, particularly blood revenge, as "mystical compensation." The group has suffered a loss for which compensation must be made. What matters is the value of the collectivum and not the value of the individual. The death of an individual signifies for primitive man not so much a personal loss as damage suffered by the group. "For the real living being is the group: individuals exist only through it. Thus the group feels itself to be directly affected, for this death means the loss of some of its substance" (p. 227). This explains, according to Lévy-Bruhl, the contradiction between the unimportance of the individual and the excitement which his death arouses among the survivors who must carry out extraordinarily burdensome mourning customs. When the death of a member of the group has to be avenged, the real and true reason is not so much fear of the soul of the deceased which demands revenge as it is the desire to restore the disturbed equilibrium of the group; and this may also result from a mere rite. Such is often the case when real vengeance is replaced by sham vengeance, as, for instance, among certain Australian tribes. Although they regard blood revenge as a compelling duty, it frequently occurs that, after having been out for a while, the expedition of revenge returns to the camp without making it clear whether the members of the other tribe responsible for the death have been killed. Nobody asks, and the matter is left undecided. "The affair is over, the act has sufficed. They do not seem to think that the dead can now take offence.—What is absolutely indispensable is not, therefore, the satisfaction to be afforded to the dead (which will be procured in any case, if there is not too much risk involved); it is a rite which shall reestablish the equilibrium of the social group, the mystic compensation for the wrong it has suffered. In a certain sense, vengeance itself may be regarded as a compensation." It is hardly probable that primitive people have any idea of a "state of equilibrium" which exists, or is supposed to exist, within the group. Such an idea, it is true, corresponds to a collectivistic view of social life. But this is rather the construction of modern social metaphysics than the expression of the collectivistic feeling of primitive man. The social character of primitive consciousness is expressed in the fact that it is thoroughly dominated by the idea of retribution. Lévy-Bruhl is certainly not right when he contrasts the existence of the group and its supposed tendency to restore the balance disturbed by the death of a member with the principle of retribution as it exists in the consciousness of primitive man. Above all, the fact that sometimes only a sham revenge is exercised must not be quoted as evidence that blood revenge does not originate principally in the belief in the death soul. Sham revenge is one of the many ways in which primitive man tries to deceive the superhuman authority; and he believes himself able to deceive this authority, although at the same time he fears it because of its superhuman powers. In this way he seeks to ease the burden which a social ideology, created by himself, imposes upon him.

41. Williams, *Orokaiva Society*, p. 170: "The expression for revenge itself is an interesting one, viz. *diroga-mine*, or an 'exchange of *diroga*,' the latter meaning the spirit of a man slain in fight in contradistinction to the spirit of one who has died in any other way."

42. Junod, *The Life of a South African Tribe*, II, 580.

43. J. Leighton Wilson, *Western Africa* (1856), p. 217.

44. Lévy-Bruhl, *The Soul of the Primitive*, pp. 228 ff.

45. Bronislaw Malinowski, "Baloma; the Spirits of the Dead in the Trobriand Islands," *Journal of the Royal Anthropological Institute of Great Britain and Ireland*, XLVI (1916), 410.

46. Richard Thurnwald, "Die Gemeinde der Banaro," *Zeitschrift f. vergleichende Rechtswissenschaft*, XXXVIII (1920), 378 ff. The same author remarks in his study *Psychologie des primitiven Menschen (Handbuch der vergl. Psychologie*, herausgegeben von Kafka), I (1922), 299, that "retribution is the basis for friendly or hostile behavior." Le Roy, *The Religion of the Primitives*, p. 165, states that "in the mind of the primitive every injury requires reparation or payment that justice may be satisfied and that the two sides of the scale, momentarily disturbed, may resume their equilibrium."

Warner, *A Black Civilization*, p. 159, writes of the Murngin, an Australian tribe: "The idea underlying most Murngin warfare is that the same injury should be inflicted upon the enemy group that one's own group has suffered. This accomplished, a clan feels satisfied; otherwise, there is a constant compulsion toward vengeance. . . . ." P. 162: "The fundamental principle underlying all the causes of Murngin warfare is that of reciprocity: if a harm has been done to an individual or a group, it is felt by the injured people that they must repay the ones who have harmed them by an injury that at least equals the one they have suffered. When the total cultural situation of Murngin life is further examined, this negative reciprocation is found to fit into a larger reciprocation. In the chapters on Murngin kinship and local organization it was seen that the foundations of these structures are built entirely on reciprocity, and that the whole civilization might be described as in dynamic equilibrium."

47. B. Malinowski, *Crime and Custom in Savage Society* (1932), pp. 22 ff. Cf. also H. Jan Hogbin, *Law and Order in Polynesia*, with an Introduction by B. Malinowski (1934), pp. xxiii ff., 83. Brinton, *The Myths of the New World*, p. 65, points out: "No mere man, least of all a savage, is kind and benevolent in spite of neglect and injury, nor is any man causelessly and ceaselessly malicious. Personal, family, or national feuds render some more inimical than others, but always from a desire to guard their own interests, never out of a delight in evil for its own sake. Thus the cruel gods of death, disease, and danger, were never of Satanic nature, while the kindliest divinities were disposed to punish, and that severely, any neglect of their ceremonies." But Brinton is not right when he adds: "Moral dualism can only arise in minds where the ideas of good and evil are not synonymous with those of pleasure and pain, for the conception of a wholly good or a wholly evil nature requires the use of these terms in their higher, ethical sense." The ethical dualism of good and evil arises from the dualism of agreeable and disagreeable, useful and harmful. In the consciousness of primitive man, the two spheres of the moral and the useful are not yet distinguished. The useful is the good and the harmful is the evil. Cf. Ernst Mosbacher, "Untersuchungen zum Suendenbegriff der Naturvoelker," *Baessler-Archiv*, XVII, Heft I (1934), 1 ff.

48. Williams, *Orokaiva Society*, p. 317.

48a. A. R. Brown, *The Andaman Islanders*, p. 237.

48b. W. Koppers, "Die Eigentumsverhältnisse bei den Yamana auf Feuerland," in *Atti del XXII Congresso Internazionale degli Americanisti* (Roma, 1928), II, 192.

P. J. Hamilton Grierson, *The Silent Trade* (1903), pp. 39 f., writes: "The practice of making a present in the expectation of receiving a suitable return seems to be well-nigh universal; and there are many instances in which a distinct understanding that an equivalent will be given prevails between donor and donee. It is true that some of the tribes to which we have referred are said to have no idea of commerce; but . . . . it may well be that refusal to trade is due, not to ignorance of trading, but fear or suspicion or misunderstanding."

Felix Somló, *Der Gueterverkehr in der Urgesellschaft* (1909), pp. 156 f., says: "Because the legal form of barter, as we know it, has not been found among these peoples, it has been concluded that the fact of exchange of goods did not exist. The gift, it is true, was found, but since in our economic life it has no great importance, it was supposed, in like manner, that it also had no importance as an idea of primitive peoples. Incidentally, it may be observed, that to denominate these primitive transactions as gifts is not accurate. Such a transaction is neither our form of gift nor our form of barter, but lies intermediate between them. It is a legal transaction rigidly circumscribed by definite rules and is the primitive form of gift and barter in the modern sense. Both have evolved out of this original undifferentiated institution. It is a mistake, therefore, to call these primitive transactions gifts. They resemble gifts in this, that at first there is a one-sided giving corresponding to a one-sided taking, and that the amount of the gift, as well as the gift itself, depends on the one-sided act of the giver. They resemble barter, however, in so far as the gift is made with the expectation of a gift in return which return gift is one of the most stringent customary duties. Custom regulates the value of the gift and the return gift by strict rules. It is therefore proper to call this legal transaction barter-gift. More important than the form, is the fact that this legal transaction is widely disseminated among primitive peoples, and has great economic significance as a means for the interchange of goods."

49. Krause, *Die Tlinkit-Indianer*, p. 168.

50. *The Poetic Edda*, ed. Henry Adams Bellows (1923), pp. 37 f., 63.

51. Marcel Mauss, "Essai sur le don: forme et raison de l'échange dans less sociétés archaiques," *L'Année sociologique*, N.S., I (1923–24), 30 ff.

52. Cf. Mauss, p. 46, n. 4.

53. Elsdon Best, "Maori Forest Lore," *Transactions of the New Zealand Institute*, XLII (1909), Part III, 439.

54. Rasmussen, *Intellectual Culture of the Iglulik Eskimos*, p. 150.

55. Thomson, I, 86.

56. Wirz, *Die Marind-anim von Hollaendisch-Sued-Neu-Guinea*, II, Part VI, 104.

57. David Boyle, "On the Paganism of the Civilized Iroquois of Ontario," *Journal of the Anthropological Institute of Great Britain and Ireland*, XXX (N.S., Vol. III [1900]), 269.

58. Albert Nicolay Gilbertson, "Some Ethical Phases of Eskimo Culture," *Journal of Religious Psychology*, VI (1913), 360.

59. Knud Rasmussen, *The People of the Polar North* (1908), p. 51.

60. Cf. above, p. 21. Significant is the following remark of Thomson, I, 123, on the fights among the Maori: "Every war had an apparent just cause. The motive may have been slight, but there was a lawfulness for it, looking at the question with the ideas of New Zealanders." Cf. also Westermarck, *The Origin and Development of the Moral Ideas*, II, 2 ff.

61. McCulloch, "Account of the Valley of Munipore and of the Hill Tribes," in *Selections from the Records of the Government of India* (Foreign Department) (1859), p. 75. Cf. Lord Avebury (John Lubbock), *Prehistoric Times* (7th ed., 1913), p. 558.

62. Best, *The Maori*, II, 232.

63. Adair, p. 158.

64. R. Karsten, *The Origin of Worship* (1905), p. 4. On p. 89 he writes: " . . . . savage worship is mainly, as we may say, a species of barter."

65. Brinton, *The Myths of the New World*, p. 294.

66. *Ibid.*, p. 297.

67. *Ibid.*, p. 298.

68. Paul Radin, "The Winnebago Tribe," *37th Annual Report of the Bureau of American Ethnology* (1923), pp. 270 ff.

69. Paul Schebesta, *Vollblutneger und Halbzwerge, Forschungen unter Waldnegern und Halbpygmaeen am Ituri in Belgisch Kongo* (1934), p. 36 (following R. Kawateis).

70. Hermann Oldenberg, *Die Religion des Veda* (1894), p. 310. With regard to the meaning of the sacrifice, Oldenberg says that it is true that "the expectancy of a gift made in return does not actually extend to the idea that God has become the debtor of men or that a

legal order above him demands payment of such a debt." But he adds that "nevertheless, considering the nature of the relationship between man and God, one believes that the latter could not fail to repay a received kindness."

71. Cassirer, *Das mythische Denken*, p. 273, remarks: "Every sacrifice includes, according to its original sense, a negative element, namely the restriction of the desire, a renunciation self-imposed by the ego." But why does the ego impose a renunciation upon itself? Obviously, in order to receive from the authority to which it sacrifices more than it renounces. Self-tormentings to which many primitive peoples subject themselves before they go hunting or fighting or after someone has died are based on the same idea, which, indeed, is the spiritual basis of all asceticism. It is anticipatory self-punishment in order to avoid a greater evil than the one voluntarily assumed, or to receive a reward which will neutralize the loss. This is the sense of all exchange.

72. Alfred Wiedemann, *The Religion of the Ancient Egyptians* (1897), p. 178.

73. M. Friedrich, "Description de l'enterrement d'un chef à Ibouzo (Niger)," *Anthropos*, II (1907), 101. Cf. Hartland, *Ritual and Belief*, pp. 184 ff.

That man exercises retribution on his gods not only by rewarding them for benefits received or to be received but also by punishing them for not granting such benefits likewise occurs among peoples with more advanced religions. In *Herodotus*, vii. 35 we read: "So when Xerxes heard of it [that the bridge had been destroyed] he was full of wrath, and straightway gave order that the Hellespont should receive three hundred lashes and that a pair of fetters should be cast into it. Nay, I have even heard it said that he bade the branders take their irons and therewith brand the Hellespont. It is certain that he commanded those who scourged the waters to utter, as they lashed them, these barbarian and wicked words: 'Thou bitter water, thy lord lays on thee this punishment because thou hast wronged him without a cause, having suffered no evil at his hands. Verily King Xerxes will cross thee, whether thou will or no. Well dost thou deserve that no man should honour thee with sacrifice; for thou art of a truth a treacherous and unsavoury river.'"

Augustus punished Neptune for the loss of his fleet by ordering that at the Circensian plays the latter's image should not be carried around with those of the other gods. Infuriated at the death of Germanicus, the Romans stoned the temples of the gods, destroyed their altars, and removed their images. Similar events took place after the murder of Caligula in order to punish the gods for having admitted such a monster to the throne. Such reactions to the superhuman authorities can be observed even among Christians. In the Middle Ages it frequently happened that the images of the saints were destroyed or thrown into rivers as punishment for not having granted the requested help. "In the first half of the sixteenth century, it was still the custom in various towns of the kingdom of Navarra in times of extraordinary dryness to carry about the image of St. Peter in solemn procession and to sing: 'St. Peter, help us,' three times. If St. Peter did not answer, the men and women shouted: 'Throw St. Peter into the river!' The clergy sought to soothe the people and to console them by saying that relief would soon arrive, but the people did not acquiesce until the clergy guaranteed the help of St. Peter." Gustav Roskoff, *Das Religionswesen der rohesten Naturvoelker* (1880), pp. 139 f.; C. Meiners, *Allgemeine kritische Geschichte der Religionen* (1806–7), I, 177 ff.

Daniel G. Brinton, *Nagualism* (1894), p. 13, writes: "The belief in a personal guardian spirit was one of the fundamental doctrines of Nagualism. . . . . In Mexico today, in addition to his special personal guardian, the native will often choose another for a limited time or for a particular purpose, and this is quite consistent with the form of Christianity he has been taught. For instance, as we are informed by an observant traveller, at New Year or at corn planting the head of a family will go to the parish church and among the various saints there displayed will select one as his guardian for the year. He will address to him his prayers for rain and sunshine, for an abundant harvest, health and prosperity, and will not neglect to back these supplications by liberal gifts. If times are good and harvest ample, the Santo is rewarded with still more gifts, and his aid is sought for another term; but if luck has been bad the Indian repairs to the church at the end of the year, bestows on his holy patron a sound cursing, calls him all the bad names he can think of, and has nothing more to do with him."

Westermarck, *Early Beliefs and Their Social Influence*, p. 28, notes: "When hard pressed, the Samoyed, after he has invoked his own deities in vain, addresses himself to the Russian god, promising to become his worshipper if he relieves him from distress; and in most cases he is said to be faithful to his promise, though he may still try to keep on good terms with his former gods by occasionally offering them a sacrifice in secret." The compensation to the Christian god consists in the fact that one becomes his adherent; the primitive Samoyed believes that the Christian deity is interested in obtaining new adherents.

74. Schultze, *Psychologie der Naturvoelker*, pp. 233, 238.

75. Lucien M. Turner, "Ethnology of the Ungava District, Hudson Bay Territory," *11th Annual Report of the Bureau of Ethnology* (1894), p. 194.

76. Schebesta, *Orang-Utan*, p. 138.

77. Kidd, p. 120.

78. *Ibid.*, pp. 89 ff.

79. Junod, *The Life of a South African Tribe*, II, 423.

80. *Ibid.*, p. 396.

81. Waldemar Bogoras, *The Chukchee: The Jessup North Pacific Expedition* ("Memoirs of the American Museum of Natural History," Vol. XI, Part II [1907]), p. 295.

82. C. K. Meek, *Tribal Studies in Northern Nigeria* (1931), II, 403.

83. C. K. Meek, *A Sudanese Kingdom: An Ethnographical Study of the Jukun-speaking Peoples of Nigeria* (1931), p. 131.

84. R. F. Fortune, *Manus Religion* ("Memoirs of the American Philosophical Society," Vol. III [1935]), pp. 8 ff.

85. Lévy-Bruhl, *Primitive Mentality*, p. 278.

In *Old New Zealand*, by a Pakeha Maori (1884), p. 105, we read: "There were in the old times two great institutions which reigned with iron rod in Maori land—the *Tapu* and the *Muru* (*Muru* in a rough way resembled damages to be paid). . . . . The offences for which people were plundered were sometimes of a nature which . . . . would seem curious. A man's ch... fell in the fire and was burnt almost to death. The father was immediately plundered to an extent that almost left him without the means of subsistence: Fishing nets, canoes, pigs, provisions—all went. His canoe upset, and he and all his family narrowly escaped drowning,—some were, perhaps, drowned. He was immediately robbed, and well pummelled with a club into the bargain, if he was not good at the science of self-defence—the club part of the ceremony being always fairly administered one against one, and after fair warning given to defend himself."

J. S. Polack, *Manners and Customs of the New Zealanders* (1840), II, 64 ff., writes: "If a man should burst his piece of ammunition while discharging it in honour of the arrival of a visitor, the weapon is instantly wrested from him, and becomes the property of the captor, for the accidental affront offered to the visitor. Should the man have received a wound in consequence, his criminality is accounted of greater magnitude, and he must be contented at the least, with the loss of his piece, and may regard himself as fortunate if he escapes a beating.—When a man enters the state of matrimony, the ceremony would not be observed with due honour, unless he allowed himself to be robbed of every article possessed by himself and the bride, every item of provision is stolen from him, and should a blanket be left to cover his personal nudity, he may thank his *Atua* [guardian spirit].—Some chiefs of high rank, on such occasions, habit themselves in the best garments they possess, and such conduct redounds greatly to their honour, as indicative of the absence of parsimony, and is reported to distant tribes as a remarkable instance of individual liberality.

The parties who undertake these burglarious excursions, must be related in some degree, but a seventieth cousin, provided he can make good his being simply a fibre of the genealogical tree, is admitted as one of the party. The alertness of the natives is particularly shown on such occasions, as much competition arises in who shall first undertake the official visit.—A similar scene takes place on the death of a wife, as if the affliction was not sufficiently overpowering. The loss of a favourite child is attended with a like wake. These visits are not confined to robbery only, as the sufferers obtain in addition a sound castigation, in which blows are often given with no sparing hand.—The rejoicing of a parent at the birth of his child, is sobered by a similar infliction, which spares neither excessive happiness nor the· most overpowering affliction.—Nor is this law confined to domestic occurrences. If one or more natives are capsized with their canoe, through stress of weather or mismanagement, the natives nearest to the place, instantly swim to the mariners, and instead of lending them assistance, appropriate to themselves every article they can lay hold of, whether paddles, or garments, then tow the canoe on shore, which they instantly make prize of, and further strip the hapless sufferers of every article of raiment, and often with the additional stimulus of a good beating.—If a chief or freedman is killed in battle, his friends immediately hasten to his plantations, and unearth every article of provisions, reducing his wives and families to destitution. An influential chief will probably appropriate to himself such of the wives of his deceased friend, as he may fancy, with a fair proportion of his slaves, and to be scrupulous in such matters, would be accounted as utterly superfluous, as the law would work in the same manner in the event of his own death."

Th. Waitz, *Anthropologie der Naturvoelker*, VI (1872), 224, writes that on the Marquesas and in New Zealand one used to plunder unfortunate men "because one regarded misfortune as a divine punishment and those inflicted by it as criminals."

Lévy-Bruhl, p. 290, remarks: ". . . . misfortune is a disqualification, and he who has been afflicted by it has at the same time suffered moral degeneration. As an object of the wrath of the unseen powers, he becomes a danger to his friends and to the social group, and they avoid his presence."

John Roscoe, *The Baganda* (1911), p. 319, says of the Baganda, a tribe in eastern Equatorial Africa, that nobody dares to save a drowning man: "They thought that the man's guardian spirit had left him to the mercy of the river-spirit, and in this way they accounted for his death."

According to Georg W. Steller, *Beschreibung von dem Lande Kamtschatka* (1774), p. 295, the natives of Kamchatka adopted even a hostile attitude toward a drowning man. If he could save himself, he was outlawed by his fellow-men.

86. The attempt to explain magic by primitive man's "egocentrism," by his alleged belief in the boundless power of his personal will over nature, the omnipotence of his wishes, is contradicted by everything we know about primitive man's mentality—above all, by his notorious lack of ego-consciousness. In magic, man turns to a superhuman—personal or impersonal—power for fulfilment of his wishes, and he does so because he does not consider himself capable of bringing about the desired effect. Alanson Skinner, "Social Life and Ceremonial Bundles of the Menomini Indians," *Anthropological Papers of the American Museum of Natural History*, XIII, Part I (1913), 132, says of the Menomini Indians: "The Menomini believe that animals of all kinds are endowed with intelligence almost equal to that of human beings and that the only reason why men are able to take them is because they are more fortunate than the beasts. . . . . Every effort was made by the Menomini to keep the supernatural powers appeased in order that they might continue their friendly aid. The actual skill of the hunter amounted to nothing if he received no assistance from above. Without such help his mere ability to approach the game, his knowledge of their haunts and his accuracy with weapons were useless. . . . . Owing to these ideas the Menomini resort to all manner of magical methods to capture their game."

The explanation of magic as the emanation of the megalomania of primitive man is, in a certain degree, connected with the tendency to separate magic from religion. Religion is characterized by the humble submission of man to the deity, imagined as an overwhelming power; magic, however, rests on man's arrogant belief to be able to exercise coercion on the powers that guide nature, to force them through specific, i.e., magic, procedures to behave according to the will of the magician. This theory is developed at length in Paul Radin's book, *Primitive Religion* (1937). Here, too, the contradiction between such an interpretation of magic and the mentality of primitive man, correctly pictured by the author, becomes clearly apparent. Primitive man's life is characterized, as Radin stresses on p. 6, by the inadequacy of his means in the fight against nature; this situation necessarily created in him "the sense of powerlessness and the feeling of insignificance." P. 7: "With fear man was born." Radin describes this fear inherent from the very beginning in primitive man as "fear inspired by a specific economic situation"; and on p. 23 he writes: "It is a very literal fear of the battle for existence under the difficult economic conditions that prevail in simple societies. The more uncertain is the food supply, the less man is technologically prepared, the greater naturally will be the feeling of insecurity and the more intense, consequently, will be the fear." Radin asserts, p. 22, "that fear is the primordial emotion with which man began." This primordial fear of primitive man is only the reverse of what Radin calls "the sense of powerlessness and the feeling of insignificance." This fact leads Radin to the following conclusion of a general psychological nature: "All this naturally led to a disorientation and disintegration of the ego. The mental correlate for such a condition is subjectivism, and subjectivism means the dominance of magic and of the most elementary forms of coercive rites. If the psychoanalysts wish to call this narcissism, there can be no legitimate objection." Since this argument is based on psychology, it must be judged from the same point of view. This means that it is incorrect to speak of a "disorientation and disintegration of the ego" of primitive man. For such a statement presumes that primitive man already possesses an ego-experience, an ego-consciousness, and a corresponding self-reliance. Only then could the ego be destroyed or dissolved. But such an ego-consciousness and self-reliance could not, according to Radin, arise in primitive man. This is an important point, since Radin's further argumentation is essentially based on this shifting of his suppositions. He may be right when he states that subjectivism is the correlate for a disintegration of the ego; such is presumably the case of narcissism among modern men. For here exists, in fact, a highly refined ego-consciousness—partly inherited, partly developed by education—which could be disintegrated by various circumstances. Here, then, could start the process which leads to that hypertrophy of the ego-consciousness which psychoanalysis calls "narcissism" and which can be explained either as an attempt at compensation or as overcompensation for some suffered rebuff. This is how Radin interprets the step from disintegration of the ego to its excess (p. 8): "It is but natural for the psyche, under such circumstances, to take refuge in compensation fantasies." But the transfer of this psychic mechanism, applicable to certain neurotics, to primitive man is quite impossible because the latter lacks the essential factor, the primary ego-consciousness and self-reliance which this process of compensation seeks to re-establish. This example shows how careful one must be with the parallelization of primitive mentality and the psychic condition of neurotics.

One of the merits of Radin's work is that he points to the importance which certain individuals have for the formation of religious ideas among primitive men; he calls them "religious formulators." On p. 15 he writes: "For a proper understanding of primitive religion, it is necessary to know not only why man postulated the supernatural and what purpose it fulfilled but also what individuals in a given society formulated it and the extent to which this formulation differed from man to man. That only a very small number of individuals in any group are interested in making an analysis of religious phenomena and that an even smaller number are qualified to do so, is patent. This is true in our own cultures and holds true to a much greater degree among primitive peoples. Although the number of religious thinkers and co-ordinators is relatively smaller in primitive societies than among ourselves, they nevertheless play an infinitely more important role." But this statement seems to be of value only if—an aspect which is not made apparent by Radin— the existence of this special group of "religious formulators" was connected with the practice of division of labor in the course of which different professions were developed. And it is admitted that this is possible only in a relatively advanced stage of social development. Undoubtedly, the influence of the professional magicians and priests on religious ideas must not be underestimated, and Radin is certainly right when he stresses that one gains a different picture of the religious ideas of a people according to whether one relies on the statements of professionals or on the corresponding accounts of an average layman. But Radin is not convincing when he asserts, on the basis of general psychological considerations, that "the task of the formulator thus becomes clear. He must—this cannot be stressed enough— free the magical act from its compulsive character" (p. 26); or when he says that "the primary function of the religious thinker" is "to mitigate the rigourousness of the coercion exercised by the ego upon the object and a granting to the object of both independence and a measure of free will" (p. 30). From a general psychological point of view—and this is the only one possible, inasmuch as one is unable to substantiate the process in question with empirical material from every people—the very opposite is the more probable. The professional magician is vitally concerned that the laymen who turn to him should believe in his decisive influence upon the superhuman authority. Hence the professional is precisely the one who is most interested in promulgating the belief that one may force the powers controlling nature to behave according to certain desires; for he himself has this capacity because he has acquired it in a specific manner. Radin rightly stresses the great influence of the personal and professional interests of these "religious formulators" upon the actual establishment of religious ideas. With reference to the relationship to the superhuman authority, these interests point to a direction the very opposite of that which Radin has to assume in order to maintain his idea of the relation between magic and religion. The intent of the professional magician is proved by his frequently observed tendency to identify himself with the superhuman authority, to make its power appear in some way as his own, and thus to produce the impression that he himself is able to bring about the desired result. The idea that the "spirit" with whose help the magician carries out his art has its abode in himself is therefore typical.

Besides, it must be observed that the relationship to the superhuman authority, in magic as elsewhere, is essentially ambivalent. Although it is true that the immediate interest of the professional magician is aimed at making the layman believe that the superhuman authority is at his disposal, he is also very much concerned in making the authority appear extremely powerful in the eyes of all believers. In these as well as in other aspects, magic as a professional system is characterized by two inconsistent tendencies. And just in this point no distinction exists between magic and religion. Certainly the development of religion is characterized by the fact that the distance between man and God is gradually increased. This distance, as expressed in terms of the power of the superhuman authority, finally reaches the stage of infinity, so that any possibility of influencing the divine will must appear incompatible with its absolute transcendency. This extreme has not yet been reached by ordinary Christianity. The achievement of such a position would mean for religion the loss of its social sense and thus its possibility of existence. But this tendency of religious development is counteracted by an opposite drift, based on the idea of divine justice. Since God rules the world justly, sin necessarily entails punishment, just as merit entails reward. It is an essentially religious idea that man, through a certain behavior pleasing to the Deity, obtains an unconditional title to a corresponding treatment from the Deity. Belief in the justice of God exercises, therefore, no less coercion upon the Deity than does the magician upon one of his "spirits." The more moral the idea of the Deity is, the more certainly it becomes subject to the law of retribution. But even if one remains aloof both from the sphere of theology—which more or less rationalizes its object—and from theological speculation about divine justice and merely seeks religion where its subjective experience is intensified to the utmost, namely, in mystics, one nevertheless constantly meets with a spiritual situation strikingly similar to the one which is regarded as characteristic of magic and which in reality is the spiritual situation of the professional magician. For the mystical experience is also characterized by the tendency of the believer to identify himself with the Deity, to let his own will coincide with the will of the Deity, and thus to force the latter to become one with the human being. This is the essence of the religion of one of the greatest mystics of all times, Master Eckehardt. In this sense Angelus Silesius, one of the most representative mystics, says (*Angelus Silesius: A Selection from the Rhymes of a German Mystic*, trans. Paul Carus [1909], pp. 15, 17):

> I know, deprived of me, God could not live a wink
> He must give up the ghost if into naught I sink.

> God is my final end; does He from me evolve,
> Then He grows out of me while I in Him dissolve.

And (*Angelus Silesius: Selections from the Cherubinic Wanderer*, translated with an Introduction by J. E. Crawford Flitch [1932], p. 119):

> God needs must do my Will, if Will in me is dead
> I write from Him His paradigm and copy-head.

If only the coercion exercised upon the superhuman authority distinguishes magic from religion, then the continuous attempts clearly to separate these two spheres must remain in vain. Cf. Hartland, *Ritual and Belief*, pp. 26 ff., 129 ff.

87. George A. Dorsey and H. R. Voth, *The Mishongnovi Ceremonies of the Snake and Antelope Fraternities* (Field Columbian Museum Pub. 66, "Anthropological Series," Vol. III, No. 3 [1902]), pp. 165–261.

88. *Ibid.*, pp. 182 ff.

89. *Ibid.*, pp. 247, 251.

90. *Ibid.*, p. 209.

91. Cf. John G. Bourke, *The Snake-Dance of the Moquis of Arizona* (1884), pp. 179–80.

92. Dorsey and Voth, p. 196.

93. A. C. Kruijt, "Regen lokken en Regenverdijven bij de Toradjas van Midden Celebes," *Tijdschrift voor Indische Taal- Land- en Volkenkunde*, XLIV (1901), 3 f.

94. George Turner, pp. 345 f.; Ernst Samter, "Altroemischer Regenzauber," *Archiv fuer Religionswissenschaft*, Vol. XXI (1922), quotes many examples of rain-magic which consist of manipulations with water, especially those where one hopes to obtain rain from the dead and therefore brings the corpse into some connection with water.

95. Sam Wide and Martin P. Nilsson, "Griechische und römische Religion," in *Einleitung in die Altertumswissenschaft*, herausgegeben von Gercke und Norden (1933), Band II, 2. Teil, p. 16, write: "When sun-heat and dryness had lasted for a long time the priest of Zeus Lycaeus, broke an oak-sprig at the latter's shrine and dipped it into a well. Soon one could perceive how the water of the well bubbled and steam came up and thickened into clouds in order to pour down later over the arcadian countryside as refreshing rain." The tree, from which the priest broke the sprig, was originally a fetish tree and the abode of the demon to whom water was offered in that way in order to receive rain from him.

Particularly informative for the importance of the idea of retribution in rain-magic is the Greek myth of the sieves of the Danaïdes. O. Gruppe, *Griechische Mythologie und Religionsgeschichte* ("Handbuch der klassischen Altertumswissenschaft," Band V, 2. Abt. [1906]), II, 831 ff., traces it to the ritual of rain-magic which consisted in the fact that girls poured water through sieves. The water was originally regarded as a gift to the death souls, as a means of placating the angered demons who hold back the rain. It was a widespread belief that dryness was caused by the thirsty death souls who sucked up both the rain clouds and the wells. The dead were imagined as thirsty and thus called ἀλίβαντες, "the dry ones," or δαναοί, "the arid ones," a word which preserved its meaning in the Danaïdes of the myth. That girls were connected with the rain-magic, which is the origin of the myth, "is probably to be explained by the fact that the souls of the ἄωροι and ἄγαμοι were regarded, above all, as the authors of aridity; therefore, a λουτροφόρος, a vase without a bottom, was placed on their grave. The legend amalgamated the girls who draw water with those whose wrath they had to soothe; the older version is probably that the Danaïdes," who had killed their bridegrooms "when, as a result of these murders, dryness befell the land, created rain through the ritual with the sieves and other ceremonies. Later, according to what appears to be a changed version of the legend, the girls were put on trial but acquitted through an ordeal. But these are new interpretations; originally, the myth referred to the ceremony of pouring out water. The gift of water, as usual with rain-sacrifices, is poured into a crevasse through which, according to the belief of those times, the thirsty death souls come to the upper world." Gruppe, who, like most of the historians of religion, is far from recognizing an ethical-juridical element in the so-called "magical" procedures, confirms by his interpretation of the Danaïdes-myth that the original intention behind this rain-magic was the placation of avenging death souls who, by inflicting dryness, exercise retribution for a crime committed on them; the water used at the rain-magic is a gift to the demons from whom one expects rain as a countergift. Gruppe, pp. 832 f., mentions a particular type of rain-magic, carried out with flowers which were important for the death cult. The similarity of this kind of magic with procedures through which infuriated and avenging death souls are to be placated is so striking that the idea of retribution as the basis of these magical operations cannot be ignored.

96. Abel Bergaigne, *La Religion védique* (1878), I, 121 ff.

97. Raoul Allier, *Magie et religion* (1935), p. 18, following Rev. W. E. Cousins, *Malagasy Customs* (Antananarivo, 1896). That the character of the thank offering is purely retributory is clear. A Vedic formula reproduced by Bergaigne, p. 141, reads: "The gods have benefited us with a fine fire; we shall honor them with a fine fire."

98. *The Jesuit Relations and Allied Documents* (1634), VI, 213.

99. Father Julius Jetté, "On the Superstitions of the Ten'a Indians (Middle Part of the Yukon Valley, Alaska)," *Anthropos*, VI (1911), 603 ff.

100. Pliny Earle Goddard, *Life and Culture of the Hupa* ("University of California Publications, American Archaeology and Ethnology," Vol. I, No. 1 [1903]), pp. 77–78.

101. Stefánsson, *My Life with the Eskimo*, p. 57.

102. Edward Moffat Weyer, *The Eskimos* (1932), p. 241.

103. George A. Dorsey, *The Pawnee; Mythology*, Part I (1906), pp. 202, 502. The buffaloes say to the boy: " 'My son, we want some good smoke.' The boy told them that he would give them tobacco, and to some of them he would blow whiffs of smoke. The Buffalo then told the boy to take a few Buffalo to the village and to have them killed. The boy took the Buffalo to the village to the people, and they killed them and sacrificed them to the gods. When the Buffalo were killed they returned to the herd and told that their meat had been put to good use and that they received smoke." Cf. also Wundt, *Mythus und Religion*, II, 173 ff.

104. Dorsey, pp. 228 ff., 505 f. The end of the story is as follows: The buffaloes say: " 'Let us now scatter all over the land, so that we will be killed by the people.' So the Buffalo scattered out over the land. . . . . The girl was taken back to the tipi and she was told to go to her people. She went to her people and here she told them that they must select a girl every year to be holy and then the Buffalo would come to the people." Cf. also Wundt, p. 176.

105. Cf. Wundt, p. 168.

106. Cf. Wundt, p. 169. Lawsuits brought against animals and their punishment by courts of the state and the church during the Middle Ages is the subject of an interesting

study by Karl von Amira, *Thierstrafen und Thierprocesse* (1891). Amira writes (pp.1 ff.): "Animals have been subjected, for damage wrought by them, to public punishment or at least to a procedure which resembled public prosecution. The state authorities have executed, on animals, the punishment of hanging, burying alive, burning, by the ordinary executioner, and this was done with observance of the same solemn and complicated ceremonies which were designated for the execution of capital punishment on men. The church authorities have excommunicated animals. This anathema was declared by a sentence which had the same form as that which was pronounced against members of the church. On the other hand the capital punishment was preceded by the regular judgment of a lay court against the animal. Both these judgments were the conclusion of regular judicial procedures. And in these, we often see the animal treated as defendant—accused, summoned to answer the accusation, defended by an appointed counsel. . . . . The secular procedure was only applied to domestic animals. . . . . Almost everywhere, the procedure took place only for the killing or wounding of human beings, and in older periods for killing *exclusively*. Where Italian law was applied, it may also—or even chiefly—be entered upon for damaging objects." The ecclesiastical procedure never took place against domestic animals. "Usually it was applied against animal species considered as vermin in daily life, such as: mice, rats, moles, insects, caterpillars, noxious larvae, snails, leeches, snakes, toads. In Canada, it is true, it was also deemed applicable against wild pigeons, in Southern France long before to storks, in Germany against sparrows, on the shores of the lake of Geneva to eels which had become noxious to the community. Generally it was an innumerable quantity which people thought they might condemn in this way. And it was not so much a damage already wrought which was to be punished, as one feared that was to be averted. The procedure thus was not vindictive or repressive but prohibitive or preventive. The people wished to protect their fertile soil, or useful water against animals appearing in great numbers by trying to beat them off. Exceptionally, other disturbances were at stake. Ecclesiastical *maledictio* or *excommunicatio* in the form of *anathema* were considered to be an adequate means. . . . . The procedure which led to the *maledictio* or *excommunicatio* of the animals is described in most of the more detailed accounts, for instance also in official legal documents, as processual. Its most noticeable peculiarity consists in that the animals are treated as the defendant party. Plaintiffs are the owners of the endangered real estate, and mostly it is the entire community which brings the suit. The case usually consists of two main parts, but they cannot always be clearly distinguished from one another. The first part of the procedure represents a litigation about the admissibility of *expulsion* of the defendant. If this demand of the plaintiff is granted, the expulsed animals may be threatened with *maledictio* or *excommunicatio*. The second part of the procedure is a dispute about the admissibility of *maledictio* or *excommunicatio* for disobeying the condemnation to expulsion."

Amira (p. 30) explains the secular punishment of animals by the influence of the Old Testament. "The Lord promised Noah and his descendants to avenge their blood not only on men, but also on all animals. To this corresponded the Laws given on Mount Sinai following which the ox who gores a man to death shall be stoned and his flesh shall not be eaten" (Gen. 9:5; Exod. 21:28–32). The ecclesiastical procedure against animals is, according to Amira (pp. 54 f.), a "trial of ghosts" (*Gespensterprocess*): "The bodies of mice, rats, moles, toads, snakes, snails, insects especially were considered as dwelling-places of souls. Already during a man's lifetime his soul may enter into such a body. After his death it may continue to err about in this shape. And in these animals there may also reside souls of demons, which, to be sure, are originally not essentially different from souls of dead people. . . . . The *condemnation* in the lawsuits against animals should be considered not so much as a condemnation of an animal than as a *magic banning of souls of men or demons*, and thus as analogous to the exorcism of spirits as demonstrated with the classic and slavic, as well as with other peoples."

107. Plutarch, *Morals*, ed. W. W. Goodwin (1883), V, 215 f. Cf. also Wundt, pp. 167, 178 f., 194 f., 293.

108. Franz Boas, "The Central Eskimo," *6th Annual Report of the Bureau of Ethnology* (1888), pp. 638 f. Cf. also the Indian tale reported by F. Boas, *Indianische Sagen von der nordpazifischen Kueste Amerikas* (1895), p. 96. Wundt, p. 167, calls both myths "very primitive stories."

109. Gordon Hall Gerould, *The Grateful Dead* (1908), p. 57.

110. Lévy-Bruhl, *La Mythologie primitive*, p. 182.

111. The material, however, does not allow the assumption that death souls are attributed to all animals without exception, although it is no simple matter to draw a line between animated and nonanimated animals. Cf. Frazer, *The Golden Bough*, Part V, Vol. II (1920), pp. 204 ff. The following examples may perhaps shed some light on this point. If, among the Dschagga, a lizard playing on the thatched roof of a hut happens to fall into the fire, extensive atonements have to be undertaken. One of these procedures is the offering of another animal, a sheep (Bruno Gutmann, *Das Recht der Dschagga* [1926], pp. 556 ff.). When the Dajak of Borneo happen to kill a crocodile, they offer as atonement a cat (F. Grabowsky, "Die Theogonie der Dajaken auf Borneo," *Internationales Archiv fuer Ethnographie*, V [1892], 119 f.). In both cases, only the consequences resulting from the death or killing of the first animal—lizard or crocodile—are feared, but one has no scruples in sacrificing the other animal—sheep or cat—in order to avoid the retribution threatening to come from the dead lizard or crocodile. And, indeed, the Dschagga believe that the death soul of an ancestor lives in the lizard. Therefore they call the animal "grandma." According to the belief of the Dajaks, a spirit, Djata, lives in the crocodile; therefore such an animal is killed only if it has itself killed a man whose relatives will exercise the legal retribution on it. No soul capable of exercising retribution is imagined in either sheep or cat. Since the Dajaks use the meat of pigs, dogs, monkeys, and deer as bait in order to catch the crocodile on which retribution is to be exercised, they do not seem to ascribe "souls" or spirits to those animals.

In addition, the killing of animals as sacrifices for deceased men must be mentioned here. The natives of the Banks Islands hang killed pigs over the grave of a deceased. They believe that, when the deceased reaches the realm of the dead, the death souls assembled there will see the sacrificed pigs and therefore esteem the new arrival. But this would imply that pigs, too, have death souls which can be seen in the other world, since their bodies remain at the grave which is in this world. This, however, is certainly not the view of the natives, for they deny the existence of death souls in pigs (Codrington, *The Melanesians*, p. 260). This may be contradictory, but it is not the only contradiction in the ideology of the belief in the soul of the dead. Even though animals—just as the women and slaves who function as sacrifices for the dead—are killed to serve the deceased in the other world, one cannot speak of death souls in the sacrificed creatures, for their survival after death has no independent importance. The personality of the deceased is extended to the creatures in his possession. Since the man survives after death, his possessions, namely, animals, slaves, and wives, have to share this survival. The same is true of the belief of certain primitive peoples that the spirits of the animals killed are in the other world at the disposal of the death soul of the killer (Tylor, I, 470). These creatures certainly do not exercise the characteristic functions of death souls to harm or help the survivors. They are by no means active souls, as those of dead men, for whom the sacrifice is intended, or those of dead animals, which are feared and venerated. But it occasionally occurs that those very animals in which human death souls are imagined are sacrificed. Thus, Peruvians used to offer llamas to their gods, although they regarded them as "holy" animals because they imagined souls of the dead to be reincarnated in them (Karsten, *The Civilization of the South American Indians*, p. 393). This presupposes a highly developed and complicated religious ideology.

112. Lichtenstein, *Travels in Southern Africa*, I, 254.

113. Edwin W. Smith and Andrew Murray Dale, *The Ila-speaking Peoples of Northern Rhodesia* (1920), I, 167 f.

114. *Ibid.*, II, 87.

115. Meek, *A Sudanese Kingdom*, p. 418.

116. Kootz-Kretschmer, *Die Safwa*, I, 145 ff.

117. J. H. Driberg, *The Lango, a Nilotic Tribe of Uganda* (1923), pp. 225 ff.

118. *Ibid.*, p. 230.

119. Rasmussen, *Intellectual Culture of the Iglulik Eskimos*, p. 56.

120. Tylor, I; 467 ff.

121. Frazer, *The Golden Bough*, Part II, pp. 190 ff.; Part V, Vol. II, pp. 204 ff.

122. Lévy-Bruhl, *Primitives and the Supernatural*, pp. 99 ff.

123. James Mooney, "Myths of the Cherokee," *19th Annual Report of the Bureau of American Ethnology* (1900), pp. 250 f.

124. Tylor, I, 468.

125. H. Vedder, *Die Bergdama* (Hamburgische Universitaet, "Abhandlungen aus dem Gebiet der Auslandskunde," Band XI, I. Teil [1923]), p. 121: "Killing a lion is indeed a happy and brave deed on the part of a man whose spear is his most effective weapon. But with the joy of victory a fear of vengeance for the 'murder' is connected. Therefore one inflicts some cuts on the upper arm of the hero; thereupon he drips some of the lion's heart blood into the wound. Thus the threatening misfortune is averted."

126. Lévy-Bruhl, p. 288.

127. L. W. Benedict, "A Study of Bagobo Ceremonial, Magic and Myth," *Annals of the New York Academy of Sciences*, XXV (1916), 238 f. M. A. Castren, *Reisen im Norden* (German translation by H. Helms, 1853), pp. 76 f., found on an expedition through Lapland that the natives of Sodankyla believed that snakes live in a society and meet each year for a court session. "The snake-chieftain does not only give judgment over snakes but his power goes even beyond the snake-society. Among other things, he inflicts punishments on men as well as upon others who have killed or injured any of his subjects." Frazer, *The Golden Bough*, Part V, Vol. II, p. 208, remarks: "Hence on the principles of his rude philosophy the primitive hunter who slays an animal believes himself exposed to the vengeance either of its disembodied spirit or of all the other animals of the same species, whom he considers as knit together, like men, by the ties of kin and the obligations of the blood feud, and therefore as bound to resent the injury done to one of their number."

128. F. W. Bain, *A Digit of the Moon and Other Love Stories from the Hindoo: Translated from the Original Manuscripts* (1910), pp. 104–8.

129. Im Thurn, p. 352.

130. Heckewelder, p. 245.

131. William Mariner, *An Account of the Natives of the Tonga Islands, in the South Pacific Ocean*, compiled and arranged by John Martin (1818), II, 221.

132. Charles Hose and W. McDougall, "The Relations between Men and Animals in Sarawak," *Journal of the Anthropological Institute of Great Britain and Ireland*, XXXI (1901), 186.

133. *Ibid.*, p. 190.

134. J. Perham, "Sea Dyak Religion," *Journal of the Straits Branch of the Royal Asiatic Society* (Singapore), No. 10 (1883), p. 221.

135. Frazer, p. 214.

136. *Ibid*

137. Edwin Sidney Hartland, *Primitive Paternity* (1909–10), I, 182.

138. Frazer, p. 216.

139. John Macrae, "Account of the Kookies or Lunctas," *Asiatic Researches*, VII (1801), 183, 189.

140. Gusidne, *Die Feuerland Indianer*, Band I: *Die Selknam*, p. 706. When a Selknam

Indian skins a fox, he carries on "a peculiar discussion with the animal. With soothing words, he tries to placate the whole community of foxes; thus he may hope to kill another one later" (p. 707).

141. Leo Sternberg, "Die Religion der Giljaken," *Archiv fuer Religionswissenschaften,* VIII (1905), 249, 260, 272. Of the South American Indians, Karsten, *The Civilization of the South American Indians,* p. 65, writes: "It is a common Indian idea that the souls of the dead preferably incarnate themselves in certain big animals and birds that normally are most used for food." Verne F. Ray, *The Sanpoil and Nespelem* ("University of Washington Publications in Anthropology," Vol. V [1932]), p. 188, says: "There was no tabu against killing one's guardian animal. On the contrary, the animal expected to be killed. A man with deer power was always a good hunter for the deer would consider it to him to be killed.

142. Emile Petitot, *Autour du grand lac des esclaves* (2d ed., 1891), p. 32.

143. F. Boas, "The Eskimo of Baffin Land and Hudson Bay," *Bulletin of the American Museum of Natural History,* XV (1907), 119 ff.

144. *Ibid.,* p. 120.

145. *Ibid.,* p. 121.

146. *Ibid.,* p. 138. Weyer, *The Eskimos,* p. 333, writes with reference to the belief of the Eskimo, that the animals have souls: "The returning souls are able to keep the other world of animals well apprised of the conduct of men on earth. As a consequence the people are constantly striving to avoid antagonizing the source of the food supply. The Eskimo . . . . does not consider that the supply of game in nature is diminished even by unrestricted slaughter. Religious rules rather than economic laws govern him in this respect. The spirits of the animals cannot be destroyed simply by killing the animals; their earthly forms represent only a transitory phase of the creatures. But failure to observe traditional rites will certainly occasion dearth of game. A slain animal must be properly treated, lest his soul return to the other world bearing a grudge." And p. 334: "The Eskimo feels it always incumbent upon him to ingratiate himself with the souls of the animals and to avoid their retaliation."

147. J. G. Frazer, *Psyche's Task* (1913), p. 45.

148. Fridtjof Nansen, *The First Crossing of Greenland* (1890), II, 329.

149. Frazer, *The Golden Bough,* Part I, Vol. I, p. 123.

150. *Ibid.,* Part II, p. 196.

151. Since the substantializing tendency does not admit a clear distinction between moral and physical-psychic qualities, the idea of retribution, which was originally in the foreground, recedes or even completely disappears from the consciousness of primitive man. Then certain procedures, particularly the tapping of blood, if carried out before such important undertakings as war and hunting expeditions, seem to have a purely hygienic character. This is how Karsten, *The Civilization of the South American Indians,* pp. 156 ff., interprets certain customs of South American Indians: "Quite commonly spread all over South America is the custom of drawing blood from the body in order to get relief in sickness, or, as it is often stated, to enhance the muscular strength of certain limbs, for instance, of the arms and the legs. That blood-letting, practiced in cases of disease, is due to magical ideas may already be inferred from the fact that, according to the Indian belief, all illnesses are directly caused by evil spirits. The spirits . . . . are supposed to enter into the system, and especially to mix in the blood, thus giving rise to ailments of different kinds and to a state of weakness in the particular part of the organism to which they have attached themselves. The Indian thinks that by bleeding that part he will rid himself of the dangerous intruder—just as sometimes he thinks it will leave his body with mere perspiration—and this belief is naturally supported by the fact that in certain cases such purgations really may give some relief. The prevalence of this idea I was myself able to observe among the Chaco tribes. Among these Indians—for instance, among the Chorotis—it is a common thing that the men bleed themselves with a thorn or a sharp splinter of wood before certain important

undertakings. Thus, they say that, by drawing blood from the arm, the limb will get more strength for pulling the bow; the practice is therefore especially resorted to before going out on a hunting expedition. If the arm fails or trembles in pulling the bow, its weakness is, according to the belief of the Chorotis, due to the presence of a *mohsek* in the blood, and they think that the evil demon will leave the body with the blood drawn." Indeed, no connection with the principle of retribution seems to exist here. But it is questionable whether such a connection would not become apparent upon closer investigation of the facts.

Among the western Equatorial pygmies, if their hunting is unsuccessful, the hunter inflicts cuts on his arms and legs, collects the blood in a cockleshell, and stains his spear and body with it. If the unsuccessfulness continues for a time, especially if the hunter keeps missing an elephant, the chieftain inflicts the cuts on the hunter, sprinkles the blood toward the four quarters of the world, and stains the hunter's spear and body. If his inability to kill an elephant is still prolonged, the hunter speaks certain words which indicate that he has made sacrifices to the animal. In other cases, he sacrifices to the "guardian spirits of the race, the clan, and the chieftain himself, i.e., the different totems" (W. Schmidt, *Der Ursprung der Gottesidee*, IV, 77). This shows clearly that the tapping of blood has, in connection with hunting, the character of expiation, especially if one keeps in mind that the blood-sacrifice takes place only when an animal offering has been without success.

152. Frazer, *The Golden Bough*, Part V, Vol. II, p. 224.

153. *Ibid.*, p. 204.

154. That totemism is connected with the peculiar idea primitive man has of conception has already been recognized by Frazer. But, according to his theory, the souls of animals, plants, and other things, the "spirits" which penetrate the body of the woman in order to be reborn by her, are not human souls. The decisive step toward the understanding of totemism is taken by Karsten, *The Origins of Religion*, p. 153, when he puts the question: "What induces these spirits to penetrate the body of a human female to be reborn as human beings?" The answer is that these spirits are human souls which had accepted the shape of animals and plants. Karsten explains this by stressing the fact that, according to the primitive view, the death soul usually assumes the shape of animals and plants. Combining this fact with primitive man's notion of conception, with his ignorance of physiological fatherhood, Karsten offers the most plausible theory of totemism which has hitherto been submitted. In his book *The Civilization of the South American Indians*, p. 435, Karsten writes: "If savages really believe that the soul, after it has left one human body in death, and before it has again taken its abode in another through a new birth, has in the meantime passed through some other form of existence, being reincarnated for instance as an animal or a plant, it is not difficult to understand why certain groups of people should reckon kinship with such natural objects. . . . . Totemism, in other words, can only arise where the doctrine of the transmigration of souls is brought into a regular system, a definite relationship being established between a whole group of kindred people and a particular species of animal or plant. The whole system, moreover, seems to be founded on that primitive theory of conception which has been discussed in the present chapter."

That the life soul which functions as a guardian spirit and also appears outside its protégé in the shape of animals or plants is a totem is presumed by Ziegler, *Ueberlieferung*, p. 157: "The totem is the external abode of life and soul of primitive man." If the totem is also recognized as the external soul of man, then it is correct to assume that the life soul existing within the body of the man is the death soul of an ancestor.

155. Theodor Koch-Grünberg, "Zum Animismus der suedamerikanischen Indianer," *Internationales Archiv fuer Ethnographie*, Suppl., XIII (1900), 14. Cf. also Karl von den Steinen, *Unter den Naturvoelkern Zentral-Brasiliens* (1894), p. 511.

156. Boas, "The Eskimo of Baffin-Land and Hudson Bay," p. 132. Rasmussen, *Intellectual Culture of the Iglulik Eskimos*, p. 107, reports an Eskimo story according to which a man was reborn in the shape of a bear in order to take revenge on his enemy.

326 SOCIETY AND NATURE

157. R. P. Trilles, *Les Pygmées de la Forêt équatoriale* ("Bibliothèque Anthropos," Vol. III [1932]), p. 460. Cf. also W. Schmidt, IV, 89.

158. Trilles, p. 430. In this connection the following custom, described by Trilles, pp. 493 ff., is of interest; its purpose is to assure the victory in an expected fight. After having been prepared by fasting, the chieftain in his dreams sees an elephant—not an ordinary one, but that elephant in which the soul of a deceased chieftain is incarnated. This elephant is sought and, if found, killed; it is recognized by the characteristics which the chieftain saw in his dream. In the ensuing song, the men address the animal as "father" or "ancestor of the clan," etc. All the warriors dip their arms into the animal's blood. But no expiation ceremony takes place. Trilles explains this by remarking that the elephant "cannot take revenge on his killers since he exposed himself to their shots and by the effusion of blood renewed the spirit of the race."

159. Ch. Keysser, "Aus dem Leben der Kai-Leute," in R. Neuhauss, *Deutsch Neu-Guinea*, III, 150 ff. Cf. also Frazer, p. 296.

160. J. Owen Dorsey, "Teton Folklore Notes," *Journal of American Folklore*, II (1889), 134.

161. H. Berkusky, "Totengeister und Ahnenkultus in Indonesien," *Archiv fuer Religionswissenschaft*, XVIII (1915), 306.

162. Warneck, *Die Religion der Batak*, p. 11.

163. Berkusky, pp. 308 f.

164. *Ibid.*, p. 309.

165. Kruijt, *Het Animisme in den Indischen Archipel*, p. 170.

166. *Ibid.*, pp. 189 ff.

167. Frazer, p. 285.

168. *Ibid.*, pp. 291 f.

169. Guenther Tessmann, "Religionsformen der Pangwe," *Zeitschrift fuer Ethnologie*, XLI (1909), 880.

170. Karsten, *The Civilization of the South American Indians*, p. 278.

171. *Ibid.*, p. 280.

172. *Ibid.*, pp. 276, 294.

173. Karsten remarks, a little more carefully (p. 294): "According to Indian theory all animals—quadrupeds, birds, reptiles, fishes, insects—possess a spirit or soul, which in essence is of the same kind as that animating man, and which survives the destruction of the body. All animals have once been men, or all men animals. This seems to be a tenet explicitly or implicitly held by all tribes. Hence the primitive view which the Indians share with most other uncivilized peoples, and which intellectually and morally places the animals on a footing of equality with man. In the practical religion or superstition of the Indians, however, only such animals play a part which, for special reasons—above all, on account of the harm that they do to man—have particularly attracted their attention. Such animals are either, in general, looked upon as the permanent or temporary reincarnations of certain human souls; or they are believed incidentally to carry the magical arrow of the sorcerers, and thus to serve as their agents in working evil. Since the magical 'arrow' is regarded as a vehicle for the sorcerer's own soul, it follows that there is no essential difference between these two sets of ideas." Karsten does not go so far as to conclude from the belief in reincarnation that the soul of the animal is identified with the death soul of the human being reincarnated in it. But in his work *The Origins of Religion*, p. 90, he says that "the soul, worshipped in animals, proves to be a human soul which in one way or another has taken up its abode in the animal in question."

174. Nieuwenhuis, *Quer durch Borneo*, I, 107.

175. Lévy-Bruhl, *Primitives and the Supernatural*, pp. 103 f.

176. Bruno Gutmann, "Die Imkerei bei den Dschagga," *Archiv fuer Anthropologie*, N.F., XIX (1922), 8 ff.

177. *Ibid.*, pp. 10 f.

178. *Ibid.*, pp. 11 f.

179. *Ibid.*, pp. 14 f.

180. *Ibid.*, p. 16.

181. *Ibid.*, pp. 20 ff.

182. R. S. Rattray, *Religion and Art in Ashanti* (1927), p. 6. For analogous customs among the Kukuyu see: C. W. Hobley, *Bantu Beliefs and Magic* (1922), pp. 31 f.; among the Baganda (Uganda): John Roscoe, *The Baganda*, p. 317.

183. Grandidier, *Ethnographie de Madagascar*, III, 308.

184. Berkusky, p. 325.

185. *Ibid.*

186. Wilhelm Mannhardt, *Wald- und Feldkulte* (2d ed., 1904), I, 10, 35.

187. Brinton, *Religions of Primitive Peoples*, p. 150.

188. Karsten, *The Civilization of the South American Indians*, pp. 304, 307.

189. Karsten, *The Origins of Religion*, p. 98.

190. *Ibid.*, p. 97.

191. Walter William Skeat and Charles Otto Blagden, *Pagan Races in the Malay Peninsula* (1906), II, 5 f.

192. The life- or birth-tree is one of the forms in which appears the widespread belief that the life soul of man, as his guardian spirit, exists outside the protected individual.

193. John Macrae, p. 189.

194. J. Spieth, *Die Religion der Eweer in Sued-Togo* ("Quellen der Religions-Geschichte," herausgegeben im Auftrag der Religionsgeschichtlichen Kommission bei der Koenigl. Gesellschaft der Wissenschaften zu Goettingen [1911]), p. 238.

195. Rasmussen, pp. 62 f.

196. The idea that illness and death are the consequences of wrong is, of course, favored by the influence of medicine men and priests. But it is hardly probable that this interpretation goes, as Radin (*Primitive Religion*, p. 71) asserts, exclusively back to the function of the "religious interpreter."

197. Best, *The Maori*, II, 32. The same author, I, 231, writes: "Whenever the Maori suffers from such visitations as an epidemic, or a failure of crops, he looks to himself for the cause thereof. He must have committed the offence for which he is being punished. It is impossible to shake their faith in this view." To this he adds: ". . . . and indeed we ourselves have retained similar beliefs; our Church teachings for centuries have been deeply affected by such superstitions."

198. Von den Steinen, p. 332.

199. Cf. above, p. 90.

200. Cf. Ph. von Martius, *Beitraege zur Ethnographie und Sprachenkunde Amerikas, zumal Brasiliens* (1867), I, 651.

201. William Curtis Farabee, *The Central Arawaks* (University of Pennsylvania, "The University Museum Anthropological Publications," Vol. IX [1918]), p. 87.

202. *Ibid.*, p. 100.

203. Koch-Gruenberg, p. 39. Grubb, *An Unknown People in an Unknown Land*, p. 161, reports of the Lenguan Indians: "Anything, therefore, in the nature of sickness or death occurring in his own district is held to be either the direct act of the *kilyikhama* [death demon] or of some unfriendly wizard from a distance." For the fact that the very primitive Fuegian Indians regard illness and death as punishment inflicted by a superhuman authority, cf. W. Schmidt, *Der Ursprung der Gottesidee*, II, 970.

204. Koch-Gruenberg, pp. 45 ff. An analogous phenomenon is the already mentioned fact that some primitive people do not help those who have met with an accident because they interpret accidents as punishments for committed wrongs. See above, p. 70. Evidence for the fact that sick people are badly treated because illness is considered to be pun-

ishment for the violation of a taboo can be found in William Ellis, *Polynesian Researches* (1831), I, 395; III, 46–48.

205. Gustaf Bolinder, *Die Indianer der tropischen Schneegebirge* (1925), p. 137.

206. Karsten, p. 241.

207. *Ibid.*, p. 242. On the importance of confession, cf. Karsten, pp. 246 ff., and above, pp. 15, 87, 99, 101, 108.

208. Cf. Steinmetz, *Ethnologische Studien zur ersten Entwicklung der Strafe*, I, 358 f.; K. Th. Preuss, "Menschenopfer und Selbstverstuemmelung bei der Totentrauer in Amerika," in *Festschrift fuer Adolf Bastian zu seinem 70. Geburtstag* (1896), p. 208; W. Schmidt, II, 794.

209. Philander Prescott, "Contributions to the History, Customs, and Opinions of the Dacota Tribe," in Henry R. Schoolcraft, *Informations respecting the History, Conditions, and Prospects of the Indian Tribes of the United States* (1852), Part II, p. 195.

210. B. W. Aginsky, "The Socio-psychological Significance of Death among the Pomo Indians," *American Imago*, Vol. I, No. 3, p. 1.

211. *Ibid.*, p. 2.

212. *Ibid.*, p. 8.

213. *Ibid.*, p. 3.

214. Krause, p. 300.

215. Wrangell, "Statistische und ethnographische Nachrichten ueber die russischen Besitzungen an der Nordwestkueste von Amerika," in Baer und Helmersen, *Beitraege zur Kenntnis des russischen Reiches* (1839), I, 104.

216. Frazer, *The Golden Bough*, Part II, p. 212.

217. Rasmussen, pp. 133 ff. Best, II, 40, 45, reports of the Maori that illnesses, since they are regarded as punishment or as crimes caused by magic, are healed by a *tohunga* (priest), who tries to find out the cause of the illness, i.e., the violation of the taboo or the magician. Consequently here, too, confession is regarded as remedy.

218. With this method of healing by the Eskimo medicine man, one may compare the incantation addressed by a Babylonian priest, on behalf of a sick person, to the deity who apparently sent the illness as punishment for a delict. Cf. Arthur Ungnad, *Die Religion der Babylonier und Assyrier* ("Religiöse Stimmen der Völker," herausgegeben von Walter Otto) (1921), p. 259. The priest enumerates various sins and asks the deity whether the ill man has committed any of them. "Did he insult his God? . . . . did he induce a judge to accept a bribe? . . . . was it an assault on his parents? . . . . did he draw a wrong borderline? . . . . etc." After this enumeration, the priest asks: "May he be redeemed from whatever has him in bonds?" This request for redemption, i.e., for extermination of the wrong, is varied; but the sense is essentially that through the abolition of the wrong, the condition for the punishment falls away and thus the end of the illness is brought about. It is significant that in another song, the sin is compared with a cord binding the culprit. The priest sings: "May the gods tear up the cord, break the ribbon, and destroy the knot of evil. . . . . May the sick live, may the seduced rise again. . . . . May his crime be pardoned and the register of his sins, crimes, and curses be thrown into the water. His sins may be redeemed, his crimes removed, his loans solved, his pains healed."

219. W. Schmidt, III, 546.

220. Koty, *Die Behandlung der Alten und Kranken bei den Naturvoelkern*, p. 328.

221. Death by violence, as already mentioned, is a social event which does not necessitate the assumption of an act by a superhuman authority. But because of his weak ego-consciousness, primitive man sometimes even ascribes results caused by himself to some "spirit" and thus believes in magic, when the evil effect is caused by some hostile party; it may happen that even death in battle, as, for instance, among the Abipones, is traced to sorcery. Cf. K. Th. Preuss, *Tod und Unsterblichkeit im Glauben der Naturvoelker* ("Sammlung gemeinverstaendlicher Vortraege," No. 146 [1930]), p. 4.

222. Kruijt, p. 256.

223. *Ibid.*, p. 366.

224. Mosbacher, p. 10. Much material can be found here for the primitive idea that illness and death are punishment for sins.

225. Warneck, *Die Religion der Batak*, p. 14.

226. *Ibid.*, pp. 12, 16.

227. *Ibid.*, pp. 13, 20.

228. Warneck, p. 7, states: "The Batak are not afraid of deceiving their gods; for instance, they sacrifice an egg and declare it to be a white buffalo. . . . . P. 20: When harvesting, they deceive them [the *begu*] by not expressing any signs of joy in order that the *begu* believe that it was a bad harvest. . . . . They offer a hen's egg and call it a pig." But: "Towards living men, however, politeness demands the opposite. When they kill a pig for a guest, they call it chicken."

229. *Annales de la propagation de la foi*, XIV (1842), 192 (P. Joseph Chevron).

230. Richard Parkinson, *Dreissig Jahre in der Suedsee* (1907), p. 189, reports: "In order to afford a woman relief when she is in labor, a man who has pity on her feigns illness, goes to the club-house, and writhes whenever he hears a cry of the laboring woman. The men come along and act as if they wanted to ease his supposed pains." Obviously, the attempt is to free the woman from pain by presenting another victim in her place. One is inclined to assume this idea of substitution, widespread among primitive peoples, also in the custom of the "Couvade."

Among the Australian Dieyerie, if a child has an accident, its relatives hit their heads with sticks and boomerangs until blood flows over their faces. Through this procedure they hope to liberate the child from its pains (S. Gason, "The Dieyerie Tribe of Australian Aborigines," in E. M. Curr, *The Australian Race* [1886–87], II, 69). It would be difficult to understand this custom, did one not keep in mind that accident and illness are widely regarded among primitive peoples as punishment inflicted by a superhuman authority. It is a substitute punishment which the relatives of the child execute upon themselves in order to make superfluous that punishment which appears in the pains of the child. In other cases similar self-tormentings and self-mutilations signify the attempt to prevent a more difficult punishment which one fears will be inflicted by the superhuman authority. Richard Andree, *Ethnographische Parallelen und Vergleiche* (1878), p. 149, explains as substitute sacrifice the action of a mother who, after having lost a child, cuts off a finger from her second child. For these substitute sacrifices, cf. Tylor, II, 400. In the case of the sacrificed finger, the substitute sacrifice has the character of substitute retribution.

The same is true for the method of healing through transfer of the illness. Andree, p. 30, mentions the following cases: "In the Bohemian Forest district, wherever someone has a fever, he goes to the forest before the sun rises, seeks a snipe-nest, takes a young snipe out, and keeps it with him for three days. After that time, he releases the snipe in the forest. Immediately he loses the fever. In Bonny, at the mouth of the Niger, a sick man attaches a living chicken to his breast over the heart; if it cries and flaps its wings, then this is considered a favorable symptom because it means that the bird has attracted the essence of the illness and thus suffers pains. The English peasant performs a similar procedure. He sews a living beetle in a linen bag and fastens it on a child suffering from whooping-cough in order that the insect attract the illness. In Voigtland, people keep cross-bills (parrot-finches) because they attract sickness. In various countries flowers from the sick-room are presented with the vile intention that the receiver will take over the illness." The idea of the transfer of illness becomes possible through the often-mentioned substantializing tendency of primitive man. But this idea is only a technical supposition. Kaplan (*Das Problem der Magie und die Psychoanalyse*) is, therefore, right when he says (p. 41): "The pathogene substance (the 'illness'), inherent in an individual, must make someone else ill; only then can the former become healthy again. This is the idea of substitution. By (direct or indirect) contagion with the sick man the other becomes identical with him and thereby

M.

replaces him. This is the true meaning of the emanation of illness." Certainly, the idea of emanation as such does not suffice to explain the mentioned events, for the mere transfer of the substance would entail the illness of both parties. The decisive thing is that the infected man replaces the man who was originally ill. This idea presupposes that illness is regarded as punishment for a wrong. Kaplan misses the decisive point. He believes that the idea of emanation is "only another expression for the idea of magic." But there is no reason to speak of magic here. The idea that qualities, forces, and conditions are substances is not "magical" at all. The assumption of a "magical" connection would be justified only in so far as primitive man's interpretation of the illness as punishment involves the relation to a superhuman authority. That the transfer of illness to someone else is not comprehended as mere substantial "contagion" but is essentially connected with the idea of retribution is borne out by the example of the man on Tahiti who was ill with leprosy. Cf. n. 246.

231. J. Mallat, *Les Philippines* (1846), II, 94.

232. William Allan Reed, *Negritos of Zambales* (1904), p. 65.

233. Robert Percival, *An Account of the Island of Ceylon* (1803), p. 195.

234. Kubary, "Die Religion der Pelauer," p. 43.

235. Codrington, p. 142.

236. William W. Gill, *Life in the Southern Isles* (n.d.), p. 183.

237. William Ellis, *Polynesian Researches*, I, 395.

238. Malinowski, *Crime and Custom in Savage Society*, pp. 87 ff., 91.

239. Fortune, *Manus Religion*, p. 8.

240. Turner, p. 272.

241. P. Josef Meier, *Mythen und Erzählungen der Küstenbewohner der Gazelle-Halbinsel (Neupommern)* ("Anthropos-Bibliothek," Band I, Heft 1 [1909]), pp. 133 ff.

242. Frazer, *The Belief in Immortality*, II, 229.

243. *Ibid.*, p. 299.

244. *Ibid.*, p. 417.

245. William Wilson, *A Missionary Voyage to the Southern Pacific Ocean* (1799), p. 278.

246. Monsord Reklaw, "Afaiau the Hermit," *Bulletin de la Société des Etudes océaniennes*, 1924, No. 9, pp. 34–35, according to Lévy-Bruhl, *Primitives and the Supernatural*, pp. 80 ff.

247. Elsdon Best, *Maori Religion and Mythology* (New Zealand Dominion Museum Bull. 10 [1924]), pp. 183, 236.

248. Van Gennep, *Mythes et légendes d'Australie*, p. li.

249. George Grey, *Journals of Two Expeditions of Discovery in North West and Western Australia*, II, 238.

250. Robert B. Smyth, *The Aborigines of Victoria* (1878), I, 444–45.

251. Strehlow, *Die Aranda- und Loritja-Staemme in Zentralaustralien*, IV/2, 20. Strehlow believes that the expedition of vengeance does not take place in order to achieve the punishment of the alleged murderer. Rather, the participants have only the desire "to soothe their grief over the death of their fellow-man in the blood of an individual of another group and to give the members of the latter cause for similar mourning." If this were true, it would be a case of absolute liability, where the sphere of those who are liable coincides with "foreigners" or "enemies." Other passages in Strehlow's work, however, admit of some doubt as to the correctness of this interpretation. First of all, the vengeance expedition seems to be desired by the dead himself. Clear symptoms of the retributory function of the death soul are shown in the customs of the natives, who obviously fear the death soul. The relatives inflict bloody wounds upon themselves, the hut of the deceased is burned down, etc. (pp. 15 ff.). Of the Loritja inhabiting the northwestern section of Australia, the following custom is reported (pp. 25 ff.). The dying man is left alone, no mourning is observed, and the corpse is not buried. As the reason for this behavior, it is stated that an unburied corpse in a state of putrefaction brings rain. But the real motive seems to be: "Since the closest relatives of the deceased were not witnesses of the death, no expedition need be sent

out to avenge his death." Presumably then, the dying man is left alone in order to avoid the
risky vengeance expedition. The idea that a putrefying corpse brings rain is a notion which
only partly excuses the behavior of the survivors. The procedure clearly shows that the dead
himself wishes to be avenged; probably, he desires the death of his murderer. Among certain tribes living north and west of the Loritja a procedure to establish the identity of the
presumed murderer is customary, and in this rite the dead man plays an essential part.
But it is to be especially observed that the Aranda, following the vengeance expedition,
carry out purification ceremonies in order not "to be killed by the friends of the killed"
(p. 23). If they assume that the death soul of the killed enemy wants to take revenge on its
murderers, then how much more reason have they to believe it of the death souls of their
own relatives. But perhaps the duty to direct vengeance against a certain group is too
troublesome. Vengeance is executed with a minimum of risk. Strehlow's report probably
represents a point of view of the Aranda which is due to a decrease of the original idea of
retribution.

252. Curr, *The Australian Race*, I, 54.
253. Baldwin Spencer and F. J. Gillen, *The Northern Tribes of Central Australia* (1904),
p. 519.
254. Le Roy, pp. 147 f.
255. *Ibid.*, p. 167.
256. Edwin W. Smith, *The Religion of Lower Races, as Illustrated by the African Bantu* (1923),
pp. 38–40.
257. E. Gottschling, "The Bavenda: A Sketch of Their History and Customs," *Journal
of the Anthropological Institute of Great Britain and Ireland*, XXXV (1905), 378.
258. Kidd, pp. 133 f., 137 ff.
259. *Ibid.*, pp. 133, 137. Chaka lived at the end of the eighteenth century.
260. Cayzac, "La Religion des Kikuyu (Afrique orientale)," pp. 310 f.
261. Baumann, *Schoepfung und Urzeit des Menschen im Mythus der afrikanischen Voelker*,
p. 296.
262. T. Winterbottom, *An Account of the Native Africans in the Neighbourhood of Sierra Leone*
(1803), I, 235 f.
263. Pechuel-Loesche, *Die Loango-Expedition*, dritte Abtheilung, Zweite Haelfte, p. 334.
264. *Ibid.*, pp. 336 ff. The author asserts, p. 338, that magic is not performed with the
aid of souls or spirits. "Witches . . . . either harm by their very nature and consequently
without knowledge and intent or else they practice witchcraft intentionally. But never do
they perform it with the help of souls or spirits, merely with substances whose harmful effect
they know, particularly poisons. . . . . Carefully prepared, these poisons even produce an
effect upon far-away objects. They destroy both body and soul." But the example given in
the text contradicts this assertion. The authority from which proceeds the punishment for
the *Tschina* violation can be imagined only as a personal being. For the primitive man who
believes this presupposes that the punishment emanates from a being who perceives the
violation of a norm and reacts against the perpetrator.

On p. 336 Pechuel-Loesche says of the *Ndodschi*, who are the worst of all witches and who
inflict all kinds of evil upon men: "One accuses less the bad man than the evil in him which
continually works itself out without his interference." Pechuel-Loesche himself calls this
"evil in man" a "horrible being" which works methodically out of the individual possessed
of it as if it were endowed with a reason and a will of its own. Thus it must be a personal
being. It is apparently only a terminological peculiarity which prevents Pechuel-Loesche
from speaking of a bad spirit.

Another example cited by the same author as evidence for the activity of sorcerers is:
"They carve . . . . a rough image which is supposed to represent a person . . . . and
throw it, with familiar curses, into the river . . . . or hold it near the fire. . . . . Just as
the image rots, disintegrates, gets charred, or withers, so the person pines away and

dies irretrievably." This is a typical case of an expression of desire by sign-language, a procedure which has the character of an action intended to be perceived by the authority to whom it is directed and who is supposed to comprehend the significance of the procedure and fulfil the desire expressed therein. As usual, the "magical" procedure is accompanied by incantations; this means that the wish is also expressed in ordinary language. The use of incantations would be senseless were they not, like prayers, directed to a superhuman being who is supposed both to understand the expressions and to fulfil them. According to Pechuel-Loesche's own account, the natives of the Loango coast believe themselves constantly surrounded by death souls and spirits. Thus they probably believe, even though they do not expressly say so, that these beings hear and understand the sign-language of their magical procedures and incantations.

In another example, Pechuel-Loesche points out (p. 339) that certain objects are discarded as if they were lost, objects which he says are "charged with disaster." Susceptible persons "catch" this evil if they graze these objects with their shadows or look at them or touch them. But if the magical substance, the "poison," is, as in an earlier mentioned example, dangerous only to that person whom the magician wishes to harm, then those who believe in this magic must suppose that the magical substance has itself powers of perception and of deliberate action. Either they attribute to the substance qualities which only personal beings can have or they assume that a personal being exists within the substance or they believe that the substance is handled by such an invisible being, a "spirit," bringing about the desired harm. It is immaterial whether the natives are fully conscious of these suppositions; they continue to use magical substances as if personal beings, invisible but powerful, and endowed with reason and will, would be effective in them or through them. Pechuel-Loesche believes (p. 347) that primitive man's magic consists in the fact "that objects have qualities which render visible things invisible because of forces inhabiting these substances." But these ideas are also possible within the sphere of a scientific view of the world, for the basic concept is that of an objective and impersonal force. It is highly improbable that primitive man should operate under such a concept. If Pechuel-Loesche intends to explain magic, especially the fetishism of the natives of Loango, by the belief of these primitives in forces inherent in the objects, he forgets that, in so doing, he has ascribed to primitive man an attitude which is not much different from scientifically rational methods. Yet only such differences justify the concepts of magic and fetishism.

As far as the particular fetishism of the Loango is concerned, Pechuel-Loesche stresses, p. 356: "Nothing in all their doings points to spirits who may have selected a magical object as an abode or were ordered to do so, and who obeyed men now." He expressly rejects the animistic theory as an explanation of fetishism. But the manner in which the natives, according to Pechuel-Loesche's own account, behave toward their fetishes shows clearly that they treat them as personal beings, endowed with reason and will, to whom they ascribe, for some reason, superhuman powers. This is especially true of the so-called "justice-fetishes," which, it is believed, are able to discover the culprit and therefore inspire with fear the individuals conscious of guilt. On p. 377 Pechuel-Loesche writes: "They serve to prevent as well as discover and punish crimes the authors of which could not be detected by man's own ingenuity. As protectors of public security, morality and the social order, as avengers of crimes, they are, so to speak, automatic prosecutors, police authorities, and executioners all in one, who begin to work as soon as payment and encouragement arouse them." On p. 359 he declares that "the natives have [in relation to the fetishes] the same feeling as we have when confronted by an electrical apparatus, the fear of receiving a shock. The fetishes, however, are not regarded as gods and these people do not imagine a spirit in them just as even timorous civilized people do not imagine a spirit in the Leyden jar." But the Leyden jar is no fetish for us because we know that everyone who touches it will receive an electric shock and because we do not believe that the Leyden jar knows who has committed theft and consequently shocks only the thief. When questioned, the natives may deny that a "spirit" lives in the fetish, but their actual attitude shows that they assume a kind of superhuman knowledge and will in the fetish which acts in such a way that the evil-doer cannot escape punishment. Therefore, Pechuel-Loesche is wrong when he considers (p. 360) as unimportant the human shape which the natives give to their fetishes. It corresponds essentially to their behavior in spreading cola nuts over their fetishes, for eating such nuts "greatly increases man's pleasure, force, and endurance."

Certain fetishes, as Pechuel-Loesche points out, serve the community "as medicine-men or as discoverers and avengers of crimes." How could this be possible unless the fetishes have the same moral and intellectual qualities which one attributes to those deities who exercise retribution? "In truth, all fetishes have the function of supplementing the activity of *Nsambi* which seems insufficient to the individual as far as his private affairs are concerned and to the community as far as public security is concerned." If the fetishes "supplement" the activities of *Nsambi*, who is a deity and as such undoubtedly a personal spiritual being, if they exercise the same functions as the latter, then how could the "force" in the fetish have other than a personal character?

In addition to justice-fetishes, there are also oracle-fetishes. The behavior toward such an oracle-fetish is described by Pechuel-Loesche as follows (p. 380): "Those who seek information from it have to approach sober, in new clothes, with their arms held out horizontally and their fingers spread out. They must also cower down and they can only hope for favorable attention from the fetish if they have kept away from their wives and from gin for three days. To the proper visitors, it manifests its opinion through its *Nganga* [fetish priest]." Such behavior in no way deviates from the behavior toward a deity. A fetish which perceives whether the human beings who approach it scrupulously observe all the regulations and which manifests its opinion through its priest is indeed something quite different from a Leyden jar or an "artificial machine," by which phrase Pechuel-Loesche tries to characterize fetishes (p. 390). There are fetishes which hate women (p. 374); others which cannot bear men, women's hair, tobacco smoke, gin, and water (p. 386). One must behave according to their tastes if one needs them. Fetishes can be insulted and may take revenge. A fetish was "grossly insulted" by a girl; it was said that she "intentionally obstructed the way" of a rolling fetish which had a globular form, that she made it run against her back; indeed, she did to it something unbelievable, namely that which necessitates the changing of children's diapers." As a result the fetish reacted with equivalent inconveniences for the community (p. 374). Is that still a Leyden jar? Pechuel-Loesche's interpretation of the fetishism of the Loango is extremely strained. He apparently wishes at all costs to oppose the animistic theory.

265. Guenther Tessmann, *Die Bubi auf Fernando Poo* ("Kulturen der Erde," Vol. XIX [1923]), pp. 107 f.

266. *Ibid.*, pp. 98, 101.

267. Tessmann denies such influences. He mentions in another work a story of the fall of man which he regards as original with the natives, although it reproduces almost the words of Genesis; cf. above, p. 161.

268. Lowie, *Primitive Religion*, p. 33.

269. Mosbacher, p. 35.

270. Vedder, *Die Bergdama*, I, 110 f., 127; II, 5.

271. Richard Lasch, *Der Eid, seine Entstehung und Beziehung zu Glaube und Brauch der Naturvoelker* (1908), p. 95.

272. Godfrey Wilson, "An African Morality," *Africa*, IX (1936), 80.

273. *Ibid.*, p. 98.

274. Meek, *A Sudanese Kingdom*, p. 246.

275. *Ibid.*, pp. 247 f.

276. C. K. Meek, *The Northern Tribes of Nigeria* (1925), p. 109.

277. C. K. Meek, *Law and Authority in a Nigerian Tribe* (1937), p. 290.

278. Rattray, *Religion and Art in Ashanti*, p. 55.

279. Henri Labouret, *Les Tribus du Rameau Lobi* ("Université de Paris, Travaux et mémoires de l'Institut d'Ethnologie," Vol. XV [1931]), p. 304.

280. Smith and Dale, I, 244 f.

281. Tylor, I, 309.

282. L. Frobenius, *Die Weltanschauung der Naturvoelker* (1898), p. 59.

283. Kruijt, p. 482.

284. A. C. Kruijt, "Measa, II," *Bijdragen tot de Taal- Land- en Volkenkunde van Nederlandsch-Indie*, LXXV (1919), 76 f. N. Adriani en Alb. C. Kruijt, *De Bare'e-sprekende Toradja's van Midden-Celebes*, II (1912), 247, quoted by Lévy-Bruhl, *Primitives and the Supernatural*, pp. 202, 203.

285. Kruijt, "Measa, III," *Bijdragen, etc.*, LXXVI (1920), 45. Smith and Dale, I, 360, speak of a case in which a claim was "brought by a man against another whose cock had committed adultery with his hen; he gravely claimed damages amounting to the value of a cow. In the event they were persuaded that the ends of justice would be met by killing and eating the cock."

286. Rasmussen, *Neue Menschen*, p. 36.

287. Cf. above, p. 101, and Krause, p. 231.

288. Castren, *Reisen im Norden*, pp. 232 f.

289. Cf., e.g., Lévy-Bruhl, *Primitive Mentality*, pp. 185 ff., 261 ff.

290. Sometimes the principle of retribution according to which evil is inflicted as the consequence of wrong does not become clearly apparent. Primarily, the reason for this is that the observer is satisfied with establishing the transcendental origin of the evil without investigating why the evil, i.e., illness, death, bad harvest, etc., has been sent by the superhuman authority—above all, by the death soul. This is, however, just the point where primitive people, always reticent in religious matters, do not readily proclaim their true opinion. Since the explorer was unable to learn the true reason why the superhuman authority inflicts misfortune upon men, he acquiesces in the statement that the spirits or death souls are "bad" and hostile to men. Thus F. E. Williams, *Orokaiva Society*, pp. 282 ff., asserts that the natives trace all misfortune, especially relative to agriculture and hunting, to the *sovai*, the death souls; but he does not investigate whether or not the idea of retribution plays any part here. Of the effect of the death souls he writes, p. 284: "Even general calamities may be ascribed to their malignancy: an earthquake, for instance, is caused by *sovai* travelling underground and presages a general sickness. One may quote the particular instance of Unina. This village used to stand on a flat hilltop, but for many years its inhabitants have been watching the ground crumble away till now their very building room is threatened. This unfortunate process they ascribe to the malice or vengeance of the *sovai* with whom they were once unwise enough to do battle in the neighbourhood. The fact that the process of detrition has apparently stopped for the present is said to be due to the intercession of one particular *sovai* who has taken pity on his old village." Since we find in Williams' book many symptoms for the retributory function of the death souls, it is more than probable that in the case in question the natives also interpret the misfortune as the "vengeance" rather than as the "malice" of an annoyed death soul. Williams stresses (pp. 308 f.) both the moral sense and the sense of justice of the natives as well as their strict obedience to the social order. He says of their "standards of morality" that "these standards, although there is no central authority to enforce them, are nevertheless observed with a large measure of fidelity; for the individual is so sunk in the social unit that he obeys its laws for the most part automatically." That the basic principle of this social order is retribution is borne out by Williams' own words, mentioned earlier. Considering the mental attitude of these natives, it seems justifiable to assume that they also interpret the acts of their *sovai* in accordance with the principle of retribution.

291. R. Thurnwald, "Neue Forschungen zum Mana-Begriff," *Archiv fuer Religionswissenschaft*, XXVII, 104.

NOTES

NOTES 335

292. A. R. Brown, *The Andaman Islanders*, pp. 152, 160.

293. Man, "On the Aboriginal Inhabitants of the Andaman Islands," p. 112.

294. R. E. Dennett, *At the Back of the Black Man's Mind* (1906), p. 52.

295. Kidd, p. 116.

296. Karsten, *The Origins of Religion*, p. 36, following Giacomo Bove, *Patagonia, Terra del Fuoco, Mari Australi* (1883), Part I, p. 139.

297. W. Schmidt, *Der Ursprung der Gottesidee*, III, 503.

298. Parkinson, *Dreissig Jahre in der Suedsee*, p. 188.

299. L. Frobenius, *Unter den unstraeflichen Aethiopen* ("Und Afrika sprach," Vol. III [1913]), p. 229.

300. Kidd, p. 118.

301. Eberhard von Sick, "Die Waniaturu (Walimi)," *Baessler Archiv*, V (1915), 55.

302. Lévy-Bruhl, *Primitives and the Supernatural*, p. 245.

303. W. Schmidt, IV, 79.

304. *Ibid.*, p. 314.

305. Paul Schebesta, *Bambuti: Die Zwerge vom Kongo* (1932), p. 222.

306. P. Schebesta, "Religioese Anschauungen der Semang ueber die Orang Kidop (die Unsterblichen)," *Archiv fuer Religionswissenschaft*, XXIV, 216 ff., 224; XXV, 31.

307. Nieuwenhuis, *Quer durch Borneo*, I, 97.

308. Parkinson, p. 187.

309. Karsten, *The Origin of Worship*, p. 19.

310. Vedder, I, 23, 27, 30, 38. In view of the clear retributory function of the divine fire, it is incomprehensible that Vedder (p. 176) says that the religion of the Bergdama "is never the origin of a moral norm." Religion and morality for the Bergdama are "two absolutely separate spheres."

311. Tylor, I, 289.

312. *Ibid.*, p. 290.

313. Dobrizhoffer, *An Account of the Abipones*, II, 85.

314. Mrs. K. Langloh Parker, *The Euahlayi Tribe* (1905), p. 98.

315. Just as A. W. Nieuwenhuis, "Die Sintflutsagen als kausallogische Naturschoepfungsmythen," in *Festschrift fuer P. W. Schmidt* (1928), pp. 515 ff. Nieuwenhuis assumes that primitive man has a strong tendency to explain natural phenomena—a statement which is highly problematical. But, even if one assumes such a tendency, one must not identify it with the tendency to causal thinking, as is done by Nieuwenhuis (p. 526). Primitive man satisfies his tendency to explanation by applying the principle of retribution and not the law of causality.

316. Lévy-Bruhl, *La Mythologie primitive*, p. 179, speaks of "etiological myths." "By referring the beings and actual events to 'precedents,' to models, to archetypes of the supernatural world, the myth does more than merely establish a causal nexus. It supplies an explanation which we would call transcendental or metaphysical"; in other words, it justifies the beings and events. When a myth seeks to justify reality it does not give more than, but something quite different from, a causal explanation. The etiological myth is not the only type which has a justifying function.

317. Cassirer, p. 134, says: "The myth represents a stage of development in which thinking does not adjust itself to the given state of things or customs or regulations, but is satisfied as soon as it succeeds somehow in transforming the present into the past. The past has no 'why'; it is itself the 'why' of all things." But this is so because the past is the lifetime of the ancestors. Cassirer himself says of the ancestor-worship of the Chinese that it expresses a conception of time in which the religious-ethical emphasis is laid neither on the future nor on the present but on the past.

318. Fortune, *Sorcerers of Dobu*, p. 262, says of the native myths of Dobu: "We have already seen that legend validates magic and that the characters of legend are often the spiritual agents which magic operates." Preuss, *Der religioese Gehalt der Mythen*, pp. 34 f.,

points out that among the Taulipang, in order to heal wounds and certain illnesses, to ease the pains of birth, and to protect men against other calamities, they tell a story that "in times of yore, certain animals, plants, and things of nature, which are personified in the tale, helped human beings for the first time." After the story is told, they speak a certain formula which expresses a faith in the benevolence of the superhuman beings who will help them again in the future. Thus for a woman in childbirth they say: "The girl of the Savanne has to call upon me if she suffers in giving birth to her son. I shall help dislodge him. She must call on me. I am the lightning. I am the drizzling rain, I am like water. I, too, am here! etc." It is difficult to understand why Preuss asserts that this formula is not an invocation of the superhuman powers. The fact that in the formula the benevolent deity presents itself as the speaker is not incompatible with the fact that the speaking of the formula implies an invocation of the deity, a request for its help. The formula is a genuine prayer. The personification of animals, plants, and natural objects in the story is also important. Obviously, the "magical" act consists in the request for help from the superhuman person. It is inconceivable how such data could be used as evidence for pre-animistic magic. In his *Lehrbuch der Voelkerkunde*, p. 93, Preuss says that one correctly understands the myth "if one regards its origin as the result of an unconscious cult. Myths did not originate in any rational tendency to explain nature, but in an experience arising from a tremendous impression which produced the idea that the superhuman personalities of primeval times created and maintained nature. Thus the stories of these personalities became the magical means of conserving the present world and its conditions both in nature and in the institutions of human society. Myths were transformed into religious cults and originally could be told only at the annual sacred festivities, the purpose of which was to maintain traditional conditions and customs, particularly those which had been instituted at the beginning of time." In the same volume, however, Thurnwald ("Geistesverfassung der Naturvoelker," p. 50) says: ". . . . many myths and tales promote the tendency to causal thinking, especially explanations relative to the origin of men, the rise of the world." Certainly these myths promote "explanations," but this does not necessitate their promoting "the tendency to causal thinking." Primitive man's tendency to explanation is—and this must be stressed again and again—satisfied by an interpretation according to social categories—above all, by the application of the principle of retribution.

319. Mrs. K. Langloh Parker, *Australian Legendary Tales* (1907), pp. 15 ff.

320. Geo. McCall Theal, *Kaffir Folk-Lore* (2d ed., 1886), pp. 78 ff.; Wundt, II, 123 f.

321. Wundt, II, 127.

322. Cf. also the tale of the Ojibwa Indians reported by W. J. Hoffman, "The Menomini Indians," *14th Annual Report of the Bureau of Ethnology* (1896), pp. 223 ff.

323. Wundt, p. 133. Wundt admits, p. 138, that the motive of vengeance already prevailed "in the earliest tales." He is right when he points out that the motive of reward came into the foreground only later, and then in a negative sense. "The avenging punishment which is inflicted upon the bad man is averted from the good man who shares the same perils. But in some very early tales this sparing of the good man has already been converted into the twofold principle of retribution according to which reward and punishment are justly distributed between good and bad individuals. Here it is often no longer the hero who exercises punishment and reward; a magical being, a demon who both avenges and rewards, looks around among men and according to their deeds grants them happiness or ruin." For tales of happiness where Wundt sees the motive of retribution, cf. pp. 134 ff., particularly the story of the Cowitchin Indians, p. 139.

324. Oscar Daehnhardt, *Natursagen* (1912), IV, 46 ff.

325. Wundt, pp. 272 ff.

326. Hugh Hastings Romilly, *From My Verandah in New Guinea* (1889), pp. 120 ff. Punishment for cannibalism is also apparently the chief motive of a Kaffir story reported by Geo. McCall Theal, *Kaffir Folk-Lore*, pp. 122 ff., which Wundt, II, 177, classifies under the

heading "Benevolent Animals": "Once in a time of famine, a woman left her home and went to live in a distant village, where she became a cannibal. She had one son, named Magoda. She ate all the people in that village except her son. Then she was compelled to hunt animals but she still caught people when she could. . . . . Her brother who had remained at home, had two daughters whom he did not treat very kindly. One day he sent them to the river for water, which they were to carry in two jugs. . . . . One of the girls fell down on a rock and broke the jug she was carrying. . . . . They walked away in the opposite direction from their home. . . . . Then they saw a fire at a distance and went to it where they saw a house. It was the house of their aunt. . . . . They went into her house where they saw a person with only one arm, one side, and one leg. . . . . When she [the cannibal] saw the children, she was very glad. She took them to her house and told them to sleep. . . . . They heard their aunt say: 'Axe, be sharp, axe, be sharp.' . . . . Afterwards when the cannibal fell asleep, they crept out, first putting two blocks of wood in their places, and ran away as fast as they could. When Nomagoda [the cannibal] awoke, she took the axe and went to kill them but the axe fell on the blocks of wood. As soon as it was day, the cannibal pursued the children. . . . . They succeeded in reaching a tall tree which they hastened to climb and hid among the branches. Nomagoda came to the tree and started to cut it down. But as soon as a chip was struck off, a bird (ntengu) sang and the chip sprang back into place. . . . . Nomagoda, who was very angry, caught the bird and swallowed it. When she put it in her mouth, one of the feathers dropped to the ground. Then she began to chop at the tree again but as soon as a chip was loosened, the feather sang. . . . . Then the chip stuck fast again. . . . . But the cannibal chopped until she sank down into the ground at the foot of the tree. The children observed three dogs as big as calves and they knew these dogs belonged to their father who was seeking them. So they called them by name, and the dogs came running to the tree and ate up the cannibal who was too tired to make her escape. Thus the children were saved and their father was so glad to get them back again that he forgave them for breaking the jug and running away." There is no doubt that benevolent animals appear in this tale. But their assistance served the purpose of executing retribution on the evil cannibal. It is interesting to note how the principle of *talio* is carried out. The cannibal herself must be eaten; but, since man-eating is prohibited to men—this is the sense of the story—dogs must be introduced to devour the criminal.

327. Wundt, pp. 248 ff.

328. Boas, *Indianische Sagen von der Nordpazifischen Kueste Amerikas*, pp. 65 ff., 68 ff.

329. Wundt, p. 180.

330. Dorsey, *The Pawnee*, I, 499 (abstract); the full story is on pp. 183 ff.

331. Cf. Daehnhardt, III, 284 ff.

332. Wundt, p. 295.

333. Cf. Wundt, pp. 309, 322 ff., 328 ff. On p. 332, he says: "Thus it is the fight of malice against innocence or boastful arrogance and pageantry against modesty and true efficiency which became the real domain of the theme of the hostile brothers and sisters." What Rasmussen, *Intellectual Culture of the Iglulik Eskimos*, p. 257, says of the stories of the Eskimos is typical: "The folk-tales, therefore, not only give an idea of the Eskimo moral code, but, viewed in the same light as themselves, afford likewise a reflection of their feelings, of what they admire and what they despise or condemn. They love strength and fearlessness, helpfulness, and kindliness. We should be kind one to another; cruelty not only hurts the person ill-treated, but recoils upon the doer. Nothing is more certain than Nemesis."

334. R. Sutherland Rattray, *Ashanti Proverbs* (1916), p. 41.

335. W. S. Phillips, *Indian Fairy Tales* (1902), pp. 60 ff.

336. Stephen Powers, *Tribes of California* (1877), pp. 70 f.

337. Boas, *Indianische Sagen von der Nordpazifischen Kueste Amerikas*, pp. 54 f.

338. P. Amaury Talbot, *In the Shadow of the Bush* (1912), pp. 370 f.

339. J. R. Wilson-Haffenden, "Notes on the Kwottos of Tato," *Journal of the African Society*, XXVII (1927–28), 144 f.

340. Jan Czekanowski, *Forschungen im Nil-Kongo-Zwischengebiet* (1924), II, 74 f.

341. Man, "On the Aboriginal Inhabitants of the Andaman Islands," pp. 166 f.

342. A. W. Howitt, "Further Notes on the Australian Class System," *Journal of the Anthropological Institute of Great Britain and Ireland*, XVIII (1889), 54.

343. Baumann, p. 335.

344. Leo Frobenius, *Atlantis, Volksmaerchen und Volksdichtungen Afrikas*, Vol. XII: *Dichtkunst der Kassaiden* (1928), p. 124.

345. Baumann, p. 338.

346. Melland, *In Witch-bound Africa*, pp. 157 f.

347. Hauptmann Kannenberg, *Mitteilungen von Forschungsreisenden und Gelehrten aus den deutschen Schutzgebieten*, XIII (1900), 153 f.

348. M. Gusinde, *Die Feuerland-Indianer*, Vol. II: *Die Yamana*, pp. 1162 f. Most of the stories of the Yamana collected by Gusinde are retribution myths, although neither the author nor the natives express this fact in the titles of the various stories. Thus a tale the essential content of which is the punishment of a wicked stepmother appears under the heading "The First Birth" (II, 1174 f.), a title which points only to a minor incident in the story.

349. Brett, *The Indian Tribes of Guiana*, pp. 390 ff.

350. Kidd, p. 105. Kidd remarks: "There are a dozen variations of this story, which is differently told by the Damaras, Zulus, Pondos, Basutos, and other tribes."

351. Gruppe, *Griechische Mythologie und Religionsgeschichte*, II, 1012, says of the Greek myths: "Sometimes pain has the function of correcting the sufferer: the Christian belief that God educates man through misfortune was also known to the Greeks. But more often the cause of the pain is the result of a violation of the divine order. Most of the tales of the classical period contain this idea. Frequently it is the maintenance of the physical order for which the heroes suffer. According to one account, the number of human beings had increased to such an extent that the earth was no longer capable of supporting them all; thereupon Zeus decided to incite a great war. In this manner the Cyprians explained the Trojan war. Ordinarily, the hero must suffer because of a violation of the ethical order. Laius was doomed to remain childless because he violated the laws of the goddess of marriage. And when Oedipus was born, he was consecrated to ruin. He did not commit any wrong; his crime was simply that he lived. The basis of the most charming Greek tales is the idea of atonement for a moral wrong which, however, need not necessarily have been committed by the one who must atone. Since the great poets were not essentially moralists, they did not expressly formulate a moral for each of their poems. They frequently indicated the moral principle only indirectly, in the same way in which life offers it to us."

352. Preuss, *Der religioese Gehalt der Mythen*, p. 17.

353. Von den Steinen, p. 372.

354. Brinton, *The Myths of the New World*, p. 152.

355. R. P. F. Francisco Ximenez, *Las Historias del origen de los Indios de esta provincia de Guatemala*, traducidas de la lengua Quiché al Castellano para mas comodidad de los ministros del S. Evangelio (1721); edited by C. Scherzer (Viena, 1857), pp. 19 f., 24 f., 47 ff.

356. Preuss, p. 15.

357. Curt Nimuendaju-Unkel, "Die Sagen von der Erschaffung und Vernichtung der Welt als Grundlage der Religion der Apapocuva-Guarani," *Zeitschrift fuer Ethnologie*, 46. Jahrg., pp. 284 ff.

358. K. Th. Preuss, *Religion und Mythologie der Uitoto*, I (1921), 117 f.

358a. *Ibid.*, pp. 53, 62, 65, 66 ff., 86 f., 110 f., 114.

358b. *Ibid.*, p. 19.

358c. *Ibid.*, pp. 54, 109.

358d. *Ibid.*, pp. 47 f.

359. *Ibid.*, p. 100.

359a. *Ibid.*, pp. 109, 72.

360. E. Casalis, *Les Bassoutos* (1859), pp. 355 f.

361. Kidd, p. 372.

362. Waitz, *Anthropologie der Naturvoelker*, VI, 94 ff., following C. O. B. Davis, *Maori Memento* (Auckland, 1855), pp. 179 ff.

363. Cf. Hermann Gunkel, *Schoepfung und Chaos in Urzeit und Endzeit* (1895), pp. 16, 21 ff.

364. *The Babylonian Epic of Creation*, transcription, translation, and commentary by S. Langdon (1923), Tablet II, pp. 116 ff.

365. Tablet IV, vss. 13 f.

366. *Ibid.*, vss. 76 ff.

367. *Ibid.*, vss. 112 ff.

368. Gunkel, pp. 24 f.

369. *Ibid.*, p. 25.

370. Cf. Daehnhardt, I, 7 ff.

371. *Ibid.*, p. 172.

372. *Ibid.*, p. 8.

373. Cf. Edw. Lehmann, "Die Perser," *Lehrbuch der Religionsgeschichte*, herausgegeben von Bertholet und Lehmann (1925), II, 233.

374. *Ibid.*, p. 221. He remarks: "Clemency and pity are out of the question; the judge is forced to stick strictly to his own law. The constitution of the world is moral, but its administration is essentially legal."

375. *Ibid.*, pp. 254 f.

376. Horatio Hale, "Huron Folk-Lore," *Journal of American Folk-Lore*, I (1888), 181 f.

377. Louis L. Meeker, "Siouan Mythological Tales," *Journal of American Folk-Lore*, XIV (1901), 161.

378. Pechuel-Loesche, *Die Loango-Expedition*, dritte Abteilung, zweite Haelfte, pp. 268 f.

379. *Ibid.*, p. 271.

380. Hesiod, *Theogony*, vss. 164 ff. (Loeb).

381. *Ibid.*, vss. 471 ff.

382. George Grey, *Polynesian Mythology*, pp. 1 ff. Cf. Tylor, I, 322 f.; further, H. Th. Fischer, *Indonesische Paradiesmythen*, pp. 320 ff.; Best, *The Maori*, I, 89 ff. Best says of the Rangi-Papa myth: "It seems that evil entered the world when the offspring of Rangi and Papa rebelled against their parents, and Tane and Whiro commenced their eternal feud, which still continues." The children of Rangi and Papa, dissatisfied with their position between their united parents, want to separate them. "It was Tane who proposed to separate them, saying: 'Let us part our parents; let us force Rangi upward, suspend him on high, and let Papa lie in space.' Most of the children agreed to this course, but Whiro and some others objected, and would have nought to do with it. This forcible separation of sky and earth is spoken of as an act of rebellion on the part of the children towards their parents, as the first act of disobedience, the first wrong committed. Already a breach had occurred between Tane and Whiro, and this was inevitable. . . . . Tane is the personified form of light, while Whiro personifies darkness and evil." Light, the principle of good, is the author of the first crime.

383. Cf. Erman, *Die Religion der Aegypter*, p. 62, who writes: "Earth and sky were not yet separated and Nut still lay on her husband Keb. Thereupon her father Shu thrust himself between them and lifted her up; and with her he lifted all the gods who had been

created until then. . . . . Nut took possession of them, counted them, and turned them into stars."

384. W. Schmidt, *Der Ursprung der Gottesidee*, IV, 107.

385. Tylor, I, 356.

386. Best, I, 134.

387. Boas, *Indianische Sagen*, pp. 37 ff.

388. Paul Ehrenreich, "Die Mythen und Legenden der suedamerikanischen Urvoclker," *Zeitschrift fuer Ethnologie*, Suppl., XXXVII (1905), 35–37.

389. Tylor, I, 354.

390. Baumann, p. 296.

391. J. B. Friedreich, *Die Weltkoerper in ihrer mythisch-symbolischen Bedeutung*, p. 264, quoted by Schultze, *Psychologie der Naturvoelker*, p. 322.

392. Gusinde, II, 1145 ff.

393. *Ibid.*, pp. 1148 ff.

394. Tylor, I, 330.

395. *Ibid.*, p. 354.

396. Van Gennep, pp. 29–30.

397. Wirz, *Die Marind-anim*, II, Part IV, 78.

398. Edward William Nelson, "The Eskimo about Bering Strait," *18th Report of the Bureau of American Ethnology* (1899), Part I, pp. 460 ff.

399. Von den Steinen, p. 375.

400. S. A. Barrett, "A Composite Myth of the Pomo Indians," *Journal of American Folk-Lore*, XIX (1906), 46 f.

401. Waldemar Bogoras, "The Folk-Lore of Northeastern Asia, as Compared with That of Northwestern America," *American Anthropologist*, N.S., IV (1902), 627.

402. Boas, *Indianische Sagen*, p. 234.

403. Th. Koch-Gruenberg, "Zwei Mythen der Arekuna Indianer," *Archiv fuer Religionswissenschaft*, XVIII (1915), 386 f.

404. Parkinson, p. 719.

405. Gusinde, II, 1216 ff.

406. Ehrenreich, p. 42.

407. Karsten, *The Civilization of the South American Indians*, p. 338.

408. Smyth, *The Aborigines of Victoria*, I, 456.

409. The examples are cited from the collection of Daehnhardt. It is significant that in this work, too, the motive of retribution is hardly noted, although it is frequently represented in the tales interpreting nature. Revenge and gratitude, punishment and reward, appear again and again.

410. James Macdonald, "Bantu Customs and Legends," *Folk-Lore*, III (1892), 355.

411. Daehnhardt, III, 502 f., following *Bulletin de la Société Neuchâteloise de Géographie*, XVI, 138.

412. S. W. Koelle, *African Native Literature* (1854), pp. 173 f.

413. Mooney, "Myths of the Cherokee," p. 293.

414. George Bird Grinnell, *Blackfoot Lodge Tales* (1892), pp. 165 f.

415. Erland Nordenskioeld, *Indianerleben* (1912), pp. 260 f.

416. Von den Steinen, p. 383.

417. Nelson, "The Eskimo about Bering Strait," p. 460.

418. Daehnhardt, III, 56, following Potanin, *Očerki Severo-Zapadnoj Mongolii* (Petersburg, 1883), IV, 181a.

419. John Batchelor, "Items of Ainu Folk-Lore," *Journal of American Folk-Lore*, VII (1894), 33 f.

420. David Brauns, *Japanische Maerchen und Sagen* (1885), pp. 64 ff., 68.

421. G. Taylor, "Folk-Lore of Aboriginal Formosa," *Folk-Lore Journal*, V (1887), 152 ff.

422. John White, *Ancient History of the Maori, His Mythology and Traditions* (Wellington, 1887), II, 120.

423. Howitt, "Further Notes on the Australian Class Systems," p. 59.

424. Smyth, *The Aborigines of Victoria*, pp. 449 ff.

425. *Ibid.*, pp. 451 ff.

426. Abstract of a paper, "The Kootenay Indians," read by E. F. Wilson, *Journal of American Folk-Lore*, III (1890), 12.

427. Emile Petitot, *Traditions indiennes du Canada Nord-Ouest* (1886), p. 389.

428. Cf. Daehnhardt, III, 175 ff.

429. Mooney, "Myths of the Cherokee," p. 288.

430. Parkinson, p. 691.

431. C. Gardner, "Folk-Lore in Mongolia," *Folk-Lore Journal*, IV (1886), 28 f.

432. Boas, *Indianische Sagen*, p. 77.

433. Daehnhardt, III, 295.

434. A. Seidel, *Anthologie aus der asiatischen Volkslitteratur* (1898), p. 8.

435. Daehnhardt, III, 295.

436. Leo Reinisch, *Die Bilin-Sprache* (1883), I, 67 f.

437. W. S. Phillips, *Indian Fairy Tales*, pp. 184 f., 188.

438. *Ibid.*, pp. 96 f. Wundt, II, 165 f., remarks correctly that the interpretation of the transformation of a man into an animal as punishment belongs to a later period, inasmuch as man originally considered the animal as an equal, even a superior, being. The principle of retribution also determines those tales in which the change appears as a delict demanding punishment. For example, cf. Wundt, pp. 198 ff.

439. Gusinde, II, 1190 ff.

440. *Ibid.*, pp. 1197 ff.

441. *Ibid.*, pp. 1201.

442. A. C. Hollis, *The Masai* (1905), pp. 271 f. Another version runs as follows: The first death occurs, but the dead can be revived. But, because of the guilt of the survivors, this possibility is lost. A myth of the Kanioka (Africa) states that originally men did not die. Once when a child died, its father asked the god Mauesse for advice; the god told him how he must act. But Mauesse also dispatched a dog to report whether men really mourned. When the dog saw that, after mourning, men laughed and played again, Mauesse inflicted death as a punishment upon men (Frobenius, *Atlantis*, XII, 174 f.). A similar tale of the Todas (southern India) is reported by W. H. R. Rivers, *The Todas* (1906), p. 400.

443. Goddard, *Life and Culture of the Hupa*, p. 75.

444. Tylor, I, 355.

445. Stephen Powers, p. 341.

446. Best, I, 144 ff. Another form of the death myth is as follows: Maui marries Rohe, a sister of the sun. Rohe dislikes her husband's ugly face. Maui forces her to change faces with him and then he kills her. Her death soul takes revenge by killing him. This is how death comes into the world. Rohe becomes the goddess of darkness. At the same time this story is an allegorical representation of one of the original ideas of mankind, namely, that death, as retribution, comes from the dead.

447. Baumann, p. 272, says of the African myths which deal with the origin of death: "A chief characteristic of all the myths of these groups is the passive role of man at the suspicious gift of mortality. The guilt rests solely upon the slowness, dressiness, daintiness of the animal which conveys the message of eternity, or upon the speed and cunning of its partner who announces mortality. But if we keep in mind that all myths take place in times of yore—sometimes even in the period of creation—and that myths originating in the south-east present animals as acting beings, frequently as the original inhabitants of the earth, then the whole problem assumes a completely different aspect." According to Baumann, these animals are the representatives of the first men.

448. Meier, *Mythen und Erzaehlungen der Kuestenbewohner der Gazelle-Halbinsel* (*Neupommern*), p. 107.

449. Parkinson, p. 683.

450. C. E. Fox, *The Threshold of the Pacific* (1924), p. 82.

451. Kidd, p. 78.

452. R. P. Colle, *Les Baluba* ("Collection de monographies ethnographiques," publiées par Cyr. van Overbergh, Vol. XI, No. 2 [1913]), pp. 519 ff.

453. Clement M. Doke, *The Lambas of Northern Rhodesia* (1931), p. 228.

454. Melland, p. 158.

455. *The Jesuit Relations and Allied Documents*, VI (1634), 159.

456. Stephen Powers, p. 293.

457. Casalis, p. 255; cf. also Carl Clemen, *Das Leben nach dem Tode im Glauben der Menschheit* (1920), pp. 18 ff.; further, Baumann, pp. 268 ff.

458. Tylor, I, 355; cf. also Baumann, p. 276. Myths in which the message is delivered by two animals, such as chameleon and lizard in the tale of the Zulu, or turtle and lizard, chameleon and snake, chameleon and hare in other tales, are based, according to Baumann, p. 276, upon an "antagonism between moon and sun beings which replaced the original· brother and sister pair." These myths must have originated in times of a "Kulturkreis" of lunarian character, for the lunar being vanquishes the solar being.

459. Meek, *Law and Authority in a Nigerian Tribe*, p. 53.

460. Baumann, pp. 280 ff. A myth of the Lunda: Nzambi, the highest being, created the first men. He prohibited one thing only: to sleep while the moon goes over the skies. One night, however, when the moon was hidden behind clouds, the first man transgressed this divine prohibition. He fell asleep and died. "Since then, everyone has died in his turn, because none can keep awake while the moon is up" (Melland, p. 164).

461. Fischer, *Indonesische Paradiesmythen*, p. 207.

462. Schebesta, *Bambuti: Die Zwerge vom Kongo*, p. 219.

463. Sarat Chandra Roy, *The Birhors* (1925), pp. 252 ff.

464. Frazer, *Folk-Lore in the Old Testament*, I (1919), p. 76, believes that the legend of the fall of man in Genesis is a version of a very old and widespread myth, the essential content of which he represents as follows: Primitive man believes that "in the beginning a perpetual renewal of youth was either appointed by a benevolent being for the human species or was actually enjoyed by them, and that but for a crime, an accident, or a blunder it would have been enjoyed by them for ever." But it must be pointed out here that for primitive mentality no clear distinction exists between "crime," "accident," and "blunder" and that the evil consequences of all these facts—which only our civilized sense of morality differentiates—are interpreted as retribution. The fact that one has to die is always, in some sense, punishment, and the cause of death a "sin." One must not, however, accept this term in the sense of Christian morality. Baumann, p. 267, correctly characterizes the African myths that deal with the origin of death as follows: "Everything that occurred in times of yore was, according to the opinion of the natives, somehow different from today. Men lived forever and did not die. They understood the language of the animals and lived with them in peace. They did not work but had plenty of food within easy reach. This guaranteed them a life without trouble. They were not yet aware of either sex or procreation; in short, all the fundamental feelings and customs characteristic of modern men were unknown to them. But one day, because of some failing, some violation of a norm, or because of curiosity or some similar bad act, they set themselves against God and He punished them in some way. All these myths form the nucleus of the African mythologies dealing with the original conditions of men. They are better developed in the dark continent than all other kinds of myths. One may label them 'legends dealing with the fall or sin of man,' if the concept of 'sin' is not used in the Christian sense only. The concept of 'sin' is familiar to every native if 'sin' means a delict against a divine or social norm. Since the delict al-

ways appears connected with its punishment, the European concept of sin is not so different from the African concept, although there is no reason to assume the influence of European ideas of morality."

465. The sin of Adam and Eve consists in the fact that they ate the fruit of the "tree of knowledge." "To know" means, in Hebrew, at the same time "to have sexual intercourse." O. Rank, *Psychoanalytische Beitraege zur Mythenforschung* (1922), pp. 74 ff., assumes as the original nucleus of the biblical myth of the fall of man the crime of incest, which Adam, son of Eve, commits with his mother, the wife of Jehovah.

466. Joseph Meier, "Kritische Bemerkungen zu J. Winthuis' Buch, 'Das Zweigeschlechterwesen,' " *Anthropos*, XXV (1930), 104.

467. Guenther Tessmann, *Die Pangwe* (1913), II, 28.

468. Charles Dundas, *Kilimanjaro and Its People* (1924), pp. 108 ff.

469. This myth, too, reminds one of the biblical story of the fall of man. Dundas considers Christian influence as improbable. James George Frazer, *The Worship of Nature*, I (1926), 223, notes: "We must not exclude the possibility that the myth originated in Africa and was thence derived, through one channel or another, by the Semites."

470. Adolf Bastian, *Geographische und ethnologische Bilder* (1873), pp. 191 ff.

471. Smyth, I, 428. The bat as a death spirit also plays a decisive role in a myth of the Euahlayi dealing with the origin of death. Cf. W. Schmidt, *Der Ursprung der Gottesidee,* III, 899.

472. Preuss, *Lehrbuch der Voelkerkunde*, p. 97.

473. Preuss bases his statement on Gusinde, I, 574 ff., 580, 907 ff. Gusinde's representation, however, does not—or at least not directly—indicate that the Selknam assume a connection between the sexual act and death. But their myths dealing with the fact that man must die show clearly the idea of retribution. True death came to this world when Kwányip, a mythical ancestor, did not allow his older brother, Aukménk, to get up after a short sleep which replaced death in those times. "One day Aukménk behaved as if he would die. Thereupon Kwányip took a coat and wrapped his brother up in it. Then he placed him on earth and covered him over. In this position, Aukménk lay there and did not move. After some days he moved a little. The younger brother noticed that. But he did not want his older brother to get up. So he rushed quickly to the spot where his brother lay. Kwányip used all his power as *xon* [magician]; he worked very hard to prevent his elder brother from getting up. . . . . Thus he remained dead. . . . . Since then, no one can rise from the grave; everyone remains dead forever. . . . ." Čenuke, another mythical ancestor, who had to wash the dead, was infuriated at Kwányip's deed and shouted: "What have you done, you evil-doer! Why did you not help your brother? He would have come to me; I would have washed him and then he would have lived gaily and youthfully! What have you done?" (Gusinde, pp. 588 f.) Thus it was apparently the crime of fratricide for which mankind was punished with death.

The Mohammedan inhabitants of Morocco have a legend according to which men did not die originally but lost their consciousness for a short time in order to be revived afterward. But the daughter of the prophet asked her father not to let revive the child of her rival. Her request was granted with God's help. But, when her own child died, she had to lose it forever, since through the fulfilment of her wish dying became a necessity by the will of God. According to Wilson D. Wallis, *Religion in Primitive Society*, p. 206, death is punishment for revengefulness, for hostile feelings toward the fellow-man. Men have to die as punishment for the fact that they wish each other death. Death is punishment for such a wish.

474. Rasmussen, *Neue Menschen*, pp. 121 f.

475. Frank H. Melland and Edward H. Cholmeley, *Through the Heart of Africa* (1912), p. 22.

476. Seligmann, *The Melanesians of British New Guinea*, p. 304.

344 SOCIETY AND NATURE

477. W. Schmidt, *Der Ursprung der Gottesidee*, II, 88 ff., 120 f., 126 f.

478. *Ibid.*, VI, 81.

479. Preuss, p. 95.

480. Walter E. Roth, "An Inquiry into the Animism and Folk-Lore of the Guiana Indians," *30th Annual Report of the Bureau of American Ethnology* (1915), p. 179. See also p. 250.

481. Gusinde, II, 1171 f.

482. Baumann, p. 328, following Perregaux in *Bulletin de la Société Neuchâteloise de Géographie*, XVII (1906), 201 ff.

483. Baumann, p. 328, following De Brandt, "Vertellingen van den Balubas," *Congo* (1922), II, 50 f.

484. Melland and Cholmeley, p. 21.

485. Father N. Stam, "Bantu Kavirondo of Mumias District (near Lake Victoria)," *Anthropos*, XIV–XV (1919–20), 979.

486. Melland, *In Witch-bound Africa*, pp. 156 f.

487. Walter E. Roth, p. 323; cf. Karsten, *The Civilization of the South American Indians*, p. 423.

488. W. Schmidt, IV, 42.

489. Frobenius, *Die Weltanschauung der Naturvoelker*, p. 321.

490. Heinz Reschke, "Die Zauberstabmythen der Batak," *Zeitschrift fuer Ethnologie*, 67. Jahrg., p. 178. Quite generally it is said here of the Indonesian paradise myths: "In innumerable versions the paradisiacal happiness of the first men is pictured again and again. This happiness lasts until the men, through their guilt, arouse the wrath of the gods. This delict (it varies in the different accounts: incest among the Batak, stench of children's excrement among the Toradja) separates men and gods, heaven and earth, and removes forever the close relationship between the two worlds. The fall of man destroys the paradisiacal condition of life; by the sweat of his brow sinful man must now struggle for his existence."

491. Brett, *The Indian Tribes of Guiana*, pp. 388 ff.

492. Karsten, p. 300.

493. Cf. Heinrich Zimmern, *Biblische und babylonische Urgeschichte* ("Der alte Orient," 2. Jahrg., Heft 3 [3d ed., 1903]), p. 32.

494. Gunkel, p. 428.

495. Cf. Zimmern, p. 33.

496. The Chaldean account of the Deluge (*Gilgamesh Epic*), translated by W. Muss-Arnolt in the *Biblical World*, III (1894), 109 ff.

497. According to Hugo Gressmann (*Das Gilgamesch Epos*, neu uebersetzt von Arthur Ungnad und gemeinverstaendlich erklaert von Hugo Gressmann [1911], p. 202), the ethical motivation already appeared very early, "if it did not exist from the very beginning." See also Friedrich Jeremias in Bertholet und Lehmann, *Lehrbuch der Religionsgeschichte*, I (1925), 598.

498. Cf. Frazer, *Folk-Lore in the Old Testament*, I, 122.

499. Heinrich Brugsch, *Die neue Weltordnung nach Vernichtung des suendigen Menschengeschlechtes* (1881), pp. 35 ff., represents the tale as follows: In the first period after the creation, the gods lived with human beings in Egypt as in paradise; the god Ra ruled as their first king. "Men were already divided into good and evil beings. The former dwelt near their god and king, Ra, and travelled with him up the Nile. The latter, afraid of the light of his eyes, fled to the mountainous parts of the desert in order to plot a conspiracy against him." Ra consequently decided to destroy these human beings. He "lets a goddess Hatter (the cosmic order) proceed from his eye, and accept the office of a goddess of vengeance. She killed the human beings whose blood covered the earth. But since there were also good men, God showed mercy, applying a peculiar way to stop the rage of the

goddess. She drank a secretly prepared drink . . . . got intoxicated and was therefore unable to recognize men. Despite the judgment which had destroyed the sinful part of mankind, the god of light no longer liked to stay on earth. He feared the human race like a contagious disease and became tired of living with them. He wanted to go where no one could reach him. With the fulfillment of his wish, a new world order began. . . . . The good men themselves took revenge on the enemies of the god of light by resorting to war against them. Ra promised to forgive them their sins for as he added in his own words: The sacrifices (the enemies of the sun-god killed by other human beings) abolished and made superfluous the further killing of bad men through divine intervention."

500. Hermann Usener, *Die Sintflutsagen* (1899), pp. 33, 47.

501. Richard Andree, *Die Flutsagen* (1891), p. 19.

502. Usener, p. 25. In the *Satapatha-Brâhmana*, translated by Julius Eggeling, I Kânda, 8 Adhyâya, I Brâhmana, 1–3 (*The Sacred Books of the East*, ed. Max Mueller, XII [1882], 216), it is said: "(1) In the morning they brought to Manu water for washing, just as now also they (are wont to) bring (water) for washing the hands. When he was washing himself, a fish came into his hands. (2) It spake to him the word, 'Rear me, I will save thee!' 'Wherefrom wilt thou save me?' 'A flood will carry away all these creatures: from that I will save thee!' 'How am I to rear thee?' (3) It said, 'As long as we are small, there is great destruction for us: fish devours fish. Thou wilt first keep me in a jar. When I outgrow that, thou wilt dig a pit and keep me in it. When I outgrow that, thou wilt take me down to the sea, for then I shall be beyond destruction.' In *The Mahabharata* the motive of retribution becomes even more apparent. There it is said (Book III: *Vana Parva*, translated into English by P. Ch. Roy [2d.; Calcutta, 1889], pp. 552 f.): "He [Manu] was the son of Vivaswan and was equal unto Brahma in glory. And he far excelled his father and grand-father in strength, in power, in fortune, as also in religious austerities. And standing on one leg and with uplifted hand, that lord of men did severe penance in the jujube forest called Visala. And there with head downwards, and with steadfast eye, he practised this rigid and severe penance for ten thousand years. And one day, whilst he was practising austerities there with wet clothes on, and matted hair on head, a fish approaching the banks of the Chirini, addressed him thus: Worshipful sir, I am a helpless little fish, I am afraid of the large ones; therefore, do thou, O great devotee, think it worth thy while to protect me from them; especially, as this fixed custom is well established amongst us, that the strong fish always prey upon the weak ones. Therefore, do thou think it fit to save me from being drowned in this sea of terrors! I shall requite thee for thy good offices." Out of gratitude the fish saved him from the deluge.

503. Frazer, I, 180. The *Zend-Avesta* contains the following story: As there was, in early times, neither disease nor death, mankind and animals increased at such an alarming rate that at intervals they had to be destroyed by hard winters. In order to secure future generations, Yima, the ruler of the world—at Ahura Mazda's command—conveyed into a square inclosure the best seeds of all living beings—men, animals, plants—so that only the best and finest might survive. "There shall be no hump-backed, none bulged forward there; no impotent, no lunatic, no poverty, no lying, no meanness, no jealousy, no decayed tooth, no leprous to be confined, nor any of the brands wherewith Angra Mainyu stamps the bodies of mortals." (*The Zend-Avesta*, Part I: *The Vendidad*, Fargard II, 29 [80]), translated by J. Darmesteter (*The Sacred Books of the East*, ed. Max Mueller, Vol. IV) (1880), p. 17. Bodily and moral deficiencies are placed on a par. Only the best deserves to be preserved. Such is the meaning of this selection. And here, too, the principle of retribution is—though not clearly—expressed.

504. Andree, p. 43.

505. Gennep, p. 45.

506. Smyth, I, 427 ff.

507. Gennep, p. 88; cf. also W. Schmidt, *Der Ursprung der Gottesidee*, III, 685.

508. Strehlow, I, 3.

509. George Taplin, *The Narrinyeri*, in J. D. Woods, *The Native Tribes of South Australia* (1879), p. 57.

510. Frazer, I, 237, following J. Chalmers and W. Wyatt Gill, *Work and Adventure in New Guinea* (1885), p. 154.

511. P. Chr. Schleiermacher, "Religioese Anschauungen und Gebraeuche der Bewohner von Berlinhafen (Deutsch-Neuguinea)," *Globus*, LXXVIII (1900), 6.

512. Thomas Williams and James Calvert, *Fiji and the Fijians* (1859), pp. 197 ff.

513. Kubary, pp. 53 ff. This myth is interesting because Kubary represents the religion of the Pelauans as though the principle of retribution did not play any role whatsoever in it.

514. William Ellis, *Polynesian Researches*, I, 386 f.

515. Andree, p. 64.

516. William Wyatt Gill, *Life in the Southern Isles*, pp. 83 f.

517. John White, *The Ancient History of the Maori*, I, 172 ff.

518. G. Grey, *Polynesian Mythology*, pp. 42 f.

519. Wilhelm von Humboldt, *Ueber die Kawi-Sprache auf der Insel Java* (1836), I, 239 ff.

520. Frazer, I, 219, following L. N. H. A. Chatelin, "Godsdienst en bijgeloof der Niassers," *Tijdschrift voor Indische Taal-, Land- en Volkenkunde*, XXVI (1881), 115.

521. Andree, p. 32.

522. Frazer, I, 222, following N. Adriani en Alb. C. Kruijt, *De Bare'e-sprekende Toradja's van Midden-Celebes* (1912), I, 20.

523. Cf. above, pp. 124–25; further, W. Schmidt, *Der Ursprung der Gottesidee*, III, 71 ff., and Nieuwenhuis, *Die Sintflutsagen als kausallogische Natur- und Schoepfungsmythen*, p. 519.

524. Frazer, I, 209, following Guerlach, "Moeurs et superstitions des sauvages Bahnars," *Les Missions catholiques*, XIX (1887), 479.

525. A. Henry, "The Lolos and Other Tribes of Western China," *Journal of the Anthropological Institute of Great Britain and Ireland*, XXXIII (1903), 105.

526. Tickell, "Memoir on the Hodésum (improperly called Kolehan)," in *Journal of the Asiatic Society of Bengal*, IX (1840), Part II, 798. See also the tale of the Mundari, a tribe of the Koles, reported by Andree, pp. 25 f.

527. Frazer, I, 198.

528. *Ibid.*, pp. 199 f.

529. Baumann, p. 307, following Emin Pascha, *Sammlung von Reisebriefen*, herausg. von Schweinfurth und Ratzel (1888), p. 469.

530. *Ibid.*, p. 307.

531. P. Amaury Talbot, *The Peoples of Southern Nigeria* (1926), III, 961 f.

532. A. B. Ellis, *The Yoruba-speaking Peoples of the Slave Coast of West Africa* (1894), p. 64.

533. Frobenius, *Atlantis*, XII, 88 f.

534. L. Tauxier, *Le Noir du Yatenga* (1917), pp. 498 f.

535. David Livingstone, *Missionary Travels and Researches in South Africa* (1858), p. 353.

536. Baumann, pp. 316 f. Baumann says, p. 322: "As far as Africa is concerned, two kinds of myths have to be distinguished, those which contain the motive of 'sin' and 'retribution' and those which lack it." But of the nine myths which in his opinion lack the motive of retribution, at least six would appear to contain it, even according to his own accounts.

1. Among the Bushmen (p. 307, following J. M. Orpen in "A Glimpse into the Mythology of the Maluti Bushmen," originally published in the *Cape Monthly Magazine*, Vol. IX [1874], reprinted in *Folk-Lore*, XXX [1919], 145 ff.): The flood is caused by snakes "out of revenge."

2. Among the Vili of Loango (p. 309; cf. John H. Weeks, *Among the Primitive Bakongo* [1914], p. 286): "The sun and moon once met together and the sun plastered some mud over a part of the moon, and thus covered up some of the light, and that is why a portion

of the moon is often in shadow. When this meeting took place, there was a flood." It is highly probable that the motive behind the sun's hostile behavior was, as in many analogous tales, vengeance.

3. Among the Ababua (p. 311, following De Calonne in *Le Mouvement sociologique internationale* [1909], X, 119): "An old woman who hoarded water kills the men who search for the liquid. The hero Mba kills the old woman. Thereupon the water flows in such quantities that it floods everything. Mba is washed away and lands on the summit of a tree." The principle of retribution appears here twice. The water woman is killed by the hero because she had retained the water and had killed those who looked for it. The flood is obviously retribution for the killing of the woman. That the avenging deed is thus avenged in turn is in accordance with the primitive idea of retribution. (A myth of a bad woman who hoards water—with a clearly pronounced motive of retribution—can also be found among the Fuegian Indians; see Gusinde, I, 613.)

4. Among the Bena-Lulua (p. 311; cf. Frobenius in *Atlantis*, XII, 157): The old water woman gives water only to him who sucks out her sores. One man does it. "Water flows in such floods that almost everyone is drowned. But the man goes on with his disgusting work and thereupon the water stops flowing." Here, too, the motive of retribution appears twice; first, when the needed water is granted as a return gift for the carrying-out of the disgusting performance; second, when the water stops flowing again as a reward for a good deed. The same motive also appears in the following tale of the Fiote (p. 311; cf. R. E. Dennett, *Notes on the Folklore of the Fjort* [1898], p. 122): "An old lady (Nzambi), after some days' journey, arrived at a town called Sinauzenzi, footsore and weary, and covered with those terrible sores which afflict a great number of negroes in the Congo district. The old woman asked for hospitality from each householder as she passed through the town but they all refused to receive her saying she was unclean. When she finally arrived at the very last house, the kind folks there took her in, nursed and cured her. . . . . When she was quite well and about to depart, she told her kind friends to pack up their trays and leave the town with her, as assuredly it was accursed and would be destroyed by Nzambi. And the night after they left, heavy rains fell, the town was submerged, and all the people drowned."

5. Among the Komililo Nandi (p. 312; cf. Ç. W. Hobley, "British East Africa: Anthropological Studies in Kavirondo and Nandi," *Journal of the Anthropological Institute of Great Britain and Ireland*, XXXIII [1903], 359): "About thirty miles east of Kisumu in Nandi country, there is a forest-clad extinct volcano named Tinderet. The Kamililo Nandi who inhabit its southern and western flanks tell a legend that high up on the mountain there is a cave in which Ilet, the spirit of the lightning, who descended there in the form of a man, took up his abode. After his descent it rained incessantly for many days, and the Oggiek or Wandorobbo hunters who lived in the forest were nearly all killed by the terrible downpour. Some of them, while searching for the cause of the rain, found Ilet in the cave and wounded him with their poisoned arrows. Thereupon he fled, and died in Arab Kibosone's country; directly he was dead, the rain ceased." Here the motive of retribution is reversed: God does not punish men with evil but men punish God because of the evil.

6. Among the Ndorobo (p. 313, following Kannenberg in *Zeitschrift fuer afrikanische und ozeanische Sprachen*, V [1900], 161) they tell that originally men lived with God in heaven; then they climbed down with him on a rope to earth. On earth god let a heavy rain fall so that the Ndorobo could no longer shoot game and had to go hungry. But a Ndorobo cut the rope and it immediately stopped raining. Since then god has lived in heaven with the human beings who remained with him. Men pay for the cessation of rain by suffering a final separation from God. This, too, is retribution.

7. Among the Ashanti (p. 313, following Edmond Perregaux, "Chez les Ashanti," *Bulletin de la Société Neuchâteloise de Géographie*, XVII [1906], 198): When the first seven human beings created by God climbed on a chain down to earth and brought fire with them, their downward climb was preceded by heavy rain which ceased only when the chain was low-

ered. When their descendants increased during the following years, they returned on the chain amidst heavy rain to heaven. The original identity of chain and rain appears clearly, according to Perregaux's representation, especially when the first seven human beings returned to heaven. "When the number of men continued to increase, the first seven men said to their children: 'As far as we are concerned, we shall return thither whence we came (to God), but you remain on earth; you will also have children and you will scatter over the earth.' As soon as they had said this, a heavy rain fell and the same chain, on which they had climbed down, took them. . . . ." The rain signifies the road from heaven to earth and back. But the myth contains still another detail (Perregaux, p. 198): "One day, unfortunately, the women while stamping their *foufou* felt embarrassed at the presence of God; they told him to go away and when he did not retire quickly enough, they hit him with their stampers. Then God, angered, retired from this world and left its direction to the spirits (fetishes). A proverb reads: Without the old woman, we would be happy." The motive of retribution appears here, too; but the myth does not belong to the flood tales.

The reason why Baumann does not always discover the motive of retribution lies in the fact that his concept of retribution is too narrow. He perceives retribution, as he says on p. 314, only where a "violation of norms" occurs. But revenge, too, is included, as well as reward for a good deed, and exchange, especially renunciation of a good as compensation for liberation from an evil. Baumann rightly asserts, p. 314, that a separation of tales interpreting the deluge as punishment from mere flood tales is impossible; "the momentum of sin is so indeterminate that in primitive stages it can hide itself in an unobtrusive way and appear as quite unimportant guilt." But punishment for sin is only one of the typical cases in which the principle of retribution is applied.

537. Gusinde, II, 1232.

538. Preuss, *Religion und Mythologie der Uitoto*, I, 60.

539. *Ibid.*, p. 61.

540. Frazer, I, 257, following P. Ehrenreich, *Beitraege zur Voelkerkunde Brasiliens* (1891), pp. 40 f.

541. A. Métraux, *La Religion des Tupinamba et ses rapports avec celle des autres tribus Tupi-Guarani* (1928), p. 44.

542. Ehrenreich, *Die Mythen und Legenden der suedamerikanischen Urvoelker*, p. 31.

543. Frazer, I, 259 f., following P. Ehrenreich, *Beitraege zur Voelkerkunde Brasiliens*, pp. 71 f.

544. Frazer, I, 261, following Rivet, "Les Indiens Jibaros," *L'Anthropologie*, XIX (1908), 236.

545. Brett, *The Indian Tribes of Guiana*, pp. 378 ff., 384.

546. *Ibid.*, p. 398.

547. Andree, p. 114, following L. F. Piedrahita, *Historia general de las conquistas del Nuevo Reyno de Granada*, p. 17, and A. v. Humboldt, *Sites des Cordillères et monuments des peuples indigènes de l'Amérique* (1869), pp. 42 f.

548. Frazer, I, 267, following H. Ternaux-Compans, *Essai sur l'ancien Cundinamarca* (Paris, n.d.), pp. 7 f.

549. William Curtis Farabee, *Indian Tribes of Eastern Peru* ("Harvard University, Papers of the Peabody Museum of American Archeology and Ethnology," Vol. X [1922]), p. 124.

550. Andree, p. 109.

551. Brinton, *The Myths of the New World*, p. 208, reproduces this part of the tale as follows: "Because they had not thought of their Mother and Father, the Heart of Heaven, whose name is Hurakan, therefore the face of the earth grew dark and a pouring rain commenced, raining by day, raining by night. Then all sorts of beings, little and great, gathered together to abuse the men to their faces; and all spoke, their mill-stones, their plates, their cups, their dogs, their hens. Said the dogs and hens, 'Very badly have you treated us,

and you have bitten us. Now we bite you in turn.' Said the mill-stones, 'Very much were we tormented by you, and daily, daily, night and day, it was squeak, squeak, screech, screech, for your sake. Now yourselves shall feel our strength, and we will grind your flesh, and make meal of your bodies,' said the mill-stones. And this is what the dogs said, 'Why did you not give us our food? No sooner did we come near than you drove us away, and the stick was always within reach when you were eating, because, forsooth, we were not able to talk. Now we will use our teeth and eat you,' said the dogs, tearing their faces. And the cups and dishes said, 'Pain and misery you gave us, smoking our tops and sides, cooking us over the fire, burning and hurting us as if we had no feeling. Now it is your turn, and you shall burn,' said the cups insultingly. Then ran the men hither and thither in despair. They climbed to the roofs of the houses, but the houses crumbled under their feet; they tried to mount to the tops of the trees, but the trees hurled them far from them; they sought refuge in the caverns, but the caverns shut before them. Thus was accomplished the ruin of this race, destined to be destroyed and overthrown; thus were they given over to destruction and contempt. And it is said that their posterity are those little monkeys who live in the woods.''

552. Bancroft, *The Native Races of the Pacific States of North America*, III, 76 f.

553. Brinton, p. 221.

554. Frazer, I, 281, following De la Borde, "Relation de l'origine, moeurs, coustumes, religion, guerres et voyages des Caraibes sauvages des Isles Antilles de l'Amérique," in *Recueil de divers voyages faits en Afrique et en l'Amerique qui n'ont point esté encore publiez* (Paris, 1684), p. 7.

555. Carl Lumholtz, *Unknown Mexico* (1902), I, 298 f.

556. W. Schmidt, *Der Ursprung der Gottesidee*, II, 40.

557. Mrs. Tilly E. Stevenson, "The Religious Life of the Zuñi Child," *5th Annual Report of the Bureau of Ethnology* (1887), p. 539; Stevenson, "The Zuñi Indians," *23rd Annual Report of the Bureau of American Ethnology* (1904), p. 61.

558. George Catlin, *O Kee-Pa: a Religious Ceremony; and Other Customs of the Mandans* (1867), pp. 1 ff.

559. Frazer, I, 288, following Father Friar Geronimo Boscana, "Chinigchinich, a Historical Account, etc., of the Acagchemem Nation," annexed to A. Robinson's *Life in California* (New York, 1846), pp. 300 f.

560. W. Schmidt, II, 510.

561. W. Matthews, "A Part of the Navajo's Mythology," *American Antiquarian*, V, No. 3 (1883), 207–13.

562. E. G. Squier, *Historical and Mythological Traditions of the Algonquins*, pp. 12 ff. (paper read before the New York Historical Society).

563. Frazer, I, 297.

564. W. H. Hooper, *Ten Months among the Tents of the Tuski* (1853), pp. 286 ff.; cf. also the tale of the Ojibway, reported by Andree, pp. 75 ff.

565. Frazer, I, 312, following E. Petitot, *Monographie des Dènè-Dindjié* (1876), p. 74.

566. J. Jetté, "On Ten'a Folk-Lore," *Journal of the Royal Anthropological Institute of Great Britain and Ireland*, XXXVIII (1908), 312 f.

567. Frazer, I, 315 f., following Petitot, *Traditions Indiennes du Canada Nord-ouest*, pp. 22–26.

568. Krause, *Die Tlinkit-Indianer*, p. 257.

569. Frazer, I, 319, following F. Boas, in "Fourth Report of the Committee on the North-western Tribes of the Dominion of Canada," *Report of the Fifty-eighth Meeting of the British Association for the Advancement of Science, held at Bath in September, 1888* (London, 1889), p. 239.

570. A. F. Chamberlain, "Report on the Kootenay Indians of South-Eastern British

Columbia," in *Eighth Report of the Committee on the North-Western Tribes of Canada* (*Report of the Sixty-second Meeting of the British Association for the Advancement of Science, held at Edinburgh, 1892*), pp. 575 f.

571. Frazer, I, 323, referring to the fact that bird and woman is used alternatively, says: "In these Indian tales no sharp line of distinction is drawn between the animal and the human personages."

572. M. Eells, "Traditions of the 'Deluge' among the Tribes of the North-West," *American Antiquarian*, I (1878–79), 70.

573. Franz Boas, *Kathlamet Texts* (Bureau of American Ethnology Bull. 26 [1901]), pp. 20 ff.

574. Andree, p. 131, finds that out of the eighty-eight tales collected by him only eight interpret the flood as a judgment proceeding from a superior being and inflicted because of sins committed by men. But the decisive element is comprehended too narrowly. What matters is whether and how far the principle of retribution plays a decisive role. From this point of view a much greater number of those tales reported by Andree are involved here. Thus, for instance, the tale of the Dajak, the *Edda* tale, the tale of the creation of the Dilolo-lake, the Montezuma tale of the Papagos, the tale of Jelch of the Tlingit, the tale of the Quiché Indians, especially the tale of the Mayscas and some other myths, reported by Andree but not counted among the retribution myths, fit into this class.

Johannes Riem, *Die Sintflut in Sage und Wissenschaft* (1925), also sets up some statistics for flood tales. Of two hundred and sixty-eight reports, the motive of retribution is only traceable, according to his opinion, in seventy-five cases. But he comprehends only those where the flood is based "on a guilt of mankind or an individual" or "on the revenge of an annoyed god." But the cases where the wrong is committed by an animal or is an act of private revenge of an individual must also be included. Further, there must be counted those cases where reward and not punishment is involved, or where the delict seems to be negligible, or where not the flood as such but rather the death it brings appears as punishment and the rescue from it as reward. That the flood is not punishment but a crime does not mean that the principle of retribution is missing, for this crime demands punishment. If one examines these reports collected by Riem from this point of view, the principle of retribution becomes manifest in more than one hundred tales. Yet Riem assumes that only eighty reports indicate any reason for the flood. In several tales reported by him the principle of retribution does not become apparent, although it exists in the reproductions of other authors. This is so in the Babylonian flood tale; here Riem says, p. 21, that the gods decided upon the flood "obviously out of mere caprice."

575. Wundt, *Mythus und Religion*, Part III, pp. 298 f., says that the older form of flood tales lacks the ethical motives, the elements of revenge, punishment, and reward. This cannot be true, at least not for the motive of revenge, since this is one of the oldest elements of mythical thinking.

CHAPTER IV

1. Cf. my essays "L'Ame et le droit," *Annuaire de l'Institut International de Philosophie du Droit et de Sociologie Juridique*, II (1936), 60 ff., and "The Soul and the Law," *Review of Religion*, I (1937), 337 ff.

2. Cf. Max Wundt, who starts his *Geschichte der griechischen Ethik* (1908), I, 5 ff., with Homer.

3. Cf. Sam Wide and Martin P. Nilsson, "Griechische und römische Religion," in *Einleitung in die Altertumswissenschaft*, ed. A. Gercke and E. Norden (4th ed., 1933), II, Part II, 2 f., 8 f. "We perceive in Greek religion two main tendencies: one is very old and popular, the other was created by Homeric culture and achieved official character. The former contains stone, tree, and animal-worship, belief in spirits and demons, magic and orgiasm, human sacrifice and other ideas and customs characteristic of primitive man. The other, however, represents rationalistic, human, and aesthetic interests. This latter tendency was apparently the stronger since it was sustained by the national consciousness and appeared emphatically in literature and art; but the former tendency was also vigorous and powerful, often influencing Homeric religion. Indeed, this religion obtained its power from the Hellenic culture and lost it when this culture broke down." Cf. also Eckart Peterich, *Die Theologie der Hellenen* (1938), pp. 12, 61, 106, 210.

4. The Homeric Zeus religion, as handed down to us in the two great epic poems, was not formed on the Greek mainland but in Asia Minor, in Ionia; and from there it decisively influenced the religion of the mother-country. The question of the relationship between Homeric religion and the religion of the immigrant Hellenes at the time when the latter conquered the aborigines, as well as the question of the relationship between the religion of these aborigines and the religion of the victors, cannot be answered here.

5. Cf. Otto Kern, *Die Religion der Griechen* (1926), I, 28, 180 ff.

6. Cf. Erwin Rohde, *Psyche, the Cult of Souls and Belief in Immortality among the Greeks*, trans. W. B. Hills (1925), pp. 156 ff. Of the epoch following Homer's era it is said: "New elements of the population came to the fore, governments began to fall and the old rule of the kings gave way to Aristocracy, Tyranny, Democracy. In friendly and (in the West especially) hostile relationship the Greeks came into contact more than formerly with foreign peoples." This development was accompanied by a renaissance of religion. "It is as though the Greeks then went through a period such as most civilized nations go through at some time or other, and such as the Greeks themselves were to repeat more than once in after centuries—a period in which the mind, after it has at least half succeeded in winning its freedom from disquieting and oppressive beliefs in invisible powers, shrinks back once more. Under the influence of adversity it feels the need of some comforting illusions behind which it may take shelter and be relieved in part of the burden of responsibility."

7. K. F. Naegelsbach, *Homerische Theologie* (2d ed., 1861), pp. 13 ff., and *Die nachhomerische Theologie des griechischen Volksglaubens* (1857), p. 40. He states that among all the qualities of the deity only the moral quality of punishing justice attested by the consciousness of the individual is maintained. "The idea of unjustly punishing deities never appears in the Greek religion."

8. Naegelsbach, *Die nachhomerische Theologie*, p. 30, and *Homerische Theologie*, pp. 31 f., where references for this assertion are mentioned. Cf. also Leopold Schmidt, *Die Ethik der alten Griechen* (1882), I, 47: "One of the firmest suppositions which the old Greeks never relinquished was the belief that a strict justice rewarding good and punishing evil ruled over the fates of men. Whatever opinion one may have of the origin of the Homeric poems, one thing is certain, their content is dominated by this idea." On p. 228 he writes:

"Although the Greeks had no idea of morally perfect deities, yet they were convinced that a divine justice tolerating no violation of order ruled over the fates of individuals as well as of peoples." Cf. also Erwin Rohde, "Die Religion der Griechen," *Kleine Schriften* (1901), II, 327: "Man may trust the gods; justice, an imperturbable justice, is the pure content of their will and government." Further, Gruppe, *Griechische Mythologie und Religionsgeschichte*, II, 1002, states: "To punish violations of the rules laid down in the world order is the highest, almost the only, moral duty of the Homeric gods." Among those elements which the Greek culture took over from the Homeric religion, we also find, besides the idea of humanly feeling gods, the "conviction of the justice and beauty of the world order" (*ibid.*, p. 1047).

9. Claudius Aelianus *Varia historia* iii. 43, trans. Thomas Stanley (1665). Cf. also M. P. Nilsson, *Die Religion der Griechen* ("Religionsgeschichtliches Lesebuch," No. 4 [1927]), p. 46. Cf. also Wilhelm Nestle, *Griechische Religiositaet von Homer bis Pindar and Aischylos* ("Die griechische Religiositaet in ihren Grundzuegen und Hauptvertretern von Homer bis Proklos I" Sammlung Göschen [1930]), p. 85.

10. *Odyssey* xxiv. 351 ff. (Loeb Classical Library).

11. Euripides *Oinomaos*, frag. 577 (J. A. Nauck, *Tragicorum Fragmenta* [1889]).

12. Cf. Kern, I, 266.

13. *Iliad* ii. 101 ff.

14. *Ibid.* 98. 196.

15. Cf. Adolf Fanta, *Der Staat in der Ilias und Odyssee* (1882), p. 49.

16. *Iliad* ii. 197 (Loeb).

17. *Ibid.* ix. 96 ff. (Loeb).

18. *Ibid.* ii. 204 ff. (Loeb).

19. *Odyssey* i. 386.

20. *Iliad* xvi. 542 (A. T. Murray in the Loeb Classical Library translates "judgments").

21. *Ibid.* xix. 181 ff. (Loeb).

22. *Odyssey* ii. 230 ff.

23. *Ibid.* iii. 244, 246 (Loeb). Verse 245, "For thrice, men say, has he been king for a generation of men," is considered interpolated. Cf. *L'Odyssee, texte établi et traduit par Victor Bérard* (2d ed., 1933), I, 64.

24. *Odyssey* iv. 690 ff. (Loeb).

25. *Ibid.* xix. 109 ff. (Loeb).

26. Cf. Georg Finsler, *Homer* (3d ed., 1924), Part I, sec. 2, pp. 178 ff., 182.

27. *Iliad* xvi. 387 ff. (Loeb).

28. *Ibid.* i. 238.

29. *Ibid.* xiii. 623 ff. (Loeb). Cf. also *ibid.* i. 159.

30. *Iliad.* iii. 320 ff. (Loeb).

31. *Ibid.* 351 ff. (Loeb).

32. *Ibid.* iv. 157 ff. (Loeb).

33. *Ibid.* viii. 22 (Loeb).

34. *Ibid.* 69 ff. (Loeb).

35. *Ibid.* xix. 418 (Loeb). In Athens a man who had risen from the dead (in case of apparent death) was not allowed to enter the sanctuary of the Erinyes (Eumenides). To rise from the dead was considered to be a kind of delict, because a violation of the law of nature. To maintain this law, conceived of as a legal norm, was the function of the Erinyes, goddesses of vengeance. Cf. Peterich, p. 224.

36. That innocent individuals are frequently made to suffer in Homer's epics is the result of the ideas of collective responsibility and absolute liability, especially hereditary liability, which dominate Homeric, as well as other primitive, morality. That these are to be regarded as thoroughly moral principles has already been stressed in another connection. Finsler, p. 177, believes that in Homer men "conclude divine wrath from misfortune. The

guilt of the unfortunate himself is not necessary." This is true. The guilt may be that of an ancestor or another member of the family, of the king or even anybody else with whom the unfortunate had some relation and who drags him along into punishment. If the Homeric man interprets every misfortune that he suffers as the effect of divine wrath, then he sees in it, even if he is not conscious of any personal guilt, a retribution justified by certain facts which may even be unknown to him. Finsler is not right, therefore, when he asserts (p. 183) that men "perceive divine wrath in their misfortunes, but not punishment." The "wrath" of the deity always has some cause, even if it is only a personal offense, insult, or violation of interest. Such a fact inevitably signifies some wrong or sin, even if committed involuntarily or unconsciously. The "wrath" of the deity, therefore, as in all primitive religions, takes the form of punishment, since it is a retributory reaction against some direct or indirect violation of the deity.

37. *Iliad* iv. 70 ff. (Loeb).

38. Finsler, p. 206.

39. Aeschylus *The Persians* 742 (Loeb).

40. Aeschylus *Niobe*, frag. 77 (156), (Loeb).

41. Cf. Nestle, pp. 125 ff.

42. Sophocles, frag. 227 (Nauck) (translation by Sir George Young in *The Dramas of Sophocles Rendered in English Verse* [Everyman's Library], p. 340).

43. *Iliad* iv. 30 ff. (Loeb).

44. *Ibid.* 37 ff. (Loeb).

45. *Ibid.* 54 ff. (Loeb).

46. *Ibid.* i. 503 ff. (Loeb).

47. *Ibid.* 218 (Loeb).

48. Euripides *Hippolytus* 1328 ff. (Loeb).

49. Cf. Nestle, p. 32. The verses from the *Iliad* (xix. 126 ff. [Loeb]) represent the anthropomorphically personified Ate as a devil whom Zeus drove out of Olympus: ". . . . wroth in his soul, and sware a mighty oath that never again unto Olympus and the starry heaven should Ate come, she that blindeth all. So said he, and whirling her in his hand flung her from the starry heaven, and quickly she came to the tilled fields of men."

50. *Odyssey* i. 32 ff. (Loeb).

51. *Ibid.* 253 ff. (Loeb).

52. *Ibid.* 267 ff. (Loeb). Cf. also *ibid.* xxii. 413.

53. *Ibid.* i. 378 ff. (Loeb).

54. *Ibid.* xiii. 213 ff. (Loeb).

55. *Ibid.* xiv. 83 ff. (Loeb).

56. *Ibid.* 283 ff. (Loeb).

57. *Ibid.* iv. 377 ff.

58. *Ibid.* 806 ff.

59. *Ibid.* xvii. 483 ff. (Loeb).

60. *Ibid.* xxii. 372 ff. (Loeb).

61. Naegelsbach, *Homerische Theologie*, pp. 31 ff., 315 ff., 345 ff., on the basis of a careful collection of references dealing with this idea, comes to the conclusion that Homeric theology adheres in principle to the idea of divine justice. Leopold Schmidt, I, 47, writes: "The Trojans must endure the punishment of the gods because one of them had wickedly violated the right of hospitality; further, they increase their guilt by the breach of a solemnly concluded treaty. For his part, Achilles, too, must atone for the excess of his revengefulness. The *Odyssey* shows even more clearly how sin does not escape its punishment and how virtue is finally rewarded."

G. W. Nitzsch, *Erklaerende Anmerkungen zu Homer's Odyssee* (1826), Vol. I, tries to clarify certain contradictions. He writes, p. 11: "If the gods sometimes appear as just, even as the representatives of eternal justice, sometimes passionate, frequently as the executors of μοῖρα

and sometimes as powerless against it; if, on the other hand, men are themselves occasionally able to determine their fate and to stop its power but sometimes resign themselves to
hostile forces without any will of their own, then these contradictions arise partly from the
conflict between human liberty and the power of fate, and partly from the anthropomorphi-
cal idea of the gods, especially the way in which the poet uses this particular idea. The
idea of divine justice obviously rules more strongly in the *Odyssey* than in the *Iliad*." Recently, however, it has been suggested that this view be abandoned. Thus, Ulrich Wilamowitz-Moellendorff, *Griechische Tragoedien* (9th ed., 1922), II, 15, shares the view that for
Homer "the moral, the good, the just, even if it has already been experienced constitutes
no characteristic of godliness. In human life, too, justice is by no means demanded." Kern,
I, 281, is also of the opinion that the idea of justice became apparent only in Hesiod's time,
but he admits that "perhaps even before Hesiod independent philosophers arrived at the
same conclusions," namely, belief in divine justice.

Finsler says that in the epic material which the poet of the *Iliad* used, or at least in certain parts of it, a firm belief in the justice of the gods is expressed; but he points out that the
poet himself describes the dominion of the gods as cruel and unjust (pp. 182, 206, 211 f.).
However, if one examines more closely those references upon which Finsler bases his theory
of the antireligious criticism of Homer, then it becomes difficult to maintain his thesis. As
proof of the fact that Homer wished to represent Zeus as an unjust god, Finsler cites the
fact that Achilles in his wrath executed only the advice of Zeus and that Zeus himself,
through Athene, induced the Trojans to break the treaty. It has already been noted in the
text that the honest belief in the justice of the deity is not shaken by the fact that all human
events, and thus also crimes committed by men, are traced to the will of the deity.

Finsler further mentions that Zeus re-established the offended honor of Achilles not in
order to punish the insolence of Agamemnon but to repay Thetis for the help she once
gave him; he wanted, however, to keep Hera from learning anything, since he feared discord in heaven. And when he attempted to fulfil the promise he had given to Thetis, he
did not tell the gods about it; he avoided the opposition "by that bombastic description of
his power." Finsler emphasizes that Hera, in order to obtain the belt of Aphrodite, with
which she intends to fascinate Zeus, availed herself of a lie, arrayed herself coquettishly,
and "then played the bashful wife before the aroused desire of Zeus." Finsler speaks here
of the "contemptible connotation" which the poet put in the verses describing "the divine
nuptials of the godly pair." In addition, Finsler points to the empty oath sworn by Hera,
frightened by the threats of the awakened Zeus; and he ascribes "petty envy" and "vanity"
to Poseidon.

In all these cases, however, there are involved only the human weaknesses which the
gods manifest in their relations with one another and which, as indicated in the text, do not
touch upon that sphere in which divine justice alone appears, namely, the relationship between god and man. The fact that in the last scene of the first book Hephaestus regards the
quarrel over mortal beings as dreadful and believes that they are not worth disturbing one's
joy for the meal (Finsler considers this as a symptom of the fact that the poet of the *Iliad*
believes in the wickedness of the gods) can be easily understood as follows: The Homeric
man believed that the gods speak contemptuously of men just as noblemen do about their
servants; certainly Homeric man never thought of regarding his gods as unjust simply because they were supposed to despise mortals. Finsler says that Zeus's "treatment of men is
more shocking inasmuch as he expressly recognizes an obligation enjoined on him through
sacrifice and prayer, an idea which did not exist before the times of our poet. Zeus says:
'Never has my altar lacked an appropriate sacrifice.' He feels the obligation but nevertheless he abandons the pious Trojan people and Hector who sacrificed so much to him both
on Ida and in the town." If the poet naïvely ascribes to the god what the Homeric man,
not less than the pious man of today, wishes, namely, that the god becomes obligated by

sacrifice and prayer, then Homer, like a pious Christian, did not dare to interpret as an injustice of the god the fact that a human being, despite sacrifice and prayer, has met with an accident. When Finsler finds Zeus "mean and disgusting," he records only his own moral judgment, and not that of Homer. Since Finsler bases his moral judgment against Zeus on the fact "that the confident hero who relies on Zeus's help is finally duped," and "the protection granted to him by the god" becomes "glittering fraud," he should also be morally indignant at the Christian God, in whose justice many a devout poet believed, whose innocent hero had, nevertheless, to fall.

Finsler says: "Only the poet of the *Iliad* created that religion which later philosophers, above all Xenophanes and Plato, regarded as so mean and for the apology of which cynics and stoics invented allegoric interpretations." The "meanness" of the Homeric gods are, however, only the inevitable consequences of anthropomorphism and are certainly as much a product of the public mind as they are the conscious work of Homer.

That justice was originally not essential to the gods of Homer is also asserted by Wide and Nilsson, pp. 24 ff.: they say that justice was added later to the concept of god by poets and philosophers, especially the Orphics. But Wide and Nilsson also admit that in Homer the gods were made "the bearers of the moral world order." M. P. Nilsson, "Die Griechen" (*Lehrbuch der Religionsgeschichte*, herausgegeben von Bertholet und Lehman, Vol. II [1925]), p. 339, believes that the Homeric gods, as gods of nature, had nothing to do with morality—rain pours down upon just as well as upon unjust beings. "Originally the human being seeks from the gods the fulfillment of his wishes and not the maintenance of morality." Among those wishes, however, the desire for retribution, for justice, plays an important part! Nilsson goes on: "The maintenance of morality is imposed upon the gods by the fact that men seek in their gods higher authority for the morals and customs of life which, according to the common belief, obligates the individual even against his own will." From this ensues the idea of a divine justice already existing in the beginnings of social life. It cannot be doubted that a strong tendency to an ideology justifying the social order, as indicated by Nilsson, must have existed in such a relatively highly developed social stage as in Homer's time. Thus Nilsson says: "On this path the Homeric man has far advanced. National ties were weak and loose but the sanctity of unwritten laws was strong." But this is nothing more than divine justice! Besides, Nilsson himself categorically asserts: "From its very beginning, Greek religion was a religion of society." Consequently, it must be a religion of justice. Nilsson also says that "the religion was always conservative" (p. 386). But this is so only because it declares the prevailing social order to be just because divinely willed.

According to W. F. Otto, *Die Goetter Griechenlands* (1929), pp. 331 ff., justice is not essential to the Greek deities. The author admits, however, that in the Homeric world one believes "in the victorious justice of Zeus." For Hesiod, he has to admit: "The peasant Hesiod, in his difficult struggle against unfaithfulness and corruption of the law, cannot conceive anything of more value to the deity than what is most sacred to himself in his existence," i.e., justice. Nevertheless, it is characteristic of the Greek spirit that it does not want happiness, but greatness: "For this human spirit which wants greatness and not happiness is the effect of a divine government different from that which peasants and citizens wish for their own existence which is directed toward possession and gain." Since Otto identifies the wish for happiness with the desire for justice, he comes to this conclusion: "The call for justice is a symptom of the fact that the human mind begins to deprive the world of its divine character. The claim for happiness which the individual believes himself to have rises above the decreasing consciousness of the divine presence." One must not consider the doctrines of the Jewish prophets and the sermons of Jesus, which center about the idea of justice, as the only religion. But neither must one commit the opposite mistake of determining the essence of religion in such a way that Jehova, whose primary characteristic is justice and who, as king, wishes the coming realm of justice to be ruled by his son, no longer appears as a true god; such a false concept renders the Jewish-Christian belief in one all-righteous God a sign which marks the beginning of the deprivation of divine character from the world.

Otto's fundamental supposition that the desire for justice, as the desire for happiness, is opposite to the ideal of greatness is more than questionable. The assumption that the Greeks were men who sought greatness rather than happiness, and therefore not justice, has no basis even if it refers only to the Homeric heroes. It is aestheticizing speculation. In addition, "greatness" is a predicate which, without any more concrete specification of the subject, is simply without meaning or significance. The "greatness" of the deity can be manifested only by its power, wisdom, kindness—and, above all, by its justice. For the fact that the specific greatness of the Greek deity consists in the justice, such an abundance of proof has been collected by former authors that Otto's thesis, counterevidence lacking, cannot be accepted. Otto himself stresses that the Greek god resembles his image, the human being. Then why should not justice, the most important good for man in his attitude toward his fellow-man, have been essential for the most human of all deities, the Greek gods?

Under the influence of Otto, Peterich tries to maintain the thesis that justice is no essential element of the Homeric religion. He even says, p. 273: "The Homeric world is an unjust one although the gods are often enough called just." But his attempt of substantiating this statement is rather artificial and not very consistent." The original justice is the justice of nature; it comes from the female, and it becomes the order of the world, the universal law in the personality of the goddess Themis. This law works in the invisible and can be understood only in the invisible. In the visible world unjustice prevails: punishment and reward are realized in the other world. The being is unjust; the coming into being is just. The male who belongs to the visible world is unjust, the female who belongs to the invisible justice and the universal law, is just. Since the Homeric world is a world of the being and the visible, a male world, it must be unjust." Peterich himself shows the important role which plays the idea of a universal order in Homer. He says expressly, p. 174: "Opis, goddess of punishment, which follows every violation of the laws appears in Iliad and Odyssey in important passages." There cannot be the slightest doubt in Homeric man's belief that retributory justice is executed in this world. And, if there is a belief in a universal world order, it must be an order of the visible world, especially in the Homeric religion, which is characterized by the complete lack of belief in retribution in another world. The identification of male, visible and unjust on the one hand, and of female, invisible and just on the other hand, has no foundation at all either in Homeric or post-Homeric religion.

The thesis that the Greek gods were amoral beings is probably connected with the doctrine, so prevalent in recent ethnology, that primitive religion had nothing to do with morality. Typical of this view is Nestle's statement (p. 12) that "originally religion and morality had nothing to do with one another. The religious behavior of primitive man was essentially amoral and selfish." But Nestle (p. 5) also points out that "religion is never the concern of one individual but always of a smaller or larger community of men." If religion is a social phenomenon, then it must be connected with morality, for morality, particularly that of primitive man, is identical with the social order. In this connection Ulrich Wilamowitz-Moellendorff, *Der Glaube der Hellenen* (1913), I, 13, is more consistent, since he considers morality, rather than religion, as a product of social life. The belief in gods arises from individual experience. "It is a fundamental fact which must never be overlooked—although this is done very often—that morality originates from communal living as distinguished from the belief in gods who are only later transformed into moral beings by men."

62. Hesiod *Works and Days* 256 (Loeb).

63. *Ibid.* 213 ff. (Loeb).

64. *Ibid.* 222 ff. (Loeb).

65. *Ibid.* 174 f. (Loeb).
66. *Ibid.* 242 ff. (Loeb).
67. *Ibid.* 249 ff. (Loeb).
68. *Ibid.* 267 ff. (Loeb).
69. *Ibid.* 123 ff. (Loeb).
70. *Ibid.* 252 ff. (Loeb).
71. *Ibid.* 276 ff. (Loeb).
72. *Ibid.* 256 ff. (Loeb).
73. *Ibid.* 258 ff. (Loeb).
74. *Luke* 16:15.
75. *Mark* 10:31.
76. Hesiod *Works and Days* 3 ff. (Loeb). Nestle, pp. 99 f., refers to Archilochus of Parus (*ca.* 650 B.C.), of whom a similar saying has been handed down to us: "One should submit everything to the gods who may elevate the humble and humiliate the great." Of Zeus the same poet says that he not only has dominion in heaven but also perceives the righteous and unrighteous acts of men and even controls might and right in the animal world. Cf. E. Diehl, *Anthologia Lyrica* (1936), frags. 58, 94.
77. Solon 4. 14 f. (in Loeb, *Elegy and Iambus*, I, 118–19).
78. *Ibid.* 13. 16 f. (Loeb, pp. 126–27).
79. Theognis 201 ff. (in Loeb, *Elegy and Iambus*, I, 252–53).
80. *Ibid.* 731 ff. (Loeb, pp. 316–17).
81. *Ibid.* 377 ff. (Loeb), pp. 274–75).
82. *Ibid.* 741 ff. (Loeb, pp. 318–19).
83. Cf. Wundt, pp. 189 f., 221 f.
84. Sophocles *Oedipus the King* 863 ff. (Loeb).
85. Aeschylus *The Persians* 853 ff. (E. H. Plumptre *Aeschylos* [1901]).
86. Aeschylus *The Suppliant Maidens* 77 ff. (Loeb).
87. *Ibid.* 395 f. (Loeb).
88. Aeschylus *The Libation-bearers* 946 ff. (Loeb).
89. Aeschylus *Agamemnon* 772 ff. (Loeb).
90. Cf. Wundt, p. 194.
91. Aeschylus *Agamemnon* 1431 ff. (Loeb).
92. *Ibid.* 1577 ff. (Loeb).
93. *Ibid.* 1608 ff. (Loeb).
94. Aeschylus *The Libation-bearers* 118 ff. (Loeb).
95. *Ibid.* 143 ff. (Loeb).
96. *Ibid.* 244 ff. (Loeb).
97. *Ibid.* 398 ff. (Loeb). It is uncertain whether these words were spoken by Orestes or Electra. The decision is for Electra in H. W. Smyth's translation (Loeb).
98. Aeschylus *The Libation-bearers* 497 ff. (Loeb).
99. *Ibid.* 639 ff. (Loeb).
100. *Ibid.* 935 ff. (Loeb).
101. *Ibid.* 987 ff. (Loeb).
102. Sophocles *Electra* 32 ff. (Loeb).
103. *Ibid.* 472 ff. (Loeb).
104. Sophocles *Antigone* 456 ff. (Loeb).
105. Aeschylus *Agamemnon* 1562 ff. (Loeb).
106. Aeschylus *The Libation-bearers* 306 ff. (Loeb).
107. Sophocles *Oedipus the King* 883 ff. (Loeb).
108. Sophocles *Oedipus at Colonus* 229 ff. (Loeb).
109. Nestle, p. 123.
110. Aeschylus *The Persians* 818 ff. (Loeb).

111. Cf. W. Christ, *Geschichte der griechischen Literatur* (Vol. VII of *Handbuch der klassischen Altertumswissenschaft*, herausgegeben von Iwan von Mueller [6th ed. 1912]), Part I, p. 342.

112. Cf., on the other hand, Wilamowitz-Moellendorff, *Griechische Tragoedien*, I, 15 f., who asserts that Sophocles never speaks of "fate as a cause, an effective force," but that for him it is "the gods, loving and hating, blessing and spoiling, heavenly and infernal beings," who act—gods "which he and his people venerated, feared, and sought to dispose favorably through sacrifices and prayers."

113. Sophocles *Oedipus the King* 273 ff. (Loeb).

114. *Ibid.* 341 (Loeb).

115. Aeschylus *Prometheus Bound* 169 ff. (Loeb).

116. *Ibid.* 103 ff. (Loeb).

117. *Ibid.* 511 ff. (Loeb).

118. Ferdinand Duemmler, *Prolegomena zu Platons Staat und der Platonischen und Aristotelischen Staatslehre* (1891), p. 14. A collection of all the Euripides references, in which the ideas that one must submit unconditionally to the laws of the state and that laws must be obeyed under all circumstances are expressed, can be found in K. Schenkl, "Die politischen Anschauungen des Euripides," *Zeitschrift fuer oesterreichische Gymnasien*, XIII (1862), 373 ff., 489.

119. Euripides *Suppliants* 549 ff. (Loeb).

120. *Ibid.* 564 f. (Loeb).

121. Euripides *Cyclops* 336 ff. (Loeb).

121a. Euripides *Electra* 737 ff. (Loeb).

122. Euripides *Electra* 954 ff. (Loeb).

123. *Ibid.* 957 ff. (Loeb).

124. Euripides *Helen* 1030 ff. (Loeb).

125. Euripides *Hecuba* 1029 ff. (Loeb).

126. *Ibid.* 1085 f. (Loeb).

127. Euripides *Archelaus*, frag. 255 (Nauck).

128. Euripides *Antiope*, frag. 233 (translated by Michael Wodhull, *The Nineteen Tragedies and Fragments of Euripides* [1809], III, 335).

129. Euripides *Phrixus*, frag. 835 (Wodhull, III, 401).

130. Euripides *Melanippe*, frag. 506 (translated by Gilbert Murray in *The Athenian Drama*, Vol. III: *Euripides* [1912], p. 330).

131. W. Nestle, *Euripides, der Dichter der griechischen Aufklaerung* (1901), p. 152.

132. Cf. Duemmler, pp. 32 f.

133. Euripides *Antiope*, frag. 222 (Wodhull, III, 335).

134. Euripides *Bellerophontes*, frag. 303 (Wodhull, III, 344).

135. Euripides *The Madness of Hercules* 777 ff. (Theodore Alois Buckley, *The Tragedies of Euripides Literally Translated or Revised* [1863]).

136. Euripides *Hippolytos Kalyptomenos*, frag. 441.

137. Euripides *Iphigeneia in Taurica* 1486 (Loeb).

138. Euripides *Alcestis* 965 ff. (Loeb).

139. Euripides *Bellerophontes*, frag. 229 (Nauck).

140. Euripides *The Madness of Hercules* 309 ff. (Loeb).

141. Euripides *Phoenix*, frag. 810 (Wodhull, III, 401).

142. Euripides *Chrysippos*, frag. 840 (Wodhull, III, 415).

143. Euripides *Helen* 711 ff. (Loeb).

144. Naegelsbach, *Nachhomerische Theologie*, p. 36.

145. *Ibid.*, p. 31.

146. In the many testimonies which we possess of the belief of the Greeks in the justice of the gods the idea of punishment plays a much more important part than the idea of reward. In the pre-Homeric worship of the dead, fear of the avenging soul which inflicts evil

upon men obviously represents the primary element, whereas hope for its protection, for the benefits to be obtained, and thus the love of it, represents a mere secondary element. The soul is a bad demon rather than a guardian spirit. This is a typical element of the soul belief of many primitive peoples. J. Carver writes in his *Travels through the Interior Parts of North America* (London, 1781), p. 388: "The human mind in its uncultivated state is apt to ascribe the extraordinary occurrences of nature, such as earthquakes, thunder, or hurricanes, to the interposition of unseen beings; the troubles and disasters also that are annexed to a savage life, the apprehensions attendant upon a precarious subsistence, and those numberless inconveniences which man in his improved state has found means to remedy, are supposed to proceed from the interposition of evil spirits; the savage consequently lives in continual apprehensions of their unkind attacks, and to avert them has recourse to charms, to the fantastic ceremonies of his priest, or the powerful influence of his *Manitous*. Fear has of course a greater share in his devotions than gratitude, and he pays more attention to deprecating the wrath of the evil than to securing the favour of the good beings." E. Bendann, in her work on *Death Customs* (1930), p. 182, remarks: "The malevolence of ghosts seems even to be more pronounced than their function as guardian spirits." The justice of the Olympic gods, too, is expressed in the punishment of evil rather than in the reward of good. Doubts in the very existence of the gods may be aroused by the fact that the evil remains unpunished, but not by the fact that the good remains unrewarded. Consequently, the ethical system which Greek theology based on the principle of justice was a system of punishment and not of reward. "In the sphere of divine justice," writes Naegelsbach in *Die nachhomerische Theologie*, pp. 37, 43, "punishment is predominant; its law is more inviolable than that of reward; in the consciousness of the people the certainty of punishment was stronger than the hope of reward." Similarly Gruppe, pp. 1003 f., points out that "before the religious revolution in the sixth century [he means the appearance of the Orphic and Pythagorean mysticism] only rarely did one hear of reward of the devout, and even if one heard of it, it appears more as the voluntary personal grace of the deity than as a title which the virtuous may claim."

Whereas religious ideology with respect to the evildoer is extremely eager to exclude the possibility that he may remain unpunished, it has the tendency with respect to the good man rather to make his reward appear superfluous. This is expressed in the doctrine that virtue insures its own reward. Even the idea occasionally appears that "it is good fortune to be virtuous. That there should be any reward for this good fortune seems so unnecessary that, reversely, the preceding virtue is regarded as compensation for the ensuing ruin" (Gruppe, p. 1004). When Hector, clad in the arms of Achilles, went into battle, Zeus decided that, as recompense for his imminent death at the hands of Achilles, he may be victorious once more (*Iliad* xvii. 206 f.).

Even in the idea of retribution realized in the other world, where imagination need not feel any restraints with regard to the joys that await good people, the element of punishment predominates. On the basis of rich historical material Leopold Schmidt asserts (I, 101) that "the phantasy of the people depicted much clearer the punishments which bad people had to expect in Hades than the rewards which good people may receive." In Homer signs of a punishing but not of a rewarding justice in the other world can be noted. The "Elysian Plain" of which Homer speaks and which one has to imagine in this world and not in Hades is not a paradise to which just people come as reward after death but a place of bliss to which certain human beings specially favored by the gods are conducted, where they live without having to die, such as Menelaus; but they are there more because of their relationship to the gods than as a result of their merits (Rohde, *Psyche*, p. 61). And, indeed, one of the pictures which Polygnotus of Thasus painted for the Lesche of the Cnidians in Delphi, namely, that which represents Odysseus in Hades, shows examples of atoning souls suffering punishment, but no hint of any reward for the just (Pausanias x. 25 ff.). As a matter of fact, punishment in the underworld was a frequent theme of painters. According to Orphic and Pythagorean belief, the sufferings which threaten the unjust, predominate over the joys which await the just (L. Schmidt, I, 101). As the law applied by the judge of the dead, Rhadamanthys, τὸ ʽΡαδαμάνθυος δίκαιον, Aristotle gives the following formula in his *Nicomachean Ethics* 1132b:

> "An a man suffer even that which he did,
> Right justice will be done."

And the principle of Pythagorean justice is: τὸ ἀντιπεπονθός, i.e., retaliation. Cf. K. F. Hermann, "Ueber Grundsaetze und Anwendung des Strafrechts im griechischen Altertum," *Abhandlungen der Kgl. Ges. der Wissensch. in Goettingen* (1855), VI, 8.

Especially in the Orphic and Pythagorean doctrine of metempsychosis is the element of punishment overstressed, since all earthly life is interpreted as punishment. True, after death the soul of the just receives a better lot in the underworld than the soul of the unjust; one also speaks of the joys of good people in the other world. But the soul does not remain in the other world; it must be reborn in order to suffer punishments again. Its real reward consists in the escape from the chain of births. As long as no documents are at hand which represent this condition as a positive well-being, one may assume that reward consists only in the negative cessation of punishment. Rohde, pp. 345, 359, who inclines toward the opposite view, admits that no Orphic fragment shows proof of a positive aspect of the negative escape from the world of birth and death. In the older Pythagorean tradition not even "the withdrawal of the soul from the κύκλος ἀνάγκης and its return to an emancipated existence as a bodiless spirit is promised to the 'Pure' " (Rohde, p. 398).

But what is the meaning of this obvious predominance of punishing over rewarding retribution in the picture of divine justice? Fundamentally both are equivalent; one is impossible without the other—indeed, one is only the consequence, only the reverse, of the other. What is the explanation for this striking one-sidedness in the religious system? We know that, of all the divine qualities, Greek popular religion adhered mainly to justice; that, in spite of so many weaknesses of the gods which the Greeks tolerated, "the idea of gods punishing unjustly did not arise" (Naegelsbach, p. 40). Why, then, is punishment for sin and not reward for merit an indispensable postulate of religion? The explanation that human conscience, from which the belief in justice arises, is a more consistent power than the imagination by which the other qualities of the human-like gods of Greece are created is not enough. Unsatisfactory, also, is the reference to the fact that evil attracts more attention than good, and the consequent necessity that punishment is much more in people's consciousness than good and its reward (L. Schmidt, I, 62). Such psychology is more than questionable. The situation is at once clarified if Greek religion is not considered an isolated system but is thought of as closely related with the socially living human beings who use the system for their self-preservation. This means that religion is comprehended as social ideology. One is forced to accept this assumption by the role which justice plays in the Greek doctrine of the gods. Justice is an essentially social category. For the individual separated from his social surroundings there is no justice. And, if religion were nothing but the relationship of this individual to his personal deity, then the latter has nothing to do with justice. That we find in the center of Greek religion the idea of justice is evidence for its social character. A religion the fundamental value of which is justice can be comprehended only as the spiritual superstructure of a social reality. This reality is represented as a coercive order of human life which has—at least in its primitive stages—the character of a punitive and not of a rewarding order. Its function consists mainly in reacting with specific coercive acts against socially harmful behavior. Law is originally criminal law. Even modern law is a social order the technique of which consists in providing sanctions; and legal sanctions are forcible deprivation of certain possessions, such as life, health, freedom, or property; their function is to inflict an evil, not to afford a benefit. So-called "private law" has, from this point of view, the same structure as criminal law. Since the Greek sees the essence of law, which for him is criminal law, in retribution, divine justice must also appear to him as retribution. The fact that in Greek religion divine justice is, above all, a punitive and not essentially a rewarding retribution signifies that divine justice mirrors and justifies positive law. Greek religion is an ideology of the Greek state which has a judicial, rather than an administrative, character. Its task was to punish those who were bad, not to reward those who were good. From the concept of the state as a legal—and that means as a punishing, not a rewarding—authority proceeds the idea, widespread as a moral principle, that the good citizen has no right to the gratitude of his government. Therefore, man has no title—or only a weak and secondary title—to the gratitude of his gods, whose justice manifests itself more in punishment than in reward.

147. Naegelsbach, p. 32; Leopold Schmidt, I, 69; Gruppe, pp. 1002 f. This last says: "Since it is presupposed that the postulates of prevailing morality are fulfilled in this world the result is that not only for the poets of the Ionic epic poems but also for all the Greeks of the classical period a delict is unfailingly although sometimes slowly punished. . . . . This principle, like others of the Homeric world, was expressly formulated only by authors living after Homer."

148. Naegelsbach, pp. 33, 355; Leopold Schmidt, I, 71 f.

149. Cf. Leopold Schmidt, I, 67.

150. Modern interpreters constantly misunderstand the facts of collective responsibility and absolute liability, self-evident for primitive man; they see in these facts nothing but a shockingly hostile attitude of the gods toward innocent people. In so doing, however, they are mistaken, for these people are "innocent" only in the sense of our morality, which is based on liability for intent and individual responsibility. This is particularly true of hereditary liability, which seems especially "unjust" to us. One may ask whether collective responsibility and absolute liability, by which both divine justice and the actual social order of primitive man are determined, are principles tending to preserve human society. The question must be answered in the affirmative, in so far as the preventive function of a social order decreeing sanctions is concerned. As far as absolute liability is concerned—and even modern criminal law does not entirely exclude it—the preventive function can easily be recognized. If one must fear punishment, even when the result is brought about involuntarily, one will be particularly careful to avoid it. When Charles Dundas, "Native Laws of Some Bantu Tribes of East Africa," *Journal of the Royal Anthropological Institute of Great Britain and Ireland*, LI (1921), 240, asked a native why they do not distinguish between murder and accidental killing, the latter answered: "If we pardon one man who kills by accident there will be nothing but accidents."

As for collective, and especially hereditary responsibility, one must keep in mind the fact that primitive man, by virtue of the thoroughly collectivistic attitude of his consciousness, will probably take an evil inflicted upon his group or descendants much harder than one which he must suffer himself. Collective responsibility, whereby a whole family or even a tribe is destroyed for the wrong of an individual, is, from an economic point of view, not a very rational social technique. But most primitive techniques are uneconomical.

151. Rohde, pp. 40 f., says that "we have no reason or excuse for attributing to this particular poet [Homer] such a desire to prove the existence of a compensatory justice in an after life." Cf. also Finsler, pp. 211 ff.

152. *Iliad* iii. 279; xix. 260.

153. Cf. Albrecht Dieterich, *Nekyia* (2d ed., 1913), pp. 54, 57; Nilsson, "Die Griechen," p. 333.

154. *Odyssey* xi. 576 ff.

155. Cf. Rohde, pp. 32 ff.; Gruppe, p. 1023; Nilsson, p. 332. Rohde and Nilsson question the Orphic influence. In the *Odyssey* xi. 568, Odysseus says he has seen Minos

adjudging punishments and rewards to the dead. Here it is evidently the deeds performed in the Hades because of which the dead are punished and rewarded, not the deeds performed during their lifetime. Cf. Peterich, p. 318.

156. *Odyssey* xi. 475–76 (Loeb). Significant are the words which the shade of Achilles speaks to Odysseus (*ibid.* 488 ff. [Loeb]): "Nay, seek not to speak soothingly to me of death, glorious Odysseus. I should choose, so I might live on earth, to serve as the hireling of another, of some portionless man whose livelihood was but small, rather than to be lord over all the dead that have perished."

157. Cf. Finsler, pp. 223 ff., 227.

158. Cf. W. F. Otto, *Die Manen* (1923), pp. 14 ff., 26, 33; also Joachim Boehme, *Die Seele und das Ich im homerischen Epos* (1929), p. 86.

Clear signs of the above-mentioned idea relating to the life soul as the guardian spirit, not identical with the man to whom it belongs, can be found among the Greeks in their belief in the life demon of man. A fragment of Menander (frag. 550) reads as follows: "By everyone of us at birth forthwith there stands a spirit, a spirit guide, beneficent, to lead us through life's mysteries" (Loeb).

Also compare Nilsson, *Die Religion der Griechen*, p. 82. A highly sublimated ethical remainder is the *Daimonion* of Socrates, that inner voice which "always forbids but never commands me to do anything which I am going to do" (Plato *Apology* 31 [Jowett]). The guardian spirit as a leader in Hades appears in Plato's *Phaedo* (107): "For after death, as they say, the genius of each individual, to whom he belonged in life, leads him to a certain place in which the dead are gathered together for judgment, whence they go into the world below, following the guide, who is appointed to conduct them from this world to the other" (Jowett).

The life soul as a leader in Hades is an idea which can be found among various primitive peoples. Thus there exists among the Sulka of the Gazelle Peninsula the custom of having two men sleep near the body of a dead man the night after his death. They do that in order that their souls may accompany the soul of the dead into the other world (Rosalind Moss, *The Life after Death in Oceania and the Malay Archipelago* [1925], p. 104). Sleeping near the dead is a custom widespread in Melanesia. Since only the life soul of the living man sleeping near the dead can guide the soul of the dead into the spirit world, one must assume that the former, rather than the latter, knows the way there. That the life soul has a special connection with the other world is also borne out by the fact that, according to a widespread idea, it goes there during dreams in order to obtain from the death souls important messages for the sleeping one. Thus G. Landtman, "Wanderings of the Dead in the Folk-Lore of the Kiwai-speaking Papuans," in *Festskrift Tillegnad Eduard Westermarck* (1912), p. 71, says: "A great number of dreams collected by me among the Kiwai people tell of wanderings to *Adiri* [i.e., the island afterworld] or of meetings with spirits of dead men, and as dreams are believed to describe the real things which the soul sees while roaming about outside the body, we understand that they must greatly influence the imagination of the people." This specific relation of the life soul as guardian spirit to the realm of the dead is very important evidence for the fact that the life soul before its incarnation into a human being was a death soul. Accordingly, it was acquainted with a sphere into which the death soul of someone just deceased was a new arrival. The other world is the real home of the soul, not only of the individual and unique soul of the pious Christian, but also of the life soul of primitive man.

159. Solon 13. 29 ff.

160. Theognis 704–10, 205 ff. Cf. also Rohde, *Psyche*, pp. 411 ff.

161. Rohde, pp. 412 ff., 421 ff., 425.

162. Naegelsbach, *Nachhomerische Theologie*, pp. 413 ff., writes: "Although death alone brings an end to all suffering it brings neither positive fortune nor happiness, but a joyless existence. It is true, however, that the Eleusinian and Orphic-Pythagorean doctrines contradict this desperate outlook of Homeric religion; fragments of these doctrines mixed with

popular (Homeric) ideas are introduced into literature by Pindar, not by the tragic poets. Although these poets amplify the Homeric idea of the other world, tragedy is silent about man's main desire, the comfort of a blessed immortality. In other words, Homeric religion still prevails." "The idea of judges of the dead cannot originate before a doctrine of rewards and punishments in the other world is developed, i.e. before the Homeric idea is mixed with Orphic and Eleusinian elements." Cf. also Leopold Schmidt, I, 97.

163. Cf. Wilamowitz-Moellendorff, *Der Glaube der Hellenen*, I, 302 ff.; Nilsson, "Die Griechen," pp. 296 ff.; Ernst Samter, *Die Religion der Griechen* (2d ed. 1925), pp. 12 ff.; Kern, *Die Religion der Griechen*, I, 28 ff.; Peterich, *Die Theologie der Hellenen*, pp. 60 ff.

164 Kern, p. 30, believes: "Whether the idea that the powers which determine and guide human lives dwell in the earth proceeds from the worship of the dead will never be explained for certain." Clearly never for certain, but nevertheless with great probability.

165. Samter, pp. 14 f.

166. The soul of the dead Patroclus appears to Achilles in a dream and says to him (*Iliad* xxiii. 70 ff. [Loeb]): "Not in my life wast thou unmindful of me, but now in my death! Bury me with all speed, that I pass within the gates of Hades. Afar do the spirits keep me aloof, the phantoms of men that have done with toils, neither suffer they me to join myself to them beyond the River, but vainly I wander through the wide-gated house of Hades."

The *Iliad* shows clear signs of an older form of soul belief originating at a time when one feared only the death souls of one's own group; for strangers and enemies, no such fear existed, and thus they recognized no duty to bury their corpses. When Agamemnon grants an armistice to the Trojans, he says (*ibid.* vii. 409 f.): "But as touching the dead I in no wise grudge that ye burn them; for to dead corpses should no man grudge, when once they are dead, the speedy consolation of fire." He thus shows clearly that it is not at all his business to "console" dead enemies. After he has triumphed over Hector, Achilles speaks (*ibid.*, xxii. 331 ff.): "Hector, thou thoughtest, I ween, whilst thou wast spoiling Patroclus, that thou wouldest be safe, and hadst no thought of me that was afar, thou fool. Far from him a helper, mightier far, was left behind at the hollow ships, even I, that have loosed thy knees. Thee shall dogs and birds rend in unseemly wise, but to him shall the Achaeans give burial." When Hector says (*ibid.* 338 f.), "I implore thee by thy life and knees and parents, suffer me not to be devoured of dogs by the ships of the Achaeans," it shows that he considers such treatment possible. But when he finally threatens (*ibid.* 358), "Bethink thee now lest haply I bring the wrath of the gods upon thee," it marks the first symptoms of an extending social consciousness the demiurge of which was no longer the wrath of the death soul of the slain enemy but a deity superior to friendship and enmity. According to a supposedly older version (cf. Finsler, Part I, sec. 1, p. 162), Achilles threw Hector's body to the dogs. The fact that in the version handed down to us he permits the old father to take the body of his son and bury it with honor is the product of a more refined sense of justice. This refinement is lacking in the case of Hector, who ordered that the head of the vanquished Patroclus be cut off and stuck on a pile before being thrown to the Trojan dogs (*Iliad* xvii. 126; xviii. 176 f.). Indeed, the idea prevails in the *Iliad* that it is the natural right of the victor to desecrate the dead body of the enemy and to cool his anger on it; neither the soul of the dead nor the gods will inflict punishment for such acts. Thus Diomedes says of the enemy whom he will kill in battle (*ibid.* xi. 394 f.): ". . . . while he, reddening the earth with his blood, rotteth away, more birds than women around him." And the Trojans killed by Agamemnon are described (*ibid.* xi. 161 f.) as "lying upon the ground dearer far to the vultures than to their wives."

The duty to bury one's own companions is also abandoned, and neither the wrath of the death soul nor the deity is operative if group members are involved who have made themselves guilty of a grave violation of the legal order. The worst crime in war is to shun battle. As a consequence, Agamemnon declares (*Iliad* ii. 391 ff.): "But whomsoever I shall see minded to tarry apart from the fight beside the beaked ships, for him shall there be no hope thereafter to escape the dogs and birds." Such is the law of war which is likewise valid for the Trojans (cf. *Iliad* xv. 348 ff.; *Odyssey* iii. 258 ff.; xxii. 30).

167. *Iliad* vi. 417 f. (Loeb).

168. *Odyssey* xxii. 411 ff. (Loeb).

169. Even in the nature of the divine gods, as pictured by the poet, one can detect the last effects of a religious belief at the center of which was the event of death. Primitive man fears death and believes that the dead person or the death soul brings it to the living. Therefore, Circe suggests to Odysseus that he turn his head away when he calls up the dead (*Odyssey* x. 529). The sight of the deity also brings death. This is apparently the reason (although the poet himself was no longer conscious of it) for Leucothea's order to Odysseus to throw her sacred veil, after he saved himself with its help, into the sea "with his face turned away"; obviously, she warns him in order that he may not see the goddess who afterward rises to the surface (Nestle, *Griechische Religiositaet*, p. 19). And for the same reason, when Thetis places before Achilles the arms forged by divine hands, it is said (*Iliad* xix. 13 ff.): "Then trembling seized all the Myrmidons, neither dared any man to look thereon, but they shrank in fear"; and (*ibid.* xx. 131): "For hard are the gods to look upon when they appear in manifest presence."

Fear is the original emotion of Homeric man toward the deity. Therefore, he immediately asks for mercy when he believes he perceives the latter, for instance, in human shape. When Athena grants Odysseus, who had appeared as a beggar, his glorious figure again, Telemachus says (*Odyssey* xvi. 181 ff.): "Of other sort thou seemest to me now, stranger, than awhile ago, and other are the garments thou hast on, and thy colour is no more the same. Verily thou art a god, one of those who hold broad heaven. Nay then, be gracious, that we may offer to thee acceptable sacrifices and golden gifts, finely wrought; but do thou spare us."

170. Aeschylus *The Libation-bearers* 323 ff. (Loeb).

171. Sophocles *Electra* 1419 ff. (Loeb).

172. Xenophon *Cyropaedia* VIII. vii. 17 (Loeb).

173. Herodotus i. 167 (Loeb).

174. Pausanias *Description of Greece* vi. 6 (Loeb). Cf. Fustel de Coulanges, *La Cité antique* (26th ed., 1920), p. 20.

175. Rohde, pp. 134 f. In the veneration of heroes Rohde perceives a "cult of ancestors," not "a cult of souls" (cf. p. 118). But the cult of ancestors is itself a form of the cult of souls. In what other form than in that of a "soul" could the dead ancestor survive? Only a belief in the soul's efficacy is the reason for the worship devoted to it. The close connection between hero veneration and death-soul worship is borne out by the fact that the hero frequently appears in the shape of a snake. Cf. J. E. Harrison, *Themis* (1912), pp. xiv, 260 ff. Miss Harrison remarks: "The hero on examination turns out to be, not a historical great man who happens to be dead, but a dead ancestor performing his due functions as such, who may in particular cases happen to have been a historical great man. As hero he is a functionary."

176. Herodotus vii. 134 f., 136 f. (Loeb). Cf. Rohde, pp. 134 ff. Other examples of heroes taking revenge and exercising retribution may be found there.

177. Samter, p. 16.

178. Cf. Kern, I, 30 ff.

179. Rohde, p. 176.

180. *Ibid.*, pp. 176 f.

181. *Ibid.*, pp. 177 ff. If, before his death, the murdered man has forgiven the murderer, the relatives have no duty of prosecution. Rohde, p. 177, interprets this fact by stating that "to such an extent was the injured soul's wish for vengeance the only point at issue, even in the legal procedure of a constitutionally governed state, and not in the least the lawless act

of the murderer as such." This is only the consequence of the principle of private prosecution which prevailed in older legal orders. The relationship to the "soul" of the murdered man is only the ideological and not the real reason. It is, therefore, not, as Rohde believes (p. 178), a reassertion of "the original claim to vengeance of the victim violently done to death—a claim closely bound up with the cult of the dead" when the state later forbids "the old custom, common in Homeric times, of buying off the blood guiltiness of the murderer by a compensatory payment made to the relatives of the dead man." It is simply the legal-technical advance toward the principle of public prosecution in modern criminal procedure, a typical stage in the evolution from blood revenge to the centralized jurisdiction of state courts. This development is accomplished independently of any belief in the soul. When Rohde says, p. 179, "The whole procedure at murder trials was directed rather to the satisfaction of invisible powers. . . . . than of the state and its living members," then he accepts as objective reality what in fact is only a subjective ideology. Indeed, the institution in question serves the state and its citizens better the more it seems to serve invisible powers.

182. Euripides *Iphigeneia in Taurica* 1223 f. (Loeb).

183. Rohde, p. 296.

184. Aeschylus *The Libation-bearers* 1048 ff.

185. *Iliad* ix. 447 f. The Erinyes appear in the myth of Cronus and Uranus in connection with the castration complex.

186. *Ibid.* 568 ff. That the mother considers the life of her brother of greater value than that of her son indicates a mother-right organization according to which the mother's brother occupies the position of authority.

187. *Ibid.* xv. 204.

188. *Ibid.* xix. 259 (Loeb). See also above, p. 212, where this passage has already been discussed.

189. *Ibid.* 264 f. (Loeb). The Erinyes as goddesses who exercise retribution for wrongs inflicted upon poor people: cf. *Odyssey* xvii. 475.

190. Aeschylus *Eumenides* 162 f. (Loeb).

191. *Ibid.* 349 ff. (Loeb).

192. *Ibid.* 365 f. (Loeb).

193. *Ibid.* 385 ff. (Loeb).

194. *Ibid.* 490 ff. (Loeb).

195. *Ibid.* 727 f. (Loeb).

196. *Ibid.* 808 f. (Loeb).

197. *Ibid.* 837 ff. (Loeb).

198. E. Rohde, pp. 178 f.

199. Heraclitus, frag. 29, in John Burnet, *Early Greek Philosophy* (4th ed., 1930), p. 135.

200. The individualized Erinys, the Demeter-Erinys (cf. Kern, I, 60), shows clearly a certain process of centralization by which the death soul becomes a personal earth-deity; it also shows the origin of Demeter in the death-soul belief.

201. Kern, I, 51.

202. Cf. Erich Kuester, *Die Schlange in der griechischen Kunst und Religion* ("Religionsgeschichtliche Versuche und Vorarbeiten," herausgegeben von Richard Wünsch und Ludwig Deubner, Band XIII, Heft 2 [1913]). The author remarks, p. 56, that the Greeks must have recognized very early the demonic nature of the snake; he explains the veneration and fear inspired by the snake here and elsewhere by its natural qualities. But this explanation does not suffice. For, on the one hand, the snake is, in fact, much less dangerous than many another animal—it appears in ancient times as a domestic animal exterminating mice, children play with it, ladies cool their necks and bosoms with it; on the other hand, it is venerated as a guardian spirit. The ambivalent attitude toward this animal is decisive for the interpretation of its function. And this ambivalence can only be understood through the belief in the soul of the dead and not through natural science. Kuester, p. 57, stresses the fact

that, although the snake has very weak vision, belief and superstition ascribe magical effect to its vision. For primitive man, the snake also has a phallic significance. Cf. Kuester, p. 49, for the same idea in antiquity. The phallic nature of the snake is closely connected with the idea of the reincarnation of a death soul which penetrates the woman's body in order to be reborn by her. Greek mythology also furnishes rich material for this view (cf. Gruppe, pp. 866 f.; Harrison, pp. 260 ff.) Miss Harrison remarks, p. 266: "Probably at first the snake was the totemistic vehicle of reincarnation and only later, when the true nature of parentage was known, identified with the φάλλος." It may be pointed out here that the sexual function of the death soul was also transferred to the Erinyes. They favor the fertility not only of the soil but also of human beings (cf. Rohde, p. 171). Since the children of the men of the tribe of the Aegidae did not survive, according to a story of Herodotus (iv. 149), they "set up . . . . a temple of the avenging spirits of Laius and Oedipus, after which the children lived." Cf. Wilamowitz-Moellendorff, *Der Glaube der Hellenen*, I, 405.

203. L. Radermacher, *Das Jenseits im Mythos der Hellenen* (1903), p. 127.

204. Rohde, p. 179. K. O. Mueller asserted in 1833 in his edition of the *Eumenides* that "the anger of the offended parents and the goddess Erinys are originally one and the same" (p. 166). B. W. Leist, *Graeco-italische Rechtsgeschichte* (1884), pp. 320 f., points out that the Erinys is not only the spirit of vengeance exercising retribution on the evildoer but also the author of the evil sentiment which confuses man's senses and gives him bad counsel. That wrong and punishment correspond to one another is expressed by the fact "that the same divine power is represented as causing the wrong and executing vengeance." The wrath, the Erinys, of the "perpetrator," is the cause of the wrong (Ate, Hybris), the wrath of the killed person is the cause of atonement. "The killed man is the demon whose vengeance does not rest until the perpetrator has, through punishment inflicted upon him, atoned for his wrong." Both the wrath of the perpetrator and that of the murdered are regarded as grave misfortunes sent by the gods. In order to express this idea, the wrath is personified as Erinys, a divine being (p. 322). Julius Lippert, *Die Religion der europaeischen Kulturvoelker* (1881), p. 367, also interprets the Erinys as a death soul.

205. The fact that in the cults of the chthonian deities the purification ceremonies are already highly developed indicates the close connection of these powers with atonement, particularly with liberation from blood guilt; moreover, the Erinyes, the typical demons of retribution, are the executive agents. Significant for the legal character of the earth-deity is the fact that the ritual lapidation of a man, frequently mentioned in the sources, was a primitive sacrifice which should be understood as a devotion to the deities of the underworld (cf. Kern, I, 31). The name of the female earth-deity in pre-Greek times is unknown. In Homer her name is Ge. Significantly, she is addressed, together with the Erinyes, in the previously mentioned oath formula. Here Zeus and Helius precede her; this may be traced to the influence of the younger Olympic gods, who tried to suppress the belief in the old earth-deity; it is probable that earlier she alone guaranteed the sacredness of the oath. Considering the great importance of the oath for the law, one can very well regard the deity protecting the oath as a deity of justice. This is borne out by the fact that Ge is the oldest oracle-deity. Just as she preceded Apollo in Delphi, she also preceded Zeus in Olympia (cf. Wilamowitz-Moellendorff, I, 205). Only because she was an old deity of justice can Hesiod (*Theogony* 135) call Themis, this purest personification of law, her daughter. Accordingly, Aeschylus identifies the two in a speech of Prometheus (*Prometheus Bound*, 211 ff.): "Full oft my mother Themis, or Earth (one form she hath but many names), had foretold to me the way in which the future was fated to come to pass." Before Apollo, she was, as Ge-Themis, the possessor of the Delphic Oracle (cf. Kern, I, 190). Considering the original identity of truth and justice, an oracle deity must also be a justice-deity. In Olympia the altar of Themis stood on the Gaion near that of Ge (Pausanias v. 14; cf. L. Preller, *Griechische Mythologie* [4th ed.; revised by Carl Robert (1894)], I, 476; Harrison, pp. 480 ff.). Therefore she is supposed to appear as a witness for Solon when the latter has to defend his dis-

burdening ordinance by which all debts were canceled. He had extricated the ὅροι, the debt-stones, from the body of black Mother Earth, Γῆ μέλαινα, into which they were pushed, apparently violating law and justice (cf. Albrecht Dieterich, *Mutter Erde* [3d ed., 1925], p. 37). In the Orphic mysteries the noephyte boasts that he is a son of Ge, which means that he is a child of law (cf. Dieterich, *Nekyia*, p. 100).

The younger Ge is called Demeter. Her byname is Erinys, the death soul exercising retribution. She is venerated as Demeter-Erinys. Wilamowitz-Moellendorff, I, 283, states: "In Erinys, that is the angered one who was later called Demeter, we must see nature which is here [not a mother but] a step-mother. This may sound too abstract but nevertheless it is the best explanation." Only one who is biased in his opinion that the oldest religion had the character of a religion of nature can assume that Demeter-Erinys was angered nature. It is the requiting law which is expressed here. Like the Erinyes, and before them the death souls, Demeter is also the guardian of the family order, the protectress of the law of marriage and by extension a deity of fertility and birth; as such, she is later a specific goddess of women. From certain Demeter cults, like the Thesmophoria, men were excluded. But the most frequent epithet of Demeter is Θεσμοφόρος, the one who establishes the law (cf. Preller-Robert, pp. 747 ff.). Θεσμοί are legal norms. It is not likely, as Wilamowitz-Moellendorff, I, 208 ff., asserts, that Demeter is called thus because she is a goddess of agriculture, which by virtue of the static quality of life requires a legal order. For nomadic hunter and cattle-breeders also have, in so far as they live socially, a legal order which plays the same role for them as for settled agricultural people. Demeter is Thesmophoros for the same reason and in the same sense as she is Erinys, because all law, especially retribution, which determined the oldest law, proceeds from her. Since she is Erinys and Thesmophoros, she is—just like her older variant, Ge—regarded as Themis' mother; this clearly stresses that the law is her function. Corresponding to the advanced social development, it is a superior and more refined law, which is more than mere revenge for murder. Society, too, has changed from a blood community into a state. One may find this idea in a myth which relates how Demeter, a mare, was mounted by Poseidon, a stallion, and gave birth to two children—one son, the cursed steed Erion, and one daughter, Themis (cf. Wilamowitz-Moellendorff, I, 283; Kern, I, 60). These two represent fierce vengeance, still preserved in the goddess Demeter-Erinys, and the milder law, Demeter-Themis. As the latter, she is not only the guardian of the family order but also the goddess of the state (cf. Kern, I, 226). If the Eleusinian mysteries apply mainly to Demeter, it is not only because she is the goddess of fertility but also because she is the protectress of justice.

As Themis, the law appears as an independent function detached from the earth-goddess. In Homer, for whom Demeter is only the goddess of fertility (*Iliad* v. 500; xiii. 322; *Odyssey* v. 125), since the function of justice had already been transferred to the Olympic gods—above all, to Zeus—Themis represents the moral-legal order (cf. Preller-Robert, p. 476). But, in accordance with the victory of the Olympic gods over the chthonian deities, she is a subordinate figure. She has a more prominent role in Hesiod (*Theogony* 901 ff.), who makes her Ge's daughter, the wife of Zeus; she gives birth to the Horae: Dike, Eunomia, and Eirene. Thus the poet illustrates allegorically the transfer of the function of law from earth to heaven. Of this Themis, Wilamowitz-Moellendorff, I, p. 207, says: "Her power consists in the fact that the θεμιστοπόλοι βασιλῆες discharge the law in their θέμιστες. Still further goes the frequently used term, ἥ θέμις ἐστίν, which comprises everything appearing as natural law, even the relationship between husband and wife." Harrison, p. 483, remarks: "These *themistes* are the ordinances of what must be done, what society compels; they are also, because what must be will be, the prophecies of what shall be in the future."

Hecate, too, whose older name was presumably Enodia and who was sometimes identified with Persephone and sometimes with Artemis (cf. Wilamowitz-Moellendorff, I, 169 ff.), appears as a deity of earth and of the dead; she, too, must have had a close relationship with the law. This is borne out by the verses, dedicated to her, from Hesiod's *Theogony*

(409–52); there she is represented as especially favored by Zeus, the highest deity of justice; it is asserted that she was highly respected even by the immortal gods (416 ff.): "For to this day, whenever any one of men on earth offers rich sacrifices and prays for favour according to custom, he calls upon Hecate. . . . . She sits by worshipful kings in judgement."

A reference in Plato's *Laws* (xi. 914) also points to the legal function of this goddess; '.ere it is said: "If a man happens to leave behind him some part of his property, whether intentionally or unintentionally, let him who may come upon the left property suffer it to remain, reflecting that such things are under the protection of the Goddess of Ways ['Eνοδία δαίμων, i.e. Hecate], and are dedicated to her by the law" (cf. Wilamowitz-Moellendorff, p. 176). This assumption must be based on a very old idea, namely, that a demon from whom the goddess Hecate later arose guarantees the inhibition of theft of lost property.

Apollo and Zeus, who were in Homeric times, as well as in the religion of later periods, the most distinguished representatives of the idea of justice, are in this, their most important function, also connected with the powers of earth. Thus, as a god of oracle and guardian of the law against murder, Apollo was the successor of an earth-deity. The avenger of all blood guilt, he killed Python, a snake demon guarding the oracles, and thus made himself guilty of shedding blood, for which, according to the Delphic tale, he underwent a long atonement (cf. Preller-Robert, pp. 238 ff., 287; Harrison, pp. 385 f.). The god who forbade and punished murder was himself forced to murder and had to be punished for it; this identification of the norm addressee and the norm authority, of the punishing god and the man to be punished, is a very old means of assuring the efficacy of a norm. As Apollo Lycius, the god was closely connected with the realm of the dead, for the wolf which was consecrated to him and which gave him his byname is a typical death-soul animal; originally, Apollo himself appears to have had the shape of a wolf (cf. Gruppe, p. 1236). Furthermore, he also appeared in the shape of a wolf as the guardian of the courts of justice (cf. Preller-Robert, pp. 253 f.). As a son of Zeus, the highest guardian of the existent social order and the divine representative of public authority, Apollo was the god of positive law and, as such, a thoroughly conservative power. The specific Apollonian norm commands obedience to the gods and to ancestral customs as well as adherence to the laws of the state (cf. Nilsson, "Die Griechen," pp. 363 ff.). Other cults than those of the Delphic god served the demands of a justice surpassing the positive law; above all, the Orphic mysteries which were centered about Dionysus, who originally, perhaps, was a god both of the earth and of the dead. Dionysus, a son of Semele, who was an earth-goddess (cf. Harrison, pp. 418 f.), frequently appeared in the shape of a snake (cf. Gruppe, p. 807; further, Gustav Anrich, *Das antike Mysterienwesen in seinem Einfluss auf das Christentum* [1894], pp. 16, 29). It is comprehensible why the priesthood of the Delphic Apollo attempted to gain control over the religious movement which manifested itself with elemental force in the Dionysian cults and which, carried to the masses of the people, could easily have assumed a revolutionary character. Dionysus was finally mastered by Apollo, and Apollonian law subdued Dionysian justice. In the Delphic religion the two were united (cf. Rohde, pp. 287 f.; Nilsson, pp. 367 ff.).

It is probable that Zeus, the powerful king of the gods, whose will Apollo knew, announced, and executed, was originally a god of the weather. Brought along by immigrating Greeks, he first settled on Olympus (cf. Kern, I, 180). Two of his oldest characteristics seem to have been truth and justice. His thunderstorm may be interpreted as punishment (cf. Leist, *Graeco-italische Rechtsgeschichte*, p. 179). It was believed that his lightning reveals the future (cf. Gruppe, p. 1109) and kills the wrongdoers. Asclepius is the object of two tales, each of which shows one of these two different but nevertheless substantially coherent functions. According to the one, he is supposed to have raised someone from the dead, an act which is regarded as crime against the prevailing order. As punishment Zeus kills him with lightning. According to the other story, Zeus splits the earth for Asclepius, so that the latter may give health-bringing oracles from the depth (Gruppe, pp. 1453 f.). In many tales lightning sent by Zeus seems to have been an instrument of retribution (cf. Rohde, p. 582). The fact that the lightning is imagined as a snake, i.e., as the abode of a demon, has therefore a particular significance and is not a mere poetic figure (cf. Gruppe, p. 807). This also explains the ambivalent significance of death through lightning. Such a death was considered not only as punishment, and thus as disgraceful, but also as the opposite, since it hallowed the victim (cf. Rohde, I, 98 f., 100 f., 166, 302, 418, 543, 581 f., for examples interpreted in this way). Although Zeus, after his entrance into Greece, where cults had earlier been performed on the hills, subdued the mountain-gods, he nevertheless associated himself with earth-gods and powers of the depth who were more firmly rooted in the consciousness of men. Zeus Trophonius, Zeus Chthonius, and Zeus Meilichius are symptoms of this process. In particular, the last one, the snake-figured god of atonement, is important in this connection, for it shows the transfer of the law function from the older to the younger deity of justice. This transfer can also be perceived in the relationship of Zeus with the goddess of earth as the older deity of justice. As Rhea, daughter of Ge, she becomes his mother; as Leto, Themis, or Hera, who was probably also an old earth-goddess, she becomes his wife (cf. Kern, I, 195, 261); or, as in the oracle of Dodona, he even takes her place. A common altar of Zeus and Demeter existed in Phlye (cf. Nilsson, p. 321; Preller-Robert, p. 147).

206. Cf. Kern, I, 28, 40, 72, 182.

207. *Odyssey* xi. 72 f. (Loeb).

208. *Iliad* ix. 632 ff. (Loeb).

209. In Homer there is no evidence of the existence of any criminal jurisdiction of the state. The centralization of criminal jurisdiction must not necessarily coincide chronologically with the broadening of the legal community beyond the family, with the establishment of the state.

210. Rohde, pp. 55 f., is, therefore, wrong when he interprets the Homeric concept of the shadow existence of the dead as an expression of resignation. Nothing was more alien to the pugnacious nature of Homeric aristocracy than resignation. Every line of the two epics shows a fervent love of life and a deep abhorrence of death. Significant is Homer's statement that Hades is the "most hated by mortals of all gods" (*Iliad* ix. 158; cf. *Iliad* xiii. 415). This is not the expression of tired resignation. If Homeric men do not believe in survival after death, it is not because of weakness. (What could prevent their fantasy from fulfilling their wishes?) They do not need such a belief, because adequate reason for any such religious ideology is lacking. These human beings, whose concept of life must not be confused with occasional tempers of the poet, are, on the whole, satisfied with their existence on earth, for they are convinced that the order of their life is good and thus just. The idea of a survival of the soul is unnecessary. For these noble people the old death soul exercising retribution has no longer any importance; its function is carried out by Zeus. On the other hand, the time has not yet arrived for the supposition of an immortal soul which suffers retribution. The social order of the state and, with it, the conviction of a realization of justice on this earth remains unshaken in the consciousness of Homeric man.

211. In the course of the ninth or eighth century B.C. the old "divine right of kings" was abolished and replaced by a government of an aristocracy which relied economically on large estates. Peasants, involved in debts and reduced to slavery, were frequently expelled from their homes and forced to emigrate. Trade and industry, too, were largely in the hands of the nobility, although the propertied middle classes slowly began to participate in government. The ruling class was a plutocracy composed of an aristocracy of birth and a money nobility. Jurisdiction was solely in the hands of this class. Violation of law in the interest of this class was the ordinary thing. Customary formation of law prevailed; this made any adaption of the legal order to prevailing social circumstances almost impossible, and consequently made it more difficult for the poor man to obtain his right. Hesiod's poetry eloquently expresses this social situation. The decisive social contrast dur-

ing the seventh and sixth centuries B.C. is between "the enslaved peasants, tenants, day-laborers, odd jobbers, and sailors, all of whom have politically no rights, and the rich people, whether their wealth was inherited or acquired through trade and commerce" (cf. Lehmann-Haupt, "Griechische Geschichte bis zur Schlacht bei Chaironea," *Einleitung in die Altertumswissenschaft* [2d ed., 1914], III, 14; cf. also K. J. Beloch, *Griechische Geschichte* [2d ed., 1912], I, 206 f., 264 ff., 347 f.). The overthrow of the aristocratic-plutocratic regime frequently does not lead to democracy but to the rule of tyrants, who declare themselves to be representatives of the subdued people. It is significant of their ideological attitude that they favored religious revivals which had their sources in the older beliefs of the people. Thus the Peisistratids supported the Orphic doctrine.

Until the seventh century B.C. the view prevailed in Greece that the law is an expression of divine will and, as such, sacred. At that time, a "far-reaching revolution" occurred. "The positive law, which prevailed in the states, was now traced to human legislation. The legal order of Homeric times revealed by the gods (ϑέμις) is replaced by statutes (ϑεσμός, νόμος), a concept entirely alien to the epic poems. Human legislation, however, can be superseded by human legislation" (Beloch, p. 351). Hence the demand for codification of the law and the advance of conscious legislation. The decisive point in this change of the idea of the law is that the latter is no longer considered as just in itself; as the realization of divine justice on earth, therefore, in so far as the legal reality is regarded as unjust, there comes into existence the need of an ideology which transfers the realization of justice, namely, retribution, into the other world. This is the specific function of the Orphic-Pythagorean doctrine.

212. According to Rohde, pp. 335 ff., 374 ff. Gruppe, pp. 862 ff., supposes that the belief in retributory justice after death and the idea of judges of the dead already existed in Cretan culture; in other words, this whole ideology proceeds from "the remotest past." Also, Peterich, p. 12, conjectures that the belief in retributory justice exercised in the other world existed in pre-Homeric religion. If the essential element of this religion was the worship of the dead, it is very unlikely that there was also a belief in retribution executed upon the dead. Worship of the dead is based on the idea that the dead is a superhuman authority punishing and rewarding the living. It is typically connected with the belief in justice realized in this world. The idea of justice realized in the other world, and that means executed upon the dead, is incompatible with true worship of the dead. It presupposes a radical change in the idea which the living have of the dead. The soul of the dead man has to be transformed from a superhuman authority, a kind of deity, efficiently interfering with the affairs of the living, into a human, although invisible and immortal, being without any influence on the living—from a subject to an object of justice.

Consequently, Rohde is right when he believes that the idea "of a compensatory justice in an after life . . . . so far as it ever became known to later Greek theology . . . . was only introduced very late, through the influence of a speculative mysticism" (pp. 40 f.). Leist, too, declares (pp. 536, 573 ff.) that the common Greek idea of justice was that the gods maintained their order—law—not in the other world but here on earth. And he sees here a contrast to the Egyptian idea according to which the real and final judgment of good and evil, the realization of justice, takes place in the other world by a court of the dead. Of Hesiod, the "first religious thinker in Europe," Kern writes, I, 266: "He did not expect reward and punishment from the other world as in the eschatology of the mysteries; this son of the soil looked full of confidence up to the summit of the Helicon on which, like on the Thessalian Olympus on the side of Zeus, who replaced the old mountain god, the goddess of justice reigns in eternity,"

213. Cf. Wundt, pp. 134 ff. Wide and Nilsson, "Griechische und römische Religion," p. 28, see a connection between the Orphic philosophy and the social revolutions of the time: "In the seventh and sixth centuries the Orphic philosophy aroused in Attica, particularly among the peasants, a great religious movement: social and economic calamity in the lower

classes may have furthered this movement. Peisistratus and his sons promoted it for political reasons" (cf. also Nilsson, "Die Griechen," p. 370). That the religious order, founded by Pythagoras, pursued political ends is well known. The close relationship between the aristocratic movement of the Pythagoreans and the Orphic philosophy can presumably be explained by the same reasons which explain why a "tyrant" like Peisistratus favored the Orphics. Nestle, *Griechische Religiositaet*, I, 56, says of the tyrants: "These men always show a strong religious ethos." But would it not be more accurate to say that they had a strong tendency to religious ideologies because they were supported by the lowest classes? It is well known that Peisistratus (cf. Nestle, p. 67), after having lost control about the middle of the sixth century, made a successful effort to regain power by having himself led back to Athens by a beautiful woman disguised as the goddess Athena. Thus he consciously abused the religious feelings of the naïve people, who became the victim of this impudent fraud.

214. Aristotle *Nicomachean Ethics* 1132b, 21 ff.; *Great Ethics* 1194a, 29 ff.; cf. Rohde, pp. 375, 397.

215. Cf. Axel W. Persson, "Der Ursprung der eleusinischen Mysterien," *Archiv fuer Religionswissenschaft*, XXI (1922), 287 ff.; Kern, I, 141.

216. Nestle, p. 59.

217. Samter, p. 27.

218. *Ibid.*, Persson, p. 300.

219. The idea, typical of primitive mentality, to escape real and heavier punishment which threatens from the superhuman authority by anticipatory self-punishment becomes clearly apparent in a story of Polycrates (Herodotus iii. 40) which is usually cited as an example of the so-called "envy of the gods." When Amasis learns of the unusual luck of Polycrates, he gives him the following advice: "Consider what you deem most precious and what you will most grieve to lose, and cast it away so that it shall never again be seen among men." When Philip of Macedonia one day received news of three fortunate events, he raised his hands toward heaven and prayed: "O God, offset all this by some moderate misfortune" (Plutarch *A Letter to Apollonius* 105 [in Loeb's *Plutarch's Moralia*, II, 125]).

220. Cf. Rohde, I, 222, 295; also Theodor Waechter, *Reinheitsvorschriften im griechischen Kult* ("Religionsgeschichtliche Versuche und Vorarbeiten," Band IX, Heft 1 [1910]), pp. 4, 9. What is the sense of mere "cultic" or "ritual" purity? Certainly not that of bodily purity, for the procedures of purification are frequently carried out with materially defiling means, such as blood, urine, etc. Thus it must have had the sense of moral-legal purity. The idea of a religious purity, as distinguished from moral-legal purity, is the problematical consequence of the sociologically impossible assumption of a religion independent of morality and law. The fact that the idea of morality and law on which the purification rites are based still has a primitive character does not imply that these rites have no connection with morality and law. Their moral-legal character is borne out by the fact that they obviously presuppose the idea of retribution. Their purpose is to escape punishment by removing its condition, namely, a wrong, a sin—shortly the evil, according to the principle of retribution. Finally, one must not overlook the fact that the crime which renders the perpetrator most "polluted" and "impure" and which requires the most severe "purification" ceremonies is everywhere, especially among the Greeks, the crime of murder.

It may, however, happen that the morality expressed in a certain religion and its rites lags behind the social reality for the ideology of which it originally came into existence, i.e., behind the actual development of the social order and the moral ideas corresponding to it; thus, a certain discord arises between the religious and civil morality, or at least between the conventional morality and that of philosophically advanced individuals. The religious ideology is more conservative than other ideologies and adjusts itself only slowly to any change in the real interests which it is supposed to serve. An example of such a difference between religious and civil morality is the following statement of Heraclitus, frags. 129, 130 (Burnet, *Early Greek Philosophy*, p. 141): "They vainly purify themselves by defiling themselves with blood, just as if one who had stepped into the mud were to wash his feet in mud. Any man who marked him doing thus would deem him mad." W. Robertson Smith, *Lectures on the Religion of the Semites* (3d ed., 1927), p. 53, writes: "Among the Semites, as among other races, religion often came to work against a higher morality, not because it was in its essence a power for evil, but because it clung to the obsolete ethical standard of a bygone stage of society."

221. O. Kern, *Orphicorum fragmenta* (1922), 32c, p. 107.

222. Kern, *Die Religion der Griechen*, II (1935), 193, writes: "The Sacrament, the magical force of Eleusinian worship, had its basis in the reproduction of the womb which the neophyte had to touch—we do not know how—in order to be reborn. Only in Eleusis was the devout regarded as a real child of the deity."

223. Cf. K. H. E. de Jong, *Das antike Mysterienwesen* (2d ed., 1919), pp. 23, 27.

224. *Hymn to Demeter* 480 ff. (in Loeb's *Hesiod, Homeric Hymns and Homerica*, p. 323).

225. Plutarch "How To Study Poetry," 21 F (in Loeb's *Plutarch's Moralia*, I, 113); cf. also Diogenes Laertius vi. 39.

226. Cf. Nestle, p. 82.

227. Cf. P. Foucart, *Les Mystères d'Eleusis* (1914), pp. 392 ff., 401 ff., 412 ff.

228. As Victor Magnien, in *Les Mystères d'Eleusis* (2d ed., 1938), pp. 208 ff., assumes.

229. Cf. Magnien, pp. 37 ff.

230. Rohde, pp. 414 ff.

231. Pindar *The Olympian Odes* ii. 56 ff. (Loeb).

232. Aeschylus *The Suppliant Maidens* 230 f. (Loeb).

233. Aeschylus *Eumenides* 258 ff. (Plumptre).

234. Cf. my essay, "Platonic Justice," *Ethics*, XLVIII (1937–38), 367 ff.

235. Cf. Rohde, pp. 467, 481 f.

236. Plato *Phaedo* 114 (Jowett).

237. *Ibid.*

238. Plato *Gorgias* 522 (Jowett).

239. Plato *The Republic* x. 608 (Jowett).

240. *Ibid.* 612.

241. *Ibid.* 612 (Jowett).

242. *Ibid.* 614 (Jowett).

243. *Ibid.* 621 (Jowett).

244. *Ibid.* vi. 509–10.

245. Plato *Phaedo* 96 ff.

246. The close connection between soul belief and the idea of justice finds negative confirmation in the philosophy of Aristotle. One of the few points in which his metaphysics differs from that of his teacher Plato is that he, in direct contradiction to Plato, maintains that justice exists only in this and not in the other world; consequently, the idea of transcendental retribution is entirely strange to him. His ethics and politics are ideologies of the concrete state and the positive law and are essentially confined to the earthly sphere. The subject of Aristotle's doctrine, which is basically optimistic, is earthly justice in which the profoundly pessimistic Plato, despite all contrary attempts, never really believed. Aristotle, therefore, had no use for the chief dogma of Plato's metaphysical ethics, the immortality of the soul. This dogma has never found its way into his system, which does not know a retribution in the other world. With Aristotle the soul—if one disregards the specifically ethical functions—is mainly a psychological-biological phenomenon; it is the vital power, the center of the capacity for nourishment, sensation, movement, etc. It is the true life soul and not the death soul which is the subject of Aristotle's psychology, a system which has not so much an ethical as a scientific character. This soul is, consequently, inseparably united with the body, and the idea that it may have a separate existence is here impossible.

It is true, however, that Aristotle did not maintain this concept of the soul throughout.

He distinguished within the soul in a broad sense a special element, the *nus*, the bearer of true thinking, which does not originate or pass away with other parts of the soul and the body connected with them. The *nus*, itself pre-existent, penetrates man from outside and has no part in his death. Thus the *nus* survives after the death of the body and its life soul. But in this postexistence it has no substance; after its separation from the body it stops thinking and loses both its memory and its consciousness. But Aristotle is not able to say where the *nus* exists after the death of the individual or what kind of existence it has. Obviously, it is only a last remainder of Platonic influence, the idea of the immortality of the soul undermined by natural scientific experience—a remnant of the metaphysical death soul reduced to an empty word. With the rejection of justice in the other world the really immortal soul substance of Platonic theology has become superfluous.

CHAPTER V

1. K. Joël, *Geschichte der antiken Philosophie* (1921), I, 258. Cf. also my article "Die Entstehung des Kausalgesetzes aus dem Vergeltungsprinzip," *Journal of Unified Science* (*Erkenntnis*), VIII (1939–40), 69 ff.

2. The elements of social interpretation in the Greek philosophy of nature may be connected with the fact that the oldest philosophers of nature were active politically. Cf. John Burnet, *Early Greek Philosophy* (4th ed., 1930), pp. 46, 52, 90 ff., 311.

3. K. Joël, *Der Ursprung der Naturphilosophie aus dem Geiste der Mystik* (1906), p. 6, writes: "No one can squeeze this innocent phrase of the poet Homer . . . . so that the water-principle of Thales will result from it. It is a long way from the personally conceived and spatially limited Oceanus to all water and even longer from all water to all being." True enough, but there is a way; and it is no longer than the one from myth (or even from mysticism) to the philosophy of nature.

4. Heraclitus, frag. 110 (in Burnet, p. 140). Cf. also Hermann Diels, *Die Fragmente der Vorsokratiker* (5th ed., 1934), Vol. I, frag. 33.

5. Joël, *Geschichte der antiken Philosophie*, I, 260.

6. Aristotle *Physics* iii. 4. 203*b*. 12 f. (Loeb).

7. Anaximenes, according to Aetius i. 3. 4 (in Burnet, p. 73). Cf. also Diels, frag. 2.

8. Cf. Wilhelm Capelle, *Die Vorsokratiker* (2d ed., 1938), No. 25, p. 97.

9. Cicero *De natura deorum* i. x (Loeb). Diogenes of Apollonia, influenced by Anaximenes, wrote (frag. 5): "And my view is, that that which has intelligence is what men call air, and that all things have their course steered by it, and that it has power over all things. For this very thing I hold to be a god, and to reach everywhere, and to dispose everything, and to be in everything . . . ." (Burnet, p. 354).

10. Joël, *Der Ursprung der Naturphilosophie aus dem Geiste der Mystik*, pp. 66 f.

11. Aristotle *De anima* i. 2. 405*a*. 19 (trans. Hicks). According to Aristotle's interpretation (*De anima* i. 2. 405*a*. 5 ff.; i. 3. 406*b*. 15 ff.; i. 5. 409*a*. 32 ff.), the soul is also in Democritus the principle or cause of motion.

12. Diogenes of Apollonia, frag. 2 (Burnet, pp. 353 f.).

13. Aristotle *De generatione et corruptione* i. 6. 322*b* (trans. H. H. Joachim).

14. Empedocles, frag. 90 (Burnet, p. 218; cf. also Diels, frag. 90).

15. Empedocles, frag. 109 (Burnet, p. 221; cf. also Diels, frag. 109).

16. Aeschylus *Agamemnon* 730 ff.

17. Heraclitus, frag. 101 (Burnet, p. 140; cf. also Diels, frag. 25).

18. Cf. above, n. 12.

19. Cf. Burnet, pp. 50 ff. Burnet says, p. 54: "The current statement that the term ἀρχή was introduced by him [Anaximander] appears to be due to a misunderstanding."

20. In medical science, justice corresponds to good health. Thus it is easy to understand that Alkmaion of Kroton, a physician intimately connected with the Pythagoreans, considered his theory of health as "isonomy" and that he observed that "most things human were two"; by this he meant, says Burnet, p. 196, that "man was made up of the hot and the cold, the moist and the dry, and the rest of the opposites. Disease was just the 'monarchy' of any one of these—the same thing that Anaximander had called 'injustice'— while health was the establishment in the body of a free government with equal laws."

21. Anaximander, frag. 1 (Diels; Burnet, p. 52).

22. Capelle, p. 75.

23. Werner Jaeger, *Paideia; the Ideals of Greek Culture*, trans. Gilbert Highet (Oxford, 1939), pp. 157 ff., says that the law referred to in the fragment of Anaximander is the law

of "polis," the Greek city-state. He points out that "Anaximander was formulating a moral, not a physical, law of nature. There is a deeply religious significance in his conception that natural phenomena are governed by a moral standard. It is not a compendious description of events, but a justification of the nature of the universe: he shows creation to be a cosmos 'writ large'—namely, a community of things under law. . . . . Anaximander's fragment shows us much of the process by which the problem of causality developed out of the problem of the ways of God to man. His idea of diké is the first stage in the projection of the life of the city-state upon the life of the universe."

24. Cassirer, *Das Mythische Denken*, p. 144, points out that in mythical thinking a connection exists "between the universal order of time which rules over all events and the eternal order of justice to which this event is subject." Thus, for instance, in the Babylonian-Assyrian religion, Marduk, the god of justice, i.e., of retribution, after his victory over Tiamat, fixes the stars as the abode of the gods and determines their course (see below, n. 41). In the Egyptian religion, the moon-deity, Toth, who, as surveyor, is both the divider of time and the lord of correct measure, functions as the scribe of the gods and, at the same time, as the judge of heaven. It was he who granted the power of utterance and of writing; and through the arts of counting and calculating he let gods and men know what belongs to them (Cassirer, p. 144). In the Chinese religion there are similar connections between the order of time and the order of justice. Cassirer also points out a connection between the order of justice and the order of time in the religion of the Indo-Germanic peoples (cf. p. 145). For the idea óf time as a goddess of retribution, cf. the above cited references of Euripides.

25. Diogenes Laertius ix. 8 (Loeb).

26. *Ibid*. ix. 7 (Loeb).

27. Heraclitus, frag. 44 (Burnet, p. 136; cf. also Diels, frag. 53).

28. Heraclitus, frag. 62 (Burnet, p. 137; cf. also Diels, frag. 80).

29. Capelle, p. 127.

30. Heraclitus, frag. 2 (Burnet, p. 133; cf. also Diels, frag. 1).

31. Diogenes Laertius ix. 7 (Loeb).

32. Aetius i. 7. 22 (H. Diels, *Doxographi Graeci* [1929], p. 303); *ibid*. 27. 1 (Diels, p. 322); *ibid*. 28. 1 (Diels, p. 323).

33. Émile Boisacq, *Dictionnaire étymologique de la langue grecque* (1916), p. 621.

34. Heraclitus, frag. 92 (Burnet, p. 139; cf. also Diels, frag. 2).

35. Heraclitus, frag. 91*b* (Burnet, p. 139; cf. also Diels, frag. 114).

36. Heraclitus, frag. 29 (Burnet, p. 135; cf. also Diels, frag. 94).

37. Heraclitus, frag. 118 (Burnet, p. 141; cf. also Diels, frag. 28).

38. Demosthenes against Aristogeiton i. 11: "And Orpheus, who revealed to us the sacred mysteries, says that the inexorable and venerable Dike, sitting beside the throne of Zeus, observes all the actions of men."

39. Capelle, No. 17, p. 39. Plato *Laws* iv. 715 (Jowett): "God, as the old tradition declares, holding in His hand the beginning, middle, and end of all that is, travels according to His nature in a straight line towards the accomplishment of His end. Justice [Dike] always accompanies Him, and is the punisher of those who fall short of the divine law." The idea of the inviolability of the universal law, conceived as the will of the deity, appears in mythical terms among the Orphics. According to Damascius (*Damascii successoris dubitationes et solutiones de primis principiis, in Platonis Parmenidem*, ed. C. Ae. Ruelle [Paris, 1889], Vol. I, 123 bis, F. 205 v., p. 317 f.), an Orphic doctrine was as follows: "In the beginning there was water and substance, from the latter, the earth was formed. Thus water and earth were the first two elements. The third originated in these two; it was a dragon with two heads, one of a bull, the other of a lion; but in the center was the face of a god, and on the shoulders were wings. He was called 'Never aging Chronos,' and also Heracles. With him was Necessity which was a being, like Adrasteia, bodyless (ἀσώματος,

corrupt form, correct: δισώματος, of double sex), and which extends through the whole universe touching its limits. Necessity is regarded as the third element. . . . . But he considers it to be of double sex, thus indicating the cause that creates everything." "Adrasteia" means the "Inexorable One" and is obviously the personification of the inviolability of the universal law, which, according to the Orphic doctrine, dominated by the idea of reward and punishment, can only be the law of retribution. It is punishment from which one cannot escape. It is significant that the "inviolability" of the universal law, the impossibility of any escape from retribution, is connected with Chronos, Time. At the end of this description of Orphic theology, one may read: "This theology praises the 'first born God' and calls him Zeus, the ruler over all things and the whole cosmos. Therefore he is also called Pan (the universal God)."

40. According to such a conception of the world, the law of gravity is a legal norm; the order of nature and the legal order are identical. In consideration of Medea's criminal plans Euripides lets the chorus say, p. 409 f. (Loeb):

"Upward and back to their fountains the sacred rivers are stealing;
Justice is turned to injustice, the order of old to confusion."

41. The inviolability of the universal law as the unshakable will of a deity of justice whose function is retribution is also to be found in the Babylonian epic of creation. The god Marduk is characterized as follows (*The Babylonian Epic of Creation*, transcription, translation, and commentary by S. Langdon):

TABLET V

1. He constructed stations for the great gods.
2. The stars their likenesses he fixed, even the Lumasi.
3. He fixed the year and designed the signs (of the zodiac).
4. For the twelve months he placed three stars each.
5. After he had defined the days of the year by signs,
6. He established the place of Nibiru to fix all of them,
7. In order that none transgress or loiter.
8. He appointed the place(s) of Enlil and Ea with him (i.e. beside the Anu way).

Marduk, the god who established the order of the cosmos and thus the order of time was the god of justice. Some of his duties were:

TABLET VII

35. He is Sagzu, knower of the thoughts of the gods, who perceived the plan.
36. Who permitted not the evil-doers to escape from him.
38. The subduer of the disobedient . . . .
39. Administrator of justice . . . .
45. Who puts an end to the totality of evil ones . . . .
132. His word is sure and his command is unalterable.
133. The utterance of his mouth no god annuls.

It has already been mentioned that Marduk is presented as an "avenger" and that his battle against Tiamat and her host as well as their annihilation are characterized as actions of retribution.

42. Joël, *Der Ursprung der Naturphilosophie aus dem Geiste der Mystik*, p. 87, says with reference to Heraclitus (frag. 29 in Burnet; frag. 94 in Diels) "that the concept of the law of nature is an anthropomorphism." It would be more correct to say that it is a "sociomorphism."

43. *Simplicii in Aristotelis Physicorum libros quattuor priores commentaria* III, 5, ed. H. Diels (*Commentaria in Aristotelem Graeca*, Vol. IX [1882], p. 480).

44. Heraclitus, frag. 22 (Burnet, p. 135; Diels, frag. 90).

45. Hippolytus "Refutation of All Heresies," ix. 5 (in *Ante-Nicene Christian Fathers*, V, 127; Diels, frags. 63–66). This description of Heraclitus' doctrine of Fire reminds one of the ethical-juristical view of the world process, characteristic of the Jewish-Christian belief in the Last Judgment. The idea therefore suggests itself to regard the description of

Hippolytus as a Christian interpretation of Heraclitus' doctrine. It cannot be denied that the unquestionably genuine fragments of Heraclitus show such a strong normative tendency. Joël, *Geschichte der antiken Philosophie*, p. 286, says of him: "He does not see, he values"; his doctrine has given Christian writers plenty of occasion for their specific interpretations; his pessimistic attitude certainly did contribute a great deal to these interpretations. His sayings about the stupidity and wickedness of men remind one of the angry orations of certain Jewish prophets. Justin called him a "Christian" before Christ. Why, then, should one not comprehend his doctrine of fire (ἐκπύρωσις) as a prophecy of a last judgment over the sinful world? This essentially normative, i.e., ethical-juristical, character of Heraclitus' conception of the world was stressed by Nietzsche ("Philosophy during the Tragic Stage of the Greeks," in *Early Greek Philosophy*, trans. M. A. Muegge, p. 97). His description of the doctrine of the Ephesian can be called in this point a congenial imitation: "I contemplate the Becoming, he exclaimed, and nobody has so attentively watched this eternal wave-surging and rhythm of things. And what do I behold? Lawfulness, infallible certainty, ever equal paths of Justice, condemning Erinyes behind all transgressions of the laws, the whole world a spectacle of a governing justice and of demoniacally omnipresent natural forces subject to justice's sway. I do not behold the punishment of that which has become, but the justification of Becoming. When has sacrilege, when has apostasy manifested itself in inviolable forms, in laws esteemed sacred? Where injustice sways, there is caprice, disorder, irregularity, contradiction; where, however, Law and Zeus's daughter, Dike, rule alone, as in this world, how could the sphere of guilt, of expiation, of judgment, and as it were the place of execution of all condemned ones, be there?" But Nietzsche overlooks the fact that Dike rules by punishing injustice; consequently one follows the pessimist Heraclitus if one assumes that "this world is a sphere of guilt."

46. Burnet, frag. 1, p. 172, translates "Avenging Justice." Cf. also Diels, frag. 1.
47. Burnet, p. 172.
48. Parmenides, frag. 8 (Burnet, p. 175; cf. also Diels, frag. 8).
49. Parmenides, frag. 8 (Burnet, p. 175; cf. also Diels, frag. 8).
50. Parmenides, frag. 8 (Burnet, p. 176; cf. also Diels, frag. 8).
51. Aeschylus *Prometheus Bound* 515 f. (Loeb).
52. Joël, *Der Ursprung der Naturphilosophie aus dem Geiste der Mystik*, p. 142, believes that the older philosophers of nature were strongly influenced by the Orphics; in fact, they "agreed so much with the Orphics, they did not need their influence." The nucleus of the Orphic doctrine is the belief in metempsychosis. And Joël asserts, p. 151, that he recognizes "in the doctrine of metempsychosis a necessary basis for the old philosophy of nature." The doctrine of metempsychosis is, however, only an ideology of the principle of retribution.
53. Empedocles, frag. 115 (Burnet, p. 222; cf. also Diels, frag. 115).
54. Diogenes Laertius viii. 77 (Loeb).
55. Aristotle *The Art of Rhetoric* I. xiii. 2 (1373b) (Loeb).
56. Cicero *The Republic* III. xi. 19 (Loeb).
57. Empedocles, frag. 136 (Burnet, p. 225; cf. also Diels, frag. 136).
58. Empedocles, frag. 137 (Burnet, pp. 225 f.; cf. also Diels, frag. 137).
59. Empedocles, frag. 135 (Burnet, p. 225; cf. also Diels, frag. 135).
60. Joël, p. 156, remarks: "The world process, in Anaximander as well as in Heraclitus, in the writings of the Pythagoreans as well as in Empedocles, is a moral one."
61. Empedocles, frag. 17 (Burnet, pp. 207 f.; cf. also Diels, frag. 17).
62. Empedocles, frag. 35 (Burnet, p. 212; cf. also Diels, p. 35).
63. Empedocles, frag. 20 (Burnet, p. 208; cf. also Diels, frag. 20).
64. Empedocles, frag. 22 (Burnet, p. 209; cf. also Diels, frag. 22).
65. Empedocles, frag. 27 (Burnet, p. 210; cf. also Diels, frag. 28).
66. Empedocles, frag. 27a (Burnet, p. 211).

· 67. "Nor had they [the dwellers in the Golden Age] any Ares for a god nor Kydoimos, no nor King Zeus nor Kronos nor Poseidon, but Kypris the Queen. . . . . Her did they propitiate with holy gifts, with painted figures and perfumes of cunning fragrancy, with offerings of pure myrrh and sweet-smelling frankincense, casting on the ground libations of brown honey. And the altar did not reek with pure bull's blood, but this was held in the greatest abomination among men, to eat the goodly limbs tearing out the life" (Empedocles, frag. 128 [Burnet, p. 224; cf. also Diels, frag. 128]).

68. Empedocles, frag. 108 (Burnet, p. 221).

69. Empedocles, frag. 130 (Burnet, p. 225).

70. Cf. F. Duemmler, *Akademika* (1889), p. 221.

71. Cf. Capelle, p. 236, n. 1.

72. Empedocles, frag. 59 (Burnet, p. 214; cf. also Diels, frag. 59).

73. Empedocles, frags. 30, 31 (Burnet, p. 211; cf. also Diels, frag. 30).

74. Aristotle *Physics* VIII. i. 252a. (Loeb).

75. Aristotle *Metaphysics* I. iv. 984b, 985a.

76. Just as Strife is wrong and at the same time punishment, Strife is not only a dividing and hence a bad, but also a uniting and hence a good, principle. Aristotle (*Metaphysics* I. iv. 985b [Loeb]) says: "Empedocles does indeed use causes to a greater degree than Anaxagoras, but not sufficiently; nor does he attain to consistency in their use. At any rate, Love often differentiates and Strife combines: because whenever the universe is differentiated into its elements by Strife, fire and each of the other elements are agglomerated into a unity; and whenever they are all combined together again by Love, the particles of each element are necessarily again differentiated."

77. Cf. above, n. 53.

78. Hippolytus vii. 17.

79. Empedocles, frag. 22 (Burnet, p. 209; cf. also Diels, frag. 22).

80. The atomists, as well as the philosophers, especially Anaximander, Heraclitus, and Aristotle, did not use the term "law of nature," although they had a clear idea of general rules determining the natural events. They did not designate these rules as "laws" (νόμοι), for in the philosophical language of the Greeks law and nature—νόμος and φύσις—were opposite (cf. Edgar Zilsel, "The Genesis of the Concept of Physical Law," *Philosophical Review*, LI [1942], pp. 249 ff.). Nevertheless, the rules determining nature were, in general, considered to be norms. Only in the atomist's concept of ἀνάγκη have the rules of nature lost any normative meaning. It is most significant that the expression "law of nature" (παρὰ τοὺς τῆς φύσεως νόμους) can be found only in Plato (*Timaeus* 83e), for Plato's philosophy is a purely theological and hence normative, moral-juristic interpretation of the universe.

81. Aristotle *De generatione animalium* 789b.

82. Plutarchi Stromat. 7 (Diels, *Doxographi Graeci*, p. 581). Cf. also Capelle, No. 48, p. 415.

83. Dionysius Alex. in Eusebius *Preparation for the Gospel* XIV. xxvii. (trans. E. H. Gifford, Part II, p. 843).

84. Plato *Protagoras* 324 (Jowett). The fact that Plato himself sticks to the doctrine of retribution proves that the theory advocated in the dialogue by Protagoras was a specifically sophistic one.

85. Aetius i. 25, 4 (Diels, p. 321; Burnet, p. 340).

86. Diels, *Die Fragmente der Vorsokratiker*, frag. 1; Burnet, p. 133.

87. Aetius i. 26. 2 (Diels, *Doxographi Graeci*, p. 321).

88. Diogenes Laertius ix. 31 ff. (Burnet, p. 338).

89. *Ibid.* ix. 7 (Loeb); cf. Heraclitus, frag. 10 (Diels).

90. *The Hibeh Papyri*, ed. B. P. Grenfell and A. S. Hunt (1906), Part I, 16, pp. 62 ff.

91. Democritus, frag. 164 (Diels).

92. Aristotle *De generatione et corruptione* i. 7. 323b.

93. Capelle, No. 37, p. 410.

94. Pliny, *Natural history* ii. 14 (Diels, 68A, 76): "Innumeros quidem credere (deos) . . . . aut, ut Democrito placuit, duos omnino, Poenam et Beneficium." "Beneficium" means "merit" as well as "reward"; the language here indicates the "equality" of the two elements connected by the principle of retribution. M. Wellmann (according to Diels, *Die Fragmente der Vorsokratiker*, Vol. II, p. 103) ascribes this fragment "to the Mendesian who, as a Pythagorean, knew the doctrine of retribution." That Bolos of Mendes, a Democritan, belonged to the school of the Pythagoreans and thus knew the doctrine of retribution is certainly not reason enough to assume an error on the part of Pliny. The doctrine of retribution, or rather the principle of retribution, as a basic norm of the whole system of ethics was a main element in Greek thinking.

95. Aristotle *Physics* II. iv. 196a (Loeb).

96. E.g., Diels, frag. 83.

97. The word αἰτία, which appears for the first time in Pindar and Aeschylus, means "guilt" here. But in Herodotus' prologue to his history it signifies "cause." In Homer the substantive, αἰτία, does not appear, but the adjective, αἴτιος, and the verb, αἰτιάομαι, are found; the former means "guilty," the latter, "to accuse," "to charge." The word is possibly related to the old Indian word *ainas*, which means "sacrilege," "sin," or "guilt" (cf. Leo Meyer, *Handbuch der griechischen Etymologie* [1901], II, 80–81). Werner Jaeger, p. 159, writes that the Greek notion "of Cause (αἰτία) was originally the same as the idea of Responsibility and was transferred from legal to physical terminology. Closely connected with this is the parallel transference of the related words, cosmos, diké, and tisis, from the sphere of law to that of nature."

CHAPTER VI

1. David Hume, *An Enquiry concerning the Human Understanding*, ed. L. A. Selby-Bigge (1894), VII, 63: "When we look about us towards external objects, and consider the opera-tion of causes, we are never able, in a single instance, to discover any power or necessary connexion; any quality, which binds the effect to the cause, and renders the one an infallible consequence of the other. We only find, that the one does actually, in fact, follow the other." "In reality, there is no part of matter, that does ever, by its sensible qualities, discover any power or energy; or give us ground to imagine, that it could produce any thing, or be fol-lowed by any other object, which we could denominate its effect." The idea of "force" in-herent in the cause which brings about the effect is only the animistic expression for the necessity of the connection between cause and effect.

2. *Ibid.*, pp. 75 f.: ". . . . that after a repetition of similar instances, the mind is carried by habit, upon the appearance of one event, to expect its usual attendant, and to believe that it will exist. This connexion, therefore, which we feel in the mind, this customary transition of the imagination from one object to its usual attendant, is the sentiment or im-pression from which we form the idea of power or necessary connexion. Nothing farther is in the case. . . . . When we say, therefore, that one object is connected with another, we mean only that they have acquired a connexion in our thought."

2a. *Ibid.*, p. 46.

3. In his essay "Bemerkungen ueber die Kraefte der unbelebten Natur," *Die Mechanik der Waerme* (1874).

4. Ernst Mach, *Die Mechanik in ihrer Entwicklung* (3d ed., 1897), pp. 493, 406.

5. Philipp Frank, *Das Kausalgesetz und seine Grenzen* (1932), p. 136.

6. *Ibid.*, pp. 136 ff. On p. 139 Frank remarks: "The respect with which philosophers use the concept of 'energy' derives to a great extent from the term, in which they may pos-sibly perceive something soul-like, 'psychoidic.' "

7. *Ibid.*, p. 140.

8. Cf., e.g., *Philosophisches Woerterbuch* by Heinrich Schmidt ("Kroeners Taschenaus-gabe," Band XIII [9th ed., 1934]), article "Energie."

9. Fritz Mauthner, *Woerterbuch der Philosophie* (1910), I, 275, strikingly remarks: "The old scholastic principle, *causa aequat effectum*, has lost its validity. Since Carnot and Clausius, we have known that with the transformation of heat into energy, a considerable amount of heat is uselessly spent and not transformed into the intended effect. If this law can be gen-eralized, the theoretical principle of the conservation of energy remains intact but the cause is no longer equal to the effect (to the effect in which we are interested); the cause is divided into two forces, one of which produces an effect, the other disappears without any useful effects being produced."

10. That the principle of the equiva ence of energies proceeds from a sphere of norma-tive thinking is also borne out by the fa-t that this principle is sometimes used as the start-ing-point of a speculation leading to this normative sphere. The view that by reference to energy the effect must be equal to the cause leads, according to Frank, p. 136, "to the as-sumption that changes at which the energy remains unchanged do not need any physical cause. Thus many hoped to have found a way by which one could comprehend the in-tervention of supernatural, spiritual factors in the world of our physical experience and could make the former compatible with the results of exact science. Such intervention is often needed to save the so-called freedom of will." The assumption of freedom of will has, since one considers it necessary for founding the ethical-juristical responsibility of the in-dividual, sense only from the point of view of normative speculation.

11. *Philosophisches Woerterbuch*, article "Kausalitaet."

12. *Ibid.*, article "Ursache."

13. Cf. Mauthner, I, 96.

14. Max Verworn, *Die Frage nach den Grenzen der Erkenntnis* (1908), pp. 15 f., 44: "Careful observation shows that an event is never produced by a single factor. If one drops the idea that an event can be produced by a single cause and acknowledges that there must be two or more causes which produce the event, then the concept of cause loses its sense and becomes identical with the concept of condition. . . . . One thing conditions the other and science can, if it wants to be exact, consist only in the establishment of the conditions of dependency. If one must have an 'ism,' it ought to be 'conditionism' and not 'causalism.' " Cf. also Mauthner, articles "Bedingung" and "Konditionismus."

15. Cf. Edgar Zilsel, "Ueber die Asymmetrie der Kausalitaet und die Einsinnigkeit der Zeit," *Die Naturwissenschaften*, XV (1927), 280 ff.

16. According to Frank, p. 142.

17. According to Frank, pp. 142 f.

18. According to Zilsel, pp. 280 f.

19. According to Zilsel, pp. 284 f.

20. Thus, e.g., M. Schlick, "Die Kausalitaet in der gegenwaertigen Physik," *Die Naturwissenschaften*, XIX (1931), 146, says: "We do not speak of causality if events exist at the same time."

21. Cf. the definition of the concept of causality in the article "Kausalitaet" in *Philosophisches Woerterbuch*.

22. Eduard May, *Die Bedeutung der Modernen Physik fuer die Theorie der Erkenntnis* (1937), pp. 80 ff., describes how in physical thinking the *propter hoc*, as well as the *post hoc*, is eliminated from the concept of causality. "If the physical time is reversible, then the causal nexus in physics must also be reversible. A mathematical relation of dependency can be read from right to left as well as from left to right; cause and effect are interchangeable." May believes that the attempts which were made in order to prevent the reversibility of the mathematical-physical causal nexus can be regarded as failures.

23. The formulation of the principle of indeterminacy, according to Max Planck, *Der Kausalbegriff in der Physik* (1932), p. 13.

24. Planck, p. 4, writes: "An event is causally determined when it can be predicted with certainty."

25. Hans Reichenbach, "Das Kausalproblem in der Physik," *Die Naturwissenschaften*, XIX (1931), 713 ff.

26. H. Bergmann, *Der Kampf um das Kausalgesetz in der juengsten Physik* ("Sammlung Vieweg," Heft 98 [1929]), p. 49; M. Schlick, *Naturphilosophie* (1925), p. 457.

27. Hans Reichenbach, "Die Kausalstruktur der Welt" in *Sitzungsberichte der Bayr. Acad. der Wiss., Math. naturw. Abt.* (1925), p. 133.

28. Grete Hermann, *Die Bedeutung der Modernen Physik fuer die Theorie der Erkenntnis* (1937), p. 43.

29. J. Loewenberg, "The Elasticity of the Idea of Causality," *University of California Publications in Philosophy*, Vol. XV (1932), p. 22.

30. Planck, pp. 5 ff., maintains, without any reference to Heisenberg's principle of indeterminacy: "It is in no case possible to predict exactly a physical event." Even when we are using the best instruments for measuring, "there is always a minimum of uncertainty." In the world of our senses no strict causality can be established. Such a causality is an hypothesis which can be applied only to the view of the world formulated by the science of physics; and this view of the world "is—to a certain extent—an arbitrary intellectual construction." A clear distinction between the world of our senses and the physical view of the world is, according to Planck, indispensable.

31. Pierre Simon Laplace, *Essai philosophique sur les probabilités* (4th ed., 1819), pp. 3–4.

32. Th. H. Huxley, *Introductory* ("Science Primers," ed. by Huxley, Roscoe, and Balfour Stewart [New York, Cincinnati, Chicago: American Book Co., n.d.]), pp. 12 ff.: "A law of man tells what we may expect society will do under certain circumstances; and a law of nature tells us what we may expect natural objects will do under certain circumstances. Each contains information addressed to our intelligence." This is not correct. The "law of man" does not tell what society *will* do but what men in society *ought* to do. The term "law," even in its juridical meaning, is ambiguous. It means the norm as the product of the law-creating process (custom or legislation), and the rule by which the jurist represents these norms, when describing the legal order. The first is addressed to our will, not to our intelligence; the latter, it is true, is addressed to our intelligence and has the character of an information. It is, however, not an information about what men *will* do but about what men *ought* to do.

Huxley points out that "the laws of nature are not the causes of the order of nature, but only our way of stating as much as we have made out of that order. Stones do not fall to the ground in consequence of the law (that anything heavy falls to the ground if it is unsupported) as people sometimes carelessly say; but the law is a way of asserting that such invariably happens when heavy bodies at the surface of the earth, stones among the rest, are free to move." This is correct; but Huxley is wrong in continuing: "The laws of nature are in fact, in this respect, similar to the laws which men make for the guidance of their conduct towards one another. There are laws about the payment of taxes, and there are laws against stealing and murder. But the law is not the cause of man's paying his taxes, nor is it the cause of his abstaining from theft and murder. The law is simply a statement of what will happen to a man if he does not pay his taxes, and if he commits theft or murder." If the law provides sanctions and if such a law becomes the contents of man's consciousness, it can very well become a motive of his behavior and hence a cause of paying his taxes and of his abstaining from theft and murder. A legislator enacts norms only because he believes that these norms, as motives in the mind of man, are capable of inducing the latter to the behavior desired by the legislator.

33. Zilsel, "The Genesis of the Concept of Physical Law," p. 247.

34. Quoted by Zilsel, p. 261.

35. William Gilbert, *De Magnete* (1600), VI, 9, 237, quoted by Zilsel, p. 261.

36. *Ibid.*, p. 263.

37. Else Wentscher, *Geschichte des Kausalproblems* (1921), pp. 6 ff., 15.

38. Zilsel, p. 266.

39. Wentscher, p. 23; Zilsel, p. 267.

40. Zilsel, p. 275. He calls our attention to the fact that the expression "law of nature" very rarely occurs in the works of Newton or in the writings of the earlier scientists of modern era. The term was not generally accepted before the end of the seventeenth century. But the idea of general rules determining the course of nature was known to philosophers and scientists of ancient Greece and in modern times at least since Galileo. Zilsel, p. 245, goes too far when saying that the concept of natural (physical) laws "was virtually unknown to antiquity and the middle ages, and that it did not arise before the middle of the seventeenth century." Zilsel himself states (p. 262), for instance, that "an abundance of physical laws is to be found in Galileo" although the latter "did not know the term 'natural law.'" The decisive question is whether the general rules according to which the scientist interprets nature are considered to be norms in the same sense as the rules of law, the legal norms. A clear distinction between laws of nature and social norms is, however, impossible so long as the idea prevails that not only society, i.e., human behavior, but also nature is determined by the omnipotent will of God. Hence, certain attempts undertaken in the seventeenth century to separate the concepts of the norm, regulating society, i.e., human behavior, and that of the rule determining natural events, had no decisive influence on the development of scientific thinking. Zilsel, p. 259, quotes Suarez, who in his *Tractatus de*

legibus (1612) "clings to the distinction between 'morals' and 'nature' and restricts the term 'law,' in its proper meaning, to the former." Suarez says, Vol. I, par. 2: "Things lacking reason properly are capable neither of law nor of obedience. In this the efficacy of divine power and natural necessity . . . . are called law by a metaphor." Zilsel, p. 273, quotes, further, Robert Boyle, who in his *Free inquiry into the vulgarly received Notion of Nature* (composed 1666; *Works* [ed. Birch], V, 170), declares the term "law," when applied to inanimate things, "an improper and figurative expression." "In the explanation," Zilsel writes, p. 273, "he strangely assumes that the law-metaphor ascribes teleological tendencies to physical objects. When an arrow, shot by a man, moves towards the mark, 'none will say that it moves by a law but by an external . . . . impulse' (p. 171). Nevertheless he himself speaks in what follows very often of the 'laws of motion prescribed by the author of things' (p. 177, cf. pp. 194, 225, 251, 252)."

41. N. Malebranche, *Search after Truth* (1694), II, 40 f.

42. Wentscher, p. 41.

43. Zilsel, p. 270. Zilsel, p. 267, refers to Patrizzi (*Nova de Universis Philosophia*, Pancosmia 12 [2d ed.; Venice, 1593), fol. 91, col. 3), who compares the stars' obeying of God's providence to maneuvering soldiers' obeying of the order of the officer.

44. Cf. Wentscher, pp. 41, 68, 76 ff.

45. George Berkeley, "A Treatise concerning the Principles of Human Knowledge," *The Works of George Berkeley*, ed. George Sampson (London, 1897), Vol. I, par. 105, pp. 225 ff.

46. Thomas Reid, "An Inquiry into the Human Mind," *The Works of Thomas Reid, D.D.: Now Fully Collected* by Sir William Hamilton (1863), I, 197 f.

47. Even in the nineteenth century some philosophers—as, for instance, Schelling and Schopenhauer—maintain that the causal nexus is established by a "will." Otto Rank, *Seelenglaube und Psychologie* (1930), p. 182, says: "The doctrine of Jesus that no sparrow falls down without God's will and the discovery of Newton that no apple could fall to the ground without cosmic laws have their source in the same voluntaristic ideology. . . . . The principle of causality and the principle of voluntarism are, at bottom, identical."

The history of the idea of causality shows why a metaphysical element, the tendency toward a transcendental authority, the will of God, is inherent in this idea, and why anti-metaphysical, positivistic, and empirical knowledge is inclined to refuse this concept or, at least, to give it a radically new interpretation. The attempt to maintain the concept of strict causality in physics leads to fictions, as, for instance, that of Laplace's "absolute intelligence." A very characteristic example is Planck's essay on the problem of causality. In order to defend this concept against certain objections, he is compelled to leave the field of science and to appeal to religion. He writes, p. 22: "We have to stick to our starting point, the statement, that an event is causally determined if it can be predicted with certainty. Otherwise we should lose our only basis. On the other hand we remain bound to the other statement that it is in no case possible to predict an event with certainty. Consequently we have to modify the first statement in order to maintain the principle of causality in nature." The modification, however, has to refer not to the content of the statement but to the subject who is capable of predicting future events. In order to be causally determined, an event need not necessarily be predicted with certainty by a human being, which is impossible. Even a scientifically schooled meteorologist, equipped with the best instruments, cannot predict today with absolute certainty the weather of tomorrow. But it is possible to assume that "an ideal spirit (idealer Geist), who knows perfectly all the physical events of today, would be capable of predicting the weather of tomorrow in all details with absolute certainty; and that applies to any other prediction of physical events." "The impossibility of predicting events with certainty" is, "from the point of view of classical as well as Quantum physics, the natural consequence of the fact that man with his organs of sense and his instruments for measuring is himself part of nature and subject to its laws from which he cannot withdraw. These are bounds which do not exist to an ideal spirit." Planck's "ideal spirit" is evidently nothing else but Laplace's "absolute intelligence." It is a philosophical disguise of the Holy Ghost. Planck writes: "We have to be on our guard against the temptation of subjecting the ideal spirit to scientific criticism." For it is a subject beyond the reach of human knowledge. The objection that the concept of such a spirit is "empty and superfluous" is encountered by Planck's assertion: "Not all statements which can not be logically substantiated, are scientifically worthless." Such a "narrow-minded formalism" chokes up just those sources "out of which such men as Galileo, Kepler, Newton and many other great physicists have fed their love for research. For all these men their devotion to science was—consciously or unconsciously—a matter of faith, of an imperturbable faith in a reasonable world order."

The "reasonable world order" is, above all, a just order. Such an order can only be the work of a superhuman being endowed with reason and will. The "faith" in such an order is the faith in God. There the close connection between the concept of strict causality and the idea of absolute reason and absolute will of God becomes very clear. The inviolable law of nature is conceivable only as an expression of divine reason and will.

However, even with the help of the Laplace-Planck fiction of an "absolute intelligence" or "ideal spirit," it is not possible to maintain the idea of strict causal determination and, hence, perfect predictability of future events. For there is no past, present, or future to an "absolute" intelligence or "ideal" spirit which is not confined within the boundaries of human knowledge; and time is only a human form of perception, one of its specific limits. Consequently, theology has to assume that God exists out of time. Hence, the concept of predictability—and that means, according to Planck, causality—is meaningless from the point of view of an "absolute intelligence" or "ideal spirit."

48. Frank, p. 287, speaks of an "antagonism" which exists between the fact that we always rely on the law of causality in practical life—even base our security on it— and the fact that it is impossible to formulate this law in a way that we can predict future events with certainty. On p. 288, however, he says that we do not rely in practical life on the "law of causality" but on special laws "which have the form of the causal law." In "practice," that means in naïve, prescientific theory, we presuppose no absolute causality but only a certain regularity. In this point there is no essential difference between civilized and primitive men or even between primitive men and animals. Their behavior is based on the observation of recurrent associations of certain events or qualities. But the trust we put in the regular course of events is sometimes violated. Things react otherwise than we expected. It is just "practice" which shows us that the regularity on which we rely is not without exceptions. In this point there exists no antagonism between "practice" and—at least modern—theory of causality.

INDEX

Reprints of Legal Classics
Published by
The Lawbook Exchange, Ltd.

A'Beckett, Gilbert Abbott. *The Comic Blackstone* [bound with] [Anstey, John]. *The Pleader's Guide, A Didactic Poem by John Surrebutter; American edition by James L. High.* With illustrations by George Cruikshank. Chicago: Callaghan & Cockcroft, 1870. xii, 376, 57, 65 pp. Reprint available December 2000 by The Lawbook Exchange, Ltd. ISBN 1-58477-104-6. Cloth. $95.

Anderson, William C. *A Dictionary of Law, Consisting of Judicial Definitions and Explanations of Words, Phrases, and Maxims, and an Exposition of the Principles of Law Comprising a Dictionary and Compendium of American and English Jurisprudence.* Chicago: T.H. Flood and Company, 1889. viii, 1140pp. Reprinted 1996 by The Lawbook Exchange, Ltd. LCCN 96-35844. ISBN 1-886363-23-4. Cloth. $125.

Austin, John. [1790-1859]. *The Province of Jurisprudence Determined.* London: John Murray, 1832. xx, 392, lxxvi pp. Reprinted 2000 by The Lawbook Exchange, Ltd. LCCN 99-33457. ISBN 1-58477-023-6. Cloth. $75.

Baldwin, Henry. *A General View of the Origin and Nature of the Constitution and Government of the United States, Deduced from the Political History and Condition of the Colonies and States, from 1774 until 1788. And the Decisions of the Supreme Court of the United States. Together with Opinions in the Cases Decided at January Term, 1837, Arising on the Restraints on the Powers of the States.* Philadelphia, Printed by J. C. Clark, 1837. v, [1], 197 p. Reprinted 2000 by The Lawbook Exchange, Ltd. LCCN 00-026728. ISBN 1-58477-098-8. Cloth. $60.

Bancroft, George. *History of the Formation of the Constitution of the United States of America. Second Edition.* New York: D. Appleton and Company, 1882. Two volumes. xxiv, 520; xiv, 501 pp. Reprinted 2000 by The Lawbook Exchange, Ltd. LCCN 99-23946. ISBN 1-58477-002-3. Cloth. $175.

Bar, Carl Ludwig von. *A History of Continental Criminal Law.* Boston: Little, Brown, and Company, 1916. lvi, 561 pp. Reprinted 1999 by The Lawbook Exchange, Ltd. LCCN 99-32341. ISBN 1-58477-013-9. Cloth. $90.

Barton, Dunbar Plunket. *Shakespeare and the Law.* With a foreword by James M. Beck. Boston: Houghton Mifflin Company, 1929. xl, 167 pp. Reprinted 1999 by The Lawbook Exchange, Ltd. LCCN 99-26602. ISBN 1-58477-000-7. Cloth. $60.

Bauer, Elizabeth Kelley. *Commentaries on the Constitution 1790-1860.* New York: Columbia University Press, 1952. 400 pp. Reprinted 1999 by The Lawbook Exchange, Ltd. LCCN 98-45409. ISBN 1-886363-66-8. Cloth. $75.

Beard, Charles Austin. *The Office of the Justice of the Peace in England, in its Origin and Development.* New York: Columbia University Press, 1904. 184, [1] pp. Reprint available November 2000 by The Lawbook Exchange, Ltd. ISBN 1-58477-102-X. Cloth. $60.

Beard, Charles. *An Economic Interpretation of the Constitution of the United States.* New York: The Macmillan Company, 1952. xxi, 330 pp. Reprint available September 2000 by The Lawbook Exchange, Ltd. LCCN 00-036834. ISBN 1-58477-111-9. Cloth. $80.

Beard, Charles A. *The Supreme Court and the Constitution.* New York: The Macmillan Company, 1912. vii, 127 pp. Reprinted 1999 by The Lawbook Exchange, Ltd. LCCN 98-50368. ISBN 1-886363-78-1. Cloth. $45.

Beck, Theodric Romeyn. *Elements of Medical Jurisprudence.* Albany: Websters and Skinners, 1823. Two volumes. xxxiv, 418; viii, [9]-471 pp. Reprinted 1997 by The Lawbook Exchange, Ltd. LCCN 96-35845. ISBN 1-886363-24-2. Cloth. $125.

Benedict, Russell. *Acts and Laws of the Thirteen Original Colonies and States: Constituting the extraordinary collection of Hon. Russell Benedict.* New York: American Art Association, 1922. [272]pp. Reprinted 1998 The Lawbook Exchange, Ltd. LC 98-20196 ISBN 1-886363-56-0. Cloth. $85.

Black, Henry Campbell. *A Dictionary of Law Containing Definitions of the Terms and Phrases of American and English Jurisprudence, Ancient and Modern. Including the Principal Terms of International, Constitutional, and Commercial Law; with a Collection of Legal Maxims and Numerous Select Titles from the Civil Law and Other Foreign Systems.* St. Paul, Minn.: West Publishing, 1891. x, 1253 pp. Reprinted 1991 by the Lawbook Exchange, Ltd. LCCN 91-62383. ISBN 0-9630106-0-3. $125.

Black, Henry Campbell. *A Law Dictionary. Containing Definitions of the Terms and Phrases of American and English Jurisprudence, Ancient and Modern. And Including the Principal Terms of International, Constitutional, Ecclesiastical and Commercial Law; and Medical Jurisprudence, with a Collection of Legal Maxims, Numerous Select Titles from the Roman, Modern Civil, Scotch, French, Spanish, and Mexican Law, and Other Foreign Systems, and a Table of Abbreviations.* St. Paul, Minn.: West Publishing, 1910. 1314 pp. Reprinted 1995 by the Lawbook Exchange, Ltd. LCCN 97-10320. ISBN 1-886363-10-2. Cloth. $150.

[Blackstone, William]. Eller, Catherine Spicer. *The William Blackstone Collection in the Yale Law Library. A Bibliographical Catalogue.* New Haven: Yale University Press, 1938. xvii, 113 pp. Reprinted 1993 by The Lawbook Exchange, Ltd. LCCN 99-38826. ISBN 0-9630106-5-4. Cloth. $50.

Bondy, William. *Separation of Governmental Powers in History, in Theory, and in the Constitutions.* New York: Columbia College, 1896. Reprinted 1999 by The Lawbook Exchange, Ltd. vi,[7]-185, [1] pp. LCCN 98-44994. ISBN 1-886363-65-X. Cloth. $65.

Bonner, Robert J. and Gertrude Smith. *The Administration of Justice from Homer to Aristotle.* Chicago: The University of Chicago Press, [1930]. Two volumes. ix, 390; vii, [320] pp. Reprint available November 2000 by The Lawbook Exchange, Ltd. ISBN 1-58477-117-8. Cloth. $160.

Bouvier, John. [1787-1851]. *Institutes of American Law New Edition by Daniel A. Gleason. In Two Volumes.* Boston: Little, Brown, & Company, 1880. lxviii, 651; iv, 798pp. Reprinted 1999 by The Lawbook Exchange, Ltd. LCCN 98-54288. ISBN 1-886363-80-3. Cloth. $250.

Bouvier, John. *A Law Dictionary Adapted to the Constitution and Laws of the United States of America, and of the Several States of the American Union; with References to the Civil and Other Systems of Foreign Law* Philadelphia: T. & J.W. Johnson, 1839. Two volumes. 559; 628 pp. Reprinted 1993 by The Lawbook Exchange, Ltd. LCCN 99-047231. ISBN 0-9630106-7-0. Cloth. $130.

[Brandeis, Louis D.]. [1856-1941]. *Brandeis on Zionism A Collection of Addresses and Statements by Louis D. Brandeis with a Foreword by Mr. Justice Felix Frankfurter.* Washington, D.C.: Zionist Organization of America, [1942]. viii, 156 pp. Reprinted 1999 by The Lawbook Exchange, Ltd. LCCN 98-49331. ISBN 1-886363-60-9. Cloth. $65.

Broom, Herbert. *A Selection of Legal Maxims, Classified and Illustrated. Eighth American, from the Fifth London Edition, with References to American Cases.* Philadelphia: T. & J.W. Johnson & Co., 1882. lxxviii, 993 [i.e. 779] pp. Reprinted 2000 by The Lawbook Exchange, Ltd. LCCN 99-049329. ISBN 1-58477-052-X. Cloth. $125.

Brown, Basil. [1860-1928]. *Law Sports at Gray's Inn (1594) Including Shakespeare's connection with the Inns of Court, the origin of the Capias Utlegatum re Coke and Bacon, Francis Bacon's connection with Warwickshire, together with a reprint of the Gesta Grayorum.* New York: [Privately Printed by the Author], 1921. xciv, 188, 88, [9] pp. LCCN 99-049829. ISBN 1-58477-056-2. Reprint available December 2000 by The Lawbook Exchange, Ltd. Cloth. $85.

Brown, Everett Somerville. *The Constitutional History of the Louisiana Purchase 1803-1812.* Berkeley: University of California Press, 1920. xi, 248 pp. Reprint available December 2000 by The Lawbook Exchange, Ltd. ISBN 1-58477-151-8. Cloth. $75.

Browne, Arthur. *A Compendious View of the Civil Law and of the Law of the Admiralty: being the substance of a course of lectures read in the University of Dublin.* New York: Halstead and Voorhies, 1840. Two volumes. xvi, 536; xi, 567 pp. Reprinted 2000 by The Lawbook Exchange, Ltd. LCCN 99-18284. ISBN 1-886363-88-9. Cloth. $175.

Buckland, W.W. *The Roman Law of Slavery: The Condition of the Slave in Private Law from Augustus to Justinian.* Cambridge: Cambridge University Press, 1908. xii, [2], 735 pp. Reprinted 2000 by The Lawbook Exchange, Ltd. LCCN 99-056922. ISBN 1-58477-068-6X. Cloth. $175.

Burrill, Alexander M. *A New Law Dictionary and Glossary: Containing Full Definitions of the Principal Terms of the Common and Civil Law; Together with Translations and Explanations of the Various Technical Phrases in Different Languages, Occurring in the Ancient and Modern Reports, and Standard Treatises; Embracing Also All the Principal Common and Civil Law Maxims. Compiled on the Basis of Spelman's Glossary, and Adapted to the Jurisprudence of the United States; with Copious Illustrations, Critical and Historical.* New York: John S. Voorhies, 1850. Two volumes. xviii, 1099 pp. Reprinted 1998 by The Lawbook Exchange, Ltd. LCCN 97-38481. ISBN 1-886363-32-3. Cloth. $175.

Bussell, F.W. *The Roman Empire. Essays on the Constitutional History from the Accession of Domitian (81 A.D.) to the Retirement of Nicephorus III. (1081 A.D.)* London: Longmans, Green, and Co., 1910. Two volumes. xiv, 402; xxiii, 521 pp. Reprinted 2000 by The Lawbook Exchange, Ltd. LCCN 99-087026. ISBN 1-58477-082-1. Cloth. $175.

Calabresi, Guido. *A Common Law for the Age of Statutes.* Cambridge: Harvard University Press, 1982. xi, 319 pp. Reprinted 2000 by The Lawbook Exchange, Ltd. LCCN 99-44889. ISBN 1-58477-040-6. Cloth. $85.

Calhoun, George M. *The Growth of Criminal Law in Ancient Greece.* Berkeley: University of California Press, 1927. x, 149 pp. LCCN 99-43192. ISBN 1-58477-037-6. Reprinted 2000 by The Lawbook Exchange, Ltd. Cloth. New. $50.

[Cardozo, Benjamin]. *Law is Justice. Notable Opinions of Mr. Justice Cardozo.* Foreword by Robert F. Wagner. Edited by A.L. Sainer. New York: Ad Press Ltd., [1938]. xvii, 441 pp. Frontis. Reprinted 1999 by The Lawbook Exchange, Ltd. LCCN 99-34154. ISBN 1-58477-010-4. Cloth. $75.

Cardozo, Benjamin. *The Paradoxes of Legal Science.* New York: Columbia University Press, 1928. v, 142 pp. Reprinted 2000 by The Lawbook Exchange, Ltd. LCCN 00-024469. ISBN 1-58477-097-X. Cloth. $75.

Chafee, Zechariah. *Free Speech in the United States.* Cambridge, Massachusetts: Harvard University Press, 1967. xviii, 634 pp. Reprint available September 2000 by The Lawbook Exchange, Ltd. LCCN 99-087317. ISBN 1-58477-085-6. Cloth. $125.

[Cherokee Laws]. *Compiled Laws of the Cherokee Nation.* Tahlequah, I.T.:National Advocate Print, 1881. 370pp. Reprinted 1998 by The Lawbook Exchange, Ltd. With a new introduction by Michael Weber. LCCN 98-12741. ISBN 1-886363-42-0. Cloth. $60.

Chipman, Nathaniel. *Principles of Government. A Treatise on Free Institutions Including the Constitution of the United States.* Burlington: Edward Smith, 1833. viii, 144, 145a-188a, [145]-330 pp. Reprint available November 2000 by The Lawbook Exchange, Ltd. LCCN 99-048863. ISBN 1-58477-046-5. Cloth. $80.

Chitwood, Oliver Perry. *Justice in Colonial Virginia.* Baltimore: Johns Hopkins Press, 1905. 123, [1] pp. Reprint available November 2000 by The Lawbook Exchange, Ltd. ISBN 1-58477-114-3. Cloth. $65.

Clark, H.B. *Biblical Law Being a text of the statutes, ordinances, and judgments established in the Holy Bible-with many allusions to secular laws-ancient, medieval, and modern-documented to the Scriptures, judicial decisions, and legal literature.* Portland, Ore.: Binfords & Mort, [1943]. . xxiv, 304 pp. LCCN 99-053316. ISBN 1-58477-062-7. Reprinted 2000 by The Lawbook Exchange, Ltd. Cloth. $75.

Cohn, Morris M. *An Introduction to the Study of the Constitution; A Study showing the Play of Physical and Social Factors in the Creation of Institutional Law* Baltimore: The Johns Hopkins Press, 1892. xi, 235 pp. Reprinted 2000 by The Lawbook Exchange, Ltd. LCCN 99-38730. ISBN 1-58477-032-5. Cloth. $50.

Coke, Edward, Sir. *The First Part of the Institutes of the Laws of England, or, A commentary upon Littleton. Not the name of the Author only, but of the Law Itself. Revised and Corrected With Additions of Notes, References, and Proper Tables, by Francis Hargrave and Charles Butler, Esqrs. Of Lincoln's Inn, Including also The Notes of Lord Chief Justice Hale and Lord Chancellor Nottingham; and An Analysis of Littleton, written by an unknown Hand in 1658-9. By Charles Butler, Esq. The Eighteenth Edition, Corrected.* London, J. & W.T. Clarke, 1823. Two volumes. ccxvi,[606]; iv, [772] pp. Reprinted 2000 by The Lawbook Exchange, Ltd. LCCN 99-41675. ISBN 1-58477-033-3. Cloth. $195.

[Continental Legal History]. *A General Survey of Events, Sources, Persons & Movements in Continental Legal History. By Various European Authors.* With an introduction by Albert Kocourek. Boston: Little, Brown, 1912. liii, 754pp. Reprinted 1998 by The Lawbook Exchange, Ltd. LCCN 98-11159. ISBN 1-886363-47-1. Cloth. $110.

Cooley, Thomas M. The General Principles of Constitutional Law in the United States of America. Boston: Little, Brown, and Company, 1880. xxxix, 376 pp.

Reprint available December 2000 by The Lawbook Exchange, Ltd. ISBN 1-58477-120-8. Cloth. $85.

Cooley, Thomas M. [1824-98]. *A Treatise on the Constitutional Limitations which Rest Upon the Legislative Power of the States of the American Union. Fifth edition.* Boston: Little, Brown, and Co., 1883. lxxxi, 886pp. Reprinted 1998 by The Lawbook Exchange, Ltd. LCCN 98-12730. ISBN 1-886363-53-6. Cloth. $120.

Cooley, Thomas McIntyre. [1824-1898]. *A Treatise on the Constitutional Limitations Which Rest Upon the Legislative Power of the States of the American Union.* [1st edition]. Boston: Little, Brown, and Co., 1868. xlvii, 720pp. Reprinted 1999 by The Lawbook Exchange, Ltd. LCCN 99-20589. ISBN 1-886363-92-7. Cloth. $95.

Corwin, Edward. *The Doctrine of Judicial Review: Its Legal and Historical Basis and Other Essays.* Princeton: Princeton University Press, 1914. ix, 178 pp. Reprinted 2000 by The Lawbook Exchange, Ltd. LCCN 99-32362. ISBN 1-58477-011-2. Cloth. $60.

Darrow, Clarence and William J. Bryan. *The World's Most Famous Court Trial. Tennessee Evolution Case. A Complete Stenographic Report of the Famous Court Test of the Anti-Evolution Act, at Dayton July 10 to 21, 1925, Including Speeches and Arguments of Attorneys.* Cincinnati: National Book Company, [1925]. [4], 339 pp. Reprinted 1997 by The Lawbook Exchange, Ltd. LCCN 97-38485. ISBN 1-886363-31-5. Cloth. $75.

Darrow, Clarence. *A Persian Pearl. And Other Essays.* East Aurora, NY: The Roycroft Shop, 1899. 175 pp. Reprinted 1997 by The Lawbook Exchange, Ltd. LCCN 97-5174. ISBN 1-886363-27-7. Cloth. $50.

Darrow, Clarence S. *An Eye for an Eye.* New York: Fox Duffield & Company, 1905. 213 pp. Reprinted 1996 by The Lawbook Exchange, Ltd. LCCN 99-047232. ISBN 1-886363-07-2. Cloth. $40.

Davis, C.K. *The Law in Shakespeare.* Washington, D.C.: Washington Law Book Co., [1883]. 303 pp. Reprinted 1999 by The Lawbook Exchange, Ltd. LCCN 98-32333. ISBN 1-886363-75-7. Cloth. $60.

Dawson, John P. *A History of Lay Judges.* Cambridge, Mass.: Harvard University Press, 1960. viii, [2], 310 pp. Reprinted 1999 by The Lawbook Exchange, Ltd. LCCN 98-50812. ISBN 1-886363-69-2. Cloth. $75.

Dodd, Walter Fairleigh. *The Revision and Amendment of State Constitutions.* Baltimore: The Johns Hopkins Press, 1910. xvii, 350 pp. Reprinted 1999 by The Lawbook Exchange, Ltd. LCCN 98-50815. ISBN 1-886363-73-0. Cloth. $65.

Duer, William Alexander. *A Course of Lectures on the Constitutional Jurisprudence of the United States; Delivered Annually in Columbia College, New York. The Second Edition, Revised, Enlarged, and Adapted to Professional as well as General Use.* Boston: Little, Brown & Co., 1856. xxiv, 545 pp. Reprinted 2000 by The Lawbook Exchange, Ltd. LCCN 99-16385. ISBN 1-58477-020-1. Cloth. $85.

Esmein, A[dhemar]. *A History of Continental Criminal Procedure with Special Reference to France. Translated by John Simpson; with an editorial preface by William E. Mikell and introductions by Norman M. Trenholme and by William Renwick Riddell.* Boston: Little, Brown and Company, 1913. xlv, 640 pp. Reprinted 2000 by The Lawbook Exchange, Ltd. LCCN 99-045906. ISBN 1-58477-042-2. Cloth. $100.

Evans, E.P. *The Criminal Prosecution and Capital Punishment of Animals.* New York: E.P. Dutton, 1906. x, 384pp. Reprinted 1998 by The Lawbook Exchange, Ltd. LCCN 98-12801. ISBN 1-886363-52-8. Cloth. $65.

Farnam, Henry W. *Chapters in the History of Social Legislation in the United States to 1860.* Washington: Carnegie Institution of Washington, 1938. xx, 496 pp. Reprinted 2000 by The Lawbook Exchange, Ltd. LCCN 99-049362. ISBN 1-58477-054-6. Cloth. $100.

[Field Codes]. [New York 1850-1865]. New York Field Codes. 1850-1865.
Vol. I. *The Code of Civil Procedure of the State of New York, Reported Complete by the Commissioners on Practice and Pleadings. 1850.*
Vol. II. *The Code of Criminal Procedure of the State of New York, Reported Complete by the Commissioners on Practice and Pleadings. 1850.*
Vol. III. *The Civil Code of the State of New York, Reported Complete by the Commissioners of the Code. 1865.*
Vol. IV. *The Penal Code of the State of New York, Reported Complete by the Commissioners of the Code. 1865.*
Vol. V. *The Political Code of the State of New York. 1860.*
With a new introduction by Michael Weber. Reprinted 1998 by The Lawbook Exchange, Ltd. Five volume series. [8], xcvi, 791; liii, [1], 486; cxii, 776; lxiv, 406, clxvii; xlvii, 607 pp. ISBN 1-886363-40-4 (set). Cloth. $495.

Finkelman, Paul, editor. *A Brief Narrative of the Case and Tryal of John Peter Zenger Printer of the New York Weekly Journal.* New York: Brandywine Press, [1997]. vii, 175 pp. Reprinted 2000 by The Lawbook Exchange, Ltd. LCCN 99-049431. ISBN 1-58477-051-1. Cloth. $50.

Finkelman, Paul. *An Imperfect Union: Slavery, Federalism and Comity.* Chapel Hill: The University of North Carolina Press, 1981. xii, 378 pp. Reprinted 2000 by The Lawbook Exchange, Ltd. LCCN 00-021509. ISBN 1-58477-092-9. Cloth. $85.

Finkelman, Paul. *Slavery in the Courtroom An Annotated Bibliography of American Cases.* Washington:Library of Congress, 1985. Illustrated. xxvii, 312pp. Reprinted 1998 by The Lawbook Exchange, Ltd. LCCN 98-11284. ISBN 1-886363-48-X. Cloth. $85.

Fisher, Sydney George. *The Evolution of the Constitution of the United States. Showing That It Is a Development of Progressive History and Not an Isolated Document Struck Off at a Given Time or an Imitation of English or Dutch Forms of Government.* Philadelphia: J.B. Lippincott, 1897. 398 pp. Reprinted 1996 by The Lawbook Exchange, Ltd. LCCN 97-41054. ISBN 1-886363-08-0. Cloth. $65.

Flanders, Henry. [1824-1911]. *A Treatise on Maritime Law* Boston: Little, Brown and Company, 1852. xvi, 444 pp. Reprinted 1999 by The Lawbook Exchange, Ltd. ISBN 1-886363-72-2. Cloth. $75.

Flanders, Henry. *An Exposition of the Constitution of the United States. Designed as a Manual of Instruction.* Philadelphia: E.H. Butler & Co., 1860. xii, 311 pp. Reprinted 1999 by The Lawbook Exchange, Ltd. LCCN 99-31594. ISBN 1-58477-014-7. Cloth. $60.

Ford, Paul Leicester. *Pamphlets on the Constitution of the United States, Published During Its Discussion by the People 1787-1788.* Brooklyn, N.Y., 1888. viii, 451 pp. Reprinted 2000 by The Lawbook Exchange, Ltd. LCCN 99-25089. ISBN 1-886363-95-1. Cloth. $75.

Forsyth, William. *The History of Lawyers. Ancient and Modern.* Boston: Estes & Lauriat, 1875. Illustrated. xvii, 404 pp. Reprinted 1996 by the Lawbook Exchange, Ltd. LCCN 95-51103. ISBN 1-886363-14-5. Cloth. $60.

Forsyth, William. *History of Trial by Jury [Second edition].* Jersey City: Frederick D. Linn, [1875]. x, 388 pp. Reprinted 1994 by The Lawbook Exchange, Ltd. LCCN 96-14505. ISBN 0-9630106-8-9. Cloth. $65.

Fortescue, Sir John. [?1394-1476?]. *The Governance of England: Otherwise Called The Difference between an Absolute and a Limited Monarchy. A Revised Text edited with Introduction, Notes, and Appendices by Charles Plummer.* London: Oxford University Press, 1885. xxiii, 387pp. Reprinted 1999 by The Lawbook Exchange, Ltd. ISBN 1-886363-79-X. Cloth. $65.

Fortescue, Sir John. *DeLaudibus Legum Angliae. A Treatise in Commendation of the Laws of England.* With Translation by Francis Gregor. Notes by Andrew Amos and a Life of the Author by Thomas (Fortescue) Lord Clermont. Cincinnati: Robert Clarke & Co., 1874. lxiv, 302 pp. Reprinted 1999 by The Lawbook Exchange, Ltd. LCCN 99-16485. ISBN 1-58477-019-8. Cloth. $65.

Foss, Edward. *A Biographical Dictionary of the Judges of England From the Conquest to the Present Time 1066-1870.* London: John Murray, 1870. xv, 792 pp. Reprinted 2000 by The Lawbook Exchange, Ltd. LCCN 99-12577. ISBN 10886363-86-2. Cloth. $100.

Freeman, A.C. *A Treatise of the Law of Judgments. Including All Final Determinations of the Rights of Parties in Actions or Proceedings at Law or in Equity. Revised, and Greatly Enlarged by Edward W. Tuttle.* San Francisco: Bancroft-Whitney, 1925. Three volumes. 1216; 1280; 1264 pp. Reprinted 1993 by The Lawbook Exchange, Ltd. LCCN 99-047228. ISBN 0-9630106-6-2. Cloth. $295.

Friedberg, Emil Albert [1837-1910]. Richter, Aemilius Ludwig [1808-1864]. *Corpus iuris canonici.-Editio Lipsiensis secunda / post Aemilii Ludouici Richteri curas ad librorum manu scriptorum et editionis Romanae fidem recognouit et adnotatione critica instruxit Aemilius Friedberg.* Leipzig : Tauchnitz, 1879-1881. Two volumes. civ, 1472 columns (736 pp.); lxxxii, 1340 columns (670 pp.) LCCN 99-088231. Reprinted 2000 by The Lawbook Exchange, Ltd. ISBN 1-58477-088-0. Cloth. $300.

Friend, Willam L. *Anglo-American Legal Bibliographies. An Annotated Guide.* Washington, D.C.: United States Government Printing Office, 1944. xii, 166 pp. Reprinted 1996 by The Lawbook Exchange, Ltd. LCCN 96-11002. ISBN 1-886363-21-8. Cloth. $65.

Fuller, Lon L. *The Law in Quest of Itself.* Boston: Beacon Press, 1966. [vi], 150 pp. Reprinted 1999 by The Lawbook Exchange, Ltd. LCCN 99-32863. ISBN 1-58477-016-3. Cloth. $45.

Futrell, William H. *The History of American Customs Jurisprudence.* New York: Published privately, 1941. 314pp. Reprinted 1998 by The Lawbook Exchange, Ltd. LCCN 98-11342. ISBN 1-886363-51-X. Cloth. $60.

Gest, John Marshall. *The Lawyer in Literature.* London: Sweet & Maxwell, Limited, 1913. xii, 249 pp. Reprinted 1999 by The Lawbook Exchange, Ltd. LCCN 99-18365. ISBN 1-886363-90-0. Cloth. $60.

Gilmore, Grant. *Security Interests in Personal Property.* Boston: Little, Brown & Company, 1965. Two volumes. xxxiv, 651; xiii, 653-1508 pp. Reprinted 1999 by The Lawbook Exchange, Ltd. LCCN 99-10258. ISBN 1-886363-81-1. Cloth. $195.

Girard, Paul F. *A Short History of Roman Law Being the First Part of his Manuel Elementaire De Droit Romain.* Translated by Augustus Henry Frazer and John Home Cameron. Toronto: Canada Law Book Company, 1906, v, 220 pp. Reprinted 2000 by The Lawbook Exchange, Ltd. LCCN 99-087383. ISBN 1-58477-078-3. Cloth. $55.

Goodhart, Arthur L. *Five Jewish Lawyers of the Common Law.* London: Oxford University Press, 1949. [4], 74 pp. Reprinted 2000 by The Lawbook Exchange, Ltd. LCCN 99-049934. ISBN 1-58477-045-7. Cloth. $60.

Greenidge, A.H.J. *The Legal Procedure of Cicero's Time.* Oxford: The Clarendon Press, 1901. xiii, 599 pp. Reprinted 2000 by The Lawbook Exchange, Ltd. LCCN 99-26771. ISBN 1-886363-99-4. Cloth. $85.

Greenleaf, Simon. *The Testimony of the Evangelists Examined by the Rules of Evidence Administered in Courts of Justice with an Appendix Containing a History of the Most Ancient Manuscript Copies of the New Testament, and a Comparison of their Text with that of the King James' Bible by Constantine Tischendorff. Also a Review of the Trial of Jesus.* New York: James Cockcroft & Company, 1874. Reprint available December 2000 by The Lawbook Exchange, Ltd.xxiii, 613 pp. LCCN 00-021510. ISBN 1-58477-020-1. Cloth. $95.

Greenleaf, Simon. *A Treatise on the Law of Evidence.* Boston: Little, Brown, and Company, 1899. Three volumes. Reprint available November 2000 by The Lawbook Exchange, Ltd. ISBN 1-58477-116-X. Cloth. $350.

Haines, Charles Grove. *The Conflict over Judicial Powers in the United States to 1870.* New York: Columbia University Press, 1909. 180 pp. Reprint available December 2000 by The Lawbook Exchange, Ltd. LCCN 99-088241. ISBN 1-58477-080-5. Cloth. $60.

Hale, Matthew. *The History and Analysis of the Common Law of England.* Stafford: J. Nutt, 1713. [x], 264, [28], 176 pp. Reprinted 2000 by The Lawbook Exchange, Ltd. LCCN 99-33739. ISBN 1-58477-024-4. Cloth. $85.

Harper, Robert Francis. *The Code of Hammurabi King of Babylon. About 2250 B.C. Autographed Text transliteration...* Chicago: The University of Chicago Press, 1904. xxviii, 194, ciii (plates) pp. London: John Murray, 1832. xx, 392, lxxvi pp. Illus. Reprinted 2000 The Lawbook Exchange, Ltd. LCCN 99-23953. ISBN 1-58477-003-1. Cloth. $75.

Harris, Virgil M. *Ancient, Curious, and Famous Wills.* Boston: Little, Brown, and Company, 1911. xiv, 472 pp. Reprinted 1999 by The Lawbook Exchange, Ltd. LCCN 99-20588. ISBN 1-886363-93-5. Cloth. $75.

Hearn, William Edward. *The Aryan Household. Its Structure and its Development. An Introduction to Comparative Jurisprudence.* London and New York: Longmans, Green, and Co., 1891. viii, 494 pp. Reprint available December 2000 by The Lawbook Exchange, Ltd. ISBN 1-58477-124-0. Cloth. $90.

Henderson, Gerard Carl. *The Position of Foreign Corporations in American Constitutional Law A Contribution to the History and Theory of Juristic Persons in Anglo-*

American Law Cambridge: Harvard University Press, 1918. xix, 199 pp. Reprinted 1999 by The Lawbook Exchange, Ltd. LCCN 99-18233. ISBN 1-886363-89-7. Cloth. $50.

Hicks, Frederick. *Men and Books Famous in the Law With an introduction by Harlan F. Stone.* Rochester, New York: Lawyers Co-operative Publishing, 1921. 259 pp. Reprinted 1992 by The Lawbook Exchange, Ltd. LCCN 92-070809. ISBN 0-9630106-2-X. Cloth. $50.

Hohfeld, Wesley. *Fundamental Legal Conceptions as Applied in Judicial Reasoning.* Edited by Walter Wheeler Cook, with a New Foreword by Arthur L. Corbin. New Haven: Yale University Press, 1964. xv, 114 pp. Reprint available November 2000 by The Lawbook Exchange, Ltd. ISBN 1-58477-162-3. Cloth. $55.

Holdsworth, William S. *Charles Dickens as a Legal Historian.* New Haven: Yale University Press, 1929. 157 pp. Reprinted 1995 by The Lawbook Exchange, Ltd. LCCN 96-46579. ISBN 1-886363-06-4. Cloth. $40.

Holdsworth, William S. *Essays in Law and History.* Edited by A.L. Goodhart and H.G. Hanbury. Oxford: At the Clarendon Press, 1946. xv, 302 pp. Reprinted 1995 by The Lawbook Exchange, Ltd. LCCN 99-047234. ISBN 1-886363-13-7. Cloth. $65.

Holdsworth, W.S. *The Historians of Anglo-American Law.* New York: Columbia University Press, 1928. 175 pp. Reprinted 1994 by The Lawbook Exchange, Ltd. ISBN 0-9630106-9-7. Cloth. $50.

Holt, W. Stull. *Treaties Defeated by the Senate. A Study of the Struggle Between President and Senate Over the Conduct of Foreign Relations.* Baltimore: The Johns Hopkins Press, 1933. vi, [1],328 pp. Reprinted 2000 by The Lawbook Exchange, Ltd. LCCN 99-39606. ISBN 1-58477-029-5. Cloth. $65.

Holthouse, Henry James. *A New Law Dictionary, Containing Explanations of Such Technical Terms and Phrases As Defined in the Works of Legal Authors, in the Practice of the Courts, and in the Parliamentary Proceedings of the Houses of Lords and Commons, To Which Is Added An Outline of An Action at Law and of A Suit in Equity. Edited, from the Second and Enlarged London Edition, With Numerous Additions, by Henry Penington.* Philadelphia: Lea and Blanchard, 1847. viii, [17]-495 pp. Reprinted 1999 by The Lawbook Exchange, Ltd. LCCN 98-49350. ISBN 1-886363-67-6. Cloth. $75.

Horton, John Theodore. *James Kent: A Study in Conservatism, 1763-1847.* New York: D. Appleton-Century Co., [1939]. xi, 354 pp. Reprinted 2000 by The Lawbook Exchange, Ltd. LCCN 99-056927. ISBN 1-58477-069-4. Cloth. $80.

Huebner, Rudolf. *A History of Germanic Private Law* Translated by Francis S. Philbrick; with an editorial preface by Ernest G. Lorenzen and introductions by Paul Vinogradoff and by William E. Walz. Boston: Little, Brown and Company, 1818. lix, 788 pp. Reprinted 2000 by The Lawbook Exchange, Ltd. LCCN 99-055138. ISBN 1-58477-065-1. Cloth. $120.

Hurst, James Willard. *Law and Social Order in the United States.* Ithaca: Cornell University Press, 1977. 318 pp. Reprinted 2000 by The Lawbook Exchange, Ltd. ISBN 1-58477-113-5. Cloth. $85.

Ilbert, Courtenay. *The Mechanics of Law Making.* New York: Columbia University Press, 1914. viii, 209 pp. Reprint available November 2000 by The Lawbook Exchange, Ltd. LCCN 99-047156. ISBN 1-58477-044-9. Cloth. $70.

Jackson, E. Hilton. *Latin for Lawyers. Containing I: A Course in Latin, with Legal Maxims and Phrases As a Basis of Instruction. II. A Collection of Over One Thousand Latin Maxims, with English Translations, Explanatory Notes, and Cross-References. III. A Vocabulary of Latin Words.* London: Sweet & Maxwell, 1915. viii, 300 pp. Reprinted 1992 by The Lawbook Exchange, Ltd. LCCN 92-074408. ISBN 0-9630106-4-6. Cloth. $50.

Jacob, Giles. [1686-1744]. *The Law Dictionary: Explaining the Rise, Progress, and Present State of the English Law; Defining and Interpreting the Terms or Words of Art; and Comprising Copious Information on the Subjects of Law, Trade, and Government. Corrected and Greatly Enlarged by T[homas] E[dlyne] Tomlins.* New York: Printed for, and Published by I. Riley, 1811. Six volumes. viii, 531; [2], 543; [2],618; [2], 472; [2], 553; [2], 471pp. Reprinted 2000 by The Lawbook Exchange, Ltd. LCCN 98-49349. ISBN 1-886363-68-4. Cloth. $495.

Jaques, E.T. *Charles Dickens in Chancery: Being an Account of his Proceedings in Respect of the "Christmas Carol" with Some Gossip in Relation to the Old Law Courts at Westminster.* London: Longmans, Green & Company, 1914. 95 pp. Reprint available December 2000 by The Lawbook Exchange, Ltd. ISBN 1-58477-106-2. Cloth. $60.

Jhering, Rudolf Von. *Law as a Means to an End.* Translated from the German by Isaac Husik with an Editorial Preface by Joseph H. Drake and with Introductions by Henry Lamm and W.M. Geldart. Boston: The Boston Book Company, 1913. lxi, 483 pp. Reprinted 1999 by The Lawbook Exchange, Ltd. LCCN 99-23754. ISBN 1-58477-009-0. Cloth. $80.

Jhering, Rudolph von. *The Struggle for Law Translated from the Fifth German Edition by John J. Lalor. Second Edition, with an Introduction by Albert Kocourek.* Chicago: Callaghan and Company, 1915. lii, 138 pp. Reprinted 1997 by The Lawbook Exchange, Ltd. LCCN 97-6826. ISBN 1-886363-25-0. Cloth. $60.

Johns, C.H.W. *Babylonian and Assyrian Laws, Contracts and Letters.* Edinburgh: T. & T. Clark, 1904. xxii, 424 pp. Reprinted 2000 by The Lawbook Exchange, Ltd. LCCN 99-32862. ISBN 1-58477-022-8. Cloth. $75.

Johns, C.H.W. , translator. *The Oldest Code of Laws in the World: The Code of Laws Promulgated by Hammurabi, King of Babylon, B.C. 2285-2242.* Edinburgh: T. & T. Clark, 1926. xii, 88 pp. Reprint available November 2000 by The Lawbook Exchange, Ltd. LCCN 99-053070. ISBN 1-58477-061-9. Cloth. $60.

Kames, Henry Home, Lord. [1696-1782]. *Historical Law Tracts. The Second Edition.* Edinburgh: A. Kincaid, 1761. xv, 463 pp. LCCN 99-43133. ISBN 1-58477-038-4. Reprinted 2000 by The Lawbook Exchange, Ltd. Cloth. $95.

Keller, Morton. *Affairs of State: Public Life in Late Nineteenth Century America.* Cambridge: Harvard University Press, 1977. ix, 631 pp. Reprinted 2000 by The Lawbook Exchange, Ltd. LCCN 99-087921. ISBN 1-58477-086-4. Cloth. $95.

Kelsen, Hans. [1881-1973]. *General Theory of Law and State.* Translated by Anders Wedberg. Cambridge: Harvard University Press, 1945. xxxiii, 516pp. Reprinted 1999 by The Lawbook Exchange, Ltd. LCCN 98-32334. ISBN 1-886363-74-9. Cloth. $75.

Kelsen, Hans. *The Law of the United Nations. A Critical Analysis of Its Fundamental Problems.* New York: Frederick A. Praeger, [1964]. xvii, 994 pp. Reprinted 2000 by The Lawbook Exchange, Ltd. ISBN 1-58477-077-5. Cloth. $125.

Kelsen, Hans. *Peace Through Law.* Chapel Hill: The University of North Carolina Press, 1944. xii, 155 pp. Reprint available September 2000 by The Lawbook Exchange, Ltd. ISBN 1-58477-103-8. Cloth. $60.

Kelsen, Hans. *Society and Nature: A Sociological Inquiry.* London: K. Kegan Paul, Trench, Trubner & Co., Ltd., [1946]. viii, 391 pp. Reprint available September 2000 by The Lawbook Exchange, Ltd. LCCN 99-054869. ISBN 1-58477-064-3. Cloth. $85.

Kelsen, Hans. *What is Justice? Justice, Law and Politics in the Mirror of Science.* Berkeley: University of California Press, 1957. [vi], 397 pp. Reprinted 2000 by The Lawbook Exchange, Ltd. ISBN 1-58477-101-1. Cloth. $95.

Kent, William. *Memoirs and Letters of James Kent, L.L.D.* Boston: Little, Brown, and Company, 1898. x, 341 pp. Reprint available December 2000 by The Lawbook Exchange, Ltd. ISBN 1-58477-100-3. Cloth. $75.

Kovalevsky, Maxime. *Modern Customs and Ancient Laws of Russia. Being the Ilchester Lectures for 1889-90.* London: David Nutt, 1891. x, 260 pp. Reprinted 2000 by The Lawbook Exchange, Ltd. LCCN 99-16487. ISBN 1-58477-017-1. Cloth. $65.

Kulsrud, Carl J. *Maritime Neutrality to 1780. A History of the Main Principles Governing Neutrality and Belligerency to 1780.* Boston: Little, Brown, and Company, 1936. x, 351 pp. Reprinted 2000 by The Lawbook Exchange, Ltd. LCCN 99-38825. ISBN 1-58477-027-9. Cloth. $65.

Langdell, C.C. [1826-1906]. *A Selection of Cases on the Law of Contracts. With References and Citations. Prepared for Use as a Text-book in Harvard Law School.* Boston: Little, Brown & Co., 1871. xvi, 1022 pp. Reprinted 1999 by The Lawbook Exchange, Ltd. LCCN 99-28293. ISBN 1-58477-001-5. Cloth. $120.

Lauterpacht, H[ersch]. *The Function of Law in the International Community.* Oxford: Clarendon Press, 1933. xxvi, 470 pp. Reprint available August 2000 by The Lawbook Exchange, Ltd. LCCN 00-022124. ISBN 1-58477-090-2. Cloth. $90.

[Legal History]. *Select Essays in Anglo-American Legal History. By Maitland, Pollock, Holmes, Beale, Holdsworth and Others.* Boston: Little, Brown, and Company, 1907. Three volumes. 847; 823; 862 pp. Reprinted 1992 by The Lawbook Exchange, Ltd. LCCN 91-77977. ISBN 0-9630106-0-1. Cloth. $195.

Lieber, Francis. *On Civil Liberty and Self-government. Enlarged edition in one volume.* Philadelphia: J.B. Lippincott & Co.. 1859. xix, [15]-629 pp. Reprint available October 2000 by The Lawbook Exchange, Ltd. LCCN 99-056928. ISBN 1-58477-070-8. Cloth. $100.

Livingston, Edward. *A System of Penal Law, for the State of Louisiana: Consisting of A Code of Crimes and Punishments, A Code of Procedure, A Code of Evidence, A Code of Reform and Prison Discipline, A Book of Definitions. Prepared Under the Authority of a Law of the Said State. To Which are Prefixed a Preliminary Report on the Plan of a Penal Code, and Introductory Reports to the Several Codes Embraced in the System of Penal Law.* Philadelphia: James Kay, Jun. & Brother, 1833. v, 745 pp. Reprinted 1999 by The Lawbook Exchange, Ltd. LCCN 99-11403. ISBN 1-886363-83-8. Cloth. $95.

Llewellyn, Karl N. *Jurisprudence. Realism in Theory and Practice.* [Chicago]: The University of Chicago Press, 1962. viii, 531 pp. Reprinted 2000 by The Lawbook Exchange, Ltd. LCCN 99-056923. ISBN 1-58477-067-8. Cloth. $95.

[Macaulay, Thomas Babington]. *A Penal Code Prepared by the Indian Law Commissioners, and published by Command of the Governor General of India in Council.* London: Pelham Richardson, Cornhill, 1838. viii, 138 pp. Reprint available December 2000 by The Lawbook Exchange, Ltd. LCCN 99-16486. ISBN 1-58477-018-X. Cloth. $65.

[MacDonell, Sir John and Edward Manson]. *Great Jurists of the World.* Edited by Sir John MacDonell and Edward Manson. With an Introduction by Van Vechten Veeder. Boston: Little, Brown, and Company, 1914. Illustrated. xxxii, 607 pp. Reprinted 1997 by The Lawbook Exchange, Ltd. LCCN 97-8298. ISBN 1-886363-28-5. Cloth. $95.

[Madison, James]. Hunt, Gaillard, Scott, James Brown. *The Debates in The Federal Convention of 1787 Which Framed the Constitution of the United States of America.* New York: Oxford University Press, 1920. xcvii, [1], 731 pp. Reprinted 1999 by The Lawbook Exchange, Ltd. LCCN 98-51911. ISBN 1-886363-77-3. Cloth. $110.

Maitland, Frederick William. *English Law and the Renaissance (The Rede Lecture for 1901) with Some Notes.* Cambridge: at the University Press, 1901. 98 pp. Reprint ed 2000 by The Lawbook Exchange, Ltd. LCCN 99-41654. ISBN 1-58477-034-1. Cloth. $60.

Maitland, Frederic William. *Roman Canon Law in the Church of England: Six Essays.* London: Methuen & Co., 1898. vii, 184 pp. Reprinted 1998 by The Lawbook Exchange, Ltd. LCCN 98-22357. ISBN 1-886363-57-9. Cloth. $65.

Maitland, Frederick W., Montague, Francis C., *A Sketch of English Legal History.* Edited with Notes and Appendices by James F. Colby. New York: G.P. Putnam's Sons, 1915. x, 234pp. Reprinted 1998 by The Lawbook Exchange, Ltd. LCCN 98-11337. ISBN 1-886363-50-1. Cloth. $50.

Mangum, Charles. *The Legal Status of the Negro.* New York: D. Appleton-Century Co., [1939]. xi, 354 pp. Reprinted 2000 by The Lawbook Exchange, Ltd. LCCN 99-056927. ISBN 1-58477-069-4. Cloth. $80.

Marke, Julius J., editor. *A Catalogue of the Law Collection at New York University With Selected Annotations.* New York: The Law Center of New York University, 1953. xxxi, 1372 pp. Reprinted 1999 by The Lawbook Exchange, Ltd. LCCN 99-19939. ISBN 1-886363-91-9. Cloth. $185.

Marsden. R.[eginald]. G.[odfrey], ed. *Documents Relating to Law and Custom of the Sea.* [n.p.]: The Navy Record Society, 1915-6. Two volumes. xxxiii, 561; xl, 457, [5] pp. Reprinted 1999 by The Lawbook Exchange, Ltd. LCCN 99-24138. ISBN 1-886363-96-X. Cloth. $175.

Marshall, John. *The Constitutional Decisions of John Marshall,* Edited, with an introductory essay by Joseph P. Cotton, Jr. New York: G.P. Putnam, 1905. Two volumes. viii, 144, 145a-188a, [145]-330 pp. Reprint available December 2000 by The Lawbook Exchange, Ltd. LCCN 99-048862. ISBN 1-58477-050-3. Cloth. $175.

[Marshall, John]. Servies, James Albert. *A Bibliography of John Marshall.* Washington: United States Commission for the Celebration of the Two Hundredth Anniversary of the Birth of John Marshall, 1956. xix, 182 pp. Reprinted 2000 by The Lawbook Exchange, Ltd. LCCN 99-088239. ISBN 1-58477-083-X. Cloth. $65.

Maxwell, W. Harold and C.R. Brown. *A Complete List of British and Colonial Law Reports and Legal Periodicals. Arranged in Alphabetical and in Chronological Order with Bibliographical Notes.* [With]: *Check List of Canadian and Newfoundland Statutes.*[Third Edition]. Toronto: The Carswell Company, Limited, 1937. viii, 141, 49 pp. Reprinted 1995 by The Lawbook Exchange, Ltd. LCCN 96-14504. ISBN 1-886363-11-0. Cloth. $70.

McCulloch, J.R. *The Works of David Ricardo, Esq., M.P. with a Notice of the Life and Writings of the Author.* London: John Murray, 1846. xxxiii, 584 pp. Reprinted 2000 by The Lawbook Exchange, Ltd. LCCN 99-39612. ISBN 1-58477-028-7. Cloth. $90.

McKechnie, William Sharp. *Magna Carta. A Commentary on the Great Charter of King John. With an Historical Introduction. Second Edition, Revised and in part Re-written.* Glasgow: James Maclehose and Sons, 1914. xvii,530, [2] pp. Reprinted 2000 by The Lawbook Exchange, Ltd. LCCN 99-38731. ISBN 1-58477-031-7. Cloth. $95.

McNamara, M. Frances. *Ragbag of Legal Quotations.* Albany: Matthew Bender & Company, 1960. xi, 334 pp. Reprinted 1992 by The Lawbook Exchange, Ltd. LCCN 92-074141. ISBN 0-9630106-3-8. Cloth. $50.

Meiklejohn, Alexander. *Free Speech and Its Relation to Self Government.* New York: Harper Brothers Publishers, [1948]. xiv, 107pp. Reprint available October 2000 by The Lawbook Exchange, Ltd. LCCN 99-87204. ISBN 1-58477-087-2. Cloth. $80.

Mendelsohn, S. *The Criminal Jurisprudence of the Ancient Hebrews. Compiled from the Talmud and other Rabbinical Writings, and Compared with Roman and English Penal Jurisprudence.* Baltimore: M. Curlander, 1891. 270 pp. Reprint available December 2000 by The Lawbook Exchange, Ltd. ISBN 1-58477-150-X. Cloth. $80.

Merriam, C.E., Jr. *History of the Theory of Sovereignty Since Rousseau.* New York: Columbia University Press, [1900]. x, [11]-233 pp. Reprinted 1999 by The Lawbook Exchange, Ltd. LCCN 98-32385. ISBN 1-886363-76-5. Cloth. $65.

Minor, Raleigh C. *Notes on the Science of Government and the Relations of the States to the United States.* [Charlottesville]: University of Virginia, 1913. x, 171 pp. Reprinted 1995 by The Lawbook Exchange, Ltd. LCCN 99-047233. ISBN 1-886363-09-9. Cloth. $40.

Moore, Blaine Free. *The Supreme Court and Unconstitutional Legislation.* New York: Columbia University Press, 1913. 158 pp. Reprint available October 2000 by The Lawbook Exchange, Ltd. ISBN 1-58477-099-6. Cloth. $60.

Morris, Thomas D. *Free Men All: The Personal Liberty Laws of the North 1780-1861.* Baltimore: The Johns Hopkins University Press, 1974. xii, 253 pp. Reprint available September 2000 by The Lawbook Exchange, Ltd. ISBN 1-58477-107-0. Cloth. $75.

Neely, Robert D. *The Lawyers of Dickens and Their Clerks.* Boston: The Christopher Publishing House, [1936]. 67pp. Reprint available December 2000 by

The Lawbook Exchange, Ltd. LCCN 00-021520. ISBN 1-58477-091-0. Cloth. $60.

Neilson, George. *Trial by Combat.* Glasgow: William Hodge & Co., 1890. xiv, 348 pp. Reprinted 2000 by The Lawbook Exchange, Ltd. LCCN 99-059101. ISBN 1-58477-075-9. Cloth. $75.

[Nichols, J.]. *A Collection of all the Wills, Now Known to Be Extant, of the Kings and Queens of England, Princes and Princesses of Wales, and every Branch of the Blood Royal, from the Reign of William the Conqueror, to that of Henry the Seventh Exclusive: With Explanatory Notes and a Glossary.* London: J. Nichols, 1780. x, 434 pp. Reprinted 1999 by The Lawbook Exchange, Ltd. LCCN 99-17114. ISBN 1-886363-87-0. Cloth. $75.

Ogle, Arthur. *The Canon Law in Mediaeval England. An Examination of William Lyndwood's "Provinciale," in Reply to the Late Professor F.W. Maitland.* London: John Murray, 1912. xv, 220 pp. Reprinted 2000 by The Lawbook Exchange, Ltd. LCCN 99-33827. ISBN 1-58477-026-0. Cloth. $65.

Perry, Ross R. *Common-law Pleading: Its History and Principles. Including Dicey's Rules Concerning Parties to Action and Stephen's Rules of Pleading.* Boston, Little, Brown and Company, 1897. xxvi, 494 pp. Reprint available October 2000 by The Lawbook Exchange, Ltd. ISBN 1-58477-105-4. Cloth. $95.

Pollock, Frederick and Frederic William Maitland. *The History of English Law before the Time of Edward I.* Cambridge: Cambridge University Press, 1898. Two volumes. xxxviii, 688; xiv, 691 pp. Reprinted 1996 by The Lawbook Exchange, Ltd. LCCN 96-16003. ISBN 1-886363-22-6. Cloth. $165.

Pollock, Sir Frederick. *The Genius of the Common Law.* New York: The Columbia University Press, 1912. vii, 141 pp. Reprinted 2000 by The Lawbook Exchange, Ltd. LCCN 99-047160. ISBN 1-58477-043-0-1. Cloth. $55.

Pomeroy, John N. *A Treatise on Equity Jurisprudence As Administered in the United States of America. Adapted for All the States and to the Union of Legal and Equitable Remedies under the Reformed Procedure.* San Francisco and New York: Bancroft-Whitney and Lawyers Cooperative, 1941. Five volumes. 914; 1134; 1063; 1104; 716 pp. Reprinted 1995 by The Lawbook Exchange, Ltd. ISBN 1-886363-05-6. Cloth. $450.

Pothier, R.J. (1699-1772)]. *Treatise on the Contract of Sale.* Translated from the French by L.S. Cushing. Boston: Charles C. Little and James Brown, 1889. xvi, 406 pp. Reprinted 2000 by The Lawbook Exchange, Ltd. LCCN 99-10260. ISBN 1-886363-82-X. Cloth. $70.

Pothier, Robert Joseph [1699-1772]. *A Treatise on the Law of Obligations, or Contracts. Translated from the French, with an Introduction, Appendix, and Notes, Illustrative of the English Law on the Subject. By William David Evans.* London: A. Strahan, 1802. Two volumes. [1], 578, [1]; iv, 715, [1]pp. Reprint available October 2000 by The Lawbook Exchange, Ltd. LCCN 99-26397. ISBN 1-886363-98-6. Cloth. $195.

Pothier, Robert Joseph [1699-1772]. *A Treatise on Obligations, Considered in a Moral and Legal View. Translated from the French of Pothier.* Translated by Francois-Xavier Martin. Newburn, N.C.: Martin & Ogden, 1802. 2 vols. in 1 book. Reprinted 2000 by The Lawbook Exchange, Ltd. With a new introduction by Warren M. Billings. LCCN 98-38360. ISBN 1-886363-62-5. Cloth. $75.

Pound, Roscoe. *Jurisprudence.* St. Paul, Minn.: West Publishing Co., 1959. Five volumes. Reprinted 2000 by The Lawbook Exchange, Ltd. ISBN 1-58477-119-4. Cloth. $495.

Powell, Chilton Latham. *English Domestic Relations 1487-1653. A Study of Matrimony and Family Life in Theory and Practice as Revealed by the Literature, Law, and History of the Period.* New York: Columbia University Press, 1917. xii, 274 pp. Reprint available October 2000 by The Lawbook Exchange, Ltd. ISBN 1-58477-096-1. Cloth. $75.

Radin, Max. *Law as Logic and Experience.* New Haven: Yale University Press, 1940. ix, [1], 171 pp. Reprinted 2000 by The Lawbook Exchange, Ltd. LCCN 99-30670. ISBN 1-58477-008-2. Cloth. $55.

Rapalje, Stewart and Lawrence, Robert L. *A Dictionary of American and English Law with Definitions of the Technical Terms of the Canon and Civil Laws. Also, Containing a Full Collection of Latin Maxims, and Citations of Upwards of Forty Thousand Reported Cases, in which Words and Phrases Have Been Judicially Defined or Construed.* Jersey City: Frederick C. Linn & Co., 1888. Two volumes. xxxviii, 1380 pp. Reprinted 1997 by The Lawbook Exchange, Ltd. LCCN 97-38484. ISBN 1-886363-33-1. Cloth. $195.

Reeve, Tapping. [1744-1823]. *The Law of Baron and Femme, of Parent and Child, Guardian and Ward, Master and Servant, and of the Powers of the Courts of Chancery; with an Essay on the Terms Heir, Heirs, Heirs of the Body. Third Edition, With Notes and References to English and American Cases by Amasa J. Parker and Charles E. Baldwin, Counselors-At-Law* Albany: William Gould, 1862. xlvi, 677pp. Reprinted 1998 by The Lawbook Exchange, Ltd. LCCN 98-36057. ISBN 1-886363-58-7. Cloth. $75.

Richards, John T. *Abraham Lincoln The Lawyer-Statesman.* Boston: Houghton Mifflin, 1916. Frontis. Illustrated. xii, 260 pp. Reprinted 1999 by The Lawbook Exchange, Ltd. LCCN 99-20587. ISBN 1-886363-94-3. Cloth. $60.

Roby, Henry John. *An Introduction to the Study of Justinian's Digest Containing an Account of its Composition and of the Jurists Used or Referred to Therein.* Cambridge: At the University Press, 1886. cclxxix pp. Reprinted 2000 by The Lawbook Exchange, Ltd. ISBN 1-58477-073-2. Cloth. $65.

Roby, Henry John. *Roman Private Law in the Times of Cicero and of the Antonines.* Cambridge: At the University Press, 1902. Two volumes. xxxii, 543; xiii, [1], 560 pp. Reprinted 2000 by The Lawbook Exchange, Ltd. ISBN 1-58477-074-0. Cloth. $180.

Sandys, Sir John Edwin. *Aristotle's Constitution of Athens. A Revised Text with an Introduction Critical and Explanatory Notes Testimonia and Indices. Second edition, Revised and Enlarged.* London: Macmillan & Co., Limited, 1902. xcii, 331 pp. Frontis. Illus. Reprinted 2000 by The Lawbook Exchange, Ltd. LCCN 99-23952. ISBN 1-58477-004-X. Cloth. $75.

Schechter, Frank I. *The Historical Foundations of the Law Relating to Trade-Marks.* New York: Columbia University Press, 1925. xxviii, 211 pp. Reprinted 2000 by The Lawbook Exchange, Ltd. LCCN 99-41673. ISBN 1-58477-035-X. Cloth. $60.

Schroeder, Theodore. *Constitutional Free Speech Defined and Defended in an Unfinished Argument in a Case of Blasphemy.* New York: Free Speech League, 1919. 456 pp. Reprint available December 2000 by The Lawbook Exchange, Ltd. LCCN 99-049361. ISBN 1-58477-053-8. Cloth. $90.

Schroeder, Theodore. *Free Speech Bibliography Including Every Discovered Attitude Toward the Problem Covering Every Method of Transmitting Ideas and Abridging Their Promulgation upon Every Subject-Matter.* New York: The H.W. Wilson Company, 1922. 456 pp. Reprint available November 2000 by The Lawbook Exchange, Ltd. LCCN 99-049361. ISBN 1-58477-053-8. Cloth. $85.

Schulte, Joh. Friedrich von. *Die Geschichte der Quellen und Literatur der canonischen Rechts.* Stuttgart: Verlag von Ferdinand Enke, 1875. Three volumes. Reprinted 2000 by The Lawbook Exchange, Ltd. LCCN 99-087494. ISBN 1-58477-089-9. Cloth. $225.

Schwartz, Bernard, editor. *The Code Napoleon and the Common-Law World. The Sesquicentennial Lectures Delivered at The Law Center of New York University December 13-15, 1954.* New York: New York University Press, 1956. x, 438pp. Reprinted 1998 by The Lawbook Exchange, Ltd. LCCN 98-34100. ISBN 1-886363-59-5. Cloth. $65.

Schwarz, Philip J. *Twice Condemned: Slaves and the Criminal Laws of Virginia, 1705-1865.* [Baton Rouge: Louisiana State University Press]. [1988]. xvi, 354pp. Reprinted 1998 by The Lawbook Exchange, Ltd. LCCN 98-4424 ISBN 1-886363-54-4. Cloth. $75.

Scott, Henry W. *The Courts of the State of New York: Their History, Development and Jurisdiction: Embracing a complete history of all the Courts and Tribunals of Justice, both Colonial and State, established from the first settlement of Manhattan Island and including the status and jurisdiction of all the Courts of the State as now constituted.* New York: Wilson Publishing Co., 1909. Reprint available December 2000 by The Lawbook Exchange, Ltd. LCCN 99-10259. ISBN 1-886363-84-6. Cloth. $95.

Scott, James Brown. *The Spanish Origin of International Law Francisco De Vitoria and His Law of Nations.* London: Humphrey Milford, 1934. 19a, 288, clviii pp. Frontispiece and portrait. Reprint available September 2000 by The Lawbook Exchange, Ltd. LCCN 00-036835. ISBN 1-58477-110-0. Cloth. $90.

Sears, John H. *Trust Estates as Business Companies.* [Second Edition]. Kansas City, Mo.: Vernon Law Book Company, 1921. xx, 782 pp. [1921]. Reprinted 1998 by The Lawbook Exchange, Ltd. LCCN 97-32423 ISBN 1-886363-41-2. Cloth. $95.

Shumaker, Walter A. *The Cyclopedic Law Dictionary Comprising the Terms and Phrases of American Jurisprudence, Including Ancient and Modern Common Law, International Law, and Numerous Select Titles from the Civil Law, the French and the Spanish Law, etc., etc. with an Exhaustive Collection of Legal Maxims. Second Edition by James C. Cahill.* Chicago: Callaghan and Company, 1922. xii, 545 pp. Reprint available October 2000 by The Lawbook Exchange, Ltd. LCCN 99-16385. ISBN 1-58477-020-1. Cloth. $150.

[St. Germain, Christopher]. [1460-1540]. *The Doctor and Student or Dialogues Between a Doctor of Divinity and a Student in the Laws of England Containing the Grounds of Those Laws Together with Questions and Cases Concerning the Equity Thereof Revised and Corrected by William Muchall, Gent. to which are added two pieces concerning Suits in Chancery by Subpoena.* Cincinnati: Robert Clarke & Co., 1874. xiv, 401pp. Reprinted 1998 by The Lawbook Exchange, Ltd. LCCN 98-11338. ISBN 1-886363-49-8. Cloth. $65.

Stammler, Rudolph. *The Theory of Justice.* Translated by Isaak Husik. New York: The Macmillan Company, 1925. xli, 591 pp. Reprinted 2000 by The Lawbook Exchange, Ltd. LCCN 99-054019. ISBN 1-58477-066-X. Cloth. $95.

Stimson, Frederic Jesup. *Glossary of Technical Terms, Phrases, and Maxims of the Common Law* Boston: Little, Brown, and Company, 1881. iv, 305pp. Reprinted 1999 by The Lawbook Exchange, Ltd. LCCN 98-50813. ISBN 1-886363-70-6. Cloth. $60.

Stimson, Frederic Jesup. *Popular Law Making, A Study of the Origin, History, and Present Tendencies of Law Making by Statute.* New York: Charles Scribner's Sons, 1910. xii, 545 pp. Reprint available December 2000 by The Lawbook Exchange, Ltd. LCCN 00-022513. ISBN 1-58477-094-5. Cloth. $85.

Stokes, I.N. Phelps. *The Iconography of Manhattan Island 1498-1909.* New York: Robert H. Dodd, 1915. Six volumes. Reprinted 1998 by The Lawbook Exchange, Ltd. LCCN 97-30604. ISBN 1-886363-30-7. Cloth. $750.

Stone, Harlan F. *Law and its Administration.* New York: Columbia University Press, 1915. vii, 232 pp. Reprint available December 2000 by The Lawbook Exchange, Ltd. LCCN 00-021508. ISBN 1-58477-093-5. Cloth. $70.

Story, Joseph. [1779-1845]. *A Familiar Exposition of the Constitution of the United States:* Containing a Brief Commentary on Every Clause, Explaining the True Nature, reasons, and Objects Thereof; Designed for the Use of School, Libraries and General Readers. With an Appendix, Containing Important Public Documents, Illustrative of the Constitution. New York: Harper & Brothers: 1865. 372 pp. Reprinted 1999 by The Lawbook Exchange, Ltd. LCCN 98-50811. ISBN 1-886363-71-4. Cloth. $60.

[Story, Joseph]. [1779-1845]. Story, William. *Life and Letters of Joseph Story, Associate Justice of the Supreme Court of the United States and Dane Professor of Law at Harvard University, edited by his son, William W. Story.* Boston: Charles C. Little and James Brown, 1851. Two volumes. xii, 574; viii, 676 pp. Frontispiece. Reprint available October 2000 by The Lawbook Exchange, Ltd. LCCN 99-058777. ISBN 1-58477-071-6. Cloth. $195.

[Story, Joseph]. Story, William W., ed. *The Miscellaneous Writings of Joseph Story, Associate Justice of the Supreme Court of the United States and Dane Professor of Law at Harvard University, edited by his son, William W. Story.* Boston: C.C. Little and J. Brown , 1852. x, 828 pp. Reprint available October 2000 by The Lawbook Exchange, Ltd. LCCN 99-058559. ISBN 1-58477-072-4. Cloth. $125.

Tayler, Thomas. *The Law Glossary: Being a Selection of the Greek, Latin, Saxon, French, Norman and Italian Sentences, Phrases, and Maxims, Found in the Leading English and American Reports, and Elementary Works.* New York: Lewis & Blood, 1856. 580 pp. Reprinted 1995 by The Lawbook Exchange, Ltd. ISBN 1-886363-12-9. Cloth. $65.

[Taylor, John]. [1753-1824]. *A Defence of the Measures of the Administration of Thomas Jefferson. By Curtius.* Washington: Samuel H. Smith, 1804. 136 pp. Reprinted 1999 by The Lawbook Exchange, Ltd. LCCN 99-24139. ISBN 1-886363-97-8. Cloth. $60.

Taylor, John. *Construction Construed and Constitutions Vindicated.* Richmond: printed by Shepherd & Pollard, 1820. iv, 344pp. Reprinted 1998 by The Lawbook Exchange, Ltd. LCCN 97-49411. ISBN 1-886363-43-9. Cloth. $65.

Taylor, John. *An Inquiry into the Principles and Policy of the Government of the United States.* Fredericksburg: Green and Cady, 1814. With an introduction by Roy

Franklin Nichols, Yale University Press, 1950. 562pp. Reprinted 1998 by The Lawbook Exchange, Ltd. LCCN 98-11147. ISBN 1-886363-46-3. Cloth. $75.

Taylor, John, of Caroline. *New Views of the Constitution of the United States.* Washington City: Printed for the Author, 1823. [4], 316pp. Reprint available December 2000 by The Lawbook Exchange, Ltd. ISBN 1-58477-079-1. Cloth. $70.

Thomson, Richard. *An Historical Essay on the Magna Charta of King John: to which are added, the Great Charter in Latin and English, the charters of liberties and confirmations, granted by Henry III and Edward I, the original Charter of the forests, and various authentic instruments connected with them: Explanatory Notes on their Several Privileges; A Descriptive Account of the Principal Originals and Editions Extant, Both in Print and Manuscript; and Other Illustrations, Derived from the Most Interesting and Authentic Sources.* London: John Major and Robert Jennings, 1829. xxxii, 612 pp. Reprinted 2000 by The Lawbook Exchange, Ltd. LCCN 99-40987. ISBN 1-58477-030-9. Cloth. $95.

Tiedeman, Christopher G. A Treatise on the Limitations of Police Power in the United States Considered from both a Civil and Criminal Standpoint. St. Louis: The F.H. Thomas Law Book Co., 1886. lxv, 662 pp. Reprint available December 2000 by The Lawbook Exchange, Ltd. ISBN 1-58477-121-6. Cloth. $110.

Townsend, William H. *Lincoln the Litigant.* Boston: Houghton Mifflin Company, 1925. [ix], [117] pp. Frontis. Illus. Reprinted 2000 by The Lawbook Exchange, Ltd. LCCN 99-16499. ISBN 1-58477-021-X. Cloth. $60.

[Trials]. [Witchcraft Trials]. *Curious Cases and Amusing Actions at Law Including Some Trials of Witches in the Seventeenth Century.* Toronto: The Carswell Co., Limited, 1916. vii, 234 pp. Reprint available October 2000 by The Lawbook Exchange, Ltd. LCCN 99-032361. ISBN 1-58477-012-0. Cloth. $65.

Tucker, Henry St. George. *Commentaries on the Laws of Virginia. Comprising the Substance of a Course of Lectures Delivered to the Winchester Law School. With an Introduction by David Cobin and Paul Finkelman.* Richmond: Shepherd and Colin, 1846. Two volumes. 34, 468; 24, 512 pp. Reprinted 1998 by The Lawbook Exchange, Ltd. LCCN 97-10313. ISBN 1-886363-26-9. Cloth. $175.

Tucker, Henry St. George. *Limitations on the Treaty-Making Power Under the Constitution of the United States.* Boston: Little, Brown, and Company, 1915. xxi, 444 pp. Reprinted 2000 by The Lawbook Exchange, Ltd. LCCN 99-31589. ISBN 1-58477-015-5. Cloth. $75.

Tucker, St. George. *Blackstone's Commentaries. With Notes of Reference to the Constitution and Laws, of the Federal Government of the United States, and of the Commonwealth of Virginia. In Five Volumes, with an Appendix to Each volume, Containing Short Tracts upon Such Subjects As Appeared Necessary to Form a Connected View of the Laws of Virginia As a Member of the Federal Union.* Philadelphia: William Young Birch and Abraham Small, 1803. Five volumes. Reprinted 1996 by The Lawbook Exchange, Ltd. LCCN 96-12566. ISBN 1-886363-15-3. Cloth. $450.

[Twiss, Sir Travers]. *The Black Book of the Admiralty, with an Appendix.* Monumenta Juridica. Edited by Sir Travers Twiss. Four volumes. 4, xciii, 491, [2]; 4, lxxxvii, 500, 31; 4, lxxxvi, 673, [1], 31; 4, clii, 559, 32 pp. LCCN 97-38809 ISBN 1-886363-39-0. 1871. Reprinted 1998 by The Lawbook Exchange, Ltd. Cloth. $495.

[Upshur, Abel Parker]. *A Brief Enquiry Into the True Nature and Character of Our Federal Government, being a review of Judge Story's Commentaries on the Constitution of the United States. By a Virginian.* Petersburg: Printed by Edmund and Julian C. Ruffin, 1840. 132pp. Reprinted 1998 by The Lawbook Exchange, Ltd. LCCN 97-11151. ISBN 1-886363-44-7. Cloth. $45.

Valmaer. [pseud]. [Ream, Michael]. *Lawyer's Code of Ethics. A Satire.* St. Louis: The F.H. Thomas Law Book Co., 1887. 143 pp. Reprint available December 2000 by The Lawbook Exchange, Ltd. LCCN 00-021508. ISBN 1-58477-093-5. Cloth. $65.

Vinogradoff, Paul. *Custom and Right.* Oslo: H. Aschehoug, 1925. 110 pp. Reprint ed 2000 by The Lawbook Exchange, Ltd. LCCN 99-0474851. ISBN 1-58477-048-1. Cloth. $45.

Vinogradoff, Paul. *Roman Law in Mediaeval Europe.* London: Harper & Brothers, 1909. 136 pp. Reprinted 2000 by The Lawbook Exchange, Ltd. LCCN 00-039068. ISBN 1-58477-109-7. Cloth. $65.

Vinogradoff, Sir Paul. *Outlines of Historical Jurisprudence.* London: Oxford University Press, 1920. Two volumes. 428; x, 315 pp. Reprinted 1999 by The Lawbook Exchange, Ltd. LCCN 98-42298. ISBN 1-886363-64-1. Cloth. $150.

Walker, James. *The Theory of the Common Law.* Boston: Little, Brown and Co., 1852. xxiv, 130pp. Reprinted 1998 by The Lawbook Exchange, Ltd. LCCN 98-9522. ISBN 1-886363-45-5. Cloth. $65.

Warren, Charles. *History of the Harvard Law School and of Early Legal Conditions in America.* New York: Lewis Publishing Company, 1908. Three volumes. xiv, 543; iv, 560; 397 pp. Illustrated. Reprinted 1999 by The Lawbook Exchange, Ltd. LCCN 99-29193. ISBN 1-58477-006-6. Cloth. $275.

White, Edw. J. *The Law in Scriptures. With Explanations of the Law Terms and Legal References in Both the Old and the New Testaments.* St. Louis: Thomas Law Book Company, 1935. xxiv, 422 pp. Reprinted 2000 by The Lawbook Exchange, Ltd. LCCN 99-059102. ISBN 1-58477-076-7. Cloth. $80.

Whiting, William. *War Powers under the Constitution of the United States. Tenth edition.* Boston: Little, Brown, and Company, 1864. xvii, 342 pp. Reprint available October 2000 by The Lawbook Exchange, Ltd. LCCN 99-049360. ISBN 1-58477-055-4. Cloth. $80.

Whitney, Henry C. *Life on the Circuit with Lincoln. With Sketches of Generals Grant, Sherman and McClellan, Judge Davis, Leonard Swett, and Other Contemporaries.* Illustrated. Boston: Estes & Lauriat, 1892. viii, 601 pp. Reprint available October 2000 by The Lawbook Exchange, Ltd. ISBN 1-58477-115-1. Cloth. $110.

Wiener, Leo. [1862-1939]. *Commentary to the Germanic Laws and Mediaeval Documents.* Cambridge: Harvard University Press, 1915. lxi, 224 pp. Reprinted 2000 by The Lawbook Exchange, Ltd. LCCN 99-23969. ISBN 1-58477-005-8. Cloth. $60.

Woodbine, George E. *Four Thirteenth Century Law Tracts. A Thesis Presented to the Faculty of the Graduate School of Yale University in Candidacy for the Degree of Doctor of Philosophy.* New Haven: Yale University Press, 1910. vi, 183 pp. Reprinted 1999 by The Lawbook Exchange, Ltd. LCCN 99-29294. ISBN 1-58477-007-4. Cloth. $50.

Woolsey, Theodore D. *Divorce and Divorce Legislation, Especially in the United States. Second Edition Revised.* New York: Charles Scribner's Sons, 1882. x, [9]-328 pp. Reprint available December 2000 by The Lawbook Exchange, Ltd. ISBN 1-58477-118-6. Cloth. $75.

[Worrall, John and Edward Brooke]. *Bibliotheca Legum Angliae. Or, a Catalogue of the Common and Statute Law Books of This Realm, and Some Others Relating Thereto: Giving an Account of Their Several Editions, Ancient Printers, Dates, and Prices, and Wherein They Differ. [With a Supplement to 1800]. Part I Compiled by John Worrall, Part II and Supplement Compiled by Edward Brooke. Parts I, II and Supplement bound in one volume.* London: Printed for Edward Brooke, 1788-1800. 316; 264; 48 pp. 1788-1800. Reprinted 1997 by The Lawbook Exchange, Ltd. LCCN 97-12962. ISBN 1-886363-29-3. Cloth. $110.

Wright, John S. *Citizenship Sovereignty.* Chicago: Published for American Citizens, the True Maintainers of State Sovereignty, 1864. Reprinted 1998 by The Lawbook Exchange, Ltd. LCCN 98-15940 ISBN 1-886363-55-2. Cloth. $65.

www.ingramcontent.com/pod-product-compliance
Lightning Source LLC
Chambersburg PA
CBHW021806270326
41932CB00007B/80